"Abiding Under the Shadow"

God's Call: To Return to Covenant
Relationship for His People

David Lebo

ISBN: 978-1-60383-223-6

Published by:
Holy Fire Publishing
717 Old Trolley Road
Attn: Suite 6, Publishing Unit #116
Summerville, SC 29485

www.ChristianPublish.com

Cover Design: Jay Cookingham

Printed in the United States of America and the United Kingdom

Dedication

In loving memory of Becky "Deborah" Hensell who interceded through the duration of the writing of this book, sometimes up to 8 hrs. in one sitting. Without her prayers, faith, and support this book would not have been possible. Only eternity will show all that she accomplished through her faithful ministry! We miss you Becky! Rest in Peace. See you again someday soon!

Thanks to Jim Hensell for all your love, prayers, encouragement, and support. You believed in me and this project while never giving up. Without you, this book would not be possible. I will be forever grateful for all you've done! You are the "HUB"!

Thanks to my wife of 23 years, Vicki, for always standing by me through all the "wilderness" years! The best is yet to come!!!

Thanks to the "Friday Night Prayer Group"... You all helped me go to "depths" that I could not have gone alone. Blessings to you all.

Thanks to Phil and Bernice Michael of "Breath of God Ministries" for helping us get "FREE"!!! (They are located in Berkeley Springs, WV.)

Thanks to Larry and Joanna Smith for your leadership and always being steadfast, immovable, unshakeable, rock solid, while having freedom to the Holy Spirit's moving!

Thanks to my mother, Delores, for being a godly example and demonstrating to me the love of Christ in action!

Table of Contents

Psalm 91
(NKJV)

He who dwells in the secret place of the Most High shall
abide under the shadow of the Almighty.
I will say of the Lord," He is my refuge and my fortress;
My God, in Him I will trust."
Surely He shall deliver you from the snare of the fowler
and from the perilous pestilence.
He shall cover you with His feathers, and under
His wings you shall take refuge;
His truth shall be your shield and buckler.
You shall not be afraid of the terror by night,
Nor of the arrow that flies by day, Nor of the pestilence that walks in darkness,
nor of the destruction that lays waste at noonday.
A thousand may fall at your side, and ten thousand at your right hand;
But it shall not come near you.
Only with your eyes shall you look, and see the reward of the wicked.
Because you have made the Lord, who is my refuge,
Even the Most High, your dwelling place,
No evil shall befall you, Nor shall any plague come near your dwelling;
For He shall give his angels charge over you,
to keep you in all your ways.
In their hands they shall bear you up,
lest you dash your foot against a stone.
You shall tread upon the lion and the cobra,
the young lion and the serpent you shall trample underfoot.
"Because he has set his love upon Me, therefore
I will deliver him; I will set him on high,
because he has known my name. He shall call upon me,
and I will answer him; I will be with
him in trouble; I will deliver him and honor him,
with long life I will satisfy him, and show him
My salvation."

Introduction

God gave this passage of scripture to me years ago to be my life verses to live by. I did not fully realize the significance or importance of what God would do with these words until years later. Since then, God has broadened my understanding and made these words come alive in greater ways than I ever thought possible.

There is more to Psalm 91 than protection, refuges, fortresses, and guardian angels. God is all these things and more; but what I want to focus on most is that the first verse speaks of a relationship that is possible between God and his people, and some of the benefits of that relationship maybe better understood as the "bridegroom" and His "bride"-- a relationship that is very close, intimate, and forever; one that shares hearts, thought, passions, desires, hopes and dreams.

Years ago I began to search my own heart trying to deal with a deep stirring, an unrest, a searching that I know now was generated by God Himself. It was an unrest saying that there had to be more to all of this; more to church, more to life, more to what I was experiencing – more to God. The God I read about in the Holy Scriptures was not the same God I was seeing in the lives of people and churches around me. I wrestled with these thoughts: "There's got to be more.", "Where's the power?", "Where's the anointing of Jesus?", "Where are the conquerors?", "Where are the healings and miracles?", and "Where is the evidence of God's word being true in the earth?" It just wasn't lining up!

I look around me and see Christians being defeated right and left. Not all, but many are living far below where God wants and needs them to be. Many are overwhelmed by depression, worry, fear, anxiety, sin, sickness, and disease. You name it. They all weigh them down; everything but what I read about that could be possible in the word of God. Something was missing.

Today, many would agree that the enemy has come in like a flood; but God is raising up His standard against it. It's time for the people of God to rise up and fight and realize who we are in Christ, and that He has created us to be sons and daughters of the Most High in all the fullness of God and reach our greatest potential in Christ. We must also know who our creator is – to really know Him in all that He is!

Everything that hinders us, holds us back, or keeps us down must go in Jesus' name. All the chains that have kept us bound for years and in the same place must be broken by the power of God. They can and will be if you let God be God in your heart and life. You can be victorious in 'Jesus' name! *Yes, you can!* You can be changed, be transformed, be different and full of God's power as He intended. The very gates of hell shall not prevail against it.

God has so much more for the child of God. We've settled for less far too long. It's time to take back what the devil has stolen from us!

We forget sometimes that we live in a world that is at war – spiritually I mean. A cosmic battle that is raging between good and evil: God vs. Satan. All around us there is evidence of a war zone with many casualties. Even Church people caught in a whirlwind of troubles so overwhelming they think: "There's no way out.", "This is all there is.", "Life will never change." Some live in a hell on earth. And yes, hell is not just for eternity.

This all has to change. The tide must turn. People's lives and souls hang in the balance – believer and unbeliever alike. People are dying in every way: physically, mentally, emotionally, and spiritually. We need God to intervene. "God help us. Pour out your spirit upon us today. Save us. Save our cities. Save our nation!"

A Season of Intercession

God directed me to a season of prayer and intercession that lasted many years, characterized by times of deep sobbing and travail for up to hours at a time. In this season, God began to speak. He began to show me some of the answers to my concerns and my heart's cry. It took some time. I could not handle it all at once, and neither will you. The Lord began it all by saying, "I am going to restore my power back into the body of Christ where it belongs!" *"Satan comes to kill, steal, and destroy." (John 10:10)*

Satan would take your very life if it were not for the grace and the mercy of God. Above all else, he wants to steal God's anointing away from His people. Why? Because, that's where the power comes from. That's were Satan is defeated and victory comes, and God's kingdom is advanced in the earth.

"The Kingdom of God suffers violence and the violent take it by force." (Matt. 11:12) That doesn't sound like most churches or people I know! Many have an "occupy until He comes" mentality and retreat behind the four walls of their churches.

We are called to be a "militant bride" able to fight spiritual wickedness in the heavenly places-- realizing "the weapons of our warfare are not carnal but mighty through God to the pulling down of strongholds." (2 Cor. 10:4). A bride full of God's power and anointing. There is no stronghold built by Satan himself that cannot be broken and demolished by the power of the living God. *"And the yoke will be destroyed because of the anointing oil." (Isaiah 10:27)*

Satan wants to keep Jesus' anointing away from the people of God, so they will be powerless to fight back. If we continue to try to fight in our own strength, we will continue to be powerless, weak, and defeated with very little results. God can do more in 5 seconds than we can do in 5 years if we let him.

Satan is much more powerful than we are, so why do we even try to fight him on our own terms, with our own weapons, our own strength, talents, or smarts? We are relying too much on ourselves and what we can do and not on God and His power alone.

God is raising up an army of believers that know who they are in Christ, and know who their God is, and are not afraid to fight and engage the enemy-- an army strong in God who is victorious with the likes of David, Joshua, Gideon, Deborah, and Jehosaphat just to name a few. There are many more in the scriptures for our example. God is the same yesterday, today, and forever. He did it once – He'll do it again-- for you and me. He can and will for those who will humble themselves before His mighty hand and will cry out with all that is within them.

Are you hungry for more of God? Are you not satisfied with your present walk with our Lord? Does it seem like something is missing? *"Blessed are those who hunger and thirst for righteousness, for they shall be filled." (Matt. 5:6).*

"Ask, and it will be given to you; seek, and you will find; knock, and it will be opened to you." (Matt. 7:7)

"You do not have because you do not ask." (Jas. 4:2)

God continued to speak to me and said, "There is more that I have for you. Come up to a higher place in me!" I responded in asking the Lord to show me how. God then led me on a two year journey that explored the very heights and the depths of God beyond my wildest imagination. At times, it was more than I could handle. God broke me, stretched me, challenged me, put me through His fire, and blessed me beyond measure. He poured out more of Himself in wave, after wave, after wave, after wave of His presence each getting stronger, and stronger, and stronger. With each wave came a fresh revelation of more of Himself, Psalm 91 being the basic foundation of it all.

I know now that there is more to God! Believe me! We have only tasted a very small portion of what God has for His people. There is so much more yet to come if you are willing to risk all that you are and all that you have to find out. Does your heart cry out for more of the Living God? Do you just want to know God for who He is and draw closer to Him?

God is calling you to get out of the "boat" and "walk out onto the water". Do something you've never done before. Leave what is safe and secure and take a big step of faith. Do you remember Peter? While walking on water himself, Jesus called out to Peter and said, "Come".

God is saying the same thing to us today. "Come, Come out! Come Out! Come out into the depths of God." Leave the shore. Leave the boat. Leave everything behind. Leave all that you can stand on or put your trust in and come out into the deep oceans of God where a whole new realm of God that you've never experienced before awaits you. Come out into the deep where you can't touch bottom, and dive down as far as you can. It's just you and God. Put all your faith and trust into Him to sustain you. He will do all the rest. There is a vast ocean of God that is largely unchartered with many mysteries yet undiscovered. Will you come out into the depths? Can you hear His voice calling you? Don't resist, don't be afraid. Come out! Time is short! Don't delay. The cost will be great; but the dividends are high!

The Laodiceans

Jesus said to the lukewarm church of the Laodicean's in Rev. 3: 14-19: *"And to the angel of the church of the Laodiceans write, These things says the Amen, the Faithful and True witness, the Beginning of the creation of God: I know your works, that you are neither cold nor hot, I could wish you were cold or hot. So then, because you are lukewarm, and neither cold nor hot, I will vomit you out of my mouth. Because you say, 'I am rich, have become wealthy, and have need of nothing' – and do not know that you are wretched, miserable, poor, blind, and naked – I counsel you to buy from me gold refined in the fire, that you may be rich; and white garments, that you may be clothed, that the shame of your nakedness may not be revealed; and anoint your eyes with eye salve, that you may see. As many as I love, I rebuke and chasten, Therefore be zealous and repent."*

They thought they had it all – the epitome of self-reliance. But in God's eyes, they were wretched, miserable, poor, blind and naked. God counseled them to buy His gold – and His gold costs! It will cost you everything that you possess. Would you be willing to trade it all for something better? It's a high price to pay; but we can't afford not to pay it! It's a matter of life and death. People's lives hang in the balance.

We need God's power back in our lives and in our churches once again to set the captive free! If you give God everything you have, He will give you everything that He has. That's the deal! And that's not a bad deal! It's that simple. *"No good thing will He withhold from those who walk uprightly." (Psalm 84:11)*

The "Ifs" and "Thens"

God is not a stingy God. He wants to give blessings and pour out of Himself upon His children; but sometimes there are blocks and hindrances in our own lives that get in the way. Many of God's promises and blessings are conditional. It's an "if" and "then" situation. We must act in obedience to God's word and do our part of the "deal". If we obey, then God can send the blessing. We need to have sensitive spiritual ears to hear clearly all that God is saying to us today, then respond by walking and living it out in obedience to His word—no matter what.

Not just when it's convenient for us or to our advantage; but all the time even if it requires great sacrifices. Some only hear what they want to hear and ignore the rest. Some may obey only in part and forget the rest. Partial obedience is still disobedience.

We need to seek God for who He is, and not just for what we can get out of Him. *"To him who knows to do good and does not do it, to him it is sin." (James 4:17)* We need to hear from heaven then do all that God asks of us. Sometimes we hear but don't act and are guilty of disobedience, laziness, and even apathy. We need to hear – then move without hesitation. We think we have all the time in the world – but we don't! God's patience with us does run out; and we will have a lot to answer for one day.

We will be able to hear God better out of that intimate relationship – the "bridegroom" and His "bride." It's all in the relationship-- how close you are to God.

The Relationship

Psalm 91:1 speaks about this very thing. "He who dwells in the secret place of the Most High, shall abide under the shadow of the Almighty." (NKJV)

Let's look at a few key words in this verse for a moment; so we can better understand the truth about this powerful verse. "He who dwells…" the word "dwells" means: to remain; to settle; as in a marriage. It is someone who remains, or settles, or lives with another as in a marriage covenant. Not just living with your boyfriend or girlfriend, but being legally married; joined together, in a covenant relationship centered around commitment and trust forever. It's not just a "fling" that you try for awhile, but a relationship for life! When you're married, you are married 24 hours a day, 7 days a week, 365 days a year – always. You live together, usually in the same house. You see each other every day, eat together, sleep together, play together, and go through "ups" and "downs" together. You don't just visit each other twice a year and then go do your own "thing". It takes a lot of time, effort, and energy to have a good marriage. You must "work" at it each and every day. The couple must develop good communication skills, being brutally honest at times with each other; working out their differences, and so on. Spiritually it's the same with our relationship with God. It takes time, effort, and energy spent towards doing some very easy disciplines such as: reading the word of God, praying, worshipping, and just spending time with Him, fellowshipping with others, etc., for us to have a really good "marriage" with God.

A man named Enoch comes to mind in the Old Testament. We don't know much about this man, but what little is mentioned of him in the scriptures is that *"Enoch walked with God"* (Gen. 5:24), and that *"he pleased God."* (Heb. 11:5).

I believe that it is by no coincidence that Enoch lived to be 365 years old before he was translated to heaven. It's very possible for every believer to walk with God 365 days a year – everyday – as closely as Enoch did in his lifetime!

The Secret Place

The next key words in our verse that we need to look at are – "the Secret Place". Where is this "secret place"? What is it referring to? And what does it have to do with me? The "secret place" was the innermost chamber in the "Tabernacle of Moses," and then later in the "Temple of Solomon." It was also called the "Most Holy Place" or the "Holy of Holies." It was the holiest place on earth. It was the place where God lived among His people – the dwelling place of "Yeshua." The "tabernacle" was "God on earth" to the Hebrew people. It was also God's pattern and protocol for how sinful man was to approach such a Most Holy God. Spiritually speaking – the pictures and principles of the tabernacle still hold true for us today, in every detail. David wrote in Psalm 27: 4, 5: *"One thing I have desired of the Lord, that I will seek; that I may dwell in the house of the Lord* all *the days of my life, to behold the beauty of the Lord and to inquire in His temple." "For in the time of trouble He shall hide me in His pavilion: in the secret place of His tabernacle He shall hide me. He shall set me high upon a rock."*

This passage of scripture says a lot about David's heart. Above all else, he wanted to live in God's house and experience Him every day of his life.

In Old Testament times, God could not dwell in the hearts of men because of sin; but today, thanks to the work Jesus Christ accomplished on the cross, God can live in the hearts of men and be with us forever. God can now live on the inside of us in all His fullness!

The "Holy of Holies" was off limits except for the high priest who went in only once a year on the "Great Day of Atonement" – risking his own life to go into the presence of the glory of God, to offer the blood of the sacrifice for the sins of the people for another year. Praise God, today, the price for sin has been paid and we are invited to enter the "Holy of Holies" – spiritually speaking – 24 hours a day, 7 days a week, and 365 days a year for the rest of our lives. But we need to examine and use God's protocol that He has given to us, pictured in the "Tabernacle of Moses", for our approach to Him still today.

All the steps are sequential. They still must be done in order. It is a progression! Many want to rush in and experience God's glory without ever first going through the brazen altar. If you want to be a person who lives in the "secret place", you must go through all the preparations first. It takes some time. It's a process – a progression – that depends on how much you invest into your relationship with God and how far you are willing to go.

You must first go through the brazen altar if you ever want to get to the innermost chambers in the tabernacle. Allow the fires of God to consume in you all that is not of Him, and offer yourselves as a "living sacrifice" unto God. (Rom. 12:2). You must be the fuel! God will be the fire! There's no other way. Only you can place yourself on that alter. No one else can do it for you. It must be an act of your own will. Place your whole heart, your entire life, everything that you are and all that you have, on the altar of God and allow the all consuming fire – God – to burn it all up! There won't be anything left of you. This is the work of God in the heart of a believer. That is exactly who He is, and so much more. He is the "refiner's fire." (Mal. 3:2). He cleanses, purifies, purges, and burns. The only way to clean gold or silver is to put it through the fire! You can clean it no other way. God wants to consume in you everything that is not of him; so that only He remains. Then you will become a "vessel of gold." That is the primary work of God in your heart and life today. Be the fuel! Be the fuel! Be the fuel! And that's just the beginning. The next station that you would come to in the tabernacle as a priest would be the brazen laver. I'll only touch on a few things here. I would encourage everyone to do an in-depth study of the "Tabernacle of

Moses". It is all still relevant today. There is so much there that we have been missing!

The brazen laver was a place all the priests could wash their hands and feet from all the "dirt" and "grime" of the day so they could be "clean". It's part of the process! We must be washed with the washing of the word of God. It's all part of God's purification for His people. He wants less of you; so there can be more of Him in your life as you draw closer to Him. We must be cleansed from all unrighteousness before we can even attempt to enter into the second chamber, or the "Holy Place" in God's order.

Many in the church today have never made it past the "Outer Court." They are only living in the vicinity of God – not as close as you can get. But, it's not all their fault. They have not been properly taught the principles that are outlined in the "Tabernacle of Moses." No matter how unpopular it may be, we need to get back to the basics of our Christianity! Repentance, humility, purification, brokenness, emptiness, sacrifice, and holiness must be preached once again from our pulpits! These principles of God have been largely lost in our modern churches today. We must get back to them—now! It is a serious day – a serious hour – time is short!

God's call is the same today as it was in Isaiah's day:

"Repent, for the Kingdom of heaven is at hand!"(Matt. 3:2) "The voice of one crying in the wilderness: Prepare the way of the Lord; make straight in the desert a highway for our God. Every valley shall be exalted and every mountain and hill brought low; The crooked places shall be made straight and the rough places smooth; The glory of the Lord shall be revealed, and all flesh shall see it together; for the mouth of the Lord has spoken." (Isaiah 40: 3-5).

The place we all need to get to is living, and dwelling, and remaining in the "secret place" of the Most High God. We need to live where God lives in all His fullness.

King David expressed his heart in Psalm 27. He longed to be with God all the time. This is possible in your life today through Jesus' work on the cross. When you except Jesus as your Lord and Savior, God begins a process of making His home in your heart and "tabernacles" with you! It's a process. It takes some time to develop, but if you allow God complete access to everything about you, He will do all the work of cleansing and purifying, and taking you to deeper

places in Him. All He needs is your permission! Let God be God in your life, and you'll be blessed beyond measure. I can guarantee it!
"You shall hide them in the secret place of your presence." (Psalm 31:20)

God wants to make His home and dwelling place in you – a place where all of His fullness, glory, and power reside. Yes, this is very possible for every believer today. This is the way Jesus has made for us. He is the Way, the Truth, and the Life! We can be filled with God's presence everyday of our lives! Not only full, but overflowing to the world around us! So, where you go-- He goes; and where you are – He is! You become God's representative in the world in all His power and glory. *Praise God!*

"El Elyon"

Let's get back to our key verse Psalm 91:1. The next phrase I want to look at with you is, "of the Most High". It is very significant that Moses chose these words to describe God here. The Hebrew words for "Most High" are "El Elyon" which means: "Possessor of Heaven and Earth." It is first mentioned in scripture in Gen. 14:18 where Abram (Abraham) meets the King of Salem by the name of Melchizedek. He was also a priest of "El Elyon." In contrast, the King of Sodom comes to Abram to strike a deal with nothing to offer, whereas the King of Salem and Priest of God brings provisions for Abram – bread and wine – and blesses him.

"Then Melchizedek King Salem brought out bread and wine; he was the priest of God Most High. And he blessed him and said: Blessed be Abram of God Most High, Possessor of heaven and earth; and blessed be God Most High, who has delivered your enemies into your hands."
Genesis 14:18-20

Three times "El Elyon" is used in this passage. Abram would not take anything from the King of Salem who was the embodiment of selfish greed and self-sufficiency of the world, and rather received provisions from the King of Salem – the priest of the Most High God. Abram discovered God as "El Elyon", and now knew Him as the possessor of heaven and earth-- the God who owns everything, and has everything that His people would ever need. He has it all   and wants to give it all to the child of God who will dwell in the secret place!

ABIDE

The next key word is "abide". This word means: "to stay permanently; to stop all night; to continue to stay; or to remain." If we dwell in the "secret place" of the Most High, we can permanently stay or remain there – all the time- under God's protection and care. We remain under His coverings, His shadow, His umbrella that embodies everything that He is! His shadow covers the earth, and that's a mighty big shadow! It's like having the largest umbrella in the world over you at all times.

Another place in scripture we find the word "abide" is in John Chapter 15. *"I am the true vine, and My Father is the vine dresser. Every branch in Me that does not bear fruit He takes away; and every branch that bears fruit He prunes, that it may bear more fruit, You are already clean because of the word which I have spoken to you. Abide in Me, and I in you. As the branch cannot bear fruit of itself, unless it abides in the vine, neither can you, unless you abide in ME. "I am the vine, you are the branches. He who abides in ME, and I in him, bears much fruit; for without Me you can do nothing. If anyone does not abide in Me, he is cast out as a branch and is withered; and they gather them and throw them into the fire, and they are burned. If you abide in ME, and My words abide in you, you will ask what you desire, and it shall be done for you."*

In verse 5, we see Jesus is the vine, and we are the branches. We must remain in Him to receive the living water that He provides and bear much fruit for the Kingdom of God. Apart from Him we will dry up and wither. We must stay connected to the life source.

This is another good picture of the relationship we must have if we want God's life giving spirit and power to flow in our lives. Verse 7 also gives us a glimpse of the power of prayer. If "you abide in Me" and "if" God's word abides in you, You can ask whatever you desire according to His written word and it shall be done for you. But this verse is conditional based upon two things: "If" you abide in Christ and "If" you know His words.

If you feel at times your prayers are just hitting the ceiling, you may have to work on your relationship with God; and take an honest assessment of where you live in relationship to where God lives. Do you live in the "Outer Court", "Inner Court", or "Most Holy Place"?

I believe very strongly that if you dwell in the "secret place" of the Most High God, or put it another way - "abide in the vine" of Christ and have a very close relationship with God – you can ask anything as it lines up with His written word – "The Holy Bible"-- and it will be done for you and it shall come to pass.

That's the power of the *"prayer of the righteous man"* as in the book of James. *"Elijah was a man with a nature like ours"*, but he had a close walk with the Lord God Almighty. That's the power of intercession. That's the power you have to pray for someone else-- for churches, for cities, and even for nations!! One person can impact the world and make a difference: *Yes he can!* God only needs just one person, who will surrender everything and say, "Here I am Lord….Send me!"

Shaddai's Shadow

The next key word to look at in Ps. 91:1 is the word "Shadow." This word has many uses and meanings. It can mean a shade cast upon a surface; a mirrored image; or a vague indication or faint suggestion of something else. It can also mean a close or constant companion.

You have probably heard it said of a child: "He's Daddy's little shadow." The boy is rarely found away from His Father. So, the child is always under the watchful care and protection of his loving father. The child looks to him for everything.

Another meaning for the word "Shadow" is to stay close to, or follow especially in secret so as to observe the movements and activities of another. In this close relationship, to be a follower of Christ, we observe who Christ is and what He did and in that process God shapes us into His same image. Lastly, it can also mean, "under the influence or domination of another." I want to be under the influence of Jesus Christ – God incarnate through His Holy Spirit – at every moment of my life as long as I live!

There's an interesting true story recorded in Acts 5:15, 16 that I think connects to all of this very well.

Verse 15… "so that they brought the sick out into the streets and laid them on beds and couches, that at least the shadow of Peter passing by might fall on some of them." Verse 16…."they were all healed."

The healing and the miraculous weren't in Peter's literal shadow, but it was in the shadow of who Peter walked with that touched everyone who came to him that day. Peter was "abiding under the Shadow of the Almighty." His shadow was an extension of the anointing power of God Himself that was on Peter's life. The power and presence of God followed Peter everywhere he went. Why? Because Peter knew how to "dwell in the secret place" of the Most High. God's power was present to do whatever was necessary, and Peter was the conduit for God to show Himself as God Almighty in the earth. Jesus' ministry, was being carried out through his obedient follower. Jesus ministry described in Isaiah 61, is meant to continue through his disciples today. This same power and presence of God can reside within His people, so that God can do these same things through us today, and show Himself as God Almighty, or in Hebrew: "El Shaddai".

This brings us to the last key word of Ps. 91:1. The word for God used here is "El Shaddai," which is also very significant. Translated as "All-Powerful" (Strongs #7706) – "shadday", it is a compound of the particle "sheh" (which or who) and "day" (sufficient). "Sheh-day" or "Shadday" is therefore: the all-sufficient God, eternally capable of being all that His people need. Other origins are to the verb "shadad" which means: "mighty or unconquerable", and also roots suggesting "mountain" indicating God's "greatness, strength and everlasting nature".

That is the God we serve: The All-Mighty, All-Powerful God who is unconquerable, capable of anything and everything! *"With God all things are possible" (Matt. 19:26).* This is who's shadow we can walk in and live in. He is everything that we need! Remember "El Elyon"? He has it all and He can give it all to the child of God who is in a covenant relationship with Him and "dwells in the secret place"; and who has made himself a "home "of the Living God. All that He is and all that He has can be poured out in and through your life! Let me put

19

this all together for you to see the truth of this verse a little more clearly.

Ps. 91:1 "He who dwells (lives all the time as in a marriage) in the secret place (the Holy of Holies where God lives) of the Most High; ("El Elyon": the possessor of Heaven and Earth: The God who owns it all) shall abide (constantly remain) under the shadow (God's umbrella, his coverings, and anointed presence) of the ALMIGHTY." ("El Shaddai": the all-sufficient God capable of being all that his people ever need).

If you live with God in a covenant relationship, He has it all and wants to give it all to you. Everything He is and everything He has is at your disposal. Every promise of God from Genesis to Revelation is a "Yes" and "Amen" for you. That's incredible but true. You can shout, "Hallelujah" if you want to here. Glory be to God!

You have to surrender everything you have and all that you are; all that you don't have and all that you are not; He wants it all! If you give Him everything – He'll give you everything that He has; and that's not a bad deal! It's as simple as that; but you have to live in the "secret place" to receive all that God has!

He wants your whole life. He will always try to get you to lay it all down. Some sadly will not; so they will never see the full benefits and blessings of God in their life. They will see some; but only to the degree that they give themselves over to God. Stop trying to hold onto your life and be in control. You'll be miserable as long as you do. Just let it all go and release it by faith into God's Hands. You'll be glad you did and you'll be blessed beyond measure.

The anointing presence and glory of God can abide with you wherever you go. It's invisible, but it casts a shadow to others and affects them in ways sometimes unknown to us. Peter's shadow – they hoped it would fall on them. Why is this in scripture? I believe there is a connection. It was the anointing power of Jesus being displayed through the power of His Holy Spirit in Peter's life.

There must be less of you to have more of God. Anointing flows out of your death! Remember the fire and the brazen altar. Altars are a place of death and a place of sacrifice. You must die to yourself to have the life of God within you. The stronger God is in you, the greater the influence and impact you will have on the world around you. **The greater the light, the longer the shadow.**

The more of God's light in you, the greater the impact on a lost and dying world. Conversely, there are no shadows on cloudy days. If you don't work on your relationship with God, there won't be much light shining out of your life, and limited influence and power to touch the lives of those around you. We all could honestly say that we need more of God in our lives--not less. We need the power and presence of God back in our lives and back in our churches once again! God, send the rain of your spirit. We need more of you – less of us. Pour in your "oil" and your "wine". We need to make room in our hearts for Him to pour in more of Himself through His precious Holy Spirit. He does not pour out His spirit indiscriminately; but only in a place where room has been made and He is invited to stay. It takes time. He needs to know that we will be responsible with what he gives us. (See. Parable of the Talents Matt: 25: 14 – 29)

Allow God to have His way in you. It doesn't all come at once, but rather through many "firings" and "fillings" (Eph. 5: 18). It's a process-- one that we must always be willing to go through. Most of us are too full of ourselves! We are always full of something. The question is: what are we full of?

New Wine Skins

I believe that God's work in us is progressive. He is always at work. For example, instead of saying, "He saved me.", that implies something in the past; something over and done with. It would be better to say, "God is saving me.", "Delivering me.", "Filling me.", "Anointing me'. This implies a work in progress. He is never truly done with us until we go home to be with the Lord. Man tends to think that he has arrived and that he knows all there is to know; but do we really know everything there is to know about a limitless God? Have we tapped out and exhausted the endless resources of God? Have we experienced all there is to God in our lifetime? The answer I must say is an empathic "NO"! In Ephesians 5:18, the bible says "*to be filled with the Spirit.*" It implies a repeated action, over, and over, and over, again. You don't just fill your car up with gas once and drive forever. It's the same here. We need to be filled continually with God's presence and spirit. Many today, rather, are running on empty and have exhausted all of their resources. With those progressive fillings, also comes progressive anointings that get stronger as we are faithful with what He gives to us.

That's the exciting part about our walk with God. It should always be fresh and exciting every day. There's always more to discover, more to fathom, more to experience. It should be the greatest adventure on which you ever embark.

"Nor do they put new wine into old wineskins, or else the wineskins break, the wine is spilled, and the wineskins are ruined. But they put new wine into new wineskins, and both are preserved" (Mat. 9:17) Wineskins are progressive too. You don't get just one and you're done. But, in fact, there are many renewals, and many transformations that await you. God will start with where you are and take you little by little to where He wants and needs you to be; but He needs your total cooperation. If you give everything to Him, He will work step-by-step to fill you with more of Himself. You can't handle it all at once, so be patient. The main thing is you're on the right road! Your life will never be the same again.

The one thing that remained in the "secret place" or the "Most Holy Place' was the "ark of the covenant." The ark was the most sacred of all the furniture in the tabernacle. It was overlaid with gold inside and out, and contained three things: the Ten Commandments, manna from heaven, and Aaron's rod that budded. The ark was the place of God's throne on earth. He lived between the cherubim and gave all His commands concerning Israel from here (Exodus 25: 20-22). It represented God's provision, power and mercy found in faithful obedience to His covenant.

The Philistines captured the ark because the Israelites failed to maintain their covenant relationship with God. Their enemy tried to steal it for their own purposes. They thought it was some secret power they could take and use for themselves. But it only backfired on them all. The ark brought great trouble to Israel's enemies and the Lord's hand was heavy upon them. Everywhere they moved it, for them, the ark only brought death, sickness, and pain. They couldn't get rid of it fast enough. After seven months they gave it back, but it still wasn't in its rightful place. It remained in a place called Kirath Jearim for 20 years, before King David brought the ark back into the capital city of Jerusalem. II Sam 6:14, 15 reads: *"David, wearing a linen ephod, dances before the Lord with all his might, while he and the entire house of Israel brought up the ark of the Lord with shouts and the sound of trumpets."* (NIV)   When you dwell in the "secret place" of the Most High and come into covenant with him, you can become an "ark" of the Living God that carries the power and presence of the Lord God Almighty. The "Ark of God" is returning to Jerusalem.

The power and presence of God is being restored to the body of Christ in our day. Satan is not afraid of us; but he is afraid of God in us. That's why he tries to keep us distracted and so busy that we don't have time to spend working on our relationship with GOD as we should -- no time to seek His face -- no time to pray or read His word. *"Man shall not live by bread alone, but by every word that precedes from the mouth of God." (Matt: 4:4)* Satan knows how to steal God's anointing power and presence away from His people, to keep us from the fullness of God and all that we should be.

Are you feeling powerless and defeated in your life today? Do you think, "There's got to be more. Is this all there is?" Are you not satisfied with life as you know it to be? I can tell you that there is definitely more to life and more to God than you would have ever dreamed possible.

The choice is yours. You decide. It's all up to you. Only you can stop the work of God in your own life. There's no one else to blame. We are without excuse. You can, and will go as far as you want to go in God. If you want to go to a higher place – you will go. I guarantee it! Just believe God and take Him at His word. Take a big step of faith and see what God will do for you, and don't give up. God is calling His people back into a covenant relationship with Him – to a place so close that they hear and obey His voice and fulfill their part of the contact-- a people who know who they are and know who God is!! God needs someone who will be a ladder from earth to heaven to bring down His mighty answers to prevailing prayer. So, what is true in the heavens can become true in the earth! Who will be a ladder from earth to heaven? Who will pay the price? Who will say, "Yes, Lord, Yes. Here I am. Send me."

If you are willing, come with me to a higher place in God, and we will fly higher where the eagles are afraid to fly?
Habakkuk 2:2, 3

"Write the vision and make it plain on tablets that he may run who reads it," for *the vision is yet for an appointed time;* *"But at the end it will speak, and it will not lie. Though it tarries, wait for it,"* *"Because it will surely come, it will not tarry."*

Prayer

Lord God, I pray for all who may embark on this journey. I pray they will leave and let go of everything to follow you and receive your best for them. Give them the strength and courage they will need to sustain them along the way. I pray they can be brutally honest with you and with themselves. May they have a hunger and a thirst for you, God, like never before. May they "wrestle" with you all night long, undaunted, unwavering, never letting go until they receive your "full" blessing. May they go through the "fire" and come out as "pure gold." May they be open to all you have for them…In Jesus Name – Amen!

The Prophetic Voice Today

"I have spoken in ages past through a voice – and that voice has been in the earth. I have hand selected men and women throughout the ages to speak 'thus saith the Lord' in the earth. You may know some of them, and some of their names you may recognize with the likes of Moses, Samuel, and Nathan. Even King David was a prophetic voice in the earth; along with Elijah, Elisha, Isaiah, Jeremiah, Ezekiel, Daniel, and all the Minor Prophets that are recorded in the Word of God. But few will realize and recognize that even after the cross; I still have my prophetic voice in the earth today!"

"The days of my Prophets have not stopped. They have not been discontinued at the cross. *'He gave some to be apostles, some to be prophets, some to be evangelists, some to be pastors and teachers.'* That is a New Testament word. It is still meant for today in your lifetime; in the year 2008."

"One of these prophetic voices in the earth today is my servant by the name of David Lebo. And the book that you are about to read has been given as a prophetic revelation to this servant to give to the rest of the world."

"What follows, as you read this book, it is 'thus saith the Lord', for my church and my bride in this day and in this hour."

"I the Lord God – I am the Bread and the Wine: that is my Word and my Spirit. They will always be in agreement to one another. There is my written word which is found in the 'Word of God' -- otherwise known as the Holy Bible; and there is my 'Rhema' word which is the spoken word of God through the Spirit of the Lord that is given to my Holy Servants – my Prophets – in the earth today."

"As you endeavor to read your way through the pages of this book, keep an open mind and an open heart to receive the fresh word of God into your life today. It is fresh food for your soul. It is fresh drink for your thirst. To Him who is thirsty, let him come and drink from the waters of life. To Him who is hungry, come; let him eat from the table of the King."

"This book is a table that is set before you that has been prepared by the King himself. This banquet – this buffet – this feast – has been prepared fresh, just for you, straight from the King's kitchen. It's always hot… it's always fresh… it's always steaming…specifically for you – My Bride – in this day and in this hour. Come and take your seat at the King's table and enjoy this spread of food that is prepared just for you.

"The Spirit of the Prophets are subject to the Prophets.' (I Cor. 14:32) My Holy Spirit testifies of Jesus. *The testimony of Jesus is the Spirit of Prophesy.'* (Rev 19:10) The Holy Spirit will speak and testify and exalt the name of Jesus."

"My Holy Spirit will speak to glorify Him and His name. My Holy Spirit will speak and testify of the same truth throughout the world. Though the person may differ, though the country may differ, and the location may differ – the content stays the same. My Holy Spirit will speak the truth and only the truth, and nothing but the truth."

"In the pages to follow, you will read the Holy Spirit testifying of the truth which will be confirmed in the written word of God time and time again."

"The truth of God is unfolding. It is a progressive revelation. Man does not know all there is to know about God. It is the Holy Spirit and Him alone that can lead you and guide you into all truth. He is the only way – for it is all spiritually discerned. *It's not by might, nor by power; but by my Spirit',* says the Lord." (Zach. 4:6).

Man needs to stop trying to figure God out all on his own, through his understanding, his knowledge, and his wisdom; and needs to begin to trust, once again, the Holy Spirit for His knowledge, His understanding, God's wisdom, and God's revelation. This book will only make sense to you as you pray and you ask the Holy Spirit to do a work in your own heart and in your own life. Without Him, this book will make no sense to you whatsoever. So, I invite you to pray this prayer with me as you continue this journey reading the pages of this book.

"Our Father who art in heaven
Hallowed be thy name
Your kingdom come
Your will be done
On earth as it is in heaven
Give us this day our daily bread
And forgive us our debts,
As we forgive our debtors.
And do not lead us into temptation.
But deliver us from the evil one.
For yours is the kingdom and the power and
the glory forever
Amen." (Mat.6:9-13)

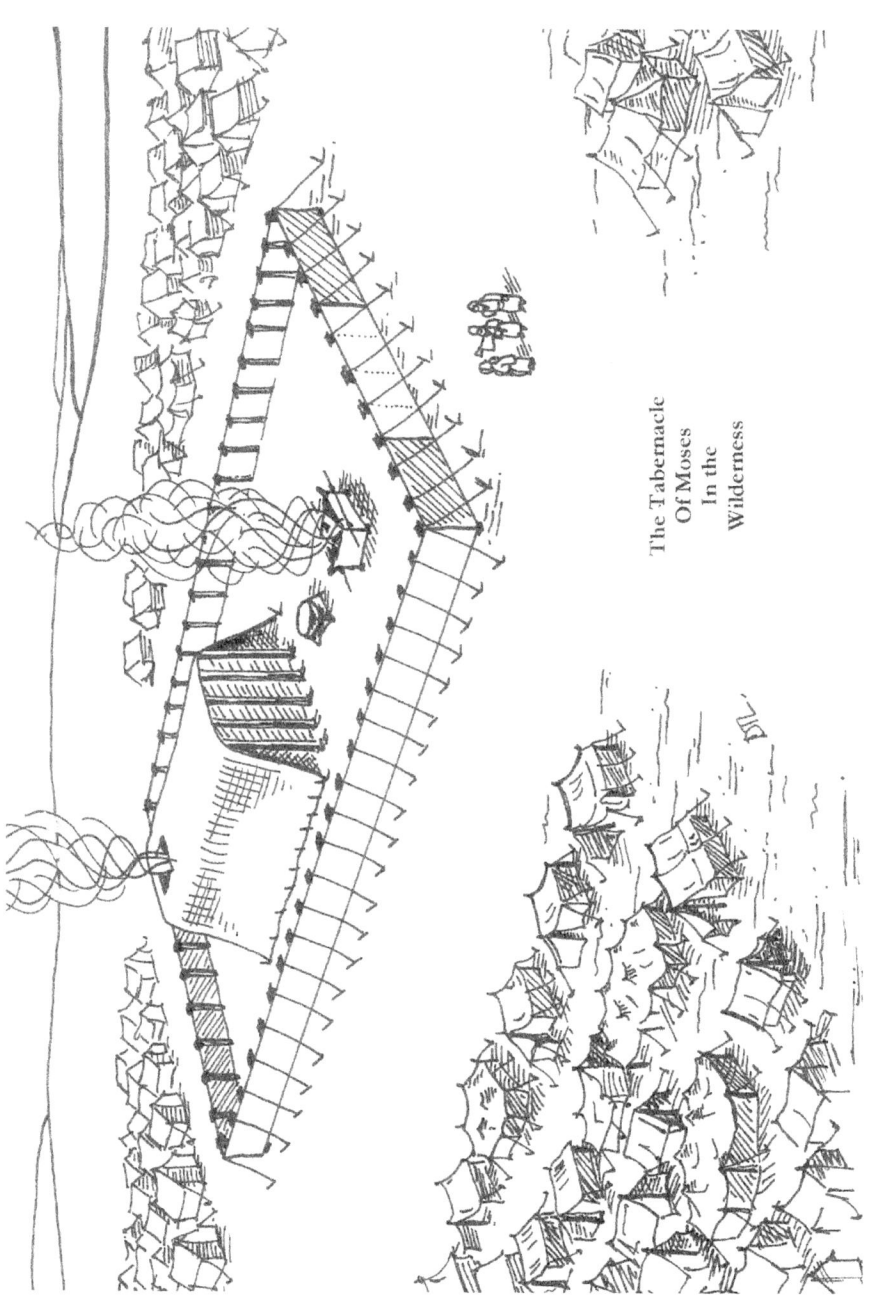

The Tabernacle
Of Moses
In the
Wilderness

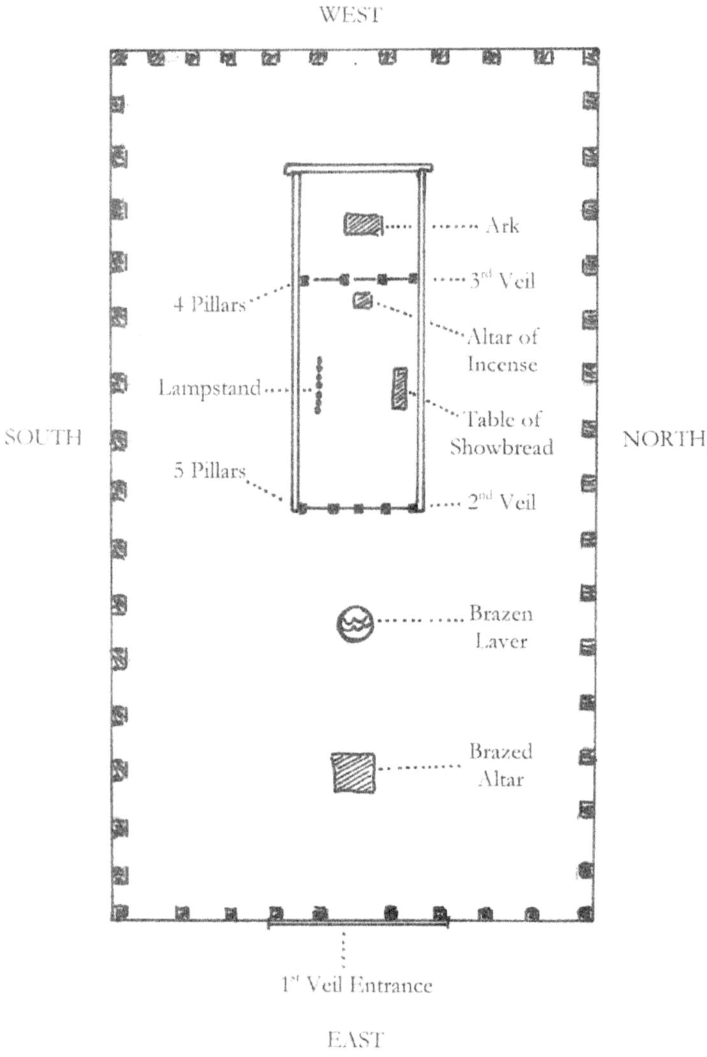

WEST

Ark

3rd Veil

4 Pillars

Altar of
Incense

Lampstand

Table of
Showbread

SOUTH
NORTH

5 Pillars

2nd Veil

Brazen
Laver

Brazed
Altar

1st Veil Entrance

EAST

Tabernacle Layout

Chapter One

It All Begins With Love

"…for God so loved the world…" Jn.3:16

The First Wave

The first wave of God's presence that came and filled the meeting room was a wave of His love. God literally filled the room with His presence. We could hardly stand up in it. We were overwhelmed by it, as if we were submerged in it – surrounded and saturated to the very cores of our being. I could literally feel God's presence and love all around me and through me; like nothing I had ever experienced before-- as if time had stopped. Every care ceased to exist, and the only thing I knew was God's love. It lasted for many hours and no one wanted to leave.

It is fitting that this journey begins with an outpouring of this love, for that is who God is. (I Jn. 4:8) He is also the Alpha and Omega – the beginning and the end of everything. So too, He is the beginning of this book. It all begins with God!

If you had to describe God with just one word, the best choice may be the word "love." This kind of heaven sent love is not of this world. It is supernatural in essence and scope. This love transcends anything and everything that we know of in this earth. It is perhaps the most powerful force on the planet.

God's love is absolutely perfect in every way. It is unconditional with no strings attached. It is never ending – the supply is limitless. It is always unfailing. It will always be there for the child of God and won't let you down. Also, God's love for us is unchanging. You can always count on it to be the same, day in and day out. This love is also sacrificial; giving up everything for the best interest of the beloved.

John 3:16 says "God so loved the world that He gave his one and only son, that whosoever believes in him shall not perish but have everlasting life."

God sacrificed His only son out of His love for the world. That's love! If we are all honest, we would all say we desperately need more of this kind of love in our lives and in our world today. There's only one place to get it. This love falls from heaven down out of the throne of God like the rains fall from the sky.

The Rain Experience

If we want more of this heaven sent love in our lives, we as God's children need to allow the rains of heaven to fall on us like never before. Over and over in scripture, rain and water are used as metaphors for God's Holy Spirit. God has often times tried to send the rain of His Spirit upon us in our churches and in our lives; but we put up our "umbrellas" and put on our "raincoats", so we don't get wet, or we quickly run for cover. When God sends rain, we must stay out in the "rain" until we are saturated with His spirit and presence to the very cores of our beings; and we can't leave until we are spiritually "soaked to the bone" with His Spirit. Every part of us must be saturated with God Himself.

So, stay out in the "rain." Throw your spiritual "umbrellas" and "raincoats" away. Don't run for cover at the first sign of rain. This is our natural tendency. Don't be in a hurry. When God sends His rain, it is very precious. You'll want to stay as long as you can. There's no where else to go that would be better then this, so you might as well be prepared to stay for a while. You'll need to stay longer than 10- 15 minutes. It may last hours! Throw your watch away too. This is the highest priority you'll ever have this side of heaven.

When you're caught up in God's presence, 5 hours will seem like 5 minutes. His time is different than ours... *"One day is as a 1,000 years"*. *(II Pet. 3:8)*

When God tries to make it rain spiritually in our churches and in our lives, we tend to run for cover. It is in our nature. The things of the flesh are in direct opposition to the things of the Spirit. We tend to reject what God wants to bless us with instead of opening our hearts and minds and receiving all that He has for us. Your flesh will be in a hurry to get to the next great priority in your busy schedules. Your flesh will say, "I don't have the time today"; or "It's a waste of time altogether." It wants to be busy "doing" rather than "soaking."

When you are in the middle of a drought, RAIN is the highest priority! It needs to be our high priority once again. When God sends his precious rain, we need to get "soaked to the bone" with His Holy Spirit. We must receive and allow God's presence to touch our lives and let God be God. Make being with Him the greatest priority that we can have, and have only a "yes" concerning everything our God has for us. We need to let God be God in our hearts and in our churches every day and every week of our lives.

The Flood

God promised that He would not flood the earth again physically in the days of Noah; but he didn't promise that He would not do it spiritually. In fact, that is exactly His plan. He is going to wipe out the wickedness in this world another way. Through the "rain" of His Spirit!

Zach. 4:6 says, "Not by might nor by power but by my spirit, says the Lord."
Hosea 6:3 says..."He will come to us like the rain, like the latter and former rain to the earth.

Isaiah 44:3 says, "For I will pour water on Him who is thirsty, and floods on the dry ground; I will pour my Spirit on your descendants."

God is in the process of flooding the earth again, but this time it's with His Holy Spirit in and through Jesus' descendants. That's us! If you are a believer and accepted Jesus as your savior and have given him your life, you are a son or daughter of the Most High God.

In the story of Noah, Gen. 7:11, there is a most powerful verse... *"On that day all the fountains of the great deep were broken up and the windowss of heaven were opened."* **Today God is breaking open the "fountains of the deep" within His people!** There are vast **"reservoirs"** of His spirit that lie deep within each and every child of God that has never been "tapped" into before. Many don't ever realize they are there. God is going to try to break them open within you and within the body of Christ worldwide. *John 7:38 says, "Out of His heart shall flow rivers of Living water."* His Spirit will flood the earth again! It's beginning to rain!! Can you hear the sounds of thunder?

As we journey through the chapters of this book, keep this "rain experience" at the forefront of your thinking and allow the Holy Spirit to saturate you with His presence and with the truth of His word. "Be soaked to the bone" with His presence!

Before the creation of the world, God has demonstrated who He is through love. He formed the earth and spoke all of creation into existence on each and every day out of His great love. Day one-- out of His love; day 2-- out of His love; day 3, day 4, day 5, and then, on the 6th day, God spoke and created man from the dust of the earth, out of His love. That's why He created the world, because of His heart of love. And God finished it all on the sixth day; but it was not good until he created man. Gen. 1:31 says, *"Then God saw everything that he had made and indeed it was very good."*

It was out of the heart of God for the creation of the world, and for man and woman to create a beautiful place for them to live. It is out of God's love that He formed them and created them – Adam and Eve. It was out of the love of God that he wanted to have a relationship with them. He wanted to talk with them and care for them, protect them, provide for them, heal them, and meet all of their needs. This is the Father's heart for His children. Just as we, in the natural, want to be good parents to our children; so it is with God for His. *"God is love."* (I Jn. 4:8). All that God has done, in every day since that day – all the days of creation – God has expressed his love for His people. In all that He does, everything is motivated by his love for His children.

God's revelation to Moses in the burning bush was that he was and still is the "I am that I am." God was saying that He would be everything to him. "I will be all that you need. I will be your provision, your protection, your guidance, a lamp to your feet and a light unto your path. I will be your everything."

Sounds like "abiding under the shadow." Doesn't it? The heart of God is for His people. Throughout history, God tried to train them in the wilderness to teach them about who He was and how they could walk with Him in a covenant relationship. All the while He had a special place set aside for them – the children of Israel – a promised land flowing with milk and honey. A land not their own. A land they did not plant nor build; but a place they could love God in return, and that God could love them and show His love to the rest of the world. He wanted to show who He was through His people, that He was a loving God who hated wickedness and despised evil, but loved righteousness, goodness and justness. He wanted people to show good to one another and to love one another throughout the world.

God tried to reveal Himself to them in those days – to set aside that land flowing with milk and honey – a land flowing with all that they needed. They needed only to walk in obedience to His law and

33

His word-- what He had instructed them to do, which was also in their best interest.

In their flesh, they could not walk in those ways. They did not listen to the voice of the Lord their God. They hardened their hearts against God. So, even in His love – He had to chastise them, discipline them, and correct them. God even had to bring, at times, his judgments upon them – all out of His love. So, they were brought into captivity into a foreign land – Babylon.

That was not God's design for them. That was not His perfect plan for them. But in this relationship that He had with them, He didn't create them to be robots, but he created them with a free will and with a heart of their own. God wanted them to love Him for who He is by choice, just as a husband loves his wife and a wife her husband. But God's call went out to them nonetheless: "Choose this day whom you will serve." God wanted them to decide which way they would go and who they would love.

So, they set aside God and went after other lovers – other gods-- and they worshipped the gods of the Canaanites, the Hittites, the Perizzites, and the Amorites – all of these other gods. They went after them. They played the harlot. They had many other lovers, all the while, breaking God's heart.

The Heart of God was broken for them in those days. So God brought about some pretty harsh judgments and sent his messengers – His prophets – to deliver sometimes very harsh words from God himself. Jeremiah's heart wept and cried over the children of Israel because the heart of God was broken. Jeremiah had the heart of God. God's heart was crushed because His people had turned their backs on Him.

God longed for them to come back to Him into His covenant relationship and would send through His prophets – throughout the Old Testament – messages that echoed: "Return unto Me, Return unto Me," says the Lord. That was the cry of God's heart in those days.

So in the days that were appointed before the foundations of the earth, God sent a baby to the little town of Bethlehem; out of His love for the world. God did not send a conquering King, but sent a baby instead. What greater expression of love could He have sent, than to send a baby to a manger? Babies are nothing but love. They are all little bundles of love-- a full expression of the heart of God.

He could have sent a conquering King, a full grown adult, and just be translated into this world; but God did not choose to do it that way. To show His love for this world, He sent a baby who would be cuddled by his mother. And even through a mother caring for her newborn baby, God expresses his love to the world. A more feminine side of God- His love, his heart, His tenderness, His mercies – all of these things are expressed through motherhood. All of these things are pictured in that little stable in Bethlehem. What a great picture of the love and heart of God.

"For God so loved the world that he gave His only begotten son, that whoever believes in Him should not perish, but have everlasting life." (Jn. 3:16)

And so God sent His son to pay the ultimate price – his one and only – to die for a people who rejected Him and who blasphemed His name, who lifted up their hearts at other alters and their high places and their Asherah poles. They worshipped at the altars of Baal. God sent His son for a people such as this, who did not deserve the love of God He had to offer. They did not deserve anything from God.

The only thing they deserved was to be wiped out from the face of the earth. And He almost did many times – to just start over. He pleaded with Moses, "Let me just wipe them all out and I'll start over with you." Moses interceded for them that day, and it was only through him that God did not do so. For they did not deserve the things God would put before them.

They did not deserve the blessings of heaven. They only deserved the punishment of Hell itself. They deserved their punishments and their captivity. They deserved what they received and more; but it was through the love of God that God wanted to bring them back.

So God sent His son Jesus Christ to die on a cross. *"For God so loved the world…"* *(John 3:16)* God gave His one and only. He gave his best in Heaven. He could have done it some other way. He could have sent a legion of Angels, but God had to send His son. And Jesus being just as the Father he said, "As you have seen me you have seen the Father." (Jn. 14:9) Jesus was God incarnate. God came down to this earth and sacrificed Himself on a cross at Calvary. *"In that while we were yet sinners Christ died for us."* (Rom. 5:8). *"He was despised, and we did*

35

not esteem Him." (Is.53:3) He paid the ultimate price. God so loved the world…and it is through His sacrifice that the entire world can be grafted in.

God chose one nation, Israel, to show who He was to a lost and dying world. And as they rejected God so He sent his son. Now the entire world can be grafted in to the family of God through faith in His son Jesus. This is God's heart for the world: that every nation, every tribe, every tongue, all people, from all over the face of the earth would be grafted into the family of God. So they can be called sons and daughters of the Most High God and be partakers of the full blessings of all of God's promises from Genesis to Revelation. The Holy Bible is an entire love revelation. It is God's love book to the world. And this is the love chapter of this book to reveal the heart of God for his people. This chapter is perhaps the greatest of them all; for everything else hinges upon this important truth.

"For God so loved the world…" (Jn. 3:16) is the basis for everything that God does. For it is through love that God gives everything to His children. And He can be the "I am that I am" for the whole wide world.

And if they come into a covenant relationship and abide in the "secret place" of the Most High God – when they do – then they are "abiding under the true shadow of the Almighty". They are coming in under the greatest "umbrella", the greatest "coverings" – all that God is and all that He can give them. They come under that and it's an "open heaven" for them. So, God can shower down His love. He can shower down His blessings. God says, "I can give them all that 'I AM.'"

God can give eternal life, salvation, deliverance, healing, blessings, and restorations to their families and to their futures. God will reverse the curse from Adam in their lives. God will be a lamp to their feet and a light to their paths. He can bring life and life more abundantly, life forevermore, unspeakable joy and full of glory. He can give new songs to sing – songs of praise in their hearts unto their God. He can deliver them out of the bondages of sin and death.

God can and will do all of these things and more. He is the "I AM that I am". The world can know God as the God that can do all things. *All things are possible with God." (Mk. 10:27)* That is the love of God for the world. That is His heart for the nations – for every tribe, every tongue, every nation, all peoples on the face of the earth – not just one nation, but all nations!!!

You must have the heart of God, and you must have and receive the love of God into your mind and spirit, and get the revelation of who He IS. So that you, too, can be beacons of light and share His love with the rest of the world. God can act sovereignly on His own, by Himself; but he chooses to carry out His plans through His people.

You must have the love of God in you and operating through you. You must have the heart of God and his love flowing as a "RIVER" in abundance. That is how God expresses His love to the world. It is through His people. There is no other way. This is how God shows all that He is-- it is through His people! If you know Jesus as your "Lord" and "Savior", then you are God's representative in the earth. You are as Jesus himself showing up in a place. God says, "Where you go – I go", and "Where you are – I am." You show Jesus to a lost and dying world. We are to be made into the image of Christ himself. *"He who dwells in the secret place of the Most High, shall abide under the shadow of the Almighty." (Ps 91:1)*

Practice doing this now from this day on, all the days of your life until God calls you home. This is something to be experienced. It won't be just words coming down out of heaven. God will put it into action. You do your part and God will do His. I guarantee it!

God has always been a very active God in his dealings with His people. He didn't just sit aside passively watching the world go around. He engaged His people. He poured out His spirit upon them and sent his blessings time and time again. So too, this book will not be just words; but you will experience it for yourself. You will live in it, and it will be active-- not passive. *"The Kingdom of God suffers violence, and the violent take it by force." (Matt. 11:12)* That is very active. *"And the gates of hell shall not stand again it." (Matt. 16:18)* That is about as active as you can get. If you come with me to a higher place, you will go and literally kick in the gates of Hell with the power of God. That's active! And you will know the truth of this verse. *Greater is he that is in you than He that is in the world!* That's the power of God.

The very foundations of hell itself will tremble for the truth that is written in this book. The world needs to hear this message! God said to me, "I am restoring my power back into the body of

Christ, where it belongs." This is what God is doing in the earth today.

Revival is coming to the world. Revival is coming! What God has begun in you, He will finish. He is your Alpha and Omega-- the beginning and the end of your faith. But all that God does in you is determined by your permission-- you're yielding to His word and His spirit and your obedience to His voice every day.

On the day God calls you home you will say as Jesus said, "It is finished." Will all that God had asked you to do have been accomplished? Will God's purposes have been done in you and through you? Will you have kept your hands to the plow and your eyes on Jesus? Will you be able to say, "I have run the race. I have fought the good fight"... with no regrets, no remorse, no looking back. Can you say in that day, "It is finished"?

You can walk in your destiny. You can "walk by my spirit", says the Lord. You can know what God's plan and His will is for your life. You don't have to stumble around for 40 years in the wilderness to find out. He will be a *"light to your path". (Ps. 119:105)* It's all in the relationship! *"Draw near to God and He will draw near to you."* Dwell in the "secret place", and you will have all the rest!

To Know This Love

"That Christ may dwell in your hearts through faith; that you, being rooted and grounded in love, my be able to comprehend with well the saints what is the width and length and depth and height – to know the love of Christ which passes knowledge; that you may be filled with all the fullness of God." Ephesians 3: 17-19

For who can know the love of God? Who can know it? Who can discern it? Who can even begin to understand it? It is not of this world. It is like nothing we have ever experienced before in the natural realm.

This love is of supernatural origin. It is a heaven sent love. Unless you know Jesus as your savior, you have never, ever, tasted of this type of love before. But, if you know Jesus as your savior, you have tasted only a taste of what this love is all about. But that is only a taste. There is so much more to know the depth, the height, the width, the length, and the expanse of this kind of love.

The author of Ephesians is speaking of the expanse of the love of God. Who can know its depths and its heights, its widths, its lengths? The author is admonishing us to go deeper in God. There is more to it than meets the eye. He is writing to the Christians at Ephesus-- Christians who have already tasted of the love of God.

"I am calling My church to the heights and the depths – to come out into the depths of My love," says the Lord. "Come out into the depths…into the deep."

God is calling all of us to come into the "deep" to experience the depths of his love; not just to know it in your mind, but to experience it in your heart!

"My people who have been called by my name…I have called you to worship me in spirit and in truth…to know me in your minds and also in your hearts in a perfect 50/50 balance, perfect balance. You'll not get out of balance, whatsoever. You'll have no fear to get out of balance, because you'll know me in spirit and in truth. You'll know the truth of my word in your mind and many know that dimension. So you can say, 'I know that God loves me. I know that in word.' But how many know that God loves them in their hearts? How many know the depths of the love of God? Are you rooted and grounded in the depths of my love?" says the Lord.

Church of the living God: Are you rooted and grounded in the depths of God's love? You see, because in that verse it is directly tied into the fullness – the fullness of the living God – to be filled…to be filled…with all the fullness of God. Are you filled with all the fullness of God today? Can you honestly ask yourself that question and say, "Yes I AM."? Are you filled? Are you filled? Are you filled today with the love of God? Do you understand the depths of His love?

If you can honestly answer that question, and if you say, "No, I don't understand it.", then come with me. Come with me! We will go to where no man has gone before. I will take you to the depths of the love of God. I will take you to the depths of His Spirit. You can know beyond the shadow of a doubt, and you can possess in your heart ----one hundred percent-- and truly know the heights, and depths, and widths, and lengths of the love of God.

It is not a question that cannot be answered; and it is not a question that can not be experienced. God wants His people to have experiences with Him! Time and time again, to come into His presence and experience the love of God and all that He is. Because, He is the ... "I am, that I am, that I am!!"

I will write on this subject just for a moment. There are many today that want to speak against experiences – experiential moments with God. God's word unto you this day is: "Be Silent! Church of the living God, if you want to be speaking against experiences – Silence!" God says, "Silence! No longer will you speak against experiences... Be silent... and in human terms... shut up ... close your mouths. I don't want to hear another word about it!" That is the heart of God.

"I want my people to experience the fullness of the living God, in all My attributes, in all that I AM." An experience with God... those in the bible that had an experience with God – they never turned back. They were changed-- transformed. They were renewed. They were not the same. They never fell away. The ones that truly had a heart experience with the Living God went on and continued their walk of faith. They shut the mouths of lions. They caused the walls of Jericho to fall down. They caused miracle after miracle after miracle. Why?

It's all recorded in the 11th Chapter of Hebrews – the FAITH chapter. All of those people "experienced" the living God. "And I want My people to 'experience' all that 'I AM.'"

"Church of the living God: What are you afraid of? What are you afraid of-- to experience the fullness of God? Are you afraid of Me? Are you afraid? Why are you afraid? I, the lord God, will tell you why."

"Adam was afraid of Me and he hid in the garden. Why? Because He had sinned against Me. I charge you this day – Church of the living God – you are afraid of me; because, you have sinned against the MOST HIGH GOD! You have sinned against Me. There is sin in your life. There is sin in your heart and you want to walk around as if there isn't. You want to walk around in your high places; looking good, smelling good, and sounding good. And in your life, you still have rotten apples in your root cellars. And you need to throw them out and get sin out of your life. Get it out! Get it out! Get it out!"

"I don't care who you are. I don't care if you are the Pastor of a 100,000 member church. This word is for you too. I don't care if you are the president of the United States of America and hold a high position in man's eyes. This word still applies to you!"

"GET IT OUT! Get the sin out of your life and listen to ME. Listen to Me. Listen to Me. It is the cries of My heart. Listen to Me and be full of My SPIRIT," says the Lord.

"Be full of the love of God. Be filled, be filled, and be filled. And if you will do that – you'll not be afraid of Me. You'll not be afraid of experiences."

"You'll not be afraid of what I will do in a church service. You'll not be afraid that I will mess it up. If you let Me be Me, if you let God be God and give me the freedom to be who "I AM", you'll not have to worry about Me messing up your pretty little services. You'll not be afraid."

"Come out into the depths of my love and My spirit," says the Lord God Almighty. "Get the sin out of your life and you'll not be afraid to come out into the depths. You'll not be afraid to let Me show up in your churches and be afraid of what I will do."

"Yes, there may have been abuses in your past....people out of balance…but if you have the spirit of the living God lining up with the truth of God in 50/50 balance…it's a perfect balance!"

"I even hold the very world from flying off its course. I have the world spinning in perfect balance on an axis from the North Pole to the south. If it varies too much in any direction, 2 to 3 degrees, the earth will not be as it is now. Scientists will say if it varies too much one way or the other the earth itself would be dramatically changed as we know it. If it got too close to the sun, just a little, it would be too hot and everything would dry up. If it was too far away everything would freeze."

"I, the lord God, who holds the universe in perfect balance, will you not give me your church services? It is a small responsibility for the MOST HIGH GOD to be in charge of. If I can order the universe and keep it in perfect balance, do you not want to entrust Me with having your services in perfect balance? Do you not think that the Most HIGH GOD can order a simple service that may last a few hours long on any given day?"

"I can order the universe from the beginning of time to the end of time. Can you give me but a few hours? Can you give me but a few moments of your time and release it unto me?", says the Lord. "It's not yours anyway! It's not yours anyway!!! It is time. It is time. Church of the living God: release all of your time unto me", says the Lord, "all of your time, 24 hours a day, 7 days a week, 365 day a year.

I want all of your time. I even want the time in your Church services. I am asking you-- Church of the living God – to release it unto me. Now, in Jesus name. And all who read this book, that admonishment goes out to you; and you will be accountable for this word. This is the word of the Living God to my church throughout the world. Release it unto me!"

"Get the sin out of your life and you won't be afraid anymore; because, perfect love casts out all fear. You're full of fear… fear of man… what they will say…what they will do… 'O my God…They may stop giving…'"

"It's time to get the sin out and you won't be afraid anymore. So, the first thing you need to do is repent. Repent! Repent, for the kingdom of God is at hand. Repent first. Get sin out and get love in! Get the love of God in!" says the Lord.

"Be filled with the love of God… filled with all the fullness of God. You'll be rooted and grounded in that love, so much so, you'll be unshakeable, immovable, and you'll be rock solid in who you are."
"You'll be rock solid in your faith. You'll have no fear of man. You'll not be afraid of the terror of night nor the arrow that flies by day. You'll not be scared of fear itself. You'll not fear "FEAR" itself."

"Church of the living God: Dwell in the secret place and you'll not be afraid of the terror of night. You'll not be afraid, period. You'll not be afraid of what man can do to you. But you'll fear God. Fear God who holds your very soul and your very life in the psalms of His hands. He is the one that can take your life at any moment. He is the one you are to fear. Fear God, Fear God, Fear God!"

"The days of fearing man are over. An admonishment to pastors and leaders all over this world: Do Not Fear Man! Fear God! Fear God! Fear God! The days of fearing man are over. Be filled to all the fullness of God! Be filled to all the fullness – to its highest degree!" If that is your hearts cry and you want God – to your highest calling – to your highest potential in God this side of Heaven…Do you? Do you?

If you say, "Yes" to that question, then read on!! If you do not and say "No" to that question, then close this book and give it to someone else who will say "Yes"!!!

So you see, church, it is crucial; it is critical that you be filled to all the fullness of God. You must get this first. You must! You must! You must get this first, before you can continue on-- before you can get anything else. And if you think, "Yea, I've already got that"... "Yea, let's move on"...check again. You've got to go back. You have to be filled to all the fullness of God to all the depths of God.

Who can know it? Who can experience it? Unless you have been to the "bottom of the sea", unless you have been down to the bottom of the "ocean", to the "rock bottom" place...only "he" can know the depths of the love of God. Only "he" can know the depths of this love. So, unless you've gone there spiritually, you have only a taste of the depths of the love of God.

God is calling the church of the living God to come out, come out, come out into the depths! And to come down, come down, come down, into the depths of the living God!

Do you want to go higher in God? You want to know God? You want to experience Him? You want to go higher, higher, and higher? The way up is down! The way up is down! You have to come down to the depths—spiritually-- to the lowest place in this world. The lowest place you can go is at the "bottom of the sea"!

This is God's call to you: Come down! Come Down! Come down into the depths of the living God. This is God's call to His one and only church in this day and in this hour. And if you will say, "Yes, Lord, Yes. I will come. I will walk on the water", you'll go to the depths!

Do you remember the day when Peter asked the Lord if he could come out of the boat and walk on the water too? That was in Peter's mind. That was something Peter thought he could do. It was not in the mind of God. But Jesus, being who He was, said, "Ok... I'll give you the opportunity. If you want to be like me and walk on water, come out. Come out. Get out of the boat. Come. Walk on water. Come see if you can do it."

But it was in the mind of God, not to let Peter walk on water that day. Because Peter tried to do it in his own strength and all within his own self, in his own mind, understanding and knowledge. It was all in the flesh! You can't walk on water in the flesh!

So, what happened? Peter began to sink. He began to go down into the depths. Before you can walk on water, you have to go down into the depths of God. You have to go down to the "bottom of the sea." And then afterwards, when you come back up; then, you can walk on water! Then you'll walk on water. Then you'll do the miraculous. Then and only then, will you be formed and shaped into the image of God's son, Jesus Christ.

Then you will be like Jesus, Himself. Then, when He calls you out, you'll walk on water, because you'll have gone to the depths. You'll have known; what is the height? What is the depth? What is the width and length of the Love of God? Because it is directly connected to you being filled, let me say that again… It is directly connected to you being filled with all the fullness of God! God says, "This is my word unto you – Church of the living God: Receive it and live. Reject it and die. There is a revival coming – a last days revival to the entire globe. This is it! And the battle cry of this revival is: Choose this day whom you will serve! CHOOSE THIS DAY WHOM YOU WILL SERVE!"

"If you remember the book of Deuteronomy, I asked the children of Israel the same thing. If you follow me and walk after my ways, and harken unto my voice and you listen to me, you will be blessed. But if you don't – you'll be under the curse. You will be under death. It is that serious church. Choose this day whom you will serve! If you serve God – it is life. If you serve yourself – it is death."

Life and death hang in the balance. Choose this day whom you will serve. If you choose life, read on. If you do not, please give this book to someone else who will!

Changing Your Thought Life

Changing your thought life is one of the most important things you'll ever do in your life. All of your old thoughts from every source must be changed and transformed… everything that you once were… all that you used to think about. Everything! Nothing escapes what I am about to tell you. All of your old thinking has to be changed and transformed. In Romans 12: 1-2, it is written…

"I beseech you therefore, brethren by the mercies of God, that you present your bodies a living sacrifice, holy, acceptable to God, which is your reasonable service. And do not be conformed to this world, but be transformed by the renewing of your mind, that you may prove what is that good and acceptable and prefect will of God."

Transformed? How? ... By the renewing of your mind. Much of your transformation will come from the renewing of your mind. So, that you may know what is that good and acceptable and perfect will of God.

Sometimes, people don't know what the will of God is for their life. Why? Romans 12: 1-2 give us a few great keys as to why? They have not offered up themselves as a living sacrifice, number one. Secondly, they have not allowed their minds to be transformed and changed. The word "repent" in the Greek is "metanoeo". It literally means: to change the way you think. You see a great part of repentance-- it is a heart change yes-- but it is the heart and mind together.

Man is a three part being: spirit, soul, and body. He is all of these things combined. He must be changed in his spirit. He also needs to be changed in his soul realm, his emotions, his thoughts; all of his carnal nature – all of it – must be changed. That is the work of God.

When you asked God into your life as Lord and Savior He came in to do a work. And when you asked God into your life that day, you didn't ask Him in to do just a partial work, a partial cleansing, or a partial transformation – Did you? When you open up the doors of your heart and you let the king of Glory come in, He comes in to be God! (See. Ps. 24)

And part of that process is changing the way you think. You are a co-laborer in the work of God in your own life and this is part of that process. You must throw out all of your old thinking. Even at times, old teachings about the word of God. Some old teachings are old manna that has been passed around for generations. Some of it isn't good. Looks good, smells good, sounds good, tastes good; but it's not good. You need to throw it out. Get rid of it! Your mind needs to be completely transformed and changed. How?

A great part of that comes from a daily diet of eating from the words of God.

"Man shall not live by bread alone, but by every word that proceeds out of the mouth of God." (Luke 4:4) Jesus instructed them to pray in this way: *"Our Father who art in heaven, Hollowed by thy name. Thy Kingdom come. Thy will be done on Earth as it is in Heaven. Give us this day our daily bread. And forgive us our debts, As we forgive out debtors. And do not lead us into*

45

temptation, But deliver us from the evil one. For yours is the Kingdom and the power and the glory forever. Amen." (Mat. 6: 9- 13)

Your daily bread is not only what you eat in the natural for your physical body, but what you eat for your spirit man as well. Many of God's people have a very poor spiritual diet that consists of a lot of junk food that doesn't take that long to prepare. It's spiritual fast food. They are on a diet of fast food. It's quick, it's easy, it's convenient; but it doesn't have a whole lot of substance to it. It doesn't have a whole lot of nutritional value to it.

"Church of the living God: where are you eating at most of the time? Is it just at a lot of fast food restaurants? That's just a lot of quick word, or is it from a gourmet buffet that takes hours to prepare? That would be like eating from the King's table-- the King of all kings and the Lord of lords. He is the greatest chef in the entire world – the entire universe." *"He has prepared a table before you even in the presence of your enemies." (See. Ps. 23:5)*

"And so you have an invitation to dine at this table. But for the most part, church of the living God, you have not accepted this invitation. You have not accepted this invitation to come and eat from My table, seated at the right hand of God, as a king, small "k", to eat at the KING's table. You have rejected the invitation, time and time again. You're too busy. Your life is filled with so many other things. You don't have the time to come and eat a good meal; to come and take a few hours and eat from my word," says the Lord.

"It will be nourishment to your bones and health to your life." (Pro. 3:8)

"The invitation is still there for you out of the heart of God. I'm calling out to you today: Church of the living God, come and sit at My table and hear of My word," says the Lord. "Eat of all the goodness of the Lord that I have for you."

From Genesis to Revelation, it's like a huge feast that has been prepared for you by the King of all kings. When was the last time you ate of this feast? When was the last time you took a bite out of the word of God? When was the last time you had a good meal from God's word-- from Genesis to Revelation. When was the last time you cracked open your bible? When was the last time you opened it up? When was the last time you even got it out?

Church, God is calling us to blow the dust off our bibles. Get it off the old book shelf, and come and eat, eat, eat! Eat a good meal for your spirit man. This good meal is more important than any meal you would eat in the natural. And we all know we love to eat in the natural. We spend a lot of time preparing meals and eating all the good foods in this life. We spend a lot of money. We'll go to fancy restaurants and fast food places like never before. There are so many fast food places now. There's one on every street corner; more so than 20-30 years ago. It is so much a part of our American culture, eating and dining out.

All of those things are great and wonderful, and they are here for us to enjoy. But when it dominates your life and you never so much as eat one word daily from the word of God, it's an abomination unto God.

You see, if you call yourself a child of God and you believe in God and you say, "Yes, I'm saved," and "I believe in God," and you called upon His name – you are required to meditate upon the word of God. It's not an option. It's a requirement. God's word to Joshua in the book of Joshua chapter 1:8 writes:

"This book of the law shall not depart from your mouth, but you shall mediate in it day and night, that you may observe to do according to all that is written in it. For then you will make your way prosperous, and then you will have good success."

It is your responsibility to meditate upon God's word. You must read it, eat of it, and feast upon it. You must take the time. It's part of your responsibility. This is part of who you are. It's your responsibility, just as God gave Adam responsibility in the Garden of Eden. You need to read the word of God every day.

Whatever is most convenient for you and there's no excuse in this. It won't hold water on the Day of Judgment. You won't say to God, "I didn't have time", or "God, but my work schedule", or "I had to leave so early"..."But God"... "But God". There won't be any "buts" on that day. This is a harsh word I know, but every child of God must make time to read the word of God every day, even if it's only for 10-15 minutes a day, whatever is most convenient for you: morning, noon, or night. And I don't think that is too much for our Lord to ask of us.

47

If you want to grow in God, if you want to discover who you are in Christ in this lifetime, if you want to discover your callings, your gifting, and your offices, if you want to walk in your destiny and not stand before God one day with great remorse and great regrets, you will simply do this one thing. READ THE WORD OF GOD EVERY DAY-- at least once a day, if not three times a day. You have three meals a day for your body, right? You should have three meals a day for your spirit man. That would be optional. That would be God's best: morning, noon, and night – 3 meals a day. If you will recall in the book of Daniel, he would pray three times a day. (See Daniel 6:10)

It's a pattern, a type, a picture for God's people today! Read the word of God at least once a day. One meal; but if you can see the benefit of this: will you give God three? Will you give God three meals a day? God has prepared a table. It's already prepared. It's a feast from Genesis to Revelation.

"I've even sent out invitations, but most of you have said you're too busy. Will you come and eat with me... dine with me?" says the Lord.

It goes by many different names, "Quiet times", "Devotionals", etc. -- whatever you want to call it. Will you come and spend time with God? That's all He wants from you is a little time… even 10-15 minutes…30 minutes? …an hour? ... whatever you can work into your life. God just wants to spend time with His kids…with His people. The invitations have gone out; but many have been sent back unopened. They are too busy.

"Can you come to the banquet? Can you come and eat from My table?" says the Lord.

Jesus' words say simply this in Luke 4: 16 – 24:

Parable of the Wedding

Then he said to him, "A certain man gave a great supper and invited many, and sent his servant at supper time to say to those who were invited, come, for all things are now ready. But they all with one accord began to make excuses. The first said to him, I have brought a piece of ground, and I must go and see it. I ask you to have me excused, And another said, "I have bought five yoke of oxen, and I am going to test them. I ask you to have me excused.' Still another said, "I have married a wife, and therefore I cannot come." So that servant came and reported these things to his master. Then the master of the house, being angry, said to his servant, "go out quickly into the streets and lanes of the city, and bring in here the poor and the maimed and the lame and the blind.' And the servant said, "Master, it is done as you commanded, and still there is room." Then the master said to the servant, "Go out into the highways and hedges, and compel them to come in, that my house may be filled. For I say to you that none of those men who were invited shall taste my supper."

"I have fields and commitments. I cannot come to the banquet." This parable is not only for the "Marriage Supper of the Lamb" that will take place in the future, but it is also for today as well.

Will you come to the table at the banquet of the Most High God? You have an invitation. Everyone in the whole world is invited to come-- over 3 billion invitations. That's a lot of invites.

How many will God receive back unopened? God has sent you one! I am sending you one right now in this book. Will you open it? Will you come to the banquet of the Most High God? Will you come or send it back unopened?

If that is your hearts cry, you may close this book now and give it to someone else who will come to this banquet! But if it is your heats cry, even to the smallest degree: Will you open the invitation? Will you read God's word at least once a day? And, will you come with me? Will you come with me to go to the heights and the higher places, where the eagles are afraid to fly? To go higher, we have to go lower!

Jesus said as recorded in these verses:

"Whoever exalts himself will be humbled,
and he who humbles himself will be exalted." (Mat. 23:12)

"Then Jesus said to His disciples, if anyone desires to come after Me, let him deny himself, and take up his cross, and follow Me. For whoever desires to save his life will lose it, but whoever loses his life for My sake will find it." (Mat. 16: 24, 25)

Will you come to this banquet? Will you read on? Will you come out into the depths and come down to the "bottom of the sea" with me? If you are willing, I will go with you. I will go with you all the way!

Who Are You?

"I am the maker of the heavens and the earth. I am the 'I AM, that I AM, that I AM.' I know who 'I am', and I want My people to know who they are. That you too can say, 'I know who I am, that I am, that I am," says the Lord.

Halleluiah! It is the most powerful revelation that any human being can discover in this lifetime! God's revelation to Moses at the burning bush was a revelation of who the "I am" was for Moses and the rest of the world. God wants all of us to have a "burning bush" experience with God so we can discover who we are in Christ, and God being our maker, creator, and Father. God wants us to be reunited into that relationship so that we all know who we are in Christ and where we fit into His kingdom dynamics.

You need to go back to the "Garden of Eden", spiritually; before sin ever entered the world. Adam knew who he was before the fall. Adam knew exactly who he was; what his calling was; and what his responsibilities were. Adam knew who he was.

Do you know who you are? Do you know what your callings are, and what your responsibilities are that have been given by the Lord God Himself. Have you had your "burning bush" revelation? Do you know who you are?

After the fall, Adam lost his identity. He did not know who he was anymore. He ran and he hid from his father and creator. He neglected his own responsibilities. Fear entered his heart. His relationship with God was broken. Adam ran in fear of his God. Before, he had no fear. He was full of the love of God. He didn't even know fear. After the fall, fear entered. He ran and hid. He didn't know who he was. He didn't know what his responsibilities were. He didn't know his calling. He was separated from the Most High God. His relationship with God was broken, and from that point on – humanity lost their identities. They didn't know who they were any longer. And it's been an age old process that God has been trying to bring them back to the same place that Adam had in the Garden.

But, I want you to know today, that through God's son, Jesus Christ, and through His sacrifice the cross, God's people can now know who they are. They can go back to the "garden" and walk with God once again in the "cool of the day", being reunited again with their creator.

Jesus Christ, himself, can reverse the curse. Reverse it all, as if sin never entered your entire life. God can reverse it all, in Jesus name. The affects of sin can be reversed, and God can restore everything back to better than its original state, back to the body of Christ and back to His people. What Satan has meant for harm – what he has tried to steal, kill and destroy from God's people – God will restore it all back to a better condition than what it was originally for those in the body of Christ.

So in this day and in this hour, God is presenting His people with a question: Do you know who you are? Who are you? And one other important question God proposed to Adam in the garden was: Where are you? God knew exactly where Adam was, but Adam, himself, did not know where he was.

Do you know where you are today with God? Where are you in your walk with the Living God? Do you know where your position is in God? How much have you grown since the first day you met God? Are you still a babe in Christ or have you grown to maturity?

Perhaps the two greatest questions I could propose to the body of Christ are: Who are you, and where are you? These are the questions that will be answered in this book: "Abiding Under The Shadow." By the time you finish this book, you'll know who you are and you'll know where you are. There will be no more doubt – no more fear. You will know your gifting, callings, offices, and your responsibilities. You'll know beyond the shadow of a doubt: what is the will of God in my life? What is that perfect and acceptable will of God in my life? You will know the answers to that question. You will know beyond the shadow of a doubt. You'll also know the "how to" of how to walk it out and put your hands to the plow. It will be for you a very practical book and a very practical word.

What to do and how to accomplish it! And so, on the last day when God calls you home, you will have no regrets and no remorse. God will look upon you and say in that day, "Well done my good and faithful servant, enter into my kingdom. Enter into the joy of the Lord."

You can walk in your destiny. You can walk in your callings. You don't have to wander in the wilderness for 40 years trying to figure it all out!

Mountains In Our Lives

"Not by might, nor by power, but by my Spirit," says the Lord. O mighty mountain…you will become level ground." (Zach. 4:6)

God is bringing down every "mountain" in the lives of His people in this day and hour. There are too many "mountains" that have been built by the hands of men. In individual's lives, in churches lives, institutions lives, in governments lives – in all the dealings of life. God is bringing them all down. There are too many to mention them all, but just to mane a few: mountains of pride are coming down in Jesus name; mountains of fear; mountains of doubt and unbelief; mountains of man's wisdom; man's understanding; and man's knowledge. Mountains of humanism: a religion that places man at the center of all things and exalts men and man's accomplishments – they are all coming down!!

There are mountains in individuals' lives of bitterness, anger, hatred, and unforgiveness, etc. They are huge obstacles that separate them from the living God. These "mountains" stand in the way of our relationship with our lord and savior Jesus Christ. And many have these obstacles and hindrances in their lives today.

Many cry out to God and say, "God, we want more of you," but they can't receive more because there is a "mountain" that stands directly between God and themselves; and they can't get over that mountain.

So, Jesus answered and said to them, "As surely, I say to you, if you have faith and do not doubt, you will not only do what was done to the fig tree, but also if you say to this mountain, 'Be removed and be cast into the sea,' it will be done. And whatever things you ask in prayer, believing, you will receive."(Mat. 21: 21,22)

You must become an active participant in the removal of your own mountains! Notice the words "if you say," "If you say"! "If you say", and that's the only way, you must speak to your mountains, in

52

your heart and in your life. The first step is to pray and ask God to help you identify what the "mountains" are in your life. Pray and search your heart *"to see if there is any wicked way in me"* (Psalms 139:24), and the light of God will shine down upon the smallest of mountains and show you what you need to confront.

The second step is that you must speak to your mountain with the power of God within you and pray your mountain down. "You say" to this mountain be removed and cast into the sea and it shall be done. Notice that Jesus makes no mention of the size of the mountain or the quantity. There can be many mountains in our lives and some seem as large as Mount Everest, but the good news is that none are too big that they can not be removed with God's help.

It is interesting to note here that Jesus uses the metaphors of a "mountain" and the "sea." What is the significance of this picture? The obstacles or hindrances being described as a "mountain" are symbols of something large and permanent that seemingly can't be removed by any natural means. Things that have to do with our "old nature" or "sinful nature" are in Adam, as he was formed from the dust of the earth, these are seen as things of the land or the earth realm. What we see, hear, smell, taste and touch is the realm that we are born into naturally.

The "sea" is the exact opposite. It is the realm of God's Holy Spirit. The Holy Spirit is described over and over in scripture as things having to do with water, as in rain, streams, rivers, and fountains. (see Hosea 6:3, Isaiah 44:3, Gen 7:11) Jesus was not from this world, but from the realms of the Spirit. If you are born again in Jesus, you can walk by His Spirit and live in and through His Spirit today. This is possible through Jesus' work on the cross. If you are living in the Spirit, it can be said that you are a "sea dweller", versus being a "land dweller" which is in Adam.

Living in the "sea" doesn't come naturally to us, but through the power of the Spirit we can live in a whole new dimension of this world in the depths of the sea. *"Old things are passed away – behold I will make all things new."*

That which is of land is of the carnal nature in Adam, and that which is water and sea is of the Holy Spirit in Jesus. You can command what is an obstacle in the flesh or carnal in Adam – what is in the natural to go into the supernatural and be engulfed by the power of God's Spirit. It will be removed from the face of the horizon as if it does not exist, as it is cast into the sea.

If you take Mount Everest, the largest mountain in the world, and if you could place it within the ocean to the deepest depths of the sea, it would still be covered with over a mile of water. Your "mountain" is still covered by the power of the Living God. Over a mile of water-- over a mile of God's Spirit! It's covered!! There is no mountain too high or too strong that has been built by the hands of men that cannot be covered by the power of God's Spirit.

In that scripture, Mathew 21: 21, 22, there are two very important keys. "You say to this mountain be removed and cast into the sea, do not doubt and have faith…" Key #1 is that "you must say". You must work together with God as a co-laborer in the work of God in your own life. God will not act sovereignly to remove your "mountain". You must speak forth the words of God Almighty in your life with your mouth, combined with the spirit of God within you. It's a combined effort. The spirit of God within you coming together with the anointed word of God on your lips speaking forth the word of God, the will of God, the thoughts of God, and the heart of God in your life. By speaking the words of God to your "mountains"-- that is the only way that they will be removed!

The second key that Jesus spoke about n Matthew 21:21, 22 is the key of faith. He said, "If you have faith and do not doubt"… "It will be done." And "whatever things you ask in prayer, believing, you will receive."

You must not doubt in your heart, but what you have asked of God believe what you say – believe what you've asked-- and it shall be done for you on earth as it is in heaven.

A Few Words About Words

Words…words…words…they are everywhere! We are bombarded in this "information age" by words from all different sources: radio, T.V., movies, people, news, media, entertainment, billboards, internet, and computers. We are literally hit with a barrage of words in our lives every day; but how many words are so unimportant? How many are really very insignificant? How many are just rubbish? ...garbage? And, I'll go even one step lower than that: How many are completely filthy and are an abomination to even fall on the ears of the saints of the living God?

God is calling us to clean up our acts! You must guard your ears, your eyes, and your heart, against what enters your temple of the living God. You should not even be hearing or setting your eyes upon some of the things that you have in your world and in your life.

Thus saith the Lord thy God, "Get it out! Get it out! Get it out of your life! 'Only the words that are true, and noble...' whatsoever things are just, and pure and lovely and of good report. If there is any virtue or anything praiseworthy, meditate on these things, (See. Phil. 4:8) -- things that are pure, lovely, and true – all that comes out of the mind of God. Think on these things. Think on these things. Church, what are you thinking about? What are you thinking on? This I my question to you this day, church of the living God. What are you thinking about?"

Words are very powerful. They are all around us. Only you can regulate what comes into your temple, what comes into your mind and your heart. This is part of your responsibility. This was also part of the responsibility that God had given to Adam in the Garden of Eden. This is part of who you are.

Adam was caretaker of his entire world. He had the responsibility for what came into his own life. He was told not to eat from the tree of the knowledge of good and evil. Evil was in this world; but he had to regulate what he allowed to enter into his being and into his life.

Eve was deceived. She allowed evil to enter her being. Then, she deceived Adam; but Adam didn't regulate it. Adam knew that there was a possibility that the apple came from the wrong tree. What apples are you eating today? Which tree are they coming from?

Church of the living God: your responsibility is to discern which tree the apples come from. They may look good, smell good, and even taste good. They may look beautiful. It looks like an apple; but it has come from the wrong tree! It is your responsibility to discern: which tree did your apple come from, the tree of life – all that is of God – or the tree of the knowledge of good and evil. Satan was in the Garden. Satan was already there. He was wrapped around a single tree. I believe he was restricted to being wrapped around only the tree of the knowledge of good and evil. These restrictions were placed upon him in the garden, by God himself.

Adam and Eve, all they needed to do was stay away from that one tree. That's all they needed to do. God is saying to us today, "Stay away from evil!" Stay away; as it pertains to entering into your own heart and life, not as it pertains to kicking in the gates of hell. Do not allow evil to enter your heart and life.

All the apples in your world can look very tempting; they can look good, smell good, and taste good. But, Satan is lurking at your door. Be careful! Ask yourself, where that apple came from before you partake of it and it enters your being!

"Church of the living God: You are eating apples from the wrong tree. You are eating an entire diet of apples from the wrong tree. Your diet is filled – as a buffet – with apples that have been taken from the wrong tree! And you're taking those just like Adam did with no discernment whatsoever... no... not even a thought as to where these apples came from!"

"You're being deceived just like Adam was deceived. You are taking them from people close to you – from your 'Eve'. Adam took from his beautiful partner. He thought she was beautiful. She looked good, smelled good, and sounded good – he never thought that deception could come through his beautiful helpmate. The one that He loved and the one He cherished."

"Church of the Living God: You still must consider the source! You are being deceived from beautiful sources. They look good, sound good, and they are beautiful in your eyes. You may even cherish these sources. You may just love them."

"I charge you this day – Church of the Living God: Even as Adam in the garden had no discernment whatsoever... Where? Where? Where? Where are your apples coming from? You must consider the source. You must check every source. If it's not from the tree of life, it's not from God. You are not to ever, absolutely never, even come near that other tree!"

"All Adam and Eve needed to do was to stay away from that tree, from that temptation, and from that evil, so it would not enter into their hearts and lives. This is God's heart. There is a world of words flying around at the speed of light all over the entire globe. What words are you eating? What words are in your diet, today? What table are you eating from? Are you eating from the King of all kings table; or are you eating the crumbs off the floor? The crumbs have gotten dirty and are only fit for the dogs of the earth."

"I am calling you to eat from the King's table which is a metaphor for eating from My word," says the Lord. "Eat from my word! I have set a table before you in the presence of your enemies. You are now seated at the right hand of God. Realize who you are in Christ! A part of who you are is that you are a 'king' that sits at the right hand of God. As a king – small 'k' – you are a King's kid that is invited to eat at your father's table. Eat the words from Heaven, from Genesis to Revelation."

"These are the words that you should live by. These are the words that you should meditate upon. These are the words that should enter into the hearts of men. These are the words that should be your very heart."

"Nothing but the word of God… Nothing but the thoughts of God… Nothing but the heart of God… Nothing but the will of God. Let My will be done in your life. What is that perfect will of God for you? You may be wondering: what is the will of God? Feast from my word. That's how you will discover it. There is no other way! You've been eating from the wrong tree! That's why you don't know what the will of God is for your life. That's why! You walk around in the darkness. That's why you don't know the callings of God upon your life."

"This may be a harsh word I know, but you're eating from the wrong tree. This is from God not man, a 'rhema word' for this day and this hour."

"Words are all around us. They are coming through your door even faster by way of the internet. Vile, vile things are being pumped into practically every house in America. Guard your doors. The internet is pumping vile things into the hearts and minds of God's people."

"Church! Church! It's time to wake up. It's time. Unplug the internet if you have to. It brings all kinds of things into your home under disguise from Satan. It looks good, sounds good, and seems beautiful; but when your back is turned – all of your family has access to the vilest things that Satan can come up with. He is feeding it to you as an apple from the tree of the knowledge of good and evil. You're eating from the wrong tree! It's a harsh word – but a harsh word nonetheless! Unplug your phone lines if you have to! Unplug the cable line! Disconnect your T.V. Disconnect your internet. It's a stumbling block to you and your family. Unplug it! Unplug it! Turn it off! Your family is eating apples from the tree of the knowledge of good and evil."

"Only this apple looks good on the outside, but an apple can be rotten at its core. It's a rotten apple! And it only takes one bad apple to spoil the whole bunch!"

In the "good old days", people would use root cellars to store up their surplus food from the previous harvest. Apples were one of the best choices, because they would keep for long periods of time through the winter months. The days of root cellars for the most part are just about over, but a great analogy lies in the "root cellar".

One bad apple can spoil the whole bunch. People would have to go down underground and check their apples to see which ones were rotten. At the very first sign of a rotten apple, they had to get rid of it... at the FIRST SIGN! FIRST SIGN! FIRST SIGN! They had to throw it out. It was only good for fertilizer at that point. They had to bury it and cover it up; only good for composting to grow more fresh crops the next year. They had to be on their guard. It was practically a daily chore for them to go down and check the root cellar. Nobody liked to do it. It could be a very creepy place: cold, dark, and damp, with spider webs all around and even possibly snakes; but an important responsibility, nonetheless.

"Part of discovering who you are is that you have the same responsibility as Adam did to check your apples in your spiritual "root cellar"! Church of the living God: I am calling you to go down and check your "root cellars". Check your apples for the first signs of rottenness. Throw them out at the first sign. Don't try to keep them. Don't try to hang on to them. Don't try to keep them in a separate bushel; a whole bushel full of rotten apples all to themselves. Don't think you can eat just a little bit now and then. Don't think you can eat just a small bite from a rotten apple, because your very life is in that apple. It will only bring sickness, disease and death. It will only roll in death, every time you try to eat from a rotten apple. You are dying a little bit every day, every day, every day, every day... and you think you can go to church and worship Me? It's an abomination unto Me!" says the Lord. "It's an abomination unto Me; and I am holding you accountable-- Church of the living God-- in the very first chapter of this book, and it only gets harder from here," says the Lord God Almighty.

"But if you want an encounter with God, and if you want to be in 'covenant relationship' with Him, then read on."

"This book will be hazardous to your life. It will literally transform and change who you are. You'll not know the old man-- who you used to be. You'll be completely changed and transformed. By the time you get done reading this book, you'll not be the same person. Your life will not be the same."

"Read on and discover who you are. Throw out all your rotten apples. Don't even try to taste them. Church, you have bushels of rotten apples hidden in your 'root cellars' where you think nobody is going to find them. You think, "Nobody goes down into my root cellar, with all the snakes and spiders and webs." You think you can hide them all down there where no one else will see."

"But you cannot escape the Lord God Almighty's presence. There is no place in this world that He will not go! He already knows that they are there. He is telling you to throw out your 'rotten apples' and check all the others too. Check for the first signs of decay, and the first signs of darkness."

"Every word that enters your life via the T.V., internet, people, radio – whatever the source – it must be filtered through God's Holy Spirit. Guard your eyes, ears and heart from what is brought into your temples. Filter all words from all media, and from all sources. What are you living on? What are you feasting upon? What table are you eating from today? Are you feasting at the tables of the 'Kings of Babylon'?"

"Daniel was a man of God who refused to eat from the king of Babylon's table; from food that could have possibly been offered up to pagan idols. He refused to eat from the food of the world-- from all the delicacies and choice foods that would be so tempting to eat. He would only eat from the food from his King's table. Church of the Living God: Are you eating from the tables of the King of Babylon – the food that this world has to offer?"

"What table are you eating from? Where did your apples come from? Did they come from the kings of Babylon or did they come from the King of kings and the Lord of lords? Which tree did your apples come from? This is the question you must ask yourself. Where did your apples come from? Even as God gave Adam that same responsibility in the garden, he needed to discern which tree his apples came from; so, too, God has given you that same job to discern for yourself before you eat of any apple in this world. No matter who gave it to you. No matter what the source may be. No matter how good it looks. No matter how close they may be to you. "Eve" looked beautiful, sounded beautiful; she was very close to Adam. He cherished her in his heart. There may be sources that you absolutely love and cherish, and you would never think they would give you a bad apple."

"You must consider every source and don't just take it all the time as if it were a good apple. It is a very high responsibility that God gave to Adam, and God gives it to you, as well. You are what you eat! Church of the Living God: you must discern which apples you eat; which apples come into your life and only you – only you – can do that job – that responsibility. No one else can do it for you. What enters into your heart, what enters into your mind, your ears, your eyes; you must discern between good and evil. You must discern which apples came from the tree of the knowledge of good and evil. That was the only evil that was in the garden! They could go anywhere else, but God warned them not to go near that tree. They had no business even going close to it. But they gave into temptation-- to curiosity-- and they ate of the wrong apple from the wrong tree!"

"So, Church of the Living God, I charge you this day: Where are your apples coming from? It is of great importance for your life. It is a matter of life and death, and for the lives of others in a lost and dying world. I am depending on you – church of God – to be filled with my power; with my love; with all that 'I AM' and take who 'I AM' to a lost and dying world; to be my representatives in the earth. I need you to be the representatives of Christ himself to a lost and dying world, and how can you be when your minds and your hearts are filled with such vile things too vile to mention? Church of the living God: You must clean up your act. Throw out that bushel of rotten apples that you have hidden in your 'root cellars'. Throw them out this day," says the Lord God Almighty, "for they will only bring you death, and sickness. They will only bring you disease; not only physically, but spiritually as well. Your entire being will die little by little with every bite you take from those rotten apples. Your entire being begins to die. It's like taking little bites of death into your being that affects your spirit, soul, mind, and body. Little by little, day by day – you don't think it's hurting you; but slowly, slowly, slowly your rolling death into your life, and you're going further and further away from the Lord your God. You're heading in the wrong direction! This is a harsh word unto you – My church – Church of the Living God. Throw away your rotten apples; for this is my word unto you this day," says the Lord God Almighty.

Giving Out The Love of God

You can't give away what you don't already first possess. You have to go to the "bottom of the sea" to understand the depths of the love of God and possess it for yourself. You have to own it! You have to be firmly rooted and grounded in the love of God. (See Eph.3: 17-19) You have to know it. You have to possess it. You have to own it. It must literally be a part of who you are. When people look at you, anyone should easily identify the love of God in you. It is to that degree, you must know the love of God. And, before you can ever begin to give it out; you have to possess it first. So, to whatever degree that you have is to the degree you can give out. So, if you only have a little, you can only give a little. It's a reaping and sowing principle. You will reap what you have sown. You can only give what has been given unto you – to the measure that God has given to you; is to the measure that you can give out. "Give and it will be given to you: good measure, pressed down, shaken together and running over will be put into your bosom. For with the same measure that you use, it will be measured back to you." (Lk. 6:38) So what you have – give away – and it will be given back to you in even greater measure! All of what you have is not meant to be kept for yourself. It's meant to be given away! How much of the love of God do you have, first, in your possession? And secondly, how much do you have to give out?

If you feel you don't have a whole lot to give, I have good news for you today. You can be filled up to overflowing and you can know the depths, and heights, and widths, and lengths of the love of God. So, get ready to be filled with the love of God. Get ready to be filled to overflowing. Get ready to be saturated in the love of God. Because, if you will say, "Yes," and come to the depths, you will be surrounded by "salt" water in the "sea." And this "salt water" will actually permeate just about anything that gets dropped into the ocean.

When you get out of the ocean you are salty. You taste salty. Ask anyone that has been in the Dead Sea. When something comes out of there, it's salty! The Dead Sea is so salty everything in it floats. But in this analogy, the love of God will permeate everything about you. The "salt water" of God's presence will permeate every part of your being and every aspect of your entire life – every area. It will trickle out and affect every area; how you relate to your wife and husband, your children, and your family, friends, neighbors and even your enemies.

Knowing the depths of God's love will affect every aspect of your life. But it is first important that we understand and receive the depths of His love. Receive it first, and then you'll be able to give even more back out. You'll be compelled by the love of God in your heart. You won't be able to contain it.

Church of the living God: Why don't we reach out more than we do to the lost and dying in this world? The ones that may go to hell that we see everyday, why don't we reach out more to them? I will propose this to you today. I will say that, perhaps, we are not filled with the love of God. Because, if you knew the depths of God's love, you – the church – would be feeding the hungry, reaching out to the lost, sheltering the homeless. You would be on the street everyday, beckoning and calling them to come in to the house of God. It would, literally, transform the way you do ministry. It would transform the way you do church. It will transform your programs; everything about the life of the church. This is how important this is.

Because, if you possess this, it will permeate everything about life as you know it now. You'll have so much love for your neighbor it will be uncomprehendable in the natural. It will be a supernatural thing. I told you the love of God was supernatural! It will break down walls between family members, and friends. It will break down walls between neighbors. It will break down walls and break chains between denominations and brothers and sisters in the Lord.

"My people who have been called by my name…" have been fighting and bickering amongst themselves for far too long, Why? They are not filled up and saturated with the love of God! It's as simple as that! I'll be very blunt and direct. This is coming straight out of heaven. They are not filled with God's love. If they were, they would not have the time to speak a single word against another brother or sister in the church today. There would be no fighting; no bickering; and no backbiting.

"Church of the living God: You're fighting the wrong battle. You're fighting amongst yourselves. You're spending too much time worrying about if every 't' is crossed and every 'i' is dotted, in the letter of your doctrines. Your eyes are on the wrong things. Look at what unites you!"

"It is the CROSS OF CHRIST!! It is the cross!!! Let's get back to the cross!! Get back to the CROSS!! At the place of the cross, God is asking you to pick up yours; for if you want to follow Christ, you have to carry your own cross. (See Lk 9:23; 14:27) Church of the living God: You are not carrying your cross. To carry your cross, you must deny yourself! You must deny yourself! You have been serving yourself for far too long. You have been serving yourselves!!! You have been eating at the tables of the 'Kings of Babylon'. The 'Kings of this world', you've been feasting at their tables. You have been in a self-preservation mode to preserve your life, to preserve your interests, to preserve your denominations; and to preserve your churches.

"I am calling you today to carry your crosses. You must deny yourselves. Deny yourselves!! Let that sink in for a moment; because, I know you haven't heard it for awhile! Deny yourself. You forget it's not about you – It's all about ME," says the Lord. "This is a serious cry and a serious call of God's heart for the church and for the world. "RETURN!! RETURN UNTO ME!!" says the Lord. "It's my heart's cry! It was the same word in the days of old-- prophet after prophet-- that I sent to my people. It's the same message; time and time again. It's the parable of the vinedresser. (see Mk. 12:1-12) I sent people time and time again, and then I sent my son. Maybe they will listen to Him. They crucified Him!!"

"They didn't even listen to my son! They did not even listen to ME, when I came down to this world. Jesus was God incarnate; God in the flesh. They did not even listen to Him. So, in this day and in this hour, the ramifications are all the more serious. I am sending forth my spirit into all the earth – the spirit of Elijah – in these days."
"Choose this day who you will serve. Return, Return unto ME," says the Lord. "Return…Return unto ME."

"I am coming back for a church that is without spot or wrinkle. Yet once more I'll shake not only the earth but also the heavens. (See Heb. 12:27) I am shaking everything," says the Lord, "absolutely

63

everything. The walls that you have built by the hands of men – they are coming down. In your churches this day: every wall, every stone that has not been laid by the master architect-- the Lord God Himself – is going to be removed."

And that is a word from the Lord! You can count on it. You can bank on it. It is a guarantee. "You live in these days. I am shaking the heavens and the earth, the sea, and dry land." (See Hag.2:6)

"I had the same message again in the New Testament in the book of Hebrews. So, you can't say, 'That's Old Testament stuff.' Church of the living God: It's a New Testament word. It's a now word!"

"I am shaking everything, and all your high walls, all your institutions, every pretty little thing you have built, if it has not been laid by the hand of God, I am sorry to say, 'It's all coming down!' It's been a waste of time. It's been a waste of your time, your efforts, and your money, if it has not been built by the Lord God Himself. He is the master builder. He is the Builder of all things." (See Heb. 3:4)

"But every now and then, My children like to get their hands into it, and they're so excited they want to jump in and work with their Dad. I like their enthusiasm; but in this case, I'm building the temple – the true Church of the Living God. I am coming back for a bride. I am coming back for one church, and this church I will build and the very gates of Hell shall not stand against it. This church – the true church – I must lay every stone – every stone."

"And you, my people, you are a 'living stone' being built into the 'House of God'-- into a habitation that contains ME, the Lord God Almighty; and only I can place that stone in this temple. No one else!"

"And all that is built in this temple must be built by ME – the Lord God on High. You see, the church I am coming back for is not a building. It's not an institution. It's a people! It's not a program! It's a people! My heart is for people-- not programs. You can throw every program out the window and I'll rewrite your programs," says the Lord. "I'll rewrite every program, if you let Me be God in the house…be God in your church services once again. I'll rewrite your programs. I'll tell you which ones can stay and which ones have to go. But the key is this: I must be God!"

"You must ask of ME – inquire of ME. Don't just do any old thing because it sounds good, looks good, smells good, tastes good and we did it 20 years ago and we are going to do it today. Throw it out the window and HEAR FROM HEAVEN! Ask ME! Inquire of ME! 'How do you want things done-- God?' Imagine that. What a great revelation. Ask God how He wants things done; And He will direct your paths. He will be a lamp to your feet and a light to your path. He will orchestrate everything. He will build the church. He'll bring growth to the church. He'll bring people in. Because, Why? I will be there. God will be there. They'll not come to hear any man speak, or to get a man's program, or hear what men have to say or any other words. They'll come to get a word from the Lord; and they'll come to be in my presence."

"That's what they need. That's what they need. I know it's a harsh word, but you've been struggling, and you've been striving for church growth. How do we get people in? How do we do this? How do we do that? What next great thing can we come up with? Simply, let ME be who "I AM" and then you can be who you are! And it is as simple as that! If I can be God in My church and in My people, then the power of the Living God can be returned to Jerusalem once again. The ark will have returned! Every church, it does not matter...Baptists, Methodist, Catholics, and Episcopalians...it does not matter. It's not a Pentecostal thing! It's not a Charismatic thing! It is a church thing-- My church."

"I'm coming back for one church. It's a people not a building. This word applies to all denominations throughout the whole world – throughout the earth!! It's not a Pentecostal thing or charismatic thing. It's a body of Christ thing! It's a 'Bride' thing!"

"Are you in the body of Christ? Will you be at the Marriage Supper of the Lamb? Will you be there? If you are, and you say you are, then this word is for you. This word I say unto my people this day – this word is for my bride. And I'm coming back for a bride, one bride, without spot or wrinkle," says the Lord.

We are in the betrothal period. It meant the same thing in the days of the Hebrews as did marriage. It was as serious as marriage itself. And in American culture today, we have lost so much as to the meaning of what marriage is to be. Satan has attacked it at its very core. But you are still in the betrothal period of the marriage supper of the lamb. It is as serious as marriage itself. And God is preparing you. Are you preparing as a bride would be for her wedding day? Are you putting on a gown that is white? Are you doing all the preparations that you should? Are you cleansing? Are you bathing? Are you cleaning yourself up? Are you getting ready for your wedding day? God needs you to have the urgency that it's your wedding day! And men, you'll have to use a little imagination, but it's a great analogy. It's the wedding day!!

I'm sure most of you have been to a wedding. If you're not married yourself, hopefully, you have at least been to one and seen all the preparations that go into a wedding. There are days, and months, and sometimes years put into planning that one wedding day.

It's the same, spiritually, with our walk with our Lord and Savior. We need to be preparing for our "Wedding Day." And with all that preparation, it's over in just a few moments. You see, you're preparing for a day to stand before a Holy God and it will all be over in a few moments. The "wedding" will have taken place. It will all be done and over with and everyone will be at the reception. Will you have made it through the doors? Will you be there for the supper?

Church of the Living God: as you take in the love of God, being of supernatural origin, you'll be reaching out with the love of God. It will transform everything about you. You're relationships will be transformed starting with your spouse, those closest to you, your children, and your grandchildren, your family, neighbors, and friends.

But the true test is this: If you have the love of God in your heart – will you love your enemies? (See Lk. 6:27 – 36) Will you love your enemies? Because if you love as the world loves what measure is that to you? What good is that? You're just as good as the world. That doesn't separate you from the world. That doesn't make you any closer to God than the rest of the world. The world loves to those degrees, but when you go to the depths, if you'll come down, after you have read this book, you'll even love your enemies. You'll do good unto them. You'll heap burning coals upon their heads (See Rom. 12:20) as a testimony against them. "Perfect love casts out all fear," (See 1 Jn. 4:18)… ALL FEAR!!! Fear of man, fear of the unknown, fear of death, fear of anything and everything, and even fear of our enemies.

God sent His son to this world as a baby to transform the world and to show the love of God in the form of a baby, so they would love one another. This is God's admonishment to the world: that they would "love one another" (See 1 Jn. 4:11).

This is the cries of God's heart that we would love one another, even your enemies. So, if you have something against your brother, what is God's call? You must go to him. Before you can even take communion, you must go to him. It is a reminder to keep everything good and everything done righteously and make it right with others.

So in this book, I'll call you in later chapters, to go make everything right before you can take communion again. You'll not have a single thought of hatred, or revenge or retaliation, for it will all be done out of the heart of God and His love. This is the true test and at the end of this book, I will ask you the same question; are you filled up to all the fullness of the love of God?

And by that last chapter, you will say, "Yes I am." You'll experience it in your heart and you'll know it in your mind, and there will be no doubt. You'll be transformed. And this is the greatest thing of all – by the end of this book – you will have had a heart transplant, where the heart of God has now become your heart.

In the book of Ezekiel, God's word says that He will give us a new heart! (See Ezek. 36:26) One that is just like His. Then you will be better conformed to the image of His son – Jesus, in every way, mind, heart and soul. You will be a representative of Jesus Christ himself, when you are finished reading this book, and you will know who you are in Christ. You'll be transformed in every area and in every way. You'll only be eating from His table, thinking only upon the words of God. You'll have His heart, and you'll know the will of God for your life and in the earth. It will not be a mystery to you.

Who can know the love of God? Who can know the mind of God? Who can know the heart of God? Except he that has been through the 'fire'; through the 'waters'; and to the 'bottom of the sea', and who has taken up his cross. It is the person who has literally done all these things in his heart and life.

He will be a vessel of gold. It is he that will know the answers to all of these questions. And you will be filled up to all the fullness of God and you can be all that you can be in the army of the living God.

You'll know who you are, and you'll be filled up to all the fullness of God this side of heaven, and you will walk in your callings, and your destiny. It will not be a mystery. You will know what is that "good, acceptable and perfect will of God" (See Rom. 12:2) in your life, in the churches life, and in the world. You'll know the will of God, because you'll have the heart of God. You'll have it all.

So, this is where we are going. This is where you are headed. If you want to come with me; come, and we'll go to a higher place, to where the eagles are afraid to fly!

God Is One

"God is the Alpha and Omega. I am the beginning of this book and I am the end of this chapter; for I am one. I AM ONE."

"There are no other gods on the face of the planet. All other gods are man made gods – little "g." I am the first and the last. I am the Alpha and Omega. I am the beginning of time and I am the end of time. I am the ancient of days. There is only one of ME. I am a three part being even as man is a three part being, and he was created in the image of God. So, too, I am three parts: Father, Son, and the Holy Spirit – each having different jobs, different responsibilities, different moving, and different applications, but all one in the same. I am a 'three-in-one' God: the trinity – Father, Son, and Holy Spirit.

"And even as we (Father, Son, and Holy Spirit) are all united together in perfect harmony, if you have seen the Son you have seen the Father. The son came to do only what the Father willed. The Holy Spirit speaks only things concerning the son to glorify His name. We are all together. All in perfect unity, and there is power in unity," says the Lord. And even in Jesus last prayer, He prayed that we would be one even as He and the Father are one! This is one of Jesus' greatest prayers! One of the most quoted of all revival scriptures is II Chronicles 7:14, 15: *"If my people who are called by my name will humble themselves and pray and seek my face and turn from their wicked ways, then I will hear from heaven, and will forgive their sin and heal their land." "Now my eyes will be open and my ears attentive to prayer made in this place."*

"Church of the living God: I charge you this day to humble yourselves in that you have not walked as one. You have spent so much time bickering and fighting; there is great division in the 'House of God'. Jesus gave a very strong warning concerning this: 'No kingdom divided against itself shall stand'. This is a harsh word. Church of the Living God, you are a divided house! You are a divided house!"

"It is time to allow Me to break down walls between denominations, between races, between peoples, and genders, and from the rich and the poor; break down walls so that my people can become one! The prayer Jesus prayed was not just some hope of a prayer that some day may take place at the culmination of the Wedding Supper of the Lamb. It was to be for NOW! It was to be for TODAY; for the church age. And Church of the Living God: You have greatly fallen short in helping to answer this prayer from my Son – Jesus – Himself. I want you to look back at this prayer once again."

*"Now I am no longer in the world, but these are in the world, and I come to you. Holy Father, keep through your name those whom you have given me, that they may be **one** as we are. (John 17:11)*
*"I do not pray for these alone, but also for those who will believe in me through their word; that they all may be **one**, as you, Father, are in me, and I in you; that they also may be **one** in us, that the world may believe that you sent me."*
*"And the glory which you gave me I have given them, that they may be **one** just as we are **one:**"*
"I in them, and you in me; that they may be made perfect in one, and that the world may know that you have sent me, and have loved them as you have loved me." (John17: 20- 23)

"Church of the living God: look at these words. Meditate upon these words. This is Jesus Christ and Him crucified; the Lord that you say that you serve. These are His words! 'I pray that…they all may be one'…"

"Are you striving to be **one** in your relationships with your brothers and sisters in Christ – with all believers; from all faiths; from all denominations; from all walks of life; all ethnic groups; and all backgrounds; from black, white, rich, poor, red, yellow, green, people…it doesn't matter the color of their skin? Are you striving and making efforts to be **one** with all of your brothers and sisters in Christ? All of them! Not just a few that you are comfortable with, that you feel good about gathering with once a week in your comfort zone. That's not what I am talking about. People from every tribe, nation, every tongue – this is the one church that I am coming back for. It will be **one** church, from all people, all nations, all tribes, and all tongues. So, if you have any problems with other people on the face of the earth: "You have a problem with me," says the Lord God

Almighty. "I have created them all in the image of God," says the Lord.

"So, I ask you this day; Church of the Living God: Search your hearts! Do you have prejudices in your hearts against your brother or your sister; regardless of age, or ethnic group, or the color of their skin, or regardless of how much money they make? Will you in this moment, allow the Living God to bring down the walls of prejudice in your life? And can you truly say that you will strive to make efforts to answer this prayer that your Lord, Himself, has prayed before He left this earth? He desires for this prayer to be answered in the church age. It wasn't some hope of a prayer that He thought could not be answered."

This is God himself praying this prayer. We must take this prayer seriously. We must look back at it once again and ask ourselves a very serious question: Am I walking as **one** with my brothers and sisters in Christ; even across denominational lines, regardless if they are Pentecostal, or considered Charismatic, or Baptist, or Methodist, or Catholic, or Protestant? Regardless of denomination!

If you are part of the Bride of Christ, then it's part of your preparation for you to be **one** with the rest of the body, even as Jesus and the Father are one. You must do anything and everything in your heart and life that will break down walls of separation in the body of Christ.

God understands why things are the way they are. Why we have so many names that differentiate between people groups and denominations. But His perfect heart is that there would be **one** church. It would be called: "Church of the living God." That would be the only denomination on the face of the earth; and it would be one wide global church, one church, one faith, one baptism, one God, and one Father who is over them all. One Lord, one Savior, who died and was crucified and who was raised and it is because He lives that we too shall live also. That is the true heart of God, and I am not saying that we will return to that state in our lifetime in the physical; but spiritually; yes it can; yes it can and yes it will.

We need to stop looking at what separates us in divisions. Man cuts it up like a "pie", and he divides it up with lines into denominations and says, 'This is Baptists. This is Methodists. This is Protestants. This is Catholics, and this is Pentecostals. God is wiping

70

away all of those lines in this day and in this hour; so that there are no lines in this "pie." No divisions in this "pie". It is one!

God says, "It's time my people who are called by my name begin to fight the right battle. You've been fighting the wrong battle. Put away your prejudices. Repent. Repent of all of them, for the Kingdom of God is at hand."

"I am uniting my church – church of the Living God: We will fight this battle under one banner! It's the banner of the Most High God! It's the banner of the KING OF KINGS and the LORD OF LORDS."

"A Kingdom divided against itself shall not stand. Are you part of the division, or are you part of the uniting? And if my people who are called by my name will humble themselves and seek my face… if you can be united as Psalm 133 so beautifully states:

'Behold how good and how pleasant it is for Brethren to dwell together in unity! It is like the precious oil upon the head, Running down on the beard, the beard of Aaron, running down on the edge of his garments. It is like the dew of Hermon, descending upon the mountains of Zion; for there the Lord commanded the Blessing – life for evermore.'"

"There is no coincidence that unity is combined with the anointing of Aaron in this Psalm. By no coincidence, with unity comes anointing! With unity comes power! One puts a thousand to flight. Two puts ten thousands to flight, and three a hundred thousand, and so on, and so on. It is exponentially powerful."

This is why Satan has been trying hard to divide the Church. He knows if he can divide us – if he can divide the forces – that is his only way to victory. And he is doing a pretty darn good job of it right now. God says, "Church of the Living God: I am calling you today to fulfill Jesus' prayer in the earth today, today! Set aside everything that would hinder; everything that would separate; every mountain; every wall; that would divide…" "And say to that Mountain, 'be removed and cast into the sea' and it shall be done." "And what are Mountains and walls in the physical will be engulfed by the power and the presence, and the spirit of the Lord God Almighty."

"Walk by My Spirit!" says the Lord. "It is possible. It is doable. You can walk by My Spirit," says the Lord. "The carnal and the spirit are in direct opposition to one another. You have been

71

walking too much in the flesh; too much in the carnal; too much on land; too much in Adam. I'm calling you to the depths. I'm calling you to leave the shore; leave everything that is secure; leave the boat; begin to walk on water. But it's my intention that you not walk on water, but even as Peter began to sink, that was My intentions for him that day! COME DOWN INTO THE DEPTHS OF THE LIVING GOD! COME DOWN INTO THE DEPTHS!" says the Lord God Almighty.

For you can't walk on water until you know the depths and the heights, the widths, and lengths of God's love, His grace, and His mercy and all the rest of who GOD is! You'll discover who He is and you'll discover who you are. He is the Alpha and Omega, the beginning and the end. He is the beginning of this book and He will be the end of this book. He is the beginning of you and He will be the end of you. He is the beginning of your faith and He is trying and pleading to work with you to come and complete the work He has begun. Will you let Him be the finisher of your faith? It takes your cooperation. It takes you doing your responsibility.

Will He finish all that He can finish in you before He calls you home? Will there be no regrets; no remorse; in that Day of Judgment? In the day that you see GOD face to face, will you be able to say, "It is finished"? Will you say in that day, "I have fought the good fight. I have finished the race"?

"This day, Church of the Living God: I am calling you to be **one** even as I and the Father are **one**. This is My charge unto you this day," says the Lord God Almighty.

Chapter Two

The Grace of God and the Power of Agreement

"…and the grace of God was upon Him." Lk.2:40
"…if two of you agree on earth concerning anything that they may ask, it will be done for them by My Father in heaven." Mat.18:19

My Grace Is Sufficient For You

"My grace is sufficient for you," says the Lord. "My grace is sufficient for you. If all I ever did was save your soul from hell, and gave you eternal life – My grace would be sufficient. That would have been enough for Me to give unto you – eternal life - but I did not stop there," says the Lord God Almighty.

"All that I give unto you; from salvation to the day I take you home and experience eternal life forever and ever; everything in between is by My grace," says the Lord God Almighty."It is by the way of grace that I give you everything. You can't earn it. You can't buy it. You can't acquire it by any means. Your good works are as filthy rags. Everything you try to do to attain it in your heart – it is as filthy rags!"

"My church needs to get a revelation of what My grace is all about. There are many today in the body of Christ that have lost that mindset. You're trying to strive your way through the kingdom. You're trying to achieve levels of greatness in my kingdom. You're wasting your time. Even once you enter the kingdom, further anointings and further giftings are all by the way of grace!"

"O, you foolish Galatians! Who has bewitched you? Who has caused you to stumble? O foolish Galatians! Has it been by works or grace? Has it been by a measure of grace that you have been saved; or has it been by your works of righteousness that you have been saved, healed, and delivered?" (see Gal. 3: 1-5)

"Church of the living God: I am calling you this day to return to a place of grace. Return unto Me," says the Lord God Almighty. "Return! Return! Return to a place of grace! Return to the cross! If you return to this place and you take up your cross and follow Me; at the foot of the cross on Calvary's hill, where Christ was crucified; this is the place I am calling My church to return to. It is a place of grace. So, as I have called you in Chapter one to come back to the cross, if you answer that cry, you'll get this revelation of grace in Chapter 2. If you have come to the foot of the cross and want to go further, you're about to receive a revelation of grace. If not, close this book and you can hand it to someone else who will. But for those that will continue on – My grace is sufficient for you this day and you're about to receive a revelation of grace that will absolutely, positively, blow your mind."

"My Grace will fall from the heavens, even as the rains fall from the sky. As the rain comes down from heaven, for My people to experience all that 'I AM that I AM'."

Hosea 6:3 says, "He will come to us like the rain, like the latter and former rain to the earth."

"I am coming in the rains of My Spirit," says The Lord, "in this day and in this hour; so My people can experience all that I AM, that I AM. Just like you can walk outside in a rain storm and 'feel' the rain hit your face, and drench you, and saturate you until you are 'soaked to the bone'; just like that – spiritually – I want My people to experience all that I AM. But in this chapter, you will experience once again My grace. I will come to you in the rains of My presence," says the Lord.

"For it is all by My spirit," says the Lord. "Zachariah 4:6 says: 'It is not by might, nor by power, but by My Spirit.' There is a dimension of who I AM that I want My people to experience! That is the realms of the spirit; but it will also line up with My word. It will line up in one hundred percent agreement with My written word. So, as this chapter is grace and agreement, all that I bring that comes in the spiritual realm will agree to My written word – to My truth."

"Those of you that are afraid of the experiential side of God-- don't be. Because, as long as it lines up perfectly with My written word; you have no fear of being out of balance. No fear whatsoever. For I am restoring My church back to a fifty -- fifty balance – a perfect balance, so that you can experience all that I AM, not just grace; but ALL that I AM, and all that I desire to give unto you this day," says the Lord God Almighty.

"I'M CALLING MY CHURCH TO RETURN TO A COVENANT RELATIONSHIP WITH ME!"

"I'm calling my church to the "Secret Place" of the Most High God. And why I have chosen *Psalm 91:1 "He who dwells in the secret place of the Most High God"*... it is for this place, the innermost chamber in the tabernacle of Moses- the Holy of Holies-- it is this room, if the high priest would make it to this inner room; so too, I am calling you church to come through the different chambers of the tabernacle. If you can get to the secret place – you enter into the chamber of the 'glory realms' of God. It is a picture of being back into a covenant relationship with the Most High God. For you see, the only thing in that chamber was the 'Ark of the Covenant'. Those very words are the 'key' to it all. There lied the 'ark'; 'the chest'; 'the box' that carried the presence of God. It was a symbol that represented the covenant or contract that God had arranged with His people –the Children of Israel. Let that sink in for a moment. It is a place of COVENANT RELATIONSHIP WITH ME," says The Lord.

"It is a place that My People who are called by My name can humble themselves and seek My face, and experience <u>all</u> that I AM, within a covenant relationship. They can experience all that 'I AM' this side of heaven. But, the contingency on this contract is that I the Lord God have signed it Myself with My precious blood of My Son; but this contract requires <u>two</u> signatures!! It requires you – My people- to walk in <u>complete</u> <u>agreement</u> with that contract. And, your obligation is simply to listen and obey the voice of the Lord thy God with all of your heart, soul, mind, and strength; and love your neighbor as yourself. Simply listen and obey the voice of the Lord. It is that simple!"

"The 'Ark of the Covenant' contained three things. It contained the 'Ten Commandments' that Moses received on Mt. Sinai. It contained some manna that fell from heaven in the wilderness – which was the bread of life that sustained them when they had no food. It also contained Aaron's rod that budded. That was symbolic of My chosen royal priesthood which you are a part of – and it also flowered and brought forth the fruit of the vine which is symbolic of the life of Christ, that He brings. Jesus came to bring men life and life more abundantly. So, if you will walk in obedience to the <u>voice</u> and the <u>word</u> of the Living God – the "rhema" word and the "logos" word – they too will also be in complete agreement to one another-- you can experience <u>all</u> that God is! It is that simple. I am calling My church in this day and in this hour to come and <u>Return To A COVENANT RELATIONSHIP</u> with the Most High God."

So, if you will come into the "secret place" and discover what that means to go "behind the veil" into the glory realms of the Lord God Himself; if you are willing to go to the place of the cross- a place of grace; and return to that place once again; you can come and go with me and I will show you the way. I will show you the way to the "Higher Places" in God; and we will fly higher than any eagle has ever flown before.

'For they that wait upon the Lord shall renew their strength; they will mount up with wings like eagles..." (Isaiah 40:31).

"AND YOU WILL FLY HIGHER THAN THE EAGLES. YOU WILL FLY HIGHER TO WHERE THE EAGLES ARE AFRAID TO FLY!"

Grace Is At The Cross!

"All that I give unto My church is through Grace. This is the avenue that it all comes through. Nothing you could do-- nothing could ever warrant any of My giftings, any of my callings, any of my offices, any of my anointings. Nothing! Nothing! Nothing!"

"It's not about you!" says the Lord.

"Church of the Living God: I want you to get that word into your spirit once again. When you come back to the place of the cross, I want you to see Jesus lifted up on a cross being crucified and you're at His feet! That's what I want you to see at the cross. It's not about you! It's about Him! Somewhere along the line – church of the Living God – you have forgotten that it is about the Lord Jesus Christ and Him crucified! He is the one who is to be exalted! He is the one who is to be lifted up! He is the one whose name is to be glorified! It's not about you!!! It's all about Him!!!! So, everything you do- **EVERYTHING** – it's not to make you look good, smell good, act good, or be accepted by people – it's not about any of that – to get the applause of man, or be in your position- it's not about that at all!"

"Church of the Living God: you need to repent of your pride and your "high places"- NOW-in Jesus' name; and fall at the feet of Jesus and ask forgiveness for your sins that you have walked in for many, many years and repent; because, it's not about you. It's not for you; to you; about you; it has nothing to do with you. You need to come back to that place, and to that mindset in your thinking and in your heart. This is the place that God wants you to return to – **the place of the cross!!**"

77

So, church of the Living God: you must come back to this place first, before we can go any further. You have to set it right with the Lord God Almighty. You have to make it right. You can't go any further in this process until you do. I told you that I was going to bring you through step by step. You have to come to this place or we can go no farther. So, those of you that can and will; lay it all down right now and pray this prayer with me.

"God, I'm sorry for all of my past sin; of times that I presumed upon the positions that you have given unto me and also the responsibilities that you have given to me. God, I am sorry and I repent, this day, for not giving you your place; for not giving you your position; for presuming upon your power and presence in our church and in our lives. God, I am sorry and I acknowledge today and realize again, that I need to come back to a place of the cross and get a new vision once again of who Jesus is and Him crucified. God, I come back to the place of that cross, 2,000 years ago at Calvary, and I fall at His feet today and I repent for all my past sins of pride. I am sorry Lord. I beg your forgiveness, and from this day forward I will give you your place. And, I acknowledge that it is all about you, and I will never again walk in those previous ways that I walked before."

"Every day, I will come to this place. Every morning I will come to the place of the cross, before I even step one foot out of bed. I will come to the place of the cross and I will submit everything unto you; and I will ask you, "Lord, what do you want this day in my life? What is your agenda? What is your agenda for my church and for my life? What is your agenda for the offices that I hold, and the anointings that you have placed in me and the giftings that you have called into my life?"

"God, what do you want me to do with this day that you have given to me? It is not my day, Lord, it is your day; and I am sorry that I have usurped your power and your time. I repent for the times that I have used your time unwisely and I have used it selfishly to build my own kingdom, my own agenda, and my own positions in my own church."

"God, I take my watch off – spiritually - and I lay it at your feet at the foot of the cross, and I give you every day from this day forward till the day you call me home. I give it all to you, Lord. Every day! Because it's yours to begin with and it's yours anyway so I give it back to you. So Lord God this day, everything that I am and all that I am not; all that I have and all that I do not have – my dreams; my hopes; my future; my ambitions – I lay them all at your feet, at the foot of this cross, and I will take up my cross daily and I will follow you! – In Jesus Name, AMEN!"

Grace Defined

There may be many definitions in the thoughts of thousands of people across the face of the earth. This word may mean different things to different people, and there may be different things that come to mind when you think of grace; but God's definition is centered around the place of the cross. And the thing I want you to have at the forefront of your thinking when you think of this word is a picture of Jesus hanging on the cross. He suffered and died a death that was not His. He was beaten almost beyond recognition. He was crowned with a crown of thorns and He was crucified on a rugged cross – one of the cruelest deaths anyone could ever go through – and He endured a punishment for a crime that He did not commit. He endured a death that He did not deserve Himself. This is God's definition and picture of grace.

This is where I want you to begin. So, throw out all of your other pictures that are associated with the word "grace", and I want you to replace them all with this picture of Christ. I know that this is a gruesome picture, and perhaps an unpleasant picture for some; but it is a picture nonetheless, that God's church needs to return to, and a word that God's church needs to return to-- to understand the full definition of what this word really means. So, we must begin here.

The word grace literally means: undeserved favor; undeserved merit; or undeserved gifts. And in the Greek the word is "charis" which means: favor, gift, or benefit; and it is where we get the word "charismatic". I know many of you are familiar with this word. It is associated with the supernatural giftings of I Corinthians 12. The prefix "charis" comes from the Greek word meaning: Grace! So, I want you to remember that everything that comes to you in your life is by way of grace -everything - absolutely everything! You must have this mindset which is the same as the mind of Christ – the mind of God. It is the understanding that you can't earn a single gift, a single blessing, a single calling, a single office or a single position. You can't strive to be better than anybody else. Oh, you can learn and study the word of God, but it is what is in the heart that counts. It's the motivation. Is it to make you look good? Or, to make you be accepted before people and man, or will you strive to read the word of God to be acceptable – "to show thyself studied and approved unto God"? You see it is the heart motive, and God knows every motive of the heart. Every single one! So, you have to look at your motives. What is the motive? Is it pure and holy before God? Or, is it tainted and corrupted, because it's been touched by man?

This is the definition of grace that we must return to! God's, grace. God's amazing grace; and it is amazing-- that old hymn that we all know and love, and have sung in our churches for decades. God's "Amazing Grace" and it is personally one of my favorites. "Amazing grace, how sweet the sound that He saved a wretch like me." This is the proper picture of what God wants His church to return to. Your righteousness is as filthy rags, and it has no merit before the King of Kings and the Lord of Lords. Even your righteous heritage – if your father was a preacher and your grandfather was a preacher, your great – grandfather was a preacher, and so on, and so on. It doesn't matter. The apostle Paul had a great heritage too, but it was as filthy rags unto God.

"I am calling those today in the earth," says the Lord God Almighty, "who have a pure heart. Who may ascend into the Hill of the Lord? Who? He that has clean hands and a pure heart, who will hearken unto the voice of the Lord thy God."

The person who will simply listen to the voice of the Lord, who will hear His "Rhema" word – fresh word in the spirit – that will line up with His "logos" word written in the Holy scriptures, and they will be in complete agreement! This person is the one! It is he that God is calling forth in these days and in this hour. It is not the person with the long heritage in their family lines – that their grandfather was a Christian and their great – great – great – great – great – great – great – great grandfather came over on the "Mayflower". It's not about all of that. In this day and hour God is calling simply the people who have a heart of gold- who have the heart of God.

Do you have the heart of God, today? Do you have a heart that beats as His beats, with His desires? ...His motives? ...His passions? ...His dreams? ...His hopes? ...and His will? If you can honestly say that you do not have all of this, there is a further work that God still needs to do in you... a further "refining"...a further "firing"...a further "cleansing process" and a further "filling" on the inside of you. If you can't say, "yes" to all of these categories (on the heart of God), then you have to go through the "fire" again. There are more "firings" for you!

I told you in the introduction that God's processes are in "multiple firings" and in "multiple fillings" so I am just telling you the truth to try to prepare you for what lies ahead. It's the only way. For if you think you have been through the fire already – think again! God will bring you through it yet again!

In Daniel chapter 3: Shadrach, Meshach, and Abednego came through a furnace that was heated up seven times hotter than normal. It's not just a onetime furnace seven times hotter. Seven is the number of "fullness and completion" and it actually refers to a number of "firings" as many as it takes! There is <u>no</u> set number! It's whatever it takes to get you to the place of fullness in God, and it is largely up to you as to how many "firings" you have to go through. You must understand it's not etched in stone. It's not some formula or some program that we just walk through and then we arrive. No. God brings you through step by step; and it's what you need specifically suited and designed, perfectly, for exactly what you need. That's how God works! That's the specific God that we serve. That's how special God can bring your "firing". He can heat it up a little hotter just as you need it or He can cut it back a little bit so the "pot" won't crack. You see, He is the "Master Potter". (see Jer.18:1-6) He is the Master! And He knows exactly what you're going through – the circumstances of life – and He uses everything to *"work together for good to those, who love God, to those who are called according to His purpose."* (Rom.8:28) HE KNOWS EXACTLY HOW HOT TO SET THE FURNACE!! Remember this word. Halleluiah!

He is just bringing you through the "firings" of God. But, if you will hang in there, if you'll go through it, the good news is this: there is a "fourth man" in the furnace with you.

It is called a "theophany" in the Old Testament-- a time when God himself came down to the earth and showed Himself. When there was somebody extra in the story – somebody special – it's a "theophany"; where God came down and you aren't quite sure if it was a man, an angel, or God Himself. And Jesus is with you now to go through the "fires" of life. I told you it wouldn't be easy. It is going to

81

be tough and hard, but the good news is Jesus goes through it all with you.

Isaiah 43:2 says, "When you pass through the waters, I will be with you; and through the rivers, they shall not overflow you. When you walk through the fire, you shall not be burned, nor shall the flame scorch you."

Christianity is not an automatic "easy street." Quite the contrary, it is almost the exact opposite. Sometimes, I think it's even harder! The cost is great. The road is hard – to carry your cross; but the good news is this: the dividends pay quite nicely. The dividends are very high! You get eternal rewards in heaven, eternal jewels in your crown and all the eternal blessings will touch you in this life – you reap the benefits of all of these things – and you'll get some material blessings as well. But, the blessings will far out weigh any of the costs. And you'll have life again flowing back in your veins, and in your life, and in your churches. You'll have the life of God flowing back in your church services, once again. You'll have God flowing in your personal life once again too. You'll have unspeakable joy, and peace, and fullness, and glory, and all of these things. All that God IS! You can put no price on these things! You can put no price on your health. People spend hundreds of thousands of dollars and the costs have thrown our insurance industry totally hay-wire, because people need healing in their body. And, I'm telling you here right now, that there is healing for the body of Christ, today, in this day and in this hour! And it won't cost you a dime, because it's all by the way of grace! It's the way of grace!

The only advice I can give you is to get into a "covenant relationship" with the Most High God! And so, if you're not in "covenant relationship" and you don't live in the "secret place" – you've got to get there! YOU'VE GOT TO GET THERE!

If you have prayed before and you haven't got your healing yet, my only advice is you've got to get to the "secret place"! Get there! Get there! Get there! Because, I will tell you this, the fullness of God lies there! And all that He IS – He can give it to you. I don't have all the answers, but I do know this answer: MY GOD HAS ALL THE ANSWERS!!! So, if I can get you from here to there – from point "A" to "B" – I will get you to where you need to be and you'll get what you need! And, the God that I serve – He'll come through for you, just as He has come through for me. Halleluiah!

God's History of Grace

"I am the same yesterday, today, and forever; the same God that you read about in My word. Church of the Living God: HEAR THIS – I am the same yesterday, today, and forever!" The same grace that God showed His people beginning with Adam and going clear through to the book of Revelation to the last person you can think of in scripture, to the last man alive, God continually showed His grace throughout history to His people. It was through His love – the heart of God – the vehicle was through the way of grace- from Adam to Paul; from Adam to John; from Adam to James – all through to the last book written in the official canon scriptures of the Holy Bible. God has shown His grace over, and over, and over again. And He has poured out His blessing, after blessing, after blessing.

God first showed His grace to Adam in the garden. He created a beautiful world out of the vehicle of grace. God gave Adam everything he needed to live – a beautiful paradise! Adam had everything he needed. He had it all!

God also showed His grace to the patriarchs: Abraham, Isaac, and Jacob; and revealed Himself to them. God showed Himself through the Priest of Melchizedek, who appeared to Abraham and brought him provisions of "bread" and "wine". He came as a messenger of the Most High God. He came out of nowhere. He was a type of Christ. He had no beginning and no end. So, God appeared to Abraham that day and continued to bless Jacob in his life. He received the blessing of the firstborn. He was God's chosen seed to show His grace to the world. And so, God continued to bless Jacob's children – the children of Israel – all 12 tribes! All of them! Every single tribe! God poured out His grace and blessings upon them all. He fed them manna in the wilderness, He gave them water, quail, fire by night – to illuminate the dark places, and cloud by day. He gave them guidance, and His glory and presence was with them. God gave them everything they needed.

And even to Moses in the burning bush, was a picture of grace to deliver His people, the children of Israel, out of the bondages of Egypt. God initiated a plan. Later God was going to wipe them all out and start over again with Moses, but it was through Moses' intercession that God spared the people and saved them all from the wrath of God. God showed them grace – blessing after blessing. They wandered in the wilderness for 40 years to experience all of the "I AM". God was trying to show them who He "IS".

So, God even gave them a pattern in the "Tabernacle of Moses" – a visual picture of Christ and His plan of redemption. The tabernacle is in every detail a picture of Christ, but also a picture and type of how man is to approach a Most Holy God. Those same principles and protocols still hold true for today! It's a way of grace from the "secret place" to the brazen altar – God to man. But from the brazen altar to the "secret place" it's a way of man's walk of faith and obedience unto the Lord. So, the entire picture of the tabernacle of Moses – piece by piece – in every detail is a visual picture for the church today, to glean from those truths of the Old Testament.

"Now all these things happened to them as examples, and they were written for our admonition, upon whom the ends of the ages have come." (ICor.10:11) The Old Testament reveals Christ for us to learn and see the deeper truths that are written in God's word. The tabernacle is a way of grace. God came down to the earth to dwell among His people. The "Tabernacle of Moses" was the "House of God" for the children of Israel. The very dwelling place of the Most High God; where He could meet with His people. But, you see there was a sin problem! How can a sinful man dwell in the same place as a Most Holy God? The tabernacle of Moses reveals unto humanity how to deal with that sin problem. And so it takes you step by step through the process of how you today, can "dwell in the secret place of the Most High God". It is possible! It is possible, today, for God and man to dwell together. Heaven and earth can come together and dwell in the same place at the same time, at the same moment! For you see, this tabernacle was a picture of Christ in every detail. Jesus was the full embodiment of grace.

"And the Word became flesh and dwelt among us and we beheld His glory, the glory as of the only begotten of the Father, full of grace and truth"..."and of His fullness we have all received, and grace for grace. "For the law was given through Moses, but grace and truth came through Jesus Christ." (John 1:14-17)

He was the full embodiment of grace. So, too, when you look at the tabernacle, it's a picture of Christ! It's an embodiment of grace. It's a visual picture of God's grace. Jesus was heaven and earth combined together! One plus one equals two! Heaven and earth came together in the life of Christ! Heaven and earth can come together in the lives of God's people! Heaven is coming down to the earth in this day and in this hour. Who will be a ladder from earth to heaven and from heaven to earth? Jacob's ladder is coming back in this day and hour. Jacob only saw a vision of the gateway to heaven – the earth realm mixing with heaven's realm. He only saw a vision, a shadow of things to come; only a portion of what was to come in the future.

"Church of the Living God: We are living in the day of Jacob's ladder – where heaven and earth can come together!" (see Gen. 28:12)

"One plus one equals two! And this being the second chapter of this book; it's by the way of grace. God is bringing down the heavens through His grace. He is rending the heavens and ringing them out with His hands as if He was wringing out a towel that has been completely saturated in His presence. He is rending the heavens in this day and in this hour; and He is sending forth the rain." (see Is. 64:1; Joel 2:23, 24)

Hosea 6:3 reads, "He will come to us like the rain, like the latter and former rain to the earth." "Church of the Living God: It is beginning to rain! He is sending not only the spring rains, but the autumn rains as well. Where people have planted for years and years in the spring – there is coming a harvest; and the harvest will be great! He is bringing the autumn rains in this day and this hour; and they will be heavy. They will be heavy." (I Kings 18:41-46)

He is rending the heavens. He is rending the heavens. But it will be for those who will go and get in the rain. Don't run from it. Run into it! Don't reject it and run away; accept it and run into it! Run into it and get "soaked to the bone" until you're saturated in God's presence. The key word is "until"-- whatever it takes. There's no formula. There's no number of how many times: three times, four times, five times, six times, seven times. Seven is the number of perfection and completion. It's whatever it takes – however many times it takes for God to perform the work He needs to do in your life. So, my advice to you is just go soak awhile! Get into God's presence and simply soak until you are saturated with His presence. Stop "doing" and start "soaking"! That is the best advice that I can give to you. And also, get into the word of God – eat "bread" and "wine" – just like the Priest of Melchizedek brought to Abraham. Eat of "bread and wine"; which is to eat of Christ the "bread of life" and drink the "wine" of His holy spirit. He is breaking open a new bottle of wine that has never been drunk before in this day and in this hour. He is bringing forth a new wine just like at the "Wedding of Cana". (see John. 2:1-11) He saved the best for last! He is bringing forth a realm of His Spirit that has never been drunk before in the earth. Halleluiah! Glory to God!

So, if you will simply just come to the wedding – you've been sent an invitation. If you'll just answer it and come; you can drink of this "new wine" that God is pouring out into the earth.

If you'll simply come; come to the waters and drink. Come into the "rains" and get "soaked to the bone". Come and do whatever it takes in your life. Be desperate for God! BE DESPERATE FOR GOD …once again! Do whatever it takes to get to the "secret place". Will you say, "God, I will do whatever it takes, and I will not stop until I get all the way to the 'secret place' – to the place of your dwelling – to the place of where you are today! Because, where you are – that's where I want to be. I don't want to just follow your trail of things that used to happen – that used to be – of some old revival somewhere. I want to be where you are now!" Halleluiah! If that's your heart's cry, come go with me.

Come! Come with me!!
I will show you the way.
I will show you the way.
Glory to God!

Grace Understood and Received

"Church of the Living God: You must come back to the cross and when you come back – get a picture and a revelation of My grace all over again. My church: you need to understand that you were saved by grace and everything that I give unto you is by the way of grace. I need you to get that revelation into your mind and into your heart; and throw out everything else that is contrary to that revelation. It is by way of grace that you are saved. It is by way of grace that you are filled. It is by way of grace that you receive the gift of the baptism of the Holy Spirit. It is by way of grace that you receive all the gifts of my spirit," says the Lord.

Every gift – gifts of prophecy is by way of grace. Every gift in I Corinthians 12, every spiritual gift listed is by way of grace. In every

86

gift listed in the New Testament, gifts of administration, gifts of encouragement, etc. they are all given by way grace. This is the place of understanding that we must return to. God's anointings are all by grace. And there's not just one – but many. They're progressive! They are all by grace! Eternal life is all by grace. You can't earn it! There's nothing you can do. It's all by grace. So, when that's understood and you return to that place it will be more easily given out and we will get to that later. But for now, you must get this revelation. You must receive this into your minds and hearts and understand it.

Who can comprehend it? Only he that comes to the place of the cross, and picks up his own cross and gets that revelation of being at the feet of Jesus. Only he can receive it! Only he can understand it. So, church this is where God wants you to come back to. He wants you to get that understanding and that picture of Jesus. Come back to His feet and look at God's grace throughout history and receive it. Understand who God is-- again! Understand that He is a God of grace and full of graciousness who loves to pour out of Himself and His blessings upon His children today!

One of the greatest pictures of grace in all of scripture is given in the life of one man in the Old Testament by the name of Mephibosheth. Not many people have ever heard of this name, nor even his life. There's not much teaching on this person today, and he is usually overlooked; but a great picture of grace nonetheless.

Mephibosheth was of the House of Saul – his crippled grandson who by all rights should have been executed by King David when he came into power. In all the uprising of the House of Saul – King David had the right to just kill them all; everyone that was in rebellion against King David. But instead, David showed tremendous grace to Mephibosheth. A beautiful picture of grace out of his love for Jonathan (Saul's son) and his respect for the King and Gods anointed. Out of David's respect for all of this and being the man of God that he was- he was a man after God's own heart – he allowed Mephibosheth to live and gave him his life back. But not only that, David could have just released him on his own accord to live out his days as best he could as a crippled peasant man perhaps begging for the rest of his life. David went beyond that. He restored all the land to Mephiboseth that belonged to his grandfather Saul and decreed that he would always eat at the King's table. And David also commanded servants to farm the land for Mephibosheth and bring in the crops so that he would be provided for. Perhaps most of all, Mephibosheth ate at David's table like one of the king's sons. (see II Sam. 9:11)

Mephibosheth was blessed beyond measure. More than he could have ever imagined. Beyond his wildest imagination, he received blessing, after blessing, after blessing-- all through the grace of the King!

And so you see, you are a picture of a modern day Mephibosheth. You are crippled in your own life and you deserve only death, but you have an invitation to eat at the King's table as a son, and eat all that you can eat; all that your heart could desire. <u>You are a Mephibosheth!</u> You have been pardoned and you, now, can eat at the King of Kings and the Lord of Lords table and eat of His food – all His word – from Genesis to Revelation. Every promise of God is at this table and you can become a partaker of this "food" by believing God's word for you and applying it to your own life.

That's just one example of grace in God's word. There are many, many more throughout the scriptures too numerous to list them all. Just one other that comes to mind is seen in the life and story of Queen Esther! She went from being a peasant girl to being a Queen – all by God's grace. You are also like a Queen Esther that is about to go before the King and if you do so presumptuously you could have the death sentence placed upon you and have your head chopped off! What a picture of grace! She entered into the King's chamber uninvited and the king showed her favor; extended his golden scepter to her and allowed her to come into his presence to hear her case. He wanted to hear what troubled her own heart, so the king gave her the time of day and listened to what she had on her mind. <u>You are like a Queen Esther</u>. The King has allowed you to come into His chamber, raise His royal scepter to you and say, "Come in my good and faithful servant. Come into my chamber and let us talk awhile. Let me hear what you would have to say. For what troubles you – troubles Me. What is on your heart is on My heart. For as you have the heart of God, it is on My heart as well. What would you like the King to do for you today?"

That is a picture of grace! And that is a picture of the grace and position that you are in today, where you can come boldly to the throne of grace. Where you can also receive mercy and not receive your death sentence and the King of Kings would listen to a man, woman, or child as agreeing as touching any one thing in the earth according to His written word – and He will do it for you! That is grace! Where you deserved death but received favor and blessing instead! That's a picture of grace. That is what Queen Esther faced. But you see, she had to prepare herself, first, before she could go into the chamber of the king. (see Esther 2:12) She couldn't go in unprepared. She had to get ready; and so it is with you. It is a picture of the church today, of how we must go through the preparations in the tabernacle of Moses before you can dwell in the "secret place" of the Most High God – into the very presence of the King himself!

You have to go through some preparations first. You can't just rush in presumptuously. There are some things you must go through before you can dwell in the same place as such a Most Holy God.

For you see, there is a sin problem and it must be reconciled. You have to go through the fire of the brazen altar. You have to go through the forgiveness of sins where the judgment of God is lifted which is the outer court and the brazen altar. Then, you have to go through the brazen laver which is the washing of the water of the word in cleansing and being purified with the word of God. Then we get to the next chamber – the Holy Place.

In this chamber only the priest could go. You had to have the garments of the priest on before you could even enter into this chamber – this second chamber on your journey to the secret place. You now have to put on the garments of the priest. "This is the realm of My Spirit," says the Lord. "These are the realms of My Holy Spirit!"

It is interesting that the same word used in the New Testament when Jesus instructed the people to wait in the upper room until they were "endued" with power from on high. That same Greek word for "endued" means: to be "clothed". For you must be "clothed" with the garments of the priesthood to enter into this chamber. If you don't have the garments of the priest on or put another way – if you are not endued with God's power from on high – if you've not "clothed" with the baptism of the Holy Spirit – you'll never enter this chamber. You'll never enter the chamber of the Holy Place. And I know that is a harsh word to some, but the buck stops here! If you think the baptism of the Holy Spirit is for yesterday or for whatever reason you don't think it's for you – you can't enter the Holy Place! And that's not just me saying that – that's God. It's all in the picture and type of the tabernacle of Moses. It's God's protocol! It's a visual picture of Christ in every detail and it's also man's approach to God that Moses made after the divine pattern. So, you'll never get to the "secret place" because you have to go through the Holy Place to get there. So, you'll never get the fullness of God unless you put on the garments of the priest. And to do that, your going to have to accept that the "Baptism of the Holy Spirit" is for you--today! It's not a Pentecostal thing or a Charismatic thing. It's a GRACE THING! And it's for the entire world –wide Church of God that He is coming back for at the culmination of the second coming of Christ! This gift is for all people from all nations, from all tribes, from all tongues, from all denominations in this day and in this hour!

Church of the Living God: God is pouring out of His Spirit in these days and He is no respecter of persons. It does not matter what denomination you are from. The baptism of the Holy Spirit is for you! Speaking in tongues is for you! You may not understand it all the way, but it's still for you, nevertheless. So, if you'll take a step of faith instead of believing a lie – you'll receive from heaven and you'll move forward and be blessed. You'll put on the garments of the priesthood and you'll enter into the next chamber. You'll enter the Holy Place where so much more awaits you, and I will get into that later on. There is so much more of God for you to experience! But, you'll never discover it because you never accepted the truth of God's word that the baptism in the spirit is for you.

The word of God says in Acts 2:38, 39 that ... *"the gift of the Holy Spirit..."* *"For the promise is to you and to your children"*... and your children's children and for every generation to come until the Lord returns!

Until you get that truth into your mind and your spirit – this is as far as you go. And if you choose not to believe it; you can close this book and give it to someone else who will. Because there is someone else out there who will believe upon the word of God and the truth of this word. Even the truth of the "Rehma word" that God is speaking as it lines up with His "Logos" or written word in these days and in these times. The baptism in the Holy Spirit is for everybody! People from all walks of life; all denominations; for rich or poor; all races, black, white, red, blue, it doesn't matter where you've come from or where you have been – it matters where you are going, and where you are headed!!!! Where are you headed?

That is the only point of significance in your life today- the only thing of significance that God looks for in you. It's not where you've been--it's where you're going! It's where you're headed that's important.

Where are you headed today?

Are you going to stop here, at the brazen laver, where you've gotten the washing of the word? You've been baptized in water in obedience unto the Lord. You've experienced salvation and gone through the Brazen Altar and your judgment has been atoned for. You've been washed and purified by God's word. Now, I charge you this day: Is this as far as you will go?

Will you close this book and never open it again? Or, will you believe on His word that the baptism in the Holy Spirit is for you? It is for you, your children, and your children's children and their children until Christ returns! The baptism in the Holy Spirit is for you today! Will you believe upon that word today? And if you do receive the promised gift – you will clothe yourself with the garments of the priesthood and you will be able to enter in to the next chamber of this progression – the Holy Place – where only the priests could go.
"You'll enter into the realms of my spirit," says the Lord.

The "Holy Place" in the tabernacle is a picture of the realms of the Holy Spirit working and operating in the church today!

"For this is My word unto you this day," says the Lord God Almighty. "Will you go to reach your full potential in God; to receive all that I have for you, and eat from the King's table as Mephibosheth did everyday of your life until the day I call you home? Will you eat from the King's table every day? You're invited to eat from the King's table. Will you open the invitation? Will you accept? Will you come and take your rightful place seated at the right hand of God at the King's table, and partake of all of His delicacies, and all of his food that is at His table? It's all set before you! From "Genesis" to "Revelation" – it is all for you! But will you eat of it today? That is my question to you this day. Will you eat all of the food that is at this table?"

If you will, continue on! If you will not; you know what to do.

Grace Given Out

When you receive and understand God's grace into your life, it is not meant for you to store it all up just for yourself. It is meant to be given back out again. And so it holds true for all that God gives to you – all that He is and all that He gives to you-- is not meant for you to store it up just for yourself; but it is to be given out again to someone

91

else. And so it is true with grace, as we come to the cross and we understand what is that good and acceptable will of God regarding grace for you – you understand it – become saturated in it – you soak in it – and now it's not time to hoard it all up, but it's time to be given back out once again.

"Church, I am calling you this day," says the Lord, "I charge you this day: you have been found wanting. You have been found lacking. This is an area that the church of the Living God has been falling short in tremendously in the body of Christ, for many, many years. Simply, to understand grace, walk in grace, and then give it back out once again."

"Church of the Living God: I am charging you this day to receive the love of God and receive the grace of God – understand it inside and out, and then walk in it – LIVE IT! Be the picture of grace to the rest of the world, even as Jesus was the full embodiment of grace Himself. So too, as you desire to be like Jesus; know that that is the goal to be shaped into the image of Christ. If you're going to be in the image of Christ, then you have to walk in grace as He did – the full embodiment of Jesus Himself. So, if you look at the life of Christ in the scriptures and all that He is and all that He did – it's all a picture of grace that you should be to the world. Jesus is a picture of the grace of God in full function to the entire world."

"And I am sorry to say that you have not been walking in the grace of God. James 4:6 says, 'God resists the proud, but gives grace to the humble.' There is a contrast here. I charge you this day: you have been walking in the former state – a state of pride and arrogance saying, 'look at us. Look at what we've got' and this verse simply states if you walk in that realm – what happens? God opposes the proud! You are in direct opposition to the Lord God Almighty. You're not walking closer to God-- you're walking further away! You're not pressing in to get into the deeper places in God, to go to the "secret place" – you're walking away. You're walking in the wrong direction."

"Church of the Living God: I charge you this day – Repent of the pride! Repent of the arrogance! It's not about you! It's all about Me!"

"If you will do this, and repent, and go to the cross, and understand the heights and depths of the grace of God and receive it into your life; then and only then are you going to be able to give it back out again to the world around you as I have called you to give."

"I have called you to be a picture of the full embodiment of Jesus Himself. You have not been representing Jesus Christ Himself very well in the earth. You are coming across more like a spoiled rotten child that has everything-- full of pride and arrogance. You're coming across to the world as a "brat" – still a child of God, but a "brat", nonetheless. Just enjoying his toys and staying in his own room, not doing any of his responsibilities or obligations. Church of the Living God: I am calling you back to a place of responsibility; a place of doing your chores; of listening to your father's voice and not being a spoiled "brat" shut up in his room!"

"Church of the Living God: I am charging you this day to walk in obedience to the Lord your God; to hear His voice and know it, and then walk in it; obey it; not just go in one ear and out the other; but to OBEY IT! Put feet in it and WALK IT OUT!"

"Church: I am calling you back to a place of the cross to receive a revelation of the grace of God – a revelation of its definition in its purest sense. And when you get that revelation you'll be able to give it back out once again as I have called you to give it out, to your brothers and sisters in Christ in the church, and also to the world-- to the lost and the dying. The ones you pass on the street everyday – all the time-- the homeless; the down and out, the drug addicts, the prostitutes, the gang members, all of these that the world would look upon as the lowly and not give them the time of day. But, My grace is sufficient for you; and My grace is sufficient for them!"

"And so, if you will walk in a place of grace, you'll be giving out all that 'I AM that I AM that I AM,' to a lost and dying world; and you'll be giving My grace to your brothers and sisters in Christ as well. You'll be giving them the opportunity to be who they are in Christ and to exercise their gifts without condemnation – exercise their gifts and callings without being called down or be put in their place. You'll be giving them grace to learn how to walk in their giftings and the grace to possibly make a mistake – God forbid – without rebuke and harsh punishments."

"You need to extend grace to them and treat them as young children who are learning how to walk in their giftings and their callings and allow them room to grow in Christ. They need to grow in their giftings because they're just young children. They need to learn how to walk and grow in those giftings as well, so that they can be a blessing to one another!"

"Church of the Living God: I charge you this day to take a second look at James 4:6: 'God resists the proud, but gives grace to the humble.' Let me say that one more time. He gives grace to whom... the humble! You must humble yourselves before the mighty hand of God. He that humbles himself, lays down his life, and takes up his cross and follows Jesus – he shall be exalted. It is he that will find life and find life more abundantly. It is in this place and in this understanding that you'll begin to experience all that God is and all that God has."

"You have been found lacking and have been found wanting, because you don't understand the grace of God. There is more that I have for you," says the Lord God Almighty. "But, you must understand this grace first in your own heart and life!"

Someone who understood grace in the Old Testament and was exemplified in their life was Joseph. Joseph was a great man of God and a great man of faith. He trusted in God even in the midst of great adversity. His very own brothers threw him in a pit and left him for dead. They would have killed him, but even they exercised a certain amount of grace so they thought the lesser would be better. So they threw him into an empty cistern and left him there to die. Then they had a better idea. "Why not make some profit?" they thought. So they sold him into a life of slavery. God had His hand upon Joseph and extended to him His grace and lead him to the very palaces of Egypt to where he held the keys to the storehouses of all the food reserves in the land. God used Joseph mightily to make that happen; and along came his brothers in the days of famine on the brink of starvation. They had to come and bow down to the very brother that they once opposed. Joseph could have sentenced them to death. Joseph had such power – second in command of all Egypt – he could have ended their very lives right then and there. But, Joseph extended God's grace to his brothers, who only once opposed him and once tried to kill him and were his enemies. He now accepted them for who they were and allowed them to experience the blessings and the grace of God in their own life that they did not deserve. So, Joseph poured out God's grace upon his brothers and gave them grain, food, and provisions, and sent word back to his father that he was still alive and well. So an entire family and nation was saved and blessed through the abundant grace that Joseph poured out so lavishly upon his brothers. This is a wonderful picture of God's grace being demonstrated in the life of one of His own. It is a picture of how we need to be today!

"Church of the Living God: I am calling you to be a 'Joseph.' He is a picture and type – a foreshadowing – of the New Testament church. You hold the keys to the storehouses to give out food in the days of famine to the world – to the lost and dying – not only your brothers and sisters, but to all! The same position Joseph held in his life, you now hold in yours!"

"But I charge you this day the words of the Living God: 'He resists the proud but gives grace to the humble.' Church: It's time to humble yourself before My mighty hand. Remember the grace of God that has been so liberally given unto you and as you have freely received – you need to freely give. So, I am calling you this day to receive my grace; an entire revelation of what that means once again!"

We sing a lot of songs about it. We sing "Amazing Grace" how sweet the sound: but how few; how few; truly understand the words of that beautiful hymn?

"Amazing Grace, how sweet the sound! It is sweet to your ears; now, you need to extend it to others so it will be sweet to theirs and be an extension of My grace to a lost and dying world. Church of the Living God: Be filled with My Grace today! " says the Lord God Almighty.

We need to get a revelation of what that word means – the grace of God. That, alone, will completely revolutionize your life and your ministry! This is just the beginning. This is just the beginning.

In the chapters ahead, I will call you to greater and greater things; where you will have to decide who you are going to serve. Are you going to serve yourself; or are you going to serve God?

And let me close this section with these words that bear repeating: "God resists the proud, but gives grace to the humble."

"Humble yourselves before My Mighty Hand," says the Lord. "Humble yourselves! Remember the grace of God that has been extended to you; so you, too, can extend it to others. For this is My word unto you this day," says the Lord God Almighty.

The Power of Agreement
1+1=2

"One plus one equals two! Simple addition, but within this equation lies the secret of power that My church needs to return to!

95

For in this day and in this hour I am calling My church back to the altars of the Living God. BACK TO THE ALTARS!! In the tabernacle of Moses, the altar of incense – rising up from man to God – was a symbol of the prayers of the saints. It is also mentioned in the book of Revelation – 'the prayers of the saints.'" (see Rev. 5:8; 8:3-4)

"But in this day and in this hour, the incense has not been burned before Me as it should. The incense is not being offered up at the altars of God. Church of the Living God: You have forsaken the altars of incense! You're not offering up prayers as you should and as are needed in this day and in this hour. You must embrace the work of the intercessor! You must embrace this ministry in this day! For without intercession – nothing happens. Without intercession – My Kingdom is not advanced in the earth. Without intercession – Satan wins. There are many battles that are being lost each and every day because My people have failed to pray as they should!"

"It is time to allow Me to light a fire in the Brazen Altar once again. The priesthood had to take the fire from the brazen altar and take it in to the golden altar of incense in the 'Tabernacle of Moses.' The priest had to take the fire of God and transfer that divine fire to combine it with their prayers at the golden altar of incense. The only way to bring back that fire, once again, is through My Spirit," says the Lord, "It is through My Spirit that ignites the fire in your prayer life."

"It is through My spirit – the realms of the spirit – that ignites fire in the prayers that are offered at the altar of incense – the prayers of the saints. They must be in complete agreement with the Holy Spirit in the earth. Complete agreement!" *"For we do not know how to pray as we ought, but the Spirit Himself makes intercession for us, with groanings which are too deep for words."* (Rom. 8:26)

"It goes beyond you! It goes beyond your comprehension! It goes beyond your understanding. It will even go beyond your language into the realms of the Spirit. You'll offer up prayers of intercession in the spirit – in tongues – in an unknown tongue and it can even go beyond that! It will go into groanings, travail and sounds! These are "the deep recesses" of intercession that you have forsaken; that you have considered strange and weird, that need to return! They are of My Spirit," says the Lord. "They need to Return. And My church: You need to listen to this word: Embrace the intercessor! Embrace this ministry; for without it – nothing happens! Get that word into your being, **for without it-- nothing happens."**

96

"You need to allow My Holy Spirit to light a fire on the inside of you, and ignite your altar of incense within you! You are an 'altar of incense'. You may not know that or realize that, but you; yourself; are an altar of incense. You are to be a vessel of gold that offers up the "prayers of the saints" within you that will rise up to the throne room of Heaven! It's a picture of the Tabernacle of Moses! It's the prayers of the saints in worship and praise unto their God!"

"Church of the Living God: I am calling you this day to realize a part of who you are is that you are an altar of incense to pray in the spirit according to the perfect will of God – to pray God's kingdom to pass in the earth."

"My Son, Jesus, is doing His part in Heaven. He is your high priest interceding at the right hand of God in the heavenlies; but I need someone to pray in the earth according to the perfect will of God and who will <u>agree</u> with God – with Jesus – in the heavenlies; and agree with My Spirit – the 3-in-1 God – who will agree with God in the earth as touching any one thing and it shall be done."

"You need to simply agree with God first and foremost, and if your life doesn't line up-- it needs to line up. If it's out of line, it needs to get back in line! If it's out of agreement with the word of God it needs to get into agreement with God, according to His perfect will as revealed in His written word!"

In God's word He declares that He is making *"every crooked way straight"*. So, everything in your life that is "crooked" and doesn't line up parallel with God's word-- is wrong! You need to look at it again and repent of it. If it's out of line, it needs to get in line. And so, God is trying to do this in your life, individually and corporately, in the church; but you have a responsibility to make sure that everything in your life lines up with God's word. Halleluiah! You need to be in 100% agreement with the word of God. That's the bottom line for your life! And so, if it's not in agreement with His word – it needs to be! That is the very first important step to a powerful prayer life! The next thing after you agree with God; then and only then, can you agree with someone else in the earth. God's word declares in Mathew 18:19, 20:

"Again, I say to you that if two of you agree on earth concerning anything that they ask, it will be done for them by My Father in heaven. For where two or three are gathered together in my name, I am there in the midst of them."

You see it takes two or three to establish the will of God, because one is open to error; two less error; and three less error. You can agree with someone else as touching any one thing in the earth according to the perfect will of God – according to what the Spirit would say-- and what the Holy Spirit knows, because He knows the perfect mind of God. He searches out the deep things of God!

I Cor. 2:10-12 says, "But God has revealed them to us through His Spirit. For the Spirit searches all things, yes the deep things of God. For what man knows the things of a man except the spirit of the man which is in him? Even so, no one knows the things of God except the Spirit of God. Now we have received, not the spirit of the world, but the Spirit who is from God, that we might know the things that have been freely given to us by God."

So, the Holy Spirit will lead you and guide you into what is that perfect, good, and acceptable will of God in the earth-- concerning all the issues of life. So, it's important; one, that you're baptized in the Holy Spirit, and two, that you speak in tongues and three that you pray in tongues so you can pray in the spirit. This is all in the "Holy Place" in the tabernacle of Moses. Remember, the "Holy Place" is the realms of the Holy Spirit! And without being "clothed" with the baptism of the Holy Spirit you can't even enter into this chamber.

"The altars of God have been forsaken! It is time to return to them once again. And this is a word from the Lord! It is time to embrace the intercessor. Allow them freedom to be who they are in Christ. Allow God freedom to be who He is – and then the church can be who she is supposed to be."

"This is My call unto My church," says the Lord, "Return to the "ALTARS' of God! I will light your fires once again! It will be divine fire; even as the priesthood would take divine fire from the brazen altar and bring it to the altar of incense and they would offer up the incense just before the veil. I will light divine fire on the inside of you; to energize your prayer life, so that you can properly offer up incense in the "Holy Place" so that your prayers can be powerful and effective!"

If you have thought in days past in your life that your prayer life just wasn't very effective, or that your prayers were just bouncing off the ceiling, I've got good news for you. The way to a powerful prayer life is one, be baptized in the Holy Spirit, two, speak in tongues

– pray in tongues and allow the Holy Spirit to pray through you! For it will not be you praying; it will be the voice of God in you – praying and speaking the perfect will of God in the earth. And the will of God will not be a mystery to you any longer, because He will reveal what is His heart, what is His will, and what is His word in the earth. The third key to a powerful prayer life is spelled out for us in the book of James. Chapter 5, verse 16 says, *"the effective, fervent prayer of a righteous man avails much."(NKJ)*

The prayers of the righteous are powerful and effective! A big key to effective prayer is your sins separate you from God. Your sins weaken your prayers. In James 5:17,18 the word of God says, *"Elijah was a man just like us. He prayed earnestly that it would not rain, and it did not rain on the land for three and a half years. Again, he prayed, and the heavens gave rain, and the earth produced its crops."* So, you, too, have the same power in prayer; but you must also be a righteous person. You must go through the process of going through the brazen altar and the brazen laver and all these things in your approach to God. And so, to get into the 'Holy Place', you would have already been through the Brazen Altar, which is symbolic of the fires of the Living God burning on the inside of you. It will burn out all sin and all that is not of you, and all that is not of God. All that is of you in your old nature, in Adam, will be gone!

"I am bringing back My power to My church, and I will bring a baptism of fire with the baptism of the Holy Spirit that will come upon My people," says the Lord God Almighty.

"I will baptize you with My Spirit and with My fire to energize your prayer life so that you can enter into the "Holy Place" to offer up prayers of intercession in the earth. And it will bring exponential power to your prayer lives – individually and corporately – as one puts a thousand to flight, two will put ten thousand , three a hundred thousand , and four a million. There is power in unity-- in corporate, unified, anointed prayer!"

"That's where the power lies! And that is what I am bringing back into My church," says the Lord God Almighty, "so, that the prayers of the righteous can be powerful and effective. I will revolutionize your prayer ministries in every church that will accept this truth!"

"You must embrace the intercessor! You must embrace the ministry of the intercessor. And if you do…if you do… look out world because your church will literally explode with God's power and presence in the earth."

"Church of the Living God: I am charging you this day. Come back to the Altars of God! Allow Me to start a fire within you so that you can offer up "prayers of the saints" in the Holy Place before the veil of God."

"Adam gave the earth away! I am taking it back through My people and through My Son Jesus Christ and His work on the cross. I am taking it back, but that's the only way."

"I am recruiting an army-- an army of the Living God --who will take their place in My kingdom and in this army. Will you take your place in the rank and file of this army? Will you take your place? Will you fall in line? Will you be a part of this army?"

"Because, the weapons of your warfare are not carnal but they are mighty through God for the pulling down of strongholds…" (II Cor. 10:4). "The weapons of your warfare, they are not of this world! You must pick them back up once again. The weapons of your warfare are not carnal – they are not of this world – they are supernatural in origin and they are supernatural in their effectiveness. And you must pick them up again! You'll discover what all of these weapons are as we go through this book and just one is the power of prayer."

"I charge you this day, Church of the Living God: Return to the altars of God! It's time to weep between the porch and the altar. It is time that My priesthood, My royal priesthood, who has been called by My name reinstitute all of your royal priestly duties, and one is to offer up the incense at the golden altar of incense in the Holy Place. RETURN BACK TO THE ALTARS OF GOD!! Burn incense, once again, before the veil. Because, as you do… A TSUNAMI OF MY SPIRIT," says the Lord, "will be unleashed in the earth, and you will be a part of that tsunami! I am bringing a move of God that has never before been seen in the earth in this day and in this hour! And I am raising up an army of intercessors who will pray in the spirit according to the perfect will of God to usher it in!"

"If My people don't pray, nothing happens! But, I am raising up an army. And it is building, and the rank and file, they are taking their place. And where they are taking their places, they are realizing who they are in Christ and the power that lies within them and that is available to them! They are taking back their world for Jesus, in their own life and in the life of their churches!"

100

"So, will you take your place today in your rank and in your file in this army? I am calling you this day to take your place. Will you take your stand and do the warfare that is necessary in this army… to pray like never before … to weep between the porch and the altar… to pray UNTIL?!! There's no formula! Just pray UNTIL! WHATEVER IT TAKES!! However many days it takes. However many times it takes. Just pray until!!"

"Would you be willing to do just that? If you are – continue on! If you are not, close this book and give it to someone else who will!"

"It's a serious day, and a serious hour! For this is God's message to His church in this day and in this hour. For this is My word unto you this day," says the Lord God Almighty.

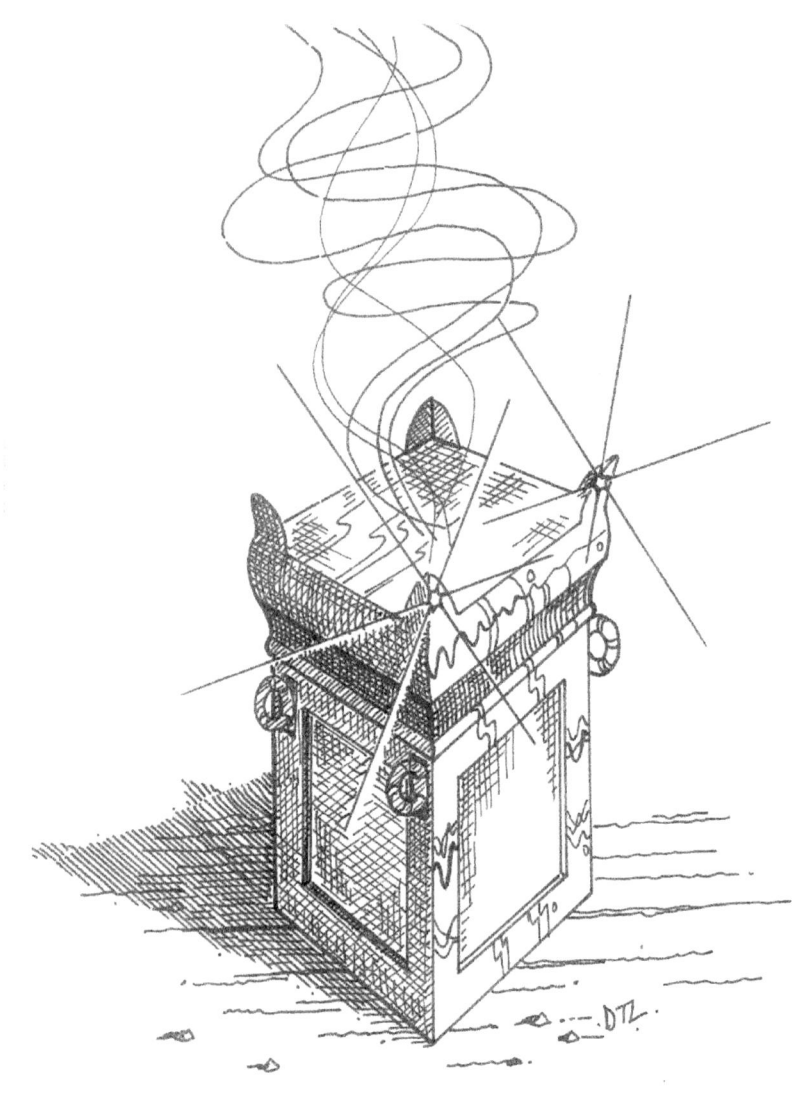

The Golden Altar of Incense

This altar was made of acacia wood overlaid with gold.
Incense was to be burned on it every morning
then again at twilight.

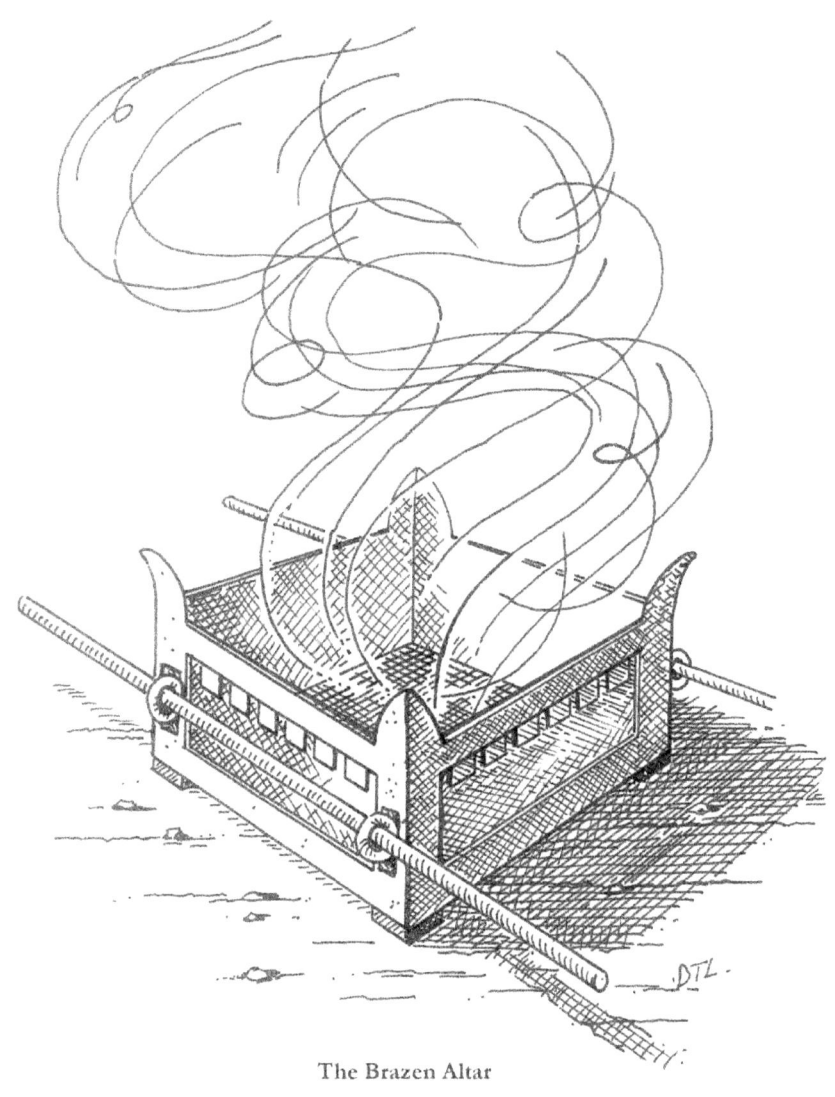

The Brazen Altar

This altar was located in the outer court where the animal
sacrifices were offered. The blood was then applied to
the four horns and set on fire.

Chapter Three

God's Mercy vs. His Judgment

"He does not treat us as our sins deserve or
repay us according to our iniquities…" Ps.103:10
"He shall take the blood and sprinkle it on the mercy
seat seven times." Lev.16:14

The Power and Strength of Three

*"Though one may be overpowered, two can defend;
a cord of three strands is not easily broken." Eccl. 4:12*

Three's are everywhere in our world today! Three's are everywhere you look! Two are good, but when a third is added it is strengthened considerably. Just think for a moment of all the three's that there are around you. They're everywhere! There are three work shifts…three domains: earth, sea, and air…three parts to a day: morning, noon, and evening…three sides to a triangle that make a very strong base: look at the pyramids of Egypt! There are three stages to maturity: childhood, adolescence, and adulthood. A three legged stool will not totter back and forth…three places awarded: first, second, and third…three metals awarded: gold, silver, and bronze. There are three primary colors from which all others can be formed. There are three time periods: past, present, and future. A third note added makes a cord that produces a more pleasant sound. Consider a cube-- there are three dimensions: length, width, and height that form a solid object. It would be interesting to list as many groups of three that you could possibly think of. Even the multiples of three are quite common in our world: 3, 6, 9, 12, 15, 18, 21, 24, 27, 30, 33, 36, 39, etc.; also three in multiples of ten: 3 x 10 = 30; 3 x 100 = 300; 3 x 1, 000 = 3,000 and so on.

These numbers are all around us in our world today, in all aspects of life. Why? Because, they originate with the creator of it all! They originate with the "originator"! The word used for God, in the very first verse of the bible, in Genesis 1:1 is the word "Elohim". *"In the beginning, God created the heavens and the earth…"* The word "Elohim" is the plural form for God and points to the triune nature of God, or the trinity. Here we see the Father, the Son, and the Holy Spirit all present at the creation of the world. So, even in the very beginning, we see a cord of three strands that originates in the Holy Trinity – the Godhead – Father, Son, and Holy Spirit. And it is from Him that all things flow. It is from Him that we get everything else. So, it is very important to recognize this connection between God and our world. These groupings of three are very strong. The verse in Eccl. 4:12 means that two are good, but when a third is added great strength and power are gained!

We can see even in the Bible itself, having a total of 66 books in all, is comprised of multiples of three. Sixty six is a multiple of three. There are 27 books to the New Testament and thirty nine to the Old – all multiples of three. Even in the framework of the word of God alone, we see that there are these cords of three strands! The number 3 and its multiples are throughout the entire Bible from beginning to end. We see many, many, groupings of three's in the word of God from cover to cover. It's loaded with three's! This is only a partial listing, so here's just a few!

There are three that testify: water, spirit, and blood (I Jn.3:8). There were three metals in the Tabernacle of Moses: gold, silver, and bronze (Ex. 25:3) ... also three colors: blue, purple, and scarlet, (Ex. 25:4)... three courts or chambers: Outer Court, Holy Place, and Most Holy Place. There were three main feasts in the Old Testament: Passover, Pentecost, and Tabernacles. (Deut. 16:16) There are three facets of man: body, soul, and spirit, (I Thes. 5:23)... three virtues: faith, hope, and love, (I Cor. 13:13)... three gifts to baby Jesus: gold, frankincense, and myrrh, (Mat. 2:11)... three aspects to the Son: Jesus is the Way, the Truth, and the Life, (Jn.14:6)... Angels cry three holies: Holy, Holy, Holy, is the Lord God Almighty, (Is. 6:3, Rev. 4:8). There were three patriarchs: Abraham, Isaac, and Jacob (Ex. 3:15). Remember, there were three Hebrew boys in the fiery furnace: Shadrach, Meshach, and Abednego. (Dan. 3:23) Esther called a three day fast before going in to see the King. Then, there are the three heavens, and the three year ministry of Jesus on earth. I think you get the picture! From cover to cover, all throughout scripture you can see this pattern of these groupings of three.

And so it is with this book: "Abiding Under the Shadow", it begins with a cord of three strands-- Chapters One, Two, and Three: the love, grace and mercy of God. These first three chapters give you a good foundation for which to build upon. Three very important aspects of God that we need to have a good understanding of for our lives. There are many, many, cords of three strands in our world and there are many that God wishes to give us depending on any given situation. He is not limited to just one cord, but God can give us many different cords of three strands as the need arises.

107

The Mercy of God

"Who can understand it? Who can know it? Who can experience it? He that comes to the cross! And again – MY CHURCH – I call you to the cross. It is a place of love, grace, and now a place of MY MERCY." I want you to get a picture of Jesus Christ and Him crucified. I want you to picture yourself, again, there that day, up on the hill of "Golgotha" – "the place of the skull". It was a place of death. The Roman Crucifixion was one of the cruelest ways of capital punishment ever to be devised by man. Jesus Christ is being crucified on that cross and you are there at the very foot of that cross. Picture yourself being there that day. It may have been a sunny day, and not a cloud in the sky, and Jesus is suffering, after he has been beaten almost beyond recognition, and the blood is flowing. There are the three that testify: the water, the blood, and the spirit (I Jn. 5:8). And there was water and blood that gushed forth from His body that day when the roman guard sunk a spear into His side to see if He was still alive. I want you to picture yourself there that day. Some of the people are crying and lamenting over His death; but others are rejoicing, laughing, and mocking at Him. They placed a crown of thorns upon God's Son's head and pronounced Him: "The King of the Jews", which prophetically – Pilate wanted to have put over Him in mockery, but in reality was a prophetic testimony in the earth of His true identity! He is the "King of the Jews". He was then, and He still is now, and He always will be!

This is a place of mercy! Because mercy – let's define mercy. It is a punishment that you should have received but you didn't get. And as you are here at this cross, the picture of mercy, realize that you should have been on this same cross. You should have been there instead of Jesus. You should have been nailed to that cross, to receive your just punishment for your sins! For you see, "the wages of sin – the payment for sin-- is death" (Rom. 6: 23). Sin must be reconciled! Sin must be reconciled! It must be paid!! The price of sin must be paid. Either you pay it, or you let someone else pay it! And that word will still hold true for those that do not accept Jesus as their savior and apply His blood to their heart. For those people, they must pay the penalty themselves, and they will. They will die, spiritually, emotionally and physically. They are dying slowly now without God, and they will die ultimately – spiritually – and they will go to hell – a place without God – to pay the full price for their own sin.

So, I charge you – the world – this day: Who? Who will pay your price? Will you pay it, or will you allow someone else to pay it for you? And the only one else that is fit, worthy, and willing to pay your death penalty for you – there is only one man willing to do that and fulfill it all – is the "God – Man" Jesus Christ! He was the only one willing, able, and fit and worthy to do it. There may be other people in the world that would lay down their life for you, but you see, they are not a fit sacrifice. They are not a worthy sacrifice, because the one that had to pay the penalty for sin, would be someone that was without sin – a perfect lamb – a perfect sacrifice-- someone that had a different nature than you. Jesus was not of this world. He was supernatural. God is His father, and He was born of the Virgin Mary. He was heaven and earth coming together for you. He was fully God and fully man – able, worthy, fit, and willing to go to the cross for you. He was the only one in the history of the world that could have gone to the cross for you. That is why Jesus is the WAY, the TRUTH, and the LIFE. He is the only way!

Some of these other religions are good in the world. They have some good moral standing and framework within them, but the one thing they all fall short in is they do not look upon a man who was sinless – who was heaven and earth combined in one body – and who died and rose again under His own power. Christianity is the only religion in the world based upon the resurrection of a man who came back from the dead under His own power. And you see, on that day He demonstrated who He was; where He came from; and that even death, hell, or the grave could not hold Him! Even death itself could not contain Him! He was more powerful than even death itself. Jesus Christ also demonstrated His power in the earth during His three year ministry. They estimate He began it at the age of thirty – which is a multiple of three – and He died at the age of thirty three. Jesus demonstrated His power in the earth over sin, sickness, disease, and death. He showed His power to raise many others from the dead also. He did miracle, after miracle, after miracle. He turned water into wine. He multiplied the bread and fish to feed the hungry, and not just a few but thousands! He commanded even the waves of the sea to be still and they were. Even the elements of nature obeyed His voice, because He created them! He could even walk on water and defy the laws of gravity. Gravity couldn't even pull Him down into the water. He defied every natural law that there is. And the one that absolutely blew everyone's mind was on the <u>third</u> day-- He rose from the grave! When Jesus died, the scriptures record that the sun was darkened for three hours and there was an earthquake. The earth itself trembled! The curtain of the temple was torn in two from top to bottom, and even the tombs were broke open and life returned to many of the holy dead, and they went and appeared to many. All of these things pointed to the fact that Jesus was truly the Son of God! And the Roman centurion guarding nearby; knew that confession and said, *"Surely He was the Son of God!"*(see Mat. 27: 45-56) All of this testified to the world, of the fact that Jesus Christ of Nazareth was who He said He was! He was, and still is, the Son of God! And He said, *"If you have seen Me, you have seen the Father".* He was not only just the Son of God – He was in complete agreement with the trinity. He was God in the flesh. He was heaven and earth that had come together!

God came down to touch humanity – to be involved with <u>their</u> creation! He didn't just stand back and watch the world go around. He engaged His creation. He engaged the cultures of the world, to reveal Himself to a lost and dying world – to reveal who He was, and is, and is to come.

This is the **picture of mercy** that the church needs to return to. And the symbol of the **cross** again is one of the most universal symbols of Christianity, but how few understand, and how few take it to heart what this symbol really means. It means someone else died for you, in your place! It's not just a pretty ornament around your neck or decoration hanging on your wall. The next time you look at a cross I want you to envision that that is where you should have been and think, "that was my cross... I should have died there instead of that innocent man." Jesus was an innocent man condemned to death for a crime that He did not commit. He only did good in the world. He took upon Himself your crime, and was punished for you. That is a picture of mercy.

So, if you have your own cross necklace and you haven't thought about it much, the next time you look at it, I want you to say to yourself, "that was my cross". That's the mercy of God. He took a punishment that was mine and gave it to someone else. That was mercy. That is mercy in your life today!

The next time you see a cross on a church, or see one sitting through a service, I want you to look at that cross and say to yourself, "that's my cross." For you see, **the death at the cross of Christ is not the death of just one man.** If you take up your cross and follow Him, **it is the death of all men!** Christianity is a calling to the cross! It represents the death of all men! And you must take up your cross and deny yourself. Jesus said; *"…whoever loses his life for my sake will find it."* (Mat. 10:39)

His kingdom is not of this world. It is directly opposite to the natural world that we live in. So, to find life in God's kingdom, you must lay down your life. You must lose it and give it all. That's what God is calling us to do today; for us to give it all to Him. Give **ALL** of our life--**all** that we are; **all** that we have; **all** that we're not; and **all** that we don't have; **all** of our dreams, our hopes, our future, our ambitions, our finances, and our desires.

I know you have heard this before, but it bears repeating. God is asking us to give it **All!** Anything you can think of, because it's not ours anymore. It's not our life. When you come to Christ, you come to Him as Lord and Savior and you ask Him to save your soul from hell. He's asking you to give your life to Him. And so when you did, and said the sinner's prayer, I believe in that day you knew what you were doing and you gave your life. But, I think it's a natural tendency over the course of life, we drift from the place of the cross and we forget that it's not about us, it's about Him; and that we are to give our lives completely – 100% - over to Jesus, because He gave His life for us.

Even in the movies when someone saves someone else from dying, they commit their life to that person, because now they are indebted to them; and they say, "oh, I owe my life to you" … "I'll serve you till the day I die" … "I owe everything that there is to you" … "I commit myself to you". In Christianity, it's the same way with Jesus and the cross. When you come to God, He gave His life for you, and all that He asks is that you give your life back to Him – in service and devotion all the days of your life. And also, do all that He says and all that He commands you to do. And you'll simply say, "Yes, Lord, Yes" … "I'll do what you ask" … "I'll do what you say." Not out of burden, but out of love and devotion and commitment; because He died in your place. And because He died, you can now live!

He not only gives you eternal life in the life hereafter; but He gives you life today! Jesus said, *"I have come that they may have life, and that they may have it more abundantly." (Jn.10:10)* You can experience this abundant life in this world, today! Now! All of your problems, all of your struggles, and all of your trials; God can turn around for good. He can reverse them all and shower blessing, upon blessing, upon blessing, down into your life-- all because Jesus died. It's all at the cross. He paid the full price to redeem man one hundred percent. It wasn't a partial payment. He didn't pay just a little bit. He paid everything He had. Why? So, that you could have everything restored back to you that you were originally meant to have. Jesus paid the full price to redeem man one hundred percent in his spirit, in his soul, and in his body. It has all been made possible. The way has been made! The deal has been struck! It has all been legally done. The wrath of God has been satisfied. In all of God's righteousness and justness, because He is the perfect judge, He has to judge sin. So legally, it has been paid up. The debt has all been paid in full. The way has been made!

I want you to keep this all in mind, as we continue on in this chapter, because we're going to talk about all of this combined. You can't talk about mercy, unless you talk about judgment as well. And you can't talk about those things without talking about Jesus' death, burial, and resurrection. And because of that, He has restored all things back to His people – to those who will simply come to Him and say, "Yes, Lord, Yes" … "I WILL follow you" … "I will do whatever you ask" …"I'll follow you to the ends of the earth" … "It's not my life anymore" … "I give it to you".

And right now, I want you to bow your head with me, as you read this book, and say this small prayer with me in these few moments. Lord, Jesus, I come to you very humbly, and I ask your forgiveness for all of my past sin, my present sin, and my future sin. I ask for your forgiveness for taking the symbol of the cross for granted. Lord Jesus, I'm sorry that I have done that, and the next time I look at the cross it will mean more to me than it has in the past. The next time I look at the cross, I will look at it as if that was my cross. Jesus took my place upon that cross and He died instead of me, and the wrath and judgment of God fell upon Him that day at "Golgatha" – on Calvary's Cross!

He took upon the wrath of God and the judgment of God on Himself – the full wrath of God! And it has all been paid. Everything is paid up in full. And it is because Jesus died and rose again that all things can be restored back to me. And God, I know now, that is mercy! I didn't get what I deserved!

And God, this day, I give you everything. I give you my life--a life for a life. Jesus, you gave me your life and now I give you my life. I want to give you everything. I may have given you everything in the past, but I may have wandered from that place. So, Lord God today, I come back to that same place, and I recommit my life to you. I rededicate my life to you. I give it all to you! All that I have, all that I am, all that I don't have, and all that I am not; all my dreams, my hopes, my ambitions, my future. I even give you all of my time, too.

Everyday from this day forward until the day you take me home. I come back to the place of this cross, and I come back to a cord of three strands that cannot be easily broken. And this cord of love, grace, and mercy, will be strong in my life. I'll not easily forget these revelations of love, grace, and mercy that have been given to me in this book.

God, I thank you for bringing me back and it's by your mercy that you do so. For you do not deal with us according to how our sins deserve, but you deal with us according to your mercy, your grace, and your love! I thank you and I give you my life once again.

And I want to continue on in this journey. I don't want to let anything stop me from receiving all that you have for me, God. I'm hungry for you, and I want everything you have for me, so that you can reveal yourself in the world today and that I can be a co–worker with you in your redemption of mankind.

God, this day, I lay everything at your feet-- at the cross of Jesus Christ – for it is in His name that we pray – AMEN.

Mercy Received – Mercy Understood!

There are many examples of people throughout history who have experienced God's abundant mercy. So many, in fact, it would take volumes of books to contain them all and write about their stories. Throughout the Old Testament, New Testament, and even throughout modern day history, it would take volumes to write about each and every one. So, just a few examples that we have already mentioned that we'll use again where now mercy is seen in the life of Mephibosheth, the life of Esther, and the lives of Joseph's brothers.

113

They all received grace as we know, but it's hard to talk about grace without talking about mercy. Because, before they received their grace – the grace of God and the blessing of God – they also experienced the mercy of God.

We'll start with the first example: Mephibosheth. Remember, He ate from the kings table – King David's table – invited to eat there all the days of His life. That was the king's promise to him. I know he lost his life later on, but it is still a picture of the church today being invited to eat from the king's table. What Mephibosheth did deserve was death, but he didn't receive the punishment that he deserved. King David showed him an abundance of mercy, not giving him what he deserved. He didn't just kill him on the spot because he was of the House of Saul. King David came into power, the reign of King Saul had declined and God's favor had shifted from Saul because he didn't walk in obedience to the Lord, and so it was transferred to King David – now God's anointed. (II Sam. 4:4,9)

Mephibosheth had received such mercy, and the same holds true for Queen Esther as she approached King Xerxes I. (Esther 5: 1-8) Her life was hanging in the balance, as she prepared herself to go before the king, anything could have happened. In her day, the king of Persia, if you went in without an invitation or appointment, he could just say, "off with their head." It was to that severity and to the utmost seriousness. But, with great courage, she had to go in to see the king, because she was going not only for herself, but for the entire nation of Israel-- for an entire people-- the Jews-- God's people. They were about to be completely annihilated by an evil plot, that was actually Satan himself, again, trying to wipe out the children of Israel – God's chosen.

So, Esther goes in to see the king, and has prepared herself for six months soaking in the oils of myrrh, and six months of perfumes and cosmetics, all just in preparation! It's a picture of the church today. So, she goes in through the chamber doors and they are opened wide and she approaches the king. Not knowing what would happen, the king extends his royal scepter to her in favor. He said to her, "Up to half of my kingdom I will give to you. What would you ask of the king today?" So, King Xerxes extended to her an abundance of mercy for she had come in unannounced. He could have killed her right then and there, or had her killed by someone else. It is a great picture of God's mercy that Esther received and then she ended up also receiving an abundance of blessing.

And we come to a third example in the lives of Joseph's brothers-- same thing-- God's pattern. They should have received, perhaps, the death penalty for all they did to Joseph. They threw him in a pit leaving him to die, and then sold him into slavery, arriving in Egypt, to Potiphar, one of Pharaoh's officials. They took his whole life away from him. Took everything he had: his family, his relationship with his father and loved ones, his surroundings, all of what he knew and was comfortable to him. He got shipped off to a foreign land and not only forced into slavery, but then was thrown into prison. Convicted of a crime he did not commit. That sounds familiar!

Joseph is also a type of Christ pictured in the Old Testament. Convicted of a crime he did not commit. Imprisoned! And those prisons, I'm sure were not like our prisons in America. Perhaps more like third world prisons ..., very, very, dark, wet, cold, and dirty. Joseph lost it all. He had reached rock bottom-- in a pit. But God brings him from pit to palace to display God's mercy to his brothers. They deserved the same thing. They deserved prison or even possibly death.

Through a series of divine events, Joseph is promoted to second in command in all of Egypt, next to Pharaoh himself. He went from prison to palace; from nothing, to having all the power. Pharaoh said to Joseph, "… *without your word, no one will lift hand or foot in all Egypt.*" (Gen. 41:44)

Incidentally, Joseph was thirty years old when he entered the service of Pharaoh, King of Egypt. (v.46) So, he had all the power to say whatever he wanted to his brothers when they came to him. He could have had them punished, thrown into prison, or even had them executed. But, he chose to show them the mercy of God, instead. He didn't have them killed, but on the contrary, he wrapped his loving arms around them and he couldn't wait to tell them who he was. Joseph said, *"I will give you the best of the land of Egypt and you can enjoy the fat of the land."* (45:18) Joseph blessed them abundantly beyond anything they could have ever expected.

All because of the love, grace, and mercy of God that was in Joseph's heart – all a type of Christ. He could demonstrate all that to his brothers with such great compassion and tender mercies – no anger; no revenge; only the mercy of God!

The word "mercy" in the Greek means: tender mercies, and to show great compassion. Joseph showed this to his brothers that day; and so too, this is what Christ shows to us. It is of tender mercies and with great compassion that we don't get what we do deserve! If you're still breathing, you have experienced God's mercy! If the ground hasn't opened up and swallowed you up for disobeying the Holy Spirit or God's law, you've experienced the mercy of God.

The word of God says in James 2:10, *"for whoever shall keep the whole law, and yet stumble in one point, he is guilty of all." "For the wages of sin is death, but the gift of God is eternal life in Christ Jesus our Lord." (Rom. 6:23)*

If you're still breathing, you've experienced God's mercy! You just need to accept Jesus as your savior, and apply by faith, what He has done on the cross for you. Believe on it, accept it, and take it into your thought processes and all that you are. Call upon the name of the Lord and then you will be saved! Saved from God's wrath; from God's eternal punishment in the lake of fire and hell itself – a place without mercy, a place without anything associated with God and His goodness that you have now experienced in this life.

Anything good in this life that you have experienced up until now is through the grace and the mercy of God. Mercy and grace combined together. It's hard to separate the two. But think on all that is good in your life – all the blessings! If you have a roof over your head, three meals a day; if you get three – most don't get that; your family; your friends; all that is good. Whatever you enjoy, it is all by the grace and mercy of God. God is calling you to Himself. And, He is pleading with you to accept His son's sacrifice in your place. He died for you so that you wouldn't have to. But His atoning work on the cross must be accepted in your life. His atoning work: His death, burial, and resurrection – you must believe it and accept it as fact, by faith, as a reality in your life. And it will begin to work for you! But, you must take a step of faith, first. So, if you haven't received Jesus as your savior; you must do so now! You must do so today!

"For whoever calls on the name of the Lord shall be saved." (Rom. 10:13)… Saved from hell itself… Saved from punishment… Saved from God's wrath, and also saved from sin and the affects of sin. You see, *"the wages of sin is death"*. The "wages" of sin in your life by you continuing to live in sin and disobedience from the Lord your God, is that you experience little bits of death in all those areas-- all of those areas of disobedience-- little bits of death roll in each and every day.

And one day, you'll experience the fullness of death, hell and the grave, because you'll be sent there!

But in the mean time, you wonder why you're struggling; trying to do it all on your own; trying to do it in the flesh, the natural, and in all of the world's wisdom. It's because it's all in the realm of sin against the knowledge of God in rebellion against God's word and God's law.

God is asking you to come into agreement with His word – the Holy Bible – and come into agreement with what He says about you; which is reality anyway. So, He looks upon you as a sinner that needs to be saved by grace. That is reality!

You should have been on that cross. So, you can either take the punishment yourself, or let someone else. And so, this day, God is calling you to let someone else! He doesn't want you to take it yourself! He doesn't want you or anyone to take it themselves. He sent His son, Jesus, to die for the whole world.

"For God so loved the world that He gave His only begotten Son, that whoever believes in Him should not perish, but have everlasting life." (Jn.3:16)

God wants you to have everlasting life. But, it's a choice! It's your choice, today! Will you choose, today, to receive God's mercy and understand it and allow Jesus to take your place on that cross? Will you apply all of that to your heart and life, today?

That is a picture of what God wants you to do today, with His son – crucified on a cross at Calvary. You must decide today. What are you going to do with Jesus? What are you going to do with Him?

The whole world must decide. They have been trying to decide what to do with Him for the last 2,000 years. But, you must personally decide what you are going to do with Him in your own life. You can't listen to what other people will say, because they won't stand with you at the Day of Judgment. They won't be there. You'll stand alone. So, you can't listen to what the world is saying about Jesus or anyone else. You must search your own heart; in your heart of hearts-- deep, deep, down inside. What is your heart saying to you? Who is Jesus? Was He the Son of God? Was He who He said He was? Did He die on a cross; that is a historical fact? Did He rise from the dead on that resurrection morning – on the third day – on that Easter Sunday morning? Did He rise from the dead to demonstrate His power even over death, hell, and the grave for you? If Jesus didn't rise from the dead then all of

Christianity is a lie and all that He said and lived for is a lie. But, He proved to the whole world that He was who He said He was. He was the Son of God-- the only man ever to come back to life under His own power. Yes, there have been others raised from the dead; but it has been by someone else. Jesus was the only man in history that came back to life under His own power!

And it should prove to you something special; something out of the ordinary; something absolutely supernatural. You should come to the same conclusion that the Roman Centurion did that day: **"*Truly this was the Son of God!*"** *(Mat.27:54)*

Jesus was who He said He was. So, I'm calling you today to a place of decision. Search your heart. Will you come to that same conclusion? "Jesus was who He said He was! And, I need to take another look at this man they called Jesus, and how He affects my life." Many others may say, "So, what?"… "But, I need to take another look. I need to take another look at this man they called Jesus… take another look at His life!"

It's all recorded in the four gospels in the New Testament, and in fact, He is seen throughout the Old Testament as well. The entire bible points to Christ! The Old Testament was a shadow of things to come; a picture and a type of the substance, or reality, of what would be. Jesus Christ and Him crucified-- the entire Old Testament-- pointed to Him. It all speaks of Him. It is all written of Him. There are many, many, types and pictures. They are all a foreshadowing of the Christ to come. So, you see, we can't just throw out the Old Testament. In fact, we need to dig into it deeper and discover the hidden truths that are written between the lines… *"Line upon line; precept upon precept."* They are all there. He is all there. We need to see Him! We need to see Jesus throughout the Old Testament. It is all written about Him and there is a great wealth of truth and a great expanse of knowledge in scripture hidden in all the types and pictures. God has given us visual pictures and parables to display, and to bring across deep, deep, spiritual truths so we can understand them easier in our lives. Jesus spoke in parables in the New Testament; where God spoke in pictures, symbols, and types in the Old Testament.

One that God has given for me to use as the writer of this book, is the "Tabernacle of Moses". I know there are many other types and other tabernacles. There is the "Tabernacle of David" and there is the more permanent "Temple of Solomon", and all these things contain great, deep, spiritual truths within them. I also understand that the "tabernacles" are an unfolding revelation throughout history beginning with Moses, then David, then Solomon, up until even the church today is a tabernacle of God – a temple of God – or a habitation of the Living God. But for this book and my purposes here, I am using the "Tabernacle of Moses"!

God is using the "Tabernacle of Moses" to bring forth this truth in this book "Abiding Under the Shadow", in this day and in this hour. And you see the "Tabernacle of Moses" is a picture of the blending of the two together: Mercy and Judgment. We see mercy shown in the third chamber, here again that number three, where the "ark of the covenant" resided, which is also the third ark mentioned in scripture. The "ark of the covenant", which we have seen before, was a chest or a box that contained the law, the manna, and the rod of Aaron. And on top of this ark there was a cover. This cover was made of solid gold and it had two cherubim, one on each side, and in between was what God called the "Mercy Seat". And it is interesting that it is called a "seat", because no one ever sat down on it!

Once a year, on the "Great Day of Atonement" the High Priest had to enter the Holy of Holies, where the Glory of God resided over the ark, and apply the blood from the animal sacrifice at the brazen altar and take it to the "mercy seat", on top of the ark. He had to make his way through the different processes and protocols to get to the Most Holy Place, or "the secret place". He would hope and pray that he had done everything right the night before so that he wouldn't drop dead in the awesome presence and glory of God. So, the High Priest would risk his own life, once a year, to offer atonement for the sins of the entire nation. When the blood was applied to the "Mercy Seat", it was transformed from a seat of judgment into a seat of mercy; and the wrath of God was satisfied for another year through the blood of the animal sacrifice that was shed.

It is very significant that the priest needed to get the blood from the brazen altar, where the judgment of God fell on the animal, and take that blood and apply it to the mercy seat! Inside the ark was the broken law of God that needed to be covered by the blood. The penalty needed to be paid!

"Without the shedding of blood there is no remission of sins."(Heb.9:22)

So, the innocent animal had to die and be the sacrifice for sin. There had to be a blood payment. Life is in the blood. So the wrath of God fell on the animal instead of the people. But, it didn't stop there. The High Priest had to take the blood and sprinkle it upon every vessel in the tabernacle and then go behind the veil into the Holy of Holies and apply the blood seven times to the top cover of the "mercy seat" on the "ark of the covenant". Seven symbolizes fullness and completion – a finished work!

Jesus, our High Priest, gave himself as a perfect sacrifice at the cross, or His brazen altar, and shed his own blood, then took it and entered the throne room of heaven or the "Holy of Holies", and applied his own blood to the "mercy seat" and satisfied the wrath of God. And now, the judgment of God does not have to fall on you! His blood must be applied by faith to your heart and to your life.

You are an "ark" of God! You are an **"ark"** of God that can be a vessel of gold to carry the power and presence of God himself in the earth today. But, you must apply the blood of Jesus' sacrifice to your heart, the completed work of Christ, who now has <u>sat</u> down at the right hand of God, seated in the heavenly places making intercession for you until He comes again.

He sat down! He sat down at the right hand of God. His work is finished! This mercy seat has now someone to occupy this throne. Jesus entered the throne of heaven and sat down on the throne of God. He sat down on the "mercy seat" because it's a finished work. It's a done deal. It's completed!

The priest in the "Tabernacle of Moses" had to remain standing the whole time while carrying out his various duties. Everything involved with the brazen altar, the brazen laver, the candlestick, the table of showbread, and the golden altar of incense – it all had to be done standing. There was no place to sit down. And they still never sat down on the ark's mercy seat, because theirs wasn't a finished work. Their work had to continue on. They had to do it every day. They had to sacrifice continually the blood of bulls and goats to satisfy the judgment of God against sin. But, now Jesus has offered himself as the perfect "Lamb of God" for the sins of the world. He was without spot or blemish – without sin. He offered his life willingly for you; all you need to do is apply the blood to your life.

God is calling us today to present our bodies a *"…living sacrifice, holy, acceptable to God, which is your reasonable service."(Rom.12:1)* As a living sacrifice, we need to visit the brazen altar in our own lives, and allow the fire of God – His "Spirit of Burning" (Is. 4:4) – to burn up all that is not God in our hearts and lives, and allow God to have His way in us. Then make our way as a holy priesthood through the duties just as they did in the Tabernacle of Moses; and do the same things – symbolically – to get to the "Holy of Holies", or the "Secret Place of the Most High".

So, it's very, very important that we study and understand these deep hidden truths in the "Tabernacle of Moses" and in some of these pictures and types; because they are all a shadow of the things that were to come, and a shadow of Jesus Himself! Now, we are living on the other side of the cross and the resurrection; but we still need to look back at these truths so we can better apply them to our lives, and better know what our responsibilities are, and what God requires of us still today!

What responsibilities do we have? By studying the "Tabernacle of Moses", it will help us to figure these things out. It gives us a visual picture and visual demonstration for us to see and look at. What was carried out in reality in those days, are still examples for us to learn from today!

So, we have gained some insight and understanding as we have looked at different aspects of the "Tabernacle of Moses". There will be more on this later as we progress.

We need to understand some of these basics – receive them, and understand them, so we can better be able to give mercy out to others, as we have been called to give.

Mercy Given Out

We must receive mercy and understand mercy ourselves before we can effectively give it out to others. We've seen some examples of mercy in the Old Testament, of people who have given out the mercy of God. David gave it to Mephiboseth; Joseph gave it to his brothers; King Xerxes gave it to Esther, and now we need to give it out to all those around us. As we have freely received, we need to freely give! (Mat.10:8)

So many times we are all guilty of judging other people, based upon what we see and quickly forget the place of the cross and what

God has so graciously given out to us. It's almost surprising to me that we look upon others in such judgmental ways and we are so quick to render judgments and condemn, and bring about a sentence as if we are the ultimate judge. That is only left for God. He is the judge and the lawgiver. He is the one that will have the final judgment for us all. So, it is not even our place to judge one another in this way.

"Church of the Living God: It is not your place to judge one another! I have not called you to be a judge. I am the Judge! I am the lawgiver. I sit on the throne in Heaven and in the Earth. That is My place to judge, and I will judge everything. I will judge you, individually; I will judge the church corporately; and I will judge the world. Everyone! They will all stand before me one day and give an account of what they did and for who they are. It is not your place to judge another human being. You've been looking with your own carnal eyes. You walk down the streets and you judge those that are homeless. You judge those that are down and out; those that have lost it all; those that are in the bad situation that they are in, whatever that may be. The 'low lifes' as you call them, I the Lord God, want to call them 'Sons and Daughters'! I died for them too! I died for them on the cross as well."

"So, the next time you look upon anyone that you may consider lower than you, if you come back to the cross, I pray you no longer have that attitude. I hope you will look upon them and give them the same mercy that you have received and the same grace of God that has been so freely given to you."

"So, Church of the Living God; I charge you this day: No longer have the attitude of giving the rich man the good seat, and the poor man the bad seat. Even as I am no respecter of persons, I want you to be the same-- no respecter of persons. You don't know which next person, who is saved and delivered, and brought out of the miry clay – the pits of hell – will be the next great evangelist in the Kingdom of God. You don't know what damage they may inflict upon the Kingdom of Darkness. I want you to look at them in this light. You are recruiting people to the army of God; from one army to another. And I want you to look upon them with the potential that I see them with--not what they are now; but what they can be and what they will be!"

"That's what I want you to see-- through the eyes of Christ. That's the perspective in your mind and in your heart that I want you

122

to have – for the world, for the lost, even for your brothers and sisters in Christ, for all of humanity, for anyone! Do not judge them!"

"For with the measure you judge, you will be judged. I haven't called you to judge. I've only called you to give out my love, my grace, and my mercy, and bring them to the cross. Be fishers of men and bring them to the cross, and I will take it from there. Pray for them. Love them. Give them mercy and grace, and I'll do the rest," says the Lord.

The Brazen Laver

To give mercy out to others, it helps to see mercy displayed throughout scripture, and one of those places, again, is pictured in the "Tabernacle of Moses". It is a shadow of Christ. So, for us to be like Christ, it helps us tremendously to look back at the tabernacle. Because the tabernacle, remember, is a picture of Christ in every detail! When you look at the tabernacle – you look at   Jesus Christ!

If you were able to see the "Tabernacle of Moses" from an aerial view, you would see that it's mapped out in the shape of a cross! Each of the tribes of Israel would each camp at a designated location; some on the North, some on the South, some on the East, and some on the West; with "God's tent"-- the tabernacle-- at the very center of it all! Even back then we see Jesus in every detail.

So, when we come to the outer court, we see the Brazen Altar and the Brazen Laver. Almost everything to do with the outer court was made of brass. Brass is symbolic for and speaks of judgment upon sin. To hold up the entire curtain of fine linen that defined the outer court, there were sixty pillars of Brass. There was the brazen altar, overlaid with brass. There was the brazen laver, which was a basin filled with water so the priests could wash their hands and feet. It was completely solid brass. All this brass speaks to us now of the ministry of the Holy Spirit in our lives. The Holy Spirit was sent to us to convict the world in regard to sin, and righteousness, and judgment. (Jn.16:8-11)

This outer court and entrance of the tabernacle with an aerial view in mind would be at the foot or base of the cross. In Dan.10:6 and Rev.1:15, we see Jesus' feet described as fine brass. So when we come into the tabernacle and begin at the brazen altar in the outer court, we are beginning at the feet of Jesus!

I want to look at the brazen laver for a few moments to help bring some understanding as to the mercy and judgment of God. Again, there were three metals in the tabernacle: gold, silver, and bronze, or brass. We are at the brass stage now. Brass speaks of the ministry of the Holy Spirit, and here at the brazen laver we see, also, the ministry of the word of God combined together. Ephesians5:26-27 says, *"that He (Jesus) might sanctify and cleanse her (the church) with* <u>*washing of water by the word,*</u> *that He might present her to Himself a glorious church, not having spot or wrinkle or any such thing, but that she should be holy and without blemish."* The laver points to judgment on sin through the word of God as it exposes things in us that don't line up with God.

The brazen laver was made of solid brass. They made it from the **"looking glasses"** of the women. These "looking glasses" were brazen mirrors, or hand mirrors, which the women gave in an offering to Moses as unto the Lord. They were today's equivalent of a "compact" or make up case used as instruments of vanity and pride; now ironically, being transformed into an instrument of washing and cleansing.

The whole idea of a mirror here is quite interesting. These polished brass hand mirrors were used much like today, to look at oneself and gaze at the beauty or the imperfections that one would see. In a mirror, we can see a true reflection of what we really look like! And so, this is the picture we see of the brazen laver and the ministry of the word of God in our lives, combined with the Holy Spirit's role. Where did the water come from? The water used in this laver, many suggest, came from the "Smitten Rock" (Ex.17:6) in the wilderness which also points to Christ. He was the "Smitten Rock". (ICor.10:4) He was beaten and bruised for us and from that "smitten rock" came forth the "water" for our cleansing.

First, we had the cleansing of the "blood" at the brazen altar; now, we have the cleansing of "water" at the brazen laver. Blood and water – just as it flowed from Jesus' side at the cross! (Jn.19:34) So, here we have the brazen laver, the washing of the word of God; the washing of Christ himself, because He is the word. (Jn.1:1)

And so, as we submit ourselves to the word of God, it has a two-fold purpose. It reveals sin as a mirror; and James speaks about this in *the New Testament. (James1:23-25) "anyone who listens to the word, but does not do what it says is like a man who looks at his face in a mirror and, after looking at himself, goes away and immediately forgets what he looks like." "…but doing it-- he will be blessed in what he does". (NIV)*

The word is our mirror! And as we look into this mirror, it reveals who we are. We get a true reflection of who we really are as God sees us – good and bad. When we read and meditate upon the word of God, it reveals who we are just as we are. And sometimes that's an ugly picture and we don't like it, and it's hard to see and deal with; but that's the ministry of the word of God in the Holy Bible; and the work of the Holy Spirit operating together in our lives. It gives us a reflection of who we really are! The priest would have to go to the brazen laver and wash his hands and his feet; and as he looked into that water, he would see a reflection of himself in the water and in the polished brass-- a reflection of who he truly was!

So daily, we need to examine ourselves and take a good look through the washing of the water of the word with the help of the convicting power of the Holy Spirit – who convicts of sin, righteousness, and judgment. We judge ourselves so God doesn't have to! We are only called to judge ourselves! You are only called to judge the man, woman, or child you see when you look in the mirror! That's the only person you are ever to judge in this world. So as we judge that person, we judge ourselves and we see all the things in us that don't line up with scripture. Then, God can help us make the necessary adjustments.

We are to help one another turn from error, in correction and in love, to build up, not to tear down, in correction to help, not in judgment to condemn, or to pass a sentencing. We need to look *"…intently into the perfect law that gives freedom"* and do what it says! (James1:25 NIV)

The word of God looks as far as the division of the *"bone and marrow"*-- into the deep, deep, places of the heart-- the deep, deep, places of your spirit. God knows who you are already; but often times you don't! You don't always see clearly enough, so things need to be revealed and reflected back at you through the word of God – the measuring rod, the plumb line, or the standard. You can see something better when you put it right next to a standard greater than what you already are. So you may say, "Oh my, I didn't know that, God, I'm sorry." It's an unfolding revelation. God brings us in slow – little by

125

little. And as with the priest, he had to wash many, many, times. He had to do it daily! So, too, we need to wash every day.

When you come to know Jesus as your savior, He doesn't do His work in you all at once. It's a process! And it is one that we must subject ourselves to every day. Spiritually speaking, we must come to this "brazen laver" every day to wash ourselves with the word of God. It is critical to your health and growth to read and meditate upon God's word daily. Everyone should read it at least a little bit – even just ten to fifteen minutes each day. Read one scripture verse a day, and say, "this is my verse for today." And if you were to memorize one verse a day, you would learn 365 new scripture verses every year! How great would that be for your life-- eating fresh manna coming down out of heaven; and washing your soul? So, as we come to the "brazen laver" or the "mirror", we see all that we truly are at the deep, deep, recesses of our being. And God, in His love and His grace, doesn't want us to stay as we are. He wants to wash and get rid of all the dirt and the filth, and all the things that are of this world – or of the earth. Because, you see, the "dirt" is from the earth realm, or the natural realm. So, we can wash and be cleansed, and get rid of all of this, so we can go farther and experience greater things of God-- things that are in the spirit realm. And we can be creatures that live in the spirit and not of the earth.

Sometimes, it is very, very, difficult to go through; but that's the work of the Holy Spirit and the word of God in our lives. That's their jobs! We need to just submit ourselves to what they are doing! Place ourselves on the brazen altar – no one else can make you go there! You have to do it willingly. No one can make you wash with water either. Just looking at water never makes you clean! It's one thing to see a truth or reflection of who you truly are, but now you have to stick your hands and feet in the water to wash and be cleansed. You have to choose to do that. You can't just see a word or a truth and expect it to work miraculously in your life. You have to apply it practically into your thinking and into your heart for everyday living. Walk in the Word moment by moment. You have to walk it out!

God just doesn't drop it all down out of heaven and make everything happen automatically in your life. You have to work some of it out yourself. You are a co-laborer with God, hand in hand. You have to work together with Him and come into agreement with His word. And that's where the renewal comes in. That's where the changing of your mind comes in. Remember, the Greek word for "repent" is metanoeo: which means to think differently. You have to change some things about yourself – all that you are! You have to come into the workings with that process, of what God wants to do in your heart and life.

The word of God shows you what you are now; what you should be, and what you can be! This is the very important ministry of the Spirit and the Word in our lives at the brazen laver, pictured in the Tabernacle of Moses. It's very important that we go back and study these things pictured for us in the tabernacle. I would encourage you all to do a study of this subject. There are many good ones out there. Look at every detail. It's fascinating what you will find! This book is not an exhaustive study for which time and space do not permit. I'll trust you to do some of that on your own. But, for these purposes, I'll just touch on some of the basics and use them as the framework to get us to the "Secret Place of the Most High." Allow the entire word of God, from Genesis to Revelation-- every word to be saturated into your being – soaked deep into your spirit!

The Holy Spirit is in complete agreement with the word of God. The ministry of the Spirit is in full agreement with the ministry of the Word. The Holy Spirit wrote the book and He will teach you the book.

"The Spirit of Truth has come; He will guide you into all truth." (Jn.16:13)

He is the revelator. He will reveal all truth to you. What you read in scripture, He will illuminate it. He'll bring light to it. He will give you the understanding. He will bring it into your heart and into your life. You can and will be all that you can be. And maybe you're not all you should be now; but God is going to shine light on who you can be!

God sees you with your greatest potential in mind – what you can be! That's how God looks at you. That is how this author looks at you as well. And I want you to obtain all that you're entitled to and experience all the fullness of God in this lifetime. And that is my goal – to get you to a place that you are receiving all that God has for you this side of heaven.

Do you want all that God has for you today? Or, do you want to settle for just part of your inheritance? If you want it all, come with me and I'll take you farther. I'll take you higher. I'll take you deeper. And, with the help of the Holy Spirit and His Word, He will reveal His truths to us – His "Rhema word", which lines up with His written "logos" word. Consider this; the word of God – His "Logos" word or His written word-- existed and was before time began. I don't know if you've ever thought about that before or not; but before the creation of the world and before time existed – the word was! Before it was ever written down, before it was in "logos" form, it was in "Rhema" form. It was in spirit form first! In the gospel of John, chapter 1:1, it says, *"the word became flesh and dwelt among us."* Jesus is the word of God. He was, and is, and is to come. And the same written word we now have in the Holy Bible for us to read and enjoy, it existed in spirit form in eternity past. And all that God is and was – He was spirit first! The word of God was in spirit form first! Then, it became "logos" word!

Now, God brings it back around and He has given unto us His spirit to clothe us and endue us with His Power from on High to be our teacher and our guide, and to reveal to us all the hidden mysteries that are within the word of God. So church, if you can handle that word, there is so much more yet to come; and we need the help of the Holy Spirit to teach us and guide us into all truth. This aspect of the Holy Spirit's ministry is pictured for us within the "Holy Place" at the "golden candlestick". These seven lamps point to the seven – fold expressions of the Holy Spirit as described in the book of Isaiah chapter eleven. It's all in the candlestick. We need the Holy Spirit to shine His light and illuminate the truth to us, today, in all His fullness; with all seven lamps being lit!

God is revealing truth to us in this day, and in this hour. It's not always a new truth that no one's ever heard before – it's just a revelation of old truth – perhaps, in a new way! Because there's so much of God – a lot of God hasn't even been revealed to us yet. We're still trying to unfold it and discover it for ourselves!

If you can handle that word, God is still somewhat of a mystery to us. We don't have Him all figured out yet. We've only just begun in this process. On the day of Pentecost, God began the birthing of the church. He began a new dimension of His power. We've only just begun to discover all of who God is. We've only just begun!

Will you come with me, church, and receive a fresh revelation of an old truth? Will you come with me and experience some fresh manna from Heaven? Will you come with me and go to a higher place in

God? But remember, to go higher, we have to go lower! If you will say, "Yes Lord, yes," then come with me and I will take you there. If you will not, you know what to do.

Resurrection and Restoration!

"THE GRAVE COUD NOT HOLD!! THE GRAVE COULD NOT HOLD ME," says the Lord. "I AM ALIVE! I AM ALIVE!" "Halleluiah"

"When you picture the cross and Jesus crucified, it's a picture of God's mercy. It's also God's judgment because He took upon your judgment. He took yours! They crucified Him that day, and they put Him in a tomb, and they rolled a large stone in front of it to keep Him in there and others out. But it could not hold ME there! IT COULD NOT HOLD!! Halleluiah! They added armed guards to guard the tomb, but it could not hold. I, the Lord God, I rolled away the stone! I brought life back into Jesus dead body, even after three days in the heart of the earth. Jesus himself prophesied of His own death, burial, and resurrection. He said, 'destroy this temple and on the third day, I will rebuild it. On the third day – I will arise!' Halleluiah!"

It's another three! The strength and power of three! It's the POWER of RESURRECTION – the Resurrection Power of the Risen Christ! If you talk about His death, you have to talk about His resurrection. On the third day, He arose from the grave. Death could not hold Him. Death did not contain Him. He demonstrated to the world that He was who He said He was. He was the Son of God, and still is today! He is alive and well, and He is seated at the right hand of God making intercession for you. He said, "I must go, so that the Holy Comforter may come."

The Holy Spirit is the third part of the trinity. He is still fully God. God is still moving in planet earth. He is still moving by His Spirit today! Is He moving in you? Is He moving in your church and in your life today?

I charge you this day: Is He having His way in your life and in your churches life today? Do you know and do you understand the resurrection power of the Living God? Do you know it? Do you know its power?

Before there's a resurrection there has to be a death! The apostle Paul describes in Phil.3:10, *"…that I may know Him and the power of His resurrection, and the fellowship of His sufferings, being conformed to His death."*

Before you can understand the power of His resurrection – there must be a death. Christ himself admonished us all to take up our cross and follow Him; but to take up our cross means to be identified with Jesus' death and burial. **We must die to ourselves!**

When you're baptized in water, which is also pictured at the brazen laver, you're baptized in the name of the Father, the Son, and the Holy Spirit. You're baptized into His death and His burial – symbolic of the old man being crucified in you-- all that is of your old nature in Adam-- born of sin. Has the old man completely died in you? Has the old man died and been crucified in your life – symbolically-- not physically. Jesus bore that for you at the cross. Jesus said,

"If anyone desires to come after Me, let him deny himself, and take up his cross, and follow Me. For whoever desires to save his life will lose it, but whoever loses his life for My sake will find it." (Mat.16:24, 25)

Have you followed Jesus today? Have you taken up your cross, today? Has death rolled in to the old man, completely? If it has, you can know the power of His resurrection! If it hasn't, there's a further work that God needs to do and it's unfolding – it's progressive! God will bring complete death to your old nature!

You see the next place Jesus went after He went to the cross, before His ascension; He also first *"descended into the lower regions of the earth"*. (seeEph.4:8, 9)

BEFORE YOU GO UP – YOU HAVE TO GO DOWN! Will you go to the depths? Will you go to the deep places of the earth?

For us to follow Jesus, you've got to go down to the depths of the earth. The word of God prophesied over seven hundred years before Christ with the *"sign of the prophet Jonah"*. *"For as Jonah was three days and three nights in the belly of the great fish, so will the Son of Man be three days and three nights in the heart of the earth." (Mat.12:40)* For the religious Pharisees and adulterous generation no other sign would be given to them. The greatest sign for all to see was that Jesus, too, would be in the *"heart of the earth"* for three days and three nights-- then rise again! He went to hell for you! Will you follow Him to the depths of the sea

130

– pictured in the life of Jonah--symbolic of a huge baptism of death to the old nature? Will you die to all that is in you? Will you die to your flesh or carnal nature, and empty yourself of all of the old; so that the new may arise?

We all are always full of something. The question is: **what are you full of?** You have to empty out of all that is not of God and go to the "depths of the sea"; which is again, like a huge baptism of water in the spirit realms. It's the death of you – to be baptized in the name of the Father, the Son, and the Holy Spirit. You are identifying with Jesus death and burial. God wants to roll in death to completely destroy your old carnal nature – in Adam. It is only he that has experienced the death of Christ that will experience the resurrection power of the risen Christ in this life. Halleluiah!

Before there's a resurrection, you have to experience a crucifixion. And you must take up your cross and be crucified with Christ; so then and only then, can you say,

"I have been crucified with Christ; it is no longer I who live, but Christ lives in me; and the life which I now live in the flesh I live by faith in the Son of God, who loved me and gave himself for me." (Gal.2:20)

To know the resurrection power of the living God, to truly, truly, know it – you must die to yourself! And then, and only then, can you truly know it. I want to tell you that today; yes, you can know of this power in your life! The same power that brought Jesus back from the dead can bring your life back from the dead. Halleluiah! Glory to God!

This same resurrection power-- the Greek word for "power" is most commonly translated as the word "dunamis". It's where we get our word "dynamite" from. It is powerful! It is explosive! It literally means: miraculous power; mighty; or to have the ability to perform miracles. This same power that was in Jesus, because of His resurrection, can now be in you! And what was once dead in you; God, can bring it all back to life.

For example, if your marriage is dying, God can make it new! If you're losing relationships, God can make them new! If you're losing your health, God can make it new! Anything and everything that you can think of in your life, you can get it all back because of the resurrection of Christ.

131

The same word "dunamis" is translated in the text of *Luke 24:49, "Behold, I send the Promise of My father upon you; but tarry in the city of Jerusalem until you are endued with <u>power</u> from on high"*; and again in *Acts 1:8, "you shall receive <u>power</u> when the Holy Spirit has come upon you…"* And one more example in *Acts 6:8, "…full of faith and power, did great wonders and signs among the people."* This same power, God is restoring back to you, individually, and back to the church, corporately. But before you can experience resurrection power, you have to experience death. You have to go through a crucifixion – spiritually.

Jesus has called us to follow Him! We must follow Him! He said, "Take up your cross", so we must take up our cross. Where did He go next? Before He went up, He went down to the lower regions of the earth – into the heart of the earth. We too, must follow Him there. We must follow Him to the "depths of the sea" just like Jonah! Where we come to the end of or the death of ourselves, and only then can we follow Him and begin to ascend upward into the Heavenly Realms to where we are seated at the right hand of God. We are seated in the heavenly places in Christ Jesus. But, before we can ascend, we have to descend. The way up is down!

God is calling us to a place of death; to a place of emptying out all that is within us – a place that is at the **"bottom of the sea"** – spiritually. Remember, I talked to you about Peter. He tried to walk on water that day in his own power and in his own strength. But, remember it wasn't God's intention for him to walk on water in that moment. Because, it was all in the mind of Peter – something he wanted to do. Jesus thought, "No, it's not your time, Peter…" "You've got to go to the depths. You've got to go down before you come up." So, what happened next? Peter began to sink; but that's exactly what God wanted him to do! He could not "walk on water" in his own strength; his own power; his own intellect; his own self. **He Could Not Do It!!**

"Church of the Living God: I'm calling you to go down. Come into the depths! Be identified with Christ's death and His burial. I'm rolling in death to you. I'm bringing a 'Spirit of Burning' and a 'Spirit of Judgment' upon sin. Remember, the Holy Spirit convicts the world of sin, righteousness, and judgment. In Isaiah 4:4, the Holy Spirit is described as a 'Spirit of Burning'. I must roll in this 'Spirit of Burning and Judgment' and death, before you can experience My Resurrection Power!"

"Church of the Living God: **You want the power without the DEATH!** You want all the miracles without the death! Church: It is a serious day! A serious hour! And this is a serious word! I call you this day to the brazen altar where you can be the sacrifice and allow the fires of God – a 'Spirit of Burning' – to come and consume <u>all</u> that is in you. Completely burn you to a crisp, until there is nothing left of you."

"Be crucified with Christ and be identified with His death and burial, and come to the 'bottom of the sea'. Empty out all that is within you. You have to come to the depths! This is My call to My church in this day and in this hour. **Come to the depths!** Come out into the deep oceans of God where there is a great vast expanse of God that awaits you-- a deep vast ocean of God that has never yet been discovered!"

"You have not tapped out the resources of God! There is so much more! Am I not endless? Does not outer space continue on forever and ever? Church: Have you come to the end of the resources of God? Have you come to the very end and extents of all that 'I AM'? The answer to that question you already know is an emphatic 'NO'."

"So, there's no other alternative but to come out into the depths, and go down into the deep places – the lower regions of the earth – the deep, deep, places of my Spirit," says the Lord God Almighty.

This great vast ocean, remember is symbolic of the realms of the Spirit. ***"Deep calls unto Deep!"*** *(Ps.42:7)* The trials of life, they are designed to overwhelm you. They are too much for you. Why? They are to drive you to your knees; to get you to see a higher power greater than yourself. They drive you to seek the Lord God Almighty, all the more. These trials in life, they are the *"waves and billows"* that sweep over you. They are designed to drive you deeper in God. Deeper than you could have ever gone without them! So, I want to encourage you today, if you don't give up and quit, and just stay on the journey – you're gonna make it!

It's just a time. It's just a season. God is saying, "Come to the depths of the Living God." He wants us all to come deeper into His realms of His Spirit and understanding of His word and know experientially how He moves! And I can guarantee you this; if you come and you reach rock bottom, there's a revelation that's awaiting that will be in later chapters that will absolutely, positively, blow your mind.

You will know the resurrection power of the Risen Savior. The same power that brought Lazarus out of the tomb will operate in your life! And it will bring you life, and power, and miracle working power back into you and to the lives of those around you. Wherever you go – God will go! Where you show up – God will show up, and He will touch lives! And He will be fully who He is; **because, you will abide under the Shadow of the Almighty.** And your shadow will be an extension of the anointing power of God operating in your life. Why? Because you live close to the Father! **You live in His shadow and yours is just an extension of His--** His power and anointing flowing through you – a vessel of gold.

"Church of the Living God: I'm calling you to the depths. I'm calling you to the depths of the sea," says the Lord.

You can walk in newness of life. You can walk in resurrection power – miracle working power. Don't let anyone else tell you that you can't. Because you can! And the same power that was demonstrated in the book of Acts can still be demonstrated in the world today! God is the same, yesterday, today and forever! He is the same. And the same power that worked in the lives of the apostles is meant to be worked in the lives of every believer on the face of the planet! If someone disagrees with you on that, just say, "That's OK, you can believe what you want; but I'm going to believe God! I believe God!" Halleluiah! Glory to God! It's all through His word!

"Your restoration--everything--was paid for at the cross. All of It! **When you think of restoration; simply put, <u>you get it all back</u>!!** Satan tries to steal, kill, and destroy everything in your life; he'll try to take it all. He would have killed you if he could. And he has tried; BUT… I, the Lord God, have paid the price for the redemption of mankind one hundred percent. All of it! Every aspect of your life has been bought and paid for by the blood of the lamb that was shed at Calvary-- by the blood of the Lamb that you apply to your heart – your 'ark of the covenant'. You apply the blood to your 'mercy seat' that turns a seat of judgment into a seat of mercy."

You are a royal priesthood! You must do this all by faith. If you have, Jesus has paid the price, a full redemption price, to buy everything back for you that Satan has tried to steal. So, everything that has been missing, everything lost, or broken, or damaged, God wants to restore it all. And not only back to its original state, but when God brings restoration, He brings it back better than it was before. He multiplies it and increases it, making it greater and better than the original – in greater measure and in abundance.

Jesus said, *"I have come that they may have life and that they may have it more abundantly." (Jn.10:10)*

God wants to pour out His abundant life upon His people. It is only limited according to the measure of our faith. That's the only limits placed upon God. He is limitless! The only restrictions placed on God are by man. So, where is your faith today? How much faith do you have? Can you believe God and what His word says? Or, will you believe man and what someone else will say to you?

Believe God! Take Him at His word! It is the gospel truth. You can take it to the bank. It comes with a guarantee! And if you will simply come into the contract – into the agreement and sign it in your blood, representing your life, the contract gets ratified in the earth for you. The deal has been met. The deal has been struck. There is an agreement. There is an accord. You come into full agreement with the word of God. It's a done deal, and the word of God, every promise from cover to cover – Genesis to Revelation – is yours! Every promise that the Lord your God has spoke concerning you – *"all will come to pass"*. All will come to pass. And the same words He uttered to Joshua, they all apply to you. Every promise will come to pass.

We see a picture of this restoration God's way illustrated for us in the Old Testament in Ex. 22:1. If someone stole an ox from you, they couldn't give just one ox back, they had to give back five. God multiplies His restoration back to you.

Even in the days of His outpouring of His spirit at Pentecost, I believe that was just the first fruits. God is bringing a move of His Spirit that is greater than the original. He is going to multiply it!

He is coming back for a glorious church, in all of her glory, without spot or wrinkle.

Church, we haven't seen anything yet! We are coming into the glory realms of God-- where the bride will come into her glory. It will all be restored in greater measure than we have seen throughout history. Get ready church. Get Ready! Do you have faith to believe that word? Do you have faith to believe it?

135

A FEW EXAMPLES

We see restoration in some other places in scripture throughout the Old Testament. Job is a great example of restoration in the life of a believer. All that the enemy had taken away, God gave it all back! And to what measure did He give? He didn't just restore it all back to its original state, He restored Job's life to twice what he had before – in a double measure, or double portion of what he had to begin with. God gave it all back and then some! He blessed Job abundantly. God poured out upon Job abundant provisions, grace, mercy and His love. Job's life is a wonderful picture of restoration-- God's way!

We can also see this type of restoration in the life of Joseph. What Satan meant for harm in Joseph's life, God turned it all completely around and used it for God's good and to the advancement of God's Kingdom. Not only to its original state, but He multiplied it! God saved Joseph and his brothers and not only them, but the entire nation of Israel along with the entire plan of redemption for the world. God saved it all and restored it all in the life of Joseph.

Joseph went from the pits of prison to the heights of the palace – from having nothing, to having it all. And that's exactly what God wants to do for each and every believer on the face of the earth. Regardless of denomination or background, if you'll simply believe God and take Him at His word, God can completely **"reverse the curse"** in your life! And what was meant for a curse against us under the law, because Jesus applied His blood to the "mercy seat" in heaven, it's no longer a curse, but now can be reversed! It can be turned around completely for good.

God can take you back to a place of restoration. It's like going back to the "Garden of Eden", spiritually, as I have mentioned before; but I'll elaborate just a little bit more. God will take you back to the "Garden of Eden" and you'll find out who you are in Christ, and where you are with God. And not only that, you'll discover what you are and what to do; in all your responsibilities in serving God, and you'll also discover some other unanswered questions of why, when, and how.

Why? You'll discover your purpose and mission in the earth. You'll discover when? Now! Now is the time. Today is the day of salvation! And you'll also discover how? How to be who you were called to be and how to accomplish your entire mission in the earth today!

You can find out all the answers to all of these things; because spiritually, you can go back to the "Garden of Eden", where everything is reversed in your life. A complete restoration, one hundred percent, in the life of the believer! Halleluiah!

God can also get you to soar up into the 'third heavens'. After you have taken up your cross, died to self, and gone to the 'bottom of the sea' – identified with Jesus death and burial, now you can ascend! You can come back up and experience the resurrection power of God, and ascend into the heavens; seated with him in the heavenly realms in Christ Jesus. Heaven and Earth can come together! You go up into the heavens, and the heavens come down! It's a "New Jerusalem"--where the heavens have come down into the earth realm and the curse is reversed! (More on this later) But for now, it is sufficient to say that in Hosea 6:2, the word of God says, "… on the **third day** He will restore us …"

On the **third day**, Jesus restored everything back to us: His church, His bride, His believers, His followers! Anyone that will call upon the name of the Lord and give their life over to God! It is a life for a life! That is what God requires of us!

I mentioned Psalm 91:1 previously: *"He that dwells in the secret place of the Most High, shall abide under the shadow of the Almighty."* For you to **get** it all – you have to **give** it all! And, God is asking you to come into a **"covenant relationship"** with Him! What does that mean again? You give your life! He is simply calling us – church – to give Him our lives: **all** that we are, **all** that we're not, **all** that we have, and **all** that we don't have. **Everything** about us! We need to hand it over! Surrender everything!

Will you surrender, this day? Will you surrender? Will you yield to what God wants to do in you and in the earth today? Will you yield to His Spirit and to His moving in your own heart?

Will you place yourself on the **"Brazen Altar"** and allow the **"Spirit of Burning"** – the spirit of fire – to come and consume everything that there is in you. And if you will, look out, because you'll experience the resurrection power – the miracle working power – of the Risen Savior-- Jesus Christ! You'll experience the "dunamis", explosive, power of God in your life. And it won't be just for you. Halleluiah!

God is calling His church to come to the depths for a reason! It's not only to bless you, but it is to bless the world! Will you take the plunge? Will you come to the depths? Will you submit yourself to the word of God and to the Holy Spirit of God? Will you say, "Yes Lord, Yes. Here I am"? If you will, I want you to pause for a moment and pray this prayer with me right now.

God, Here I am. I place myself on the "brazen altar" of God, and I want you God to come down as an all–consuming fire and burn out of me all that should not be. Completely consume me, so that there's nothing left of me and all that there is left **– is you!**

And Lord God, as I will take up my cross and follow you, I will follow you to the **"depths of the sea".** I will take the plunge, as Peter did, and I will begin to sink and go down to the depths. **Deep calls unto Deep!**

God, I will yield to what your spirit is doing in my life. I will yield to what your spirit is saying in my life. You're calling me to the depths. And this day, I will say, "Yes Lord, Yes." If you'll call me, I'll come! It's exactly what Peter did that day. He began to come to Jesus; and Jesus called him out to the depths and he began to sink!

God, I will sink down to the "depths of the sea" – a picture of death, humility, and emptiness. I will empty out of all that is in me – everything, completely, and allow you to do what you want in my life, and I will die to myself. And it is in that place, that I can experience your resurrection power in my life.

God, I want your resurrection power in my life. I want your restoration also, but I realize before I get restoration, I have to die to myself.

So, Lord, this day, I die to myself, again! And I will die daily and pick up my cross daily, and I will read your word daily. And I will experience you in times of refreshing in worshiping you in spirit and in truth. I'll come to the "brazen laver" daily to wash myself of this world – to wash off the dirt and the filth that should not be in my life, or in any child of God.

God, I humbly come to you this day. Have your way in me. Have your way with me! I give you everything. I want all that you have for me in this life-- **Complete Restoration**. Complete **Everything!** I want to walk in my callings, my giftings, and my offices. I want to help you accomplish your mission in this world. I want to take my place in the rank and file of the army of God. I want everything that you have for me in this life. I want it all! And I'll not let you go until you bless me. **I'll be a Jacob.** I'll wrestle with you all night long, until I am changed and transformed, and my walk will never be the same! God, I give you everything this day. I humbly submit myself to your leadings and your callings, and your yearnings. I submit to you pulling on my heart strings, Lord. I feel you pulling on them now, and I want to obey! I want to obey you in everything! In Jesus name, amen!

If that is your hearts cry, come, go with me and we'll go to a higher place. If that is not, you can close this book and give it to someone else.

And now, I must close with a word of warning. The word of God declares in the book of Deut. 28:23, "…and your heavens which are over your head shall be bronze…" if his children do not walk in obedience unto His voice. The heavens will be as brass! And brass speaks of judgment. I don't think any of us wants the judgment of God to fall upon us to any degree. But, it's the word of God. We, the church, must walk in obedience to God's word, no matter how big or how small. We need to obey anytime the Lord tells us to do something. It is very, very important!

Moses didn't see the fullness of the promise land, nor was he allowed to enter it, because of his disobedience. You may say, "Wow, that's severe! God, that's being really harsh, don't you think?" But, God just wants us to trust and obey; it's a picture of the responsibility that He is calling into our lives.

We must obey the word of God. We must also learn to hear His voice and hear His Spirit speaking to us daily, and then we must walk in it-- whatever He says--whatever it may be. We should not think about it and wonder, "Well, I'll do that when I get around to it, or I might do that later on."

"So, Walk By My Spirit," says the Lord.
"Walk By My Word."
"Obey My Voice.

If you will simply do just that; I, the Lord God, will take care of all the rest! I will take care of all the rest! If you will obey and listen to My voice, I promise you that I will pour out such a blessing you will not be able to contain it all. It will, literally, spill out of your life and bless all of those around you. It will absolutely, positively, blow your mind! I'll take you into a new realm of My Spirit – a new dimension of My power that you, yourself, have never known. But also, I'm bringing

139

My church into a realm of My Spirit that has never been known in the earth before. It is greater and better than all the last outpourings of My Spirit."

"Church of the Living God: It is the 'eleventh hour'! Time is short! I'm pouring out of My Spirit like never before, in this day and in this hour. You live in a very, very, exciting time in our history! The word of God is unfolding before our very eyes! I'm calling all those who will listen and who will hearken unto the voice of the Lord their God – people from all nations, all tribes, and all tongues. Will you hearken? Will you listen? Will you hear the voice of the Lord your God, and what His Spirit is saying to His church in these days? Will you hear? Will you listen? Will you hear what the spirit is saying in these last days?"

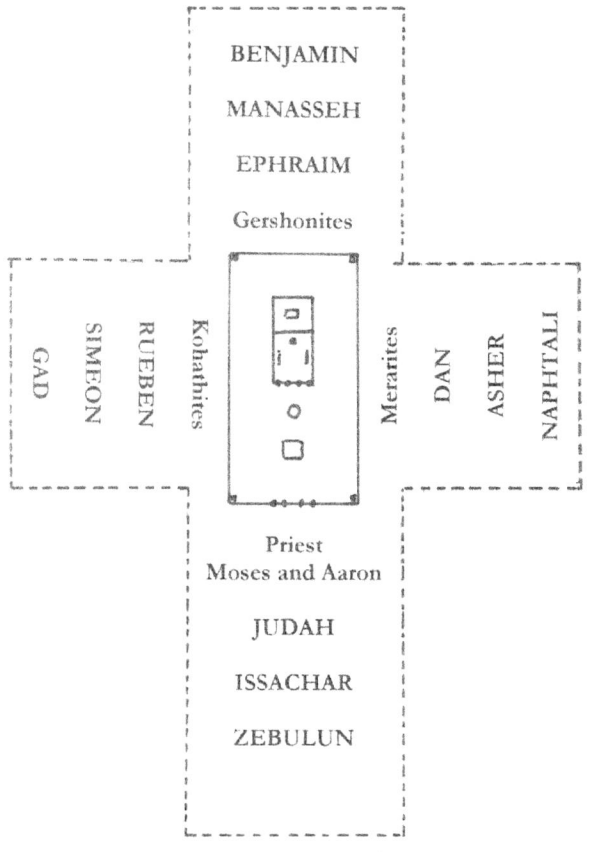

Ariel view of the Camp of Israel
in the shape of a cross; 1,400 yrs. before there
ever was a cross! All of the tabernacle,
in every detail is a picture of Christ!

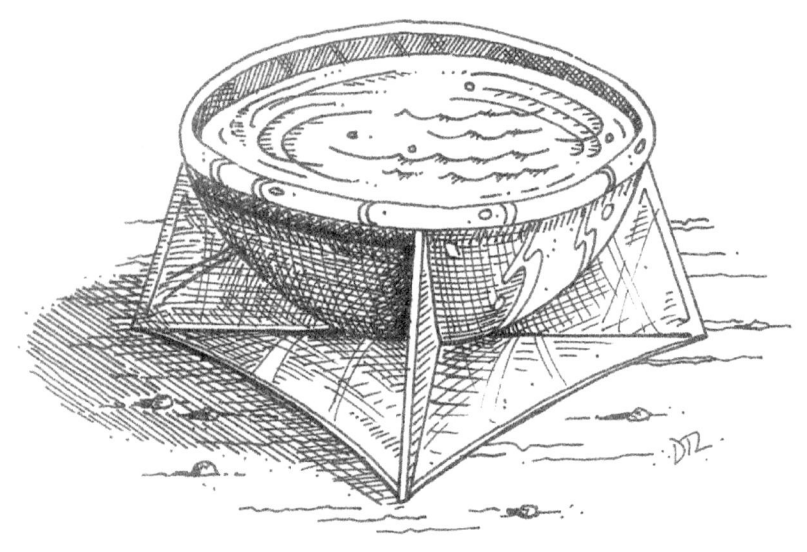

The Brazen Laver

This basin is where the priest would come
to wash his hands and feet in the waters of cleansing.
The water is believed to come from the smitten rock.

Chapter Four

Freedom for The Captives

*"It was for freedom that Christ
has set us free." Gal.5:1*

Let Freedom Reign

"I am the King!"
"I am the King!"
"I am the King!"
says the Lord God Almighty.

"The plaque above my head on my cross that day read: 'This is the King of the Jews.' Pilate had it put there, and it spoke prophetically that that is who 'I AM'. Part of who 'I AM, that I AM, that I AM" is that I am the ruling, reigning, King of the universe. I rule and reign in the universe – the entire universe. It includes the heavens and the earth. Adam gave it away. I took it back on the cross at Calvary. I not only died on the cross, I spent three days in the lower regions of the earth – in the heart of the earth-- as the 'sign of Jonah'. Even as Jonah spent three days and three nights in the belly of a fish, it was a prophetic picture pointing to the son of man who would also spend three days and three nights in the heart of the earth."

"I want my people to remember, Eph. 4: 8-9; because after I went to the cross, where did I go? I went to the lower regions of the earth. It means I went down to hell. I went to hell for you," says the Lord God Almighty, "to redeem a fallen world and a fallen creation – to redeem it all – 100%-- to buy it all back – 100%. For you see, before I ascended, I descended and I kicked in hell's gates, and I took back the keys of death, hell, and the grave. Remember, Adam gave it away. He gave his power and authority away to Satan which is symbolic of him having the keys. That's why I had to go there with my full power and my full authority from the Father, himself, from the very throne of heaven. I, Jesus, had it all in heaven-- left it all and came to earth. I gave it all and died for you. I went to hell and got it all back; then I ascended to heaven and now I can give it all back to my sons and daughters as their inheritance!"

You see, someone died and left you something-- **Your Inheritance**! If you've accepted Christ as your Lord and Savior, you are a descendant of Christ! You are a son or daughter of the Most High God! Jesus died and left you something. He has it all! If you'll come into a **covenant relationship** with Jesus Christ, He died and left you something. And the something that He died for and left you **– is everything**! Everything that He is and everything that He has! **He**

has it all and wants to give it all to you! He is El Elyon and He is also, El Shaddai!

"So, I the Lord God took the keys to death, hell, and the grave. I took the authority back from Satan, himself, that keeps my people bound." The word of God declares, *"when He ascended on high he lead captives in His train…"* (Eph. 4:7, NIV) and… *"He led captivity captive".* (NKJ) Jesus took the power to hold away from Satan. I want you to get that into your spirit. Jesus took the power to hold!

"Hells gates are no longer locked," says the Lord. "They are unlocked because My son died, went to hell, kicked in hell's gates, took the keys from Satan himself, and then ascended up into the heavenly realms seated at the right hand of the Father, now, interceding for you. That's reality! That's the word of God! That is truth! And the truth shall set you free."

"But some of My people, even in the church today, have believed a lie and come under an illusion that hell's gates are still closed and locked. They appear closed. They think, "This is as good as it gets." "This is all there is." "This is how life will be as I know it." "I have to live with this disease." "I have to live with this problem." "I have to live with life the way it is." But you see, they live in an illusion; and they have believed a lie. Satan is the "father of lies." That's all he is, and that's all that he can do now. The only power that he has is to lie and get people to think that the lie is the truth. And I want you to get that and understand that just for a moment."

"Because, **reality is the way you perceive it to be**. Reality to you is the way you think it is. Satan has tremendous power and hold over this creation. He is *"the prince and the power of the air."* (Eph. 2:2) But the only power that He has, that he utilizes with such great efficiency, is that he tries to get My people to believe a lie, even just a small twisted lie."

"**A half truth is still a whole lie.** He's been using the same tactics for ages. He even tempted Jesus, the son of God in the wilderness by using the word of God against Him. Even going back further than that, to the temptation in the Garden of Eden, he used the word of God against Eve and said, "Did God really say…?" and then quoted the word of the Lord just to introduce a little doubt -- a little question. He twists the word of God just a little bit to keep My people in captivity behind hell's gates with only the power of a lie."

145

"But I want you to know today, Isaiah chapter 61, still holds true today! *'The Spirit of the Sovereign Lord is upon me…'* The same anointing that was upon My son Jesus needs to be upon My sons and daughters of the Most High God. They need to realize who they are as a descendant of Jesus! You are a son or a daughter of the Most High God, and you carry the same anointing that was in His family line. It is still for you today and can be upon all of His sons and daughters. Now this same anointing is described here in Isaiah 61: 1-6. Read this portion of scripture with yourself in mind!

Isaiah 61: 1-6

1) *"The Spirit of the Sovereign Lord is on **ME**, because the Lord has anointed **me** to preach good news to the poor. He has sent **me** to bind up the brokenhearted, to proclaim freedom for the captives and release from darkness for the prisoners, 2) to proclaim the year of the Lord's favor, and the day of vengeance of our God, to comfort all who mourn, 3) and provide for them who grieve in Zion – to bestow on them a crown of beauty instead of ashes, the oil of gladness instead of mourning, and a garment of praise instead of a spirit of despair. They will be called oaks of righteousness, a planting of the Lord for the display of his splendor. 4) They will rebuild the ancient ruins and restore the places long devastated; they will renew the ruined cities that have been devastated for generations. 5) Aliens will shepherd your flocks; foreigners will work your fields and vineyards. 6) And you will be called priests of the Lord; you will be named ministers of our God. (NIV)*

You are "priests of the Lord" and you are named "ministers of our God." That is another part of who you are. God has called us all to be a "Royal Priesthood", and a "Holy Nation" unto our God – a chosen generation. (I Pet. 2:9) The same anointing that was upon Jesus is to be upon His sons and daughters; and we are to carry out His same ministry in the world today!

Freedom Isn't Free

Let freedom reign in all the earth. Let freedom reign! But in order for that to be so; for that to be true; there has to be a price that is paid. We see it paralleled in the natural realm along with the spiritual realm as well.

Once a year, we celebrate "Memorial Day" in memory of all the fallen soldiers that have given their lives while fighting in the many battles throughout our history for the freedom of our country. We, as a nation, have paid a very high price to enjoy the freedoms that we have here in this country – the United States of America. There have been thousands of brave men and now women that have fought for their country and given of themselves and paid the ultimate price for our freedom. And we thank you, and we honor you, along with your families for the sacrifices that have been made. Freedom isn't free!

And with that in mind, we also can remember another fallen hero, another fallen soldier, that paid the ultimate price, for He too, gave His life on a cross at Calvary for you. He paid the ultimate price for your freedom, and this freedom is even more important than any other. I can honestly say that we all should look to Jesus as being our greatest hero! He fought in the greatest war in the history of the world; and the good news is: He won! He won in the greatest and most important battle that has ever been waged. **He has won! He has won!**

Jesus descended into the lower regions of the earth; and He was there for three days and three nights. What did He do there? He fought a battle against Satan himself. He fought in the spirit realm for three days and three nights and He won, and He kicked in Hell's gates! And you don't think that Satan was going to give up those keys lightly do you? But with the power and anointing of God, Jesus fought this great battle and waged warfare against Satan himself and took the keys that were in his grasp that he was holding on to so tightly. Jesus had defeated him in every way. Jesus has won! And He didn't stay there. He ascended back to the earth for forty days appearing to many and talking with His disciples.

"There was a violent earthquake, for an angel of the Lord…rolled back the stone…and said, 'He is not here; he has risen, just as He said.'" (Mat. 28:6). He appeared to over 500 people in this earth to prove to the entire world that He was who He said He was. Even the dead came back to life. Some of the graves of the saints were opened up and those who had died were raised to life and appeared to many in the Holy City. He showed himself to all the apostles and many other close followers. He even walked through walls and was willing to allow Thomas to put his

hand into His side so that he would believe. *"Jesus did many other miraculous signs in the presence of his disciples which are not recorded in this book."* (John 20:30)

Jesus took captivity captive and then He ascended up into the heavenly realms. *"When He ascended on high, he lead captives in his train, and gave gifts to men….to fill the whole universe. He gave some to be apostles, some to be prophets, some to be evangelists, and some to be pastors and teachers."* (Eph. 4:8, 10, 11) That was the beginnings of the church and the church age, and He could freely give gifts unto men.

You can experience this freedom that Jesus purchased for you. He died and went to hell – took the keys – the power to hold you – and now can set the captive free. You can experience freedom from your own prison, freedom from sin, freedom from death, hell, and the grave. You can also have freedom from Satan himself, and all of this world system.

But, it just all doesn't happen overnight all at one time or all in one day. It's a process. Some faster than others, but it takes a little time and participation on your part.

On the day that you knew Jesus Christ as your Lord and Savior, something happened in your heart and in your life – a change occurred. You knew God as the God of your salvation. But you and the church, worldwide, still need to know God as their "Deliverer." It all just doesn't happen, magically all in one day. You have to walk it out, step by step, day by day, little by little. And it is largely up to you. You must engage the process and ask the Lord your God to set you free from all that binds you – from all that holds you – to set you free from your prison – whatever that may be. Whatever area in your life Satan still holds you down in, you need to ask God to set you free and then you need to walk it out day by day. Get into the word of God and proclaim the truth of His word and "the truth shall set you free"… in Jesus name.

Deliverance has gotten a bad rap in our modern day church. Satan would want you to feel like you are the only one in the world that needs it. He wants us all to have images of Hollywood movies and "Hocus – Pocus" to scare us and send fear into the hearts of God's people. Satan wants you to be afraid and he wants to keep you in ignorance. *"It is for a lack of knowledge that my people perish."* (See Hosea 4:6)

148

So, I want you to know today that deliverance is a good word, not a bad word. And also it usually comes little by little, day by day, that you experience from the day of salvation till the day God takes you home in greater and greater degrees of freedom. It's a progressive work. It's a process. But, you must engage the process and you must allow God to do what He wants to do in your heart and in your life. Turn everything over to God!

So, you really, one, must learn that deliverance is good for you – that it's a good word. It is for you today. Then secondly, you need to ask God for it. And then, you have to walk it out day by day, little by little in progressive degrees with God helping you every step of the way. The other thing you need to know is that we're all in this together! *"No temptation has overtaken you except such as is common to man."* (I Cor. 10:13). **We're all in the same boat and we all need it!** Each and every one of us needs deliverance and that in itself is a huge word. Because it seems in today's modern church, it's a bad word and everyone's afraid to talk about it. But there are real life issues that people are dealing with and they need real life answers.

And all of life's answers are found in Jesus. One of the greatest aspects of His anointed ministry in Isaiah 61 is to set the captive free. Remember, the reality is that we all were once in the kingdom of darkness; but now we have been translated into the Kingdom of Light and have entered into God's Kingdom under His rulership. We sometimes forget about where we have come from.

We, the church, also forget about where we have come from. We were once in the Kingdom of Darkness that Satan rules and controls. He was once considered our father, and we were held under his influence. We forget about that! (See. Jn. 8:44)

Even if you are born into God's Kingdom from birth and walked with God all your life, you still have an old nature that is born in Adam that has its connections with the kingdom of darkness. So, in some small degree or another, we are all in the same boat! And you see, that is a truth that will set you free! Satan wants to keep you in the lie that you're the only one in the world that needs deliverance. He does a really good job of keeping us in our prisons just by simply lying to us all the time. *"When he lies, he speaks his native language, for he is a liar and a father of lies…"* (John 8:44, NIV)

So, today, right now, this is a freeing word for us all – a freeing truth. I am proclaiming the truth today, that we all need deliverance.

We all do! When you look around and see everyone else from the sinner on the street to even your brothers and sisters in Christ in church – everyone in this world needs deliverance from sin, Satan, and this world system!

Even in the Lord's Prayer, God instructed us to pray in this way:

"Our Father in Heaven;
Hollowed be your name
Your Kingdom come.
Your will be done on earth as it is
in Heaven.
Give us this day our daily bread.
And forgive us our debts,
as we forgive our debtors
And do not lead us into temptation,
But deliver us from the evil one.
For yours is the kingdom and the
power and the glory forever. Amen "(Mat. 6: 9-13)

Here we see that the Lord Jesus Christ instructed us to pray for deliverance! It must be important! Pray for deliverance! Have we lost sight of this important ministry – church? Have we lost sight of the fact that even Jesus – God incarnate – instructed us to pray for deliverance? It is for all of us, and especially in the times that we live in today!

Satan is busy, busy, busy, trying to lock up the church behind hell's gates in many different facets and aspects of life – in any way that he can. Jesus wants to set the captives free. He wants to set the church free! Because, even the church is held captive in some degree or another and we'll see that a little later on.

Even in Psalm 91, verse 13, it describes the power and position that you now hold in Christ. ***"You*** *shall* ***tread*** *upon the lion and the cobra, the young lion and* ***the serpent*** *you shall trample under foot."* Satan is under your feet! If you have come into the Kingdom, Satan is under your feet! You must realize this is the power and authority you have as a child of the Almighty! This is a truth you must believe! This word is for you!

150

"He who is in you is greater than he who is in the world." (I Jn. 4:4) God wants to work with you to set you free and to make sure Satan is under your feet. God wants to make that a reality in your own life today. You can trample upon the lion, the cobra and the serpent! You can be strong in Christ and be more than a conqueror! You can have victory today! I want to finish this section and close with these encouraging words. Satan is a defeated foe! He is defeated! He is defeated!

Deliverance! Deliverance! Deliverance!

"It's a battle cry of the ages! It is timeless! The same battle cry that I had in days past is the same battle cry that I have in this day and in this hour. I brought about a great deliverance that day when the children of Israel crossed the Red Sea upon dry ground. It's a picture of the church today! As you look at this story, you must put yourself in the same shoes that the children of Israel were in that day. They had the Red Sea in front of them and the Egyptian Army, Pharaoh, and all his chariots hot on their trail. They had no where to go. But, I, the Lord God, was a pillar of cloud by day and a fire by night. I was a wall of fire and cloud between them all night long. Then Moses, a type of Christ, raised his staff and stretched out his hand over the Red Sea, and I rolled back the waters on their behalf."

It's a picture of the church; and it's a picture of you! And you see, they had to walk it out. They had to walk, step by step, through the bottom of the sea so that they could attain their own deliverance! If they just stood still, it would have been one of the greatest annihilations and slaughters in the history of mankind, and the story would have ended there. But they didn't stand still! They had to move. They had to walk it out!

So, step by step, they walked their way to freedom! They walked their way to deliverance! And I think many of you know the story. We're very familiar with the life of Moses and the Exodus, the Passover, and the crossing of the Red Sea. God drove back the waters for the Israelites. They rolled back all night long; and the same water that saved the children of Israel – destroyed the entire Egyptian army! Pharaoh and all his chariots, horseman, and troops – simply put – the enemy was destroyed! It's a picture of you and all of your enemies

151

being destroyed. And in this story, where did they end up? We have to look at Exodus 15: "The Song of Moses!" And as we read that chapter, we discover in this great song of deliverance that

"…the Horse and it's rider he has hurled into the sea. The Lord is a warrior; the Lord is his name. Pharaoh's chariots and his army he has hurled into the sea. The best of Pharaoh's officers are drowned in the Red Sea. The deep waters have covered them; they sank to the depths like a stone."(v. 1-5, NIV)

The enemy was completely destroyed and annihilated. *"The horse and its rider"* and *"Pharaoh's army"* are symbolic of all of your enemies that are trying to destroy you that have their roots with Satan himself.

Think of all your enemies that you may still be battling in your life today and what they may be. And I don't mean external enemies-- I mean internal. And those are greater than any of your external enemies. I mean like 'spirits of fear' that just grip your heart and hold you captive in your own prison, so much so you're afraid to do anything. You're afraid to take a single step. You can't even walk through a parted 'Red Sea' with the enemy hot on your trail. I'm talking about things like: anger, hatred, bitterness, unforgiveness, and fear of rejection, envy, jealousy, pride, prejudice, and poverty – a poverty mentality, even sickness and disease. Perhaps you have believed a lie that healing is not for you today. And maybe someone said to you, "You just have to live with it." "It's your burden to bear." It's not your burden to bear; because Christ, He bore it for you. Healing is in the atonement! Jesus paid a full price to redeem man 100% -- spirit, soul and body! *"By His stripes we are healed."* (Isa. 53:5) I know the subject of healing for the body is very controversial today; but I must still believe what God's word says, and I must still in obedience pray for the sick that they may be healed.

Take a step of faith with me and believe God, and begin to move in His direction! Just like the children of Israel had to move. They had to walk it out step by step. You need to believe the truth of God's word and walk in it. Believe it! You see, the "spirit of fear" can hold you captive so you don't do anything. You're afraid and Satan's got you just where he wants you, and he's hot on your trail.

But, I want you to know that deliverance is still necessary today, and it is for you! And the same song that was sung in the earth in Exodus chapter 15 – that same song is still sung today! And you too can sing your own song – your song of deliverance in your heart and life today. You can sing it afresh and anew in your own life. You can sing your own version of "The Song of Moses" with all your own words; and sing, "God has set me free this day!"… "Halleluiah"… if you'll just believe God.

The same water that saves you – destroys your enemies! That's why it so important to go to the "depths of the sea". That's why God is calling us to go deeper in Him – to come to the "bottom of the sea". It's like a huge baptism in the Holy Spirit. Remember, water is a symbol of the Holy Spirit. It's a huge baptism where you die to yourself, and you die to all that is in you-- all that is in your old nature. If you come to the end of you, it will be the beginning of God. And all your enemies will be destroyed in the process!

Moses was a great "deliverer" of Israel. God had raised him up as a great man of God to go and speak before Pharaoh. He went back to Pharaoh many times and said these simple words that still apply today: "Let my people go. Let my people go!" God through His spirit is saying the same thing today to Satan himself, "Let my people go!"

And as for the children of Israel, they were delivered out of Egypt and eventually made it to the Promised Land. Symbolically, "Egypt" is the land of bondage – the land of captivity – and the land of sin. It is representative of our sin nature and how, in Adam, we are held in bondage and held captive to sin. We are a slave to sin in Adam. But, God today is interested in getting "Egypt" out of you. And when He sets you free from all the old and brings you to the death of yourself, it will be the life of God in you and you will truly be set free.

That's why it's so important to come to the cross and then go to the "bottom of the sea" – to come down into the depths of God. It is there in that place that you'll identify with the death and burial of Christ, and you will have emptied out of all that is inside of you. There will be nothing left of you! You will be completely emptied out of yourself, and all that is left in you will be fully God.

We are always full of something! The question is: What are we full of? What are you full of today? So, we'll come to the depths and the death of you, and it will be the life of God.

"In this day and in this hour, I am pouring out my Spirit like never before," says the Lord God Almighty. "And I am asking you

153

this day even as I asked Job the question: Have you walked in the recesses of the deep? Have you come to the depths of my Spirit?" says the Lord. "Because, if you come to the depths, it will be the complete death of you and the complete life of God. I am pouring out my Spirit in these days. Will you, today, allow Me to do what I need to do in your life? Will you yield to my Spirit?" says the Lord God Almighty. "Will you yield to all that I want to do in your life?"

"I, the Lord God, am a gentleman. I will not barge in. I will not kick in the door of your heart." Revelation 3:20 says, *I stand at the door and knock. If anyone hears My voice and opens the door, I will come in and eat with him and he with Me.' I* stand at the door of your heart and I am knocking – now. Will you have enough courage to simply, open the door?"

"If you do and open the door of your heart and let Me in, I'll set you free! I will set you free from all that keeps you bound-- from all that holds you back-- from all that hinders you. Satan has no authority over you once you become a child of God. That's why it's important to come to the cross and accept Jesus as your savior; because you come in under My protections and My covenant. I'm calling you this day church."

"Have you walked in the recesses of the deep? Have you walked in the recesses of the deep? Come into the depths of My Spirit," says the Lord. "There is more that I have for you! Greater freedom; newness of life; resurrection power; blessings upon blessings forevermore; it's all in My Spirit! But you have to open the door of your heart and you have to believe My word, and you have to go to the depths, and die to yourself. You have to take up your cross and follow ME. TAKE UP YOUR CROSS AND FOLLOW ME. TAKE UP YOUR CROSS AND FOLLOW ME. This is my word unto you this day," says the Lord God Almighty.

The Walls of Jericho

And the walls came tumbling down! The walls of Jericho came crashing down that day. It was thought that the walls of Jericho were impregnable, unconquerable, and indestructible. They were thirty feet high and twenty feet thick, built on approximately eight acres of land. A literal fortress in its day! It was thought that it could never be

154

defeated. That was the mindset in the natural. But the mindset in the spiritual – God had a different plan. God had an unusual battle plan that day. A supernatural strategy, that was not devised in the heart of man, but was devised in the heart of God. He spoke to Joshua, the leader of the Children of Israel and successor to Moses, and gave him in complete detail the entire battle plan. They were to march around this entire fortress once every day for six days in a row while the priests would blow the trumpets continually, but not another sound could be uttered; not a single word spoken. They must remain in complete silence. With an armed guard out in front, and then the seven priests blowing seven trumpets of ram's horns followed by the ark of the Lord's covenant, which was symbolic of the power and presence of God among His people, then followed by the rest of the armed men, they marched.

"*And on the seventh day, they got up at day break and marched around the city seven times.*" (Joshua 6:15) Seven priests, blowing seven ram's horns, marching around the city seven times on the seventh day, sounded the trumpet blast and then Joshua, at the precise moment, gave the command for the people to "shout". "*For the Lord has given you the city!*" (v.16). God's anointed leader knew now is the time – lift up your voice! They all did in obedience to the Lord's command, and with their loud shout unto God in the precise moment; the walls of Jericho came crashing down! The greatest of enemy strongholds – the greatest of enemy fortresses came crashing down that day. There is no enemy fortress, no enemy stronghold that Satan holds today, that cannot be destroyed by the anointed power of the Living God.

Let's look at a few key ingredients to this unusual battle plan. They had to walk together as one-- in unity. They all had to do what they were told to do. They had to be unified and committed to the battle plan. They had to be of one mind, one purpose, one heart, and one mission. They all knew that was their mission – to take Jericho. Miraculously enough, they had to be silent for the whole time, which is a miracle in itself; because that would be very, very, difficult to do, especially on the seventh day to march around the city seven times – a fortress that took up eight acres, without saying a word, without uttering a single word of complaint, or grumble a single negative word! God wanted silence! Sometimes in our lives, God wants our silence on certain things too. It's better for us not to say anything at all.

They all walked in unity that day and they also walked in obedience to the Lord their God's battle plan. They didn't think about how strange it was or how weird it was; they may have thought about it for a moment, at first; but they didn't dwell on it, and it didn't stop them from carrying it out and putting feet into it or walking in obedience to the Lord's commands.

So, we can learn a very valuable lesson from this: no matter what the Lord says – no matter what-- when we know it's God – Do it! Put feet in it! Walk it out! Listen to it! Don't stand still.

Don't think it over. Don't debate about it with God, or even argue with God. Don't reason it out. Don't try to make sense of it all. God may give you some **unusual battle plans** in your life, and you see, that's the nature of God. Because, if it's never been done before, you have to trust God and walk in obedience to **what God's doing now** in your situation. It may not be the same as it was done yesterday, or the same as someone else did it in the past; because, we need to learn and be trained how to walk in obedience and listen to the voice of the Lord our God. We must listen and walk in obedience to His word no matter what it is-- no matter how great or small. And it usually starts in the small things and then it mushrooms into the bigger things. He that is faithful in the little things, God will make you ruler over many things (Mat. 25:21). So, if you're not faithful in the small things, God will not trust you with more! It is very, very important to walk in obedience in the little things... little things... little things. God is into the little things-- even if it doesn't sound rational-- even if it doesn't sound reasonable. The walls came tumbling down that day at the battle of Jericho through a supernatural battle plan that God had devised. It was not conceived in the minds of men. It was supernatural in origin, in effectiveness, in power, and in scope.

"But, I the Lord God could have done it on the first day! I am all powerful. I am the creator of the ends of the earth. I can do anything, but I chose not to do it on the first day all by Myself. I chose to engage my people so they would be a part of what I was doing in the earth."

So, God gave them a supernatural battle plan, one that did not rely on their numbers, their strength, their wisdom, their energy or their resources. They had to rely on their God, and trust in God's battle plan, in God's wisdom, God's knowledge, God's understanding, God's might and power – all of the seven-fold dimensions of the Holy

156

Spirit. They had to trust in every aspect of who the Holy Spirit is today. They had to place their trust in their supernatural God. And many of them may not have had the faith to believe that, but Joshua did. The leader that received the battle plan believed it! And He got everyone else to believe as well. And that speaks a lot to us today.

We need to get behind our leaders when they hear from God and they have a word from God, as long as it lines up with the written word of God. We need to believe them. We need to trust in them and walk with them, and be unified with the vision that God gives to His leaders, if it comes from God.

At Jericho, they walked in unity and obedience. And as they did, the power of God came upon them as a corporate anointing. This story demonstrates to us what a corporate anointing can accomplish.

One can chase a thousand or two can put ten thousand to flight, three a hundred thousand, and four a million. However you do the math, it comes in exponential power, each time increasing the effectiveness of all the others. What kind of power comes when the people of God walk in unity? Think about that for moment! Imagine it! Unity brings exponential power! (See Deut. 32:30, Joshua 23:10). And what looks impossible becomes possible. All things are possible with God!! **"ALL THINGS ARE POSSIBLE WITH GOD."** (Mk. 10:27). And what looks impossible for the children of Israel that day at the city of Jericho – the greatest fortress in their day – it was completely destroyed. God, miraculously, brought about a complete deliverance! Seven, Seven, Seven, look at all the sevens: seven priests, seven trumpets, on the seventh day marching around the city seven times. It's a picture of fullness and completion. God wants to bring about a full and complete deliverance in our hearts and in our lives still today-- deliverance from everything that is not of God. Everything that is in our old nature, in Adam, that has its roots in the Kingdom of darkness. God wants us to be totally free from all of it. *"If the son sets you free, you will be free indeed."* (Jn. 8:36). God wants you to experience complete deliverance and freedom in your heart and life from all that is not God. That is the truth! And remember, **"...the truth will set you free."** (Jn. 8:32)

So, one, you have to know that's for you, and you can say, "That word is for me." Then secondly, believe it! Know that word is for you! And third, walk in it-- practice believing it each and everyday for the rest of you life. Just like they had to walk through the Red Sea and walk around the city of Jericho; we, too, have to walk things out in our own lives – it's a picture of the day by day events in our lives – moment by moment, minute by minute. We need to hang on to what the word of God says to us and be transformed by it, in the midst of the trials and struggles of life that we will face that will test our faith.

Another Key!

We need to look at another key element in this story of the battle of Jericho. When they lifted up their voices, they lifted up a shout unto God. The seventh time around, when the priests sounded the trumpet blast, Joshua commanded the people, *"Shout! For the Lord has given you the city!"* (Joshua 6:16). They supplied the shout! God supplied the power! **Obedience turns the heart of God!** When we do simply what God asks us to do, it releases God's power in the earth!

They lifted up their voices, that day, in obedience onto the Lord their God through directions given by their leader Joshua. They lifted up a shout of praise unto their God – a battle cry. They were entering their military war campaign. They were at war! You are also at war with the kingdom of darkness. And it is necessary in this day and in this hour; God is asking us again to lift up our voices and to not hold back!!

Says the Spirit of the Lord, "Church of the Living God: It's time to shout!! THE TIMES OF SILENCE ARE OVER! THE TIMES OF SILENCE ARE OVER!! It's time to lift up your voice like never before! Shout unto God with the voice of triumph! Lift up your voice with a shout of praise unto our God. It's a "Shabach" of praise unto our God. Halleluiah! And if you will, the Holy Spirit will combine with that shout of praise, and enemy strongholds will come crashing down, not only in your life, but in the lives of those around you; and also, in the lives of people all across the face of the earth."

"It's time – my church – it's time to lift up your voices like never before! Don't hold back! Don't be afraid of volume in your church," says the Lord.

"Leaders and Pastors: **Don't be afraid of unusual battle plans!** Halleluiah! Even as I gave Joshua an unusual battle plan, I will also give you unusual battle plans. That's the importance of hearing My voice daily! **Every service has a different battle plan!** You have to listen to ME to get the battle plan. And that means you have to trust, and you have to listen, and you have to be close and you have to hear. Because every service I'll give you a new plan. It won't be your plan, it will be My plan," says the Lord.

"All my leaders have to be in a place that they can hear ME! I'm calling you all to the **Secret Place of the Most High God**! Not only the lay people, but the leaders – first and foremost! I'm calling you to the secret place – into the very presence of the living God-- behind the veil. Stop being satisfied with just living in the Holy Place. **Come in behind the veil.** I'm calling you-- leaders of my church worldwide-- to come in behind the veil. Come in behind the veil! IT'S WHERE YOU NEED TO BE! IT'S WHERE YOU NEED TO LIVE. And in this place, I'll give you supernatural battle plans."

There are seven Hebrew words for praise. And one of them is the word "Shabach." "They lifted up a 'Shabach' of praise at the battle of Jericho, and combined with My Spirit," says the Lord God Almighty, "it brought down the walls of Jericho and they came crashing down." Halleluiah! ("Shabach" (strong's #7623) means: to address in a loud tone; loud; glory; praise; triumph.)

"So, too, in your life, Psalm 47:1 says, 'Shout to God with the voice of triumph.' I charge you this day. Lift up your voice. Shout unto God. Don't be silent anymore! **Blow a trumpet in ZION. Sound the Alarm on My Holy Mountain!** Lift up your voice and shout out a battle cry; because it's a battle cry of the ages. You are at war, and I'm calling an army together from the four corners of the earth. Will you be in this army?" says the Lord God Almighty. "Will you be in this army of the Living God? Will you experience great victory in your own life, and in the life of the church and in the life of the Kingdom – worldwide? Will you see 'thy Kingdom come, thy will be done on earth as it is in heaven?' Will you see – thy kingdom come? Will you see it in your life, and in the lives of those around you? Will you see it come to pass?"

"I'm calling you this day – church – part of who you are is that you are a **warrior** in the army of the Living God. Will you take your place in the rank and file of this army? Will you accept your place and position? Will you come into submission unto other people's authority over you? There is a rank and file in this army. There are those that are over you, and there are some that are under. Will you take your place and not struggle for position in this army?"

"Church: this is my word unto you this day, and this may be a harsh word to some. Stop trying to fight for position in this army! Be satisfied where you're at and with what you have. It is a high calling. Be delivered of the pride and the jealousy that rages within your soul. Do not be envious of those that may be over you, or that may have more power and influence than you. Lay it all down this day. Lay it all down. It is of the flesh. It is of the carnal nature. It is in Adam, and it needs to be crucified this day," says the Lord God Almighty. "It needs to be crucified this day. Because, Satan has been using it against you! He's been using it against you all this time. So, you must lay it down this day," says the Lord.

Rahab

Another picture we see, that applies to the New Testament Church at the battle of Jericho, is seen in the life of "Rahab". Not many people would think much of Rahab. The world would consider her to be one of the "low-lifes" in our day. She was a prostitute. Some would not think much of her; but God did; because, she put her faith in God when the spies came to scout out the city. Rahab believed God. She put her faith in the God of the Hebrews! She believed, and she was saved, and delivered! Her life is a type and picture of the New Testament church today!

"Church of the Living God: You've prostituted yourself and you have played the harlot. You have had many lovers! YOU HAVE PLAYED THE HARLOT! And it's time to repent! Seek after your first love. Come back to ME," says the Lord your God. "Fall in love with ME, all over again. Fall in love with ME once again. You've broken My heart," says the Lord. "I'm coming back for a bride, a glorious bride who is without spot or wrinkle, who is clothed in garments of white. I'm not coming back for a harlot!"

"Church of the Living God: **REPENT**! You have had many lovers of your soul. You have loved your money instead of ME," says the Lord. "You've put your money before me. It has become an idol in your life. You have put careers, and positions, and status, and respect from man, all over ME. It's time that you put ME FIRST, again, in your life. It's time that you put me first! Return to your first love. Return to your first love!" says the Lord God Almighty.

160

"'Rahab', a picture of the New Testament Church, was locked up, sealed up, held captive in an enemy stronghold. My church today is still held captive in many aspects and walks of life. The enemy has kept you bound and locked up. But in this day and in this hour, I am setting "RAHAB" free! I am setting 'Rahab' free!" says the Lord. Halleluiah!

"The Spirit of the Lord is coming in great power and in great might. Even as in the days of Jericho, I am unleashing My power in the earth that will break all enemy strongholds and they will come crumbling down. I will break every yoke of bondage, and I will set every captive free. There is no enemy stronghold that I will not destroy! There is a **'yoke breaking anointing'** that is being released in the heavens that is coming down into the earth realm. And it's coming through my people," says the Lord God Almighty, "and it is being released in this day and in this hour – **A YOKE BREAKING ANOINTING!"**

A "yoke" is a symbol of bondage. It's what they used in biblical times to join two oxen together to plow the fields. It was a very strong frame of wood usually resting upon the neck of the animal and held in position by heavy bands. It was designed to hold the oxen together. That's a "YOKE." It would bind them so strongly together that it made it almost impossible for the oxen to break free! The oxen would need some outside help! That's the picture of what a "yoke" is and when God speaks of the "yoke", that's what we need to keep in mind.

"I am breaking every 'YOKE' of bondage in this day and in this hour. And I am setting the captive free; and I am also setting My 'RAHAB' free; because, if you remember, Rahab put a scarlet cord out her window. She and her household were saved that day and set free from an enemy stronghold. They were the only ones that were saved in the entire fortress; because, they put out the scarlet cord. It's symbolic of the blood of Jesus Christ and the Passover lamb. If you'll identify with Jesus' blood and the 'Passover Lamb', His death, and His burial – there is resurrection power coming your way! But, you have to identify with the scarlet cord. That's what saved her. That's what set her free! They knew to set her free. How? They saw the scarlet cord! When the armies of Heaven come marching through, will they see your 'scarlet cord' hanging out your window? Because, the armies of heaven are coming, and they are combined with the armies of My

161

people," says the Lord your God. "The armies of heaven are coming, even as in the day of Jericho. There is an army of heaven that is coming for you, to help set you free. You see, you can be a 'Rahab' to any degree in your life. You are still held captive in an enemy stronghold."

"The armies of God are coming! Will they see your scarlet cord? Are you identified with the blood of Jesus – the blood of the Passover Lamb – who was slain for you? Do you believe that word? Are you identified with Jesus' blood, His death, and His burial?"

"If you are, and if you will put out your scarlet cord today, be ready, because the armies of God are headed your way. And it is coming," says the Lord your God. "It is coming! And when they arrive – be ready; because, in that day and in that hour, I the Lord God, will bring about a supernatural deliverance in your life-- and not only yours-- but your churches life, and throughout the world."

"Will you put out your scarlet cord today and say, 'I need help, set me free!' There is a breaker anointing that has been released in the earth – **A YOKE BREAKING ANOINTING** that will break every enemy stronghold, just as in the days of Jericho, and bring the walls of bondage crumbling down and set the captives free. Halleluiah! It has been unleashed in the earth! It can not be stopped! It will not be stopped!" says the Lord God Almighty.

"You will be affected by it one way or the other. Glory to God. Halleluiah! Throw your scarlet cord out the window and be set free this day. Let it be a blessing to you. Embrace it. Receive it. Believe it! It's the word of God."

"Jesus Christ, himself, carried the breaker anointing to set the captive free. That same anointing is being released through the modern day church. And, when I say, 'church', I mean the people of God – the bride of Christ. Will you be in the bride of Christ? Do you consider yourself a part of the bride? If you do, receive the word of God and receive deliverance today from all that holds you back-- from all that hinders you. This is what I am doing in the earth today," says the Lord God Almighty.

Let God Be God

Let God be God! Halleluiah! We need to give God the freedom to be who He is; and then, He will give us the freedom to be who we are! We need to set God free! We have held God captive for far too long. Ironically, God limits Himself tremendously in power to move in the earth depending on what His people will believe and what they will allow Him to do. For decades and even for centuries, **we - the church – have been holding God – himself – back!** If you can handle that word – it's true! And the truth shall set you free! We need to LET GOD BE GOD!!!

Give Him the freedom in your own life and also in your churches life; and then that will, in turn, impact the world. And then, God can better establish His Kingdom and advance His cause throughout the earth. Then the Lord's Prayer, as you well know, as He prayed,

"LET THY KINGDOM COME!"
"LET THY KINGDOM COME!"
"LET THY KINGDOM COME!"

"Let thy will be done, on earth as it is in heaven." (Mat. 6:10). Halleluiah! "The only way the Kingdom of God can be advanced in the earth, is through My people," says the Lord. "There is no other way!! I have no other plan. It's the only way! Adam gave it away; but I'm taking it back through my Son Jesus, through His work on the cross, then through My people!"

Will you let God be God in your heart and life today? It must begin with you! Halleluiah! The journey of a thousand miles begins with one step. The changing of the world begins with changing you! Halleluiah! LET REVIVAL BEGIN IN YOU!! LET IT BEGIN IN YOU! You have no excuse! No one else will stand with you in the Day of Judgment. Will you listen to what the Spirit says in these days?

To Him who has ears to hear…
To Him who has ears to hear…
To Him who has ears to hear...

let him hear what the Spirit of God is saying in these days. Will you let God be God in your life today? … Now? …In this Moment?

... As you read this book, right now? If you will, pray this prayer with me right now, in Jesus Name!

Prayer

God: I am sorry that I have not allowed you to be God in My life. God, I repent and humble myself before your mighty hand this day. I humbly come to you and ask your forgiveness for all my past sin, for all my present sin, and all my future sin. I ask you God to wash me clean, afresh and anew today. Wash me in your blood. Wash me in the blood of Jesus that cleanses me from all sin, and wash me in the water of your word – your "logos" word and your "Rhema" word. Wash me in your word today. God, I am sorry for not letting you be you. I release you to do what you want to do in my life today. And I will yield to your Spirit. I will yield to your presence. I will yield to your word; I will listen, and walk in obedience unto your word and your calling in my life. Even like the army of Israel at Jericho that day, as they walked around the city in obedience unto your word; so too, I will walk in obedience unto your word, Lord. No matter how unusual the word may be, no matter how strange the battle plan, God, I will listen and I will obey. I will trust and obey. I give you everything in my life, Lord. Set me free! Set me, this "Rahab," held captive in an enemy stronghold – all that would keep me captive behind hell's gates. Set me free God, today, from all the lies of the enemy that I have been listening to; for that is the only power that he has to hold me. He has to resort to speaking lies, and I choose, this day, not to believe his lies anymore. I choose to believe the truth which is in your word. I believe your written word – your "Holy Bible". So, this day from Genesis to Revelation, I believe it is all for me. I give you my entire life and I give you the freedom to be fully God in my life. Be God in my life, Lord; and I will yield and submit to the moving and the workings of your Holy Spirit in my life today, in Jesus name – AMEN and AMEN.

If you have prayed this prayer, get ready, get ready, get ready; because, God "*...stands at the door and knocks, if anyone hears my voice and opens the door, I will come in and eat with him, and he with me.*" (Rev. 3:20)

If you hear His voice and you open the door of your heart, He is coming in; and God is going to do a complete work in you. And He is going to set you free to be who you were meant to be! Halleluiah! He will set you free from all of the old, and bring you into all the new.

You can be all you can be in the army of God. And you will be uniquely you, with all of your gifts, callings, and abilities. Only you can be you and fulfill the purposes of God in your life. Only God has called you to do what you are going to do. We need to erase an old mentality that God will just raise up somebody else to take your place. No, not necessarily! I have to believe that some things will just go undone. If you don't do it; no one else will – and it creates a void. There's a space. There is a "stone" not laid in the wall of the temple of God. There is something not done. So, only you can do what God has called you to do. You are special and you have a special assignment! Only you have the unique gifting, talents, and anointings that God has placed in you to equip you for every good work in Christ. You have a mission, and only you can fulfill that mission in the earth today.

It is very important that you are set free, so all the giftings and the callings of God are freely expressed in you to be a blessing to you and be a blessing to the church; and then, in turn, be a blessing to the world around you. There must be freedom of praise and worship in you – gifts of song and dance – and a freedom to express all of God's supernatural spiritual gifts as mentioned in I Cor. 12. All of these Gifts! The church must allow the expression of all these giftings so our warfare can be effective. They are for us today! Don't believe a lie. They are for you to experience and be a blessing to you, and not only to you, but to bless others around you: prophecy, words of wisdom, words of knowledge, gifts of healing, ect. All nine have been given to the church to be utilized with power to impact a lost and dying world. They are extremely valuable. They are crucial, and they are critical. And these "grace – gifts" or "charis – gifts" need to be released in each and every believer in the body of Christ on the face of the planet.

We need more power and more weapons fighting for us and with us – not less! We need all the weapons of our warfare released with complete freedom to wage effective warfare against Satan and the forces of evil in this present age.

There are vast reservoirs of God's Spirit that lie deep within each and every believer that have never been tapped into before. They need to be accessed so they can freely flow like a giant, rushing river of God's Spirit and be a blessing in the earth. You'll be able to discover fully who you are and also be able to walk in your destiny and fulfill the plan of God in your own life. You'll also realize, for some of you, the offices that you may hold in God's five fold ministry.

"When he ascended on high he led captives in this train and gave gifts to men." (Eph. 4:8) *"He gave some to be apostles, some to be prophets, some to be evangelists, and some to be pastors and teachers, to prepare God's people for works of service, so that the body of Christ may be built up."* (V.11) They are all gifts that Jesus died and paid for, then went to hell for, so that they could be given and established in the church as part of His government; and then, released into the earth for this day and this hour! *"Give and it will be given to you. A good measure, pressed down, shaken together and running over, will be poured into your lap. For with the measure you use, it will be measured to you."* (Luke 6:38 NIV)

This verse does not only apply to money and finances; but rather, it is a Kingdom principle that works with Kingdom dynamics. It works supernaturally throughout God's entire Kingdom. **Very simply stated, to the degree that you give yourself over to God is to the measure that God will give back to you!**

So, it's all up to you as to how far you go! I can try to encourage you, admonish you, and push you to higher places, but unless you are willing to go – you'll never go. You'll never get to new places in Him. God is limited to what you will allow Him to do in your heart and life, and how much you pursue the Kingdom of God. Much of our life comes down to our daily disciplines. How much do you read the word of God? How much time do you spend in prayer just talking to God? Just being with Him? … How about worshipping Him? Do you really want to get to know your creator, the Almighty, who is capable of anything? Are you hungry for more of Him, or are you full and satisfied?

What you give to the Kingdom is what you'll get back in return! It's a Kingdom principle. It works every time! It's a Kingdom word. I didn't write it. It's the word of God. So, to the degree you give yourself over to God is to the degree that you will get Him back in return!

It's all up to you. Will you come further in your walk with God? Will you come to the depths? Will you come to the greatest of heights, and fly higher where the eagles are afraid to fly? Will you

166

come with ME? I can only give you an invitation. You must say in your heart, "Yes Lord, Yes. I will go. I'll do whatever it takes. Lord. I'll pay any price." I promise you this: the cost may be great, but the dividends are high! They are out of this world. Halleluiah!

You can choose where you want to live in God. Do you want to live on the east side of the Jordan with the tribes of Reuben, Gad, and the half-tribe of Manasseh? Or do you want to go in and gain the full blessing and inherit the full Promised Land? (See Numbers 32:19) There will be some that may even discourage you from doing so! (See Numbers 32:7)

All the abundance of all that God is – **All that HE IS** – awaits you! Is that what you want? I'm here to tell you how to get **all** that God **is**. Will you come with me, and fight your battle of "Jericho" and continue to fight in your spiritual warfare campaign to possess your promised land today? I told you it wouldn't be easy. There are some battles to fight! But know this: "I, the Lord, God, I will fight for you!"

The battle is not yours, but the battle is the Lord's. And as long as you yield your vessel to the workings of God, He will fight for you! Your part is to yield, submit, pray, give your total life and being over to God, and just do all the little things to walk it out day by day. You'll possess your promised land step by step; moment by moment; day by day!

Remember, it's a process. You won't get there over night; but you will begin to see the difference in your life. You will walk it out – step by step. It's going to take some energy on your part, and you have to learn how to be a warrior in the armies of Heaven! That is part of who you are – a warrior – and we will look at that more later! You will learn how to fight and possess your promised land, and I want you to realize and know today that it is very doable! It can be achieved. We can inherit the "Promised Land" this side of heaven. You don't have to die and go to heaven to experience all of the "Promised Land". The "Promised Land" can come to you!

Freedom in the Church

"Let God be God" – not only individually, but corporately! We need to give God the freedom to do what He wants to do in our midst! Not what we want; but what God wants-- and not just once in

167

a while, but everyday of our lives. Every time we - the body of Christ – gathers together; every service; not just one revival service once a month, or once a quarter, or once a year, or five nights a year – EVERY SERVICE-- we need to give over to the Lord our God!

"Church of the Living God: What are you afraid of? Are you afraid of what God will do? Are you afraid of Me?" says the Lord. "You are bound by spirits of fear? I have not given you a spirit of fear leading again to bondage; but I have given you a spirit of power, love and a sound mind. Will you give Me the freedom in your service and let ME be ME – Let God be God? Will you give Me my freedom? And if you will, I will give you your freedom in return. Because, whom the Son sets free – He is free indeed. You are bound by spirits of fear! You are a 'Rahab' locked up behind 'Jericho walls'! And this day, you need to be set free from that bondage."

"Do not be afraid of what I, the Lord God, will do in your midst. Come and wait upon Me. Wait upon Me in silence, even as the people of Israel did in the day of Jericho. Wait upon Me in silence. And it doesn't matter for how long. Don't be in a hurry! **Don't be uncomfortable with silence.** Just wait. **Wait!** It's not about your agenda, it's about My agenda! Will you let ME – the King of all Kings – be the King in your midst? Will you let the King come in and do what He wants to do in your services and in your churches this day?"

"Church of the Living God, I charge you this day: RELEASE ME TODAY! RELEASE ME! LET ME GO! You've been trying to contain ME and put ME in a box and keep ME confined for generations! My word unto you this day, church of the Living God – worldwide – Let ME GO! Even as Moses went to Pharaoh and said, "Let MY People Go!", and I brought about a great deliverance for the Children of Israel that day. I am asking you now – church – to LET ME GO!"

"Let ME go and let Me be free to be who 'I AM' in your midst. If you will and agree with that word, I the Lord God am about to bring the greatest move of God that you have ever seen on the face of the earth. It is coming! It is coming! The question is: Will you be apart of it? Will you see it? Will you experience it? Will you know it? Will you be a half-tribe and live on the east side of the Jordan, or will you be a full-tribe and come into the fullness of all that God has for you? That is what is at stake. Do you want the fullness of God? Do you want to see all that I AM and all that I can do in this world and in this

168

life? If you do – church leaders-- say, "Yes Lord, Yes." Hearken unto the voice of the Lord your God; you're under a great responsibility and thus a greater judgment."

"I, the Lord God, need you to listen to My voice! Hear what the Spirit is saying in these days. Listen! Don't brush it off. Listen with all that is within you; for this word is true, and this word shall prove faithful." Halleluiah!

"Give Me freedom in your services – every single one! Give Me the freedom to be who I AM, and do all that I want to do and all that I can do. I want to heal you. I want to touch you. I want to deliver you. I want to come in and absolutely blow your minds with the Power of God."

"Eye has not seen, nor ear has heard, nor has entered into the heart of man the things which I hold and have in store for those who will listen unto MY VOICE! This is my call unto My Church in this day and this hour. I want to be all that I AM; so that you can be all that YOU ARE," says the Lord. "Let Me say that one more time. **I want to be all that I AM**, so that **you can be all that YOU ARE!"**

"But, unless you release ME and let Me Go and allow Me to be God in your midst, you'll still be held captive. You'll still be a 'Rahab' held behind 'Jericho walls'. Will you release Me today and simply let ME go? I, the Lord God, I beg you to let me go…Let me go….Let me go!!!!"

"If you do… If you let Me go, and that's a big "IF", you can see the "if" and "then" principle all throughout scripture. "If" my people do this – "then" I will do this. It's an "if" and "then" principle! If you let me go, I will release such a move of God in the earth so powerful that you have never experienced before! No one has on the face of the earth, and My people will be set free! There will be new anointings for praise and worship, song and dance, even new anointings to preach, and for the prophetic, and also revelation of my word," says the Lord.

"There are new anointings that haven't even been received yet. You don't even know of them yet – anointings for healing and miracles, signs, and wonders that will absolutely blow your mind. Your carnal mind cannot comprehend what I hold in store for you. And, if you will simply, LET ME GO – it will be unleashed into the four corners of the world. It will impact as far as the east is from the west, and the north is from the south – in all four directions! **It's a global**

message for all peoples! The glory of God will cover the earth! The glory of God resided in the 'Holy of Holies' or the 'Secret Place' of the Most High God, where the 'Ark of the Covenant' was kept. The glory dwelt between the cherubim-- the glory of God in all His fullness, and all that He is, and was, and is to come. I resided behind the veil in the 'Secret Place' of the Most High. In the pattern given to Moses, the dimensions of the Most Holy Place were in a perfect square. It's symbolic of the four corners of the earth! My glory is intended to extend out in all directions to cover all the earth-- the same glory of God that dwelt in the "Secret Place!"

"**If my people** will make the journey to the "Secret Place", and **get in covenant** with ME to be a habitation for their God and give me **everything** that they are – **I'll give them everything that I AM!** The glory of God will dwell within the tabernacle of My people; and in this way, the glory of God will cover the earth."

It is an unfolding revelation of the tabernacle in scripture from the Tabernacle of Moses, to the Tabernacle of David, to the Temple of Solomon, to the New Testament Church, and to you in this day and in this hour. This message and power is to extend to the four corners of the earth. Even as in the book of Acts Jesus said, "You will receive power when the Holy Spirit comes on you and you will be my witnesses in Jerusalem and in all Judea, and Samaria, and to the ends of the earth. It's also a four stage process – locally, regionally, nationally, then to the ends of the earth!

It is interesting that in the "Tabernacle of Moses" we see this four square pattern repeated over and over throughout-- from the brazen altar, to the golden altar of incense, to the priest's breast plate, to the veil, and the door were all four square. Most importantly, the Holy of Holies was also a four square dimension where God lived among His people. This all speaks of that global message, and also points to the "NEW JERUSALEM" that we read of in Revelation Chapters 21 and 22. *"And I heard a loud voice from heaven saying, 'The tabernacle of God is with men, and He will dwell with then, and they shall be His people. God himself will be with them and be their God.'"* (Rev. 21:3)

It's a four square city *"as long as it is wide."* (V.16) **It's a now vision! It's a now word! It's a now revelation!** The veil has been torn in two! We can go behind the veil! There are futuristic dimensions to that vision; but there is also a **"today" dimension to**

170

that vision. The **"New Jerusalem"** is for today as well-- where heaven and earth come together!

"Church of the Living God: **Heaven's coming down! Heaven's coming down into the Earth! And it's coming down through My people!** Jacob saw a vision of the gateway to Heaven with the angels of God ascending and descending. It's a Jacob's ladder! He only saw a shadow of things that were yet to come. **Jacob's ladder is for today!** It's an open heaven! An "Open Heaven" is in Deut. 28:12-- the "obedience" chapter. So, **"if"** my people who are called by My name will humble themselves and pray and seek my face, I the Lord God, will answer from heaven. I will heal their land and I will answer their cry. It's an open heaven! It's and "if" and "then" principle." **Obedience turns the heart of God!** God needs someone in the earth to ratify the contract. He signed it in His blood, now you must sign it in your blood – not literal blood-- but representative of your life-- the giving of yourself and your entire life over to God. If you do, you've entered the "New Jerusalem"!!! Heaven and earth comes together! The King is in His court, and He issues out His decrees and His word, and whatever He speaks becomes true in the earth. It is! It is! It is!"

"Church of the living God, I am asking you to simply: **LET ME GO. LET ME GO. LET ME GO--** to be free to be who **I AM**, so I can set you free to be who **YOU ARE**! This is my word unto you this day," says the Lord God Almighty.

Chapter Five

God's Five Fold Ministry

"When He ascended of high,
He lead captivity captive,
and gave gifts to men." Eph.4:8

Let God arise!

Let God arise, in you, and let his enemies be scattered! You are an "Ark of God" – a vessel of gold – to carry the power and the presence of the living God. Every time the ark would move, Moses would say those words. It was prophetic pointing to you being the "Ark of God"-- a vessel of gold – one that has been through the fire. The only way to clean gold is to put it through the fire! And you must go through the fire to be a vessel of gold. And if you do, you become an "Ark of God", able to carry the power and the presence of God in the earth. "So, let God arise, in you," says the Lord. "Let God arise, in you, and then your enemies will be scattered!"

You see, that was a prophetic word, even in the days of Moses, pointing thousands of years into the future to the church age. So this word is for you, for such a time as this: "You are an 'Ark of God'"; and also; "Let God arise in you and let your enemies be scattered!"

"So, it all falls down to you and your responsibilities. I, the Lord God, can do nothing unless you allow me to. I can do absolutely nothing without your say so. I must have your permission! You are without excuse. No more excuses. No more pointing of the finger. You control everything that I will do in you," says the Lord God Almighty. "You can blame no other person or no other thing on the face of the earth. All I need from you is a 'Yes Lord, Yes…Yes Lord, Yes… Do in me all that you desire to do and I will submit to you, and I will yield to your will in my life.' That is an open vessel! That is a yielded vessel! That's all I need! And if I get that from you; if you will say those words, I, the Lord God, will open the windows of heaven and pour out a blessing in you, so much so, you'll not be able to contain it all. So, get ready. Get ready to receive from on high all that the Lord thy God has for you in this life. If you do not yield to the Lord your God, the purposes of God and the callings of God will never be fulfilled in your life. You'll never attain or reach the fullness of God in this lifetime. You never will! Because, I need your cooperation in the earth and in your life – on the inside of you – in your heart, in your mind, and in your spirit-- everything about you must be yielded and submitted to the will of God in your life. So this is my word unto you this day: Let God ARISE IN YOU, AND LET HIS ENEMIES BE SCATTERED," for thus saith the Lord Thy God.

The Government of God
(Ephesians 4: 8:13)

"When He ascended on high, He led captives in his train and gave gifts to men. What does 'He ascended' mean except that he also descended to the lower earthly regions? He who descended is the very one who ascended higher than all the heavens, in order to fill the whole universe. It was he who gave some to be apostles, some to be prophets, some to be evangelists, and some to be pastors and teachers, to prepare God's people for works of service, so that the body of Christ may be built up until we all reach unity in the faith and in the knowledge of the Son in God, and become mature, attaining to the whole measure of the fullness of Christ." (Eph 4: 8-13)

"'When he ascended on high he gave gifts unto men.' I, the Lord God, I ascended; but I also descended into the lower regions of the earth. I went to hell, kicked in hell's gates, took the keys directly back from Satan himself which is all the power and authority in this lifetime. I took back the power to hold. I took captivity captive. Halleluiah! Then I ascended back to the earth realm, and I appeared to over five hundred people in this world. I even appeared to Thomas, walked through walls and had him stick his fingers in my side. I ate with them, bread and fish, to prove to them that I, the Lord God, had risen. 'He is alive! He is alive!' is the testimony that I wanted to speak to them that day. 'He is alive. He has risen!' But I also ascended into the heavenly realms and when I ascended I said in that day, 'I must leave so that the Holy comforter may come.' And in that day and in that moment, when I ascended into the heavens, I released giftings into the earth. Halleluiah!" *"And the government will be upon his shoulder. …Upon the throne of DAVID and over his Kingdom, to order it and establish it with judgment and justice from that time forward, even forever. The zeal of the Lord of hosts will perform this." (Isaiah 9: 6,7)*

"'The government will be upon his shoulder.' In that day, I established My government in the earth. It began in my earthly walk, because I was the fullness of God in the earth, and I gave my power and authority to the twelve apostles. They were the foundations of the apostles and prophets added to the foundation laid in the Old Testament. I was laying yet another foundation of the twelve apostles, and then I gave my power to the twenty – to send them out, all before my death, burial, and resurrection. But in that day and in the moment,

175

I the Lord God said that I would leave so that the Holy comforter may come. And it is through the Holy Spirit –within the church age – that the gift of the Holy Spirit must be received in the church. Halleluiah! The gift of the Holy Spirit is for all people-- all nations, all tribes, all tongues, and all denominations. It is a gift for you, and every generation after you-- to your children, and your children's children, and your children's, children's children. He is for all generations until I return. It is so very important. It is crucial. It is critical that the church of the Living God receive this truth. **The baptism in the Holy Ghost is for all believers, for this day and in this hour.** It's not a denominational thing. It's not a Pentecostal thing. It's not a charismatic thing. **It's a Bride of Christ thing!** It is a **gift** that I have given to my church," says the Lord, "for all people, for all time!" Halleluiah!

"So, with that also, is the giftings in Eph 4: 8 -13. I have given some to be apostles, some to be prophets, evangelists, pastors, and teachers. It is My government in the earth-- the government of God in the earth-- not Man's government but God's government!" Halleluiah!

"NOT MAN's GOVERNMENT, BUT GOD'S GOVERNMENT! Let God arise and let His enemies be scattered! Let God's government in all of His entirety – all that God is – Let Him ARISE! We need to let God's government arise in the earth. For you see, that is a part of who He is – it's His government! It's all that He is – and He gave some to be apostles, prophets, evangelists, pastors, and teachers. It's all of who He is, and it's all throughout scripture – and we'll see that later on. It's the pattern. It's the protocol. It's the type. God's the same yesterday, today, and forever. He existed in eternity past, present, and He'll exist in eternity future. This is all coming from God. God set it up a long time ago and He gave us some pictures to look at so we can see His five– fold ministry far back into eternity past, before Eph. 4: 8-13 was ever written. God was, and He "IS", and He shall be! So what we see in Eph. 4: 8-13, it already was, and it still is today, and it shall be in the future."

"So, church of the Living God: It is time to reinstitute what has already been-- what has already been established-- what has already been a pattern in my written word. **It needs to be reestablished in My church**, in this day and in this hour. Church of the Living God: You have departed from My pattern! You have departed from My

176

blueprint! You have gotten away from the government of God. It is My established order!"

"IT CANNOT CHANGE! And it will not change for any man. NO MAN CAN CHANGE THE ORDER OF GOD! No man can change this order. When you depart from this order or this blueprint – it does not work. **It does not work!"**

"Church of the Living God: You wonder why you are struggling. Why are you faltering? Why are we not as fruitful as we need to be or want to be? You've departed from the pattern! You've departed from the blueprint! You're only utilizing, perhaps, two offices of the five-fold ministry: pastors and teachers. You're trying to build it all on just pastors and teachers. It's 2/5ths. You need to have 5/5 ths, for 5/5ths makes up the whole! You need them all this day. **You need all FIVE: Apostles, Prophets, Evangelists, Pastors and Teachers!** You need all five," says the Lord. "And some would say, 'The days of the apostles are over', but I the Lord God, today, give you a fresh word. Apostles are still for today! I established the original 12 in my earth walk, but when I ascended, why did I include apostles in the giftings? I would have only said, 'Pastors and Teachers.' If apostles were over, I would have never included that word in written scripture. **Apostles are still for today!** They are a gift to the church, to be released in the earth. You must have ALL FIVE. You need the apostle to govern, and to establish new works, and to build and establish my government in the earth. And also, the prophet is still for today. They are included in Eph. 4: 8 – 13, in that portion of scripture. Prophets are still for today! It is building upon the prophets of old that we see in the Old Testament. They are still for today. And one a little more accepted is the office of evangelist, but they are fading fast. My church has been gripped with fear. Pastors are afraid to allow other preachers to come in and take their pulpits. They have a spirit of fear. They need to allow the evangelist to come in and do what he has been called to do-- to help establish my Kingdom in the earth." *"And the government will be upon His shoulder. And His name will be called Wonderful, Counselor, Mighty God, Everlasting Father, Prince of Peace."* (Isa.9:6)

"Even in My names – it's a five-fold name of Christ! We see again God's five-fold dimension and His five-fold Kingdom. Even in His very names, we see a five-fold dimension of Christ."

The government of God will be established in the earth one way or the other, and the gates of hell shall not stand against it. Every anointing in Christ that He carried is meant to be given back down into the church in all the fullness of God that he carried during his lifetime. Jesus was the embodiment of the Lord God Almighty Himself – God incarnate. He is "Emanuel", which means: "God with us". The fullness of God, in that same measure, is to be poured out into the church today – now!

But it is poured out through God's order – through His blueprint. Remember, anointing flows down. So, all that was in Christ Jesus must flow down to the 12 apostles, then the 20, a good foundation, then to His fivefold ministry.

The very next thing He did, when Jesus left this earth, He established His 5 – fold ministry to be poured out in the earth through the church. Then, from fivefold ministry, it must flow down from there into the rest of the body of Christ.

"Why are you lacking anointing? Why are you lacking giftings? Why are you not seeing all that you desire to see in the church? A part of this answer lies in this mystery. It has been a mystery to a large part of my church for centuries, but I am unveiling this mystery and this revelation in this day and in this hour. You must have fivefold ministry built up within your church. Accept it. Receive it. Allow God to raise up leaders within the church that only God will raise up. It's not who man calls, but who God calls!"

There are 3 major anointings of Christ that you also see in the Old Testament pattern. In the Old Testament only a king, a priest, or a prophet could be anointed – that was a shadow of things to come. Those three anointings were combined in the ministry and in the full body of Christ himself. He carried all three anointings: the kingly anointing, the priestly anointing, and the prophetic anointing. It was all in Christ. And those major three are to be released into the body of Christ today. You carry a kingly anointing, a priestly anointing, and a prophetic anointing, whether you know it or not. You are called to be kings and priests, and ministers unto your God.

"In the Kingly anointing, it carries all authority and all power in the earth. You see, the King – he had the final say. There was no one more powerful than the King in the earth. That speaks of the power and authority that I have given to my church when I gave them the keys to the Kingdom. On that day, I spoke to Peter, and it is

178

interesting his name 'Petros' in the Greek literally means: small stone; and I declared upon this rock I will build My church and what I meant in that passage was Peter's confession. He was asked, 'Who do you say I am?' And Peter said, 'You are Christ, the Son of the Living God. You are the Christ!' And upon this confession, 'You are the Christ', I will build my church and upon this rock, 'Petra', which means: massive rock, 'Upon this rock I will build My church…'" (Mat. 16:13-19)

"For you see, Christ is the massive rock. He is the chief cornerstone. He is the ROCK UPON WHICH I STAND. He is the chief cornerstone in the building of my spiritual house--the precious cornerstone-- the most important of all stones in any foundation. The cornerstone was the largest, most beautiful, and most ornate stone that drew the most attention. Jesus is the cornerstone. He was chief among all other 'stones' in the foundations of the 12 apostles and the prophets in the days of old. And it is upon this rock that I will build my church, and I have given to them the keys to the Kingdom. I didn't just give them to Peter that day; I was giving them to the 'Petra'-- to the rock-- to my spiritual house with the same confession--that I am building in this church age. I gave the 'Keys to the Kingdom' to My church."

"So, Church of the Living God: If you didn't know it before, you hold the keys to the Kingdom. You have the power that is supreme over all other powers in the earth. It is represented in the kingly anointing that you carry. There is nothing more powerful in the earth; which means all other powers are subordinate to that power. Which also means in the scriptures, Satan is under your feet. That's what that means. He is beneath you. He is under you in power, in authority, and in dominion. You see, Adam had full reign over this entire world. It was given to Him from above. Anointing flows down. Adam ruled and reigned in the earth. Adam gave it away to Satan. Satan ruled, rejected God, and did what he wanted for a while – for a time. Adam gave it away, but I took it back though My Son and now it's through My Church. I am still taking the world back; but it is through My people," says the Lord God. "There is only one way. It is through My people – to reestablish My Kingdom in the earth. You see, it's not an earthly kingdom. I have long said, 'My Kingdom is not of this world.' It is a spiritual kingdom. My Church: You need to look spiritually. You are a spiritual house that I am building up. Jesus is the chief cornerstone. The 12 apostles are one foundation added to

179

the prophets of old. Fivefold ministry is the pillars that I, the Lord God have raised up that are seen in the tabernacle of Moses. You couldn't even get into the Holy Place without passing between the five pillars. It's a picture of fivefold ministry."

"And we will see also, I'm putting a covering on it all. There are also five coverings – five porches. So, I put a roof on it all. Then I also lay up the walls. Because, you-- my church – every believer-- is a 'living stone' being placed by the hand of God and Him alone, in the walls of God's spiritual house."

"And you see it's a "New Jerusalem" in the earth! You are a spiritual Israel! You are a spiritual Jew! Stop looking in the natural. Start looking in the spiritual," says the Lord. "You see, in I Cor. 15:46 what happened in the natural, it happened in the natural first, then the spiritual. It's a pattern. It's a type. It's a shadow. I showed it all in the physical recorded throughout the whole entire Old Testament. You see pictures time and time again: the nation of Israel, the Tabernacle of Moses, the Tabernacle of David, and the Temple of Solomon. In everything, it was in the natural first. It all played out and these are recorded for our examples that we may learn from them. So all of the Old Testament has been written, not to be forgotten and said of: "This is Old Testament stuff." But rather, it is written for your example, for you to learn from today. There is a wealth of treasures and mysteries of my Kingdom that are hidden and woven throughout the Old Testament."

"So, it's time to get back into the Old Testament, to sharpen our swords again, and get into the meat of the word and the mysteries of my Kingdom," says the Lord God Almighty.

"All that I am, that I AM, that I AM, **ALL** that I AM – I want to give to my church in this day and in this hour. If you'll only follow the pattern-- follow the blueprint. That's what I've been trying to show you throughout this book using the 'Tabernacle of Moses'. If you will go through the protocol and the patterns of what was established in the 'Tabernacle of Moses'. You must go through the door of the outer court, then to the brazen altar, then the brazen laver. Then, you enter through the first "veil" past the five pillars into the Holy Place; which now you're in the Holy Spirit realm with the lampstand, the table of showbread, and the golden altar of incense. There you pass through the second veil into the Holy of Holies – the secret place-- into the glory realms of God where the "Ark of the

Covenant" was kept. If you'll come into covenant with Me," says the Lord God on High, "and apply the blood of the lamb to your heart. You are the **"Ark of God"!** When you go through this pattern and go through these steps, you can become an "ARK" of the Living God-- Halleluiah – that carries the glory, the power, and the presence of the Living God. **You carry all that I AM!!!** All that I AM is meant for the church today. But you see, it all must be poured out through My established government in the earth! Even as there are natural ranks and positions that you identify with in the natural realm – you have Prime Ministers, and Presidents, and leaders over nations. Then you have people under them. You have the vice president, then you have the cabinet, and congress, then governors over all the states, then you even have state cabinets, and also local authorities. Power and authority flows down! Anointing flows down! What is true in the natural is also true in the spiritual."

"I, the Lord God, cause nations to rise and fall. They only carry what power I give to them. So, even their power is given to them by Me-- the Lord God on High. Halleluiah! Glory to God! We forget also that in My Kingdom – spiritually – power flows down! Anointing flows down! You have natural government. You also have spiritual government. We forget that."

"God the Father gave all that He is to Jesus. He was God incarnate in the earth. Jesus then passed it down to the 12 apostles. That is why their lives were so powerful. They carried the full anointing of God in their lives. Jesus – He ascended and He gave gifts to men. The power of God was given to the church through His fivefold ministry. That's the next level of power in God's government. It always flows down! Then from there it goes down into the church. Why do you lack in power? Why do you lack in giftings? **YOU'RE BYPASSING THE GOVERNMENT OF GOD!** It should be of no surprise. You cannot bypass the government of God in the earth. It's already been established from eternity past. It's a pattern. It's the blueprint. If you try to bypass it, it will fail. It will fail!"

If you try to bypass fivefold ministry in the earth and in your church, and if you say, "that is not for today"; you will not have the power of God be unleashed in your midst – ever-- never – ever. You'll have a trickle; but you'll never have the fullness. You will never have the fullness of God. And I know that is a hard word for some, but it is the truth nevertheless.

So, if you will humble yourself before the mighty hand of God, receive His truth into your heart and life, walk it out, accept it, and apply it into your life and into your ministry; get ready! Get ready! Because God will open up the windows of heaven and He will pour out so much of Himself upon you that you'll not be able to contain it all. He will absolutely, positively, blow your minds! And the full power of God that resided in His Son – all 3 anointings- the Kingly, Priestly, and Prophetic – will flow into your church and into the body of Christ like never before, such as the world has never seen. And all it will take is for you to receive this word of God. Receive it. Study it. Look at it. Research it! See if what I have said already in this chapter, lines up with the written word of God. Prove it! And it shall be found faithful. This word shall be found faithful!

And if you'll humble yourself and allow this word to permeate your being, God will shine the light of His truth down upon you, and it will literally change your life and your ministry. It will also change the world. Halleluiah!

But, it's all up to you. It's all up to you! "Will you let God arise in you, this day," says the Lord God Almighty, "and cause his enemies to be scattered?"

Word to the World

Let God Arise, and let His enemies be scattered! Halleluiah! Glory! Glory! Moses declared those words in his day in the natural. It not only speaks of the letting God arise in you and your enemies in you being scattered – it has a twofold dimension with it also. If you let God arise in you and lift up a shout of praise unto God, it releases God's power into the natural realm that is around you as well.

"Even as in the days of Jericho, an anointed shout caused the walls to fall down; it's a picture of every demonic stronghold crumbling and falling over nations, over regions, over states, and over churches. So, when you let God arise in you, it not only affects you, it affects the world and I can unleash my power in the earth," says the Lord God Almighty!

"And it also causes demons to tremble! Satan has a fivefold dimension to his kingdom as well. So, church of the Living God: You better have your fivefold kingdom, and your fivefold ministry established in your church, or you will be over run – literally over run by the enemy! Satan has his fivefold kingdom as well and you can see it outlined in Eph. 6:12: principalities, powers, rulers of darkness, spiritual wickedness in high places and Satan himself. It's a fivefold kingdom of demonic power and presence in the earth. Satan has his FIVE--- We better have our FIVE!"

God arise, and reestablish your fivefold ministry within your Kingdom! This word is for the entire church worldwide. For thus saith the Lord thy God, the creator of the ends of the earth, "There is no search in My understanding. Who is like Me that would counsel Me and give Me instruction? Were you there when I laid the foundations of the earth? Were you there when I stretched out the heavens and put the stars in place? Were you there when I raised the mountains and I lowered the valleys? Were you there when I filled the seas with a tear from my eye? Were you there when I spoke light and light was? Were you there when I created all the animals in this beautiful world of mine? Were you there on the sixth day in the garden when I took dust from the earth – mere dust from the earth-- and formed man? Who is like Me that would counsel Me?" says the Lord. "Who is man that he would try to instruct Me, and counsel Me, and give Me understanding? Can you add anything to my knowledge? Can you add anything to My wisdom? Is there anything at all that you could give Me that would add to what I already have? Is there anything?"

"I, the Lord God, I need **NO** counsel from you – this day," says the Lord. "I need no understanding from you," says the Lord. "I need no knowledge from you," says the Lord. "I need absolutely nothing from you that you could give me except-- **yourself.** That's all that I need from you – is your vessel – your willing heart – your openness to just let Me do what I need to do in you. And then and only then can I do what I want to do in the world today. So, if you want to see a move of God in the world-- it must begin with you!"

"So, all that I have – I want to give to the body of Christ-- today! But, you must – you must-- open the door of your heart and let ME in to you. So, that I can inhabit your temple – your tabernacle – and you can be an "ARK" of God that can carry the power of God in the earth. So wherever you go –I go!   WHEREVER YOU GO – I GO!!!"

"If you'll come to the 'secret place', if you'll come with me and take my hand and go further in God, if you'll not be satisfied to just hang out in the outer court or just mill around in the Holy Place. You know of My giftings. You know of My supernatural gifts. It's all in the Holy Place and you can rejoice in that and making it that far. **But, there's more!** There's more! There's more! But you have to press in. There's more than just the giftings. There's more than just the praise and the worship. There's more than just the table of showbread, the golden altar of incense, and the golden lampstand. I'm calling you this day: The "veil" has been torn! I want you to get that. THE VEIL HAS BEEN TORN IN TWO!!! WHY? So, you can come into the 'Glory realms of God'-- today! It's not just for a futuristic millennial period of Christ and Him coming back and establishing a new heaven and a new earth. The glory realms of God are for today. You can come in past the veil and experience all that I AM, that I AM. You can experience the glory – THE GLORY – THE GLORY – of God in the earth-- today!! Halleluiah! Glory to God!"

The Holy of Holies was a four square room where the Ark of the Covenant was kept in the Tabernacle of Moses. It is a picture that is timeless! It has no beginning or end. The symbolism has no end! Even though we don't have a physical tabernacle any more, you can't just throw away the picture, and the meaning, and the symbolism behind it all. It points to a four square city of a four square "NEW JERUSALM" in Revelation 21. It also points to a four square dimension of the four corners of the earth. It's global. This "NEW JERUSALEM" city is global!

"It's a spiritual house. Remember, first came the natural, then the spiritual. First came the pattern-- then the substance! FIRST came the blueprint-- then the fulfillment. Christ came to fulfill it all, not to abolish any one letter of the law. But Jesus said, "I came to fulfill every letter of the law…" and it was meant to continue on throughout eternity until the Lord returns!"

"Until there is a new dimension of my Kingdom established. The "New Jerusalem" is still for today, and many, many, many people miss this truth." But it's all throughout scripture and the pattern we see in the Tabernacle of Moses, in every detail, is meant for our examples that we may learn and be blessed from these scriptures today.

This is why it is so important to still study the Old Testament; to look at every detail; every pattern, every shadow – everything! Why?

Because it all points to Christ. Everything that was ever written was written of Christ – it points to Him, it speaks of Him, it goes to Him – it glorifies Him.

John chapter one, verse one: *"In the beginning was the word and the word was with God, and the word was God, and the word became flesh and dwelt among us."* Jesus was the word. The word became flesh and dwelt among us. The word Jesus became flesh. He became "Emmanuel": God with us. So the word you have today in the Holy canon scriptures of the Holy Bible, every word, when you read it and think of it – it is Christ! It is Jesus! It is Him personified in parables, in pictures, in types, and in shadows.

And then when He came to the earth, He became the substances of all things in His earthly walk. He was everything that God is, and was, and is to come. And when He left this world He said, *"I must leave that the Holy Spirit may come."*

"The fullness of the spirit that was in Jesus is meant to come down and be in you in this lifetime, in this dimension, in this day and in this hour-- in its entirety—in all its fullness. He carried the full anointing of God in every dimension, in every gifting, in every detail. And the fullness of God is meant to be given down into My church into every believer – every "living stone" to build up God's spiritual house – His "New Jerusalem" in this day and in this hour. **You are spiritual 'Israel'!** You are spiritual 'Jerusalem'. You are spiritually 'Jewish', for you have been grafted into the olive tree."

"Yes, I, the Lord God, have a plan for natural Israel as well; and every kingdom will fall into my plan for the end times. And natural Israel, there will be a day that she will return to Me and call upon Me as 'Messiah' as a nation."

"It is in my word. My word prophesies of that day, and that day shall be. But for this day, you have been grafted in, so that my power and glory could not only be revealed through one nation, it could be revealed through **all** nations. And you are a part of that plan of redemption in the earth. Halleluiah!"

"So, this is a worldwide message to every church that will call upon the name of the God of the Hebrews – who will call upon the name of 'Yahweh'! You are spiritual Israel. You are spiritually Jewish. You have been grafted in. You HAVE BEEN GRAFTED IN! Accept it. Receive it and the truth shall set you free! The truth shall set you free! So, get ready. Get ready. Get ready. If you'll receive all

185

of this word, all that I AM, that I AM, that I AM, can be poured out into my people."

"'If my people, who are called by my name will humble themselves and seek my face and pray…' I Chron. 7:14 is perhaps the most famous of all revival scriptures. I will use it yet one more time. 'If my people, who are called by my name will humble themselves and pray and seek my face…' 'If' they will humble themselves, 'if' they will seek my face, 'if' they will pray unto ME," says the Lord, "then" I, the Lord God on High – if you give ME all that you have – I'll give you all that I have!"

"That's the covenant that I have written. THAT IS THE COVENANT….that I have written!!!"
"IT CAN NOT BE CHANGED!!!!!"
"IT WILL NOT BE CHANGED!!!!!"
"IT IS! IT HAS BEEN ESTABLISHED! It cannot be changed. You can come no other way. Jesus is the Way, the Truth, and the Life. No man comes to the Father except by Him! You have to come through Christ. You have to come through Jesus, in His entirety. He is the word. He is every word. The word became flesh and dwelt among us. He had the first word and He will have the last word. And you can no longer ignore all of His words in between. You must stop ignoring every word in between – His revelation-- His scriptures. It all speaks of Christ."

"Church of the Living God, worldwide: Stop ignoring God's word – His present day manna. Every word was written of Him. Every word speaks of Him. It points to Him. It comes from Him, to you, through you, and back to Him – full circle. There were four rings on the Ark of the Covenant that they slipped the poles through to carry it with because they weren't allowed to even touch it. The four rings speak of this very truth – full circle – from God, to you, through you, and back to God. It's a never ending circle. And it's a never ending circle of my anointing power. It comes from God the Father through my anointed government. It must come through the pattern – the protocol-- the blueprint. It flows down. Anointing flows down and it must flow down through my pattern that's already been established from eternity past. It cannot be changed. And if you will accept this word, it will flow through you with new power, in greater ways, and in new dimensions. And it will all flow back with glory and praise unto the Lord Jesus Christ – to Him be the honor, to Him be

186

the glory! No other flesh will glory in His presence. It all flows from Him, and through you and back to Him."

"You see, you're part of His 7th day creation. You are the finished work of God. He rested on the 7th day in Genesis at the natural creation of this world. He didn't do anything else on the 7th day. Why? It was reserved for Him to complete His creation in you – in Jesus! Jesus is the perfect 7th day man. He was completely full and complete with all that God is and was and is to come. He was the fullness of God that came down into the earth. He was full and complete! He was the 7th day man-- the 7th day creation!"

"And all that He was, and is, and is to come, flows down into you and through you, so that now you can be the 7th day creation of the Most High God. You go from a 6th day man in Adam, who is lacking, who is incomplete, to a 7th day man in Jesus where you are full and complete, not lacking any one thing in your life. This is my power. This is my glory."

"I'm coming back for a bride, not a beat- up battered bride, but one that is glorious that is arrayed in all of her splendor. I'm coming back for a glorious church. Will you be a part of this glorious church, today? Will you be a part of the bride of Christ? If you say, 'YES, I want to be a part of that bride,' then allow My word to penetrate your heart and life. Allow my living word to come into your very being and become a part of who you are. Receive it implanted and allow my word to take root in your heart. Have my word fall upon good soil, so that it may grow and flourish, and bring life and fruit into your life."

"Church of the Living God: These are serious days. It's a serious hour. I, the Lord God, speak My fresh manna from Heaven to my worldwide global church. I am coming back for a glorious bride; for one church-- one body. Will you be a part of this living church of this glorious bride? Search your heart this day! Will you be a part of this bride? For this is My word unto you this day," says the Lord God Almighty.

Satan Has His Five

"Finally, my brethren, be strong in the Lord and in the power of His might. Put on the whole armor of God, that you may be able to stand against the wiles of the devil. For we do not wrestle against flesh and blood, but against principalities,

against the rulers of the darkness of this age, against spiritual hosts of wickedness in the heavenly places." (Then Satan himself who is ruler over them all.) (Eph.6: 10 – 12)

Satan has his five. Church: We better get our five! It's a pattern all throughout scripture. It's a type. We can see it time and time again in various places. Abram fought in the Valley of Siddim and was later approached by the King of Sodom who represented an alliance of **five** kings. This king wanted to make a deal. (Gen. 14)

"Even back in the days of Abram (Abraham), he had to war and fight against the kings of this world, and he overcame them and was victorious. Why? He was My chosen vessel. He had the anointing and blessing of God upon His life, and a promise that He would be the father of many nations. And even My promise and My words to Abraham speaks into eternity future. Abraham is our father. He is the father of the Jews, but He is also your father too. Why?"

"Because, you have been grafted in! He would be a father of many nations; so spiritually, I am raising up my kingdoms in the earth-- My nations who will humble themselves and seek after me, so that they will become godly nations; ones that call upon the name of 'Jehovah' and 'Yahweh' – the God of the Hebrews. That they will be nations who listen to My voice; who look unto ME for all their direction; that their leaders look to ME for their wisdom, their counsel, their might, their understanding, and that the governments of the earth in the kingdoms and the nations of this world can turn and be godly nations!"

"*'A Father of many nations'… 'that nations would rise and fall'…* I, the Lord God will cause nations to rise and fall. If they are evil nations they will incur the judgment of God. If they are a godly nation, and they seek my face, they come in under my protections-- my covenant – my coverings. So even in the days of Abram, I had my hand upon him. He warred and fought against the enemy with his own men. Routing them, he recovered all the plunder and the people that had been taken in the previous battle, including his nephew Lot. Four other kings had ruled the whole territory for 12 years until the alliance of **five** kings rebelled in the 13th year at the Valley of Siddim, and Abram coming to their rescue. God was with Abram. Throughout Old Testament history, we see this pattern with national Israel."

"As I began to form them as a young nation, I sent Abraham to a land that he did not know of, nor even knew how to get there. All through history we see this pattern. Moses warred against the **five** Kings of the Midianites. (Num. 31:8) Then Joshua, all through the days of entering the Promised Land and the land of the Philistines, Israel was constantly attacked by the people of that land. In Josh. 10:16, Joshua killed the **five** Amorite Kings. Israel was tormented by **five** Philistine Lords (Josh. 13:3) and **five** cities. (I Sam. 6) And perhaps the greatest picture of them all, we see more **fives** in the battle of David and Goliath. We know by scripture in II Sam 21:22, that there were four brothers of **Goliath** – the descendants of Rapha-- making **five** giants in all." (also mentioned in Deut. 9:2)

"Satan has his **five** – we must have **God's five** operating in the church and in the earth—today! It is a desperate hour! We need all that God has for us to fight this battle – not LESS! We need more of God and all that He has available to us; and a very important, major part of that is to have His fivefold ministry in operation."

"Without it the Church will be overrun! Church of the Living God: You have held to a form of godliness, but you have denied the power there of. Where is your power? Why are you lacking? Why? You have not allowed My fivefold ministry to be raised up in your midst. You must allow ME, the Lord God on High, to raise up My fivefold ministry within your churches in the earth. They are all represented in the **five** pillars in the Tabernacle of Moses; but they are too heavy for men to lift up. I, the Lord God, must raise up men and women of God to fulfill these offices of God that I call—only whom I choose. It is not your choice. It is not man's choice to fill these offices in God's government in the earth. You see, I, the Lord God, must choose."

Man has been trying to choose the anointed ones all through the entire history of Israel. King Saul was man's choice – not God's. Another example, Jesse, the father of David, tried to bring all seven of his son's before Samuel – God's anointed prophet. You see, God anointed Samuel in the earth. Anointing flows down! So it must have come through Samuel, God's anointed prophet, for the next king to be chosen.

So Samuel came to Jesse's house that day and he basically said in paraphrasing, "Where are your sons?" And it is interesting enough Jesse brought the first born – the oldest – Eliab to Samuel. Even

Samuel thought He was the one. If Jesse had his way that day, his oldest son would have been anointed King of Israel, and it would have been a very big mistake, because none of them had the heart of God. So, Jesse brought each of the seven sons before Samuel – one after the other – all seven. And it was not even in Jesse's intention that day, to bring David before Samuel; because, David wasn't much in Jesse's eyes. He was the youngest and the smallest. He was even tending the sheep which was the lowest job of all for anyone to be assigned. That job was given to the lowest member of your house.

Jesse didn't even want to bring David before Samuel. So, Samuel got through all seven sons and continually said, "no he's not the one; no he's no the one." Finally, Samuel asked, "Are these all the sons you have? Jesse – do you have any more sons? Do you have any more here?" Because Samuel knew God had sent him there that day to anoint the next King of Israel. Surely, he must have been there. Jesse said, "Yeah, there's just little David. He's out attending to the sheep." Samuel said, "Go get him. We will wait here. We'll not even sit down until he gets here!" Why? HE WAS THE KING! Samuel would not even sit down because the King was coming! THE KING WAS COMING! Halleluiah! He had a sense in the spirit that this was going to be the one. Samuel did not hesitate; he looked upon little David and the Lord said, "Yes, anoint him. He is the one!"

So Samuel poured out from his horn of oil. Anointing flows down! He had a horn of oil… the horn was taken from an animal which is symbolic of the strength of that animal; and speaks of power and anointing to rule. The death of the animal would provide the horn for the oil—a vessel. Samuel poured out the full anointing of God upon David that day; so, David would become the next King of Israel. That would not be the only anointing that David would receive in his lifetime. There were several anointings of David. He carried with him all three anointings of Christ – the Kingly, the Priestly, and the Prophetic. And the covenant with David which God had made with him was that, his Kingdom, there would be no end.

For you see, you are kings and priests of the Lord God Almighty. You are to establish the kingdom and carry the kingly anointing that was upon David, in the earth today. King David's Kingdom was perhaps the greatest, most powerful, and most glorious of all in Israel. Solomon's was very glorious and full of splendor, but David's was perhaps the most powerful.

You, too, carry this same kingly anointing in the earth today. And it is interesting that David was the eighth son of Jesse. We will get into this more a little later on in the following chapters, but just a little nugget of truth for you now. David was the eighth son of Jesse. You're a 6th day creation in Adam. You're a 7th day creation in Christ, when you have the fullness of God. And then, you're an 8th day creation as a "new beginning" and possessing an "overflow" into the church age. The first day of the new week is the 8th day! It's a "new beginning"-- a "new age." So, you carry this same anointing that was upon the "eighth day son" of Jesse – as an "8th day" man, woman, or child in the earth today, as a new beginning!

"So the same anointing that was upon King David is upon you and My church in the earth, today. He carried all the fullness of God in the earth. It was upon King David, and continued through his family line. It was passed down through the line of David until we get to Jesus. Then Jesus still carried the kingly anointing of King David and it is an overflow to you as an "eighth day man" – an "eighth day creation", in Christ, in the earth today!

So, all those anointings – the kingly, (II Sam 5:3), the priestly, and the prophetic (Acts 2:30) we see operating in David's life. In the book of the Psalms, David wrote many under the anointing of the Holy Spirit. He had an anointing for praise and worship. He had the anointing of the priesthood to come before God in the tabernacle. We see David placing the Ark of the Covenant in his tabernacle with no veil. (II Sam. 6:17) He wore a linen ephod as a priest. (v14) He offered burnt and peace offerings before the Lord – the priestly sacrifices. (v17) He gave the priestly blessings to the people. (6:18; Num. 6:24 - 27) David officiated as King-Priest after the order of Melchisedek. (I Chron. 15:29; 16:1-3) Only three people carried all three anointings in one: Moses, David and Jesus – each builders of a tabernacle!

1) The Prophetic Anointing – Ministers the word of the Lord.
2) The Kingly Anointing – Ministers the power; ruling and reining; God's authority.
3) The Priestly Anointing – Ministry of reconciliation; intercession; prayer; worship and praise unto God.

All three anointings of David are meant to come into the church today. It will be a Kingdom that will never end! It is a spiritual Kingdom, a spiritual house, a spiritual Israel, a spiritually Jewish nation-- a holy nation unto God. It is a "New Jerusalem" in the earth!

191

And it is a picture, a pattern, and a type that we see all throughout scripture. It's an everlasting Kingdom. Jesus brought it in His earth walk. He gave His authority to His apostles, and then to His fivefold ministry, and then released it into the earth to every believer that comes into His Kingdom – every believer-- not just a few special, anointed, people. It is to come down to, and move through, every believer! Anointing flows down! Remember, from Samuel to King David and his family line – from Jesus – to the 12 – to fivefold ministry – down to all the "living stones" in the church today, the ones that have been anointed by Jesus himself – not by man.

"Man tries to anoint the 'sons of Jesse'. In like fashion, the church today is still trying to anoint the 'sons of Jesse' as the anointed of God. They are acting as David's father to try to anoint whoever they think is best; whoever they think is the wisest, or most beautiful, or the most handsome, and bring them before the prophets of God to be anointed. You must go through God's order! It has to come down through God himself and who He chooses. Even today, the church must anoint only those who God chooses for leadership. And sadly enough, there are some today that still try to anoint people that have not been anointed by God, and sometimes their ministries fail. Why? Their work has not been blessed and anointed by God himself. And I know that is a hard word for some. But, you must accept and take your place in the rank and file of My Kingdom," says the Lord. "I must place the 'stones'. Remember that word. I must place the stones! I am the architect. I am the builder of this house. I MUST PLACE THE STONES! IT IS MY HOUSE! It is MY NEW JERUSALEM. I must place the stones--not man." *"Once more I will shake heaven and earth, the sea and dry land; and I will shake all nations, and they shall come to the desire of all nations, and I will fill this temple with glory," says the Lord of hosts. "The glory of this latter temple shall be greater than the former."* (Hag. 2:6, 7, 9)

"See that you do not refuse Him who speaks. For if they did not escape who refused Him who spoke on earth, much more shall we not escape if we turn away from Him who speaks from heaven. Whose voice then shook the earth; but now He has promised, saying 'Yet once more I shake not only the earth, but also heaven.' Now this, 'Yet once more,' indicates the removal of those things that are being shaken, as of things that are made, that the things which cannot be shaken may remain."

192

"Therefore, since we are receiving a Kingdom which cannot be shaken, let us have grace by which we may serve God acceptably with reverence and godly rear. For our God is a consuming fire!" (Hebrews 12: 25-29)

"All that can be shaken will be shaken. Everything that has not been placed by the hand of God will fall! It is coming down. It is coming down!" says the Lord God Almighty. "You have placed many stones in the walls of your kingdoms – My church – and you have tried to build them up and help me in this process. I, the Lord God, need no help in this process. In fact, I ask you not to lay these stones," says the Lord. "They must be laid by my hand. So, in this day, get ready – for I am causing a shaking in the land. I am causing a shaking in the earth. Everything that is not laid by my hand will come down," says the Lord God Almighty.

"For this Kingdom – this "New Jerusalem"-- must be laid by My hand," says the Lord. "And this "New Jerusalem" **IS** for today." This New Jerusalem **IS** for today!

David and Goliath
(I Samuel 17: 1-58)

The story of David and Goliath, perhaps is one of the most well know stories in all of history, that we all know and love because it has such a great ending. However, some of the details may have been overlooked.

Israel had been tormented by the Philistines for years and years; and there were some descendants of the Anakites that had teamed up with the Philistines to fight for them. They were a large race; a race of giants that were good in warfare and intimidation. Their race was almost completely annihilated and wiped out. Only a small remnant remained – the descendants of Rapha – the descendants of the Anakites. They happened to live in the land of Philistia, and they combined forces with the people there-- the Philistines. During this time, in King David's day, a young shepherd boy keeping his flocks is just anointed the next king of Israel. And from that day, you'll read in scripture, the Spirit of the Lord came upon David in power from that very moment on.

193

The day Samuel anointed David, the Spirit of the Lord came upon David in power and shortly after that we see the picture of David and Goliath, and of Israel and the Philistines. It was much more than a battle between one boy and one giant. It was much more than a battle between one nation of Israel verses another.

It was a battle all right-- God verses Satan! It was a battle of the ages. For you see, if the nation of Israel had lost, they would have gone into slavery and subjection unto a heathen nation of the Philistines. So, how dramatic is that, on this battlefield that the Philistines send out one giant named Goliath and they boiled it all down to one fight; and if any one man could defeat this one giant – to the victor goes the spoils. The loser would serve the winner and be submissive to whatever they asked. Freedom would be lost!

Everything was at stake here-- everything: the future of Israel, David's Kingdom, and the line in the genealogy of David. Everything was at stake. So there is much more going on here than just one boy verses one giant – it was the Kingdom of God verses the Kingdom of Satan himself.

So, the full anointing of God that was put on a shepherd boy was brought to the battlefield that day. Young David carried the full anointing of God Most High. He was sent there by his father Jesse to bring his brothers some bread and provisions to strengthen them for the battle to come. He was really sent there almost by accident in the natural; but it was for such a time as this.

In the precise moment, God Almighty sent David to the battle. Why? Because He carried the full anointing of God that no one else carried! And it was passed down to him by the prophet Samuel.

Saul didn't carry it. David's brothers didn't carry it. Just a little boy-- a picture of all things --that God would send a small boy to fight a giant; so that it wouldn't be by their might, or by their own power, or by the strength of their numbers that victory would come. A small boy – and he is the only one that shows up and professes the words of the Lord. He prophetically proclaims the word of God in the earth on that battlefield. He says, *"For who is this uncircumcised Philistine, that he should defy the armies of the living God."* (I Sam. 17:26) He is the only one there that rises up and proclaims the word of the Lord. Why? He carried the prophetic anointing of God!

So, David is one boy, verses one giant. And so Goliath comes and he taunts the armies of Israel for forty days, every morning and evening he would take his stand. All of Israel, for the most part are just scared out of their wits. They don't know what to do. They were stalled out. They had no clue what to do next; and along comes this little shepherd boy. They tried to put Saul's armor on him. The King had the best armor in the battle. They tried to give David the best armor of what man could come up with; but he couldn't even move in it, so he took it all back off.

What does David do then? David runs to the stream-- a picture of water, and the Holy Spirit-- and He gathers **five** stones from the river. David went to the river! We, too, need to run to the river once again-- The River of God! And in that "River of God" there will be those **five** stones. It's a symbol of God's **five-fold ministry in the hands of the king**. David grabbed his **five** stones—a picture of the fullness of God combined with fivefold ministry and the government of God.

DAVID RAN TO THE RIVER! We, too, need to run to the "River" and gather God's **five** stones. Those **five** stones will be "a stone of stumbling and a rock of offense" to the world; but they will also be powerful weapons of our warfare. These **five** stones were the weapons of David's warfare in that moment against Goliath. So, HE RAN TO THE RIVER! We need to run to the river. He gathered the **five** stones and his sling and went forward to fight this giant – Goliath, that stood over 9' 9" tall. A giant in any day – he was from the descendants of Rapha or the Anakites that are mentioned in Deut. 9:2. Goliath was not the only one left, as we see mentioned in II Sam. 21:22. All of Goliath's four brothers are mentioned here, and all four were killed at the hands of David and his fighting men. Satan does have his five!

So, here we have one boy verses one giant-- one boy representing the entire Kingdom of God in the earth, and one giant representing the entire Kingdom of Satan in the earth. It was more than just a little boy fighting a very large giant. Everything was on the line that day.

David brought the full anointing of God with him. He had just been anointed by Samuel, God's anointed prophet. He went to the River of God to get his **five** stones. He carried the full power of fivefold ministry and God's government in the earth!

It was God's five verses Satan's five! Goliath was just the representative of the entire kingdom of darkness in the earth. David

195

was just the representation of all the fullness that God had in store that day. You see, its pictures and symbols! It was more than just what meets the eye. Satan will always send his five! We, the church, need to send our five! Always!! It's a picture. It's a pattern. It's a type. And we see it here in this famous story of David and Goliath.

We all know the ending. David only needed one stone. One stone miraculously guided by God himself. It plunged into Goliath's forehead and he fell to the ground dead. Then, David, having no sword of his own, took the sword of the enemy and cut off his head. God brought about a great victory that day for the nation of Israel and it began the ascension of King David to His rightful throne because he was God's anointed.

You see, Saul was man's choice. David was God's choice! And we see God's anointing upon the life of David throughout His entire lifetime. He wasn't a perfect man; but when he sinned he was repentant and turned his heart toward God again. He always inquired of Lord and was a man after God's own heart, and he always went back to the Lord His God.

For you see, it is essential that we have fivefold ministry in the church, today. We must have ALL FIVE: Apostles, Prophets, Evangelists, Pastors, and Teachers; because Satan has his five. It's a pattern. It's a type. It's a shadow; and it is for us today to see here in scripture a truth and a reality of what we war against today.

"For the weapons of our warfare are not carnal but mighty in God for pulling down strongholds." (II Cor. 10:4) The weapons of our warfare, they are many, and we will discuss some of those later on. But the full armor of God includes the shield of faith, the sword of the Spirit and all of those things listed in Eph. 6:14 – 18. But what I want to focus on in this chapter is another weapon of our warfare being the **five** stones of David that we need to use in every church today. They need to be reinstituted and put back in place in the government of God – in God's church today. This is a very important word, and I want every church leader all over the face of the earth to hear this word. Satan has his five. We must have our five. You must allow God to raise up, within your church, pillars, that also speak of the fivefold ministry – that we see in the Tabernacle of Moses holding up the first veil to the Holy Place. Allow God to raise up these pillars in the church. Why? Eph. 4:12:

196

"...for the equipping of the saints for the work of the ministry, for the edifying of the body of Christ." This is where the equipping comes in. This is where the giftings flow down. You see, it all flows down. It must come from God's established order. It must come from God's established government in the earth. It's already been established. It is the pattern. It is the blue-print. It is the protocol.

The only way to defeat Satan's kingdom – the principalities, the rulers, the powers, the spiritual wickedness in high places and Satan himself – the only way to defeat them and their fivefold kingdom is through God's fivefold ministry that God has ordained for the church age for such a time as this. It is crucial. It is critical. You must allow God to raise up His government in the earth!

David and Goliath's battle was not only fought on one battlefield for that day but all of Goliath's brothers were also killed by David's fighting men-- that we see later on in scripture. Every one of his brothers that even tried to avenge Goliath's death, every one, was cut down and destroyed by an anointed fighting warrior in God's Kingdom. Each and everyone were destroyed. "I am establishing my government in the earth," says the Lord your God. "The Kingdoms of this world shall become the Kingdoms of our God. My government shall be established in the earth one way of the other. The question is: Will you be a part of it? Will you receive this word and allow it to penetrate your heart? Receive the truth of this word. It is from the Lord your God, the creator of the ends of the earth. It is a desperate hour. It is the eleventh hour. Time is short."

Satan is bringing his five with all that he can, in all of his fury. We must bring God's five in all of God's power and glory to combat the spiritual **"fives of darkness"** in this world. This is a very, very, important word. We **must** reestablish God's five-fold ministry in the earth today.

Will you let God arise, in you, and let his enemies be scattered? If you do – they will be. If you don't – they won't!

A Cloud The Size of A Man's Hand
(I Kings 18: 1-46)

It was a showdown of the ages: Elijah verses the Prophets of Baal. Mt Carmel was the setting and they had assembled all of Israel

197

there to see it. The prophet Elijah, being the gentleman that he was, allowed the prophets of Baal to call on their god first. *"The god who answers by fire, He is God."* (I Kings 18:24) The prophets of Baal prayed. They danced. They shouted and even cut themselves which was their custom, until their blood flowed to get an answer from their gods. They did all they could do to call upon their gods, to see what would happen. And Elijah patiently waited, and waited, and at one point even mocked them saying, "Shout louder, perhaps he is in deep thought, busy, or traveling, or maybe he is asleep and needs to be awakened." All day long they continued in their frenzy for hours and hours, but there was no response. No one answered them; no god paid any attention to them.

Elijah repaired the altar of the Lord which was in ruins, because of Israel's state of apostasy. He took 12 stones, one for each tribe of the sons of Jacob, or "Israel", to repair the altar. He then prepared the sacrifice! He arranged the wood, the bull, and even dug a trench around the entire altar. Then he did one very unusual thing – he saturated it all with water. They filled four large jars with water and poured them all out three times over till the water ran down and even filled up the trench. Why? It would be even harder to start a fire on a water-logged sacrifice and a greater testament to His God. Israel was in the midst of a great drought that had lasted 3 ½ years that the Lord God had brought upon them in judgment for abandoning the Lord's commands. And only at the word of the prophet Elijah would it begin to rain again. They had sought after Elijah to kill him and destroy him for what He had done. Probably to get him to reverse it, and then kill him, so it wouldn't ever happen again. But before this, Elijah had gone into hiding. After many days, God had said to him, "Go and present yourself to Ahab." (v.18:1)

Elijah prayed that day at Mt. Carmel, and then the fire of the Lord fell from heaven. It consumed the entire sacrifice, the wood, the stones, and the soil, and even evaporated all the water in the trench. Then all of Israel called upon the Lord as their God, while Elijah commanded them to siege all 450 prophets of Baal and 400 prophets of Asherah, who had eaten at Jezebel's table and led Israel astray. Elijah had them brought down to the Kishon Valley where they killed every single one in obedience to the Law of Moses.(see Dt. 15: 6-9)

It was another battle of the ages. Good versus evil--God verses Satan. You see, Baalism had taken over in Israel, the equivalent of satanic worship today, even in the midst of God's chosen people. How easy it is for Satan to slip in and corrupt even God's chosen. How much more important it is for us to be on the alert, and to fight, and to have God's anointing from heaven upon us in this day and in this hour.

How much more do we need God's power in our lives and in our churches today? Elijah won a great victory that day for the Kingdom of God, and after the great victory, Ahab was about to go on his way to feast and drink, but Elijah stayed back and remained for a moment. He waited upon God and prayed at the top of Mt. Carmel bending down to the ground with his face between his knees.

He told his servant to *"go and look toward the sea."* "There is nothing there," he replied. So, Elijah told his servant to "go back" seven times and look towards the sea. LOOK TOWARDS THE SEA. LOOK TOWARDS THE SEA! Do you see anything? Is there anything beginning to form?

You see, Elijah had the word from God, that it would begin to rain again only at His word. He had the prophetic word for himself for this situation. But he still had to pray it through. He still bowed down and prayed to his God for that word to come to pass. So in the fullness and completion of time, seven times he bowed down and he prayed. Seven times he sent his servant to look towards the sea. "Go back", Elijah said. "Go Back. Go Back. Go Back." And patiently, seven times his servant did. And on the seventh time he came back and said, *"I see a cloud the size of a man's hand rising from the sea."* "I SEE A CLOUD THE SIZE OF A MAN'S HAND!"

It was a sign to Elijah that the promise of God was going to come to pass. It was a sign of rain. That servant could have come back and said anything. "I see a cloud the size of a melon." He could have used any other word, but we must look at the words that were used in this text. He used the words "as small as a <u>man's hand</u>". Why?

It's a symbol of fivefold ministry and the right hand of God. The power and authority that comes from God himself, and flows through fivefold ministry, and then down into the body and then into the earth. And then what follows in this story? Elijah sends his servant to tell King Ahab, even in a word of faith because it had not been raining at all yet; and he says to him, *"Go tell Ahab, hitch up your chariot and go before the rain stops you,"* because travel would be very tough soon.

And then, the heavens broke open and brought forth the rain! Ahab was bogged down in this chariot for a deluge began to fall. The skies grew black with clouds, the wind began to blow, a great storm arose, and a heavy rain followed, ending a three and a half year drought.

"Church of the Living God: Its beginning to rain! IT'S BEGINNING TO RAIN! HALLELUIA! I am pouring out My Spirit in the earth, and it's falling through the **clouds** of five-fold ministry," says the Lord God Almighty. "I prophesied in My Word in Joel chapter two – that afterwards, I will pour out My Spirit on all people, upon the young and upon the old, men, women and upon all flesh – everyone-- each and every one! I am beginning to bring forth My rain in the earth, in this day and in this hour. But how much it rains depends on you!"

HOW MUCH IT RAINS DEPENDS ON YOU! How you respond to the word of the Lord. You see, it's not all just written in stone, or in concrete. It's not all just automatic! It doesn't just happen. God needs our participation in all His plans of redemption in the earth. We must respond to what God is saying to us today. We must respond favorably, and say, "Lord God, have your way."

How much it rains depends on us!!! You see, sometimes we think it's all separated and God's just going to pour out the rain independently. We all anticipate it with great expectation and we think: "Yes, God's going to pour out His Spirit." Yes, He has promised that, but it is conditional. It's an "if" and "then" principle: "if" we respond to God; "if" we humble ourselves; "if" we receive the word – engrafted; "if" we receive this word. I Kings chapter 18 is a picture. There's a cloud – it's the size of a man's hand. The hand has five fingers – it's a symbol and picture of five-fold ministry. It's in the heavens. It's a cloud that brings forth the rain! Anointing flows down from God to Jesus through God's government in the earth. In I Kings 18:44, Elijah's servant says that he sees a cloud the size of a man's hand. It is very significant that he uses those words. The rain came through a cloud that had the hand of God in it, with five fingers. We are created in God's image. It came directly from God's right hand – the right hand of power and authority and blessing.

It all flows down through five-fold ministry. Church: We need to get this! We need to get this one! This is major! It is critical! It is crucial! The heavy rain that came that day for Elijah came out of a cloud; it began with a small cloud the size of a man's hand. We cannot by-pass the fivefold ministry of God! It is His established government! His established order! It all flows down from heaven! If we want all the fullness of God, we will accept this word, and we will accept and establish God's order in our lives and in our churches lives.

Elijah bowed down and prayed seven times before the rains came. It's a picture of fullness. Do you want the fullness of God in your life today? Do you want the fullness of God in your church? Do you want it for the city that you live in, or the country that you live in, or the world that you live in? Do you want all that God has for you in this day and in this hour?

We see the full power and authority of God and favor upon Elijah. He was perhaps the greatest prophet that ever lived. There's not a lot written about him in scripture, but we do see miracle, after miracle, after miracle, happening in Elijah's life. Why? He was God's anointed and he carried the full anointing of God himself in the earth to combat the evil forces of darkness. Elijah battled the kingdoms of darkness in this world, and at times, he thought he stood alone and was the only one left. But God spoke to him and said that He had reserved 7,000-- all whose knees have not bowed down to Baal.

"In this day and in this hour, I also have My reserve – my remnant – that have not bowed their knees to Baal, that have not compromised. This is the day of My remnant," says the Lord God Almighty.

"This is the day of my remnant. And I am calling you forth in this day and in this hour, to be My Elijah's in the earth. Will you be My Elijah's, to carry the full anointing of God, to speak forth my prophetic word in the earth, to say 'thus saith the Lord'? These are the days of my Elijahs," says the Lord. "Even the spirit of Elijah had been resurrected – remember Elijah was taken up into heaven in a whirlwind and chariots of fire and did not see death. The same spirit of Elijah had come down in Jesus day—the prophetic voice of God in the earth. He was the frontrunner for Jesus' ministry – John the Baptist! That same spirit is being resurrected again in this day and in this hour to carry on the prophetic, and also the priestly anointing that was transferred from John the Baptist to Jesus at the river Jordan that day. So now Jesus is our high priest, and it has been transferred to us, so we now are the Royal Priesthood unto God and a holy nation.

So you too are even called to carry out miracles in this life. He even raised the dead! Elijah had been staying with the widow at Zarephath and her son after the Brook Cherith had dried up from the drought. God had sent him there. The boy became ill after Elijah had increased her jar of oil and jar of flour immeasurably. They would never run out until the rains came! It was a miracle. He gave them unlimited provisions for them to live on-- a never ending supply of oil! And so a little while later, the son became ill, grew worse and worse, and eventually died.

The widow tried to blame Elijah for this tragedy; but Elijah said, "Give me your son." And so he took the boy to the upper room where he was staying, and laid him on his bed. He stretched himself out on the boy three times and cried out to the Lord, "O Lord, my God, let this boy's life return to him!" These three times speaks of resurrection. Elijah laid his entire body upon the young boy that day, and I believe it is likened to the body of Christ – the fullness of the body of Christ was being laid out upon that boy-- three times for resurrection power. Then the Lord heard Elijah's cry and the breath of God came back into that young boy's body and he lived again. He was raised to life that day. "That's the resurrection power of Christ! And that is the same power that I intend for my church to carry in this day and in this hour," says the Lord.

We see miracle after miracle in Elijah's life, from shutting up the heavens to speaking forth the rain. He even called fire down from heaven and destroyed two armies of Ahaziah's fighting men. The King sent out two dispatches of fifty men just to get one man – Elijah. Elijah answered the captain and said, *"If I am a man of God, may fire come down from heaven and consume you and your fifty men."* (II Kings 1:10) The fire fell and consumed every single one – twice. Not just once – but twice! And then a third company of fifty men was sent out to bring Elijah back to King Ahaziah. This time the captain begged Elijah, falling on his knees before him, "Please man of God, do not harm us or kill us, but please come with us for the King wants to see you today." Then an angel of the Lord said for Elijah to go down with them and not be afraid. And so he went to see King Ahaziah, and at Elijah's word, for consulting Baal-Zebub, the god of Ekron, he pronounced this judgment of God upon him. *"Because you have done this, you will never leave the bed you are lying on. You will certainly die! So he died according to the word of the Lord that Elijah had spoken."* (II Kings 1: 16, 17)

202

Elijah also pronounced judgments upon King Ahab and his wife Jezebel for their wickedness and by his word, it was, and they both died violent deaths!

"I am doing the same thing in the earth today. You are my Elijah's, and at your word so shall it be. As you abide in me and My word abides in you," says the Lord God Almighty, "and you eat of My flesh and drink of My blood, under My anointing, as it lines up with My written word, ask whatever you desire and it shall be done for you. You are my 'kings' – small 'k' – and you are to carry out my power and my authority in the earth today. You are My Elijah's in this day and in this hour."

"Will you receive all that I have for you?" says the Lord. "Will you receive the fullness of God that Christ carried? He carried the anointing of God without measure – the fullness of God. That's what I want to give to you today – the fullness of God without measure – unlimited anointing in your life today – a jar of oil that never runs out. Will you simply receive this word of the Lord this day?" says the Lord God Almighty, the creator of the ends of the earth.

Pool of Bethesda
(John 5:1-14)

In the gospel of John, there is a great picture of God's fivefold ministry that many, perhaps would miss in a fast reading. But if you read through it again, you'll discover that this particular pool in Jerusalem near the Sheep Gate was surrounded by "five covered porches" or "colonnades" depending on the translation.

"These **FIVE** porches are My five coverings," says the Lord God Almighty, "in fivefold ministry. And in that day, the angel would come down into the pool and stir the waters, and the lame, the blind, and the paralyzed would all lie there waiting for that moment when that one angel sent from God would stir the waters so they could jump in and be healed. There was one catch. You had to be the first one in. In that day, there was one man in particular who had been an invalid for thirty eight years. He could not make it into the pool fast enough to be the first one in. So then, Jesus came by that special day and He noticed this one man laying by the pool and He asked him the question, "Do you want to be made well?" And the sick man replied,

"I have no man to put me into the pool when the water is stirred." This man is much like the church today, who gives excuse, after excuse, why they can't jump into the pool. Because in this day and in this hour, there are no excuses! All excuses have been eliminated! Why? Because in this day and in this hour, Jesus **is** the pool; and the pool now comes to you. TODAY, THE POOL COMES TO YOU!! HALLELUIA!!"

"And I, the Lord God, am stirring the waters in this day and in this hour. I am not just sending My angel, not just one angel; but I, the Lord God, am stirring the waters-- but it is through My FIVEFOLD Ministry – My FIVE-FOLD COVERINGS! It's a picture of the church. Can you see it? The pool of Bethesda has **five** coverings or **five** porches, and it is a pool of MY Spirit," says the Lord. "It's the Holy Spirit – a container of my Holy Spirit! It's a picture of My church. It's a pool, a container, a vessel of My Holy Spirit without measure that I am stirring!"

"And each and every one of My believers in the church today that can jump into the 'pool' can receive what they need and be healed in this day and in this hour."

The lame man by the pool of Bethesda did not jump into the pool of water; but instead, jumped into the "pool" of Jesus. And Jesus said to him, "Rise, take up your bed and walk." This happened on the Sabbath day. You see, Jesus is the perfect 7th day Sabbath man in the earth. He is the pool! The pool came to the lame man. Jesus is the 7th day man – the fullness of God in the earth-- and He comes to you today to bring you rest, to bring you the true Sabbath day rest. So you can become a 7th day creation in Jesus and become full and complete in Him. Remember, He is the 7th day man in the earth – the fullness of God. When you come into Jesus, you can be full and complete not lacking any one thing! There will be more on this later. Halleluiah!

We see here in this Pool of Bethesda, that this is a picture of **five**fold ministry or **five** coverings over a pool of water, where a multitude of people are trying to get what they need-- if they can just get in. You see, Jesus is the pool today! Will you come to Jesus today? Will you come to the pool? And will you come into God's government, and into His **fivefold** ministry – His **five** porches? It's God's government. It's God's order. It's God's pattern. Will you allow it to be established in your life and in the church today? "Jump into Jesus and get all that you need! Jump into Jesus," says the Lord

204

God Almighty, "He is the Pool of Bethesda and He carries all that you need."

"I am building My 'Pools of Bethesda' all across this world in this day and in this hour. They have a pool of my Holy Spirit-- a pool of My anointing power for miracles to be released that has no limit," says the Lord God Almighty.

"And this pool is underneath My **five** porches," says the Lord. "It is my fivefold ministry-- part of my government in the earth. Will you help establish these 'Pools of Bethesda' all across the globe? Will you be a part of this? And if you will say, "Yes, Lord. Yes I will. I will allow you to raise up fivefold ministry in our midst. And if you say, "Yes Lord yes", God says, "Yes, I will. I will. I will raise up the 'Pool of Bethesda' all over again in this day and in this hour." Every believer on the face of the earth can go to a "Pool of Bethesda" and jump into it and receive all that they need.

"You see, I am releasing gifts of miracles, supernatural signs and wonders, and gifts of healing in this day and in this hour-- more than has ever been released before. I, the Lord God, if you say, "Yes, Lord yes", get ready, get ready. I will absolutely, positively, blow your carnal minds. I will absolutely blow your mind with what I am about to do in the earth-- miracle after miracle, after miracle. It will not matter the condition of the body. It will not matter that it has been dead for three or four days. It will not matter. Do not look with the sight of your eyes. If their condition bothers you, close your eyes and call upon God for more faith, to believe My word."

"And this is my word unto you this day: I am building My 'Pools of Bethesda' in My 'New Jerusalem' by the Sheep Gate in this day and in this hour. Will you be a part of this building? Will you be a part of this release of My power and My anointing in the earth today? Open your heart this day," says the Lord. "Open your heart, and receive My word engrafted into your spirit. Let it become apart of who you are, and the truth shall set you free. The truth shall set you free! For this is my word unto you this day," says the Lord God Almighty.

The Holy Anointing Oil
(Exodus 30: 22-33)

It is by no coincidence that the holy anointing oil of God outlined in the book of Exodus chapter 30 is made up of **five** principle spices – a holy anointing recipe! It is another important **five** in the Kingdom of God. Even the holy anointing oil itself was made up of **five principle spices**: 500 shekels of liquid **myrrh**, 250 shekels of **cinnamon**, another 250 shekels of **sweet smelling cane**, 500 shekels of **cassia**, and one hin of **olive oil**.

The holy anointing oil is symbolic of the ministry of the Holy Spirit in our lives who anoints us to minister. We can do nothing without him-- nothing without this oil. Jesus said, "I am the vine and you are the branches. He who abides in me, and I in him, bears much fruit." (Jn. 15:5) Apart from God, if we are cut off, the flow of life ceases to be. If we're cut off, the flow from the life of the vine ceases to flow into our lives and makes it impossible for us to bear fruit at all!

It's the same picture of the holy anointing oil that flows down out of heaven. The anointing flows down. Remember, **the anointing flows down!** In Exodus 30, they are instructed to anoint the entire tabernacle, the Ark of the Covenant, and all of the furniture, every single piece, the brazen altar, the brazen laver, the golden lampstand, the table of showbread, the golden altar of incense – every single piece of furniture must be anointed. Why? Because they were all used for the service of God, and all the utensils included: the meat forks, dishes, wick trimmers and trays, the fire pans ect. – everything in the service of God had to be anointed. When someone or something was anointed it meant that they were consecrated unto God and set apart "that they may be most holy." (v. 29)

"This day and in this hour, you are called to be a royal priesthood unto me. You are called to be set apart from the world to be consecrated in the service of the King. So, even as I am holy, you too, are to be holy."

"As obedient children, do not conform to the evil desires you had when you lived in ignorance. But just as he who called you is holy, so be holy in all you do; for it is written: Be holy, because I am holy." (Peter 1: 14-16)

206

"Aaron and all of his sons also had to be anointed so that they could minister as priests unto the Lord in the tabernacle service. And this holy anointing oil could only be put upon a **priest**-- **no one else!** And you see, you have been called to be a priest in the service of the King, in the government of God and carry God's full anointing in the earth. So, apart from the anointing of God, you can do nothing. Apart from the anointing, you can do nothing. For it is by My Spirit," says the Lord.

"Church of the Living God: You have been adding to and taking from My 'Holy Anointing Oil' recipe. In the days of Moses, these instructions were given so that this recipe was never to be tampered with, never to be changed, never to be added to or taken away from, and it carried a very severe penalty. They were to be cut off from their people."

"This was the equivalent of death in that day; because to be cut off meant you were put outside of the walls of the city and forgotten; and you were subject to the enemies attack and all that could come against you. There were many more dangers in their day than there are in ours today. We are a little more secure today, and to be cut off doesn't seem to be a big deal to us; but to them it was a matter of life and death!"

"Even still today, it is a matter of life and death – spiritually – for you have been tainting and corrupting My holy anointing oil. You have been adding to it and taking away from it. It has become corrupted, tainted, and changed. Its purity has been lost. Its power and effectiveness has also been lost, along with its potency. It's no longer pure! IT IS NO LONGER PURE! THE ANOINTING OIL THAT YOU'RE POURING OUT HAS BEEN TAINTED. IT IS CORRUPTED! It has so much mixture of man in it, there is very little left of the original recipe! There is very little left of God Most High. Church of the living God, I am calling you this day: You must clean up your act! Let my anointing oil flow down out of Heaven – PURE and HOLY. Receive it – Pure and Holy! It must flow down out of Heaven directly. It must flow from God the Father, to Jesus Christ Himself, to his five-fold ministry, then to the body of Christ. You can't make up your own oil recipe. You can't make up your own anointing!"

"You cannot CREATE THE ANOINTING! You CANNOT CREATE THE ANOINTING OF GOD! You can only take each ingredient in obedience to God as He designates – as He instructs – to combine these spices together to form the anointing oil of God!"

"Church of the Living God: Stop trying to add to it! Stop trying to take away from it! And simply just receive it from heaven as God originated, as God instructed man to do. It's a holy anointing oil recipe straight out of heaven. We cannot tamper with the anointing and use it for ourselves. God's anointing is not for you; it is for Him. God will give you the recipe. God will give you the combination of principle spices. God will give you the combination of things, and people, and aspects of ministry you are to combine to bring certain spices and anointing together and then it will be powerful. Then it will be potent, and it will be pure. It will be effective; because, it won't be tainted or corrupted by man. You all must get your recipe from the Lord your God. You must get your recipe from Jesus himself. He'll show you who is a principle spice in His Holy anointing oil recipe for your church. He'll show you who are the anointed leaders? Who are the anointed ministers? Who does God call? Who does God raise up?"

"IT'S GOD'S RECIPE! It's God's mixture! Leave it alone. Don't try to add to it, or to make it better or bigger. You see, that is the mistake that man makes. He thinks bigger is always better. Bigger is not always better."

"You may have heard the old phrase: Less is more! Sometimes with God – less is more. So those of you that are few in number, be not discouraged, and be not dismayed; because I, the Lord your God, will pour out my Holy anointing oil upon you and it will be more powerful, more potent than you have ever experienced before in your life. And though you are small now – you will be great among the nations. Because I, the Lord God, will pour out My holy anointing oil upon you – even as Samuel poured out his horn of oil upon David as a young boy who would later be King of Israel. From that day forward, the Spirit of the Lord came upon David in power and in great might. So too, My Holy Spirit shall come upon you," says the Lord, "and you will carry the Kingly anointing, the Priestly anointing, and the Prophetic anointing – all three that were in the line of David and also all that was in Jesus' life and in His earthly walk. All of this is meant to be in My church today!"

"Receive this word unto yourselves this day. Receive it into your heart and into your life. Receive it engrafted into your body and being, so that it may become a part of who you are; because, the truth shall set you free, and this is the truth of the Living God. And it is also the truth of God that is backed up by his written word in His holy scriptures," for thus saith the Lord your God.

Five Wise Virgins
(Mat. 25: 1-13)

"Then the kingdom of heaven shall be likened to ten virgins, who took their lamps, and went out to meet the bridegroom. Now five of them were wise, and five were foolish. Those who were foolish took their lamps and took no oil with them, but the wise took oil in their vessels with their lamps. But while the bridegroom was delayed, they all slumbered and slept. And at midnight a cry was heard: 'Behold, the bridegroom is coming; go out to meet Him!' Then all those virgins arose, and trimmed their lamps. And the foolish said to the wise, 'Give us some of your oil; for our lamps are going out.' But the wise answered, saying,' No, lest there should not be enough for us and you; but go rather to those who sell, and buy for yourselves. And while they went to buy, the bridegroom came; and those who were ready went in with him to the wedding; and the door was shut. Afterwards the other virgins came also, saying, 'Lord, Lord, open to us!' But he answered and said, 'Assuredly, I say to you, I do not know you.' Watch therefore, for you know neither the day nor the hour in which the son of man is coming."

There were **five** foolish and there were **five** wise. Five foolish virgins that only had their lamps with no oil in reserve; but there were also FIVE WISE. Why were they described as wise? Because they had extra vessels of oil along with the lamps that they had that were lit, so that they could be ready just in case they had to wait awhile for the bridegroom to come. And in verse 4, we can see that the bridegroom was delayed for a certain period of time. They had no idea when he would come. And as the bridegroom was delayed, they all laid down and they went to sleep.

And after a certain time had passed and when they least expected it, at the midnight hour, "a cry was heard: Behold, the bridegroom is coming; go out to meet him." (v.6)

"BEHOLD THE BRIDEGROOM COMES!"

"HALLELUIAH!"

"BEHOLD THE BRIDEGEGOOM COMES!"

"We will hear those words someday: 'Behold the bridegroom comes.' Will you be ready?" says the Lord God Almighty. "Will you be a virgin that is wise and has extra oil in reserve, or will you be a foolish virgin that has no extra oil whatsoever, and is only going on what they can contain and what they hold, right now?"

Their lamps were lit, but they were quickly going out. And in this parable, what do we see? 'Behold the Bridegroom comes!' Five were ready, five were not; and the ones that were not were scrambling. They were in a frenzy. They were worried, and they spoke to the five wise and said, "Give us some of your oil, for our lamps are going out." (V.8) Please can we have some?

And the five wise said, "No, you must go and buy your own for there will not be enough for us." So as they went on their way to buy more oil, the bridegroom came and the five wise that were ready went in to the wedding and the door was shut.

Then the five foolish returned; and as much as they wanted to go in, they could not for the door had been closed. They could not enter into the wedding! They were foolish virgins. They were not ready for the bridegroom to come.

"Church of the Living God: in this day and in this hour, I'm calling you to be ready. Be ready! Be ready! Which of the 10 virgins will you be part of-- the wise or the foolish? Will you live on only what you have? So many of you are running on just what you have! You have had one experience with God. You've gotten a little oil in your lamp; but your lamp has to be lit, so it burns and gets used up. So you must have refillings of God. There must be refillings of His holy anointing oil flowing in you life. You can't go on just a onetime experience with God. That's not going to cut it! It's not going to work. So many of you are just running on what you have – just a little bit of oil that God gave you a long time ago."

"It's time. It is time. It is time, to receive all that God has for you, to jump in the pool and get wet all over again and get a taste of God's Holy anointing power once again in your life."

"Remember, our walks with God are progressive. The anointings of God are progressive. You don't just get one 'wine skin' and you're done. My holy anointing 'Oil' and My holy anointing "Wine" is meant to be poured out in your life to be used up for the purposes and the workings in the service of God. I don't give it to you to horde it up; I give it to you to use it."

"Remember, Ephesians 4: 8-12: God's five-fold ministry. Verse 12 says, '...to equip the saints for the work of the ministry, for the edifying of the body of Christ.' My holy anointing oil flows down out of heaven, and it is to equip you for the works of service. It is to empower you to go in My Kingly anointing, My Priestly anointing, and My Prophetic anointing-- to be My Elijah's in this world-- to go in the power of Elijah even to do miracles in this day." Halleluiah. Glory to God.

"It's not just a onetime filling. In Ephesians 5:18, where I command you to "be filled" with My Spirit-- it means progressively. It refers to "multiple" fillings! It's not just a onetime filling."

"Church of the Living God: this day, be filled with My Spirit," says the Lord, "CONTINUALLY IN A NEVER ENDING MEASURE! As it flows down and you use it up, there is a fresh 'River of God' that is flowing down back into your life that is uninterrupted."

"You see, that's the River of God that flows! It's the same river of God that flows in the 'NEW JERUSALEM'. It is meant to flow in you continually and to be never ending; because, it comes from a source that is never ending. If it comes from man, it will run out; because man's resources are limited. God's resources are unlimited."

"So when we get our anointing oil from heaven, it never runs out! There's a never ending supply of My holy anointing oil waiting in heaven to be pour out into the earth; but it must be poured out through My protocol – through My Government – through My pattern – through My blueprint. It must flow down! Down out of Heaven, through My Son, then through five-fold ministry, and then down into My 'Living Stones'. Every believer is to be a 'living stone' in the house of God."

"You see, this house that I am building is a spiritual house. It is a spiritual 'Israel'. It is a spiritual 'Jerusalem'. There is a natural Jerusalem and there is also a spiritual 'Jerusalem'. Halleluiah. And I have plans for both," says the Lord God Almighty. "But you have not come to a house that has been made by the hands of men; you have come to a temple – a holy temple of God-- that is being built by the hands of the Living God. Every 'stone' is being laid by His hand – every stone, every stone, every stone!"

"You have come to a spiritual house, to a 'NEW JERUSALEM', to be My holy kings, and My holy priests, and My holy

211

prophets in this Kingdom. Halleluiah; and to this Kingdom there shall be no end. It's the government of God established in the earth."

"Jesus started it over 2,000 years ago with His earth walk. He was the fullness of God manifested in the earth – 'Emmanuel': God INCARNATE. God came to this earth. He had it all. He left it all in heaven; gave it all at the cross, so that He could give it all to you, and to His church, in this church age-- now!" says the Lord God Almighty.

"If you abide in Me and My words abide in you, ask whatever you desire and it shall be done for you. Eat of My flesh and drink of My blood," says the Lord. "Eat of My word this day," says the Lord God Almighty. Halleluiah! "My word is life. It is food. It is Manna-- straight out of heaven! If you will eat of this manna, it will be life to your bones – life! I have come to give men life and life more abundantly."

"If you eat anything that is added to that, it can be death to you. I set before you this day: life and death. Which will you choose this day? Which will you choose?"

"Will you be one of the five foolish virgins or one of the five wise virgins? Who will you be? Who will you be? I charge you this day: Will you be one of the FIVE WISE VIRGINS that were ready and had extra oil in their vessels along with their lamps? They had an abundance! They had more than enough!"

"Will you be a vessel of abundance this day in the earth? Will you be a vessel that is overflowing with my Spirit," says the Lord. "Will you be an eighth day creation? Will you be one of the eighth sons of Jesse, and carry the full anointing of Jesus himself in the earth today? For this is My word unto you this day," says the Lord God Almighty.

Chapter Six

The Significance of Six

"Let Us make man in Our image,
according to Our likeness…then God
saw everything that He had made
and indeed it was very good. So the evening
and the morning were the sixth day."
Gen.1:26, 31

Six is the Number of Man

"In the beginning, God created the heavens and the earth! In the beginning, I created the heavens and the earth by My mighty hand, and by My great power. In the beginning, I spoke light and light was. I raised the mountains and lowered the valleys. I spoke each day of creation and it was; and on the sixth day I created man, and I saw that it was very good. It was a very significant day, because then, it was very good."

So, all the beauty that we can enjoy in our world today – nothing comes close to the beauty that God saw within man – within woman and within children. Nothing comes close to the beauty and splendor of God's creation that He made on the sixth day. It has held a special place in the heart of God for all of creation; for all of eternity. So God formed Adam out of the dust of the earth; and He formed Eve out of a rib from Adam. Then Adam said, *"This is now bone of my bones and flesh of my flesh."* (Gen.2:23) You see, Adam had a wife. The first man and the first woman, they were united together in holy matrimony. Everything in the garden was holy – completely holy, perfect, and complete. They did not lack any one thing in the garden. They could experience the complete glory of God – in all that God was, and is, and is to come – His complete existence. They knew it. They could walk in it and fellowship with God in the "cool of the day". Everything was perfect. They could walk in the glory of God. They were only told not to do just one thing – eat from the tree of the knowledge of good and evil. If they would have just stayed away and listened, they would have lived in this paradise forever and ever; because they could eat from the tree of life. "I wanted them to eat of that tree – this tree of life – forever and ever. That was My intention for all of mankind," says the Lord God Almighty. "My intentions for Adam and all of man – every woman – every child was that they loved Me forever in a perfect utopia, a paradise, where they had all that they needed."

But even before this time, we have to go back into eternity past a little bit farther. There was a high cherub that was in charge of all praise in heaven; but then he fell like lightening from heaven down to the earth. (Luke 10:18) He wanted to ascend up into the throne of God and be just like God; and so, Lucifer was kicked out of the heavens and cast down to the earth.

In Isaiah 14:12-15, the prophet writes: *"How you are fallen from heaven, O Lucifer, son of the morning! How you are cut down to the ground, you who weakened the nations! For you have said in your heart: 'I will ascend into heaven. I will exalt my throne above the stars of God; I will also sit on the mount of the congregation, on the farthest sides of the north; I will ascend above the heights of the clouds; I will make myself like the Most High.' Yet you shall be brought down to Sheol, to the lowest depths of the Pit."*

This fallen angel in charge of praise left heaven with a third of all the angels – fallen angels- that today we describe as demons. Yes, he is alive and well in planet earth today, and he was also alive in the Garden of Eden. He was crafty, slick, and sly more than all the other beasts of the earth. So this serpent (Satan) came along, and I believe he had only limited parameters in the garden and was restricted to the tree of the knowledge of good and evil. If Adam and Eve would have just stayed away; but they saw that the fruit was *"good for food and pleasing to the eye, and also desirable for gaining wisdom"*; and did not discern which tree the apple came from. And so, they saw it was good, and they ate it; but it was an apple from the wrong tree!

The serpent had a little discourse with Eve and said to her, "Did God really say, 'You must not eat from any tree in the garden?'" He invoked doubt and unbelief into Eve's mind. Then she did not know for sure where this apple had come from. He caused her to question God's original command to them concerning the fruit. The serpent also said, "You will not surely die, for God knows that when you eat of it your eyes will be opened, and you will be like God, knowing good and evil."

The wise thing to do would have been to throw it down, step on it, trample it, and remember what God had said. And if there was any doubt at all, do not proceed any further. But Eve did not use her God given discernment, ate of this apple, was deceived, and then she also went to Adam to get him to eat of the same fruit. Adam, also, did not use his God given discernment, ate the fruit and did not question: "Eve, where did this come from?" or "Eve, where did you get this apple?" "Which tree did it come from?" "You don't remember; God said that we could not eat from the tree of the knowledge of good and evil." But Adam, too, was deceived by her beauty and he partook of the same fruit – the same apple from the same tree.

215

Satan was very cunning and very crafty. He deceived Adam and Eve simply by twisting the truth and changing the word of God just a little bit, and he introduced the thoughts of doubt and called into question what God had said originally. Did God say? Did God say?

And you see, Satan has been doing this same thing ever since throughout history for thousands of years. He has been using the same tactics; and you think we would be getting a handle on that by now. It's so simple, yet so hard and difficult; and we, too, can easily be deceived all over again, and again, simply by not recognizing the truth in the word of God.

So all of mankind, from Adam to Jesus, to today, through all of Adam's genealogy as he populated the world, through Noah and his line, through all of his sons-- all of mankind has fallen under this same curse.

God pronounced a curse upon all three: Adam and Eve, the serpent, and within that was a curse upon the whole world that we see today. We are all under the same curse as we are born naturally into this world. We are under the curse of Adam and Eve, and Satan, and the world. For you see, the curses came at the fall of man. So in Adam, we are under the curse. The curse upon Adam was that he would toil and sweat to bring forth fruit from the ground where before it was easy. He had all that he needed – piece of cake. He still had to work. He was given responsibility and dominion in the earth, but his labor was very enjoyable. It was very relaxing and fruit for food came with great ease, but now it was going to be difficult. "Thorns and thistles" would grow from the ground; and it would be very, very, difficult now to bring forth food from the earth. It would come by the sweat of his brow and his toil with great labor and hardship; and we can see that in our lives today.

So, the point I want to bring across to you, for the purposes of this book, is that all of man is under the curse – every man, woman, and child that is ever born naturally are all under these same fallen conditions, and not only that, our relationship with God was severed. Perhaps the greatest thing that happened – the greatest punishment – was that Adam would no longer walk with God in the cool of the day in the Garden of Eden. He was kicked out of the garden – out of his paradise. The world would undergo changes and his relationship with God was lost – they were separated. He no longer experienced the glory of God. He no longer had everything he needed.

216

When you're born into this world now, every baby is lacking and wanting. They are crying immediately, because they're hungry and they need food, or they need to be held and they need love and attention, support, and encouragement. Babies come into this world completely helpless – completely lacking in every dimension; and they rely solely upon their God given parents for everything. The parents are a type of "god" to them.

God has instituted the family to provide for babies needs so that they would be brought up in the way that they should go, and get all that they need. That's the God given institution of marriage-- to fill the voids brought about by the curse.

With the original sin of Adam, he became the "son of sin", the "son of disobedience", the "son of perdition", or the "son of lawlessness". All of these things came into his spirit in that moment – in that day. His relationship with God was totally destroyed. He was now a son of disobedience, and he would always have the tendency to do what was wrong!

When children come into this world, you don't have to teach them what is wrong. Their natural tendency is to always do what is wrong; and if they are never trained and taught what is right, some children would never learn what is right. So, it is embedded in the nature of man a tendency to do the wrong thing.

Even as sin came through the first Adam, he was the son of lawlessness, the son of perdition, the fall came, the curse came; his relationship with God was lost. In the second Adam, the second son of God, Jesus Christ himself, He was and is the son of obedience. He was the son of faith that walked in complete fullness of the law. He listened to the Father in every regard in his entire life. He lived a completely sinless life. God was his Father just as with Adam, but how could he walk a sinless life? How? Because God made a promise in Genesis 3:15 in His pronouncement of the curse to Satan himself – to the serpent, He said, *"And I will put enmity between you and the woman, and between your seed and her seed; He shall bruise your head; and you shall bruise his heel."* (NKJV)

Even in Genesis 3:15, when God is about to kick them out of the garden, God institutes a plan of redemption; a plan of getting all that was lost back. And you see, that plan; that enmity was that God would come down and He would bring a separation between the natural seed of man – passed down through Adam – to create the

Messiah. Jesus had no earthly father. God interrupted the line and genealogy of Adam; and did a miraculous thing. Jesus was born of the Virgin Mary, and God was his father. So, Jesus did not have the same nature of man--the number six-- in him. He did not have the fallen nature – the fallen capacity to always do the wrong thing. He had the full nature of God in His life and in His being. Remember, Jesus was God incarnate in the earth. He was God—"Emmanuel": God with us; the fullness of God in all that He is, and was, and is to come.

Jesus said, "If you have seen me, you have seen the father." He was the son of God, yes, but He was also the fullness of God and the completeness of God in the earth. He was the Father, the Son, and the Holy Spirit; the trinity of God all in one human form; so that we could see Him and behold His glory in the earth. So you see, the glory of God came back down into the earth. John 1:14 says, *The word became flesh and made His dwelling among us. We have seen His glory, the glory of the one and only who came from the Father, full of grace and truth."*

And some knew Him not; and completely missed Him in the flesh. They were looking for Him in the natural. They were looking for a king to overthrow the Roman Empire and establish His natural kingdom in the earth; just like King David and King Solomon had in former days of Israel's glory years. Israel's glory, in Christ, is in you today!

Jesus said, "My kingdom is not of this world." (Jn. 18:36) If they knew that, they would have received Him, and received all that He had to give. But the world was still bound to this fallen nature in Adam-- this carnal thinking-- all because of one man. All because of one man's disobedience, death came to all. You see, death came not only physically in that we are mortal and we will all die; but death also came to our minds and our spirits. Our spirits died and our minds died. We could no longer think righteously the way God thought. We couldn't behold his glory and think on all of His wonderful things in the garden.

So our fallen state was not only physical, as death came we would all die and not live forever, but it also came to us spiritually, and mentally—it came to all three: Spirit, Soul, and Body. Man is a three part being just like God is a three part God.

In Adam, we are fallen in all of those areas. We are a sixth day creation in Adam in the natural. That means we are a six in our spirit, a six in our minds-- our soul realm-- and we are a six in our body.

218

Completely lost! Completely separated from God our Father-- our Creator! We are "animal- like" in nature. In Jeremiah 17:9, the word of God describes the human heart as *"deceitful above all things, and desperately wicked. Who can know it?"* Only God knows! It is capable of horrific things left unchecked. We can see this truth unveiled to us very easily; all we need to do is pick up a newspaper, or turn on our television sets and watch any news broadcast on any channel to see the great atrocities that the human spirit is capable of -- great genocides and holocausts throughout history-- and even in our day today.

We have not improved in this area through science, philosophy, government, humanism; or through any other created thing, nor through our advanced civilizations. We are still "animal- like" in our fallen nature – regardless of our technology, or our great sophistication. Without God, we quickly revert back to an "animal— like" nature that is capable of horrific sins against its own species.

We are one of the few species in the earth that will absolutely destroy its own lines of creative reproduction. Left unchecked, I believe at one point man could completely wipe himself out. We have the capability. We have the nuclear, atomic, and hydrogen bombs; with the push of a button we could eliminate this world-- in our great wisdom. It would come at a cost of our complete annihilation and destruction – if left unchecked, in the flesh, in our world today. If we rely on ourselves, we may end up destroying what God has created! And what God created in six days, man will end up destroying in one second with the push of a button.

So, if you can receive that word, it is very easy to see in our world. If we can even look into ourselves knowing without God, we can be capable of great sin and great crimes against humanity if it all went unchecked. Without God, we are capable of great disobedience and horrific sin against everyone around us, and against our world.

And you see, that's how life goes. When there's too much sin and flesh in a person's life, they'll respond in that nature; and they will usually wind up doing the wrong thing. And much of their life, in all of its chaos, and in all of its problems and trials, comes because it's self inflicted; because the enemy came along and used the same lie on them and said, "Did God Say?" And you see, they're in their fallen nature. But God, through Christ, sent His word! *"The word became flesh and dwelt among us and we beheld His glory"*. And the same word that God used and said, "Light" – and light was. It was His Rhema word. It was not yet written in book form. That same word came in the body of Jesus Christ; and it walked the earth. He was the word, is the word, became flesh – dwelt among us, and He is the word to come. He had the first word and He will have the last word, and all the words in between. We've been given the written word of God – the Holy Bible. A good acronym for "B, I, B, L, E", is "Basic Instructions Before Leaving Earth". It contains everything we need pertaining to life and godliness to give us instructions and guidance in this world; and if we will simply do what it says and be a son of obedience, our lives will be completely changed and transformed. We can walk with God once again, just like in the Garden of Eden in the "cool of the day" like Adam did almost four thousand years ago. What Adam lost – we can get it all back. We can behold the glory of God in our lives today; in this day and in this hour. We can walk with God as Adam walked with God, and as Enoch walked with God.

Jesus walked with God. It was all the same lineage of Adam straight down to Jesus. We see a line of faith trying to be preserved in the earth. God had a plan! He began it in Gen. 3:15. *"And I will put enmity between you the woman, and between your seed and her seed. He shall bruise your head, and you shall bruise his heel."*

This is part of the curse upon Satan himself! What does that speak of? It speaks of the Messiah – Jesus Christ! Satan is under our feet – in Christ. And Jesus will bruise his heel, stomping upon Satan's head in this day and in this hour. Adam gave it away. We can get it all back; if we'll simply walk in obedience to the second Adam – Jesus Christ and Him crucified – to His entire word, His entire written word, from Genesis to Revelation. If we will listen to it, if we'll read it, hear it, receive it, and then walk in it.

Sometimes we read it, listen to it, but we don't receive it and then, we don't walk in it. When we eat His "flesh" and drink His "blood", that means it goes into our being to such a degree – just like when you eat a hamburger – it becomes a part of who you are. Just as you receive the bread and the wine of communion, you are saying that you agree with what He has done completely. Remember, Jesus is the "Bread of Life". He is the "manna from heaven". You are eating of His bread – His word – and you receive His words in their entirety; not picking and choosing what you will obey and what you'll not obey-- all of it-- in its entirety. You're entering into an agreement. Whether you know it or not, you're saying, "I will be a son of obedience." You are entering into a **covenantal agreement** by eating the "bread and wine" of communion, and we will touch on more of that later. But I'm trying to get you to see that you are in the sixth day creation of God in Adam from the beginning of time. God created Adam, on the sixth day. You are a sixth day creation in your fallen state, and in your fallen nature.

So you are a **six** in your spirit, a **six** in your soul, and a **six** in your body without God! And it's only by the grace of God and His introduction of His son Jesus into the earth, that you can have any hope of being delivered out of that condition – from being a **666**, to being a **777**!

Seven in scripture speaks of the fullness and completion of God. It's one of God's favorite numbers; and we see this number all throughout scripture. Why? It is a special number. It's God's number. Jesus was totally God, in all His fullness, in the earth. He was full. He was a seven! He was and always is-- complete! So in Christ, you can be a seven in all areas of your life. The scriptures reveal that you are a three part being: spirit, soul, and body. (I Thes.5:23)

You can be a seven in your spirit, a seven in your soul, and a seven in your body being fully redeemed, and all that God is in His word can be a reality in your life today!

I want to give you a little equation that sums it up very nicely. Let's think about and consider the number one for a moment. The number of God is "one", that we have already discussed back in chapter one. He is "One"! There is only one God. There are no other gods before Him. One is the completion of all things! The number one speaks of wholeness. It cannot be divided or separated by any other whole number without producing a fraction. It is also the beginning of all numbers.

Now we know that man is the number of six. He was created on the sixth day. So, God plus man equals fullness, completeness, and perfection. One plus six equals seven. Then, the inverse of this equation, mathematically works in the same way. The number seven – the fullness, completeness, and perfection of all things – which was Jesus himself-- seven minus one (God) equals six (the number of fallen man).

So you have, Jesus being the 7, - 1, being God, or
Jesus the God – man, minus God, then
You have Adam being fallen man which is a 6.

221

7 – 1 = 6 or Completeness, Fullness, and Perfection – God = fallen man!

Adam lost it all. He lost the glory. He was full. He was the first Adam. He was full just like Jesus was full. Adam was like Jesus in the Garden of Eden. Scripture speaks very strongly of two people: the first Adam, and the second Adam - Adam and Jesus. Adam had it all in the beginning. He was full, complete and perfect, and he walked with God. 7 – 1 = 6. When he sinned, he lost it all. His relationship with God was severed. If you take away God then man is fallen; totally fallen! He is a six! He is a six in his spirit, a six in his soul, and a six in his body; capable of great horrific sins even against his own kind; and he can destroy this world left unchecked. Remember this simple equation: 7 – 1 = 6. But also remember the inverse of this equation. We are a six in our fallen nature in Adam... 6 + 1 = 7; the fullness, completion, and the perfection of God's creation. Six plus God equals fullness. We can be full again in Jesus! Where we were lacking as a baby and needed everything in this world, we can now be full and complete, not lacking any one thing in our lives in Jesus Christ.

Six is the Number of Labor

"Even back before the dawning of time, six was the number of labor; in eternity past. I the Lord God, I created the heavens and the earth and all that is in them; all that is above the earth, beneath the earth, and in the earth. I created it all – all of it – in six days! In the days of creation, in its perfect state and condition, I created it all in six days."

"I created man on the sixth day and saw that it was very good. Then I rested from all of My labors on the seventh day and declared it a holy day unto man. The seventh day – it always was holy; it always is holy; and always will be holy!" says the Lord. "Spiritually – it will always be holy!"

"For you see, since the beginning of time, I have no end or beginning. There is no time in this dimension – in My dimension – in My spiritual dimension! Even in the garden, time was to continue on throughout eternity in that condition. And as man fell, and his relationship with ME was lost, I set in motion a plan from the beginning of time. That plan always was, always is, and always will be.

222

It shall never be thwarted. It shall never be over thrown. It shall never be changed. It is! It is! It is! And Satan has tried to thwart those plans and stop the plan of God in the earth; but he will never succeed. He cannot and will not. He has tried his best, many, many, times; but I, the Lord God always prevail. I always prevail. And I even use what he has meant for harm and I turn it around on him, and use it completely against him to his own demise. This is the workings of God. My thoughts are not your thoughts, neither are My ways your ways, nor is My time your time," says the Lord.

"As a day is as a thousand years unto you- a thousand years is as one day to me – not just literally, but figuratively. A thousand upon a thousand days; upon a thousand days will be as one of My days. With Me there is no time. It is not measured in the same way, as it is with you. For as man fell, he fell from My graces and My glory; from all that I had for him. And I have tried all these years to teach him to walk in My ways; and to reveal Myself to him – progressively – little by little – day by day. My plan of redemption has been unveiling since Genesis 3:15 till now. It's been an unfolding revelation throughout the history of mankind. In the days of the patriarchs, and all down through history and in the nation of Israel – what I have shown in the natural has come in the natural first, then the spiritual. And you see, all these things have been written for your example," says the Lord. "Why? In symbols, pictures, types, and shadows – figuratively speaking – so I can reveal Myself all over again to a lost humanity."

"And we see in scripture, as God rested on the seventh day, so too it should be in the earth. I, the Lord God, will train man as he was created in My image. He too would work for 6 days, and keep the seventh day as a holy day. And I gave them a Sabbath day rest even as I, the Lord God, rested in the heavens; so too, it should be true in the earth. What is true in the heavens will always come down to be true in the earth. I the Lord God will always be working to bring My will to be true in the earth; but I need man's cooperation and his obedience. So, I instituted the Sabbath day and to keep it holy. It was a holy day as unto the Lord."

And also in scripture, we see the number six being associated with labor in the life of Jacob. He had to work for his flocks to acquire them from Laban, for six years; then it was a full completion of his labor, and then he was allowed to leave and be free. But he worked for six years by the sweat of his brow in all his toil. Even a Hebrew servant had to work six years to reach the fulfillment of their agreement and then they were set free on the seventh year; but they had to work those six years for their master. So we can see all these sixes associated with labor in the word of God. Noah worked on the enormous ark for many, many, years, and then when he was 600 years old, he finally entered the ark and his work was finished.

"So, I have tried to teach all of mankind that you have six days to work and you will bring forth the fruit of the vine by the sweat of your labor, which is also very significant. But the seventh day, it shall be holy as unto the Lord. It is the seventh day."

"Church of the Living God: You have missed it! The Sabbath Day is not by the letter of the law. It is not you trying to strive to be holy! All of your fleshly achievements – they must die. They must die. The Sabbath Day was, and is, and will be a holy day as unto the Lord. But that day-- it came down to the earth in the form of My Son. Jesus was, and is, and always will be the complete fulfillment of everything in the Sabbath Day—or the seventh day. Man has tried to keep the Sabbath in their flesh; to keep that day holy and not mess it up. In the days of old, the Hebrews would always try, to the best of his ability, not to sin and to keep the law on that day; and also, not to do any work-- to do as little as possible in fear not to sin against the Most High God. To do any work on the Sabbath would mean the death penalty!"

"You can never work your way to holiness! Jesus, himself, was the complete holy day in the earth! He is the "Ancient of Days". He is the holiest of all days; eternity past into eternity future. He is the Sabbath Day – the embodiment of the holiness of God, in the earth. He was the Sabbath in His earth walk. He was in eternity past. He is now, still today. TODAY, HE IS THE SABBATH DAY!! He is "The Holy Day"-- now, and He will be in all the days – a thousand, upon a thousand days into the future. That has never changed. It always was and always will be. HE WILL ALWAYS BE THE SEVENTH DAY SABBATH DAY – a holy day unto the Lord."

Jesus, in His earth walk, was God's finished work in the earth that God had reserved at the beginning of creation. God rested from all His labors. Why? He still had more work to do! And it points to Christ. God came down to this world to finish what He didn't finish in the first week! God himself came down to this earth for a season – a season of days. It was His representation of all that He was, and all that

He is, and all that He will be! Jesus, Himself, was, and is, and will be—always-- the full representation of God in the earth.

We forget sometimes that Jesus was fully God in the earth. So, it's like God himself coming down to be with His creation and be among men. God came down to do a work and do it in such a way that it was completely holy – to demonstrate to all of mankind – He was the God-Man. He was sinless. He kept the law perfectly, made no mistakes-- Jesus was the God-Man. He kept every day as a holy day unto the Lord. And He said this remarkable statement: He said, "He was Lord of the Sabbath".

They tried to trick him and then even kill him, because Jesus would heal people on the Sabbath day. They were looking at it in the letter of the law and saying, "No, you can't do anything on the Sabbath day... It is unlawful". He said *"So the Son of Man is Lord even of the Sabbath."* (Mk.2:27, 28)

"I AM LORD OF THE SABBATH!"

"I AM LORD OF ALL DAYS!"

"You see, they did not know to whom they were speaking. **He was the Sabbath! He is the Sabbath; and He always will be the Sabbath!** He is the holiest of all days. He is the 'Ancient of Days'. He is a thousand upon a thousand days. There is no time in the spirit! There is no time. A thousand years is as one day to Me. It does not matter. There are no time limits. I've only given man limits and the measurements of time. It is for man's benefit-- not for mine. The Sabbath was for man's benefit, not mine. That's when Jesus said, 'the Sabbath was made for man, not man for the Sabbath'."

The Sabbath, he meant, was for man's benefit that would be shortly revealed in the earth. God was bringing it all back. All that Adam lost, God was bringing it back in His Son – Jesus. So you can be full and complete, in Jesus, and every day can be a "holy day" in your life, and you can walk as God intended for you to walk in the earth. And all that God asks of you – it can be; because God has made a way. And there are no excuses. God still wants His children to walk in holiness! Even in the New Testament, in I Peter 1:15, 16, it says, *"But just as He who called you is holy, so be holy in all you do; for it is written: Be holy, because I am holy."*

If we come into Jesus, everyday becomes our "Sabbath Day Rest" in God. No more striving to attain anything from God. We can be holy in every day and not be a son of disobedience anymore – or a son of lawlessness – but a son of the Most High God – a "son of obedience and a son of righteousness". So all that was given to Jesus can be imputed into us; and we can receive a new nature and a new life, and be born again as a descendant of Jesus, and take on his divine-like nature – his divine being – his divine character – so that all that He was and is, can be in us. So, we are God's seventh day work – in Christ – in the earth. It's not by our works of righteousness; but God's work-- in us-- through His Holy Spirit as we yield to Him!

When Jesus came to do his work, it was all for us. He didn't come to be served as a king, He came to serve and to do His work. And so He did, and when it was all completed on the cross, what did He say? He said, "It is finished." He gave up His spirit and He died. In the natural, what He came to do was finished; but in the spiritual, even then, He descended into the lower regions of the earth to take back the keys from Satan himself. Then, He returned and appeared in the earth and showed himself to over five hundred people for forty days and forty nights before He ascended up into the heavens.

"The work that God is doing now is still very active-- for He is still working today; but it is in you," says the Lord God Almighty.

In two dimensions: in you and also in the world. His plan of redemption is going to play out with all the nations, with all their rising and falling, and with the culmination of time. It will all come to fruition – a fulfillment – a completion.

But in His work, He is working two fold; in the natural, but also in the spiritual. He provides for you in the natural with a roof over your head and food on your table. That's miracles from God too; but He also has another work:

"You are the seventh day work of God in the earth!"

In Jesus Christ, we can be a finished work – a completed work – a full work. Philippians 1:6 says, *"He who began a good work in you will carry it on to completion until the day of Christ Jesus."* What God has begun, He will also finish. He had the first word-- He'll have the last word. He began a work in you-- He will also complete it. He is the author and the finisher of your faith. He is the beginning of you, and He will be the end of you. He is the beginning of your faith, and He will be the end of your faith.

The question only remains: will you participate in the work of God-- in you-- and in the world today? It just doesn't fall down out of heaven, or just happen by accident. We can't just sit around and watch the world go around. We must engage the work that God is doing in our hearts and lives.

"Arise, O Mighty Warriors! Take your stand and your positions in My kingdom," says the Lord. "Allow Me to put your swords to the grindstone and sharpen your swords. It is a day of battle," says the Lord God Almighty. "Brush the dust off the armor that I have already given you."

"BRUSH THE DUST OFF OF YOUR ARMOR AND PUT IT ON"!! "IT'S TIME TO FIGHT"

"It is time to fight!" says the Lord God Almighty. "You have been sitting around idle and not doing anything but eating, and eating, and eating of my word, and getting fatter, and fatter, and fatter. You are guilty of the sin of gluttony – spiritually! You boast in all your knowledge and in all your books. You have been eating, and eating, and eating, and basking in all of the great knowledge that you have acquired <u>about</u> God. But it's time; this day you must begin to put it to use! It's one thing to know things about God; but I only give them to you to use, or they will be taken away."

Remember the parable of the talents where what was given was used and it was multiplied. It was their responsibility to multiply it in the earth. And the one that just buried it and hid it… what happened? It was taken away and given to the others. And that seems very unfair, but it's a spiritual truth that we must understand. Use it or lose it! It's very simple. "Use it or lose it!" says the Lord God Almighty.

"God, in these days, is speaking very frankly and very clearly. It's not about the numbers of My words, because messages can get lost trying to be colorful, or sounding good, so that people will want to digest it. Those days are over. In these days, God is speaking very frankly and very clearly in fewer words so that the message doesn't get misconstrued or misinterpreted." **"Use it or lose it!"**

"This is My Word unto you this day, Church of the Living God, Church of My World Wide Bride of Christ: "Stop sitting around being idle and complacent, eating in all the goodness of My Kingdom, but only eating it for yourself. There is still a root of selfishness within you that needs to be cut off! And even in this day, in this hour, I curse every root of selfishness in Jesus name! Every deep root, so that it can not draw water and life into it ever again. And as these roots die, I will grow new roots-- Roots of My character," says the Lord. "Roots of My virtues and all that I am. And you see, those roots draw the life giving

227

water to the plant and to the vine and bring forth much fruit. So, you not only have to abide in the vine, you have to have good, strong, healthy roots in the plant of your being," says the Lord God Almighty.

"Six, being the number of 'Labor', I also have this against you: You have not had your hands to the plow. In plowing, you have to look forward and not look back. You have forsaken My plow," says the Lord. "You're sitting idle and you gave fallen asleep in the work of the kingdom. You have not only looked back and looked in all other directions, you have fallen asleep in the fields! And there sits My plow and My yoke of oxen. The fields are not getting plowed. The harvest is not being brought in. Look up to the fields for they are white for harvest. Pray to the Lord of the Harvest to send out laborers. The harvest is great, but the laborers are few. They are few!"

"Church of the Living God: I am recruiting laborers to this harvest field. Will you wake up, put your hands to the plow once again, speak to the oxen, and work together to plow these fields and bring in this harvest. Your work is not yet over, just as mine is not over."

The Sabbath Day is a good day to rest and devote the day to the Lord. It is good for your health and physical body, for spending time with family, and for getting closer to God and all of those things; but more importantly, we have missed a deeper spiritual truth that has been … it has been … "it is" … before the beginning of time-- that **Jesus is the Sabbath Day!** He is the complete fulfillment of the Sabbath Day. He is the Holy of Holies – the perfect God-Man in the earth. He satisfied the fulfillment of the law to every letter; not only the law of the Sabbath, but every law. He is the Sabbath Day; the complete holiest of all days; but He takes it one step further: He was, and is, and is to come; the holiest of every day – a thousand upon a thousand days into eternity past and eternity future!

He is the Holy Day! And all that He is-- is to be given unto us in Jesus. So, we can enter our Sabbath day rest – our completeness, our *fullness, our perfection in Christ. We can be all that we were ever* meant to be in Jesus, and we can go back to the "Garden of Eden" having our relationship with God being fully restored. We can walk with God, even as Adam walked with God, in the "cool of the day"!

Adam experienced all the glory of God. So too, we can experience **all** of the glory of God, find out who we are in Christ before sin ever entered our life, and reverse the curse-- in Jesus!

Remember this word: In Jesus-- the curse can be reversed – completely!

The Number of the Beast

We have seen in scripture that six is the number of man. Six is also the number of labor; but now, here we see another dimension and connection that the Lord has written and weaved throughout the scriptures with this little number "six". It also has a connection with the number of the "beast". We are all very familiar with this series of numbers. It is the same number repeated three times over: it is "666" or the "number of the beast"; that we see in Revelation 13:18. *"This calls for wisdom. If anyone has insight, let him calculate the number of the beast, for it is man's number. His number is six, six, six."* In that same verse, we see that this number is the number of man – the number six – but it is repeated three times in a row for a series of three sixes. There is a connection here that I believe a lot of people have missed for generations, and there may be a deeper truth to bring us greater insight, if you'll receive it.

We see this number – six, six, six. It is the number of man repeated three times. Three is a number of God, so we get the number of the beast by the two numbers of man and God coming together in the same series! The beast will one day be a man in the earth that raises himself up to be like God. We can all receive the idea that there is a future fulfillment of that truth in the days ahead as history unfolds. There will be one man to fulfill that revelation in the natural realm.

But also, there is a deeper revelation in a spiritual truth as God often times does; there is a natural fulfillment and then there is a spiritual fulfillment of that same word. There is a spiritual fulfillment of this word in connecting these two thoughts and ideas – these two numbers – the number of man with the number of the beast— together.

In a fallen state, the man in you- in Adam- is a six in your spirit, a six in your soul, and a six in your body- a 666. You see, at the fall of man – man set himself up to be like God. In the garden, part of the temptation was that you will be like God. Satan deceived Eve and he said, "O, that if you will eat of this tree you will be **like God** knowing the difference between good and evil." So, in that temptation

229

there was a draw, something very, very, tempting and satisfying, and alluring that they would be like God.

So, what Satan has tried to be – he wanted to be like God too: but he fell. Then, he tried to set man up to be like God and tempt them with the same thing, so they fell – man fell. It's the sin of pride! Ever since then, man has set himself up to be, in many ways, the center of the universe. We exalt self! Mankind has exalted himself all throughout history. We can see this idea very strongly in the Greek and Roman cultures and even in ours today. Humanism and many of the philosophies that have been passed down to us in our modern culture came from the Greeks, and the Romans, and many pagan cultures throughout history. There have been many men that have raised themselves up to be like a god. We can see this recorded throughout scripture as well.

This original temptation came from a beast. It was a serpent in the garden-- Satan embodying himself in the serpent. The symbolism is very important. And when that curse came, all the beasts of the earth were cursed and Satan lower than all of them. He would crawl on his belly, eat the dust of the earth; and he would be beneath all of them. So he is really under all of creation. He is at the lowest of his low; but he still tries -yet today- to exalt himself into places that are only reserved for true divinity – the true God – the one and only true God. So he has been tempting man with the same sin: the sin of pride and with the sin of selfishness throughout the world and in the earth today. We see it all throughout history.

In scripture, one of the places we see the number six repeated again with this same idea; that is perhaps one of the best examples, if you remember, is in the book of Daniel. King Nebuchadnezzar raised up a golden image that stood sixty cubits high and six cubits wide. Here we see the number six again; six times ten; or any multiple of a number is significant.

It was a golden image, and he was the king of Babylon. It is the land of sin – the land of wickedness – the land of rebellion against God in scripture. We see this described for us later in the book of Revelation: "O, Babylon has fallen". All of this world system will fall one day, but it is still in our midst today. And so it was in the days of Daniel, King Nebuchadnezzar raised up this golden image to get all of Babylon to bow down and worship this image. And if you remember, there were three Hebrew boys that we commonly know as Shadrach,

Meshach, and Abednego which were actually their Babylonian names – not their Hebrew names; and we still know them by these names today. They were thrown into a fiery furnace for not bowing down to this golden image.

"Church of the Living God: I, the Lord thy God, the creator of the ends of the earth, I will not bow to anyone or anything; nor any other gods that ever were, that are, or shall be. You shall place no other gods before you – one of My Ten Commandments. You have bowed down to the golden image of Nebuchadnezzar. It is the epitome of pride and self – exaltation. King Nebuchadnezer said, 'look at me, look at what I have created'." *"Is not this great Babylon that I have built for a royal dwelling by my mighty power and for the honor of my majesty?" (Dan.4:30)*

It is by his confession that the judgment of God could fall upon him. *"Out of the abundance of the heart the mouth speaks." (Mat.12:34)* What was in his heart was full of pride and self – exaltation and the epitome of that was that he built this golden image. He wanted his entire kingdom to bow down and worship it. He really wanted the worship.

You see, today, Satan still wants our worship. He wants to be like God. King Nebuchadnezzar wanted to be like a god… same temptation… self – exaltation. He wanted to be the highest – the Most High – the greatest, the most powerful, the strongest. Man's temptation today is to do the same thing. There is a lot of fighting that goes on in regard to just this one sin – for position – for power – for self exaltation – to be the best – to be the greatest – to be the highest – to be the smartest – the wisest – the most knowledgeable – and the list goes on, and on, and on. It's the same sin! And here we see it perfectly in the life of Nebuchadnezzar. If you remember that story, without going into every detail, judgment came upon King Nebuchadnezzar for his pride. He had a dream. No one in all his kingdom could tell him what his dream meant. No one knew. No one understood. There was no knowledge – no wisdom – no understanding. But they had a young man that they had brought into their kingdom. He was a Hebrew. He was from the nation of Israel, and perhaps from the descendants of King Hezekiah. He was royalty. His name was Daniel. He came from a background of great prominence and education. Even his body – his physical appearance was not marred by physical labor, so he was taken into the counsel of the king during the "Babylonian Captivity" that the

Israelites were under for up to seventy years. He was from a prominent family of royalty within the kingdom of Israel. He ate well. He was taught well. He learned well, and had a wonderful background.

King Nebuchadnezzar was very wise in doing this: he recruited these young, well-educated, prominent Hebrew men into his service at the palace (after the fall of Jerusalem). There was no one found like them. In all matters of wisdom and understanding, the king found them to be ten times better than all in his land. He also wanted them to learn all the ways of Babylon, and teach them the language and literature of the Chaldeans to become more like them. So, they had to adapt to some degree just to live there. Even their names were changed.

Daniel's name was changed to Belteshazzar. Daniel's friends: Shadrach, Meshach, and Abednego-- changed from Hananiah, Mishael, and Azariah— they were given these new names to try and give them new identities. But they tried to draw the line and wouldn't allow this culture to influence who they really were. They wanted to keep their Hebraic roots and identities for that is who they were – their true identity! So, they drew the line at worshiping this golden image. That was too much! They would never bow down to this golden image or any other for that matter. The Babylonians could change their names, but not their hearts! They were still Hebrew!

King Nebuchadnezzar wanted everyone's worship so badly. He wanted all the kingdom to exalt him as the greatest of all. And for his pride, he had this dream; and Daniel was the only one who could interpret this dream. No one else could; but this young, smart, well educated prophet of God. This interpreter of dreams came before this great king and pronounced the interpretation to his king even in an apologetic way, and a great judgment came to King Nebuchadnezzar for his prideful heart.

Do you remember the story? What happened? His dream was fulfilled and came true. He became like a beast of the earth and he would walk around on all fours as a beast of burden – like cattle. He would eat grass like cows and the dew of heaven would fall upon him until his hair grew like the feathers of an eagle, and his fingers and toe nails would grow like the claws of a bird. (see Dan.4:33) Sounds like a beast to me.

And here we see the sin of pride and self-exaltation meeting the judgment of God in the earth. Here we see a very vivid picture of this truth in reality – a man becoming a beast. And so for three and a half years, he ate the grass of the earth just like cattle – a beast of burden. Here we can see a combination of this idea of the beast and man coming together in one person. And the good news was that it was only until the day that he humbled himself and acknowledged the Most High. God would give his kingdom back to him and he did for a short time afterwards. So, King Nebuchadnezzar repented and his kingdom was restored back to him even greater than it was before; because God had even raised him up to be a king for such a time as this. God had a purpose in his rulership as He does all kingdoms and all rulers of the earth. For God causes all kingdoms to rise and fall; and all leaders to rise and fall, even for just a short time, to accomplish His purposes in the earth.

Before the king's dream and judgment, the Hebrew boys would not bow and give worship or homage to this great golden image. Their attitude was that their God would save them, but even if He did not they would not serve any other gods, nor worship them even unto death. "Do what you need to do," they thought. Furious at their attitudes, King Nebuchadnezzar ordered the furnace to be heated up seven times hotter than normal and threw the three Hebrew boys into the furnace. Do you remember what happened? There was a fourth man in the furnace; one *"like a son of the gods."* (Dan.3:25) It was Jesus himself. He was the fourth man in the furnace!

And then God brought them through the fire, and they came out unharmed, and not even a *"hair on their heads were singed; their robes not scorched, and there was no smell of fire on them."* (v.27) They were untouched in the natural; but their spirit man went through the fire, and was burned to a crisp! Then, King Nebuchadnezer gave glory and honor to the God of the Hebrews in his lifetime.

This beast idea continues even on into the days of King Darius the Mede. The Medo – Persian army took over Babylon and so the kings changed. Still in a state of captivity, Daniel, also known as Belteshazzar, was under attack from the enemy and being persecuted as well. They could not get his worship either. Satan tried to trip him up, and so they issued an edict making it illegal to pray to any other god or man but King Darius for thirty days. But Daniel continued to pray three times a day while facing towards Jerusalem from an upstairs room with the windows opened. This edict stated anyone caught praying would be thrown into the Lion's Den. (Dan.6)

And so here again, Daniel now is thrown into the Lions Den for refusing to obey what Satan had tried to force him to do. He did not think of himself, and would only bow down to his God. There are several other examples in scripture where the beast is always trying to get our worship – Satan, himself, through that sin of pride. Even worshiping ourselves, in a sense, we are worshiping the image of the beast. It's self-exaltation and self-pride through our old nature in Adam. Remember the golden calf in the days of Moses, when he came down out of the mountain. They had worshipped the golden calf almost immediately. Moses had been delayed and they just needed to worship something, so they made a golden calf. It was a golden beast.

Later in the Book of Esther, we see a man named Mordecai that would not bow down to the wicked Haman. For this, Haman sought a way to destroy all of Mordecai's people – the Jews. It is a picture again, of Satan himself, trying to get our worship, and becoming so enraged if he doesn't get it. And we can even go a step further, to Jesus and His temptation in the wilderness. Satan tried to tempt Jesus saying, "If you will bow down and worship me, I'll give you all the kingdoms of the earth." But, they really weren't even his to give. He was trying to tempt Jesus into bowing down and worshiping him; and to thwart God's plan in the earth, and the work of God that Jesus would accomplish on the cross. Satan has tried to stop it many times. Why? He wants to be worshiped. He wants to be the Most High God. He wants to be worshipped in the earth, for this time, in this dispensation. He is the prince of this world, and he has very limited rulership and authority. There is very little that he can do. One of his greatest tools that he uses with the utmost efficiency is the lie.

He is the "Father of lies". He's been twisting the truth for thousands of years since the beginning in the garden. He will twist the truth just a little bit, to get us to believe a lie, and tempt us to do the wrong thing. He will tempt us to worship ourselves – to be self centered and self-exalting. When we come into this world, this is our nature. We are very selfish. Babies are very interested in only what they need, and if that goes unchecked by the Lord and His nature, we will grow up to be very selfish people. I'm sure we all know a few folks that have grown up to be like that. But in Jesus' kingdom, we deny self, and through His work in us, we only worship God, and we will not bow down to any other gods in this world.

But you see, Satan has tripped us up, and he has tempted us. We do exalt ourselves many, many, times, over and over again, in many, many, ways. We think we are the center of the universe and that we are the most important thing; so we only look after ourselves. And you see, that's the whole process that God brings us through. It should be less of us and more of Him-- less of the beast and more of God in us-- less of our old nature and more of God's nature in us.

In the Ten Commandments, God had proclaimed to all of the world: "There should be no other gods before Me." No other gods. Satan has become more subtle than just creating a golden calf image and placing it before us, and then we bow down to it. He has become so much more subtle than that. Now, he gets us to bow down and worship other things in our lives. And this may be a hard word for some, but the truth of it is, we worship the created rather than the creator! You'll find that in Romans, chapter one. They were guilty of worshiping created idols that were made by the hands of men. They made a golden calf and worshiped it. But now, we worship things that are also made by the hands of men. We worship our houses, our cars-- anything and everything you can think of in our lives that we place to be more important than God-- becomes an idol to us in our hearts.

The images of gold are significant, because gold was used as a means of trading in the past – silver and gold. We have a gold backing now, but we trade with paper money. In a very large sense, we worship our money! It goes back to our labor for six days, what we have done, and what we have toiled and worked hard for.

But it all comes through God; and we forget that sometimes. And then, we see what we have attained and use it on ourselves. It's a form of worship! You see, worship is more than just singing a song, or a hymn, or a song of praise to God. Worship is everything that we are: our careers, the things that we work for, the work of our hands, every aspect of life needs to be in worship unto our Lord and Savior.

And so, when we give of our money, our tithe, and our offerings, those things are an act of worship unto God. It shouldn't be something done begrudgingly, or even that we skimp on and hold back from God. Because, where our hearts are- generally speaking- that will be where our money goes! You can look at this truth: if we look at our check books and see what we spend our money on, usually that is where our heart is. And in a sense, we worship our gold and our silver.

We watch the stock market to see how it's going to rise and fall, and everything hinges on that.

We came into this world lacking and wanting, and we still want more! Our flesh tends to want more, and more, and more, and it's never satisfied. We want more money; an abundance of it. And then, more is never enough, and so we want more; and then we spend, and we buy, and we get things more expensive than we used to be able to afford, and then after awhile those things "rust and moths destroys" and they get all worn out, and then we want more. And you see, this way we are never satisfied, and the human heart still wants more.

But the greatest form of worship is when we give all of our hearts to God – every aspect – even yielding what we labor for six days for-- that was part of the curse – now becomes a blessing in our lives. And now, in Christ, we should freely give to God all that we are – including the fruit of our labors – we should give to God. It's a kingdom dynamic!

"Give and it will be given unto you, pressed down, shaken together and running over, will be poured into your lap. For with the measure you use, it will be measured to you". (Lk.6:38)

So, even our finances …

"Church of the Living God: Why are we lacking? Why are we found wanting? It is because we do not worship God with all that we are and all that we have! We have been worshiping at the golden images of King Nebuchadnezzar. We have been bowing down to the idols created by men – by the hands of men-- and worshiping the created rather than the creator."

"So, Church of the Living God, I charge you this day: A check in your spirit. Will you be like Shadrach, Meshach, and Abednego, and not bow to any image of gold that Satan will try to put in front of you? Will you not bow to any other gods in this life? Remember, God's Ten Commandments – the first one God said, *'You shall have no other gods before me.'"* (Ex. 20:3)

These are the gods and the images in our lives – the idols – the graven images. All the things that we love that we put in front of God. Our hearts devotion is for those things instead of for God. A good test to see where you are at is to imagine if everything was taken away.

236

Where would you be? Would you fall apart, crumble, and cry for an eternity, and think all is lost?

There was a man in scripture that this had happened to. Job was a man just like us, and he was tested. In his day of testing and the day of trial ... God gives and God takes away... When it's taken away, what remains? Will it be of God's kingdom? Will it be something of eternity, where neither moth nor rust can corrupt?

"Seek ye first the Kingdom of God and all of His righteousness and everything else shall be added unto you.' You haven't been seeking the kingdom first. You've had many other interests, and many other gods before Me-- many other lovers! It's the same picture!"

"Church of the Living God: I'm calling you to return to your first love. Return to Your First Love! The Ten Commandments were summed up into two, in the New Testament. If you could simply do these two things, the letter of the law – all ten – they were combined and fulfilled in these two:

"Love the Lord thy God with all your heart, and with all your soul, and with all your mind; and love your neighbor as yourself." (Mat. 22:37-40)

If you do these two things, Jesus said that you have fulfilled all of the law and the prophets. God wants our hearts, one hundred percent, sole devotion to God, in all of its entirety: all that we are, all that we touch, all that we have, and all that we think--ALL OF IT. And we give out of all that we are unto God as an act of worship.

We give our tithes and offerings unto God for His work, to help complete His work in the earth. So you can be a part of His plan. You can't out give God. It's a kingdom dynamic. You give spiritually of yourself, and in the physical, of all that you are. *"Give and it will be given to you; good measure, pressed down, shaken together, and running over..."* (Lk.6:38)

You may say, "I don't have much to give"; but God says, "Give what you've got, and I'll multiply it back." Remember the five loaves of bread and the two fish that the young boy brought to Jesus. We bring what we have, then God multiplies it back out in the earth; and He can feed the five thousand and also the three thousand!

"Church of the Living God: Why are you lacking? Why are you in want? You haven't given Me everything. You haven't given Me your whole heart, your whole life, all of your worship. It has been divided!

You have been worshiping the created rather than the creator. Get rid of the idols and the images – the golden images of Nebuchadnezzar-- in your life. Anything that your heart loves, if it were taken away, would you be devastated? It can be anything-- whatever you put your heart, your devotion, and your money into, along with your hard work and toil. It's what you work and toil for, and what your money buys – you must check – because that is what you worship."

And it can be way out of balance from what God wants. God wants to bless the work of your hands. But it is to extend His kingdom. We have to be about our Father's business. We have to be thinking about Kingdom things, again!

"Church of the Living God: I'm calling you back to Kingdom thinking, Kingdom work, and if you claim to be a child of God, you have a responsibility: financially and spiritually, mentally and emotionally, and in all aspects of life, to give to the Kingdom. You can be used in all of these different dimensions in the earth, so that God's Kingdom can come down into the earth. It's in the Lord's Prayer! Jesus instructed His disciples to pray:

"Our Father in Heaven, Hallowed be Your Name.
Your kingdom come. *Your will be done*
on earth as it is in heaven." (Mat. 6:9, 10)

It just doesn't get done by itself. And God has only chosen to use His people to carry out His purposes in the earth. It's His only plan. You are a part of that plan; and unless you realize and fulfill your responsibility in the earth, a large part of that plan never gets done. It never gets accomplished.

"So, this day, Church of the Living God: I am asking you to check your hearts; check your spirits; check your soul. It's good, every now and then, to do a heart check. Where are you today? Where are you today? Are you giving God all of your hearts devotion, and worship, or are you worshiping other things in your life? Check your checkbook! Where is your money flowing into? That's where your heart is!"

"I, the Lord God, am asking you lovingly, patiently, to draw you unto Myself. You need to take a second look at these issues in your life. You must be about Kingdom business. Why are you lacking? Why are you found wanting? It's because you have not given of

238

yourself fully in all these areas, to release My power into the body of Christ in this day and in this hour. If you give Me all that you are and all that you have, I will give you all that I AM and all that I have," says the Lord.

"And if you'll come into 'Covenant Relationship' with Me, that's the covenant – life for a life! I signed it in My blood; now, you sign it in your blood. You give Me your whole life – everything, and I'll give you all that I AM, that I AM, that I AM."

"For this is My word unto you this day," says the Lord God Almighty.

Six Fingers and Six Toes

One of Goliath's brothers had six fingers and six toes on each hand and each foot. Why? Why is this shown in scripture? It could be easily overlooked. But as we have discussed before in chapter five, God has His five and Satan has his five. And when David fought the battle with Goliath that day, he wasn't just fighting one giant. Goliath was just the representation of the entire kingdom of darkness in the earth.

David had his five stones, representing God's fivefold ministry. Goliath had his four brothers, representing Satan's five-point kingdom. Remember, even in satanic worship, they use the five pointed star. Satan does have a fivefold dimension as we have already discussed. But here, we see one of Goliath's brothers – very significant – he is described in scripture as just being the "huge man". He is the only one of the five that is not described by name. Why? There is great significance to every detail in all of scripture! We must pay attention to details!

This man had no name. He is described as "huge man", having six fingers and six toes on each hand and foot. We see again the number of man repeated four times in the body of this giant. So all that he touched, and all that he walked in, was also cursed by a six. Here is a picture of universal man being under the curse in all that he touches, and all that he walks in, everyday. All of mankind is under the curse of Adam, represented in the number six!

Feet are symbolic of an earth walk; of things we have to walk in and live in day by day; moment by moment. This "huge man" had six toes on each foot, so all that he walked in everyday of his life – he was under the curse – under a six, six, six, in his spirit, in his soul, and in his body – the natural man under Adam.

But here, we see four sixes. Why four sixes? Well, he had two hands and two feet – all that he touched and all that he walked in – but if you add them up: it's six, plus six, plus six, plus six, equals twenty four. $(6 + 6 + 6 + 6 = 24)$

Man is under the curse twenty four hours a day, seven days a week, and three hundred sixty five days a year. All men are under the curse of Adam. He cannot escape it. There is no way out; except through the way God has made; through His way – God's way. *"Jesus is the Way, the Truth, and the Life; No man comes to the Father except through Him."* (Jn.14:16)

It is through Jesus' blood and Him crucified! Jesus paid the price; paid it all on the cross at Calvary; so, that you can be set free from your bondage of sin and death; and from your bondage of the curse of the law, and all that came with it at the fall of man. Adam lost it all; but God can give it all back to you through His son – Jesus Christ. So the six that you know in your spirit, the six that you know in your soul, and the six that you have in your body can all be redeemed by the blood of the LAMB. The price was paid for you at Calvary, through the death, burial, and resurrection of Christ. This curse can be reversed!

Twenty four speaks of a number of time. There are twenty four hours in a day--a multiple of six. There's God's time, and then there's man's time. God's time is endless. There is no beginning and no end. It is measureless! God does not measure time as man measures time. It is a great mystery that may be revealed. But God has given man a measure of time and as we look at how we measure this time, at our clocks in our day, we see many sixes. There are sixty seconds in a minute. There are sixty minutes in an hour. There are twenty four hours in a day. There are twelve hours of daylight and twelve hours of night. It's all multiples of six. It is the time dimension of man. There are also twelve months to one full year, another multiple of six. Two times six equals twelve. Six is the basis for the measurement of time in the earth for man.

So, in this giant, he is the representation of all men – universal man - having no name; and all men are under the fall of the curse in all that they do, and in all that they walk in, day by day. Their hands and their feet are all under a curse; and they live in a curse twenty four hours a day, seven days a week in every day. We can see this pictured in this one "huge man" – this brother of Goliath. And it is interesting to note that all of these giants were slain in scripture in II Samuel 21:22. We see that all four were killed, but it doesn't say how. They were killed by members of David's fighting men-- anointed fighting men-- that were in service to King David. This is very significant.

So, we need to go back and put a few pictures together. David is fighting Goliath – a representation of good versus evil – five stones versus five brothers all together. In that day and in that hour, when David fought Goliath; you remember, he could not fight the battle with the armor of Saul upon his body. It was too cumbersome for him to use. He couldn't get around. He couldn't move. He had to take it back off. What did he do? He went to the stream--went to the river – the water – grabbed five smooth stones that probably did fly better, but there's a deeper truth here that we have seen. It's five-fold ministry in the hands of the King!

David killed Goliath with one of those stones. He never needed all five. The stone was divinely guided to the forehead of Goliath; and Goliath fell to the earth. And scripture backs this up: when Goliath fell to the ground, he was already dead! (see I Sam.17:49,50)

So why did David take the sword of Goliath and cut his head off? There is a deeper truth pictured here in this story that we need to understand. The picture of a sword cutting off the flesh of a giant! *"It is not by might, nor by power but by My Spirit,"* says the Lord. (Zach.4:6) The "sword" in scripture is the word of God. And we see here, by the word of God an enemy was slain.

Goliath boasted of great things that day on the battlefield. He boasted in great pride and arrogance to bring down this young shepherd boy. Goliath despised him and said, *"Am I a dog that you come at me with sticks? Come here and I'll give your flesh to the birds of the air and the beasts of the field."* (ISam.17:43, 44)

But David spoke his words – anointed words – by the Spirit of the Lord that had been placed within him at the anointing of Samuel the prophet. Everyone else was dismayed and terrified. But David said, *"Who is this underlined uncircumcised Philistine that he should defy the armies of the living God?"* (v.26) *"I come to you in the name of the Lord of Hosts, the God of the armies of Israel, whom you have defied. This day the Lord will deliver you into*

241

my hand, and I will strike you and take your head from you... for the battle is the Lord's, and He will give you into our hands." (v.45,46,47) David spoke out the anointed word of God that day, and it was the anointed word that brought down Goliath in the spirit. It even guided his stone from his sling to hit Goliath perfectly in the forehead. That's what killed Goliath that day. It was the power of God. He was already dead as he hit the ground.

So why do we see this picture of little David taking this huge sword from this giant, Goliath, to cut his head off? Why? It's a picture of the cutting away of the flesh by the sword of the Lord. David took the sword for himself, so it no longer belonged to Goliath. It was Goliath's sword, but it was David's reward or trophy for his great victory that day. We see in scripture he takes it with him and places the sword in his tent as a trophy and it becomes the sword of David in his possession.

So, David took his own sword that he took from the enemy, and what the enemy meant for harm, he turned it around and used it for the enemy's destruction. David "circumcised" his head completely off for his thoughts and words that Goliath had spoken against the armies of the Living God. This is a picture of a cutting away of the flesh by the sword of God in a universal man that is under the curse-- under the law-- in his fallen state. Goliath's brother had six fingers and six toes on each hand and foot, and he too was killed. He was fallen in everything that he touched and did, and all that he walked in. It's a picture of fallen man having his flesh cut away. Why his head? We need a circumcision of our hearts in every dimension of our lives – spirit, soul, and body!

Circumcision was a sign in the natural, in Abraham's day, that they would be the children of God, and faithful to the covenantal relationship with God. Today, it is a circumcision of the heart. It's not a circumcision in the natural realm; it's a circumcision in the spirit realm.

And we need a circumcision of our spirit and our souls, which includes our minds, a cutting away of all that is of our flesh nature-- all that is in Adam – all that is of our carnal mind and our carnal nature.

So, here we see a complete beheading of the carnal mind in Goliath! His thoughts did not line up with God's. Sometimes in our lives, we need a complete beheading of our carnal mind. That's what God wants. That's what God desires; for us to put off the carnal mind

242

and put on the mind of Christ; to take on His thoughts, His words, so that they become a part of our being and part of who we are! So, here we see that it's a circumcision of the flesh, of our complete and total old nature, which includes all of our old mind sets and carnal thinking. Nothing in our carnal nature and our carnal mind will benefit our spirit man. The two are in direct opposition to one another. We must be redeemed fully in our spirit, in our soul, and in our body.

This circumcision of the heart means all flesh; not just in the foreskins of our male sex organs like in the days of Abraham, in the Old Testament. That was a sign to the world for them that they were set apart, and were to live a life in obedience to their God, separated from sin and all that was unholy in the world. They were the children of God, and in the covenant of Abraham.

In this day and in this hour, it is a circumcision of the heart that means all of our being. All of who we are. And it's not just one organ, but all organs; in all of our being – spirit, soul, and body – all that we are. So all acts of the flesh need to be cut off and separated for us to become holy. And so, God says, *"Be holy even as I am holy."* *(1Pet.1:16)* And you see, that is attainable. God never asks us to do anything that He has not already made a way for us to walk in it.

So what He asks us to do, it can be accomplished if we do it God's way. In this life, we can be 99.9% pure and holy as God perfects his nature in us, and we can walk the walk we're supposed to walk in cooperation with God. We can reach the fullness of God in this lifetime and be all that we were meant to be! Less of us and more of Him; but it may come at a bit of a price for us! We need to renew our minds with the word of God. *"Be transformed by the renewing of our minds".* (Rom. 12:2)

I know a lot of people don't like to hear that, but a lot of their old thinking needs to get thrown out the window. Half of what they do know isn't true anyway, and they desperately need to get the truth of the living God straight out of the written word of God, backed up by the Spirit of God with His anointing upon it! That may be a hard word for some, but we do need our heads cut off! Our carnal mind needs to go away – completely! It's a circumcision of the mind along with all flesh in this New Covenant that we need to enter into in Christ – a removal of all the old flesh nature that we are born into naturally.

The first sign of circumcision was given in the days of Abram when God promised, *"I will make you a father of many nations and your offspring will outnumber the stars of heaven."* Abram believed God in faith that He would be faithful to perform His word and fulfill His promises. God also had promised land to His descendants and that He would be their God. As a sign to all the world of this covenantal agreement between these two parties, and that they were bound to one another, was the circumcision of all the males. It was a sign or mark that they had accepted the terms of the agreement, and by faith would keep their own covenantal obligations.

God changed Abram's name to Abraham which means: "father of many." With this distinguishing mark, one could tell whether or not someone was a Jew and worshiped the God of Abraham and was one of his descendents. This was performed in the natural, but with deep spiritual implications.

In Gen.17:11, we can read of this "sign of the covenant" – a cutting away of the flesh. In verse 12, every male who was eight days old must be circumcised in obedience to this covenant agreement. If not, they would be cut off from their people because they would have broken God's covenant in the earth and did not recognize the relationship. God even tried to kill Moses for not circumcising his son while he was staying in Midian. (Ex.4:24)

The sign was at the male sex reproductive organ. Why? It's only seen in intimacy at times of close relationship. It speaks of the Covenant Relationship between God and His people, and also implies the idea of reproduction. His promise to Abraham, when he was ninety-nine years old was, *"I will make you a father of many nations",* even at a time when he had no children, no descendants, no heir to all that he had or to carry on his family line. And to even make matters worse, his wife Sarah, at the age of ninety, was barren. She was past the years of child bearing for her life. But nevertheless, the promise came through the Spirit and not in the flesh!

They tried to fulfill it in the flesh, and they got an Ishmael, the son of Hagar. They tried to help God out and made a great mistake that has caused severe ramifications even in our time to this very day. But God had a plan! The promise would come through the Spirit. The Lord said that Sarah would conceive and have a son, even past the years of child bearing; and she was to call him Isaac. "Is anything too hard for the Lord?" (v.18)

God said to Abraham, *"I will make you very fruitful; I will make nations of you, and kings will come from you. I will establish My covenant as an everlasting covenant between me and you and your descendants after you for the generations to come to be your God and the God of your descendants after you."(Gen.17:6, 7)*

God established a covenant (or contract) with Abraham, and made him several promises. The sign of the covenant was a cutting away of the male sex organ. There was blood involved and a cutting away of some flesh that died. They were to do this throughout all their generations to come. So they could reproduce what had been started in the earth and to preserve a godly line of people among all humanity in the natural realm that were in covenant with God Most High. God's promise to Abraham was that *"Kings will come from you."* (v.6) There have been many kings to come in the natural, but there was one king in particular that God spoke of that day. It was the King of all kings, and the Lord of all lords. Jesus Christ of Nazareth would come from this same family line, and be a blessing to all the nations of the earth.

Spiritually – we have come into this same covenant through Jesus Christ our Messiah; through the circumcising of our hearts and the cutting away of our flesh – spiritually – of all that is in Adam – all that is in our old nature. We are coming into a New Covenantal agreement with God. He will be our God-- that's His promise; and we need to love Him, and listen to Him, and obey His voice. That's our obligation.

And the New Covenant is this: God has given us all that He can do in the finished work of Christ. He signed this new contract in His blood that He shed on Calvary's cross. Now, we need to sign this contract in our blood-- a circumcision of the heart. The only thing that we can give to God is our entire life and our entire being-- that involves our entire existence. That's all God wants from us. He just wants us! He wants our life. All that we are! He simply wants our life, and for us to have an intimate relationship with our creator – it's the bridegroom and bride!

So, if you will circumcise your heart, and you are willing to allow God to cut away all of your flesh; the first one was done by the hands of men; the second one is done by the hands of God. God comes and circumcises all of our flesh off our entire body – spiritually speaking.

Circumcision was a requirement to partake of the Passover meal in the Old Testament. Even today, it is a requirement to partake of the Lords table or communion in our day. To be a believer, you

245

have a circumcision of the heart that has begun by the hand of God, but you need to allow God to complete the work in you that He has begun, so you can be full in this lifetime.

There is even an Old Testament promise in Deut.30:6, *"The Lord your God will circumcise your hearts and the hearts of your descendents so that you may love Him with all your hearts and with all your soul and live."*

We are those descendants that are to love Him with all of our heart, with all of our soul and lives! We are the spiritual descendants of Abraham; and the spiritual descendants of Jesus, himself-- children of faith--children of the Spirit! "For a Jew is not one that is only one outwardly, but a Jew is one – inwardly – a circumcision of the heart, by the spirit; not by a written code or the letter of the law, but it is by God's Spirit," says the Lord God Almighty.

God cuts away the flesh of our being and it's all done by His hand; no other man can do this work in the earth. Nothing we can do, nothing that we can try to attain, can ever accomplish a circumcision of our flesh in this life.

Paul writes about this very thing in Rom. 2:28, 29. It is a sign to the world for us. How will the world know us? It is by our holy living and our changed hearts. It becomes an outward sign and evidence that we are in a covenantal agreement with our Lord and Savior Jesus Christ the Messiah; the Most High God. And that we are participants of the divine nature-- on the inside of us-- not on the outside; and that we are the descendants of Christ to be multiplied in the earth. What is in the natural; it is in the natural first as a symbol, a type, or a picture-- a shadow of things to come in the spirit.

In Paul's letter to the Galatians he writes in chapter six concerning a great debate over this subject of circumcision-- if a believer should have it done or not. And to sum up that debate, Paul instructs the Galatian believers that circumcision means nothing… *"what counts is a new creation."*(v.15) And also in Phil.3:3, *"it is we who are the circumcision, we who worship by the Spirit of God; who glory in Christ Jesus, and who put no confidence in the flesh…"*

Finally, in Colossians 2:11, Paul writes again, *"In Him you were also circumcised, in the putting off of the sinful nature, not with a circumcision done by the hands of men but with the circumcision done by Christ."*

You see, Christ does the work of cutting away our old rebellious nature that does all the wrong things, and gives us a new nature that is one after the divine nature of Christ that He displayed in the earth during His earth-walk and ministry. A changed heart – now that's a miracle!

"For behold, I make all things new – all the old has passed away – behold, I make all things new," says the Lord God Almighty. "I am making all things new, in this day and in this hour; and that includes your flesh nature. It must be cut away by the hand of God and die. It is a work that must be done by My Spirit. But you must avail yourself to Me," says the Lord. "You must yield to My Spirit. Yield to the workings of God and the leadings of God in your life and simply yield and say, 'Yes Lord, Yes. Here I am. Do all that you want to do in me', and present yourself – your body as a living sacrifice, holy and acceptable unto God."

This process is progressive! You don't come into holiness all in the first day. Spiritually you do in the heavens, but what is true in the heavens needs to come down and play itself out to be true in the earth. It's a process!

So, to walk in holiness, you have to walk it out day by day, in repentance and in humility, in patience, in longsuffering, in trials and in testings, in tribulations, and through all of these things-- the work of God gets completed in your heart and in your life in this lifetime.

"So, it's not where you've been. It's not what's in your past. The biggest question is: Where are you headed? What road are you on and where are you going? It's in the journey. It's not where you've been. It's where you're going, and what road you are on to get there! What road are you on this day?"

"Church of the Living God: What road are you traveling down in this day and in this hour? Many of you may have been walking with Me at one point in your life, but you've traveled down the wrong road. You've taken a detour! It's time to get back on the highway to heaven," says the Lord God Almighty. "I am making every crooked way straight. Every rough place smooth… Every mountain will be brought low and every valley will be raised up. This is a word for your life. Everything that has tried to exalt itself and been a mountain in your life, God is bringing down. Every valley that has been inadequate and been lacking, I am filling up. It's all level ground at the cross. It's all level ground at the cross."

"Will you, this day, subject yourselves to the sword of the Lord … to the sword of David? Even as in the day he fought the giant Goliath. Will you subject yourself to the sword of the Lord, which is the word of God, and allow it to cut away your flesh – all flesh that is in Adam in your old nature; so that you can be transformed and renewed and be made a new creation in Christ? It all just doesn't happen automatically. You are part of the process. You must submit yourself to the workings of God in your life. Remember this word: your response determines your future, each and every day! You can take a left turn or a right turn. You can do a one hundred and eighty degree turn and go completely away from Me; but it is your choice. I will never override your free will choice."

"So, if you will say 'Yes Lord, Yes. I will submit myself – and subject myself to the entire word of God – all of it – not just parts of it!' You can't just pick out certain parts of the word of God. It's the whole loaf of bread. You can't just pick and choose. In God's economy, it's all or nothing. That's what He wants. If you pick and choose, you're just going to get what you get; and that's as far as you will go. But who wants to eat crumbs from the floor like a dog, when you can eat from the table of the King as royalty?"

"You've been given an invitation. Will you come and eat from this table?" says the Lord God Almighty. "Will you come and eat of My word – My bread – and drink My wine," says the Lord, "and come into a covenantal agreement with Me? Will you eat from the Kings table today? Will you eat from My entire word – My entire bread that I have for you? Jesus is the 'Bread of Life'. Will you eat of His flesh and drink of His blood? If you do, you enter into a covenantal agreement with the Most High God. And you can be a son of obedience in this day and in this hour. You can walk by My Word, and in My Spirit," says the Lord God Almighty.

Two Piles of Six

Every exact detail of the tabernacle of Moses was given by divine pattern. There was nothing left to conjecture or to guessing in the mind of man. Nothing was left to the imagination, and there was no room for creativity here in these blueprints for this tabernacle. Moses had to obey God in every detail. What was in the mind of God was given to him through the Spirit of God in a divine pattern. And Moses being the man of faith that he was, inspected all the workings of the tabernacle before they were set up to make sure that they were all made by the divine pattern. Everything in the tabernacle of Moses, in every detail, is there for a reason – every detail. In a quick reading, it just seems like a temporary building or tent like structure that could be taken down quickly and transported – a temporary temple – which they could carry while going through their wilderness journey until they could reach and arrive at their promised land. But, there is more to it than what meets the eye!

One of the pieces of furniture that we have not yet discussed in this book – we have a couple more yet to go - is the **"Table of Showbread"**. This table was always placed on the north side of the "Holy Place". And in this "Holy Place", it would be the second chamber that you would enter into. The first one is the outer court that anyone could go into. The second one is the "Holy Place" that only a priest could go into, and then the third place was the "Most Holy Place", that we have discussed, or the "Secret Place", that only the high priest could enter and then only once a year.

But this place where the Table of Showbread was kept, was in the Holy Place, and this is where we will discuss some very important truths that are hidden within this piece of furniture in the Tabernacle of Moses.

To describe this table, it was a golden table. Everything in this chamber had to be golden. We have the golden candlestick. We have the golden table of showbread, and we have the golden altar of incense. The golden table was always placed on the north side, the golden candlestick on the south side, and the golden altar on the west side; and the veil or door to enter facing east. Every time they set the tabernacle up – everything would be placed in its proper place and location as God had described.

This table was made of "Shittim" wood overlaid with gold. These two elements are combined in this divine pattern. Wood speaks of humanity – something of the earth – and points to the humanity of Christ. It was then overlaid with gold that speaks of divinity or the divine nature of Christ. Two elements are combined together to make this one table. Christ was both fully man and fully God. The two were combined into one flesh – one body – one man – the man Jesus Christ; and He walked the earth over two thousand years ago in His earthly ministry. This symbolism all points to Christ.

Upon this table would be placed twelve loaves of bread. Scripture describes it as "rows"; but literally would mean more accurately that they would be placed in "piles". (No yeast, so it wouldn't rise-- it was a flat bread or a "matsa".) So, we have a picture of "two piles of six"; a pile of six breads, and then another pile of six breads. We have a six and another six, side by side; one for each tribe of the children of Israel, so that all the tribes were represented before the Lord in the "Holy Place". This bread was placed there continually. It was to be there always as an everlasting covenant, and as a sign of that covenant, that it would never end; that God would establish through His Son Jesus Christ, through the ages, and forever.

In this table, we also see that there were "bowls and covers" which were actually cups of wine. (Ex: 25-29) We see the combination of bread and wine at this table! The scripture says that it was strong wine that was to be poured out as a libation offering before the Lord. (Num.28:7) This was the drink offering of outpoured wine that was solely used at this table. And we see in all the other ministrations of the priesthood during the Passover and with each animal offered, there was a libation drink offering that was poured out onto the ground. It was not to be drunk; but it was to be poured out as an offering.

So in these two elements, the bread and the wine, we see them as being connected to something else that is very familiar to most of us. It is all pointing to the "Table of the Lord" that we see in the New Testament that was instituted by Jesus Christ, himself.

Within this table, we see **"two piles of six"** loaves of bread that are piled up side by side; a pile of six beside another six. Numerically, if we put a six beside another six, we get sixty six. Which interestingly enough – I believe there is a connection here – there are sixty six books of the bible from Genesis to Revelation. The entire word of God is represented at this table – every word. The entire sixty six books of the bible are represented here in the **bread!**

Jesus is the **"Bread of Life"**. It's one of the seven **"I AM"** statements that Jesus made in His earthly walk and ministry recorded in the gospel of John. (We will get into some of this later in chapter seven.) One of these "I AM" statements is: "I am the Bread of Life". He was the manna that fell down out of heaven on the seventh day. Remember, the Israelites in the wilderness could only gather the manna for six days; and they would gather a double portion on the sixth day. There again, you see two sixes on the sixth day; enough for the seventh day. Then, they were to rest from their labors on the seventh day- the Sabbath day. There was no manna on the seventh day;

250

this all points to Jesus being the seventh day Sabbath manna that came down out of heaven. He came directly from the throne room of heaven. Do you see the pictures? Do you see them all lining up? He is the seventh day manna, fresh out of heaven. He was fully God and fully man combined into one body – one flesh – one life.

John chapter 1:1, *"In the beginning was the word and the word was with God and the word was God … and the word became flesh and dwelt among us …"*(v.14) Jesus was the word of God coming down out of heaven into the earth. That's the symbolism. That's the picture. So, we see Jesus in His fullness – in His entirety – the complete word of God is represented here at the table of showbread; clear back almost 1,500 years before Christ ever walked the earth. It was a shadow of things to come!

Remember, God had a plan. Genesis 3:15, *"I will put enmity between you and the woman and between your seed and her seed; He will bruise your head, and you will bruise His heel."*(NKJV) Satan is under Jesus' feet! God was sending His son to come to the earth to fulfill His plan of redemption to gain back a lost and dying world; so that our fellowship with God could be restored. Remember, it was broken at the fall of Adam.

And here at this table, we see that the priest would come and partake of this bread and pour out these libation offerings, the drink offerings unto the Lord, pouring the wine out on the ground. We see that this is a picture of Christ. He is the" Bread of Life." (Jn. 6:35) The bread and the wine represent a covenantal agreement. The wine is also symbolic of Jesus' blood that was poured out for the sins of the world!

The priest would come and partake of this bread that is also known as "face bread" or the "bread of the presence". He could eat the bread, but he had to pour out the wine as a libation. In so doing, the priest was coming into a covenantal agreement representing all the people, all the twelve tribes of the nation of Israel, before God. Remember, the priests were the representatives of all the people. All the people could not come into that "Holy Place". It would be impractical, and also, they were not holy. God had a holy priesthood set apart in the tribe of the Levites, along with Moses and Aaron, and his four sons. That was the priesthood to carry out all the necessary functions and duties surrounding their relationship with God.

And only those of the priesthood could eat of this bread and could even stand in this holy place. The symbolism is quite obvious

251

here. You, today, have been called, and any and all believers have been called, to be a royal priesthood unto God. You are called to partake of this table – the bread and the wine; but it's not at the table of showbread, for that is no longer in existence. Jesus brings many of these thoughts together. Do you remember the last supper? There have been many famous paintings about this subject: Jesus at His last supper with His twelve disciples reclined at a table. It's all a picture of the Passover meal – the last one that Jesus would ever eat of – as all good Jews did every year. Once a year, they would partake of the Passover meal that was instituted in the days of Moses just before their great deliverance out of Egypt.

It is at this Passover meal that Jesus combines a lot of thoughts together. He was the lamb symbolically at this Passover for He was about to die. In the precise timing of all this, Jesus Christ died on Passover. He was the lamb. And He took the unleavened bread that had no yeast in it symbolizing His own sinless life. He took the bread and broke it and said, *"Take, eat; this is My body which is broken for you; do this in remembrance of Me."* (ICor.11:24) It was His body that was broken, and beaten, and bruised, and torn. He was tortured – literally tortured-- for you and me. Then He went to the cross – one of the cruelest punishments that could ever be inflicted upon anyone – the Roman crucifixion. And He died for all of mankind; everyone, so that we could be reunited with our creator. After the bread, He took the wine and said, *"This cup is the New Covenant in My blood; this do, as often as you drink it, in remembrance of Me."*(v.25) The wine of the cup is symbolic of Jesus blood which was poured out as a libation offering for you. You see, Jesus is the lamb! He is the bread! He is the wine!

It is very interesting, in the Old Testament, you had to be circumcised to partake of the Passover, so that meant you had to be a Jew in covenant with Yahweh with very few exceptions. Bring that thought up to the New Testament and our day, as we have discussed, it is a circumcision of the flesh and of the heart in all areas of our lives.

So to partake of this communion meal, you must be, number one, a believer in the Lord Jesus Christ, but that also means that God has circumcised your heart and at least has begun that work in you. And that work is a process that will continue on; of which, you will be a participant. God will continually circumcise your flesh, to cut it off from your being, so it's no longer even a part of you; and then that flesh will die. If you cut off flesh from your body, that flesh will die.

252

You see, that's the symbolism. That's what God desires in us. All that is in Adam; all that is of our old nature; all that is of our flesh is to be cut off.

This is the picture here at the table of showbread; and even Communion. **When you are taking communion**, you are entering into a **covenantal agreement** with God! There are many today that do not even realize what they are doing when they take communion. The act of communion alone won't save you. No ritual that we could ever do will save us. It must be combined with faith. *"For Abraham believed God and it was reckoned to him as righteousness."* (Gen.15:6)

"Church of the Living God: We need to know and take knowledge of what we are doing. There are many sick among you! Why? You partake of the Lords communion unworthily; which means irreverently, which means you don't know what you're doing and you throw it around like some common thing-- and say the same thing over and over again. You cannot partake of this bread and this wine unless you are circumcised! And if you are not, you are taking it unworthily."

"Church of the Living God: There are many sick among you, because you take it unworthily. You take it unknowingly. You take it in ignorance. You take it being uncircumcised of heart. You're too full of YOURSELF! You have not allowed the sword of My word to come and cut off from your being all that is in Adam – all that is in your flesh – all that is in your old nature. You are acting as an uncircumcised Philistine! You need your heads cut off! All of your old mind sets and old patterns of thinking, in the carnal mind, needs to be cut completely off!"

Circumcision is of the heart, but that means your total being – your total essence of who you are. It was a sign of the Old Testament Covenant of all Israelites in their body. It's not a bodily circumcision in this New Covenant. Man is a three part being – spirit, soul, and body. The body, in the natural, has already been done, as a shadow of things to come. The two left remaining – areas of life – are the soul realm and the spirit realm. It's all of our being-- which includes our minds. *"… that you present your bodies a living sacrifice, holy, acceptable to God… be transformed by the renewing of your mind…"* (Rom. 12:1,2)

There is a renewing of the mind that comes into play. WE MUST PUT ON THE MIND OF CHRIST; which means eating and partaking of the word of God from Genesis to Revelation. Eating the "Bread" of God! We need to ingest it – take it into our being – then digest it into our being – and that takes awhile. It takes some time to digest that dinner you just ate in the natural. You need to digest the word of God also. It's a process! Just like eating in the natural is a process; eating in the spiritual is a process. There is a digestive process that takes place where the word-- or the bread-- becomes a part of who we are!

"Church of the Living God: We need to be changed. We need to be transformed in our spirit, in our soul, and in our body. But sometimes it never gets down to our bodies to manifest in our bodies! Why? Our spirits aren't changed. Our souls aren't changed. The soul realm is the realm of the mind and the emotions. It rarely gets down to our bodies."

I Thes.5:23 shows us that we are a three part being in that order: spirit, soul and body. Most importantly, God wants to redeem our spirit man and He wants to give you eternal life; and only some ever get that far. They barely make it into the kingdom. Some walk a little further with God and God begins to heal their soul realm – all the deep hurts in their hearts and beings. Jesus was "…wounded for our transgressions…and bruised for our iniquities." (Is.53:5) A wound usually inflicts a bruise upon the body. Many of us walk around all beat up with bruises from things that have happened to us in the past. God wants to heal those things, but it takes some time. There is time involved in all of these things.

God wants to heal our innermost beings; and bring an inner healing to the soul realms of our lives. You see, God wants to fix and heal **all** of us. Every part of who we are. It is a holistic type of thinking and way of looking at things, which is also how the Hebrews looked at life. They had a holistic view of life. Jesus came down right in the midst of that culture. He didn't come down into the Roman culture or the Greek culture which separated all of these three parts of our beings. These did not have a holistic view of life.

God is interested in the whole man. But it is a process and to get down to the body … "Why are there many sick among you?" Because you partake unworthily of the Lord's Table. You're not worthy because you're not circumcised. You had to be circumcised to partake of Passover in the Old Testament. This is a New Testament Passover -- Communion with the Lord! Jesus Christ died on Passover. He was the Lamb. He instituted this communion as a Passover – last supper-- that was intended for all of His disciples throughout the generations. But you see, you had to be circumcised to partake of Passover. It was a separation between the Israelites and the Egyptians so that all of the first born males of the Israelites would be saved from the death angel that came at the tenth plague.

Even today, it is a separation between the believers and the world today. You are Spiritual Israel, because you are a Jew spiritually and you are of the nation of Israel spiritually, for you have been grafted in as a descendant of Abraham and as a descendant of Christ. Even as they came out of Egypt in the great Exodus, there was not one among them that was feeble. They came out in health. Their clothes and their shoes did not wear out. God divinely took care of them and met all their needs. He wanted to show them that He was the God of the Hebrews and still the God of Abraham, Isaac, and Jacob – otherwise known as "Yahweh".

When Moses had his encounter with God in the Midian desert at the Burning Bush, the bush was miraculously not consumed. God revealed Himself to Moses and gave him a mission to accomplish in the earth. And Moses said, "When I go, who should I say has sent me?" Then God said, "Tell them the I AM has sent you. The I AM, that I AM, that I AM has sent you." This is where we see the name "Yahweh". The name describes the total essence of all that God is. He is the "I AM" that "I AM". And you see, Jesus had seven "I AM" statements in the gospel of John. Jesus, too, was God incarnate. He was the "I AM".

He had seven "I AM" statements pointing to the fullness and completion of God in all that He is. God wants us to experience that today. But to do that, we need to know what we are getting ourselves into. So, when you partake of communion once a month, once a week, four times a year, or every time you gather; the most important thing is every time you do, it's not just a ritual, but that you know what you're doing.

You are entering into a covenant agreement with God! Bread and wine speaks of covenant. We see it at Passover, at the table of showbread, with Abraham and Melchizedek, at the last supper-- all throughout scripture the symbols of bread and wine are mentioned. You are eating at the Lord's Table. David spoke of this in Psalms 23:5: *"You prepare a table before me in the presence of my enemies."* When you are coming to the Lord's Table, partaking of the bread and the wine, you are entering into a covenantal agreement with God identifying with His

255

death, burial, and resurrection. You are believing on the Lord Jesus Christ by faith that He has done these things for you- participating in the benefits of His sacrificial death, and that you are going to do your part of this covenantal agreement.

God has done all that He is supposed to do and He has signed this agreement in His blood. Jesus said, "This is a new covenant-- a new agreement. This is My body that is broken for you; this is the blood of My covenant that has been spilled for you." He signed it in His blood; now **when you partake of this communion** you are saying, "God, I will sign the agreement in my blood; representative of my life. I am giving you my life; my whole entire life, all that I am, and I will live by your word."

You see, it's a New Testament Passover. You are also saying that you are subjecting yourself and partaking of the entire word of God and it's affects upon your life; and you are opening up the gates of your heart and accepting **all of the word** of God into your being! Eating the bread – Jesus is the bread that fell down out of heaven— you are symbolically **eating all of the word** of God and **believing all of the word** for you!

"Man shall not live by bread alone, but by every word that proceeds out of the mouth of God." (Deut.8:3) That is what is happening when you are partaking of communion! You are entering into a **covenantal agreement** with God. Unless you're willing to lay it all down – don't take it. It's not just a ritual that if you take it, you're saved, or that you hope you're saved, or that you do it in remembrance of Jesus body and what He did. Yes, we do remember Him, but it's more than that! It's more than just a memorial to say, "Yes God, we remember your death".

We are to remember it all the days of our life! This is a covenant agreement that we do remember the Lord's death. But you see, we are also to proclaim it. We are to proclaim the Lord's death until He comes! But we are to do it every day of our life! Proclaim the Lord's death until He comes! It speaks of the covenantal agreement that you are entering into; all the days of your life-- not just one day a week, on Sunday, or once a month, or twice a year, or however many times you go to church. It's not just for Easter and Christmas, because there are those who do that.

This is an agreement – **a spiritual agreement** that you are entering into that you are to proclaim the Lord's death every day of your life until He comes. You see, it's deeper than just a memorial – **it's a covenantal relationship!** Remember, circumcision was done in the flesh to the male reproductive organ. Why? It has implications to the **descendants** of Abraham, but it also has implications of intimacy. It was only ever seen in times of intimate relationship and is symbolic of our relationship between God and man. It's a circumcision of the heart – of our flesh. Why? It speaks of that intimate, close relationship that we are to have with our Creator.

Remember, we are the "Bride of Christ". God is preparing a Bride for His wedding day; for a consummation of the marriage at the wedding supper of the Lamb. He is preparing us for that day, for the ultimate time of great intimacy; but we can still enjoy a betrothal period just as they did in the Hebrew culture. To be betrothed was as serious as being married. It was a covenantal agreement that said you were reserved for one person; and it was taken a lot more seriously than it is in our American culture today.

This is looked upon very lightly in our modern day culture. And we throw it around like it's nothing. But God has created it to be a holy institution between one man and one woman in holy matrimony. Why? It is the highest institution on earth that represents the relationship between God and His creation - the bridegroom and the bride. It is Most Holy! And it is to remain Most Holy.

Satan has tried to corrupt that relationship for decades, and he is doing a very good job of destroying the institution of marriage. That is why we must fight for this institution and the sanctity of marriage, because it has been ordained by God himself. We see it all throughout scripture. It's a picture of the bridegroom and His bride.

Will you allow God to circumcise your heart and cut away all flesh in your spirit realm and your soul realm-- that includes your mind? Literally cut off your entire carnal mind and "behead" the old carnal mind with all of its old patterns of thinking.

It's a circumcision of the heart –**all flesh**-- and it's done by the hands of God, not by the hands of men. The first one was done by the hands of men. The second one is done by the hands of God. Will you allow the word of God – the sword of His Spirit to come and cut away from you all that should not belong in you? And then only through that process can you enter into intimate times with the Lord.

You see, because when we go before a Holy God, even in the days of old, when the high priest went into the "Holy of Holies", he needed to make sure that he did everything absolutely correct as he was instructed to do, or he would die. He would literally fall over dead, and they would have to drag him out by the rope that was tied around his ankle.

When we come into the presence of such a Holy God – our flesh must die. So, the death of you is the life of God! It's a lot of these concepts put together; and God has given us many pictures to see the same thing. God puts all these things together for us. *"But the natural man does not receive the things of the Spirit of God for they are foolishness to him; nor can he know them because they are spiritually discerned."* (I Cor.2:14)

The spirit mind and the natural mind – the things of the spirit and the things of the natural or the flesh – they are in direct opposition to one another. If they would have known the Lord, and would have known in the spirit, they would not have crucified Him. They did not know Him or have fellowship with Him. No relationship. The word for fellowship and communion in the Greek is the word "Koinonia".

Communion at the Lord's Table and the Table of Showbread were all about "Koinonia" or fellowship – spending time to get to know God. This word "Koinonia" carries the thought a little bit deeper. It literally means fellowship to such intimacy as to have sexual intercourse as we see in the marriage institution of God. So, to know God really means to know Him in this great degree of intimacy… to know Him that deeply, just as a husband and wife can know one another, and they become one. It's a picture of the covenant that God wants with His people. We can know God very intimately. We can know His heart, His will, His mind, ect., just like a couple in the natural – a man and a woman-- can know one another. Just as in this natural relationship, we too, can know God in the spirit.

To give you a few examples of this in the New Testament, Jesus said, *"Many will say to Me in that day, 'Lord, Lord, have we not prophesied in your name, cast out demons in your name, and done many wonders in your name?' And then I will declare to them, 'I never knew you; depart from Me…'"* (Mat. 7:22-23) They didn't have the fellowship or the relationship. It's all about relationship! We see this again on the road to Emmaus. This man came upon these two men while walking along the road talking about the events that had recently taken place. This man asked them about what they were discussing. They replied, *"about this Jesus of Nazareth, He was a prophet, powerful in word and deed before God and all the people. The chief priests and our rulers handed Him over to be crucified and*

258

we had hoped He was the one who would redeem Israel. It's been days since this all happened and even the tomb is empty. There is no body." As they walked along, this first man spoke to them with great wisdom and understanding concerning all the scriptures beginning with Moses and on through the prophets. They were so impressed by him and his teaching that they asked him to stay with them awhile. So they sat down for a meal, which is very important in Jewish culture: a Jew and a Gentile could not even eat together.

"When he was at the table with them, he took the bread, gave thanks, broke it and began to give it to them. Then their eyes were opened and they recognized **(knew)** *Him, and He disappeared from their sight."* (Luke24:30, 31 NIV) He vanished before their very eyes! Their eyes were opened and they **knew** Him. They knew who He was and it was revealed to them that this man was the Lord of Glory that had been crucified and risen. This man was Jesus of Nazareth of whom they had spoke about! **They knew Him!** It is very significant that they **knew** Him in that precise moment – **at the breaking of the bread.** Why? It speaks of the "Koinonia": communion or fellowship that we are to have at the Lords table.

We can know Jesus Christ and Him crucified. We have our relationship restored back to its fullest measure; and even in greater ways than we had originally. Remember, when God restores something, He multiplies and increases it. So, we can go spiritually back to the Garden of Eden and walk with God in the cool of the day, and know God to His fullest.

We can know Him as the "I AM", that "I AM"-- The God of the Hebrews: "YAHWEH"! We can know Him as the "I AM that I AM". He is our everything! And if we know Him in that way, and we enter into that covenantal relationship where God has done His part of the bargain, the agreement, the deal, the contract, and we do what we are required to do, which is giving Him our life, but that means everything that we are. Everything: all that we are and all that we're not, all that we have, and all that we don't have, all of our dreams, our hopes, our desires, everything about us; even our careers, our money, our finances, our wealth; because has not all this been given to you by the Father of Light? Every good blessing comes down from the Father. We need to just give it all back to Him!

You see, that's what God wants from us today. The subtitle of this book is-- **God's Call: To Return to Covenant Relationship for**

259

His People! That's what God is doing today. He's calling us all back to the original agreement, to this original, New Covenant, agreement that Jesus established at the last supper – and through His death, burial, and resurrection. That's what He meant – that we have to give it all – all of ourselves. I know that may be a hard word for some; but why are you lacking? Why are you in want? It is to the measure that you give it shall be given back unto you.

You haven't given your full self. You haven't given everything. And God is only obligated to give back to the measure that you give. Why are there many sick among you? Why? You haven't given everything that you have to God. You have strayed away from the original agreement. And I will say this: that is a very dangerous place to be.

God is calling us back in repentance. Lord God, forgive us for missing it. Forgive us for straying away. Forgive us for leaving our first love; for we have played the harlot, and we have gone after many other lovers in this world. We have been enticed by all the wealth in this world. We have been tempted by the enemy and drawn away. Remember Satan is craftier than all the other beasts of the earth. He was the serpent in the garden and he deceived Eve very craftily and in a very cunning way.

Church of the Living God: Satan is very good at what he does. And it doesn't take much for him to come and lie to us, and deceive us, and pull us away from our relationship with our creator. That's his purpose and intentions. He wants to rob, kill, and destroy what God has created, and what God has intended. He wants to destroy the fellowship that we once had in the garden. He wants to see us lost for all eternity; and in the process, he wants us to worship him. Worship the created rather than the creator!

And if we do that, worship the created and all the things of this world, we are ultimately worshiping Satan himself. He is the full embodiment of pride. He wants our worship; and we, in that way, when we serve ourselves and all the things of this world system and we worship things rather than the creator – we are truly worshiping the beast. And if we put ourselves in the center of the universe and worship ourselves, we are truly worshiping the image of the beast.

And I know that is a hard word for some, but you must search your heart and search the word. Search the scriptures. It is a truth of God, nevertheless.

Get Out Your Spiritual Shovels

Get out your spiritual shovels. It's time to dig! Halleluiah! Man tries to bury, to cover up, and to hide. Even in the days of Adam, when he sinned in the garden, what did he do? He ran. He hid. He was ashamed. He did not want to see God face to face, because of what he did. And so, too, it holds true with even mankind today. We're still doing the same thing! We sin. We mess up. We disobey God, and we run away. We hide from God because we're ashamed of what we've done. We don't want anyone else to know; so we bury it, keeping it hidden in secret. We cover it up, and over time, we just throw more dirt on it thinking that's going to keep it there, hidden, and in the dark.

That's man's way! But God's way is entirely different. When we mess up, we don't just run away; but we come back to the foot of the cross! I Jn.1:9 says, *"If we confess our sins, He is faithful and just to forgive us our sins and to cleanse us from all unrighteousness."* That's God's Way!

God has made a provision for if and when we do mess up and sin against Him. And that should be in progressively smaller and smaller ways as you walk with God. Your relationship with God should be a progressive climb upward into higher and higher places in Christ; as the old carnal nature diminishes and the divine nature increases. You should sin less and less in your life until you attain 99.9% holiness in this lifetime; and it can be achieved. You can walk in holiness! You can walk in obedience! You can hear the voice of God!

"For My sheep know My voice. I call unto them and they hear, and they listen, and they obey, and they do what I tell them. I have made a way! And that way is Jesus Christ. He is the Way, the Truth, and the Life. No man comes to the Father except by Him."

Jesus said, "I am the door of the sheep. All who ever came before Me are thieves and robbers, but the sheep did not hear them. I am the door. If anyone enters by Me, he will be saved, and will go in and out and find pasture." (Jn.10:7-9)

The Tabernacle of Moses also had three doors or veils into the three chambers. To proceed deeper into the tabernacle with each new chamber you had to enter through a "door". You couldn't sneak in the back or underneath the "linen curtain" to get into this house of God. You must enter God's prescribes way. If you don't do it by God's pattern – IT DOES NOT WORK!!

God has made the pattern. God has made the blueprint. God has made the plan. YOU CAN NOT MAKE YOUR OWN PLAN!

You cannot come by your own way. Mankind can never dictate to God how they will come to God. Many, many people try to strike a deal with God and say, "God, if you'll only do this for me, I'll give you my whole life. I'll do this for you. I'll do that for you." They promise the sun and the moon. They give great promises to God in trying to coerce God into doing what they want.

"I, the Lord God, I hear this time and time again. My creation – mankind – comes to Me over and over to try to strike their deal. But I have already made a way. I have determined a plan from before the foundations of the world in eternity past. It was already set. I made a way." Even in Genesis 3:15, we see the promise of the Messiah. He is the Way! You must come through the door – through the veil of Jesus Christ and Him crucified – His death, burial, and resurrection. You must believe on the Lord Jesus Christ and you shall be saved! He is the only Way, the Truth, and the Life. He is the truth – the total truth; and He is also the life – the total life.

So, if you come God's way and receive all of God's truth, you'll get all of God's life in return! Jesus said, "I am the Way, the Truth, and the Life. I have come to give men life and life more abundantly." He wants to pour out of all that He is into His creation; but we must come through the **"WAY"** that God has prescribed!

Man tries to bury it – to hide it; even when they come and they ask forgiveness for the wrongs that they have done, they still try to bury it. They don't deal with it in God's prescribed way. They don't take it one step further.

In scripture, it says to confess our sins to one another, and sometimes you may have to speak it out and bring it to light, and go and tell someone else – another important relationship in your life. "I want you to know something I've done that I'm not proud of. The Lord's putting it in my heart that I need to tell you."

In that type of confession, there is great healing. God may lead you to go to someone and say to them, "I forgive you", or vice versa. They may need to ask forgiveness from you. And then God can restore the relationship. But you see, if those things are buried and just forgotten about and we only go to God and think everything else is fine, we are only deceiving ourselves, because it's not God's prescribed way.

God is into and all about relationships – relationships with the Father and relationships with one another. If you look at the cross, and use that as a symbol for this analogy; the horizontal cross beam represents all our horizontal relationships that we need to keep in a good and upright way, then our vertical relationship will be much, much, better; and be clear and clean.

So, God is saying for us today as a very good analogy, to keep all of our horizontal relationships good with our fellow man. For how can we not keep those good and upright with our brothers that we can see, if we can't keep those right, how can we keep our relationship with our Father in Heaven who we can't see!

So, even before you bring your gift to the altar, there is instruction in scripture that says to go and make things right. And part of partaking of the Lord's Table – the bread and the wine – unworthily also means; if you have something against your brother or vice versa, you've got to go make it right before you partake of the Lord's communion-- **because you are offering the gift of yourself!** (Mat. 5:23, 24)

Because, this is why: How can you have "communion" and fellowship with your brother who you see; if that relationship is broken, then how can you have full fellowship with your Father in heaven whom you can't see? So God instructs us to go and make everything right. Keep our horizontal relationships good, proper and upright. When everything is good between your fellow man, then your relationship with God will be in its fullest measure. So, the next time, before you take communion, check your spirit. Make sure you are a circumcised "Jew" ready to enter a **covenantal agreement** with God; and that also, you will check in your spirit and go to your brother or sister that perhaps you have sinned against. If there are hurts there and wounds still there, go make it right. Ask their forgiveness or even tell them, "You know, this is how you hurt me," or "You really hurt me when you said that." Make it right on your end of the relationship! The rest is up to them. Whatever they do with it is entirely up to them. You can't control that. But what you can control, and what is your responsibility is that you must go and make everything good with your brother or sister. Do this **before** you partake of the Lord's Communion.

That is God's check, but there's a deep spiritual truth in that; and that's in the symbol of the cross. If we desire to be close to God, it will be a stumbling block and a hindrance to us if our relationships with our brothers are not good, upright, and renewed—maintained in God's prescribed way.

If your brother sins against you, "How many times, Lord, should I forgive my brother?" Jesus said, "Seventy times seven." We see the sevens in those numbers – not a literal seventy times seven or four hundred ninety times... no, it is symbolic of ... always... full and complete forgiveness!

How many times do I forgive my brother who sins against me? Every time! Why? It frees you up from bitterness, and from anger, or hatred. It frees you up! But it doesn't mean for you to be a door mat for anyone to continually sin against you. No, that's not what its saying; because we should even make those things right and say, "You know, you cannot do this anymore. You cannot behave this way anymore." And in a spirit of correction, we can teach and help others in their walk with God. Keeping our relationships good with our fellow man frees us up from the bondages of unforgiveness, hatred, and bitterness.

All these things are relational things that we have with other people in our lives that God places there: with our husbands, wives, children, our family, our friends, and our co-workers. It's all relational!

God is a very relational God. **So, if we keep our horizontals right, our vertical will be right!** And then, we will be closer to God in our lives, and the desires of our heart can come true.

So, getting back to our spiritual shovels: At times we need to go back and dig up what we've buried, and deal with them properly-- God's way. Face reality. Face the truth of it. Don't run from it. Don't hide from it. Confess it and deal with it God's way. And then, when it's uncovered, God's holy fire is going to come down and consume it and completely destroy it, so that it will be non-existent. It won't ever be there anymore. You see, if it's just buried, it's still alive. We think we've given it a proper funeral and its dead, but in reality, it's only buried alive. **It still has life – it's just buried alive!**

This is where Satan can still use it against us, and bring it back to us, time and time again. It's always there affecting how we live. We relive old hurts over, and over, and over again. It's like a broken record that just gets replayed over and over. And all those hurts, and heartaches, and bad feelings – the bitterness, the hatred, the anger— everything-- all just keeps coming back. We can't seem to get free from it. Why? It's still alive. Why? We never dealt with it God's way!

Man's way is just to cover it up and bury it. Man's way says, "Time heals all wounds." But I'm here to tell you today that time **does not** heal all wounds. It's a lie from the pits of hell, and Satan would want you to believe that lie.

Time does not heal all wounds! In fact, it only makes it worse. It's the complete opposite of the truth. The reality is, the more time that goes by, and the more dirt we throw on it, the deeper it gets! Then, there's more and more dirt piled on top of it, and it just gets deeper and deeper into our spirit. Then, it gets harder to deal with – harder to uncover – with more work involved with our "spiritual shovels" to uncover it. It's going to be even more painful as time goes by.

So, God's way is to bring His fire down from heaven. God is into cremation instead of burial! He wants to bring His fire down out of heaven and consume everything in our lives that Satan could use against us that is in our old man – our old nature – all our old sins, old habits, all our old mind sets, and old beliefs. All that we are, and all that we were, in Adam. God wants to bring His fire to it all! God is into cremation instead of burial! He is an all-consuming fire; but He needs our cooperation. We need to be willing to get our shovels out. Get them out of the shed and start digging. Start uncovering all the past wrongs that Satan uses against us that literally holds us back from going any further in God.

We need to pray and seek God and ask Him for inner healing, that God will heal those wounds, and give us the strength and the courage to go back and uncover these issues in our lives God's way! We must be brutally honest with ourselves, with God, and with others.

There's one old saying that is true: "Honesty is the best policy." That one is true; because that comes from the heart of God. The truth shall set you free! When you see it as God sees it in a righteous way at the truth of the matter – in reality – that is the truth; and you deal with it as the truth of it is – the truth shall set you free. Glory to God!

God operates in the realm of light, and what is kept in darkness is kept in secret and is hidden. So when it is revealed and brought out into the open and there is knowledge – and it's confessed-- that's symbolic of God bringing His light upon it.

So, when you uncover something, and you get your spiritual shovel out, it's no longer buried and kept in darkness, but now the sun

265

can shine down upon it. It's no longer buried; it's now on the surface. God can bring His light and the truth of His word to it; and He deals with it properly and He sends His all-consuming fire down upon it and burns it up, and destroys it, so it's not there anymore. Then Satan can no longer use it against us. All of our old wounds and hurts can be healed and restored. Where we were once bruised in our soul realm – Jesus was bruised for our iniquities – for the deep, deep bruises and wounds of our spirit – God wants to heal all of those things as well. He wants to heal us in all areas: spirit, soul, and body, to be a complete man, in wholeness, and restore everything back to us that has been lost.

Sometimes we are healed in our spirit, but not in our soul realm; and then not in our bodies. So we look something like a seven, six, six or a seven, seven, six-- in our spirit, soul, and body. God wants us to be a seven, seven, seven – fully complete and whole-- receiving all that God has intended for us, today, in our lives.

You can only go as far as you want to go. Let me say that again. You can only go as far as **you** want to go. This may be a hard word for some, but it all stops here. This is as far as you can go, if you're not willing to get out your spiritual shovel! Get it out of the shed and brush the dust off of it, clean it up, and get it ready to be used; and go through this process of inner healing. This is as far as you can go in God. It's that important. God wants us to go back and deal with everything in our life. Why? To deal with everything in a righteous way – Gods way! Why? So, Satan can't use it against us!

He is repeatedly beating us up – reminding us again, and again, and again – wounding us over, and over, and over again with the same old stuff! He has beaten us up until we are just a beaten, battered, broken, wounded bride that's walking around barely even crawling.

"Not a picture of the glorious bride that I am coming back for," says the Lord God Almighty. "You're beat up. You're battered. You're wounded. You're barely crawling around. Your white dress is stained and soiled. It's ripped. It's torn. And you're not ready for the wedding! This is part of your preparation. I'm coming back for a glorious bride – one without spot or wrinkle. Will you be a part of that bride this day?" says the Lord God Almighty. Will you allow My holy fires to fall down out of heaven to consume your sacrifice, which is your entire life and being?"

266

"Even as in the days of Elijah, on the top of Mt. Carmel, it a show down of the ages: God verses Satan – the prophet of God verses the prophets of Baal and Ashera – one verses eight hundred and fifty. It was a showdown of the ages! And it has implications for you this day," says the Lord God Almighty.

"Will you be the sacrifice and place yourself on the altar of God; to allow the fires of God to come down out of heaven and consume you in your entirety-- everything that there is about you? Are you willing to allow your life to be subjected to the fire of God – to burn up in you all that should not belong – everything – the wood, the stones, even the water in the trench? It even burned up the soil. It's everything from the earth realm-- everything that is in Adam."

"Adam was formed from the dust of the earth. It speaks of all that is in our carnal nature and in our flesh. It all has to be burned up! Different picture – same concept… Circumcision is the cutting away of the flesh… different picture – same idea."

"Elijah poured buckets of water– four buckets on the sacrifice three times over, for a total of **twelve** buckets in all. Why? Twelve buckets of water speaks of God's government in the earth, Apostolic Authority, and the New Jerusalem. **The fullness of God needs to saturate the sacrifice!** God intends for us to be **saturated** in the fullness of God!"

"Will you allow yourself to be saturated in My Holy Presence?" says the Lord. "Will you allow yourself to be saturated with My Holy Spirit, place yourself on the altar of God, and yield to all that My Spirit wants to do in your life? If you will simply do that, be submissive, be yielding, be humble, and give Me everything you've got – I the Lord God will send fire from Heaven and consume your life and consume it totally-- everything about you! Everything about your old nature in Adam – all of your old being will be completely consumed by ME the Lord God on High. Is that what you want? Is that your heart's desire this day?" says the Lord God Almighty.

If it is, you can go no further until you get your spiritual shovel out. Go back-- no matter how painful – no matter how hard. God will give you the strength and courage to sort through some of these issues in your life that were never dealt with GOD'S WAY.

"Time does not heal all wounds. That is a lie. God heals all wounds! But I can't heal those wounds if you keep them from Me. I need to shine My light down upon them; so that I can touch them and heal your past. Bring all your heartaches and wounds to the foot of the cross. Don't bury them. Don't run and hide, and cover them up. Bring them to the cross and reveal them to Me," says the Lord your God.

"Confess your sins to Me, and confess your sins to one another where it is applicable; where I will lead you and guide you. You must have all your horizontal relationships right before your vertical can be right."

"I, the Lord God, will give you the strength and the courage to do all of these things; so that complete- one hundred percent- healing can come to your soul realm, to your mind, and to your heart. And I will heal all the past wounds that have ever been inflicted upon your life. And I will reverse their damage that has been brought against you. And every sin that anyone has ever committed against you will have no more affect upon you; and the curse that comes with all of that can be reversed in Jesus Christ, in His Name, and by His blood." *'They overcame him by the blood of the Lamb and by the word of their testimony…'* (Rev.12:11)

"Come to the foot of the cross and speak the word of your testimony unto ME, the Lord your God. Speak to Me what is on your heart and mind. All the things that you are concerned with, I, the Lord God, am concerned with as well. So come before Me this day, and present your case. Present to Me all that has wounded you in the past, all that makes your heart break, and all that makes you cry. Come and bring it all to Me. Don't run and hide. Don't bury them and try to hide them from Me. Come and present your case before Me, and, I the Lord God, **as you see the truth as it is**, and you **deal** with it **as it is,** the truth shall set you free."

"THE TRUTH SHALL SET YOU FREE!"
"THE TRUTH SHALL SET YOU FREE!"

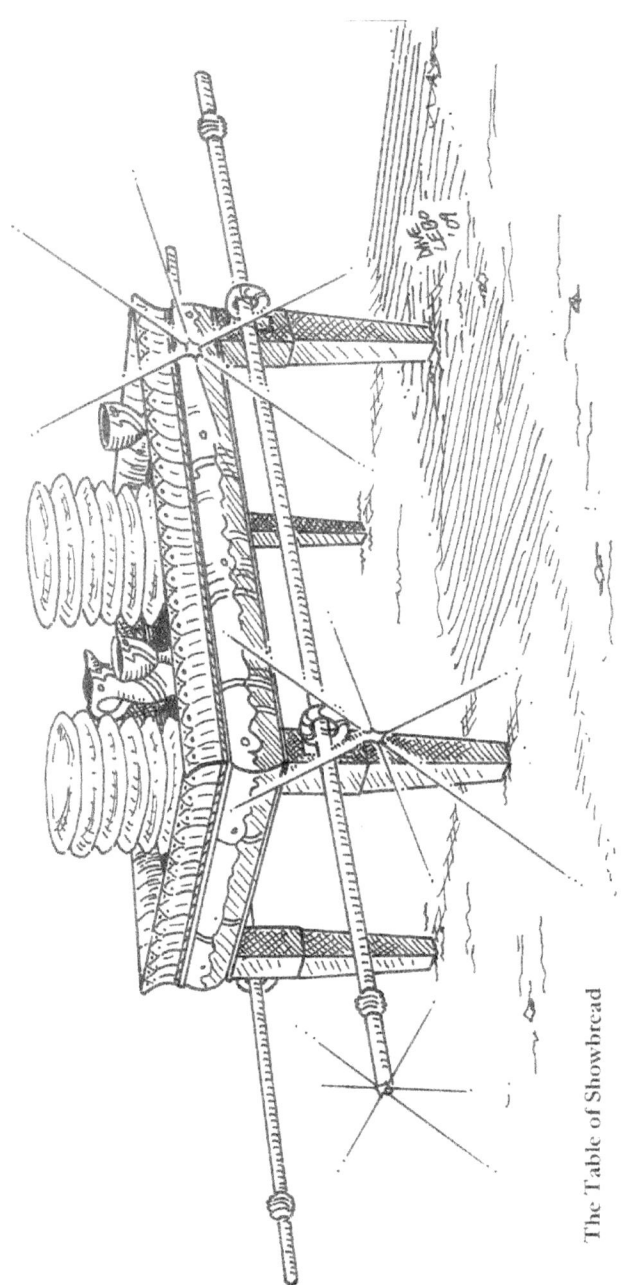

The Table of Showbread

This golden table is where the 12 loaves of bread were presented always in God's presence along with the wine for the libation. It's Bread and Wine!

269

Chapter Seven

The Number of Fullness And Completion

"...to know the love of Christ which passes knowledge; that you may be filled with all the fullness of God." Eph.3:19

"Before the beginning of time, I was. Before the beginning of you, I was. Before the end of time, I AM; and before the end of time, I will be. I am the fullness of all things," says the Lord God Almighty. "I am the fullness of all things. The totality of everything put together all wrapped up into one. Before there was anything, I AM. Before the creation of the world, I AM. Before the division of light and dark, of daytime and night time, I AM. Before all the creation of the earth, when I raised the mountains and lowered the valleys, when I formed all the animals and the birds and fish, I AM. Before I formed man on the sixth day of creation, I AM."

"And on the seventh day, Halleluiah, I AM, that I AM, that I AM."" I AM THE SEVENTH DAY! I AM THE SEVENTH DAY!" "I am the fullness of everything-- everything-- the complete fullness of the universe-- everything known to man and everything unknown. If you can grasp this concept in your mind, it's brought by the Spirit of the Lord, and only discerned by the Spirit."

"I am the fullness of everything in its totality; which means: I AM THE SEVENTH DAY – ALWAYS!!!   I am the seventh day in eternity past. I am the seventh day in eternity present. And I am the seventh day in eternity future. I always was, and always will be the Seventh Day!" Halleluiah. Glory to God!

"Seven represents the fullness and completeness, and the perfection of all things. You see a 'seven' in the seven days of creation at the beginning, and you see many, many 'sevens' in the book of Revelation at the completeness, the fullness, and at the end of all things – in the summation of time – in the end of this dispensation and at the beginning of the next."

"There are many sevens all throughout the holy scriptures from Genesis to Revelation. Seven is perhaps one of the most used numbers in all of scripture next to the number one, which speaks of ME, I the Lord God, the creator of the heavens and the earth. I am one!"

"But in the beginning, I divided time for man's sake, not for My sake. Remember, My time is not your time, and a thousand years is as one day. You're not in the same time zone as God is. Halleluiah! A thousand upon a thousand years is as one day to God. For eternity; there is no time. It goes on forever in both directions – eternity past and eternity future; but for man, I divided the days into seven days; and one can see 'sevens' all throughout scripture, time and time again."

It's very significant when there are numbers used. It's not by accident. Any time you read the scriptures, be aware of the numbers that are mentioned.

"In our natural world during the days of creation, I spoke, 'light', and light was. I spoke and formed the earth and all of the planets."   We see the number seven in this creation in the natural. Even today, there are seven major continents in the world. It's evidence of our creator. It was once said that if a sailor sailed across the world he would have sailed the "seven seas". There are seven major bodies of water; many, many more in modern times that have been named since then; but still a basis of "seven seas" in our oceans. Musically, there are seven notes, A – G that in any combination of those notes gives us all the beautiful melodies of all the songs in all their different varieties. They are all made up of just seven notes.

Even artistically speaking, in the colors of the rainbow and in the full spectrum of color, there are only seven colors. Some of you may remember the acronym: R.O.Y.G.B.I.V. from your art classes. Red, orange, yellow, green, blue, indigo, and violet: they are all colors of the full spectrum. Perfect light – pure light – when it is run through a prism reflects the full spectrum of color on a wall or a ceiling. Remember when you were a kid, playing those games hanging prisms and looking at all the beautiful light and color on the wall? All seven of those colors are present in pure light. And you see, that all reflects the creator, for "God is light and in Him is no darkness at all." (IJn.1:5) It's symbolic of the presence of God in all His fullness. All that He "IS" dwells in pure light; and we can see Him revealed in these seven full colors of the spectrum and the rainbow that corresponds to the seven-fold dimension of the Holy Spirit.

Even as man measures a full week, it's seven days. Everyone lives every day, week by week, year by year; but it's all broken down into a weekly measurement of time – seven days.

We hear the expression, "We all live week to week". It's all broken down into the number seven. It gives evidence of our creator. Even in time, and that seventh day is very, very, significant; because, God is the seventh day. God is built right into our weekly time cycles-- every seven days! Remember back in the Book of Genesis during the days of creation, God came to the seventh day... what did He do? He rested and then He blessed it; and it was Holy! It was the only day of the week that was blessed and holy.

This number "seven" comes from the Hebrew word "shevah" or from the root word "savah" which means: to be "full" or "satisfied", and it is derived also from the word "shaba" which means to be "complete".

So, when we get that Hebrew understanding of this number, we see how it links with the fullness of all things, and that God is the fullness and completion of all things.

GOD IS THE NUMBER SEVEN!

It is perhaps His favorite number – SEVEN. You see, because all things are in Him; and He is the fullness of **all** things. So, the number seven represents that thought and that idea. **Everything is in God.** It always was, always will be, and always is-- even today. But to give us some understanding of this word and how it applies to us today, God was always the seventh day – the fullness of all things. So, then He sent His son Jesus to the earth.

He is the "I AM, that I AM, that I AM."

He is "YAHWEH" incarnate. Remember, He was fully God and fully man in the same body. So, God came down to the earth; and God is the fullness of all things. So too, Christ is the fullness of all things. In Jesus Christ, we, too, can become full, complete, and satisfied; and not lacking in any one thing. He came to this earth, born of the virgin Mary, fulfilled the law to every letter and every detail, lived a perfect life, was sinless, then died on a cross for you and me; so that all of the fullness that He possessed could be transferred to us!

Jesus Christ is the "Seventh Day"; and in Christ you, too, can be a "Seventh Day Creation". You can be a seven in your spirit, a seven in your soul, and a seven in your body.

We can find the number seven all throughout scripture, from Genesis to Revelation and everywhere in between, in many, many, different applications. The number seven and its multiples are used close to six hundred times in the bible. Remember, Christ is the "Word". He is the fullness of the word; so, all of the word of God points to Christ-- Himself... all of it...in its entirety. It all speaks of Christ! So, when you're reading the bible and you're looking at a particular story, or ceremony, or feast, in every detail, it all points to an application of Christ, an aspect of Christ that is being revealed. That's how complicated He is, because there's so much in Him. It's hard for us to understand all of Him at one time. So, we are all learning. We're all growing. We're all trying to draw closer to Christ. We're on this journey until we are taken home. We should be rediscovering fresh revelation, and fresh manna, along the way. It should always be exciting, new, and fresh. There is so much to God, our walks with Him should never get old or boring.

As you have read through the scriptures, you can most likely recall many sevens in all the different stories. Just a few examples listed here briefly are: a total of seven individual feasts in the Old Testament; Jacob worked seven years for each wife – Leah and Rachael; Pharaoh's dream, interpreted by Joseph, had seven cows eaten by seven cows with seven years of plenty and famine. Even multiples of seven: Daniel's prayer was held up 21 days in the heavens by the Prince of Persia; Moses father –in-law, the priest of Midian, had seven daughters. One of the most famous of all that we are very familiar with is the battle of Jericho. Joshua marched around the city seven times on the seventh day with seven trumpets blown by seven priests. It's a picture of fullness and completion.

All throughout scripture we can see many sevens: Three Hebrew boys in the fiery furnace heated up seven times hotter; Elijah prayed seven times to fulfill the word of God that had already been given to him. In the Tabernacle of Moses, we find the seven lamps of the candlestick that corresponds to the seven fold expressions of the Holy Spirit recorded in Isaiah chapter eleven, and also in Revelation chapter three-- the seven spirits of God that are around His throne.

Jesus spoke on "How many times should I forgive my brother?" Seventy times seven: it's complete forgiveness. Solomon took seven years to complete the temple. God is building a temple today, but it is a temple of people. We as believers are a part of God's tabernacle – His house – His temple – His habitation today. You, as a believer in Christ, are a part of the larger, corporate, dwelling place of God.

There are seven abominations that anger God, in the book of Proverbs. Also, the high priest would apply the blood to the Ark of the Covenant seven times on the Day of Atonement. Many, many, times we can find this number "seven" throughout scripture.

All of these numbers are there for a reason. They're not just plopped in there for no reason at all. We need to begin to look at details, details, details. We also need to begin to put some pictures together, from Genesis to Revelation, and all throughout the scriptures. The Old Testament wasn't just written for those people way back when. They are still written for our examples today, and we need to go back as the church of God and begin to take a second look at all of these pictures in the Old Testament. Because, why? They all speak of Christ. They all point to Christ. If we want a deeper understanding and revelation of Christ and have a deeper relationship with our God, we will look at these deeper truths and pictures that reveal God. They are all there for us! Remember, the word became flesh and dwelt among us. Jesus is every written word in every book of the bible – all sixty six. I know we all have our favorite books and our favorite chapters; but remember, it's all pointing to Christ.

So, I challenge you to begin to read some books of the Bible that you may even shy away from, because they're too hard, or they speak of something you don't want to read, or maybe is not very happy to read about. All of it points to Christ! So, I challenge you: read some of the Minor Prophets and even some of the harder books like Ezekiel and Daniel. Read them. Pray through them. Ask the Lord to shine His Holy Spirit down upon you and give you illumination to understand these words from God. Because, I'm telling you – Church – we are really missing a lot of the meat of the word through these deeper truths revealed in the Old Testament. We need to go back and re-read them, and rediscover some things that, in some cases, have totally been missed. We tend to get locked in and focus on some of the same things over and over. We also seem to focus on the New Testament and just forget the rest. But the Old Testament is much bigger than the New Testament. So, I feel in my heart, we are really missing a lot. And God wants us to pick our bibles back up; but this time, open it to the Old Testament and realize it's not just for those folks way back when. It is for you today. It is for you today! There is an abundance of fresh manna awaiting you in the Old Testament!

Jesus Is The Perfect Seven

"I AM the I AM, that I AM." As God gave that revelation to Moses, God was fully there. All of God was there in the burning bush: God the Father, God the Son, and God the Holy Spirit. Even as they were altogether in Genesis at Creation as revealed in the word

"Eloheim" being the plural form of God; so, too, the word "Eloheim" has connections with the word "Yahweh".

And in this burning bush, God is, and He was, and He always will be. That same revelation given to Moses: the "I AM that I AM" is given again in the person of Jesus. He came to this earth as "Emmanuel": God with us. He was God incarnate. Jesus spoke seven times in the gospel of John:

1.   I am the Bread of Life. (Jn. 6:35)
2.   I am the Light of the World. (8:12)
3.   I am the Gate. (10:9)
4.   I am the Good Shepherd. (10:11,14)
5.   I am the Resurrection and the Life. (11:25)
6.   I am the Way, the Truth, and the Life. (14:6)
7.   I am the True Vine. (15:1-5)

This is the only gospel that records this aspect of God. Jesus is "Yahweh" incarnate, would be a better way to describe this personality of God. This Hebrew name for God, it may be best said, that it is God's proper name. One of the earliest revelations given of who God is was given to Moses at the burning bush. And Moses didn't even quite know who He was. Moses had a personal one-on-one encounter with the Most High God in all of His fullness, in all that He was, and is, and is to come. He is "Yahweh". This name comes from the Hebrew verb which means: "to be" or "to live"; and it has direct ties with the idea of life itself.

All throughout scripture when you see the word "Lord" translated in all capitals it would be better translated as "Yahweh". And I think that we do ourselves a great disservice by not translating all of the names for God as they should be in scripture as Yahweh or Eloheim, or El Shaddai, or El Elyon, or Jehovah Nissi, or Jehovah Rophe, and others. We need to resurrect all of God's names again, and begin to teach the body of Christ this diversity in who God is that is revealed through His many names, because each one speaks of a different personality and activity of God that has been lost. So, if we have only one word for God, it takes away from all of these other descriptions and pictures of who God really is!

Jesus: He is "Yahweh" incarnate. He is the fullness of God. All that God is—everything-- is also in His son Jesus Christ. It is through Jesus that makes all that God is available to us today! Jesus is God coming to the earth. Sometimes I think we lose sight of that fact.

Yes, He was God's son, but He was not anything less. He was not lower than God the Father-- not lower in any way, shape, or form. He was fully God in the earth. So, all that God is, Jesus was and is: in all of God's aspects, His omniscience, His being all-powerful, all-knowing, without beginning or end. He is the alpha and omega. Everything you can think of. He was without sin in the world, born of the Virgin Mary. His father was God himself, while His mother was fully a woman. Jesus was fully God, and fully a man in His earthly life.

Remember, in Genesis 3:15 God's promise to the serpent was that *"I will place enmity between you and the woman, and between your seed and her seed."* It's the promise of the Messiah! The flesh nature would be interrupted. It was stopped in Jesus. He would no longer carry the nature of Adam – his father, in all of its falleness, in all of its wickedness, and in all of its corruption.

Jesus could only do good in His lifetime. Whatever He heard the Father saying and doing, that's what He would do. Jesus only ever did good in the world and only ever spoke good. If they would have seen Him for who He was, they would not have crucified the Lord of Glory. But what Satan meant for harm, God would turn it all for good. God had a plan all along!

Jesus is the fullness of all things. He was present at creation. We see this in the word "Eloheim". Then He came to the earth in the fullness of God. He was able to speak even to the storm and calm it. His disciples marveled, "Even the waves obey Him". Who is this man? There was no sickness or disease that was beyond His power to heal or touch. Every single person that came to Christ-- all were healed. Jesus never turned anyone away that wanted to be touched by God. He never turned them away without receiving what they needed.

He is the fullness of all things – everything-- perfectly holy-- perfectly sinless. He was, and is, and is to come, the fullness of all things. He fulfilled the law to its very letter. He fulfilled everything that He was sent to do. He accomplished His mission. He completed the work that He was sent to do, and He did all of that work for you and I.

Jesus came not to be set up as an earthly king and overthrow the Roman government or any others in the world. You see, they were looking for the messiah to do just that in the natural. That's why they missed Him.

Jesus said, "My kingdom is not of this world". In fact, "the kingdom of God", Jesus said, "is within you", a very simple yet profound statement. They were looking for the kingdom to come in a physical sense, but this kingdom Jesus would bring lies within the hearts of all men. It is a spiritual kingdom and it's a spiritual work that He does within the life of every believer.

It's interesting that all the physical temples have been destroyed. You see, God is building a new temple, a new tabernacle, a new habitation that He can live in and dwell in. That habitation happens to be the individual believer and also the body of Christ corporately. God wants to make His abode – His dwelling place in your heart and life; and He wants to come in all His fullness – in His entirety. He wants to come in and take over-- everything; because He's the king, and everything else is subordinate to Him. That's the process in the life of the believer. We are all on this journey together. And if you have become saved and asked Jesus into your heart, God has begun a process in you-- of coming and setting up His kingship in your life and taking over. He wants to rule and reign in your heart and life. Life is all about us relinquishing our control over to Him; and that's a process that takes some time. It doesn't all happen overnight. We still try to hang on to things, but then we begin to understand and realize: **"Hey wow, God wants it all!"**

He does His work little by little as we can handle it and as we grow in God. It's that whole process of taking the Promised Land – little by little – step by step – battle by battle. We are all going to have our battles in this life till the day we die. That's not ever going to stop. But, the good news is that we get the victory through our Lord Jesus Christ. And in every battle that we face, we can be victorious; and, yes, we can be "Overcomers" by His Spirit!

"...we do not war according to the flesh. For The weapons of our warfare are not carnal, but mighty in God for pulling down strongholds." (I Cor. 10:3, 4)

So, for anything that you may face in your life, God has an answer. And if you'll battle your way through it, you can be an overcomer. You can be victorious! God has given us everything pertaining to life and godliness. (II Pet. 1:3) He's given us everything we need, including His very own Spirit. Jesus said, *"...if I do not go away, the Helper will not come to you; but if I depart, I will send Him to you."* (Jn.16:7)

He's not only given us the word of God, He's given us the author of the word. He will be the teacher of the word, and He will

279

lead us and guide us into all the great mysteries in the word of God-- the things that we don't understand. It all comes through spiritual discernment. You see, we have to begin to ask the Holy Spirit to enlighten the word of God to us. And the things that we don't understand, we ask Him to reveal these deeper truths and these mysteries to us so we can get His wisdom, knowledge, and understanding of them. That is a promise in the word of God. The Holy Spirit will be your teacher and lead you into all truth! (Jn. 16:13)

And yes, there are great teachers in the kingdom. Yes, learn from them. There are great apostles in the kingdom – learn from them. There are evangelists, pastors and prophets in the five-fold ministry – learn from them. But don't rely on them exclusively for your complete diet. Take what they say and praise God. That's one meal. But to get three meals a day, you need to learn how to fish on your own and not have people give you fish all the time. This is available to every child of God. The Holy Spirit will lead you and guide you into all truth.

Every answer that you need – "God IS". Every problem that you face in your life today – "God IS". For every obstacle, every hindrance, every wall, and even bigger-- every mountain – God is your answer to everything that you face in your life today!

So, no matter what life may throw at you, no matter what Satan may throw at you, or what other people may throw at you, you can stand firm and be strong, full in God, having everything that you need to travel through this life's journey, and to make it home to the wedding supper of the lamb. You have everything that you need available to you.

In the pages to follow, we are going to discover how all of this fullness of God that is in the Father, the Son, and the Holy Spirit can trickle down and be a positive force and reality in your life.

God is the Living God. He died physically, but He rose again, and He is alive today. Though you may not see Him as often as you would like, or hear His audible voice as you would like, or even have Him send signs down out of heaven as you would like – **HE STILL IS.** He is ALIVE and well today, and He is concerned about every detail of your life and with what is happening on planet earth. He has not forgotten you. He has not forgotten the plans that He has for you, and He has not forgotten about the plans that He has in a broader spectrum for this nation and for this world. He holds everything in the palms of His hands; and He will fulfill everything in His written word in His time. He had the first word and He will have the last word; and not one word in between, of His, will fall to the ground.

"For as the rain comes down, and the snow from heaven, and do not return there, but water the earth, and make it bring forth and bud, that it may give seed to the sower and bread to the eater, so shall My word be that goes forth from My mouth; it shall not return to Me void, but it shall accomplish what I please, and it shall prosper in the thing for which I sent it." (Is.55:10, 11)

I want to encourage you today with this word: You will find Him and see Him if you seek for Him with all of your heart. Stop looking with your eyes, and ears, and all of your physical senses. Stop trying to figure God out before you trust Him. If you will pray to Him and ask Him to reveal Himself to you – He will. There is a faith work that He wants to do in your heart. If you only have a very small measure of faith, or you feel like you don't have hardly any at all, begin with that, and pray to God and say, "Lord, increase my faith", just as the disciples did. "God, increase my faith. I want to know you more. I want to see you in my life more."

If you will pray just that simple little prayer, God will come in and He will honor that prayer. Because Revelation 3:20 says, *"I stand at the door and knock. If anyone hears My voice and opens the door, I will come in and eat with him, and he with Me."*

Will you simply do just that? He's knocking on the door of your heart. Will you open the door and let Him in today? Will you accept Jesus and all that He has done for you into your life and say, "Yes, Lord, Yes. I believe you and I want all that you have for me in my life. I accept you and I accept everything you've done for me, and I want you to come and live in my heart today and be Lord of My life."

Will you do that today? He will come in, in all that He is, and in all of His fullness. It can be yours in this lifetime! You don't have to die and cross over to be in the "Promised Land". You can be in the "Promised Land" of God, today-- in this lifetime-- and experience all that God has for you and His people—now!

You Are The Seventh Day Creation

"All that I AM is yours. Halleluiah! Somebody died and left you something. Your inheritance as a son or daughter of the Most High God – as a descendant of Christ Himself-- IS EVERYTHING! All that I AM, that I AM, that I AM, is yours-- this day," says the Lord God Almighty. Halleluiah! Glory to God.

"My Son Jesus, He came down to this earth to complete a work that I did not finish at creation. I reserved the seventh day for no work. Why? Because I knew man would fall. I had a plan. My plan of redemption was a plan in eternity past. I reserved the seventh day as a day of no work and for rest, and I declared it to be a holy, blessed day in the earth. Why? Because, I was going to send MY SON down to this earth to complete a work that I had begun."

"My 'Seventh Day' work, spiritually, is in Jesus Christ. All the work that He accomplished in His earth walk, He came to do for you. And even now, I am completing a work in you that is an extension of His earthly ministry in the earth in this world-- through My Holy Spirit," says the Lord God Almighty.

"So, I have a work to do in you through My Spirit", says the Lord. "This is an extension of the work that Christ did in the earth; which is also an extension of the work that I did in the first week at the beginning. So, the work that I desire to do in the human heart is My 'Seventh Day Work'. *He who has begun a good work in you will complete it until the day of Jesus Christ.*" (Phil.1:6)

"GOD IS THE BEGINNING OF YOU AND HE WILL BE THE END OF YOU.   HE IS THE BEGINNING OF YOUR FAITH, AND HE WILL BE THE END OF YOUR FAITH."

When you came to know Christ as your Lord and Savior, that was just the beginning. God began a work in you that day. He is going to work on you in many, many, different facets and ways. Every day afterwards, He's going to put you through the fire. He's going to put you on the anvil and bring the hammer of His word. He's going to hammer on you and hammer you out!

Gold comes from the earth. It's pretty much unusable as it is. It's just a rough rock – a metal in the earth. But it's rare; it's precious; and we value it very highly. It must be subjected to fire. The only way to clean gold is to put it through the fire. It's the only way to burn out every impurity-- every piece of dirt that is of the earth. It also needs to be hammered. In scripture, you see several times some things referred to as a "beaten work". It had to be hammered. They would use it in gold overlays-- very thin applications so it could be laid over something else and made into something beautiful. So, for you to be a vessel of gold as God desires, you're going to have to be subjected to the "hammer" and the "fire". (Jer. 23:29)

You see, that's a process that God brings every believer through. He doesn't do all of His work on the very first day that you come to know Christ. We get impatient, and we want it all now. We all want it quick. We live in a microwave world where you push a button and get what you want. Remember, God's time is not our time.

IT TAKES TIME to form a diamond in the heart of the earth. That same diamond a little earlier was a lump of coal; but it is formed with great heat and pressure. So when you're under pressure and the trials of life and the sufferings of God come your way, you're being put through the fire. It is to accomplish God's purposes in you!

In I Peter1:6,7, he writes, *"In this you greatly rejoice though now for a little while you may have had to suffer grief in all kinds of trials, these have come so that your faith – of greater worth than gold which perishes even though refined by fire – may be proved genuine and may result in praise, glory, and honor when Jesus Christ is revealed."*

It's in the mysteries of God that He does His work. Sometimes the greatest times of our lives with the greatest spiritual growth comes out of the hardest testings, the deepest sufferings, the most difficult tribulations, and the greatest of trials. We're going to see this in scripture a little later on.

God is trying to form you into a "vessel of gold" to carry His divine presence and glory in the earth. He is going to burn up all the wood, the stubble, the hay, the chaff – everything – the rocks, even the dirt – everything that is of this world-- pictures of an earthly nature in Adam. Remember, Adam was formed from the dust of the earth, so the things of the earth realm speak of that nature – things in the natural realm. God wants to get rid of all of that and to do so, there are different processes that He will bring us through; but the ultimate goal is to bring you in and make you into that vessel of gold.

If you remember, the Ark of the Covenant was one of these vessels. It was made of Shittim wood of the earth overlaid with gold.

This pointed to Christ having two natures, being fully man and fully God. The wood is of the earth realm and speaks of His human nature, while the gold overlay speaks of His divine nature being fully God.

We're in the same boat. We have two natures as well. We have an old nature – our flesh nature in Adam – and we have a divine nature that has begun to grow in us. God wants His nature to arise in us and be one hundred percent full and complete. The other nature in Adam that we were born with needs to go down to zero percent; or as close to zero as we can get in this lifetime. That is the process that God works in us. We may never reach a full zero percent, but maybe a tenth of one percent.

Theoretically speaking, that's what we need to progress towards. That is the truth of His word, and we need to walk and move in that direction. God has made a way! So what we cannot do – could never do in ourselves – God sent His son – HE DID THE WORK THAT WE COULD NEVER DO!! HALLELUIA!!!

He went to the cross and was crucified in our place; so we could be reunited with our creator-- with our Father in heaven. We could never do that. We were in the world... lost... floundering around... looking for ways to get reunited with our heavenly Father. And man throughout history has tried many, many, ways to get back in touch with God to no avail.

And I'm here to tell you today that none of them work. God made **the** way; and that way is Jesus Christ and Him crucified!

HE IS THE WAY, THE TRUTH, AND THE LIFE; NO MAN COMES TO THE FATHER BUT BY HIM. YOU CANNOT WORK YOUR WAY TO HOLINESS. You cannot work your way back to fullness or completeness.

Why are you lacking? Why are you wanting? Why are you not satisfied? You have to come God's way! You've been striving to come your own way. YOU CAN'T COME YOUR WAY! You've got to come God's way. It's His pattern – His blueprint – His plan of redemption. You must come by the way of the cross and believe on the Lord Jesus Christ and you shall be saved. That's the beginning of it all. You must – for all other processes in your life that God wants to do – you must always do it God's way.

And as for our flesh nature, I'm sorry to say, it has to come through the fire, and through the water of cleansing, and also be subjected to the hammer of God's word as in Jeremiah 23:29. *"Is not*

My word like a fire", says the Lord, *"and like a hammer that breaks the rock in pieces?"* The word beats upon us with such force it breaks every rock to pieces that was set up in our life as a stronghold of the enemy. There is no easy way to get rid of our carnal nature – our flesh – our carnal mind or anything in Adam. It will be a hard way to come; but if you give it all up and continue to repent and seek God – spiritually speaking – it all comes easy. When you know the principles of surrender, brokenness, humility, longsuffering and the purposes of trials and testings – God is at work in all of these things and He's going to do a work in you if you respond in the appropriate way. You have one of two choices to make: When tough times come, you can cut and run, and it will only get harder; or you can press in and get a hold of God and draw closer to Him, then He will bring His "Refiner's Fire" in you.

But, the choice is yours. You can go one way or the other. I pray that you choose life, because it is a life and death situation. If you choose to cut and run, it will mean death to you spiritually, physically, emotionally, and in every other way in your life-- you'll see death roll in. But if you choose God, He is going to bring life to the situation, in every way: spiritually, emotionally, mentally and physically – in every aspect of life. God will bring nothing but life, life, life; so you can be a **seven** in your spirit, a **seven** in your soul, and a **seven** in your body. You'll be a **777—complete wholeness!**

And with that series of numbers, we see the number seven repeated three times over. Remember, three speaks of God and the trinity, and we see that seven is the number of fullness and completion. It's God working His divine nature in you in every aspect of life to where you can be a full seven, seven, seven – a "Seventh Day Creation" in that day. You can experience all three sevens on the same day—the seventh day!

We can see many pictures in scripture of this seven fold fullness of God that He wants for His people. One of the most well known stories in scripture has to be the battle of Jericho. We've even had that story in this book in previous chapters and you're all very familiar with the story by now I'm sure, so we'll just cut to the highlights.

In this story, we had seen the complete deliverance for the body of Christ and for the individual believer. There are many sevens pictured here. They marched around the city seven times on the

285

seventh day, blowing seven trumpets of ram's horns by seven priests with the Ark of the Covenant going before them.

You are a "Seventh Day Creation". You have **complete deliverance** at your disposal. If you'll just learn how to walk in it day by day, even as they had to walk around the city of Jericho once a day for six days and then on the seventh day, they had to walk seven times around the city. You must walk it out step by step, day by day.

If it doesn't come the first day, it may come the second day. You see with God, we must just believe His word. We don't know when it's coming, but we must walk in that direction. There is complete deliverance waiting for the child of God; today. I know that word deliverance scares a lot of people, but I want you to know today that it's a word to be embraced, not to be afraid of. Welcome it! It's a good thing! We should pray to the Lord our God that He would deliver us from all evil. In fact, it is in the Lord's Prayer where He instructed His disciples to pray: "...deliver us from the evil one." (Mat 6:13) That's not only external evil – it's internal also-- all of our old nature in Adam that Satan can use against us and use as instruments of sin in the world instead of instruments of righteousness.

The next picture we can see in scripture is that of a **complete atonement.** The high priest had to enter into the Holy of Holies only once a year on the Great Day of Atonement for the sins of the nation. He had to apply the blood from the sacrifice that was slain in the outer court at the brazen altar and bring the blood and transfer it to the Ark of the Covenant. But he had to apply it **seven** times to the mercy seat! What is the significance of this you may ask? It pointed to Christ and the perfect, complete atonement that He would pay for on the cross at Calvary. He paid a full price. He didn't pay just half the price or just part of the price – just a little bit for your spirit or a little bit for your soul. He paid the full price so that the total man can be bought back – so you can be redeemed- 100%. He paid the full price at Calvary. These applications of the blood on the mercy seat coincide with the bleedings of Christ. It is said that Jesus Christ had seven bleeding spots on His body in all His sufferings. I believe that these two ideas go together here; and it's a perfect picture of complete atonement. Christ had bleeding on His back from the whipping, bleeding on His head from the crown of thorns, both hands and both feet from the nails at the cross, and one final spear in His side from the guard checking to see if He was still alive. He had seven bleeding locations altogether on

286

His body, that I believe reveals to us this same picture of complete atonement.

Complete atonement – you see, many would believe that God is only concerned about our spirit man. But we have to take it another step further. God is also concerned about the soul realm of our being – our thoughts, our emotions, our intellect, our ego – all of these things. God wants to heal these things as well – a complete inner healing of every area of our being. And then lastly, some may not believe that God has made a way and a provision for the **complete healing** of our bodies. That is also in the atonement. A good picture of this in the scriptures is seen in the life of Naaman where the number seven is repeated again in II Kings chapter five. Naaman was the commander of the army of the king of Aram. He was not even a Hebrew; but he had heard of the man of God by the name of Elisha. A young Israelite girl who served Naaman's wife advised him to go see this man of God in hopes that he would heal Naaman of his leprosy.

Elisha had told him to do an unusual thing: *"Go wash yourself* **seven** *times in the Jordan, and your flesh will be restored and you will be cleansed."*(II Kings5:10 NIV) But Naaman became angry at this order. He didn't want to go jump in this muddy Jordan River to be healed. That sounded too crazy! He didn't want God to do it that way. So Naaman's servants helped him out with his conflict and advised him to just listen and obey what Elisha had told him to do. Just do it!

A lot of times we do the same and question God's ways and means. We want to do it our way; or we have a preconceived idea on how God's going to do something. Simply put, if we will just walk in obedience to what God says – that's the simplest way I can put it. **Do What He Says!** Walk in obedience; and if it's God, it's going to happen.

So here Naaman listens to Elisha-- the man of God. He goes and jumps in the Jordan River how many times? It was **seven** times: a picture of fullness and completion. Naaman – on the seventh time receives his full healing and *"his flesh was restored and became clean like that of a young boy."*(v.14) He was healed of leprosy which was considered a very dreaded disease in those days.

There are many other pictures of sevens in the word of God. One is complete prayer in the life of Elijah at Mt. Carmel at the showdown of the ages. He had gone up against the prophets of Baal and Asherah when he called down fire from heaven to consume the

287

sacrifice. God had promised that the rains would come. So shortly after this, Elijah didn't stand idly by and watch the world go around and wait for the clouds. No, what did Elijah do? He bowed his face to the ground with His face between his knees, and prayed **seven** times. It's another picture of fullness and completion: **Complete intercession.**

He prayed **until** the promise came. We need to stay on the course that leads us to the fulfillment of the word. We need to pray **until** the promise of God comes to pass. Many give up before the promise comes. Many quit and give up on the word – on the promise. I want to encourage you today. If the Lord has given you a personal promise, don't give up on it. You have got to pray **until**. *"Has He said, and will He not do?" (Num.23:19)*

Get with some anointed people that will pray with you and believe God. Remember chapter two and the power of agreement. The church needs to bring back the emphasis of prayer and intercession. Embrace the intercessor! The prayer meeting can be the most powerful, most important meeting that you'll ever have. Because without prayer – nothing happens! WITHOUT PRAYER – NOTHING HAPPENS!

Another picture we see in scripture is **complete purification** with the three Hebrew boys in the fiery furnace. This is perhaps one of the most important of all that many would like to avoid; but we must go through the fire. We've touched on it in previous chapters. The three Hebrew boys dancing in the fire – there's a fourth man in the fire. That fourth man in the fire is Jesus Christ himself. Old Nebuchadnezer heated up their furnace seven times hotter.

Sometimes Satan himself will try to heat up your furnace. Old Nebuchadnezer – he was a type of anti-Christ in the Old Testament. Satan, himself, will come along and try to heat up your furnace. And you may wonder: "Why Lord, why? Why am I facing what I am facing?" But God, in His infinite wisdom, has a plan for you, and He knows it involves a refiner's fire. And you're going to come out of that fire as a vessel of gold. Remember, Shadrach, Meshach and Abednego came out of that fire without even a hair on their heads being singed. But their inner man- their spirit man was burned to a crisp! Halleluiah!

You see, that's the workings of God. He wants to burn everything in us completely to a crisp that is not God. And I know many of you may be foreign to that concept; but that is the truth of

God's word, nevertheless. **God is in the fire business!** He is an all consuming fire. He is the fire! What Satan meant for harm, God will turn completely around. He will reverse it – completely – and then use it against him later. So, that fiery trial that you are facing right now, God's going to turn it for good; and there will be a blessing when you come out of the fire. It will be for the furtherance and the advancement of the kingdom in you and also on the outside of you. We're going to talk more about this a little later on.

We can also see a picture of **complete forgiveness** that Jesus gave in this example. How many times do I forgive my brother? Jesus answered, "seventy times seven". It's not a literal seventy times seven; but used figuratively, it means: as many times as it takes. It's the number of fullness, completion and perfection. Remember, Jesus also said, *"…if you do not forgive, neither will your Father in heaven forgive your trespasses."* (Mk.11:26) So, it's directly tied in to our forgiveness that we receive from our Heavenly Father.

There is also in scripture the picture of **complete consecration** unto God. I'll use this example of the life of Samson. Samson had seven locks of uncut hair—an outward sign of what was supposed to be an inward devotion. Not many people may know that or remember that about him, but you can read it for yourself in Judges16:19. This number again is very significant. Samson was a Nazarite from birth set apart unto God to live a life of holiness. We know that Samson failed many, many, times and he didn't fully complete the work that God had given him to do. Quite a sad story actually.

There is not any one of us, I'm sure, that would want to stand before God one day, and know that we didn't finish everything that God had put our hands to. But I want you to know today that we can finish the work that God gives us to do. We can be successful. We can be victorious in Christ, and see the promises of God fulfilled in our lives. We'll talk about Samson more a little later on as well.

I want you to know that you can be a **777**, in your spirit, soul, and body; and you can be full, complete, perfect and satisfied in every way, shape, and form in your entire life and being. Everything that God IS-- we can be too! All that He has can be ours!

Somebody died and left you something, and that inheritance is yours-- today-- this side of heaven. You don't have to die to get it all. But it is reserved for you, and it is kept , and it includes complete

289

healing of your inner man, your mental state of being, throwing out all of the old mindsets, and even includes the healing of your physical body – any and all diseases no matter how big or small.

But there are some deep, deep, truths that the body of Christ needs to break into that they have been ignoring for many, many, years. And you are suffering the consequences of it. Why are you lacking? Why are you found wanting? Why are you not satisfied? Because you're not doing it God's way. You're trying to do it your way. And until you are broken of that, this is as far as you go.

Unless you are willing to be broken of all of your past ideologies and old forms of teaching, dead religion, and the traditions of men – if you're not willing to let loose of all of that – this is as far as you go. But if you're willing to come further, I'll take you further and deeper than you ever thought imaginable!

There is a "Promised Land" of God this side of heaven that He wants His people to experience-- now! Today! So, if you'll come with me, we'll go to the deeper places. We'll go to the higher places-- where the eagles are afraid to fly!

Seven Lamps

"Church of the Living God: Where are your 'Seven Lamps'? Where are they? You are to have all seven lamps lit with wicks trimmed, and lamps filled with oil to be burning continually! They are NOT BURNING CONTINUALLY! You're letting them go out, and you're fumbling around in the dark just trying to light one or two; and you're not filling them all with oil as I have commanded My priesthood to do."

"Your **WICKS** – ALL SEVEN – need trimmed! They have been just smoking, and smoking, and smoking. There is no light. It is but a small glow – an ember-- and it's about to go out! Allow ME, the Lord Your God, to come and trim your wicks, and fill your lamps with the oil of My anointing so that your lamps can shine brightly as I have called you to shine."

"Church of the Living God: You have been living in a realm of My Spirit in the Holy Place, but this place – it has been dark. You have not lit all seven lamps and kept the wicks trimmed; so that your lamps will shine brightly unto the Lord."

You see, the priest, he had to do everything in the Holy Place by lamp light. There was absolutely no sunlight in this chamber. So he had to minister at the Table of Showbread by lamplight, and break the bread and pour out the libation offering unto the Lord. He had to offer up incense at the golden altar, solely by lamplight. He had to take the blood of the sacrifice into the third chamber by lamplight. Everything that He did, He did by divine fire that came from the Brazen Altar. Remember, the glory of God fell at the Tabernacle in the Holy of Holies, and then it shot out from there and consumed the sacrifice on the Brazen Altar. God started the fire; but it was up to the priesthood to maintain the fire. The lamps were to continually burn throughout their generations.

"God has lit the fire of the church on the day of Pentecost, but it's up to My Royal Priesthood – it's up to you – to keep the fire burning! Church of the Living God, I charge you this day: You have allowed the fires of God in the Holy Place on this lampstand to almost go out. They are down to a glowing ember, and there has been nothing but smoke coming off of your lampstand."

"I HAVE NOT CALLED YOU TO BE SMOKE; BUT TO BE A LIGHT TO THE WORLD. YOU'RE LIGHT IS ABOUT TO GO OUT! It is time, My church and My people, that you allow ME, the Lord your God, to come and trim your wicks. You see, I am your high priest. I must trim your wicks and fill your lamps with oil. It's a two-fold process. You must do your responsibility, and you must allow ME to do mine. Subject yourself in humility, in brokenness, and in repentance, to come and allow ME to do the work that I need to do in you," says the Lord God Almighty.

"Come and enter into times of My presence," says the Lord, "that I may fill you with more of My anointing oil down out of heaven. That is your responsibility. You must enter into times of worship and praise, and just being alone with Me," says the Lord God Almighty.

"I charge you this day: It is a great responsibility. You must – YOU MUST KEEP YOUR LIGHT SHINING. Don't get lazy and allow these lamps to go out to where you're nothing but a smoldering ember. Church of the Living God, I charge you this day: Throw out everything else that is not of Me – all of man's understanding, man's revelation, man's tradition, and man's illumination. There is no natural light in the Holy Place. I'm calling you to a place where you can receive My revelation fully from My SPIRIT," says the Lord God Almighty.

The seven lamps are an expression of the seven fold spirits of God that are around the throne of God all of the time – in eternity past and eternity future. They are the seven fold spirits of God: the spirit of wisdom, understanding, counsel, power, and of knowledge, and of the fear of the Lord. Also, the spirit of the Lord will rest on him. (Is. 11:1,2)

"Church of the Living God: You must once again rely on My Holy Spirit illumination to lead you and guide you into all truth." Remember the lampstand was a *"beaten work of pure gold"*. It had three shafts on each side, and on each shaft was a series of three – a bud, a flower, and an almond; and on the central shaft there was four series of three. Three fours are twelve. So if you total them all up, three nines are twenty seven, there are twenty seven on each side, equals fifty four, plus twelve from the center equals sixty six. How many books of the bible are there? We see this picture again: sixty six books of the bible. It's **complete illumination** – full illumination of all the scriptures!

We need the Holy Spirit's illumination of scripture once again in our lives and in our churches today. We need to quit relying on yesterday's illumination – on yesterday's bread – on yesterday's manna. God wants us to receive fresh manna every day. Every day of our life we can have a fresh revelation of the word of God for our lives and for our churches. Every day should be the gathering of fresh manna from heaven!

Remember, Jesus is the "Seventh Day Manna" out of Heaven. There was no manna on the seventh day in the wilderness as seen in Exodus 16. Jesus is our seventh day manna. He is our daily bread. It's the Lord's Prayer again: *"Give us this day our daily bread"*, not just physically, but spiritually. *"For man shall not live by bread alone, but by every word that proceeds out of the mouth of God."* (Deut.8:3)

"We need the Holy Spirit's help and His illumination of His word. HE WROTE THE BOOK! HE CAN TEACH IT! HE CAN EXPLAIN IT! HE CAN REVEAL IT TO US!" says the Lord God Almighty.

There are aspects of God and deeper truths of God that we haven't even tapped into yet. "Church of the Living God: You need to hear this word. It is a very, very, important word. To Him that has ears to hear, let him hear what the Spirit is saying in these days. You need to hear this word. The ways of man, and the illuminations of man, need to be thrown away. You've been relying too much on man's

292

wisdom, man's knowledge, man's understanding, man's revelation, man's power, and man's might. You need to get back to the Holy Place – spiritually, where you are surrounded by darkness and there is no natural sunlight that comes into this chamber of the Holy Place. Then you must light the lamps of the lampstand – representative of My seven-fold expressions of the Holy Spirit in the earth. They are only to be filled with olive oil-- My holy anointing recipe – clear oil of pressed olives for the lamps."

Where does this olive oil come from? The word "Gethsemane" means: "oil or oil press". Jesus Christ prayed in the garden of "Gethsemane". He went there to make preparations for the cross. He cried, and He prayed tears of blood in such agony of heart for what He was about to face for you and I. It was through His body being "pressed" and beaten, and Him dying for us, that we get this precious holy anointing oil that can flow through the Holy Spirit of God. Jesus said, "I must go so that the holy comforter may come." He sent the holy comforter at a very high price. He was beaten, bruised, tortured, and hung on a cross – perhaps the worst, most painful, horrific death anyone could ever endure. He died such a death for you and me, so that we can receive the fullness of the Spirit of God.

This may be new revelation for some, but there is one Holy Spirit with seven expressions of that same spirit of God, and they are around the throne of heaven all the time. That same expression of the spirit is given in Isaiah 11:2 in describing the anointed ministry of Jesus Christ himself; and that same ministry is to be carried out in the earth today through us.

Church of the Living God: We must get back to relying on the Holy Spirit for all of our wisdom, our knowledge, our understanding, and all our illumination of the scriptures. We need to get back to Him being our teacher and our guide.

God's word says in Psalm 119:105, *"Your word is a lamp to my feet and a light for my path."* That light is the seven fold lampstand or "menorah" in Jewish terms that stood in the Holy Place of the Tabernacle of Moses. We need to get back to understanding these seven fold expressions of the Holy Spirit of God. We need to get to know who He is again, afresh and anew. He is the third person of the trinity, and He, too, is fully God; and He is the one that is finishing God's "Seventh Day Creations" in the earth.

Jesus finished His earth walk. He said, "I must go so that the Holy Comforter may come." The Holy Spirit of God, today, is moving in planet earth. He is fully God. So, when you hear that the Holy Spirit is moving and working in any given place or service, it is fully God moving among His people in a "Spiritual Tabernacle" that is created by everyone who will call upon the name of the Lord. They have been "grafted in" as a son or a daughter of the Most High God.

"You are to be a 'light of the world.' (Mat.5:14-16) You are to 'walk as children of light'. (Eph.5:13-14) This is My command unto you this day: Walk as children of Light. Allow Me to trim your wicks and keep the fires burning in your life," says the Lord God Almighty. "It was the responsibility of the priest to keep the fire burning. This is your responsibility in your life today. I lit the fire," says the Lord. "I lit the fire. Now, you – only you – can keep it burning," says the Lord God Almighty.

Seven Locks

Samson is a great figure in the Old Testament, and we all can identify with his story. Most of us have heard it many times over, for it has been repeated throughout the course of history. There contains in His life, a very familiar story to us all: the one of "Samson and Delilah" with his very long hair, and his great feats of strength and power that he displayed throughout his lifetime.

But many do not know or have overlooked the detail in scripture that is twice mentioned in Judges chapter 16, of the fact that Samson had **seven** braids, or seven locks of hair that were very long. Many do not realize why he would have had such long hair, or even why the seven locks.

Samson was a Nazarite from birth; and it was quite a miraculous story, early on, in the beginning of his life. His mother and father were visited by an angel of the Lord, and they were quite surprised. The angel said to his mother, *"You are sterile and childless, but you are going to conceive and have a son."* (Judges 13:3) Samson was another promised son that God had great plans for. The angel had come down and spoke to Manoah and his wife concerning how to raise this child and to instruct him, teaching him all the parameters that he should not cross as a Nazarite. These Nazarite vows were given back in the days of Moses. (Num.6) One could become a Nazarite for any length of time, while it was to be a period of devotion and consecration, set apart unto the Lord.

There were certain things that they could do and could not do. One that was very important in the life of a Nazarite was that they couldn't drink wine or fermented drink, or anything else that came from the grape vine-- not even so much as a raisin or a grape seed. They were to just stay away from it. And also, they were never allowed to touch a dead body, even if it was in their own family. To come too close would risk becoming defiled by death. These vows were normally totally voluntary. It was all their choice to show Israel, through their lifestyle, the highest standards of holiness, sanctity, and commitment to the Lord.

The Hebrew word for Nazarite comes from the word "nazar" which means: "to set apart". During this period of separation, they were not to have any razor touch their head and let their hair grow long as a sign or symbol of their consecration – an outward evidence of an inner devotion – for they must be holy unto the Lord.

And if they messed up and sinned against their vow and to God, they had to shave their head, offer a sin offering, and then go through a seven day period of cleansing and start their time all over again. When their time was completely over, they would shave their head as a final culmination and burn their hair under the sacrifice of the fellowship offering.

Samson was a Nazarite from birth. He really didn't have a choice in the matter. In his case, his was involuntary; but God had a special plan for him. Samson had a marvelous beginning. He had the blessing of God and the Spirit of God stirring him, and also the appearance of an angel to his parents at his birth, and a great promise from God: that He would begin the deliverance of Israel from the hands of their enemy the Philistines. He was born into a time when Israel was in a state of great apostasy, and as a nation had fallen into the hands of the Philistines for forty years during the time of the Judges. He could have brought about a great deliverance for His people; but Samson, all through his lifetime, flirted with disaster. He was never fully devoted to God in his heart, and kept going against the word of God and even the word of his parents. He demanded a Philistine wife against his parent's wishes and against the Law of Moses among other things. (Deut.7:3)

The Spirit of the Lord, supernaturally, would come upon him in great power and in great might, and at one point, he even tore a lion apart with his bare hands. But on the way back down that same road, he touched the dead body of that lion to get honey out of the carcass. (Judges14:9) His desire for food was greater and went beyond his vow to the Lord. Then again a little later on in another instance, he grabbed a fresh jawbone of a donkey and killed a thousand men. He was not to touch death.

So, over and over, Samson continued to break his vows to the Lord and his dedication and consecration unto God was not near what it should have been. It's really quite the sad testimony here for the life of Samson. He flirted, time and time again, with disaster in many different ways.

One very well known time is seen in the famous story of Samson and Delilah. The rulers of the Philistines wanted to find out the secret of his great strength, subdue him, and then capture him; because to look at him one would not realize where his strength came from. It was supernatural not natural. Scripture points to the evidence that he was just a normal man like everyone else. It was a mystery to them all. Samson's great strength was not his own, but was the direct result of the Spirit of the Living God enduing him with power – a spiritual source not a physical source! So, they set a trap for him, and bribed Delilah with a large sum of silver to discover the secret of his great strength. For you see, Samson had fallen in love with Delilah. Three times Samson tricked her and would not divulge the mystery of his great strength. But, on the fourth time, he finally gave in to her prodding's and her beauty. She was on the side of the Philistines and only wanted her reward money.

Samson gave in, his own flesh being very weak. He told her in Judges 16:17, *"No razor has ever been used on my head … if my head were shaved my strength would leave me; and I would become as weak as any other man"*. His long hair was a sign to the world that he was a Nazarite; an outward appearance of something that was internal. He should have been completely dedicated and consecrated unto the Lord. What God could have done with him if he had been.

"Church of the Living God: I HAVE CALLED YOU ALSO TO BE A NAZARITE-- to be holy, separated, and consecrated, unto the Lord your God; and to be completely dedicated unto Me. If you will be, the spirit of the Lord will come upon you as well; and you, too, will tear the lion in half with your bare hands!"

"Satan roars about as a 'lion' seeking whom he may devour; but he will not devour you, for the Spirit of the Lord will rise up on the inside of you, and you will tear the lion in two and destroy Satan himself – for he is under your feet. Halleluiah! Greater is He that is in you, then he that is in the world."

The life of Samson is a very sad testimony, for he never accomplished everything that God wanted him to do. He was to bring about the deliverance of an entire nation, Israel, from the oppression of their enemies; but instead was preoccupied with his own desires. **Samson was a very selfish man – full of himself!** He always had his own interests in mind and heart – only what he wanted: if he was hungry, or if he was angry, or if he was in love, or wanted this woman, or that woman. He was more concerned with satisfying his own sexual passions and his fleshly nature than pleasing his Holy God.

Throughout his lifetime, Samson had many confrontations with the Philistines. Which is what God wanted; but all of his motives were very wrong – completely wrong. He was not led by the Spirit of God. It was all for revenge and motivated out of a heart of anger and fury just to get even. He was uncontrollable! The Spirit of the Lord would come upon him and God still used him in great and mighty ways; but it only consisted of sporadic exploits against this pagan nation. His disobedience eventually caught up with him in a big way. He flirted with disaster one too many times. The Philistines shaved off all seven locks of his hair while he was sleeping in Delilah's lap. And the scriptures say, *"He did not know that the Lord had departed from him."*(v.20) He had no real relationship with His God. His strength was gone! They seized him, then gouged out his eyes, and took him to a place called Gaza where they bound him with bronze shackles and forced him to grind grain at a grinding wheel in prison. Grinding all day long, blind and in prison, he finally began to see! In this process, through his sufferings, his trials, and his testings as Samson went around and around this grinding wheel, as a slave and prisoner of His enemies, God was at work!

For the first time we see in Samson's life evidence that he began to humble himself while God was doing a work on the inside of his heart. Bound with bronze shackles, which remember, bronze is a symbol of judgment; Samson was enduring the judgment of God for all of his disobedience against the word and the will of God for his life.

As he went around and around, he was being humbled more and more. During this time, his hair began to grow back-- the outward sign of an inward devotion. As his hair came back, so did his relationship with God; and for the first time in his life he could truly say that he had that relationship. But it came through great trials, sufferings, and even judgment. But it didn't have to be that way. Almost all of Samson's trouble in his life was self-inflicted; running outside the will of God. Sounds familiar doesn't it!

But if we can walk and live how God wants us to and listen to the voice of the Lord our God, we can avoid many, many, hardships and disappointments in our lifetime. Not to say that things won't get tough at times, or there won't be a trial or a test. No. I'm not saying that. But they will be minimized, and you won't wander in the wilderness for forty years as a consequence of your own doing. You can reach the "Promised Land" in this life. You can avoid a lot of heartaches, pain, trouble, and tears, if you will just obey the Lord and do what He tells you to do.

Back to Samson again: while enduring through prison, Samson was called out by the Philistines to a festival held in the temple of Dagon their god where thousands had gathered for the celebration. Samson was their "trophy" to show off, so they made him perform and entertain them while praising their god for delivering him into their hands. They were all in very high spirits that day. The temple was very crowded with over three thousand on the roof alone. Scripture doesn't say how many were in the main halls but it seems to be a "standing room only" crowd.

Samson, leaning against the main pillars, prayed one last prayer, *"O, Sovereign Lord, remember me. O God, please strengthen me just once more, and let me with one blow get revenge on the Philistines for my two eyes. Let me die with the Philistines."* (16:28, 30 NIV) He still had revenge and wrong motives in his heart; but God honored his prayer anyway for Israel's sake! He had some faith building in his heart, and a true connection with His God began to develop. He pushed with all his might against the two central pillars of the temple, by the Spirit of the Lord, and it came crashing down. His strength returned because of his devotion to God. That's what God was trying to teach him all along.

He failed miserably in showing a life of holiness unto God, to Israel, and to the rest of the world. He never did fully accomplish what God wanted him to do, nor in the ways God wanted to do it; but he did kill more in his death than he did during his life. There is a spiritual lesson in that for all of us. Through the death of ourselves, God destroys our enemies! When we can die completely to self and totally serve the Lord, we will cause greater destruction to the enemy's fortresses, and help bring down his kingdom!

I don't know about you, but I want to be counted among those who listen to the Lord and fulfill all that God has called me to do, and complete my mission while I'm here in this world. I don't want to be like a Samson that only fulfills part, or just some, or none. Even as in Samson's life, our strength and power – our "**seven locks of hair**" – needs to come from an inner devotion and consecration unto the Lord. Remember, the word "Nazarite" means: to be set apart. And the number **seven** is a picture of fullness and completion – **complete consecration.** God is calling each and every one of us to be set apart; in the world but not of the world!

"The Spirit of the Lord is upon Me to preach the good news to the poor.' It's Isaiah 61. The Spirit of the Lord will come upon you in power and might to finish Jesus' ministry in the earth, if you'll be consecrated unto Me," says the Lord your God.

"NO CONSECRATION – NO POWER!! It's as simple as that. So I'm calling you this day, Church of the Living God: Come back to a place of consecration and dedication, and of being separated from the world. You can be in the world but not of the world; be set apart as a holy nation – a royal priesthood-- unto Me-- separated spiritually – not physically. Then when you're separated spiritually you can go back and impact your world physically. Why? Because, you'll carry the power and presence of the Living God. YOU'LL CARRY THE POWER! And you can be that vessel of gold – that "**Ark**" **of the Living God**-- just like the Ark of the Covenant."

The Ark was kept in the Most Holy Place. The glory hovered over the Ark above the Mercy-Seat, and between the Cherubim. God lived in the Holy of Holies. That was His habitation. He wants to make you a habitation of the Most High God; and when God comes in to live on the inside of you, He is going to clean up house. He will get rid of everything that is not of Him. He is going to set your house in order and put everything in its place. Nothing will be hidden from His sight.

He'll even check all of the closets, and clean out all of the junk, and all the garbage, and throw it all away. He'll also check in to your favorite room where you've said, "O, God, don't go in there!" He must go even in that room, and even the garage, where you keep all of your junk. He's going to clean it all up, if you want to be a habitation for the Lord. He comes to live, and eat, and have His being, in your house.

"So this day, I charge you, Church the Living God: RETURN TO YOUR FIRST LOVE! Remember the excitement and the joy of the Lord, of what it was like the very first day you came to God; because, every day can be as fresh as that day. It's a new day! It's the dawning of a new day! Your walk with Me does not have to be old and boring, and dull, and stale, but it can be fresh, and new, and alive, and vibrant, and exhilarating!"

"LIFE CAN BE A GREAT ADVENTURE!" HALLELUIAH!

"This is what I want you to return to. Return to your first love. There is more that I have for you," says the Lord God Almighty. "You can be full: a **seven** in your spirit, a **seven** in your soul, and a **seven** in your body. That is the truth of the word of God, if you'll believe it, receive it, and walk in it. In the days ahead, step by step, day by day, week by week, you're going to walk in it; and you're going to rediscover an old relationship that will get set on fire for the kingdom of God." Halleluiah!

Face the Fire!

(It's the only way – like it or not!)   (Rev.3:18; Mal.3:2)

"I have a fan in My hand, and I am fanning the flames of an old relationship that you once had. I'm calling you back to your first love," says the Lord God Almighty. "There is a flame that lies deep within you, and it may just be a smoldering ember that is about to go out; but I, the Lord God, just in the nick of time, I AM FANNING MY FLAME TO BLOW THE SPIRIT OF THE LORD AND THE BREATH OF GOD UPON THIS EMBER, so that it may be fanned and become a mighty forest fire in My Spirit," says the Lord God Almighty.

He who has begun a good work in you will also bring it to completion and fruition and fullness. (seePhil.1:6) God began a work in you. He wants to complete it; and He's going to bring you through whatever you need to go through in order to finish it; and a lot of it is up to you – what you go through – and how you respond. Remember this word again! YOUR RESPONSE DETERMINES YOUR FUTURE!

So, if you get on track with God, you may avoid a lot of pitfalls, heartaches, valleys and dark places. It's all up to you! God is going to bring us all through the fire, one way or the other! There's no way to avoid it! Like it or not, we've got to go through the fire. That's God's Way!

We see the picture of the Brazen Altar in the Tabernacle of Moses. You are the living sacrifice. It must be burned up! We see another example with Elijah on Mt. Carmel. Fire fell from heaven and consumed the sacrifice. Everything was burned up – completely everything! Shadrach, Meshach, and Abednego in the fiery furnace of Nebuchadnezzar heated up seven times hotter. Not a hair on their head was singed but everything on the inside was charred to a crisp – completely burned up! That's what God's all about! He is an All-Consuming fire! (see Deut.4:24)

That brings us to one very important reference to fire, and that is found in Revelation 3:18. God counsels all of us to come buy gold, refined in the fire. It was a word to the church of Laodicea. They were neither cold nor hot. They were just lukewarm. GOD IS ABOUT TO SPIT THEM OUT OF HIS MOUTH!! For they say, "I am rich and have acquired great wealth, and I don't need a thing." It was the epitome of self-righteousness and self-existence. They had it all. They didn't even need God anymore. But, they didn't realize that in God's eyes, and the truth of it all was, they were wretched, pitiful, poor, blind, and naked. What a very harsh description of this church in the book of Revelation. And sadly, I think this church has great parallels to the church today, especially, the church in America.

"WE HAVE IT ALL." "We've got EVERYTHING", or so we think we do. In our pride, in all of our wealth, and in all the blessings that God has so graciously poured out upon us, we have just accumulated as much as we possibly could. We've just STORED IT ALL UP! WE HAVE TO BUILD BIGGER BARNS because of all of our stuff! God says, "Your barns are empty; but My barn's are full."

In God's eyes, we're wretched, poor, pitiful, blind and naked, because in our self-righteousness and self-existence we have nothing; and we lose sight of the fact that all this good stuff came from God himself, and all the blessings of life are from Him. Every good thing comes down from the Father of Lights – every blessing. And if we fail to acknowledge that, we're in big trouble!

"Church of the Living God: Come buy 'Gold' refined in the fire. This 'Gold' – it will cost you – it will cost you everything you've got; and IF YOU'RE WILLING TO GIVE ME EVERYTHING YOU'VE GOT – I'LL GIVE YOU EVERYTHING THAT I HAVE! Halleluiah! And then, you will be rich and wealthy; but you'll be rich and wealthy in Me – spiritually. And all that I can give to you, IT IS WORTH MORE THAN ALL THE WEALTH IN THE WORLD -- ALL THE SILVER AND GOLD THAT YOU CAN COLLECT and put into one place. What I can give you is worth more than all of that put together! This is the gold that I want you to buy!" says the Lord God Almighty.

"Church of the Living God: You can't afford not to buy it! Because, spiritually, you are pitiful, you are poor, you are blind, and you are naked. You cannot even see where you are going; and you can't even see the fact that you're naked – no clothes on whatsoever – none of My clothes – none of My priestly garments – none of My kingly attire – none of My prophetic attire. You're completely naked! You have no robes of righteousness, no gowns of white, no garments of praise—nothing. YOU'RE COMPLETELY NAKED; which means you have put on nothing of Me. This **'gold'** costs, and it will cost you everything you've got. But if you will give Me everything you've got – I'll give you everything that I've got! And then, you will have **'My Gold'**-- the most valuable gold on the face to the planet. You see, gold is the symbol of deity and of the kingship. You are kings and priests of the Most High God."

"YOU ARE A KING IN MY KINGDOM! START ACTING LIKE ONE! HALLELUIAH!"

"YOU ARE A KING, a priest, and a prophet – the three annointings of Christ should all flow in My body-- My church-- in this day, and in this hour. Come buy 'gold' refined in the fire. I am an all-consuming fire," says the Lord God Almighty. "I am the Refiners Fire!"

"WHO CAN ENDURE THE DAY OF HIS COMING? And who can stand when He appears? For He is like a refiner's fire and like launderer's soap. He will sit as a refiner and a purifier of silver. He will purify the sons of Levi and purge them as gold and silver." (Mal.3:2)

"YOU ARE THE LEVITES OF THE MOST HIGH GOD! You are the royal priesthood unto God. Do you think you can walk in any way short of a priesthood? All that I had asked them to do in the Old Testament – symbolically – I ask the same thing of you today. Be thou holy, even as I am Holy," says the Lord God Almighty.

"It is possible, today, for that verse to be fulfilled in you," says the Lord God Almighty. "I have made a way. I have given you everything that you need. You have My Spirit-- My word-- everything pertaining to life and godliness – I have given it all to you. It is available to you today! You can have all that I AM!"

One, if you can know that it is for you and available!

Two, if you can grab a hold of it by faith and say, "Yes that is for me".

Then thirdly, simply walk in obedience to the word of God in your life day by day.

*"The words of the Lord are pure words, like silver tried in a furnace of earth, purified **seven** times."* (Ps.12:6) It is **perfect**. It is **complete**. It is **FULL**. **Every word in the Word of God is for you, today!** Halleluiah!

Don't believe a lie, or someone saying to you, "O, that's not for you", or believe the Father of lies where he'll try to twist the word of God and say, "Did God say?" and bring doubt and unbelief into your heart.

I encourage you this day: *"Believe on the Lord Jesus Christ, and you will be saved."* (Acts16:31) Believe on the Lord! Believe His word – every single word from Genesis to Revelation. It's **all** for you! Halleluiah! And if you will believe that, receive it into your heart, begin to walk it out in obedience every day, and pray until you begin to see the promises of God fulfilled in your life – you can be a **seven** in your spirit, a **seven** in your soul, and a **seven** in your body. **It is the promise of God!**

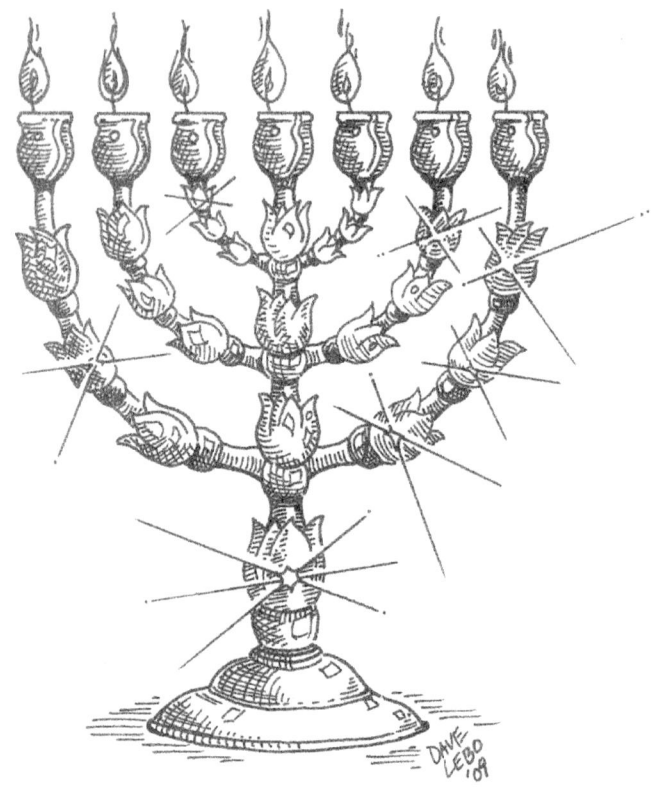

The Lampstand

One piece of gold of hammered work with
burning olive oil provided the only light
in the Holy Place for the priest to minister.
It was to burn continually – never to go out!

304

Chapter Eight

More than Enough

"I have come that they may
have life, and that they may have
it more abundantly." Jn. 10:10

My Cup Runs Over
(Ps.23:5)

"I have more than enough. I have too much. I have an excess. I have an abundance; so much so, I've got to give it away!" How many of us would love to be able to say those words? "GOD, I'VE GOT TOO MUCH! I'VE GOT TO GIVE SOME AWAY." You see, that's the place God wants all of His people to LIVE IN--to experience, and to STAY IN!!!

Church of the Living God; we've got to get there and God wants us to stay there, never to leave! It is "Promised Land" living at its best. We are to not only enter and live there, but we are meant to stay there ALL THE DAYS OF OUR LIVES; not just one day a week; not just one week out of the year; and not even a few months out of the year; but twenty four hours a day, seven days a week, three hundred sixty five days a year-- **every year**. Halleluiah! It's the year of Jubilee! Every 50th year in Israel was called the "Year of Jubilee"; literally: "the time of shouting". It was a year of celebration: slaves were set free, debts were cancelled, land was returned, inheritances restored, and liberty was proclaimed throughout the land with the sounds of trumpet blasts from the ram's horns, on the great Day of Atonement. Truly a cause for shouting! Liberty coincides with the work of the High Priest on that sacred of all days. All the liberties of the "Year of Jubilee" are now made available to us, through the atoning work of Christ on the cross! Jesus is the 50th year!

The year of Jubilee is not just every fiftieth year anymore. **It is the fullness and completion of all weeks** – the fullness and completion of time. It is seven full weeks of seven years. Count off seven Sabbaths of years, or **seven times seven** years, up until the forty ninth year; and when you break into the fiftieth year, it's the year of Jubilee. (see Lev. 25:8) It's the year of complete fullness and abundance which is in Christ Jesus our Risen Savior – our Risen Lord. So now, every year can be a year of Jubilee for the bride of Christ, today! Christ is our Jubilee!

The Hebrew word for eight is "shemonah". It comes from the root word "shamen" which means: rich, fat, plenteous, and it carries the idea of plumpness as if a surplus above the perfect seven. I want to give you a simple equation again, that illustrates this principle very well: **7+1=8.**

Seven is the fullness of God, while **one** is the number of God. So the fullness of God plus more of God equals an excess of God, or abundance. **Eight** is representative of abundance, a surplus, more than enough, having too much, an overflow, or having extra.

The number eight, in scripture, also carries the idea of "New Beginnings". We can see this illustrated many times throughout the bible. There were eight people saved on Noah's Ark from the judgment of God, and then through Noah's family, God began a new world. (Peter3:20) David was the eighth son of Jesse that God used to begin a new dynasty. (ISam.16:10-11) The eighth day is the first day of a new week. Circumcision was performed on the eighth day of life on all the males. It was the sign of the Covenant or the beginning of a new relationship between man and their God.

In the natural, we see that an eighth note completes an octave but that eighth note starts a whole new series of notes: A-G-A. The eighth color of a rainbow begins a new spectrum. What we see in the natural is also paralleled in the spiritual.

Many may not have heard it explained this way, but Jesus rose from the grave on the eighth day of the week and started a "new beginning". It was the beginnings of the church of the Living God and made it possible for the outpouring of His Holy Spirit in the earth at the day of Pentecost – fifty days after Passover-- which corresponds also to the fiftieth year of Jubilee! It's the Resurrection Power of God that makes it all possible.

God wants us to experience this "Resurrection Power" in our lives; this surplus; this abundance; this overflow of having too much; and to start a "new beginning" in our lives. The process has begun if you have accepted Jesus as your Lord and Savior. That is the "new beginning".

"Church of the Living God: Many of you have begun this new beginning, but so many of you ARE DRY AND BARREN, AND LIVE IN A WASTELAND – A WILDERNESS. YOU'RE LIVING IN THE DESERT, VOID OF RAIN AND WATER. You're like a dry and thirsty land that is devoid of life. You're ground is hard and cracked open, and has been baked by the sun; but deep, deep, down inside of you – YOU STILL CRY OUT FOR RAIN!"

"YOU NEED GOD TO COME AND POUR OUT OF HIS SPIRIT INTO YOUR LIFE. YOU NEED THE RAINS OF GOD'S PRESENCE TO COME AND SATURATE YOUR DRY AND

THIRSTY LAND; and then stay in it for days, upon days, upon days until that cracked ground begins to absorb all of that water and can become whole again. Continue to stay in it, and stay, and stay, and stay until YOU HAVE TOO MUCH – until the water begins to puddle and form pools of water, and then pools begin to form brooks, then brooks form creeks, and then creeks to streams, to rivers."

There is a verse in Ecclesiastes1:7 that says, *"All the rivers run into the sea; yet the sea is not full"*. It's a picture of God. It all comes from God, goes through God, and then goes back to God in a full cycle. And God wants your river to flow into the ocean in a never ending cycle of His presence and His Spirit.

As the rivers flow into the ocean, there is a vast evaporation that takes place continually every day. Millions of gallons of water evaporate into the heavens and form the clouds once again. AND THEN GOD CAN SEND FORTH HIS RAIN into the earth. It's a never ending supply, so you never have to worry about a drought ever again, in the kingdom of God.

There is a place that God wants His people to dwell. It is "Promised Land" living, with streams, fountains, and brooks. It's where God sends forth His rain that brings forth the "new wine", the "grain", and the "oil" in abundance. It's a place where there's an abundance of everything!

"ALL THAT I AM, that I AM, that I AM is awaiting you, in this land," says the Lord Almighty, "and it is awaiting you this day. If you will take a step of faith, continue on this journey reading this book from cover to cover, allowing the rains of His presence to sink into your being, and if you'll allow it to be absorbed into you, it will spring forth life. And you'll enter into a new life, a new walk, and new dimensions that you have only dreamed of. This is My word unto you, this day: If you will but only take that step of faith and open wide the gates of your heart and let the King of Glory come in; I promise you, you will not be disappointed and you will live in a land where you can say, 'I HAVE TOO MUCH. I HAVE TO GIVE SOME AWAY!'"

There Is a River

"There is a river, whose streams make glad the City of God, the Holy Place where the Most High dwells." (Ps.46:4) (NIV)

"There is a river that flows from the City of God and the Holy Place where the Most High dwells. WHEREVER I LIVE: THERE IS A RIVER; a river of life that flows. I lived in the garden – there was a river. I lived in the temple – there was a river. And I live in the Holy City, the New Jerusalem; and in that city – there is a river! All of these rivers in scripture – IT'S THE SAME RIVER! Halleluiah! IT'S WHERE I LIVE!! It's the River of Life! It began all life and watered all life in the garden. In Ezekiel, on its banks, it brought forth life; and also in the New Jerusalem. Wherever the water would go, it brought forth life."

"Church of the Living God: This word is for the worldwide church – the body of Christ. I, the Lord God, I AM THE RIVER! I AM the 'River of Life'. It is a symbol of My presence, and My Spirit in the earth." "Church of the Living God: To have a river flowing in you – you need to have an abundance-- an overflow. This day, I have this against you: YOU HAVE DAMMED UP MY RIVER!!... To where it is, and now has become, a stagnant lake. IT HAS BECOME POLLUTED, overgrown with algae and plants; and it is choking itself off from the life that it should have. Rivers are intended to flow. They must always be moving forward! Mankind likes to dam them up for one reason or another: for power, for recreation, for wildlife, for resorts, for pleasure, and for luxury. Mankind is drawn to the waters in the natural – to lakefront property – to oceanfront property. We need water to live. We need to drink it. We love to play in it, to swim in it, to live by it, and to explore it; but spiritually and also naturally, the oceans are the last great frontier. We know less about the oceans than we do outer space. It is the last great frontier; and Church of the Living God, it is the same spiritually. We know very little about the oceans."

There are vast oceans of God that are awaiting our exploration! GOD IS WAITING FOR US TO COME TO THE OCEANS OF GOD; but there's only one way to get there and it is through the rivers. You have to have an abundance to have a river; and as Ecc.1:7 says, *"All the rivers run into the sea, yet the sea is not full."*

"Church of the Living God: You need to break down your 'dams' and allow My 'River of Life' to flow once again – allow My Spirit to flow in your midst once again." *"There is a river whose streams make glad the City of God, the Holy Place where the Most High Dwells."* (Ps.46:4) "These streams – it makes glad the City of God."

309

"Church of the Living God: You have grieved My heart. My heart is broken because you have dammed up My River without My consent. You've tried to manipulate the Holy Spirit! You try to contain Him and get Him to do what you want Him to do. And you have tried to build lakefront properties along this dammed up river for your enjoyment and for man's own pleasures."

"Church of the Living God: I have this against you. The Holy Spirit is not for you – you are for Him! YOU ARE FOR HIM! You are to flow in this River where He wants you to flow, and go where He wants you to go; not vice versa. I charge you this day: Break down your dams! They are not by My design!"

"BREAK DOWN YOUR DAMS, and sell your lakefront property! It is not My design; it is not my intentions; and let My River flow once again. But you must flow where the river flows, and you must flow how the river flows; and with each wave, with each current, you must relinquish your control of the Holy Spirit and die to yourself to where He controls you--- you don't control Him."

"Relinquish everything to His control, and He will take you to the oceans! He will take you to the 'sea' and to the 'depths of God'; where all the mysteries of God that we cannot even yet fathom await us! Church of the Living God: There is a river that lies within you. Jesus said, *'Out of his innermost being shall flow rivers of living water.'* (John7:38) There is a mighty rushing river of God that lies deep, deep, within you that you have not yet seen nor heard. IT WILL BE THE SOUND OF A MIGHTY RUSHING RIVER, that has never before been heard in the earth nor has been imagined."

"I am pouring out My Spirit in these days," says the Lord God Almighty. "It is beginning to rain in the earth; but it is raining upon a dry and thirsty land. And it will take some time for that ground to absorb the water and to become soft, and pliable, and workable again. But know this, as you allow My rains to fall, the ground will become soft and saturated with My presence," says the Lord. "And in due time, the ground will not be able to absorb the abundance of water; and puddles will begin to form, and then brooks, and streams, and creeks, and then – yes – RIVERS will begin to form! And all of those rivers will begin to flow into the sea!"

"I charge you this day: There is a 'Tidal Wave' of My Presence that is about to hit the globe! I AM UNLEASHING A TSUNAMI OF MY SPIRIT IN THESE DAYS," says the Lord God Almighty, "a powerful wave, upon wave, upon wave, upon wave of My Spirit. IF MAN WILL NOT COME TO THE SEA – SPIRITUALLY – I WILL BRING THE SEA TO THEM AND I WILL FLOOD THE GROUNDS AND I WILL FLOOD THE EARTH!" says the Lord God Almighty.

"I AM POURING OUT MY SPIRIT IN THESE DAYS, to not only bring the rains of My presence, the former and the latter rains, but I am 'BREAKING OPEN FOUNTAINS OF THE DEEP' in My people, to cause a TSUNAMI of My Spirit to go forth in all directions- - to flood the earth with My presence," says the Lord God Almighty.

"Church of the Living God: All streams and all rivers, they flow into the oceans. I, the Lord, God, am calling you – let your rivers flow into the oceans. LET YOUR RIVERS FLOW ONCE AGAIN! BREAK UP ALL YOUR DAMS! SELL YOUR LAKEFRONT PROPERTIES; AND COME LIVE IN THE SEA! LIVE IN THE SEA!!! This is where I want you to live. You've had it all wrong. Come, come, to the depths. Come to the deep! This is My call in this day, and in this hour. Will you hear the voice of the Lord Your God? To him who has ears to hear, let him hear what the spirit is saying in these days. *There is a river whose streams make glad the City of God – the Holy Place where the Most High Dwells.*'" (Psalms46:4)

"I live in the river," says the Lord God Almighty. "I AM THE RIVER! I AM He who was, and who is, and who is to come. I am He who was – the river in the Garden of Eden where it all began; and that river separated into four headwaters – symbolic of the four corners of the earth; and it watered everything in the garden and it brought life to that garden; because I LIVED THERE!"

"Ezekiel saw a vision of a river flowing out from the threshold of the temple. At first, it was ankle-deep, then it was knee-deep, and then the further and further away from the temple He got, the river got deeper and deeper. Then it was waist deep. Then He said that it was too deep to cross; and 'deep enough to swim in.'" (47:5)

"And in this vision, even this river flowed into the sea. And what happened when it emptied into the sea? All the water there became fresh and swarms of living creatures would live in this sea. And wherever this river flowed it would bring life to everything. And that once which was dead – it would bring life! Swarms of fish would live there of many, many, kinds; and it would also bring life to the fruit trees that grew along its banks. Their leaves would not wither, nor

311

would their fruit fail, but every month they would bear fruit. Why? Because, the water from the sanctuary flowed there. Their fruit would serve as food and their leaves for healing!" (v12)

"IT'S ALL THE SAME RIVER! The river in Revelation 22 – it's the same river. The angel showed John, in the spirit, a river of the 'Water of Life' as clear as crystal flowing from the throne of God and of the Lamb, down the middle of the great street of the city! It's the NEW JERUSALEM – the City of God."

"IT'S WHERE I LIVE!"   "IT'S THE SAME RIVER!"

"It's a different dimension of time. I AM He who was. I AM He who IS; and I AM He who IS TO COME. THE TABERNACLE OF GOD IS NOW AMONG MEN!!!"

In Jesus' day He said, "Destroy this temple, and I will raise it again in three days." Jesus is now building the "NEW JERUSALEM TEMPLE" of His people. The old temple was destroyed. Halleluiah! God no longer lives in a temple made by men; but He lives in a temple whose "stones" are laid by the hand of God. He is building a "New Jerusalem Temple" – an entire city made of "little temples". You are a "temple" of the Living God – the place where God lives, and dwells, and moves, and has His being. And each and every little temple that comes together, corporately, builds a "New Jerusalem".

We can see in Revelation 22 there are similarities and parallels with this same river. *On each side of the river stood the tree of life, bearing twelve crops of fruit, yielding its fruit every month. And the leaves of the tree are for the healing of the nations."(v.2)* Notice that this portion of scripture is written in the present tense – "are for" the healing of the nations. Not "will be"-- "are for"-- NOW! Halleluiah! *"No longer will there be any curse. The throne of God and the Lamb will be in the city, and His servants will serve Him." (v.3) "They will see His face, and His name will be on their foreheads."(v4)*

In this city, we serve the King. When Jesus was crucified, there was a plaque that was fastened to His cross: *"He is Jesus of Nazareth, the King of the Jews."* (John19:19) Pilate had it intentionally placed there against the wishes of the chief priests of the Jews. But Pilate did not even know; prophetically, it was placed there on His cross – because that was giving Him His true identity! And it began when He died and the earth shook with a violent earth quake, and darkness came over the face of the earth. Something had occurred that day. Halleluiah! Glory to God! The temple shook and the veil was rent in two. It was in that day that Jesus established His kingdom in the earth.

312

"He who has begun a good work in you will complete it until the day of Jesus Christ." (Phil. 4:6)   He is building a church. He is building a tabernacle. He is building a temple – a place that He can live in and dwell in; and that place is in you; and also, in and among His people today – NOW; not going to be – NOW! Halleluiah! We will touch on this more in Chapter 12, but this is just a little nugget of truth for you to meditate on and to help prepare you for the word to come.

"There is a RIVER whose STREAMS make glad the City of God, the Holy Place where the Most High Dwells." (Psalms 46:4)

Where do you live today? Do you live in the desert? Do you live in the waste lands? Or, do you live in the river? If you live in the river, all rivers flow into the sea. This is where God is trying to get His people to come to; so that they flow with the currents, wherever the Holy Spirit may take them, and wind up in the deep vast oceans of God. IT'S TO THE OCEAN!!!!

Church – we haven't arrived yet. There is so much more! There's more! There's more! And if we'll ride the currents of these rivers of God – God wants to take us there. But, we can't resist. We can't dam up the river, try to enjoy it just for ourselves, and build our resorts along the banks. God is saying in this day and in this hour, "BREAK DOWN YOUR DAMS – THERE'S MORE!" We have not arrived yet! We've got to flow with what the Holy Spirit is doing in these days. We must stop trying to control Him, and stop telling Him what to do. We've got it all wrong. We've got it backwards! We have got to start listening and saying, "God, what do you want? What do you want us to do? We'll do whatever you ask of us!" That is what God wants us to return to: a place of humility, a place of brokenness, a place of complete abandonment unto the Lord Our God and His purposes for our lives to where we relinquish all control of our life over to Him. **IT'S NOT OUR LIFE ANYMORE!**

If you are a Christian, you are required by God to give your life away. You may not realize that. No one may have ever told you that before; but it's a life for a life. Jesus gave His life for you; now, the least that you can do is give your entire – one hundred percent – complete, life and being over – just hand it all over-- to the Lord God Almighty. Let Him have all control over it; and then, you trust Him for the outcome. And that's the **FAITH WALK!** Stop trying to figure everything out yourself. Stop trying to live on the land, where everything is secure, firm, and familiar, and leave it all - leave the shore and everything that you know, and come out into the oceans of God – out into the deep, deep, depths of His presence and His Spirit. That is where the Lord is calling each and every member of His body and His church worldwide – globally-- in this day and in this hour.

"Church of the Living God: Will you listen to what the Spirit of the Lord is saying in these days? Will you listen? It is a serious day. It is a serious hour. There is no time for games. There is no time for fooling around or for wasting God's precious time and also wasting your time."

"Time is running out! Choose this day whom you will serve. If God be God, serve Him. If Baal be god, serve him. It's a showdown of the ages! **CHOOSE THIS DAY WHOM YOU WILL SERVE!** If God be God, serve Him!"

Floods upon the Dry Ground
(ISAIAH 44:3)

"Even as in the days of Noah, when I brought forth an abundance of rain, the sky broke open and the rains began to fall for forty days and forty nights. I flooded the earth because its wickedness was so great, and not only that – I broke open the fountains of the great deep and THERE WAS TOO MUCH WATER!"

"Judgment came upon the earth against all wickedness; for the earth was full of corruption and violence, and man's heart was wicked, and *every inclination of the thoughts of his heart was only evil all the time*." (Gen.6:5,11)

"And I, the Lord God, was grieved that I had even made man. And I spoke to a man named 'Noah' that found favor in My eyes. He was a righteous man and blameless among His people; and Noah walked with God." (Genesis 6:9)

"So, I had instructed Noah to build an ark made of gopher wood. It would have great capacity to hold seven of every clean animal and two of every unclean animal – four hundred fifty feet long, seventy five feet wide, and forty five feet high, with three decks. This ark would foreshadow the coming of My Son – Jesus Christ – into the earth. This ark is a type of Christ. THIS ARK, IT SAVED THE RIGHTEOUS, through the waters – the waters of My Spirit brought blessing to the righteous in the ark, but destroyed all the wickedness in the earth. It was an abundance of rain – an abundance of water."

"You need too much water to form a river. And then when there is too much – rivers swell their banks and turn into a flood. Also in the natural, I can bring My hurricane to flood the earth; or I can bring a tsunami of My Spirit," says the Lord.

"In these days and in this hour-- spiritually – I am bringing both – the rains of My Spirit – but I am also breaking open the fountains of the deep and the vast oceans of God that lie deep within My people to cause a **spiritual tsunami** of My presence," says the Lord, "to flood the earth again!"

"I promised Noah and all the inhabitants of the earth that I would not flood it again in the physical. And I placed this sign of that covenant in the clouds of the heavens – a rainbow – as a reminder to ME and all the world that I would not flood the world again to wipe out wickedness; but I never promised that I would not do it spiritually. In fact, that is exactly My plan!" (see Gen. 9:12-17)

"There is a river whose streams make glad the City of God, the Holy Place where the Most High Dwells."(Psalms 46:4) If you will dwell in the "Secret Place" of the Most High God – it is a place where the Most High Dwells. Out of your innermost being shall flow "Rivers of Living Waters", but all rivers flow into the oceans. (Ecc.1:7) God is calling us to the sea. As we come to the sea and are obedient to the voice of the Lord Our God, God is going to begin to reveal Himself to us in ways that will absolutely, positively, blow our minds!

"GOD IS GOING TO BREAK OPEN THE FOUNTAINS OF THE DEEP THAT LIE WITHIN YOU , and cause a TSUNAMI – a Tidal Wave of His Spirit – so much so; that THE WORLD HAS NEVER SEEN BEFORE, in the history of mankind. There is a move of God that is coming to this earth that eyes have not seen, nor ear heard, nor has ever even entered into the heart of man what God has in store."

"Church of the Living God: Prepare yourselves. Prepare ye the way of the Lord. Make a Highway for our God. Open wide the gates of your heart; so that the King of Glory may come in. Open wide the gates of your heart. Receive the word of God implanted into your being, so much so, that it becomes a part of who you are. Believe It!"

"Faith comes by hearing and hearing the word of God. This is the word of God for this day – for this time-- for this hour! Will you

315

jump into the river of God and allow it to take you to the great vast oceans of God? THEY ARE WAITING! THEY ARE WAITING FOR YOU TO COME!"

There is a T-shirt that I saw once that read these words: "The world is covered with 70% water – RACE YOU TO IT!" Spiritually, we should race each other to the oceans of God.

Isaiah 42:10 says, *"You who go down to the sea"*. There is a vast ocean of God awaiting us that has largely been unexplored. RACE YOU TO IT! BE A SEA DWELLER-- not a land dweller! COME WITH ME. LET'S RUN! RUN! RUN, with all that is within you. Let us run to the sea, dive in, and go to the depths to where we die to ourselves, take up our cross, and follow Him. It is in this place, if you will come to where you die to yourself completely, the death of you is the life of God!

Isaiah 44:3 says, *"I will pour water on him who is thirsty, and FLOODS on the dry ground, I will pour My Spirit on your **descendants** and My blessing on your offspring."*

We are the descendants of Jacob. We are the descendants of Israel. God promises to pour out of Himself in His Spirit, and in His presence, upon all flesh.

Joel 2:28 says, *"I will pour out My Spirit on all people. Your sons and your daughters will prophesy, your old men will dream dreams, your young men will see visions. Even on My servants, both men and women I will pour out My Spirit in those days. I will show wonders in the heavens and on the earth. Everyone who calls upon the name of the Lord will be saved." (v.32)*

Many are familiar with that portion of scripture, but maybe not so familiar – if you back up just a few verses and notice in verses 12, 13, 15, and 17. There is a contingency placed upon that promise. Verse twelve begins with: if we return to Him with all of our hearts, rend our hearts not our garments, with fasting, weeping, and mourning. Declare a Holy Fast and call a sacred assembly. Priests weep between the porch and the altar: "Spare your people." Then, God will take pity on His people and pour out His Spirit. Listen to this description of what follows.

316

(v.19) "Then the Lord will reply to them: 'I am sending you grain, new wine and oil, enough to satisfy you fully...'! (v.22) "trees are bearing their fruit; the fig tree and the vine yield their riches." (v.23) "He sends you abundant showers..." (v.24) "...threshing floors will be filled with grain; the vats will overflow with new wine and oil." (v.26) "You will have plenty to eat, until you are full..."

"It's an "If' and "then" promise. It is conditional. In a word it means: REPENT! REPENT! Rend your hearts – not your garments! Not what is outward; but what is inward-- for I, the Lord God, look upon the heart. I, the Lord God, see your pride. I see your boasting. It is an abomination unto Me. I am calling you this day to declare a Holy Fast. Call a sacred assembly. Weep, and cry, and mourn. You are My priests. Have you forsaken the altars of the Living God? Is there no crying? Is there no mourning in Zion?"

"Church of the Living God: You say you want more of Me, but I want more of you! It is conditional. It is contingent on the covenant – on the contract – on the agreement. And the contract is simply this: Life for a life. I want it all! You can't hold on to the things that you love or the things you don't want Me to see, or be a part of. You have to give Me everything. That's the contract. That's the covenant. That's the agreement!"

"And to the measure you give -- give and it shall be given unto you – pressed down, good measure, overflowing – and to the measure that you use – it shall be given back unto you. That is a Kingdom principle including finances, but it goes well beyond money-- BEYOND FINANCES!!"

"You look at only money and have applied that verse so you can be blessed financially; but I counsel you, again, come buy 'gold refined in the fire'. It is gold that is more precious and more costly than all the gold in the world combined. This is the gold that I need you to buy!   RETURN TO THE ALTAR OF GOD! THE ALTAR WAS IN FRONT OF THE VEIL just before you went into the Holy of Holies – the Most Holy of all places. My priesthood, I'm calling you again: you must offer up incense – the prayers of the saints. And you-- My priests-- My royal priesthood – that includes everybody – all believers from all nations, from all tribes, from all peoples – you must weep between the porch and the altar and intercede for the world. Remember chapter two – 'without intercession nothing happens'! This call is not placed upon just a few, or little old ladies that are great

317

prayer warriors. Not to take away from them, but it's not just their calling."

"IF YOU WANT TO BE GREAT IN THE KINGDOM," Jesus said, *"You must be the servant of all."* If you want to be first – you've got to be last. *"But many who are first will be last and the last first."* (Mat. 19:30) "Jesus Christ did not come to this world to be served as an ordinary king. He came to serve and lay down His life for the world. If you want to be great in the Kingdom, you've got to lay down your life, take up your cross, and follow Jesus. You have to walk as He walked. Walk in His footsteps, which include at times: agonizing travail, weeping, mourning, fasting and prayer. There's no way around it. To go up in My Kingdom, you must go down; then you will go forward on your knees."

"Church of the Living God: We must get back to a place of repentance, humility, and BROKENESS!" 'Who may ascend into the hill of the Lord? Or who may stand in His holy place? He that has clean hands and a pure heart…' (Ps.24:3, 4) "I dwell in the high and holy place, with him who has a contrite and humble spirit…" (Is. 57:15)

"This word is given for correction, for admonishment, and to lift you up. Yes, and at times I discipline those that I love. If I did not discipline you, you would know then that you were in great trouble. But, this word is given for correction, teaching, and for training in righteousness."

"You have drifted far from where you have once started. You must return to the beginning basics of the early church: the breaking of bread, devoted to the Apostles teaching, to fasting and to prayer. Get back to the basics. Forget all the fluff, the bells and the whistles-- all the extras-- that are leaving very little fruit. I'm calling you back to the basics!"

"Be My Royal Priesthood once again. Go through the steps outlined as a pattern in the Tabernacle of Moses: from the brazen altar, to the brazen laver, to the Holy Place and all of these details – in every step are principles for the church today-- to get us to the place where we need to be – living and dwelling in the secret place of the Most High God!"

And so, the contract is simply this: If we give God all that we have and all that we are – God will give us, in return, all that He is and all that He has! That is the covenant that we must return to! This is the relationship that God wants us to have as His bride – as the body of Christ in this day and in this hour. We have forsaken our first love. God is instructing us today to return to our first love as the bride of Christ – which is a covenantal relationship – a marriage which will be culminated at the marriage supper of the Lamb one day in the not too distant future. But until then, this is our betrothal period; and we are promised to only one love. We are to remain faithful to Him and all He has called us to do. This is the heartbeat of God. This is His very heart for His people in this day and in this hour.

And if we will do just that, return to Him with all of our hearts; then He promised in His word that He will pour out His Spirit upon all flesh, and He will bring floods of His living water upon the dry ground.

The prophet Isaiah writes: *"The Lord will surely comfort Zion and will look with compassion on all her ruins; He will make her deserts like Eden, her wastelands like the garden of the Lord. Joy and gladness will be found in her, thanksgiving and the sound of singing." (Is. 51:3) (NIV)*

"There is a river whose streams make glad the City of God, the Holy Place, where the Most High Dwells" (Psalms 46:4)

"When the River returns, joy and singing will also return. I, the Lord God, am restoring the places long devastated; the cities that have been laid waste in ruin. I am pouring floods upon the dry ground. I am turning deserts into streams of My living water to cause them to flourish. I am restoring everything in this day and in this hour – everything! The places long devastated, I am rebuilding," says the Lord God Almighty.

"Church of the Living God: Heed the voice of the Lord your God. Listen to this word. Do not ignore what the Spirit of the Lord is saying in these days. It is a serious day. It is a serious hour. THE BLOOD OF THE PEOPLE WILL BE UPON YOU! You must listen. Receive it. Absorb it. Digest it, and let it become a part of who you are. Let faith arise in your heart, and then begin to walk in it, move in it, and live in it. Halleluiah! LIVE IN THE RIVER! LIVE IN THE RIVER! LIVE IN THE RIVER!"

Open the Storehouses
(Deut. 28:12)

"THERE IS A FAMINE IN THE LAND! *'Not a famine of food or a thirst for water, but a famine of hearing the words of the Lord.'* (Amos 8:11) THERE IS A FAMINE IN THE LAND! People are desperate for hearing the 'Rhema' word – the fresh manna from heaven – a word for today, for their situation, for what they are going through to deal with the problems of this world. Amos 8:12 says, *'men will stagger from sea to sea and wander from north to east, searching for the word of the Lord, but they will not find it.'(NIV)* THERE IS A FAMINE IN THE LAND! MEN ARE STAGGERING FROM SEA TO SEA AND WANDERING all across the face of this earth. People who are lost and hungry, and who are thirsty; but they find nothing to eat – nothing to drink."

"Church of the Living God: IT IS TIME. IT IS TIME to realize who you are and what position you hold. You are as a **'Joseph'** – second in command of all of Egypt (the kingdom) and you hold the keys to the storehouses. There was a famine in the land in the days of Joseph. It was a worldwide famine. People from all the countries of the known world came to Joseph for food. By the wisdom of the Lord and Joseph's ability to interpret dreams, he knew the future. He knew that there would be seven years of abundance followed by seven years of famine. So with God's help, he put in place a plan to store up huge quantities of grain; so much so, that he stopped keeping records of it, for it was 'beyond measure'. (Gen. 41:49) And in that day and in that hour, when it was necessary to do so, Joseph opened the storehouses and sold grain to all the other countries because famine was severe in all the world."

"IT IS THE SAME SITUATION IN OUR WORLD TODAY."

"Church of the Living God: You have stored up, and stored up, the grain of the bread of My Word for years, and years, and years. It is time. It is time to open up the storehouses," says the Lord God Almighty.

"You hold the keys to the storehouses of heaven! You have at your disposal an abundance of bread that you have been holding on to for yourself. It is not time to store it up for yourself – to be fat-- to be plump. I give you an abundance only to give it out and to share with others. If you remember the little boy that brought his five loaves and his two fish to Jesus. He didn't hoard it up for himself. He could have taken it and just enjoyed his own lunch and let everyone else go hungry. But he didn't. He brought his lunch to Jesus. He gave Him all that He had: five loaves of barley and two fish. We all know the story. Jesus multiplied it back out and He fed over five thousand men, plus women and children, which could total over twenty five thousand strong." God multiplied it back out and fed the hungry crowds on two different occasions, and each time there was an abundance, or a surplus, that was left over. There was too much. Normally, we don't like to eat leftovers; but I'll take GOD'S LEFTOVERS ANY TIME! God is the God of LEFTOVERS! He loves to give until there's more than enough!

"Church of the Living God: I, the Lord thy God, I have blessed you – My BRIDE – tremendously, abundantly, beyond more than you could ever think or imagine. But, it is in the heart of God that I want to bless you even more. But as I do, so much so, that your barns will be overflowing and your vats will brim over with new wine. It is not only given to you just to store it up. I give you an abundance to give it back out, and to be a blessing to the rest of the world."

And remember, this is kingdom dynamics: *"Give and it will be given to you; good measure, pressed down, shaken together and running over will be put into your bosom. For with the same measure that you use, it will be measured back to you."* (Luke 6:38)

You have heard it once said, "You can't out give God." This is true in all areas of life; not only financial, but relational, material, in business, in spiritual blessing, praying for others, in speaking a kind word to someone; in just giving what you have like the little boy with the five loaves and the two fish. "GIVE WHAT YOU'VE GOT," the Lord says. "GIVE WHAT YOU'VE GOT!" And God will give back to you immeasurably – beyond measure.

"Church of the Living God: I charge you this day – give liberally! Give abundantly! Give lavishly! Don't try to hoard it all up for yourself! You see, that is a problem in My church worldwide today. YOU'RE TOO STINGY!"

"It shows a lack of faith that you can't trust Me for tomorrow; for does not tomorrow have enough care of its own? Trust Me for Today; for do I not care for the sparrows and the lilies of the field? Are they not adorned with greater glory than even the glory of Solomon's temple? How much more are you worth than they? I will care for you. I will provide for you. I will be your daily bread. I will be your sunshine and your night. I will be your food and your water. I will be your clothing and your house. I'll be your everything! I'll supply for you all your needs in the natural and also in the spiritual. I'll be your everything. But, I charge you this day; Church of the Living God: You must give Me everything that you are, all that you have, and all that you're not – your dreams, your hopes, your future, your goals – everything! And even test Me in this," says the Lord Thy God. *"Bring the whole tithe into the storehouse, that there may be food in My House. Test Me in this,"* says the Lord God Almighty, *"and see if I will not throw open the floodgates of heaven and pour out so much blessing that you will not have room enough for it."* (Mal. 3:10)

"Church of the Living God: I have blessed you abundantly beyond measure, and I have called you in obedience to only give Me ten percent – to walk in obedience unto My word. The promise is contingent on your obedience. My word declares, 'Bring the whole tithe into the storehouse…' It's an 'If' and 'then' promise!"

"Church of the Living God-- worldwide: I challenge you this day – if you are not tithing a full ten percent of the blessing of God in your life – I challenge you this day to begin to do so. To walk in obedience to My word and test Me in this," says the Lord, "will I not throw open the flood gates of heaven and pour out a blessing upon you; so much so, you'll not have room enough to contain it all."

Remember, "Open Heavens" are in the obedience chapter of the word of God: Deut. 28. "If you diligently obey the voice of the Lord Your God to observe carefully all His commandments…"-- the promises that follow are this:

"I will set you high above all nations of the earth…and blessings shall come upon you…"

"…blessed in the city…and country." (v.3) "The fruit of your womb…your crops…your livestock be blessed…when you come in…and when you go out." (v.4-6) "…enemies will be defeated…" (v.7) "…establish you as His holy people…" (v.9) "… blessings on your barns …" (v.8)

"Your barns will be overflowing! Halleluiah! Why? Because your barns will be My barns, when you walk in disobedience to Me," says the Lord, "your barns are empty and My barns are full. When you walk in obedience, all that is in My BARNS gets transferred to your barns and then your barns become full."

"It's a symbol of the storehouses of heaven! All that I have, I give unto you," says the Lord, "if you will follow after Me and fully obey My word. But to obey My word, you must love Me. So if you love Me with all of your heart, your soul, mind and strength – you'll simply do what I say. You'll simply do all that I ask of you," says the Lord. "And My commands are not burdensome and they will not make you weary. In fact, they are designed to bless you all the more. It's a kingdom dynamic! It's a kingdom principle."

"You'll lend to nations and borrow from none."(v.12) "You'll be the head and not the tail." (v.13) "I will open the heavens, the storehouses of My bounty, I will send rain upon your land in season and to bless all the works of your hands," says the Lord God Almighty. (v.12)

Proverbs 3:9-10 says, *"Honor the Lord with your wealth with the first fruits of all your crops,* THEN YOUR **BARNS** WILL BE FILLED TO **OVERFLOWING**; *and your vats will* **brim over** *with new wine."*
I Sam.2:30 says, *"Those who honor Me, I will honor".*

When you walk in obedience to the Lord thy God, it creates a situation – an environment in your life where there are "OPEN HEAVENS" over you all the time: twenty four hours a day, seven days a week, and three hundred sixty five days a year. Obedience creates an "Open Heaven" over your entire life and your entire being.

Jacob saw a picture of this in a dream in Genesis 28:10-17. It was the "Gateway to Heaven". He saw a stairway resting on the earth reaching to the heavens and the angels of God were ascending and descending upon it. And above it stood the Lord and He said, "I AM the Lord, the God of Abraham and Isaac." God renews the same covenant with His son Jacob. He promises him the land again and that his descendants will dwell in the land on which he was lying, (v.13) and be a nation all to themselves. Jacob said, *"How awesome is this place! This is none other than the house of God; this is the gate of heaven."* (v17)

"Church of the Living God: You, too, can have an "OPEN HEAVEN" that is unleashed over your life, if you'll simply walk in obedience to the Lord thy God. And the angels of God will ascend and descend and bring down the blessings of God and take up the prayers of the saints. I want to pour out into My people; so much so, that they'll not be able to contain it all; and so they have an abundance, an excess, more than enough, to give away!"

Walk in obedience unto the Lord. Jesus took the Ten Commandments and condensed them into two! *"Love the Lord your God with all your heart, soul, and mind… and love your neighbor as yourself."* (Mat. 22:37-40) Jesus also said, *"If you love Me, you will obey what I command."* (Jn. 14:15) So, it is simply this: LOVE THE LORD and DO what He says!

Live in the "River", and do what the Holy Spirit is telling you to do. If it's to give something to someone – give it! If the Lord tells you to do something – do it! It's as simple as that. Walk in obedience to everything that you find in the word of God – from Genesis to Revelation. Live in obedience to it. Be a doer of the word and not merely a hearer only.

"This is Promised Land living," says the Lord God Almighty. "And, you don't have to die and cross on over to live in the 'Promised Land'. That 'Promised Land' was for Jacob's descendants. Jacob's descendants are you and I, if you have called upon the name of the Lord Jesus Christ and have accepted Him in your heart, repented of your sins, and now you live for him. This is 'Promised Land' living. Deut. 8:7-10, gives us a good description of this Promised Land that is part of our inheritance. It would be a 'good land', a land with 'brooks and water, of fountains and springs that flow out of valleys and hills', and land of 'wheat and barley', of 'vines and fig trees and pomegranates', a land of 'olive oil and honey', a land in which you will eat 'bread without scarcity', 'in which you will lack nothing' …and you would eat until you were 'full'; and you would be a blessing to the Lord."

You can choose to live in this land today. Some, however, have chosen to live on the east side of the Jordan and have not crossed over into this Promised Land. It is all up to you. You can either eat from the King's table, or eat crumbs from the floor that are only fit for dogs. I don't know about you, but I want to eat from the King's table, and receive all that God has for me in this lifetime.

Ephesians 3:20 says, *"Now to Him who is able to do immeasurably more than all we ask or imagine according to His power that is at work in us."* It is according to the power that is at work in us. It is conditional – to the degree that we are obedient to the Lord, and to the degree of our closeness in our relationship with God.

God is calling you to live in the secret place of the Most High God. Will you, today, listen to the voice of the Lord your God, and simply do what He tells you to do? Put feet into it. Walk in it. Walk it out. Remember, we have to walk it out, day by day. And if you are willing to do that, you will live in your "Promised Land", and you will have an abundance-- an excess – an overflow. You'll have too much, and you'll have to give it all away; but it will only come back to you and be multiplied back into your life.

That's how God does things! He doesn't just give it back to you to where it's the same as what you had before; He gives back in abundance. You can't out-give God. So, I challenge you today, to give of all that you have – your talents, your gifts, your time, your material possessions, your heart, your prayers, your praise, your worship, your gifts in the body. If it's teaching-- teach with all you've got – with all that is within you. If it's preaching – preach. If it's prophesying – prophesy. If it's giving to the poor – give. Whatever your giftings are – do it as unto the Lord with all that is within you.

Give of your heart and your passion. Give of everything and God will give back into you more than you could ever handle-- more than you could ever imagine. The Lord your God will open the floodgates of heaven and pour out His blessings upon you; so much so, that you'll not have room enough to contain them all.

I Am The Resurrection And The Life
(John 11:25)

"I am the resurrection and the life. He who believes in Me will live, even though he dies; and whoever lives and believes in Me will never die. I am nothing but LIFE! In ME, there is no death. The two cannot stay together. Halleluiah! Glory to God!"

"I, the Lord, God, came down to this earth, and walked among men in the form of My Son, Jesus Christ. I was beaten. I was bruised. I was tortured, and I was nailed to a cross-- all for you. And Jesus Christ became separated from His Father in Heaven for a brief moment. He cried out in a loud voice, *My God, My God, why have you forsaken Me?"* (Mat.27:46)

There was a separation for a moment. Why? There had to be. For Jesus to experience death, He had to be separated from the life of God-- separated from Himself – if you will. It is a hard truth to understand.

"I died, experienced death, and even was separated from God and took upon the punishment of all men. I died and went to hell for all of mankind. I became separated from the Father; but it was only for just three days; and ON THE THIRD DAY I ROSE FROM THE DEAD; and life came back into my dead body."

It was on the first day of the week, (Mat. 28:1) or the eighth day. And interestingly enough, there are eight other recorded resurrections in the word of God: three in the Old Testament and five in the New Testament.

The three in the Old Testament, all three, involve Elijah and Elisha. The first one mentioned is the son of the widow of Zarapheth where Elijah prayed and laid on the boy three times; and on the third time, the boy was resurrected back to life. (I Kings 17:17-25) The second one recorded is the son of the woman of Shunem. This young man was raised by Elijah's successor Elisha and he did it in a similar way as Elijah had done. (II Kings 4:8-37) The third was a man raised as the Israelites were burying a dead man. They threw his body into Elisha's tomb; and when the body touched Elisha's bones, the man came back to life and stood up on his feet. (II Kings 13:20-21)

The other five are written in the New Testament, and I will briefly mention all five. The first is the daughter of Jarius in Mark 5:35. This little girl was twelve years old. She was the daughter of a synagogue ruler. Jesus said to him, "Don't be afraid; just believe." (v36) Jesus put everyone else out, except the parents and the disciples who were with Him, for laughing at Jesus' statement that "the child is not dead but asleep". (v39) He took the girl by the hand and said to her, "get up"! She came back to life, got up, and walked around.

The second was the son of the widow of Nain, in Luke 7:11-18. Jesus just touched a coffin at a funeral and said, "Arise", and the man sat up and began to talk.

The third is probably the most well known of them all-- a man by the name of "Lazarus" recorded in John 11. Jesus loved him and his family very deeply; but it is interesting in scripture that He delayed even two more days to get to where Lazarus was. Jesus said, "I am the resurrection and the life. Lazarus, come forth. Take off the grave clothes!" Life came back into a dead body that day, for God displayed His power in the earth.

The fourth was Dorcus in Acts 9:36. Peter sent them all out of the room as well, then he knelt and prayed and he simply said, "Get up"; and life came back into her body.

The fifth is a bit of an unusual story. The Apostle Paul was teaching at a very late hour; and a man named "Eutychus" went to sleep and fell out of a window in an upper room. Paul went down, put his arms around him and said, "He's Alive!" Then, they all went back upstairs and continued to listen to Paul's teaching until daybreak. (Acts. 20:7-11)

God wants to bring His resurrection power into our lives as well. And what does that mean to experience this resurrection power? The number eight, as we had learned earlier, carries with it the connotation of "New Beginnings". When you come to know Christ, God has given you a "new beginning". You have become "born again"; as Jesus explained to Nicodemus in John 3. But, that is just the beginning of a process. God doesn't give you all of it the first day. It's a process that you have to walk out and grow in. But, in this process, God does promise: *"If anyone is in Christ, he is a new creation; old things have passed away; behold, all things have become new."* (II Cor. 5:17)

In Christ-- you have to hear this church -- In Christ, "all things have become new" -- not will be-- have become new! We need to begin to walk in that kind of mentality. The promise is for you now! "Church of the Living God: I am the resurrection and the Life. I am calling you forth even as I have called Lazarus out of the tomb; to experience My 'resurrection power', and a 'new beginning'. I gave Lazarus a 'new beginning' that day when life came into a dead body. The areas of your life that have still had touches of death in them; I, the Lord God, want to bring life back into every one of them. ALL THINGS HAVE BECOME NEW!"

"You can experience resurrection power in all aspects of life. And those things that have appeared to be dead, those dead bones in your being, you need to throw them into Elisha's tomb, and the Spirit of the Living God will come upon those areas and bring life back into those dead bones-- those portions of your being and portions of your life that have still had aspects of death in them."

"I'm going to resurrect them. You see, I the Lord God am nothing but LIFE! When My life begins to flow in you as a mighty rushing river, and you go and live in the depths of the sea; the sea has been rid of death. There is no death there; only life, nothing but life-- nothing but Life! It's Resurrection Power! Just as we have seen in the rivers. Wherever the river flows, it brings life – the complete opposite of death. As it flows, it will always rid itself of death." "So I charge you this day, church of the Living God: as you begin to soak in the rains of My presence and the rivers begin to flow in your life and you live where God lives, the life of God will begin to flow in every aspect of your life."

In this river, there will be everything! Everything is in the river. You'll begin to experience new life, new power to walk, a new attitude, a new outlook on life, a new faith, even new thoughts and a new mind, and new strength-- anything and everything that you can imagine. I have made just a small listing of things that have come to mind. You'll begin to walk in new heights, new depths, new dimensions, and new realms. It will be a new day-- a new dawn. You'll have new health, new happiness, new joy, new peace, new love, new talk, new tongues, new songs, new wine, new oil, new anointings; because you'll be in a new covenant, a new contract, a new agreement. You'll have a new name and a new identity. You'll be a new man, a new woman, or a new child. You will literally not be the same person when this resurrection power takes its hold and the river begins to flow; and you'll become a "sea dweller" instead of a "land dweller".

Even as in Revelation 21, in talking about the "New Jerusalem", in verse 5: *"He who was seated on the throne said, 'I AM MAKING EVERYTHING NEW!'"*

The Tabernacle of God is now among men. When you live where God lives – you'll have nothing but life flowing in your life. Nothing but LIFE! Nothing but LIFE!

You Are an Eighth Son of Jesse
(I Sam. 16:10-13)

DAVID was the eighth son of Jesse. Jesse had seven of his sons pass before Samuel. If it was up to Jesse, his first born son would have been the next king of Israel. Jesse didn't even think enough to have his eighth son come before Samuel – the prophet of God-- who had come there, directed by God, to anoint the next king. But, each son passed before him that day and he knew; "No, this is not the one, this is not the one". And so he asked Jesse, "Do you have any more sons?" "There is still the youngest," Jesse answered, "but he is tending the sheep." Samuel said, "Send for him. We will not sit down until he arrives".

328

In that day, Samuel took his "horn of oil" that came from an animal; no sacrifice-- no horn; no sacrifice – no oil. Jesus Christ was the "LAMB" that was slain. He was the sacrifice that brings forth God's Holy Anointing Oil.

Samuel anointed David that day and the scriptures say, *"The Spirit of the Lord came upon David from that day forward".* (v13) The full anointing of God rested upon David from that very moment on.

David was later anointed two more times following this anointing. Once, when he became king of Judah; and then, also, when he became king over all of Israel. Those three anointings in the physical correspond to the three anointings that he received, spiritually, the very first time he was anointed. They were symbolic of the three anointings that he carried from the very first time.

In the Old Testament, only a king, a priest, or a prophet could be anointed – all of which are a foreshadowing of the ministry of Jesus Christ to come many years later.

Also, man was to never try and mix these anointings into the same person. If one were to presume upon God in that way, judgment awaited them. We see this in the life of King Saul who tried to offer sacrifices instead of waiting for Samuel. Saul forfeited his kingdom. (I Sam. 13:14) Also, King Uzziah burned incense in the temple and was struck with leprosy for the rest of his life. (I Chron. 26:15-21; Is. 6:1)

But as we see in the life of David, he was not judged for mixing these three anointings in His life; because he was divinely appointed to carry all three in his lifetime.

The dominate anointing in David's life, we all could guess, was the kingly anointing. He ruled and reigned over the kingdom of Judah and all of Israel for a total of forty years from the age of thirty to seventy. He also carried the prophetic anointing that we are all familiar with because he wrote the majority of the Psalms. Some are prophetic in nature; many times written of King Jesus the Messiah – the King of all kings. (see Ps. 2, 72, 89, 110)

David, also, as a young boy prophesied the words of the Lord to Goliath; and I believe it was the anointed word that killed Goliath that day. David was the only one present operating in the spirit. Acts 2:29, 30 states that David was a prophet of the Lord. But the one that not many may realize is that David also carried the "Priestly Anointing" – the ministry of reconciliation. It's not seen in his life until David's physical third anointing, after David captures the city of Zion and he sets up the Tabernacle. He begins to exercise the priestly functions and duties of the Old Testament priests; that were formerly forbidden by a king to do.

David wore a linen ephod as a priest in II Sam. 6:14. He also set the Ark of the Covenant in the Tabernacle that he himself had pitched for it. (v17) David offered burnt offerings and peace offerings before the Lord that were the priestly sacrifices. He blessed the people in the name of the Lord of Hosts; which was the priestly blessing. (II Sam. 6:18; Num. 6:24-27) David in his lifetime officiated as the king-priest in the same order of the king-priest Malchizedek, (I Chron. 15:27; 16:13) which is of great significance. It was all to foreshadow the coming of one of his descendants – Jesus Christ, Himself. Jesus would be anointed also, in all three of these ways.

There were only three people in history that carried all three anointings; and it is interesting to note that they were all builders of tabernacles-- the dwelling place of the Most High God! Moses carried all three. He was the ruler of the nation. He began the priesthood; and he was a prophet or a spokesman for the Lord God Almighty to the rest of the people.

Secondly, King David carried all three. The third person is Jesus Christ, Himself – who is now, today, building His true Tabernacle made of "living stones"—a symbol of all the true believers being built up into a holy tabernacle of the Living God.

Which brings it all down to you! You are an eighth son of Jesse, which means that you too, carry the same anointings that the eighth son of Jesse did: the kingly anointing; the priestly anointing, and the prophetic anointing. These three are meant to be carried out in the body of Christ today, in this day and in this hour.   It's Isaiah 61! *"The Spirit of the Lord is upon me because He has anointed me to preach good news to the poor; He has sent me to bind up the broken hearted, to proclaim freedom for the captives, and release from darkness for the prisoners, to proclaim the year of the Lords favor and the day of vengeance of our God, to comfort all who mourn, and provide for those who grieve in ZION – to bestow on them a crown of beauty instead of ashes; the oil of gladness, instead of mourning, and a garment of praise instead of a spirit of despair. They will be called oaks of righteousness, a planting of the Lord for the display of His splendor."* (Is. 61:1-3)

You have been called to carry the same anointing that the Lord Jesus carried in His lifetime. Jesus said, "I must go so the Holy Comforter may come." The Holy Spirit is continuing Jesus' work that

He could not finish in the three years of His earthly ministry. But, He is continuing it, in this day and in this hour, through His people.

"Church of the Living God: I am calling you to put on the garments of praise instead of a spirit of despair, garments of salvation, and robes of righteousness. It's all in Isaiah 61. When you're putting on 'garments', you are putting on ME," says the Lord God Almighty.

"There are garments of the Kingship just as in Joseph's day. You are putting on ME and that aspect of ME; to rule and reign, and administer My power over the enemy. I'm calling you to put on the garments of the priesthood! You're putting on ME and an aspect of who I AM. I'm calling you, once again, to be a Royal Priesthood unto ME. Symbolically, to wear the tunic, the breastplate, the turban, the ephod, and the sash: all of these – symbolically – to carry out the priestly ministrations in My Holy Temple; to act as mediator and intercessor, and to offer up the prayers of the saints, and to worship Me and praise Me. You have the ministry of reconciliation for all the people unto their God; to bring that relationship back together again. You've been called to put on the garments of the priest!"

"You've also been called to put on the garments of the prophet. You may ask, 'What are the garments of the prophet?' One of the greatest prophets who ever lived was Elijah. He never saw death, because God took him. He was translated up into heaven. And that same power of Elijah as prophesied would return back into the earth. A partial fulfillment of that was in the life of John the Baptist. Both men possessed the prophetic voice of the Holy Spirit in the earth."

John was one that was called to be in the wilderness. He was the voice of one crying in the wilderness: "prepare ye the way of the Lord. Make a Highway for God." What did he wear? He wore a garment of camel's hair. He was a wild man that ate locusts and honey in the desert. He was different. He had forsaken his former priestly garments and man's calling. Why? Because it all had become corrupted and so he went out into the wilderness to be separated from the established order and be alone with God.

God's anointing was placed upon John before he was ever born. The angel Gabriel had visited his father Zacharias the priest while he was ministering at the golden altar of incense; and spoke to him many things concerning his son. The angel said, "And he will turn many of the children of Israel to the Lord their God. He will also go before Him in the spirit and power of Elijah, 'to turn the hearts of the fathers to their children', and the disobedient to the wisdom of the just, to make ready a people prepared for the Lord." (Luke 1:16-17)

The spirit of Elijah (the Holy Spirit's prophesying power)--that same power-- rested upon John the Baptist. He was a forerunner, of Jesus Christ the Messiah.

"I have called you to be a spokesman and a forerunner of the King of kings and the Lord of lords; to speak forth the words of the Lord; and declare these same words; and be a voice of one crying in the wilderness: *Prepare the way of the Lord; make straight in the desert a highway for our God.*'" (Is. 40:3) "I have called each and every believer to be a forerunner – a spokesman in the earth – to speak forth the words of God; as a forerunner of God Himself as He begins to show up all over the world in power and in great might."

"These are the days of My Elijahs," says the Lord God Almighty. John was dressed in camel's hair--the garments of the skins of an animal. He was one crying in the wilderness. He was a "living tabernacle" of the Most High God in the wilderness. The Tabernacle of Moses was designed with an outer tent-like covering over the Holy Place and the Most Holy Place made of animal skins-- the place where God lived.

The first clothing ever seen in scripture that God supplied to Adam and Eve was made from animal skins. In the garden, Adam experienced and carried the glory of God before the fall. But when Adam sinned … ADAM LOST THE GLORY! He became naked and ashamed, and was separated from God; but then God supplied through the sacrifice of an animal – clothing! He gave His glory back; to preserve it, and for man to be a "tabernacle" of the Most High God once again!

God made those first garments of animal skins. Today, God is trying to do the same thing for us. He is making spiritual garments once again for us to put on! So that we, too, can know our true identity of who we are in Christ. We have been called to be kings, priests, and prophets. And one step further, we are called to be warriors in God's Kingdom. Halleluiah! Put on the full armor of God in all of its array – every element. When we do, we are putting on God in a different aspect and personality of who He is.

All these garments in scripture are virtues of God and qualities of godliness that we are to possess to be formed into His image. Are we not to be formed into His image and become just like Jesus Christ?

"Even as I called Lazarus out of the tomb, and I told them to take off the 'grave clothes'; so too this day, I call you Church of the Living God: take off your grave clothes and put on the garments of praise for a spirit of heaviness. Wrap yourselves in robes of righteousness. PUT ON ME, THE LIVING GOD in every aspect and all of My fullness – all that I AM, that I AM, that I AM is intended to be displayed in the earth through My people," says the Lord God Almighty. "But, you must put them all on! You must wear them; so they become part of who you are!"

Revelation 16:15 says, *"Behold I am coming as a thief. Blessed is he who watches, and keeps his garments, lest he walk naked and they see his shame."*

Revelation 7:9 says, *"a great multitude standing before the throne clothed with white robes."*

"How shall I find you at the day of My appearing?" says the Lord God Almighty. Naked and barren, without any clothes at all; or will I find you wrapped in robes of righteousness, and garments of praise, and clothed with white robes, and all the aspects of who I AM? Is that how I will find you?"

"I charge you this day," says the Lord, "Those that are naked – be clothed with Me. Those that are clothed already, but have filthy garments – clean up your garments – wash them so they may be white again. I am coming back for a 'Bride' that is clothed in 'garments of white'. There will be no filthiness in her whatsoever. White robes are symbolic of nothing but God – of purity, holiness, and of righteousness, and being in a right relationship with the Lord their God; with no defilement at all. I, the Lord God, when I return, what will I find you wearing? What will I find you wearing?"

Chapter Nine

All Nine

"But the fruit of the Spirit is love, joy, peace,
longsuffering, kindness, goodness, faithfulness,
gentleness, self-control. Against such there
is no law." Gal. 5:22,23

"There are diversities of gifts, but the same Spirit.
There are differences of ministries, but the same Lord.
and there are diversities of activities, but it is the same
God who works all in all. But the manifestation of the Spirit
is given to each one for the profit of all." ICor.12:4-7

GAZED, AMAZED, and BEWILDERED!
(Acts 2:15)

It was nine o'clock a.m., early on that Pentecost morning. People from all over the known world were gathered in Jerusalem for the Feast of Pentecost, also known as the "Feast of Weeks." People from every nation, every tribe, from many languages, gathered together in obedience to their God, and came to Jerusalem to celebrate the feast of Pentecost. It was the second of the main festivals that the Jews were to celebrate every year: the first was Passover, the second was Pentecost, and the third was Tabernacles.

Pentecost occurred exactly seven weeks and a day after "firstfruits", or fifty days in all. The Greek prefix "pente" means: fifty. First fruits came at the end of Passover. Jesus was resurrected on "firstfruits". He was the "firstfruits" raised from the dead meaning that there were many more to follow. He was resurrected from the dead in hopes that we may be also. And if you are a believer in Christ and call upon His name, you can trust and be assured that you too will rise from the dead and gain eternal life.

Jesus has made a way where there was no way. A short time before this eventful day, Jesus had instructed His disciples and His apostles to wait until they were endued with power from on high. He had given them a promise in Acts 1: 5, 8. *"For John truly baptized with water, but you shall be baptized with the Holy Spirit not many days from now. But, you shall receive power when the Holy Spirit has come upon you; and you shall be witnesses to Me in Jerusalem, and in all Judea and Samaria, and to the end of the earth."* They were to "wait for the promise of the Father" (v4) until they were endued with power from on high. So there were about one hundred and twenty, as the scriptures say, that waited in this upper room during one of the hours of prayer – nine o'clock a.m. A devout Jew would pray three times a day: nine a.m., noon, and again at three o'clock p.m. Acts 2:1-4 says, *"When the Day of Pentecost had fully come, they were all with one accord in one place. And suddenly there came a sound from heaven, as of a rushing wind and it filled the whole house where they were sitting. Then there appeared to them divided tongues, as of fire, and one sat upon each of them. And they were all filled with the Holy Spirit and began to speak with other tongues, as the Spirit gave them utterance."* So they were all together in one accord, in one place. And where the place that they were staying – it was shaken and the Holy Spirit came down upon them. And they saw upon each one of them tongues of fire, and they began to speak in another language. It was a heavenly language – a language of angels.

This outpouring had never before occurred in the history of mankind. It was new. It was fresh. It was a supernatural phenomenon. It could not be explained. Some had no idea. Some gazed at them in amazement and were absolutely bewildered. They had absolutely no idea what was going on. They were perplexed. They marveled. The bible describes the scene with words such as these. They had no idea what was happening, but they knew it was something special and that it was supernatural. Others looked upon the scene and mocked them, and thought that they were all drunk with new wine.

But Peter, the apostle that had denied Christ three times before the rooster crowed, and a short time before was afraid to publically confess that he even associated with Jesus Christ of Nazareth; but on this day, he spoke up in a loud voice. He raised his voice and said, *"Men of Judea and all who dwell in Jerusalem, let this be known to you, and heed my words. For these are not drunk, as you suppose, since it is only the third hour of the day."* (9:00 a.m.) (Acts *2:14, 15*) *But what you now see: This is that! "This is what was spoken by the Prophet Joel." (v16) "And it shall come to pass in the last days; says God, that I will pour out My Spirit on all flesh; your sons and daughters shall prophesy, your young men shall see visions, your old men shall dream dreams. And on My menservants and on My maidservants I will pour out My Spirit in those days; And they shall prophesy." (v.17, 18)*

Peter preached the very first sermon of the Church Age. It was the beginning of a whole new dimension that the world had never seen before. It would be known as the "Age of the Spirit", when God would begin to pour out His Spirit on all mankind.

Man for the first time in the history of the world, could now become a tabernacle or a dwelling place of the Most High God. You see, before God could only dwell in tents or in a temple made by the hands of men. But now God would reside in temples made by the hands of God-Himself. It would be reversed. So what God has fashioned, formed, and made in the likeness of man, in us; we are now the tabernacles and the temples of the Most High God-- a place where He can live.

And because of Jesus Christ's work on the cross and what He accomplished at Calvary, now God's Holy Spirit, the third person of the trinity, can now come and take up his residence within man's heart

– within each and every one of us – to whom all who will call upon the name of the Lord.

The people looking on said to Peter and the rest of the Apostles, *"What shall we do?"* (v37) Then Peter, in this famous sermon instructed the people saying simply, *"Repent, and let every one of you be baptized in the name of Jesus Christ for the remission of sins; and you shall receive the gift of the Holy Spirit."* (v38)

Today, the world is still amazed, and they gaze, and they look upon this supernatural phenomenon with such bewilderment. Even now, today, the world is still confused about this supernatural event. But know this: it is still occurring today! It never stopped! It never ceased! *"For the promise is to you and to your children and to all who are afar off as many as the Lord our God will call."* (v39) This element of Peter's sermon still applies today!

"Church of the Living God: You have gazed; you have been amazed, and you have been bewildered at this supernatural phenomenon. I, the Lord God, I don't want you to be in confusion about what this means. I don't want you to be in the dark. Satan has caused confusion for hundreds of years regarding what has happened on this one day – the "Day of Pentecost."

"Peter gave the only explanation that there was. He said in short, "This is that." This is that which was spoken of through the prophet Joel: *'In the last days, I will pour out My Spirit upon all flesh.'* ALL FLESH! I, the Lord God, I leave no one out: the young, the old, the rich, the poor, male or female. It does not matter. All flesh means all flesh, and it still means that today. It means ALL FLESH: ALL DENOMINATIONS, ALL CHURCHES, from the north, the south, the east, and the west – worldwide. This word is for every believer, every church and every denomination!" Halleluiah!

"You'll have to change your doctrines if you have to; because, this word is for you! The Holy Spirit is intended to be a great blessing to My people," says the Lord God Almighty. "It is given as a great gift unto you with the sign of speaking in an unknown language – an unknown tongue. It is meant to edify you, and to build you up, and to admonish you." Paul writes in the New Testament: *"he who speaks in an unknown tongue edifies himself."* (I Cor. 14:4) You can build yourself up in your holy faith by speaking in tongues quietly in your own prayer time. That is one use of this gifting.

There are other times in a corporate service that one, or two, or three may speak in a loud tongue, but he that interprets edifies the church. It's another use of the gifting of this supernatural phenomenon. It is given to build up the church; to give them revelation; to give what the Spirit of the Lord may say to them in that moment; to give them a "Rhema" word, or fresh manna straight out of Heaven from the very mind of God for that day.

"Church of the Living God: Many of you have been deceived for generations in thinking that this gift is not for you. Satan has come in and blinded you to the truth. You have said in the past that this gifting has ceased – that this gifting has stopped. I, the Lord God, want to inform you today, it has NOT CEASED! It has not stopped! My word never says that it would cease or stop. I, the Lord God, want to lovingly correct you today to the truth. Knowledge has not ceased – in the context of that scripture. Knowledge continues. And in the fullness of time, when they are no longer needed, only then shall they (tongues) cease. When Jesus Christ returns for the second time, then they will cease. Because then, we will all speak the same language again."

"Let My Spirit fall from Heaven. Let the Rains of My presence rain down upon you once again-- regardless of denomination; regardless of what you've been taught before; regardless of your doctrine. If you seek Me, you will find Me; if you seek for Me with all of your heart."

"I am looking for a people who are hungry for God once again. I am looking for the hungry and the thirsty, to give out bread and wine in this day and in this hour. The bread and the wine is symbolic of My word and My Spirit-- Word and Spirit in fifty-fifty balance. If you're not in fifty-fifty balance of those two things – you're out of balance; and you need to return to fifty percent Word and fifty percent Spirit. And if you are out of balance in either way, you need to return to that perfect heavenly balance that I, the Lord God, have intended for My church to experience, in this day and in this hour."

"The day of Pentecost was a great, supernatural outpouring of My Spirit. It was the beginning of the Church Age. It was not meant to discontinue, or be stopped by any man or demon in hell. It is meant to continue on as a gift, as a blessing, as a weapon of power, to be used with great wisdom and stewardship within My church, until My son Jesus returns again – until the second coming of Christ."

"So, Church of the Living God, those reading this book: you must rethink your theology, your doctrines, your traditions of men, what your father believed, what your father's father believed and so on. Not just because it's tradition, but if you will search your heart and seek after the truth, the truth shall set you free."

"In this day and in this hour, I am pouring out of My Spirit upon the hungry-- upon the thirsty. Those who will say within themselves that they want all of God no matter what that means. Those that will reach a point of total abandonment, and leave everything in this world behind, to run after God with a heart set on fire with a passion for Him. If that is you, you will seek after the truth and you will find it; and you will find God in that truth and He will baptize you with His Holy Spirit and fire with the evidence of speaking in tongues."

You'll enter into a whole new realm of His Spirit. You'll enter into the realm of the "Holy Place" in the Tabernacle of Moses. He will lead you and guide you into all truth. He wrote the book, and He will teach you the book. He will be a witness when others speak to you the truth; and you will come under the Apostles teaching, and to the breaking of bread, and to prayer, and fellowship-- all those things that the early church did!

"Church of the Living God: We need to return to the basics-- the basics of what the Apostles did. They taught the truth of the word. They had fellowship and times of waiting upon God. They broke bread together. They came into covenant with God, and with one another. They gave their entire life over to the Most High God. That's what covenant means. That's what this New Covenant is all about. We give of our entire life – one hundred percent-- over to God. Complete abandonment to the purposes of God. They also gathered together in prayer."

"Church of the Living God: We need to return to all of these basics; and if we will and if you will; I challenge you this day: Will you return to the basics as outlined in Acts 2:42? If you will come back to these basics, I promise you this: the place where you are standing, it will be shaken, and a mighty rushing wind will come into that room, and the presence of the Living God will come in and take up His residence among you, and supernatural signs and wonders, and supernatural displays, of the outpouring of His Spirit will occur. But that's okay, because remember the verse: 'God takes the foolish things of this world to confound the wise.' It will appear at times foolish in the flesh, the natural, and in the carnal-- to the church and to the world. It will be unexplainable in the carnal. They will say, 'Wow, what is that?', and you can simply say, 'This is that. This is what was spoken of through the prophet Joel.' You can say exactly the same thing that Peter said. It was the only explanation that he could offer. Why? It was a spiritual explanation. It was in the mind of Christ. **This is that!** And, that's the only explanation that you can offer-- what was spoken of 835 years earlier through the prophet Joel. That God will pour out His Spirit upon all flesh. It can only be spiritually discerned. It can only be spiritually understood. For it is only by My Spirit," says the Lord.

"Church of the Living God, throughout all denominations: Stop trying to look at the baptism in the Holy Spirit in the natural, or in the carnal and explain it away, or reason it away. Humble yourself before the mighty hand of God. Allow Him to break you, to sift you, and to shake you through all of the extras that we have added, through all of the junk and the garbage that is not of God. Allow God to sift through it all, and get you to a place of hearing from the Most High God directly. And you, if you will seek Him with all of your heart, you will find Him and Him alone; and it will be void of all of the extras of what man has tried to add."

"Church of the Living God, I charge you this day: will you seek God with all of your heart with all of your soul, and with all of your mind? Will you seek Him and love Him with all that is within you? Will you run after Him with all that you have with complete abandonment – with a complete hunger and thirst after the things of God once again? Or are you completely full, satisfied and content, and have all that you would ever want or desire? If that's the case, you can stay exactly where you are every day for the rest of your life. You can be fat, full, plump, content, and stay in the same place that you always have been and never move forward if that's what you want."

But if you're like me, and you want all that God has for you in this lifetime, and you'll not look in the natural or the carnal, and if you'll not listen to people around you and what man may say, and that you will look forward and keep your eyes fixed upon Jesus – the author and finisher of your faith-- and look at Him and Him alone, not being side tracked to the right or to the left; and run full force with all that you have straight towards Jesus and say, "I want all that you have for me God." Come with me and we will go to a Higher Place. I'll take you

341

to a deeper place in God. Remember, to go up in God you have to go down. So the way up is down. I'll take you to the depths!

I'll take you to the depths! Are you ready? If you are and can say, "Yes, Lord. Yes"-- turn the page! And you can come with me to a higher place and we will go where the eagles are afraid to fly!

Restoring the Balance
(Ex. 25:31-40)

"Church of the Living God: I, the Lord God, I am restoring the perfect balance of My gifts and My fruits to the body of Christ in this day and in this hour. Church of the Living God: You have been way out of balance in both directions. I have pictured for you, in scripture, the golden lampstand first seen in the Tabernacle of Moses. It is a representation of My church. They are the light of the world also pictured in the book of Revelation. But there is more to the seven lamps of this lampstand. There is more than the sixty six ornaments totaled in all, corresponding to the sixty six books of the Bible that we had seen in chapter seven."

There is more to this piece of furniture that was fashioned out of a single piece of gold in Moses day. If you will look with me once again at this beautiful, golden piece of furniture that we do not have the privilege of looking at an original in our day, but it is described in detail in Exodus chapter 25, for us to look at and to learn from.

It was fashioned out of one piece of gold – the symbol of unity that needs to be in the body of Christ. Jesus prayed, *"That they may be one just as we are one ..."* (John 17:22) It was part of His last prayer here on this earth. It was very significant and carried great importance. Jesus didn't think of it in light terms but counted it as a very serious matter, because He included it in the last prayer He would pray before leaving this world. This prayer can be fulfilled in our lives today!

Church of the Living God: We need to come together for such a time as this. It is a desperate hour. We need to put aside all the differences that separate us. We need to put aside denominational differences, doctrinal differences and come together with what unites us. We are all serving the same God; with the same mission, and with the same purpose. United we stand-- divided we fall. Jesus said these very words, in His teachings to the multitude, *"If a kingdom is divided against itself, that kingdom cannot stand."* (Mk. 3:24)

"Church of the Living God: the **lampstand** represents **you** – the church. The very first thing about it was it was made out of one piece of gold. It is to be united. This is my charge to you this day: this is chapter one stuff, being repeated again! You must come together! You must come together! You must come together! This is from the very heart of God. The lampstand was fashioned out of one piece of gold. It was a beaten work. It was a hammered work. The anointings of God come from the sufferings of Christ. The anointing oil that flowed in it came from '…pure oil of pressed olives for the light, to make the lamps burn continually.'" (Lev. 24:2)

The olives had to be pressed, as we have seen before, the name "Gethsemane" from the "Garden of Gethsemane" means: "olive press". It was where Jesus prayed and endured that long night of anguished prayer in His sufferings. He prayed, "Father, if it is your will, take this cup away from Me; nevertheless not My will, but yours, be done." (Luke 22:42)

It was through His sufferings and His crucifixion, His death, burial, and resurrection that our anointing comes and flows. That's the only way we can get it; identifying with the sufferings of Christ; taking up our cross, and dying to ourselves, so that the anointing may flow; so we can be a light to the world and express the seven fold dimensions of the Holy Spirit; as outlined in Isaiah chapter 11 and Revelation chapter 3.

But there is more to this lampstand, as we have seen before, there were sixty six ornaments that covered the entire lampstand (counting every branch). There were three sets of three on each side branch, with nine individual ornaments on each branch, or nine sets of ornaments on each side. And as it was fashioned and designed by God-- it was symmetrical – perfectly balanced – the same on one side as it was on the other. It is a picture of something. What could that be? We turn to the New Testament for the answer to that question.

In I Cor. 12 and Gal. 5, we see that there are nine gifts listed and there are nine fruits listed. So as the church of Christ shines it's light in the world, and the lampstand is a picture of the church, in that same picture, there is a perfect balance of gifts and fruits that are and should be in that shining of the light of the gospel of Jesus Christ. All of that light can only come from the oil. The oil is the anointing, and out of that, flows the gifts and the fruits in perfect balance.

"Church of the Living God: You have been out of balance. If you have too much fruit and no gifts, the lampstand falls over and gives no light. If you have too much gifts and no fruit, you're out of balance and the lampstand falls over and there is no light."

Jesus said, "You are the light of the world. A city that is set on a hill cannot be hidden. Nor do they light a lamp and put it under a basket, but on a lampstand and it gives light to all who are in the house. Let your light shine before men, that they may see your good works and glorify your Father in heaven." (Mat. 5:14-16)

You see in the picture of all that light emitting from the golden lampstand there are nine sets of ornaments on one side, and nine sets of ornaments on the other side. It's a picture of the balance between gifts and fruits. It's what God intends. It is what He has designed to be within the church. We can't pick and choose what we want to keep and throw the rest away. God did not intend for us to only have one gift, or two gifts, or three and then only one, two, or three fruits on the other side. He wants all nine – **ALL NINE** GIFTS and **ALL NINE** FRUITS-- working together in perfect balance, perfect harmony, and perfect symmetry. That's the picture of the church. We must return to this picture. They are intended to bless not only us, but then to bless the entire world as well.

Paul writes, in the New Testament, a perfect example of this. I Cor. 12 is the gift chapter followed by I Cor. 13, which is the love chapter, and then chapter 14 talks about the gifts again-- its gifts, fruit, and then gifts. So, the fruit chapter is sandwiched directly in between the gift chapters as Paul is discussing the workings of the Spirit at the church of Corinth.

It reminds me of yet another picture, in a different place in scripture, in the description of the priestly garments, which happen to be the only set of garments that God Himself designed in the entire bible. God Himself designed the high priests clothing even down to his underwear. And everything is there for a reason – every detail.

I would like to bring your attention to the ephod and the bottom hem. God specifically instructed there to be on that hem a golden bell, then a pomegranate, a bell, a pomegranate, a bell, a pomegranate, in a series all the way around the hem of that garment.

Why? It is a picture of this same idea in the New Testament of a gift and a fruit, a gift and a fruit, a gift and a fruit. If the fruit was not there the bells would clang together. Paul said, *"Though I speak with tongues of men and of angles, but have not love; I have become a sounding brass or a clanging cymbal."* (I Cor. 13:1) If you have gifts and no fruit, you are nothing but noise. You see, the fruit is there on the hem of the garment so that the bell sounds as a bell should, with a clear sounding word. It's a clear sound! It's understood as a bell! It's identified as a bell, and you know it's the bell of the priest's garments. When he went in behind the veil, they could still hear him in there moving around; and then when he came back out, they could hear the sound and it was a good sign that he didn't fall over dead.

"Church of the Living God: Jesus is your High Priest. He entered into the Holy of Holies, the throne room of heaven, and applied His own blood to the Ark of the Covenant to set you free and to make a way where there was no way; so that you too, now, can come into the very throne room of God, past the veil, into the Holy of Holies. It's God's throne in the earth – the Glory of God – all that He is! His entire essence is in the Secret Place."

"Church of the Living God: Do not be satisfied living in the Holy Place – in the realm of My Spirit – in the realm of the Lampstand; where all of My giftings and all of My fruits have been available. You've got to press in. There's more. There's another chamber for you to discover. I'm calling you in, to go beyond the veil and enter the Secret Place of the Most High God – into the Holy of Holies – into the presence of the Living God where His glory and His essence reside. This is all that He "IS". It's His throne room in the earth. You need to press in. Take what you know and have experienced; don't throw it away, just add to it. Press in! Press in!

Just like the woman with the issue of blood that needed to press through the crowd. Expend a little bit of energy. Get past the resistance and be determined to touch the hem of His garment. She needed to press in!

"Church of the Living God: You need to press in and touch the Hem of His garment. Why? Jesus is our High Priest. All the gifts are on His hem. All the fruits are on His hem in perfect fifty-fifty balance. Gifts of miracles are on the hem. Gifts of healing are on the hem. Gifts of prophecy are on the hem of Jesus' garment. It's a clear sounding word-- the ringing of a bell-- a clear sounding word! All it takes is just one word from Jesus to change a whole situation. All it takes is JUST ONE WORD!"

In this woman's case, it took no words. All she needed to do was press in and touch the hem. And she thought to herself, *"If only I may touch His garment, I shall be made well."* (Mat. 9:21) And Jesus said to her, *"Your faith has made you well."* (v.22) Flowing out of that hem of His garment was the anointing of the Most Holy One. It's the anointing of God flowing out through the church.

On the Day of Pentecost they were all together in one place, in one mind, and in one accord. The lampstand was made of one piece of gold of a beaten work. If we can come together in unity and stop beating each other up, stabbing each other in the back, being jealous of one another's anointings, and accept one another as we are and as God uses us, in the diversities of gifting and in the varieties of gifting as mentioned in I Cor. 12:4-7 (NKJ); there will be an outward flow of God's power through His church as we have never seen before. Psalm 133 says, *"How pleasant it is for brethren to dwell together in unity. It is like the precious oil upon the head, running down on the beard, the beard of Aaron, running down on the edge of his garments."* (v.1, 2) The unity is associated with the anointing! If we can come together and be as one, allow God to be God, don't put God in a box and try to tell Him what to do, allow Him to have the freedom to be who He is, and then He can allow us to have the freedom to be who we are. There will be an outward flow of God's precious holy anointing oil in and through the church in the fullness that God intended it to flow in; and it will be in perfect balance as well.

We don't have to be afraid of any one gift that God may have for us. We tend to be afraid of some of the giftings. We're not so much afraid of the fruit but we are of the giftings; because they are different. They **amaze** us; they **marvel** us; and we are **bewildered** by them; because we can't understand them in the natural. But if we will cross over into the realm of the spirit and allow the Holy Spirit, who is the author and the finisher of them all, He will teach us how to move in them. He'll teach us how to operate in them, and we don't need to be afraid of the gifts at all ever again!

If they are a little bit different, a little louder, a little longer, a little more unusual; maybe you've never seen it done in that way before – that's okay! Let God be God! Let God be God throughout the whole body of Christ. Don't be afraid of the anointings and the giftings of God. And when we come together, every piece of the body: the hand, the foot, the eyes, the ears, the arm, the leg, the mouth; they all form one body and it's the body of Christ; and then, He is all together lovely! (Song of Songs 5:16) He is all together beautiful!

"Church of the Living God; I admonish you this day: We need to come together as one accepting **all** the gifts and **all** the fruits in perfect balance. We need to have love for one another. Love for one another's gifting and diversities of gifting, and don't be so quick to judge and say, 'That's not God'… or 'That's not the way God has done it in the past'… or 'That's not the way that I have seen it before'. Because, I am speaking this word in love: God is going to begin to do greater, more unusual things than we have ever seen before. Expect the unusual! The Day of Pentecost was unusual. God's moving and God's workings are not always what we would consider or what we are used to seeing in the past. Why? I believe it's to keep us on our toes, and keep us walking by faith. It's to keep us walking and living in the Spirit; so that God's in control and we're not! We have to come by way of faith, walking in the Spirit, and allowing God to do what He wants."

Moses thought that he would just hit the rock, because he hit the rock before. God told him to speak to the rock the second time. He gave up the Promised Land because he didn't walk in obedience to his Lord and his God.

You see, we have to do it the way God wants. Each and every time, relinquish our agendas for any given service or meeting and say, "King of kings and Lord of lords: Come take your throne and do it your way – whatever that may be."

And you see, this way, you have to listen to the Spirit, and know the mind of the Spirit at any given moment. That's the place we need to get to. That is "Secret Place" living! That is "Holy of Holies" living; where it's the death of you, and the complete life of God. Not what you want, but what He wants—where all of your flesh is crucified!

You see, dead men see God. It's the death of your flesh; and I mean all of it, absolutely ALL OF IT! So, if you're offended by someone speaking in tongues; you're not dead yet. If you're not offended by someone speaking in tongues; but it's too loud or too long; you're not dead yet.

EXPECT THE SUPERNATURAL! EXPECT THE UNUSUAL!

A word in Isaiah 8:6-8, the children of Israel had rejected the *"gentle waters of Shiloh"*. If you reject the "gentle waters of Shiloh" – a calm, nice, peaceful move of the Spirit-- God's going to bring the "mighty rushing waters of the Euphrates" and it's only going to get more intense from there.

"Church of the Living God: Stop rejecting what God wants to bring! STOP REJECTING WHAT GOD WANTS TO BRING; because as you do, it's going to get more intense. He's going to get louder, not quieter! He's going to get longer not shorter! The children of Israel begged Moses for God not to speak to them because they could not endure it. THEY COULD NOT ENDURE GOD SPEAKING DIRECTLY TO THEM! Why? Their flesh could not endure it! If you can't endure God's voice speaking to you, you're walking with too much in the flesh. There's too much still left of you, and you need to go to the cross yet again and be crucified with Christ, take up your cross, and follow Him. You need to go to the brazen altar and be that living sacrifice and allow God's Spirit to burn up everything until there is nothing left-- absolutely nothing left of you!"

I know this is a harsh word to some; but it is the truth of the gospel of Jesus Christ nevertheless. I'm going to give it to you straight. And I told you at times this book will be hard. If you can receive that word – receive it into your heart – go a little bit further – even into your stomach and digest it, and allow it to become a part of who you are. It will radically change your life forever. You will not be the same, and your life will not be the same either. To all who will hear what the Spirit of the Lord is saying in these days; who will put aside every encumbrance, every hindrance, and run this race with endurance: Will you hear what the Holy Spirit is saying to you in these days? If you will, come go with me. Come! Let us go to a higher place!

I Love My Garden
(Isaiah 5:7)

"I, the Lord God, I love My garden! I planted a garden in the beginning. You know it as the Garden of Eden. I put many, many, beautiful things in this garden, and I was not pleased until I placed man there, then it was very good! Even now you, My church, are a garden of the Lord." Isaiah 5:7 reads *"The vineyard of the Lord Almighty is the house of Israel, and the men of Judah are the garden of His delight."* (NKJ) "You are My Garden," says the Lord God Almighty. "In the parable of the tenants, I built a wall around it, dug a winepress, and built a watchtower to protect it and watch over it."

Jesus used this allegory in John 15: He said "I am the vine, you are the branches. My Father is the vinedresser." He comes along and He prunes you, and He prunes you some more, and then He prunes you even more. Why? So that you will produce fruit. God is not interested in just a bunch of leaves growing on His vines. His goal is fruit, fruit, and more fruit! He will cut away from you anything that would rob precious energy, or sunlight, or be any kind of diversion, or take away from the fruit production in your life.

So anything that you don't need, it is His job, His nature, to come and cut it off of you. That's what God does! We should expect nothing less from our Father in heaven; after all -- He is the vinedresser!!

The trouble comes when we resist and say, "No God, No... No God... Not that branch! No, don't cut that one! Oh God, why did you have to go and cut that one off; I really liked that branch." You see, it doesn't matter what we like, or what we want, or what we want to hold on to. It just doesn't matter. You have been crucified with Christ. Your life is no longer your own. When you accepted Christ you gave your life away.

So, we need to be open minded and open hearted, and allow God to come and cut off any branch that does not bear any fruit or enough fruit. If He wants to cut it off, let Him cut it off; because ultimately, it will be for your benefit, your health, and be a blessing to you; so that you will produce even more fruit.

If you can receive this word, it may be different than what you have heard in the past; but I want you to consider it nonetheless.

What is fruit? Many have asked this question and have had different answers given to them. **Fruit is the visible, tangible, fulfillment of God's word in the life of a believer!** That is a Holy Ghost definition! You see, the Lord your God has planted a vineyard. He does so with the seed of the word. Let's go to the parable of the sower in Mark ch.4. There were four different kinds of soil. If the seed fell on good soil, and the seed took – it would begin to grow. And if that vine grew well enough, Jesus said it would bring forth either thirty fold fruit, sixty fold, or one hundred fold. The farmer planted the seed, but just didn't know how much of a harvest he would get in return. The seed is the planting in hopes of a harvest! You just don't know how much. It's variable and changing depending on the different circumstances that arise, and conditions that come into play, regarding the care of that vine. But God loves His vineyard. He loves His garden. He built a wall around it. He built a watchtower to keep the enemy out of it, and to make sure that it's growing as it should.

"Stay in the vineyard! Abide in God! Stay inside the four walls! This is the only place that you can be fully protected from the wiles of the enemy. God will protect His vines; so that the enemy cannot come in and cut them down and destroy His vineyard; or even steal the seed that has been planted in you."

"I the Lord God, I love My Garden. I care for it! I protect it! I watch over it! I make it rain in the seasons to water the earth, and I bring forth the sunlight to cause the vines to grow. I even cultivate the soil and crush the rocks to pieces, so that they may add nutrients to the soil. What was once rocky soil, I can come and pulverize the rocks with My word and turn it into a powder; and then, it becomes fertilizer for the soil. (see Jer.23:29) My word… is like a hammer that breaks the rocks to pieces."

"I fertilize the soil… I pull the weeds in this vineyard that would come in and grow, and choke the very life out of the vine – the worries and the cares of this life. All the things that would distract you from your relationship with the Lord your God, I pull them out; so that they are not a problem to you in your life anymore."

"You see, I am trying to produce as much fruit as possible on every vine. I am calling you in to the Secret Place of the Most High God: 'Outer Court living' is thirty fold production. 'Holy Place living' is sixty fold production. 'Secret Place living' is one hundred fold production."

It is one hundred percent of the word of God being fulfilled in the life of a believer. It is one hundred fold blessing. One hundred is the number representative of heavens fullness, heaven's completeness, and heaven's divine standard. That is "Secret Place" living! That is what God is trying to do in your life. Some choose to live in the "Outer Court" and they will only see a partial fulfillment of the word of God in their life. Some will choose to live in the "Holy Place" and it will only be partial – a little over fifty percent – or one half the word of God – or sixty fold production. The Lord wants to bring about the entire fulfillment of His word to you – His "Rhema" word and His "Logos" word-- from Genesis to Revelation-- all of His spoken word to you and all of His written word to you – every promise! He wants to bring them all to pass in your life-- today.

But it will only come about if you allow Him to do what He wants to do in your life. Let Him be the vinedresser – come in – cut off – and prune – all the unnecessary things out of your life, and expose you to the SON...S-O-N; allow the rains of His presence to water you and saturate your soil, so that His life can flow into your vine and out into the branches and then to the fruit. Allow God to weed the soil and also bring the hammer of His word to you. In all these things, He is trying to produce the fulfillment of the word of God in your life! But it's all up to you as to what you allow Him to do in your life!

How much rain do you get? How much sun (son) do you get? How many weeds do you have growing next to you? How many dead branches or unproductive branches do you have growing on your vine that rob vital energy from the fruit? How many rocks do you have in your soil? How much fertilizer are you getting? How much nutrition and food are you getting? All these variables and factors determine how much fruit the farmer harvests and how much production does he yield for each seed that He planted!

The Kingdom of God is like a farmer that sows seed in His field as described in the Parable of the Sower. (Mk. 4) He takes the seed. He scatters it upon the ground. There are different conditions of the soil that exist, and different circumstances that the seed encounters. One, the birds come and steal it away. Two, there are rocky places where there is not much soil. The seed sprang up quickly and began to grow, but when the sun came out the plants were scorched and withered because the roots weren't deep enough. Thirdly, some of the seed fell among thorns and the plants were choked out. And the fourth and final lasting condition is the seed fell on good soil. This is the condition that God wants us to have. He wants to take care of it, give it good soil, plenty of rain, plenty of sunshine, plenty of fertilizer, prune the vines, weed the grounds and do all these things to produce one hundred fold fruit in the life of every believer.

There is then, growing on your vine, a crop of mature fruit; one for every promise in the word of God – one for every promise! So if you can get a picture of that, your vine would have thousands of fruit growing on it with every promise in the word of God being fulfilled in your life. Maybe not all at one time but they will be formed through a process that takes time, in different seasons of your life. They will be developing, maturing, and growing; and then one day there's the hope of the mature fruit that can be picked from your vine!

Proverbs 11:30 reads, *"The fruit of the righteous is a tree of life."* This may be another concept that you have never heard of before, but you actually become a "tree of life" that's just like the one back in the Garden of Eden. Other people can pick the fruit off of your tree; because they can see the visible, tangible, evidence of the word of God coming to pass in your life, and they can reap a blessing from the seed that was sown in you. They can eat and enjoy the fruit of it. It's good for food. It looks good. It tasted good. It smells good. It nourishes them and gives them a blessing; and then, guess what? There's a seed in the fruit! And most of us probably spit out the seeds that we can, but in the animal kingdom the whole fruit is eaten, seed and all.

So as someone eats the whole fruit and all, the seed gets planted into another life and begins the process all over again. There is the planting of the seed again. If enough seed gets eaten, it will begin to take root. Then, they will begin to grow a whole new vine themselves; and the process starts all over again. MORE VINES for the vineyard!

Psalm 91:2 gives us a picture of the Lord our God being our "refuge" and our "fortress". Psalm 144:2 says, "He is our 'high tower'". It's the same picture. God is our "Fortress". He is our "high tower". He has built a wall around us to protect us and to watch over us. We are His vineyard-- the garden of His delight. You see, it's also a picture of the New Jerusalem. In this place in the New Testament, there were four walls, and God is in the midst of these four walls. It's "Secret Place" living!

Church of the Living God: We've got to get to the "Secret Place" of the Most High God. In this place, the word of God – it is! **IT IS! IT IS!** You will have entered into the "IS" realm of God. It is heaven coming down into the earth where the Lord Jesus prayed, *"Thy will be done on earth as it is in heaven."* It is Jacob's ladder! It's a New Jerusalem! It's heaven coming down to the earth! It is *"Thy will be done on earth as it is in heaven."* It is the fulfillment of the word of God in the life of a believer. It is the word of God becoming a reality in that life--

in someone who will only believe God: listen, believe, and obey. Just believe His word! It is "Secret Place" living.

God is trying to bring heaven down into the earth to where His word shall be fulfilled and become a reality in our lives. *"He is watching over His word to perform it…"* (Jer. 1:12) to cause it to come to pass. But, it takes someone who will believe His word. It takes someone who will have the faith to trust God; who will walk by faith and not by sight; not look at what you see or what you hear and just fully – one hundred percent-- believe God!

The word of God can be a reality in the life of any child of God who will simply believe, take God at His word, and "abide in the vine". You see, that's "Secret Place" living. That's pressing in to one hundred fold fruit. Abiding in the vine! That's abiding and remaining in the courtyard of the vineyard with the walls all around you. That is having a close intimate relationship with the Lord your God. It's a "New Jerusalem" in the earth.

We have to stop doing it our way, and begin to do it God's way. It's all outlined in the Tabernacle of Moses where there is "Outer Court", "Holy Place" and "Secret Place" living. We have to begin to do it God's way. It's His pattern-- His protocol. Stop living in the "Outer Court" and live in the "Secret Place". We have to get to where God lives. There's more! Press in!

"Church of the Living God: When I pass by you, will I find any fruit on your fig tree? Will I find any fulfillment of the word of God in your life? You know what happened when Jesus passed by the fig tree and saw no fruit on it. He cursed it and it withered. It completely dried up. It is a picture of enduring the judgment of God for what you have been given. You have been given much. Good seed, plenty of water, plenty of sunlight, exposure to the Son – S-O-N! You have been well cultivated, and well weeded. How much fruit will there be on your vines?"

"Church of the Living God: I am hoping for one hundred fold fruit production on My vines. That is My goal and My heart's desire, to see My vineyard flourish and bring forth an abundance of fruit. *"You will know them by their fruit."* (Mat. 7:16) It is the fulfillment and the maturing of the seed; and it must go through many, many, different stages of growth, processes, and seasons."

It must be developed and nourished, and that is where you come in. You must allow yourself to be saturated in the presence of

353

God; watered by the rains of His Spirit; be exposed to the SON; allow yourself to be hammered by God's word, so that all of your rocks will be crushed into a powder, and then act as a fertilizer for your soil, and be assimilated in that soil; so that you can grow and flourish; have all your weeds pulled out; and be subject to much pruning. All these things are variables and things that you have as your responsibility in the Kingdom of God. Remember, we are co-workers with God. He cannot do anything in your life unless you allow Him to do what He wants; and you listen to Him. So if He says, "spend longer times in the rains of My Presence," you do it! You don't ask questions. You don't argue. You just do it. If He says, "You need a little more exposure to the son – S-O-N, you just do it! You spend more time with Jesus. You have longer quiet times and prayer times, or devotionals alone with God. If He says, "Read My Word more", that's being subject to the hammer; and then you simply do what He says. **Listen, believe, and do!** It's as simple as that!

If you will do just that, in using this analogy of the vineyard, and allow yourself to undergo all of these processes, the fruit will be a natural outgrowth of all of these processes along with the care that the Lord wants to give you. But you have your responsibilities as well. Don't venture outside the courtyard. Don't allow your vines to grow out there; because the enemy will cut down your vines – chop them off. God does not intend for that to happen.

You see, that is "Secret Place" living. That's "Abiding under the Shadow of the Almighty". It's where you live under the greatest protections and coverings – the largest umbrella-- in the universe. You are under God's divine care. All the protections and the promises of God are yours. Why? Because you "abide in the vine" and you have a close, intimate, relationship with your Heavenly Father. That is "Abiding under the Shadow". That is "Secret Place" living. But that's the only place where all of heaven and all of God's word is applied to you.

So allow yourself to undergo all of these processes in abundance, and the word of God will be fulfilled in your life. The seed that has been planted will grow into a mature vine. It will blossom and begin to form fruit on the vine; and even though it may be small fruit at first, they will grow to maturity and then that fruit will be the complete fulfillment of the word of God in your life. It is the visual evidence of the life that is lived "Abiding in the Vine". And then someone else can come along and pick your fruit, be nourished by it, and it will be a blessing to them. "A tree is known by its fruit." (Mat. 12:33)

How much fruit do you have on your vine? Where are your fruits? Where is the fulfillment of the word of God in your life? Are you living it? Are you experiencing it? Are you a living testimony? The world is dying to see a "living epistle" in you – that this word of God and this Christianity works! *"For the time has come for judgment to begin at the House of God..."* (I Pet. 4:17)

The world is longing to see someone who will believe their God and His word, and where it becomes a reality in their life. God is raising up a people who will do simply this: believe God – just believe Him-- and take Him at His word!

Conceived By the Holy Ghost
(Gen. 12:1-3)

"Abraham was My chosen vessel. He was a man of faith, honor, and integrity. I chose Him from the line of Shem – one of Noah's three sons. It would be a righteous-line through whom the Messiah would eventually come from. I, the Lord God, I appeared to Abraham when he was seventy five years old. I spoke to Him and said, *"Leave your country, your people, and your father's household and go to the land I will show you. I will make you into a great nation and I will bless you; I will make your name great, and you will be a blessing. I will bless those who bless you, and whoever curses you I will curse; and all peoples on earth will be blessed through you."*(Genesis 12:1-3)

There was this one problem: His wife Sarai was barren and she had no children-- none whatsoever-- no one in line to be the heir of everything that they owned-- no one to carry on the family name. There was no heir. There was no son or daughter. No hope of the future.

"But, I the Lord God, I had conceived in Him that day – a word from God – a promise that I fully intended to fulfill one day in the earth-- in My time!" says the Lord. "You see, My time is not Man's time. My ways are not your ways. And in 'Secret Place Living' – it is a place of intimacy. It is a place of closeness with the Lord your God, having fellowship with Him. The Greek word used for fellowship is

"Koinonia" which carries with it connotations of sexual relations. And it is in this place – in "Secret Place Living" that the promises of God are placed within your spirit – deep, deep into the heart of your being."

And that which is in you is conceived by the Holy Spirit. And it is in this place that the Lord your God places the seeds of His word in you concerning your future, your purpose, and your mission in this life. They are conceived by the Holy Spirit; and they begin to grow in you, just as a little baby will begin to develop on the inside of its mother's womb.

And it doesn't matter whether you are male or female. You see, in New Testament covenant the circumcision of the heart is for all people. It's no longer just the males that are circumcised – it is both the males and the females. So, God does not look upon gender in this case. All can be conceived by the Holy Ghost. It is just an analogy that pictures for us the intimacy and the close relationship that we can have with our creator. It is a tangible, physical picture of something in the natural that portrays what happens in the spiritual better than anything else.

Remember, what happens in the natural is also paralleled in the spiritual. So, we can take the simple idea of pregnancy and the gestational period that a woman goes through, and relate it to a very deep spiritual truth.

In the natural, a woman's gestational period is normally nine months, corresponding to chapter nine and the Holy Spirit. But in the spirit realm, a thousand years is as a day and one day as a thousand years. So time is completely different in the spirit realm. And you see, God is in that time zone! So, what is conceived in us may take a lot longer than just nine months to develop and be brought to delivery.

In Abraham's case, it took twenty five years! He was seventy five years old when the first promise came; but he was one hundred years old when it was fulfilled. God appeared again to Abram, his first name when he was ninety nine years old, and established His covenant with His servant. (Gen. 17:4-7) God said, *I will make you a father of many nations*" and changed his name to Abraham - "Father of many"- the sign of that covenant being circumcision. It was the cutting away of his flesh. He had to undergo that to be in the covenant, and for God to fulfill His word in his life. That's what he had to do as a sign to say that God was His God. And it is interesting to note that right after the circumcision of his flesh the promise was fulfilled.

In our life, it's the same way today! We must undergo the circumcision of the heart and the cutting away of all of our flesh for the promises of God to be fulfilled in our life. And if and when we allow God to do that, we're in a better position for that promise to come to pass. It's the way God works. The flesh must die for the spirit to live!

Abraham was one hundred years old when his wife Sarah gave birth to their son Issac. God changed Sarai's name as well to Sarah, which means: "Mother of Nations". He was their promised son, where all things would be fulfilled through Issac and his line, right down through to Jesus Christ – himself – the King of all kings.

God had said to Abram, *"Look up at the heavens and count the stars – if indeed you can count them."* Your descendants will outnumber the stars! He was giving that promise to a man whose wife was barren and past the age of child-bearing when he was seventy five years old!

They both laughed at the promise of God; because in the natural it just couldn't happen. It was totally impossible! There was no way it could be fulfilled in the flesh. They tried to fulfill the promise of God on their own and got an Ishmael… totally messed everything up! God still blessed Ishmael, but it was not God's pattern. It was not God's way. It was not His will for their lives. They tried to fulfill the promise of God in the flesh, in their own power, their own way, and totally messed it up – in tremendous proportions.

So, God kept waiting and waiting. Why? He was instilling faith in their hearts. "Will you believe the promise of God? Will you believe what I have said to you? Will you believe what I have said to you no matter how it all looks? Will you believe?"

God later challenged Abraham. He said, "Go sacrifice the promise". Take Isaac up to the mountain and sacrifice him. Would he be willing to do that, and give it all back to God? He was testing Abraham. Was faith building in his heart and in his life?

Abraham listened. He obeyed God. He believed God. They began to walk up the mountain when Isaac asked, "But where is the lamb for the burnt offering?" Abraham answered, "God himself will provide the lamb for the burnt offering, my son." He was walking by faith, not by sight. And just as he was about to kill Issac, the angel of the Lord stopped him. God provided a ram that was caught in the thickets to be sacrificed instead of Isaac. The "ram" was a type of Christ – a substitutionary death for Isaac's life. God made a way, just

357

as he does for each and every one of us. God provides His son Jesus Christ as the "Way" – the Lamb of God-- that takes away the sins of the world. He died in our place. Everything looked impossible! The death and the barrenness of the womb represents all the ways and the means of man that could never fulfill or accomplish the promise of God. It can only come through the work of the Spirit! *"It's not by might, nor by power, but by My Spirit," says the Lord."* (Zach. 4:6)

Earlier, Abraham even asked God, "Can you not bless Ishmael?" implying that maybe God could just fulfill the promise through him since he was already born. God said, "Yes, I'll bless him; but I have another way. You will receive the promised son." God told Abraham, "I will return to you at the appointed time next year and Sarah will have a son." His wife would give birth to the promised son – Isaac. God would be faithful to His promise and fulfill all that he had spoken to Abraham.

There are many of you that have been to the "Secret Place" and who have lived there awhile, who have stayed and remained, who are hungry for God, who have conceived by the Holy Spirit, a purpose, a mission, a divine plan for your life. And you have waited, and you have waited, and you have waited – maybe, some for years. I personally, had waited twenty years before I had actually begun to see the fulfillment of the promise of God in my life. Some gestational periods may be shorter, some longer. But the key to all of this is that you must still continue to believe God for that promised "child" – that promised blessing-- that promised mission or purpose.

Continue to believe God no matter what everything else looks like. You see, as you are carrying this baby many things could happen. Even in the natural as women are carrying a baby, they need to take good care of themselves. Get the proper rest and the proper diet, eat all the proper foods, and go to the doctor to get checked out. Just like all of these things in the natural, we need to take care of ourselves and this "baby" in the spiritual.

We must get the proper diet and nutrition, exercise, and rest, etc. We need to take care of this "baby" that is growing within us, so that we can carry it to a "full term". Then, it can be birthed into the earth in its proper time, on its proper "birthday"; so that all the world can rejoice with us and celebrate the birth of this "child"!

If we don't take care of ourselves, we could have a miscarriage; and what was conceived in us from the Holy Ghost could be lost. Or, we could give birth to it too soon – rush the process – and it would be a premature birth – it could live awhile – people could see it, marvel at it, rejoice for awhile, be blessed by it; but then it could die a premature birth and not survive, because it wasn't developed enough. It wasn't time yet!

And then lastly, we could give up altogether – throw in the towel, and "abort" the promise – "the baby" – and say, "Forget it … it's been too long in coming. It's too hard to carry this 'baby' anymore. I've been waiting way too long for this promise. I must not have heard God right.   I heard wrong." And then, we "abort" the "baby" ourselves and give up on the promise. We kill it. We destroy it all by ourselves. But, if we will carry it to "full term" and take care of it – take care of the word of God – the promise – that has been conceived in our "womb", and continue to have faith and believe God – God will bring forth the fulfillment of the promise and the word that He has spoken concerning us, all in His perfect time.

"Church of the Living God: that which is in you is conceived by the Holy Ghost. There are ministries that I am developing within you that you must take care of—it's a 'baby' – a 'ministry'. You can't see it yet. It hasn't been birthed into the earth yet; but nevertheless, even as in the natural, a pregnant woman must take care of herself. So you too, must take care of yourself and the 'baby'. That is part of your responsibility of seeing that it is birthed into the earth. You have to protect it, take care of it, nurture it, get the proper rest, nutrition, exercise, anything and everything that you can think of to take care of this 'baby'. You have to protect it in your comings and your goings. So you won't fall down and even miscarry in that way. Also, protect it from others trying to destroy this 'child'."

You see, Satan has done this all along throughout history. He has tried to kill babies in their infancy to stop the plans and the purposes of God in the earth from being fulfilled. Remember Moses and Jesus? He'll do the same thing to you. He'll try to kill your "baby" before it's ever born, or get it to be born too soon, be premature, and not survive. He'll try to get you to miscarry; hit you with something; or to get you to fall down and miscarry; or to get you to be so discouraged that you'll want to abort it yourself and say, "I don't want this 'baby' anymore. Just forget it". You see, those things can happen, because we're in this thing together with God. He has His role to play, and we have our role to play. It's our responsibility to take care of the word of God: the promises, the purposes, the missions, and the ministries of God, that have been conceived in us and carry them – for how long?

Until it's ready! In the natural, babies come when they are ready! The baby decides when to come along. With God, we can't try to rush it. We can't force it. And when that baby is ready to come, it will come; and nothing can stop it. Spiritually, it's the same way with ministries, the purpose of God, or the mission of God for you in your life.

If you take care of it, and protect it, and you don't "abort it" yourself, that "baby" is going to grow and be developed. You may be able to help determine how fast or slow it's developing by how you're caring for it, and caring for yourself. So, you're in it together with God; and when it's fully ready, it will come and be birthed into the earth on that right day at the perfect time, on its appropriate "birthday". And you will fulfill God's purpose, His plan, and His mission for your life; and the ministry that is within you will be given birth into the earth.

Other people will also celebrate the "birth" of your "baby" and rejoice in its arrival. The "baby" will be a blessing to many in the earth. You see, that's how God works! All of us are called to be ministers of the Most High God. All of us have a ministry to some extent or another.

All babies come in different sizes, shapes, and colors, and looks, and facets, and diversities, and variations! It's the same with ministries, but none are less loved by our Father in heaven! All are important. All are prized! All are valuable! None is more important than the other. None is greater or higher than any other. All have equal value at the foot of the cross!

So, if you have not conceived by the Holy Ghost yet, you need to get to the "Secret Place"; because we all have a ministry. We all have a purpose, a plan, and a mission, in this life that God wants to birth in us; but we must carry it through to full term, then that ministry can be birthed into the earth.

God will be birthing new ministries in our day and in our time. Will you be one who will go to the "Secret Place" …a place of intimacy and closeness with our God and be "conceived" by the Holy Ghost and then carry it to "full term"… that you know, that you know, that you know, what God had spoken to you? There will be a witness of the spirit, and it will be confirmed to you many, many times

360

over – not just once, but two, three, four, times-- up to as many times as you need it confirmed – until it's ready to be birthed into the earth! It may be five years, it may be ten, it may be twenty, or it could be longer; but, if you will take care of it as you would a natural baby – and carry it through until full term-- it will be birthed into the earth one day!

Are You Living On the East Side?
(Joshua 13:8; Numbers 32)

"Church of the Living God: Are you living on the east side, or are you ready to cross over the Jordan River and live on the west side, and enter a land with fountains, and springs, and brooks, with wheat and barley, and vines, and fig trees, a land of olive oil and honey, a land in which you will eat bread without scarcity, in which you will lack nothing."

It's the description of the Promised Land in Deut. 8:7; a place flowing with milk and honey; a place that you will lack absolutely nothing. Sounds like a place that I would like to live in! It is "Promised Land Living" at its best! It is also "Secret Place Living" at its best!

The closer you get to God, the greater the fulfillment of the word of God in your life. Don't settle for anything less than one hundred percent fulfillment of the word of God in your life. Don't settle for less!

In the days of Moses as they were about to enter into the Promised Land, they sent a team of twelve spies to scout out the land for forty days, that the Lord God had promised them. Only two spies, Joshua and Caleb, came back with a good report. All the other ones, the other ten, came back with a bad report. And in that bad report, they described people that were bigger and stronger than they were, a land that devours those that live in it. "We're like grasshoppers compared to them," they said. But there were two: Joshua and Caleb...

Caleb silenced all the people and said, "We should go up and take possession of the land for we can certainly do it." Joshua and Caleb spoke words of faith, hope, and promise. Their reward for their good report was that they could enter the land that they had scouted out. The rest, because of their doubt, their unbelief, and because of believing the bad report, all those twenty years of age and older would fall and die in the desert. They would never see the promise of God

361

fulfilled in their life. Even, their great leader Moses would never enter the Promised Land. He would see it from a distance, but he would never enter it because of his disobedience to God.

In those days and in that time, there were two and a half tribes of the children of Israel – the tribe of Gad, Reuben, and half of the tribe of Manasseh-- that decided that the land on the East side of the Jordan was good enough for them. They had large herds of livestock and that land happened to be good for grazing. They thought, "This is far enough. This is good enough for us. We can stay here. It's been a long journey. We're tired. We're half worn out. Let's just stay here. We're close enough." So, they asked Moses, the leader of God's people, if he would allow them to stay there and for that land to become their inheritance.

Moses had seen this kind of thing before – this kind of discouragement. He said to them, *"Why do you discourage the Israelites from going over into the land the Lord has given them?"* (Num. 32:7) It was the same as in the days of the twelve spies. He said, "Shall your countrymen go to war while you sit here?" They replied, "It would not be fair for all of us not to fight with you; but let us build cities and pens for our livestock, and allow our women and children to stay behind, and we will come back to them after all the tribes receive their inheritance. We still want this land! We still want to stay here!"

They still insisted to stay on the East side of the Jordan River. We can stay there too if we want, but the Lord our God has a much better land for us if we'll be willing to fight for it and go in and possess the land. The other nine and a half tribes, they went in with Joshua as their military leader and they fought battle after battle, and they did possess the land that God had wanted for them. But only nine and a half tribes went in and possessed the fullness of all that God had for them.

You can stay on the "East Side" if you want to, but I don't know about you, I want all that God has for me. I want to go in and possess the land – all of it – a land flowing with milk and honey, with springs and fountains, and brooks, and bread without scarcity. I want everything that God has for me; so I'm going in and enter the land. Will you go with me and possess that land?

"Do not believe a bad report!" says the Lord God Almighty. "Satan himself will try to spread lies among the camp, and spread rumors and false-hoods, to discourage God's people from going

362

further in their walk with God and from going deeper. For whatever reason, the people spread a bad report about the Promised Land. They said the people are too big, too strong, and the land devours those living in it. It was all lies!"

"Church of the Living God: Be careful! Be aware of the enemy! He is the father of lies, and he will try to spread his lies any way that he can to discourage and deceive God's people from receiving the truth and receiving all the promises of God, and then discouraging them from possessing the full, entire, "Promised Land" of God that is available in this lifetime."

We do not have to cross over and die, and then go to heaven, to possess the "Promised Land". The "Promised Land" is for here and now, in this lifetime; to be experienced and to be a reality in our lives. We can experience all that God has for us. We need to go for God's best and live on the "West Side"! In looking at the Tabernacle of Moses, the entrance always faced to the east. You would have to head west if you would make your way into the deeper chambers of the tabernacle. The Most Holy Place where God's glory dwelt was always on the west side of the tabernacle. That's where God is calling us to come to today!

"HEAD WEST!" HALLELUIAH! "GO WEST! GO WEST!" It is God's word to us today. "GO WEST!" It is "Promised Land" living, and it is "Secret Place" living at its best!

Do not settle for living on the "East Side" of the Jordan. There is a vast ocean of God with many deep mysteries long yet to be discovered that are awaiting us; so we can experience all that God has, and it's all on the West Side of the Jordan. It's in the "Secret Place" of the Most High!

Psalms 91:1 says, *"He who dwells in the secret place of the Most High, shall abide under the shadow of the Almighty."* God's calling us to the secret place. It is a place where the Most High dwells. The glory of God lives there and resides there. It is His complete essence of all that He is.

Do you want all of God today for your life, and receive it in this life time? If you will give God all that you are and all that you have, all that you are not, and all that you don't have; your dreams, your hopes, your future… everything… If you give Him everything, He is obligated by His covenant – life for a life – to give you everything that He has! That is "Secret Place" living. It's the throne of God where the Ark of the Covenant was kept. The Ark is a symbol of the covenant between our God and His people today. It is "New Testament living" at its best: Life for a life.

The contract has been signed by Jesus Christ Himself with His blood that He shed on the cross at Calvary. He now needs that contract or covenant signed with another signature, and it has to be symbolically signed in your blood; which is representative of your entire life and your entire being – all that you are – everything! If you'll be willing to give Him that, He'll give you all that He is. It is one hundred fold blessing and fruitfulness of the Kingdom of God!

"The kingdoms of this world have become the kingdoms of our Lord and His Christ, and He shall reign forever and ever." (Rev. 11:15) It's where the Kingdom of God has now become the Kingdom in the earth. HEAVEN'S COMING DOWN!   HEAVEN'S COMING DOWN!

Heaven's coming down into the earth realm. It's Jacob's ladder! It's "Secret Place" living! It's a "New Jerusalem". It is the one hundred percent fulfillment of the word of God in the believer's life. Don't settle for anything less! DO NOT SETTLE FOR ANYTHING LESS. It is your complete inheritance as a son or a daughter of the Most High God. You are a descendant of Abraham. You are a descendant of Isaac. You are a descendant of Jesus Christ of Nazareth. You are a child of the Most High God. Someone died and left you something; and that something is the fulfillment of every word that God has ever spoken concerning His children from Genesis to Revelation!!!!

The choice is yours. It's all up to you. Do you want to live in the "Outer Court", the "Holy Place", or the "Secret Place"? Do you want to live on the "East Side of the Jordan" or do you want to cross over and live in the vast oceans of God – the "Promised Land"-- that the Lord your God has given you. It's your inheritance! It's up to you whether you want to receive it or not, enjoy it or not, and whether or not you want to spend it in this lifetime. The choice is yours. It's all up to you!

Where Are the Other Nine?
(Luke 17:11-19)

"Now on His way to Jerusalem, Jesus traveled along the border between Samaria and Galilee. As He was going into a village, ten men who had leprosy met Him.

They stood at a distance and called out in a loud voice, 'Jesus, Master, have pity on us!'"

When He saw them, He said, "Go show yourselves to the priest." And as they went, they were cleansed. One of them, when he saw he was healed, came back, praising God in a loud voice. He threw himself at Jesus' feet and thanked Him — and he was a Samaritan.

Jesus asked, "Were not all ten cleansed? Where are the other nine? Was no one found to return and give praise to God except this foreigner?" Then He said to him, "Rise and go; your faith has made you well."

"Church of the Living God: Where are the other nine? Jesus Christ Himself, God in the earth, asked them, to all who would hear Him: 'Where are the other nine?' I charge you this day, Church of the Living God: I ask you the same question, 'Where are the other nine?' Have I not done many great things for you? Have I not saved you from the fires of hell itself? Have I not set you free from being captivity's captive, and from Satan's power? I have translated you from the kingdom of darkness and into the kingdom of light. Have I not fed you? Have I not clothed you? Have I not cared for you? Have I not given you a roof over your head, a warm fire in your fireplace? Have I not given you people to love and to care for? And Have I not given you those who would love you and care for you in return?"

"Consider the lilies of the fields, have I not cared for them and are not you more valuable than they are? They are arrayed in all of My splendor, greater than Solomon's Temple. And so too, have I not arrayed you more glorious than Solomon's Temple to be wrapped in My robes of righteousness and arrayed in all of My splendor," says the Lord, " to be clothed with garments of praise and to shine forth the glories of God in the earth. Have I not done all these things for you?

"But, where are you? Where are the other nine? Only one has returned to thank Me and he has fallen at My feet," says the Lord. "And to top it all off, he is a Samaritan! He is a foreigner!"

"Church of the Living God: You are not foreigners! But, you are children of the Most High God. Are you not to return to Me and do the same thing that this man has done, and bow at the feet of Jesus in thanksgiving and praise unto your God?"

"Church of the Living God: You have taken so much for granted that you have forgotten your first love. I'm calling you this day to return to an intimate place-- a place of closeness and intimacy with

Me. I'm calling you to the "Secret Place" where you "abide in the vine", and to where I abide in you and you in Me, and we become one."

"You are 'bone of My bone' and 'flesh of My flesh'. You are My 'bride'. Adam had a bride. Eve was bone of His bone and flesh of his flesh. You are the bride of Christ. You are 'bone of His bone' and 'flesh of His flesh'. You have been taken and fashioned from His side to be one with Him and to take on His nature--to be as one – united of the same mind, same purpose, same desires, same goals, and same mission."

"This is the place I'm calling you to. Return to your first love, and fall in love with Jesus all over again. Come and spend the time with Him. Thank Him for all the good blessings that He has called into your life. Spend time in His presence. Develop that intimate relationship with Him! Don't just come to God when you need something! Don't just come to Him when you need a miracle, and then when He gives you that miracle, you run off never to return!"

"I, the Lord God, I am asking you this day just as Jesus asked in His day: Where are the other nine? I want you to come back and sit at My feet awhile and spend time with Me; so I may love you, and care for you, and protect you. It's 'Secret Place' living! It's 'Abiding Under the Shadow of the Almighty'! And you can have the greatest umbrella and the greatest protections over you in the entire universe, and it's only found for those who will live in the 'Secret Place'!"

Will you come back to your first love and come into a place of intimacy again? Will you enter in past the veil into the Holy of Holies-- into the "Secret Place" of the Most High God? If you will, you will abide under the Shadow of the Almighty! Don't wait until you need that miracle to come and get to know Jesus in your life. Today is the day of salvation! Today is the day to begin that new, fresh, intimate relationship all over again.

Don't wait another moment! Do it now! And if you will, pray this prayer with me:

Lord Jesus, I am sorry for not giving you the time that I should; for not coming back to you and falling at your feet and worshiping you, and spending time with you. God, I'm sorry for just taking the blessings of God for granted to where it's not enough; and I just keep taking, and taking, and taking, and I don't give anything back.

God, I am sorry that I have lost my first love. So, I come back to you now, and I fall at your feet and I ask your forgiveness; and I repent of my former ways; and I want to get to know you all over again. I want to fall in love with you all over again; and know you as I did the very first day that I asked you into my life. Amen.

If you will pray this simple prayer, the Lord God – He will forgive you and cleanse you from all unrighteousness. He will cast your sins as far as the east is from the west, and He will remember them no more.

And though your robes may have been stained and they are crimson red, He will make them as white as snow! I John 1:9 says, *"If we confess our sins, He is faithful and just to forgive us our sins and to cleanse us from all unrighteousness."* If you will simply do just that, your forgiven; and you begin a whole new relationship with the Lord your God. It's not too late to begin today.

So, come with me – we'll go to a higher place!

Such As I Have
(Acts 3:1-26)

It was the ninth hour of the day. Peter and John were going up to the temple in Jerusalem that day. It was the hour of prayer. They came across a man who had been crippled from birth that never walked in his entire life. He was over forty years of age.

This man had wanted to acquire alms for the poor. He had been placed there every day – day in and day out. It was his livelihood. It's all he knew how to do-- beg for a little silver or a little gold. Maybe just a portion of someone's offering that they were taking to the temple – in hopes that they would give some of it to a poor, crippled man in need. He was hoping to get just a little bit more so he could survive another day. He lived a very low life and existence in this culture. He was looked down upon from society. They did not think much of the cripples, or the leapers.

But for this man, on this day, his life was about to change forever. He was about to encounter two men that had been with Jesus – two ambassadors of the Kingdom of the Most High God – the Kingdom of God in the earth. He looked to them with one thing on his mind-- to get a little bit of silver or a little bit of gold; but what he got was more valuable than he could ever have imagined.

Peter and John came up to this lame man and Peter said, *"Silver and gold I do not have; but what I do have, I give you. In the name of Jesus Christ of Nazareth, rise up and walk."* (Acts 3:6) He took him by the right hand and helped him up, and *"immediately his feet and ankle bones received strength. So he, leaping up, stood and walked"*.   Then he went with them into the temple courts, *"walking, leaping, and praising God."* (v.7,8) This man walked for the first time in His whole life. He never even learned how and yet he was jumping, and leaping, and praising God for the miracle that he had just received.

You see Peter and John, they had no material silver or gold to give, but they had a "divine spiritual gold" that they had acquired from their Most Heavenly Father! Revelation 3:18 says, *"I counsel you to buy from Me gold refined in the fire..."* It is Jesus' words to the church of Laodicea, and it is still God's word to us today.

God is saying to us, "I counsel you to buy gold refined in the fire." It's "Secret Place Living". It's the "Ark of the Covenant." The "Ark" was overlaid with gold – just pure gold – along with the "Mercy Seat". It's the throne of God in the earth.

Peter and John were speaking out the King's decrees in the earth and saying, "Thus saith the Lord, 'Arise and walk!'" That is "Secret Place" living! They had acquired and purchased this divine gold from the Most High God. It **cost** them everything that they had.

Jesus said, *"I tell you the truth... and everyone who has left houses, or brothers, or sisters, or father, or mother, or children, or fields, for My sake will receive a hundred times as much and will inherit eternal life."* (Mat. 19:29,30) It's "Secret Place" blessing!

Peter and John were "Arks of the Covenant." They were carriers of the glory; the presence and the power of God in the earth. God wants each and every one of us to be the very same thing – "ARKS OF THE COVENANT" – "VESSELS OF GOLD"--to carry the power and presence of the Living God in the earth today.   In becoming "arks", we would have acquired this gold by giving God everything that we have – all that we are; all that we're not; and all that we have; and all that we don't have – our dreams, our hopes, out future – all of it. You see, when we give God everything, then He gives us His divine gold that has been refined in the fire!

368

Remember, the only way to clean gold is to put it through the fire. So as we come through our trials, and our testings, and our sufferings – through that process-- and we press in through it all – we go deeper in God than we had ever thought imaginable. And through the process, we are becoming closer, and closer, and closer, to our Heavenly Father; and we are coming closer and closer into "Secret Place Living". If it wasn't for the fire and the trials, we wouldn't go as far as we could have without them.

So, we can consider it all joy when we encounter various trials! We know what God is doing. He is perfecting our faith. He is producing in us perseverance and endurance, and He is making us "vessels of gold" refined in the fire. So that someday, we can say even as Peter did, "Such as I have, I give unto you. Arise and walk, in the name of Jesus."

You see, you can't give away what you first don't possess. So you have to have it first before you can give it away. And God wants us to have an abundance of all that He "IS" and all that He has; so that we can give it away to everyone that we come in contact with.

It's not just for us to horde it up, receive the blessing just for ourselves, and hold on to it. Yes, we can receive the blessing; but we're going to have so much, we're going to have to give some away. And that is "Secret Place Living" at its best!

The Priests and the Sadducees were greatly disturbed at Peter and John's teaching and their proclaiming of Jesus' resurrection. They put them in jail until the next day when they could be questioned, and they asked, *"By what power or what name did you do this?"* (Acts 4:7) Then Peter, filled with the Holy Spirit, responded, *"Rulers and elders of the people! If we are being called to account today for an act of kindness shown to a cripple and are asked how he was healed, then know this, you and all the people of Israel: It is by the name of Jesus Christ of Nazareth, whom you crucified but whom God raised from the dead, that this man stands before you healed."* (v.8-10) They added, *"Salvation is found in no one else, for there is no other name under heaven given to men by which we must be saved."* (v.12)

The Priests and the Sadducees commanded them not to speak or teach at all, anymore, in the name of Jesus. But Peter and John boldly replied, *"Judge for yourselves whether it is right in God's sight to obey you rather than God. For we cannot help speaking about what we have seen and heard."* (v.18-20) *"After further threats, they let them go."* (v.21)

They went back to their own people and they had a prayer meeting. They prayed, *"Sovereign Lord, consider their threats and enable your servants to speak your word with great boldness. Stretch out your hand to heal and perform miraculous signs and wonders through the name of your holy servant Jesus."* (4:29-30)

"After they prayed, the place where they were meeting was shaken; and they were all filled with the Holy Spirit and spoke the word of God boldly." (v.31)

"With great power the apostles continued to testify to the resurrection of the Lord Jesus and much grace was upon them all." (v.33)

"People brought the sick into the streets and laid them on beds and mats so that at least Peter's shadow might fall on some of them as he passed by."

"Crowds gathered also from the towns around Jerusalem, bringing their sick and those tormented by evil spirits, and all of them were healed." (Acts 5:15-16)

Peter, Peter, Peter!! He dwelt in the "Secret Place" of the Most High; and he abided under the shadow of the Almighty. It was not Peter's shadow that healed everyone that day; it was the shadow of whom Peter walked in! He abided under the shadow of the Almighty. He was under the greatest coverings in the universe of the Lord His God. It was the power and the anointing of God upon Peter's life that day that had healed all those that they had brought to him.

God wants to do the very same thing through His body – through His church—through you-- in this day and in this hour. He wants to make each and every believer carriers of the divine presence. He wants to make each and every believer an "Ark of the Covenant" – a "vessel of GOLD"-- to carry the power and presence of the Living God into the world, into the streets, into the highways and byways – not just in the church; but to break out of the four walls of the church and take it to the streets – into the shopping malls, and into the plazas. Wherever you may go as an "Ark of the Covenant"-- a vessel of gold-- you carry the power and the presence of the Living God with you.

But, remember, you can't give away what you don't have. So, you must first "purchase" this gold – pay the price-- no matter how high it is. We can't afford not to pay it; because people are dying. People are drowning. People's lives are being destroyed, and some are going straight to hell. They are counting on us to acquire this gold and to pay the price that we need to pay, no matter what it is. It's the highest price that you'll ever pay. But, you'll reap the highest benefits that you could ever imagine! The cost is great, but the dividends are high!

Will you buy this "Gold" from the Lord your God that has been refined in the fire and pay the price? And that price is everything … everything … everything …!!!

Will you pay the price today? If you will, you too can be a carrier of the presence – an "Ark of the Covenant" – and carry the power, and glory, and the presence of the Living God to a lost and dying world.

Chapter Ten

A Tsunami of God's Spirit

"The Lord on high is mightier than the noise of many waters, than the mighty waves of the sea." Ps.93:4

Mans Responsibility to God and
Number of Trials and Testings
(Deut. 8:12)

"I am the Lord God, the creator of the ends of the earth. Who is like Me? I, the Lord God, have given you-- all mankind-- everything that you need pertaining to life and godliness. I have spoken My words out of Heaven in days past, in days present, and in the days ahead. I am the same yesterday, today, and forever. (Hebrews 12:26) My voice – it shook the earth, and I spoke as thunder loud. In the days of Mt. Sinai, when Moses went up into the mountain to speak with Me, there were flashes of lightening, and thunder, and the very earth – it shook-- at the sound of My voice and all the people were afraid. But My servant Moses, I instructed Him in the third month on the third day that they had left Egypt, I called Moses up into the mountain. Why? To receive the greatest revelation from God that they had ever heard to that date. Moses would receive the law and all the Ten Commandments written by the finger of God to instruct them in the ways that they should live and walk; to counsel them and teach them concerning all the things of life."

"I gave them a moral law, summed up in the Ten Commandments. I gave them civil laws that would govern them in their society, and also gave them some ceremonial laws that would establish their religious institutions, and their sacrificial system. All of these things, I gave to them on that day. It is everything they needed pertaining to life and godliness."

The number ten has long been a symbol of God's requirements for His people, and the Ten Commandments are a very well known symbol of what God has asked of all of mankind. We are all very familiar with the Ten Commandments. Their influence has touched almost every nation in the world. If you speak of them, most will know what they stand for. This number ten is symbolic of "mans responsibility to God", and what we are required to do for Him. It's also the number of "trials and testings".

Jesus, being fully God in the earth, as complicated as all of the law was, simplified it for us today. In the New Testament, Jesus said you will have fulfilled all the law and the prophets if you simply do these two things – these two commandments: "Love the Lord your God with all your heart, with all your soul, with all your mind… and love your neighbor as yourself." (Mat. 22:37,39) If you will do those things, you will have fulfilled all the others.

You see, it's the law of the Spirit; for the Spirit brings freedom. Now it is a law that is written upon the tablets of your heart; not on tablets of stone anymore; and that you will simply obey whatever the Lord may say to you, out of a heart of love for your creator. And you will fulfill the law, because it's a law that's written on the tablet of your heart; and you'll instinctively do the things of the law. It won't be a forced requirement that goes against your nature; it will be a part of your nature. It is a part of who you are; because now, you have a new nature. If you have been born of the Spirit, you are a child of God of the Spirit; and you will do instinctively the things of the law, and you will fulfill the law summed up in those two laws that Jesus had given. That's the law of the Spirit!

The number ten is also the number of "trials and testings" that we can see over and over mentioned in scripture. Even the Ten Commandments were a test of Israel to see whether or not they could keep God's commands. (Deut.8:12) The number ten is the number of divine law and order that God had established for the nation of Israel.

Another example of these trials and testings we find in the book of Daniel chapter 1:12-14. It was a testing period requested by Daniel and the three Hebrew boys concerning their special diet. Daniel said to the guard, "test your servants for ten days … give us nothing but vegetables to eat and water to drink. Then compare our appearance with that of the young men who eat the royal food" …he agreed and tested them for ten days.

Also with the number ten is directly linked to the Hebrew word for ten: "eser" from the root "asar" which means: to accumulate, to tithe, or to take or give a tenth-- giving a tenth of all that you have – all of your firstfruits unto God. It's a test of our trust and obedience unto God to see whether we will trust God with our finances, because it all comes from Him anyway.

In Malachi 3:10, concerning the idea of tithing, this is one area that we are instructed to test God Himself. God's word says, *"Bring the whole tithe into the storehouse… and test Me in this and see if I will not throw open the floodgates of heaven and pour out so much blessing that you will not have room enough for it."(NIV)* We are to test God to see if He is faithful to His word. It's an "if" and "then" promise! If we do our part, then God will do His part.

"Ten" was also the number of times that Israel had tested God. Numbers 14:22, 23 says, "…disobeyed Me and tested Me ten times" and not one of them will ever see the land I promised them. The young nation of Israel tested God ten times in the wilderness wanderings, and they failed every single time. "Test Me in this," says the Lord. 'Test Me' in this: Bring the whole tithe into the storehouse and see if I will not throw open the floodgates of heaven and pour out such a tremendous blessing upon you that you will not have room enough to contain it all."

"Church of the Living God, I will say unto you this day: You have not been faithful to bring the whole tithe into the storehouse. Why are you lacking? Why are you in want? Church of the Living God: Malachi 3:10 – "Test Me in this," says the Lord God Almighty. "Will I not be faithful to give you all that you need or could ever imagine?"

"Test Me!" says the Lord. "Will I not be faithful to My word? Bring the whole tithe into the storehouse. Give Me a tenth of all that you make, because is not all of it given to you by the hand of God? Are not all of your blessings – do they not all come from the Father of Lights. All that you have and all that you are – it all comes from Me! And I only ask you to give a tenth of that. Why? To test you in your obedience unto My word, and if you will walk in obedience unto My word," says the Lord, "and in turn, you will test Me to see if I will be found faithful to My word."

"You have not tested Me in this, and I, in turn have not opened the flood gates of heaven. There is so much more that I have to give unto you. But you won't trust Me with ten percent of what I give to you. How can I trust you with more?"

We see in scripture, also, that Job was tested and tried ten times by his friends in Job 19:3, "ten times now you have reproached me…" In another example, Jacob had his wages changed by Laban ten times in Geneses 31:7 while Jacob was working for Rachael's hand in marriage. In the parable of the virgins, they were all tested by the delay of the bridegroom. Every one of them fell asleep. And how many virgins were there? There were ten! (Mat. 25:1) Lastly, we also read that God had brought ten plagues upon the land of Egypt, in the book of Exodus, to try and test Pharaoh before he would let the children of Israel go. All throughout scripture we can see that this number ten is directly correlated with times of trials and testings; as it is recorded throughout history, so too it is still true today.

And as we come to chapter ten in this book, "Abiding Under the Shadow", it is the chapter perhaps that will "try" you and "test" you – the reader – the most. For this chapter alone will require more of you than any other previous chapter. It will require greater commitment, dedication, endurance, perseverance, and strength – more than any other chapter or any other request that I have brought before you. It will challenge you to the utmost. It will challenge you to climb to greater heights in God; higher than you have ever gone before. But to go higher, remember, we have to go lower!

In this chapter, I will challenge you to come to the complete, undeniable, end of yourself. Are you prepared to die completely to yourself, and all that you thought you were, in the person that you assumed that you were, the person that everyone else thinks you are; and give up completely all that you have – your dreams, your hopes, your future, your plans – everything!? I challenge you, right now, before we go any further: Are you willing to give up everything to follow Jesus?

If you are, come with me. I am taking you to the lowest and darkest of all the dark places of the earth. I am taking you to a place that will cause the very gates of hell to be shaken to its core! Will you come with me to this place? Will you come and give God your all? Because, if you say, "Yes. Yes Lord, Yes." the world as you know it will never be the same.

Ten To Two
(Mat. 22:34-40; Mk.12:28-31)

"In the days of Moses, I called him up into the mountain and I gave him the Ten Commandments for the world, written by the finger of God upon two tablets of stone. I also instructed Moses about everything concerning the tabernacle, the priesthood, and all the furniture that would be placed within this tabernacle."

One of those pieces of furniture was the "Ark of the Covenant"; and that ark – it was to be kept within the Holy of Holies – the third chamber of the tabernacle of Moses – the innermost room of this temporary, traveling, house of God. It was the dwelling place of "Yeshua".

Within this golden "Ark of the Covenant", these tablets of stone were kept along with a pot of manna from heaven that fell in the wilderness, and also Aaron's rod that budded.

You see, these Ten Commandments were given within the context of a covenantal relationship – of a Heavenly Father with His earthly children. Likewise, those Ten Commandments also hold true for today, but they have been reduced to simply two commandments in the New Testament – TEN to TWO!

Jesus had said in His teachings that all the law and the prophets shall be fulfilled if you can do just these two things. We have already mentioned them and touched on them: Love the Lord your God with all your heart, soul, mind, and strength and love your neighbor as yourself. (Mat. 22:34, Mk. 12:30, 31) If you do these two things … you will have fulfilled all of the law.

"This day, I call you, My church, up into the Mountain of God. Even as I called Moses up into Mt Sinai, I call you – church of the Living God – come, come, come up into Mount Zion, the city of the King of all kings, and the Lord of all lords. I call you into this mountain to come into a covenantal relationship with Me; just as I was calling the children of Israel to come into that covenantal relationship; so too, I am calling you this day."

"But the words of God are no longer written on the tablets of stone. They are now written on the tablets of your heart," says the Lord God Almighty.

For thus saith the Lord, "All of My word from Genesis to Revelation shall be written upon your heart. It's the fresh manna. The same manna that fell in the wilderness – it still falls today. But remember, Jesus is the seventh day manna, and you are an Ark of the Covenant, and you contain this fresh manna – this fresh word. Jesus, remember, He is the living word.

"In the beginning was the Word and the Word was with God, and the Word was God. He was in the beginning with God." (Jn.1:1-2)

The word of God, in its entirety, is written upon the tablets of your heart, and you will obey the things of this law – instinctively, because you have been born from above. You are a new creation. You have a new father. You've been translated from the kingdom of darkness into the kingdom of light.

And now, you'll not struggle to obey the letter of the law as the Old Testament was given; but now you'll do the things – instinctively

378

of the law. You'll want to love thy neighbor. You'll want to not covet anything your neighbor has. You'll want to not commit adultery, or steal, or lie, or bear false witness, because it will not be a part of your new nature.

Jesus came to fulfill the law. He fulfilled every letter, dotted every "i", and crossed every "t". He is the fulfillment of every word that God has ever spoken; and now, He has fulfilled it in and through His people.

You have become an "ark of gold" – an "Ark of the Covenant" in New Testament terms. You contain the same three things that the old "Ark of the Covenant" contained: the law of God written upon the tablets of your heart; fresh manna that fell from heaven; and also the rod of Aaron that budded.

"You are a chosen, royal priesthood unto Me, just as Aaron was in the Old Testament to carry out your priestly duties in the earth. I have called you to be a royal priesthood-- a chosen nation. Remember the priesthood was in charge of the tabernacle and all of its functions; to carry it from place to place, to offer sacrifices, to offer prayers and intercession, to be a light in the world, to give out the bread and the wine of the Table of Showbread. I have called you to administer all these things concerning the Tabernacle of Moses, but now it's in symbolic language. You won't resurrect the old Tabernacle of Moses, but you will participate in each function of each station— spiritually! The same things the royal priesthood had to go through in the days of old, symbolically-- My church – I still call you to go through the same things today."

"So, put yourselves on the brazen altar and be a living sacrifice unto Me, holy and acceptable, which is your reasonable service, and then wash in the brazen laver. Wash in the water of My word, and be cleansed and purified from all unrighteousness, from all sin, to be holy even as I am holy," says the Lord God Almighty. "This is what I have called you to: to be baptized in My Holy Spirit and fire so you may enter into the Holy Place … to trim the wicks and light the lampstand to minister at the table of showbread and move on to the golden altar of incense. This is what I've called you to be. This is a great part of who you are – you're identity-- to come in behind the veil. Not just once a year; but every day, every moment, of every day."

You can live in the "Holy of Holies" twenty four hours a day, seven days a week, and three hundred sixty five days a year, for the rest of your life.

You can live in the "Secret Place" of the Most High God ... in the Holy of Holies or the Most Holy Place. It's the same place that the Lord God Almighty lives; and you can live with Him and abide in His presence wherever you go in this life. "Wherever you go – I GO!"

"That is where I have called you to be: To live and to move in the "Secret Place" of the Most High God. Contrary to popular opinion, you don't come here and visit just once in awhile, once a week, once a quarter, once a year; and then you have to leave again to go out and minister to the world. No. You can minister to the world from this place; because this place is wherever you go. Wherever you go – I go, and the power and the presence of the Lord your God follows you all the days of your life."

That is being an "Ark of the Covenant"-- a vessel of gold. Because, whenever it moved the glory of God would move; and it was the throne of God in the earth.

And so, if you are an "Ark of the Covenant" you are a throne of God in the earth, and wherever you go – He goes-- and the glory of God moves with you. The power and presence of God does not have to leave you. You see, it's a place that follows you. You carry it with you.

The "Secret Place" used to be only in one place in the earth at any one time. Now it's everywhere in the earth. It's wherever you are, if you're abiding in God in a covenantal relationship with Him where you should be. To be a disciple of Christ ... to be a follower of Christ... wherever He goes – you go!

The greatest commandment is to love the Lord thy God with all your heart, soul, mind, and strength. "To love God" ... but Jesus said, "If you love Me you will obey My word!" So we follow God and obey God out of a heart of love, not out of a heart of obligation with any resentment or doing things begrudgingly, forced out of duty, or something we have to do.

We want to do it! We long to do it! We love to do it! And that is the heart change that Jesus brings. We obey God out of a heart of love. So all that He asks of us we will do – whatever it is. That is being a true disciple and a follower of Christ. Whatever He asks you to do, specifically, even individually, very personally, in your life—you will do out of a heart of love!

If He would ask of you to leave everything and go to the ends of the earth and be a missionary to tell people about Jesus … you'll do it, out of a heart of love. That is a true disciple of Christ. He may not ask everyone to do that and go to the ends of the earth for Him, but all of us must come to a place in our hearts that whatever He would ask, we would do.

This is the place that I am inviting you to come to. It's a place that is the end of you. The complete death of you is the full life of God. This is the place that I am calling you to come to. So, come with Me. Will you listen to God and do all that He asks, and all that He requires of you – whatever it may be?

He is calling each and every one of us to a place of death. So I invite all of you – the worldwide church of God – to come and place yourselves on the brazen altar of God where the fire of God will come down out of heaven and consume everything that there is about you in the flesh, in the natural, and in the carnal. There will be nothing left of you and that's the way God wants it to be.

He's called you to be a living sacrifice. Will you come and lay yourself on the brazen altar of God – symbolically-- and give up everything that you are and all that you have? Just let it all go for God and say, "Lord, here I am. Whatever you want is what I want. And whatever you say-- I will obey."

Will you come to that place? This is the place that God is calling all of us to come to. And if you will simply do just that … He will do all the rest! He will do all the rest!

Come To the Depths
(Mat.14:22-36)

God is calling! God is calling out to each one of us: Come to the depths! Will you come? Will you listen? Will you obey what the Lord thy God would say to you in this day and in this hour? Will you leave the shore; the land; the carnal; the natural; and all that you find familiar? Will you get in that boat and come out into the vast oceans of God? Come out into the deep waters and then once you're there, will you climb out of that boat? Will you leave all that is secure and safe; and obey the Lord's command to come?

Peter was in the same predicament that day. The Lord Jesus was off by Himself praying in a mountain and He had told the disciples to go on ahead with the intentions of catching up to them later. It was a God set-up! God had a plan. God had a lesson – a teaching – something that He wanted all of us to see. It wasn't just for Peter that day.

The waves, they began to grow rough and stormy, and their situation became uncertain. Fear set in to the disciples. They looked across the sea and they thought they saw an image walking on the water. "A ghost," they cried. They were terrified. They were afraid. Jesus said, "Take courage it is I; don't be afraid." Then Peter replied, "Lord, if it's you, tell me to come to you on the water." Jesus granted his request even though it was in the mind and heart of Peter. The idea did not originate in the mind of Christ! Jesus said to Peter, "Come".

Peter did have a measure of faith to get out of that boat and begin to walk on water; but it was too much for Peter, and that was exactly what Jesus wanted him to know. Peter could not do it in and of himself! He could not do it if it was his idea, his thought, or his intention. It was not birthed out of the heart of God in that moment, for Peter to walk on water that day.

Peter did exactly what the Lord wanted to show them all. He began to sink. And in this picture, God gives us a lesson for all of us today: Apart from Him we can do nothing. We cannot do the miraculous in the natural or in the carnal. Anything that is of ourselves we cannot do. Peter had a few things to learn still in his walk with God. Jesus wanted him to sink to the depths of the sea! And it's exactly the same place He is calling each and every one of us to come to.

Come to the depths of the Living God! We've been on the shore, and in the land of the natural for far too long! Remember, land is a symbol of the natural realm, the earth realm or the carnal realm. The sea is the realm of the Spirit! God is calling us to the realm of the Spirit, symbolic of coming and diving into the depths of the sea and sinking down, down, down, down, down, as far as humanly possible-- actually, to the very bottom of the ocean. It's the lowest of lowest places that anyone could ever go in this world without going underground!

He's calling us to the depths of the sea. Will you come out, leave the shore, get in the boat, come out into the deep waters, and then go one step further – take a big step of faith and leave the boat and dive into the depths of the sea?

COME DOWN TO THE DEPTHS!!!!!

Not even in the shallow waters, because some of us have been in the shallow waters for far too long. There's more that God has for you! There is more that God has. He's calling us to listen to His voice. Obey whatever He tells us to do.

I want you to know today, God's call to us ... to all who will hear ... to all who will listen ... and obey is simply: "Come to the depths." Dive into the vast oceans of God. Let everything else go, and at the bottom of the sea is the complete death of you; but it will be the full life of God.

Peter gets a bad rap for not walking on water that day. Jesus said, "You of little faith, why did you doubt?" And we assume right away that somehow Peter failed the test. Jesus was trying to show Peter that he didn't have the faith that it required to do the miraculous. But, Peter did exactly what God wanted him to do. He mustered up what faith he did have and he got out of that boat to try to do what Jesus did; but it was not the right time.

Peter had not died completely to himself yet. And he would have to undergo several more tests before he was ready to do the miraculous. Peter had to sink into the depths of the sea; and I will show you in this chapter how that parallels the death of the old nature and the old man.

Once you come to the depths and die completely to yourself; then, you can ascend back up to the surface and walk on water. You can do the miraculous, because why? At the death of you – as you decrease – God increases and that includes all that God is!

You see, faith is supernatural. It's not natural. You can't get faith on the land. You have to get faith in the sea realm. And when you come back up and you can walk on water, you will have the faith of Jesus Himself. All that God is and all that He has, He wants to give to His children. And that includes even His FAITH ... to have the faith of God Himself ... in the earth!

And I know that may sound like a new and different concept to some, but it is the truth nevertheless. And I will show you in the

383

pages to come, if you will just simply read on with an open mind and an open heart.

Will you come to the depths? Will you come with Me and I will show you a higher place? But remember, to go higher we have to go lower.

Come To the Bottom Of the Sea
(Job 38:16, 17)

The lowest of lowest places on the face of the earth without going underground is at the bottom of the sea. It also happens to be one of the darkest of darkest places that anyone could ever go. It also happens to be a place, when you get done going through this process, it will cause the very foundations of hell itself to be shaken. Remember, the way up is down!

Jesus had instructed his disciples, *"He that exalts himself shall be humbled, but he that humbles himself shall be exalted."* (Mat. 23:12) The way up is down! We need to humble ourselves before the mighty hand of God. So as we have dived into this vast ocean of God we are sinking down, down, down, further and further – the further you go the more of yourself has to die. The further you go, the more has to be emptied out of you, to where you reach a point of one hundred percent total emptiness. There's nothing left of you! This process will test you beyond anything else that you will ever go through.

You see, it's the war between the flesh and the spirit. It may not happen overnight. In fact, it probably won't. It will take great perseverance, endurance, longsuffering, stamina, and godly strength to get you to the bottom. In fact, it will require at least a small group of others to help push you there. You'll go further in a group than you will ever go on your own. Because, it's going to take other people's encouragement, and them pushing you to greater depths, than you've ever gone before; and I mean that literally.

You'll have to endure times with God that will be longer than you have ever thought imaginable; and in those times, the heavy, weighty, presence of God will come upon you as you are broken with repentance. You'll be driven to your knees and fall prostrate, flat out, to the floor. And experientially, you will feel the heavy, weighty, presence of the Living God upon your physical body. It can be

384

characterized with times of groaning, travail, crying, and sobbing. Why? Because you'll be dying to yourself!

Dying to yourself… and even the picture of dying never seems pleasant to us, and there is a certain part of that, that won't be to your natural, carnal, flesh man. Because the spirit and the flesh, they war against one another. But to the "Spirit Man" it's going to mean life, and resurrection power, and anointing. But it won't be easy! It's not for the faint-hearted. It's not for the weak. It's not for those who will give up easy. But, if you will make that dive, and you will hang on to God, and you have a group of people that will encourage you to continue on this journey … you will make it to the bottom of the sea. You will make it to a place that you have died completely to yourself!

And the only thing that exists at these depths is the Lord God Almighty Himself. This is the place that we are going that God is calling us to. As a disciple of Christ, we all want to follow Jesus. And you say, "Well, did Jesus go to the bottom of the sea?" I want to tell you today that in a sense He did; and I'll tell you how.

The Scribes and Pharisees came to Jesus and asked for a miraculous sign, then Jesus answered, *"A wicked and adulterous generation asks for a miraculous sign! But none will be given it except the sign of the prophet Jonah."* (Mat.12:38-40) He compared Himself to the life experiences of the prophet Jonah, which is a well known story. Most of us know what happened to Jonah. He tried to run from the will of God for his life, and take a ship in the complete opposite direction from where God wanted him to go. He ended up being thrown overboard into the depths of the sea. And God provided, perhaps, a whale to come by and swallow him up for three days and three nights. Jonah was in the heart of the sea.

Jesus compared His very life … He said in effect, "the next sign that I'm going to give you is My death, burial, and resurrection". He compared it to the life experience of the prophet Jonah. So, in His death, burial, and resurrection Jesus went to the cross and He died. What do the scriptures say? Before He ascended, He also descended into the lower regions of the earth. (Ephesians 4:9) So, He went to the very gates of hell, took the keys from Satan himself; the power and authority to hold all of mankind, and then ascended back to earth, and then, up into the heavens.

He walked among us for forty days and forty nights. His body came back to life and then He ascended to the Father and was nslated into the heavens. So, I will present to you today as a follower of Christ we must follow Him in His footsteps. We must go to the cross and take up our crosses – deny ourselves-- take up our cross and follow Him. Where did He go next? He descended into the lower regions of the earth. We must do that as well. We must descend into the lower regions of the earth!

It's like a huge baptism into the heart of the sea, to sink down into the depths of the ocean, until we hit "rock bottom". That's as low as we can go! And in so doing, it is the death of us! Taking up our cross and following Him.

Psalms 42:7 says, *"Deep calls unto deep."* That verse was quoted from the book of Jonah 2:3. Jonah is quoted as saying, *"You hurled me into the deep, into the very heart of the seas, and the currents swirled about me; all your waves and breakers swept over me...the deep surrounded me."* (v.5)

You see, all of our trials, and testings, and sufferings in this life are designed to sweep over us and overwhelm us to be too much for us. Why? Because, they drive us deeper and push us closer to God. You'll go deeper and farther in your walk with God through the trials beyond your wildest imagination. It must come through trial. You'll never go as deep as you could have without the trials.

So, you can have two reactions to the things that life throws at you. You can give up and quit or go deeper. And I'm sure most of us would just want to go deeper in God. We don't want to quit or give up. We don't want to give up on God, so we have to go deeper in Him.

To give you an idea of where we are headed using a natural setting, the deepest place in the ocean was fairly recently discovered in 1951 in the South Pacific Ocean off the Marianna's Islands. It's in a place called the Marianna's Trench. It is 35,838 feet deep. It takes five hours to free fall to the very bottom. It's over seven miles down, and over a mile deeper than Mount Everest is tall. At these depths, the amount of water that would be over you is at 16,883 pounds per square inch of pressure. That would break almost everything into oblivion. The oceanographers refer to this region of the earth as the "Abyssal Zones" or the "Great Abyss". It's the areas just above the sea floor. All light is lost around eight hundred to one thousand feet down. There is no light here at these depths!

This is the place that God is calling us to go. And in the natural, we see a picture of this that parallels many spiritual truths in this analogy. At these depths you will be completely, one hundred percent, empty; and you will be completely, one hundred percent, broken into a million pieces. And the heavy, heavy, weighty, presence of God will absolutely obliterate everything that has to do with your carnal, fleshly, Adamic nature.

Doesn't sound very appealing to our flesh; but it does to our spirit. If we want to do what God is asking us to do, this is exactly the place that we must come to – a place of emptiness, brokenness, humility, and death. Col.3:3 says, *"for you died, and your life is hidden with Christ in God."*

Gal. 2:20 reads, *"I am crucified with Christ; it is no longer I who live, but Christ lives in me, and the life which I now live in the flesh I live by faith in the Son of God who loved me and gave Himself for me."*

You see, especially the church in America, we forget about a crucified lifestyle. Remember, the cross is not the death of one man – it's the death of all men. Jesus said, *"If anyone would come after Me, he must deny himself and take up his cross and follow Me."* (Mat. 16:24)

We don't know a lot about dying to ourselves in America. At times it seems to be all about us. It's the "Me" generation. "Have it your way". And at times, we have become just a bunch of spoiled brats waiting for the next thing that we can get from God. And we are clueless when it comes to a crucified lifestyle. But, that is Christianity! That is the Jesus I know from Nazareth. This is the gospel that He has brought.

Matthew 16:25 says, *"For whoever wants to save his life, will lose it, but whoever loses his life for Me will find it."(NIV)* So, it is losing our life – giving up of our life for Him; that is what we are called to do!

"Church of the Living God: You are too full of yourself! Empty out of yourself all that is not of Me," says the Lord Your God. "Remember the principles of humility, brokenness, and emptiness. Take up your cross and follow Me. It's not about you! It's NOT ABOUT you; and what you want: your hopes, your dreams, your desires, your plans, your future; none of it! It's all about coming to a place of submission and saying, 'God, I give You my life.' You must remember, it's a life for a life. I gave you My life so that you can live. Now you must give your life so that I may live! In the life that I now live, I live through My people. The complete death of you is the full life of God!"

"Church of the Living God: I have called you to die to yourself completely, fully, one hundred percent. Not in part. Not in just a small percentage, so you can stay alive in other areas of your life and have it your way."

"YOU CAN'T HAVE IT BOTH WAYS!"

"YOU CANNOT LIVE ON THE LAND AND LIVE IN THE SEA AT THE SAME TIME!"

"It's got to be one or the other! This is a serious call and it goes out into all the world to every church, every tribe, every people, every nation, and every tongue … to all who can hear and have ears to hear what the Spirit is saying in these days."

"I'm calling you to a place of complete, one hundred percent, DEATH-- the death of you-- so that I may live. Church of the Living God: there has been way too much of you still alive within My body, within My church, and within My bride. You must come to the depths! If you choose to follow Me, you truly have no other choice. No matter how painful it may be to your flesh, to your carnal nature, or whatever you may have to give up. I'm calling you to the bottom of the sea! It is the lowest, darkest place on the face of the planet."

"He who humbles himself will be exalted." (Lk. 14:11) It is a place of one hundred percent humility before God; one hundred percent, complete abandonment unto God; one hundred percent complete end of you; and the realization that you must die to self. And you do it in every practical sense of the word. You do it, and experientially in the Spirit, you experience it, and you come to the bottom of the sea. And that is the place that it becomes a reality! It's not just in theory, or doctrine, or thought; but it becomes a reality. You have died to yourself.

"This is the place that I am calling every believer on the face of the planet to come to in every aspect of life: theologically, doctrinally, and experientially, in Spirit and Truth. And it's symbolic of you being crucified with Christ, taking up your cross, denying yourself, and following after JESUS. It may be the hardest thing that you ever do in your lifetime … to your flesh."

But, I assure you, in the Spirit, it will be the most rewarding and the most fulfilling thing that you will ever do. Because, when this process is over, the anointing of God will come upon you in such greater measure that your mind cannot fully comprehend. Your life will not be the same. The lives of those around you will not be the same, and the world that you live in – life – will not be the same. And as more and more people begin to experience this truth, the church of the Living God will begin to be what God has called her to be; and we will literally change the world as we know it for the Kingdom of God.

All God needs is for you to say, "Yes, Lord. Yes." All He needs is your consent to say, "Yes Lord, Here I am. I will obey your call. I will go wherever you want me to go. I will dive into the vast oceans of God and allow you, Lord, to push me down into the depths of God further than I have ever gone before until I hit rock bottom – the "Bottom of the SEA"! I am willing, Lord, for you to take me to these depths. I will go."

Will you pray that small simple prayer today and say, "Yes, Lord. Yes, I want to go to the depths of God. I want to go to the bottom of the sea. I want to die completely to myself. I'm tired of battling this flesh. I'm tired of battling myself. Will you please destroy my "self"? Put an end to this carnal nature-- this carnal flesh-- that I have been locked into."

It is at these depths that you will win this battle! You will die to yourself. Your flesh will be crucified, all of your enemies will be defeated, and you will live a victorious life that you have longed to live. You will carry the power, and presence, and the anointing of GOD. Wherever you go – He will go; and signs and wonders will follow you all the days of your life. And you will look and behold the beauty of the Lord and see His goodness in everything that you do. It will radically change your life as you now know it.

If you want change, if you want victory, if you want more of God, if you want more of the power and presence of the Living God flowing out of you and in your life, come with me. Continue to read this book with an open mind and an open heart. Come with me and turn the page.

The Horse and It's Rider
(Exodus 15)

Looking back historically, there were some other people that were also at the **"bottom of the sea"**! We have to take a look back some 3,500 years ago to the true story of the Red Sea Crossing! The children of Israel had been kept in bondage in Egypt for 430 years to the day. God had brought **ten** plagues against the land of Egypt, with the final one being the death of all the firstborn. Pharaoh summoned Moses and Aaron and said, *"Leave My people, you and the Israelites! Go, worship the Lord as you have requested. Take your flocks and herds ... and go"* (Exodus 12:31,32) The Egyptians urged them to leave quickly *"for otherwise"*, they said, *"We will all die!"* They gave the Israelites what they asked for: articles of silver and gold, and clothing. *"They plundered the Egyptians."* (v.35, 36)

God did not lead them through the Philistine country, though that was shorter. For God said, "If they face war, they might change their minds and return to Egypt." So, God led His people around by the desert road toward the Red Sea; a pillar of cloud by day and a pillar of fire by night – over two million people! The Lord spoke to Moses and said, *"Camp between Migdol and the sea ... I will harden Pharaoh's heart and he will pursue you ... But I will gain glory for myself through Pharaoh and all his army. The Egyptians will know that I AM the LORD."* (see ch.14)

Pharaoh changed his mind and said, "What have we done?" He made ready six hundred of his choice chariots along with all the other chariots of Egypt – all his horses, chariots, horsemen, and troops – all pursued the Israelites and overtook them as they camped by the sea.

The Israelites were terrified as this great army marched towards them. They said to Moses, *"Were there no graves in Egypt that you brought us to the desert to die? It would have been better for us to serve the Egyptians then to die in the desert."* (Ex.14:12)

Moses answered the people, *"Do not be afraid. Stand firm and you will see the deliverance the Lord will bring you today. The Egyptians you see today you will never see again. The Lord will fight for you; you need only to be still."* (v.13,14)

The Lord told them to move! *"Raise your staff and stretch out your hand over the sea to divide the water so that the Israelites can go through the sea on dry ground." (v.16)* An angel of God, along with the pillar of cloud, stood between them and the armies of Egypt all night long as the Lord drove back the sea with a strong east wind and turned it into dry land. The waters were divided, and they walked through on the BOTTOM OF THE SEA! The Egyptian army followed them into the sea, and the Lord threw them into confusion and made the wheels of their chariots come off. They said, "Retreat! The Lord their God is fighting for them." *"Moses stretched out his hand over the sea and at daybreak the sea went back into its place."(v.27)* All of the army that followed them into the sea were completely destroyed ... *"not one of them survived"*. (v.28)

The Israelites saw God's great power displayed for them and feared God, and put their trust in Him and His servant Moses. The water had saved them, but it destroyed their enemies! Then Moses and the Israelites sang a song of celebration to the Lord on the other side, accompanied by tambourines and dancing! This song is recorded in Exodus Chapter 15. It would be good to read the whole chapter, but I will touch on just a few highlights.

The Song of Moses and Miriam! A Song of Deliverance! Exodus 15:1-5 reads:

v.1 "I will sing to the Lord, for He is highly exalted. The horse and it's rider he has hurled into the sea."

v.2 "The Lord is my strength and my song; he has become my salvation. He is My God, and I will praise Him, My father's God, and I will exalt Him".

v.3 "The Lord is a warrior; the Lord is His name."

v.4 "Pharaoh's chariots and his army He has hurled into the sea. The best of Pharaoh's officers are drowned in the Red Sea."

v.5 "The deep waters have covered them; they sank to the depths like a stone."

v.7 "you threw down those who opposed you ..."

v.8 "the deep waters congealed in the heart of the sea."

v.10 "the sea covered them. They sank like lead in the mighty waters."

v.16 "they will be as still as a stone."

Miriam, Aaron's sister, joined in with all the women dancing and shaking tambourines. She sang to them:

v.21..."Sing to the Lord, for He is highly exalted. The Horse and Its Rider He has hurled into the sea."

The entire nation of Israel was at the **bottom of the sea!** God had baptized the whole nation all at one time – over two million strong --at the bottom of the Red Sea. The same water that saved them-- destroyed their enemies! We are spiritual ISRAEL! We are God's chosen. We are His people. This is a picture of spiritual Israel at the bottom of the sea. When you hit the bottom of the ocean and die to yourself – one hundred percent – all of your enemies are dead at the bottom of the sea. It's the same picture.

The Song of Moses: "the horse and its rider"... "have been hurled into the sea". The Horse and its rider" are symbolic of every one of your enemies that would come chasing after you to destroy you in your spirit, in your soul, or in your body. Every single one has been drowned at the bottom of the sea.

"They sank to the depths like a stone." **One of your greatest enemies ... Is you**!! So you become like a **"stone"** in the natural, in your flesh, your carnal man, your Adamic nature. For when you have died, one of your greatest enemies – you, self, your flesh, your carnal nature-- it all has died. It is an enemy that wars against your spirit man!

When you die to yourself, and "self" – one of your greatest enemies-- becomes like a "stone", then you become a "stone of stumbling" and a "rock of offense"; and you will truly become like Jesus in the world. The complete death of you is the full life of God! Not only the death of you as your greatest enemy, once that enemy is defeated, all the other enemies are defeated as well. Anything and everything that you can think of: be it fear, anger, hatred, lust, cancer, and disease. Any and all diseases – they are destroyed at these depths!

"The horse and its rider has been hurled into the sea." "They sank to the depths as a stone". Cancer does not live at these depths! Sugar diabetes does not live at these depths! Hatred, anger, jealousy, wrath, lust – all sin-- does not live at these depths! **The only thing that lives here ... Is GOD!** Only God!! In the darkest of darkest places, He is still GOD! Before there was ever light, before He ever spoke and said, "Let there be light", and light was. In all of the darkness, He was, and always is—GOD! In your darkest day and in your darkest hour, HE IS STILL GOD! He is the God of the day, and still the God of the Night! There is no darkness in God, but God is still in the darkness! There's a difference! And at these depths ... there is only God: His holiness, His righteousness, His purity, every aspect and virtue of GOD is here; and all that is left in you, all that is left is only GOD – that's it! Nothing else lives at these depths. EVERYTHING ELSE IS DESTROYED!!!!!

This is a place that complete darkness surrounds you. There's nothing else here, but God alone. There is only the wonderful, thick, heavy, weighty, presence, and the awesomeness of GOD. You can't see a thing at these depths. There is no light here! But you don't need to, because at these depths you walk by faith not by sight!

WALK BY FAITH, NOT BY SIGHT!! Even when you are surrounded by pitch blackness, it's OK. Just close your eyes and walk by faith. You don't need to see where you're going. Our sight just gets in the way. At these depths, all you will need is faith.   In the realms of the miraculous, all you need is faith. You won't need to see where you are going.

Job 22:11 says, *"...darkness so that you cannot see and an abundance of water covers you."*

(12:22) *"He uncovers deep things out of darkness and brings the shadow of death to light."*

(23:17) *"I was not cut off from the presence of darkness, and He did not hide deep darkness from my face."*

The further you go down into the depths of God the more you will die to yourself until there's nothing left of you!

Genesis 49:25 reads, *"...Blessings of the Deep that lie beneath."*

The "Blessings of the Deep" are that you die to yourself; perhaps, your greatest enemy that you will ever face, and all of your other enemies are dead and destroyed at these depths as well! When you die to yourself you become a "rock of offense" and a "stone of stumbling" just as Jesus was. (I Pet. 2:8) And when you hit the bottom of the sea, you are as a "rock" that creates such an impact that it causes an underwater, spiritual, earthquake that shakes the very foundations of hell itself. Everything is shaken!

"EVERYTHING IS SHAKEN AT THESE DEPTHS! Why? Because, the contract has been ratified in the earth! If someone will go, and obey My voice, and go to the depths of the sea, and die to themselves, and give Me their life fully – it's life for a life – that's the Covenant! That's the contract! I signed it in My Blood, now I need someone to sign it in their blood symbolic of their life. Life for a life! And if that contract – that agreement – if it has been met – it has been completed in the earth – I, the Lord God, am obligated to fulfill My word and My contract in the earth, and I will be their God. This is 'ABIDING UNDER THE SHADOW OF THE ALMIGHTY!' This is living in the 'Secret Place' – the 'Holy of Holies'-- the place where God dwells. You give Me all that you have-- then I'll give you all that I have," says the Lord God Almighty!

Satan is not afraid of you; but he is afraid of God in you - in power, and in anointing, and in great might. He is afraid of someone that will come to the depths, and go to the bottom of the sea. Why? It ratifies the contract. It ratifies the covenant. IT CAUSES HEAVEN TO BEGIN TO COME DOWN INTO THE EARTH! Halleluiah! Glory to God! It causes God's word to begin to come true in the earth. Why? Because, someone paid the price. Someone walked in full obedience to what the Lord required of them! And the foundations of hell itself are shaken to its very core.

Haggai 2:6-9 says, *"This is what the Sovereign Lord says: I will once more shake the heavens and the earth, the sea and the dry land. I will shake all nations ... and I will fill this house with glory. The glory of this present house will be greater than the glory of the former house."*

Hebrews 12:26-29 says, *"...and at that time His voice shook the earth"*, (at Mt. Sinai) but now He has promised, *"Once more I will shake not only the earth but also the heavens. The words "once more" indicate the removing of what can be shaken, that is, created things, so that what cannot be shaken may remain." "Therefore, since we are receiving a kingdom that cannot be shaken, let us be thankful, so worship God acceptably with reverence and awe, for our God is a consuming fire."*

"Church of the Living God: I am shaking everything. It has already begun. It has already begun. Why? Because, I have at least one person who has been to the depths, and has sank like a 'stone', and died to himself; and he has hit the bottom of the sea and caused an underwater earthquake that will shake the very foundations of hell itself. I AM SHAKING EVERYTHING!" says the Lord God Almighty. "Everything ... especially My church. And all that they have tried to build is coming down. Every stone that has not been laid by the hand of God-- in this tabernacle-- in this temple-- it is coming down. All of Man's ways, all of man's traditions, every institution – it will be shaken! Why? So that the only thing left will be that which is built by the hand of the Lord, and what He wants in His temple-- in His tabernacle."

Remember, He is the architect. He is the Master Builder. He has the plan and the blueprint. Man has only gotten in the way. Man has only fouled things up. God needs for man to get out of the way – to completely die to their greatest enemy that they would ever face.

All of mankind needs to die to themselves! Then, and only then, can they experience true victory in their lives. Then, and only then, can they truly be an overcomer. Then, and only then, will they see all their other enemies destroyed around them. The process has already begun!

It only takes one "rock" to hit the "bottom of the sea" to cause an underwater earthquake that will shake the world. God needs only one person who will obey His call to come to the depths and completely die to themselves, and be filled with all the fullness of God.

Someone has to go! If no one pays the price – if no one goes and there are no "rocks" – there are no earthquakes! Just as God had asked Job, *"Have you journeyed to the springs of the sea, or walked in the recesses of the deep?* (Job 38:16) *Have the gates of death been shown to you?"* (v.17) Will you come to the recesses of the deep and die to yourself? The cost is very, very, high; but the dividends are out of this world! Will you come to the depths, today? Will you let everything else go in your life? Let it all go! Let it all go! I promise you it will be well worth the journey!

Prepare! Prepare!
For a Tsunami Is About To Hit!
(Genesis 7:11)

You have your warning! On December 26, 2004, at 7:58 am, the people of Indonesia and the surrounding countries did not have the luxury of such a warning. In our lifetime, the worst, most devastating tsunami hit the province of Ache in Indonesia directly, with catastrophic results. A 9.3 magnitude earthquake occurred at the bottom of the Indian Ocean just off their coast. That earthquake triggered the most powerful tsunami that the world has ever seen in recorded history. In just a matter of hours, it had impacted over twelve countries. Shock waves were felt around the world. The hardest hit countries were Indonesia, Sri Lanka, India, Thailand, and Myanmar (Burma). The tsunami traveled sixteen hours, as far as Africa's east coast some 5,300 miles away. It was even detected as far north as British Columbia, Canada! It has taken a devastating toll in many ways: in loss of life, humanitarian aid, economically, culturally, socially, and even geographically. Recovery from this tsunami may take decades, and its affects may be felt forever.

More than 230,000 people were killed with an estimated 1.69 million people displaced. It is the deadliest tsunami on record. Here are a few statistics to give you a better idea of this tsunami's power.

- It travels 500-800 miles per hour in the open sea with only a ripple on the surface-- gone almost undetected.
- When it hits the shore it has slowed to 10-20 miles per hour; but the wave compresses and piles up higher and higher.
- Wave heights can reach 20ft. to100ft. tall
- It reaches inland 1.5 to 2 miles.
- Tsunami's generally occur in successive waves up to 3 and 4 arriving ½ hour apart, sometimes more and more powerful as the waves come in with smaller waves occurring all day long.
- Its estimated energy release is more than 1,500 times that of the Hiroshima Atomic Bomb.
- It caused the whole planet to wobble 2.5 inches.
- It slightly altered the earth's rotation.
- It affected time.
- It changed the geography of some coastlines.
- It went out into all directions; North, South, East, and West.
- It had global impact.
- It could not be stopped – only detected!

What occurs in the natural is, often times, a good metaphor to help us understand things that occur spiritually with amazing comparisons. How powerful is God? What is God capable of?

I don't know if even a "tsunami" metaphor comes close; but it's the best way that I know of to describe what God is doing now.

When a believer hits the **"bottom of the sea"** and dies to their self like a **"stone",** and death rolls in to their greatest enemy – their self. That "stone" hits the bottom of the sea with such great impact it causes an **"underwater earthquake"** that causes a chain reaction, that triggers a **"spiritual tsunami"** that begins to rise to the surface and is sent out into all directions, to the four corners of the earth.

And this **spiritual tsunami**, just as the natural tsunami's cause great destruction, in the same way, this tsunami will cause **catastrophic destruction to the kingdom of darkness!** Every stronghold of Satan will be destroyed - in people, in cities, in churches, in states, in regions, and in nations. No stronghold of Satan will be able to remain intact when this **"tsunami"** comes through.

And it's coming in **successive waves**-- wave, upon wave, upon wave! And it will be relentless with this tsunami. **It will not stop.** It has already been released into the earth. And it will hit other people, churches, cities, regions, and nations. And then, in turn, this tsunami will be released out of those people; and so on, and so on, and so on.

These waves will have a **global impact.** Just as the natural tsunami affected the world in 2004, this tsunami will also have global impact. It will hit every nation; every tribe; every tongue; every people on the face of the planet. It will trigger the greatest revival that the world has ever seen throughout the history of all of mankind. *"Eye has not seen, nor ear heard, nor have entered into the heart of man, the things which God has prepared for those who love Him."* (I Cor. 2:9)

Just as natural tsunamis can be created from underwater earthquakes, so it is true with spiritual ones. When any believer hits the "bottom of the sea" and they die to their self completely, they hit the bottom of the sea like a "stone", and that impact creates this spiritual, underwater, earthquake that begins a chain reaction, and causes a "tsunami" of God's Spirit and Power to be released in them, and through them, in all directions throughout the world.

There is a verse, Genesis 7:11 that was given concerning the days of Noah, when God was going to flood the earth. God promised that He was never going to flood the earth again in the natural; but He never promised He wouldn't in the spiritual. And this time, it's coming in the form of a tsunami!

One of the most devastating effects of a tsunami is the flooding of the coastal areas. Likewise in the spiritual, God is going to flood the earth again with His power and His presence. Only this time it is through a "tsunami" being released through His people. It only takes one person – one "rock" – one "stone" – to create a "spiritual tsunami".

When that someone hits the "bottom of the sea" it causes the "fountains of the deep" to be broken up on the inside of them. **There are mass reservoirs of God's Spirit and power that have never been tapped into before deep inside our beings.** They exist in every believer on the face of the planet; but few are ever accessed. Many never realize they are there?

When you hit "rock bottom" and you die to yourself, and the only thing that is left in you is God, God breaks open the "fountains of the deep" on the inside of you. It's the power and potential of the Living God to rise up on the inside of you like a "tsunami wave" of His Spirit in the earth!

And that's just the metaphor for the power, the presence, and the anointing of God that is available in every life-- in every believer. Whosoever shall call upon the name of the Lord and come into a **covenantal agreement** with their God and give Him all that He desires. That is the Power of God unleashed in the life of a believer. That is what's coming!

I am warning you this day. This is what is coming. Halleluiah! Glory to God! You cannot run. You cannot hide. You can only prepare for the impact. So the best thing you can do is stand and say, "God, here I am. Hit me with this tsunami of Your Spirit, and force out of me all that should not belong-- all that is not of you."

You see, in turn, you are drug out into the depths of the sea, and it washes everyone else that wants to go out into the sea. "The waves and the billows"… they sweep over you to overwhelm you and take you to the depths to where you, in turn, die to yourself and trigger another tsunami in your life to affect all the other lives around you. And so what is created is wave, upon wave, upon wave, upon wave, of God's Power; and it will affect the entire world. *"The Kingdom of heaven suffers violence, and the violent take it by force."* (Mat. 11:12) Are you willing to go to the darkest of darkest places on this earth? Are you willing to go to the lowest of lowest places?

"Church of the Living God: You have lived many, many, years in places of comfort and security. You have lived behind the four walls of your steeples. You have lived in houses of comfort. You have eaten until you are full, fat, and lazy; and you have fallen asleep. Can you be awakened from your slumber? Will you hear what the Spirit is saying in these days? Can I shake you to wake you?"

CAN I SHAKE YOU TO WAKE YOU?!!" "I AM SHAKING "EVERYTHING!!! ABSOLUTELY EVERYTHING!" Why? "It's for your own good. You have been asleep for far too long. You have said, 'Yes', to go to the pleasant places … to the comfortable places … to the pretty places; but will you say, 'Yes', to the darkest of darkest places where there is no light? Will you come to the lowest place on the earth?"

"Do you carry, and do you possess, the power and the anointing of God to go and kick in hell's gates and cause the very foundations of hell itself to tremble?"

"WILL HELL TREMBLE IN YOUR PRESENCE?"

"If not, you need to come to the bottom of the sea, and come to the death of yourself."

"SELF IS YOUR GREATEST ENEMY!!!"

"Will you take up your cross and follow Me? If you will say, 'Yes', and come to the depths of God, to the very 'bottom of the sea', and sink like a 'stone', the impact of that stone will cause a "spiritual tsunami" to be released in the earth in your life; and God will break open the "fountains of the deep" on the inside of you!"

There are reservoirs of God's Spirit of power, and potential, and anointing, that lies on the inside of you that have never been tapped into before. And all it takes is for someone to push you to greater depths than you've ever gone before. Come. Will you go? Come with me! I will push you to the depths to where there will be nothing left of you, and all that is left is only God.

"You will have decreased and I, the Lord Your God will have increased. I AM THE TSUNAMI!" says the Lord Your God. "I AM THE TSUNAMI! I AM THE WAVE! I AM THE BREAKER!"

Psalms 93:4 says, *The Lord on high is **Mightier** than the noise of many waters, than the **mighty waves of the sea**.*" (NKJV)

"I, the Lord God, am mightier than the mighty waves of a tsunami! I am causing a tsunami wave of My Spirit to come up from the depths of the sea, to cause catastrophic destruction to the kingdoms of darkness in this world, and nothing of this kingdom will be left standing."

Micah 2:12, 13 reads,

"I will surely gather all of you, O Jacob; I will surely bring together the remnant of Israel". "I will bring them together like sheep in a pen, like a flock in its pasture; the place will throng with people. One who breaks open the way will go up before them; They will break through the gate and go out. Their king will pass through before them, the Lord at their head."

"This is the 'breaker anointing'!"

"I AM THE BREAKER," says the Lord Your God.

"I AM THE WAVE. I AM THE TSUNAMI."

There is a two-fold application to this revelation: on the outside of you and on the inside of you. Already on the outside, it has begun. It has occurred, and the tsunami has been released in the earth and is about to hit where you live. Halleluiah! It is causing absolute destruction to Satan's fortresses in the spirit realm. And the other application is that the "tsunami" has been released in you; and all of your enemies have been destroyed. And you can say, "God, here I am. Let your tsunami wave come and hit me, and force out of me all that should not belong."

"If you go to the depths, there will be a **'breaker anointing of God'** released in your life." Micah 2:13 reads, *"One who breaks open the way will go up before them."* "You have to go down before you can go up. When you come up from the depths of the sea, you'll carry a 'breaker anointing of God'. It only takes one to get it all started!" *"They will break through the gate and go out. Their king will pass through before them, the Lord at their head."* "When you went to the "bottom of the sea", you caused the very foundations of hell itself to be shaken. You will carry the power and the anointing to "break through" the very gates of hell to set the captive free, with the Lord Your God – He will pass through ahead of you leading the way."

"God is the Tsunami! He is the breaker waves! This may be new to most of you. Some of you will reject this; but many more will accept it! As this tsunami of God comes through and causes destruction to Satan's kingdom, there will be tremendous **blessing** in its wake, and in its wake will be the **glory** of God."

"**This tsunami cannot be stopped.** It can only be detected, and only a warning can be sounded! It is coming fast. It is coming furiously, swiftly, and powerfully! This revival will be global, and it will be the greatest the world has ever seen. It will change the face of the earth as we know it."

But someone has to go to the bottom of the sea to create it, die to self and give their life fully over to God and obey His voice completely! This is being in a "covenant relationship" with our creator; doing simply whatever He asks.

If you give Him everything you've got – He will give you everything He's got! That's the deal! The contract has been ratified in the earth and nothing can hold back God's hand. He is obligated by His justness and righteousness to fulfill His word in the earth. It's an "if" and "then" principle. And God never breaks a contract!

THE TSUNAMI – IT IS COMING! IT IS COMING! EVERYONE MUST PREPARE FOR IT TO HIT!It is about to hit where you live. Will you stand and allow God to do what He wants to do in your life? Will you stand and allow this **"TSUNAMI"** to force out of you all that should not belong – all that is not God?

Will you allow this "Tsunami" to drag you under into the depths of God to the very "bottom of the sea" where you too can die to yourself – your greatest enemy – and sink like a "stone"? And then you, yourself, cause another underwater earthquake, and then the tsunami begins all over again; and yet another wave is generated; and yet another wave is created; and so on, and so on.

THIS IS YOUR WARNING! Halleluiah! You cannot run. You cannot hide. You can only brace yourself for the impact! For it is coming to a city near you.

Ride the Wave
(Gal. 5:16)

Once the "tsunami" is created in your life and God breaks open the **"fountains of the deep"** within you that have lied dormant for years upon years; all you simply have to do is "RIDE THE WAVE" of God's Spirit – a tsunami of His Spirit of what He is doing in the earth today. Remember, **God is the "Tsunami"**. God is the **"Breaker"**. He is the **"Wave"**. It's a metaphor for us moving in the Spirit and living in the Spirit realm.

We have left the shore. We have left the land. We have taken a dive deep into the ocean – down into the depths. It is the world of the Spirit! God wants us to leave the realm of the land-- the carnal realm-- the flesh realm. It is symbolic of coming into the oceans of God; and when you do and you come up from the deep, you carry the "breaker anointing" with the power and presence of God Almighty – to break through the very gates of hell in this world – strongholds of the enemy – they will not be able to stand in the presence and power of what God is doing in the earth.

Hell itself has been shaken. It is trembling. But as you move in the spirit, and live in the spirit, and you die to self, God will do it all in you and through you. Remember, He is the wave! Are we not admonished in the New Testament in Galatians 5:16 to "live by the Spirit" and "walk in the Spirit"? (v.25)   It is as if we are **"expert surfers"** of the Most High God navigating all the waves of His Spirit;

moving in different ways, in different giftings, in different styles and variations; but we are all riding the same wave!

It's all the same wave! We may just surf it a little bit differently. And you'll ride this wave in a different style, being used in different giftings and different variations, all of the same spirit. But God will show you, teach you, and lead you, as to how you are to **"surf"**. He will go up before you. He will show you how to navigate these waves and how to be an "expert surfer" in His Kingdom!

I Cor. 2:9-12 says, *"… eye has not seen nor ear heard, nor have entered into the heart of man the things which God has prepared for those who love Him." **"But God has revealed them to us through His Spirit."** He has revealed it to us by His Spirit! " For the Spirit searches all things, yes, the deep things of God …no one knows the thoughts of God except the Spirit of God … that we may understand what God has freely given us."*

The Spirit of the Lord searches the mind of God and reveals the deep things of God that lie within His heart. Who can know the mind of God except the Spirit of God, and who can know the mind of God except the one who searches out His word in the scriptures as they line up with God's Holy Spirit?

It is the Holy Spirit that will lead you and guide you. He is the WAVE! He will be the force to propel you to where He wants you to go. He will teach you and guide you into all of God's truth. He testifies of Jesus Christ, and Him crucified, and Him risen, and no one else! The Holy Spirit has a seven-fold application within Himself: the Spirit of <u>wisdom</u>, of <u>knowledge</u>, of <u>understanding</u>, and of <u>counsel</u>, <u>might</u>, and the <u>fear of the Lord,</u> all within the <u>Spirit</u> of the Lord. (Isaiah 11:2) (Rev.3:1)

You'll know where to go, what to do, which way to turn. If you live in the spirit, you'll not get side tracked. You'll not waste a lot of time doing something in your own self, in your own way, or in your own strength, and have nothing come of it. You can live in God's plan step by step, day by day, and year by year, and walk in God's plan, and purpose, and mission for your life. You can know the mind of God and what He wants you to do!

Throw out your agendas. Throw out your plans. It's not about what you want; it's what He wants! God does not exist for you; but you exist for Him. You don't control Him; He should control you!

Every thought can be taken captive to the obedience of Christ. It is possible for all your thoughts to line up with the word of God… All of your thoughts…All of your actions…All of your deeds…

"Live in the Spirit of God! You can walk by My Spirit," says the Lord. "It's not by might, nor by power, but by My Spirit," says the Lord God Almighty. "The problem has been, there has been far too much flesh, far too much carnality, and far too much of **'self'** in the way!"

We've got to get it out of the way. And as we do, we can "ABIDE IN THE VINE", and live in the "SECRET PLACE" of the Most High God, where all of the promises of God can come true in the earth. HEAVEN'S COMING DOWN! Heaven is coming down into the earth! Halleluiah! Glory to God! In this realm, all things are possible. In this realm, ALL THINGS ARE POSSIBLE! To them who will believe, this is the realm of miracles. When you come up from "bottom of the sea" and a "tsunami" has been unleashed in your life – NOW – YOU CAN WALK ON WATER! Now you can do the impossible! Now you can do the greater works that Jesus has done. Simply, "RIDE THE WAVE" of His Spirit. Enjoy His presence. Enjoy what He is doing in the earth and in your life and …

… **"RIDE THE WAVE"** !!!!!!!

Become a part of what He is doing in the earth today. Don't try to go your own way, because that will come to nothing. Live by the Spirit! Follow His leadings! Just simply, **"RIDE THE WAVE"**, and be an **"EXPERT SURFER"** in the Kingdom of God!

Ride the wave of what God is doing in the earth today!

The Ark of the Covenant

A box of Acacia wood overlaid with gold inside and out, contained the 10 commandments, manna, and Aaron's rod. It represented God's throne in the earth and was kept in the Most Holy Place or the "Secret Place".

Chapter Eleven

Gone On Ahead

"Joseph had been taken down to Egypt." Gen. 39:1

LAWLESSNESS and DISORDER
(Jud. 17:6)

The number eleven in the bible, symbolically, has its associations with the words and the concepts of incompleteness, disorganization, and disintegration. Also, in other places in scripture it is referenced to the ideas of lawlessness, sin, disorder, and the antichrist.

We will first begin with the ideas of "incompleteness". It's just a little bit shy – not quite enough. Eleven hours is one hour short of a full time cycle for a full day, or a complete night. Eleven is also, as we well know, one short of a full dozen. It is a very familiar picture. When you buy eggs at the grocery store, you buy them – how? You buy them by the dozen. We live our days and our nights all by the time clock as the hours tick by. We may arise at six, seven, or eight in the morning. We have lunch around twelve noon. We get home from work around six p.m. It's a full day cycle! And then some of us may go to bed at twelve midnight and rise again at six a.m. You see, the Jews also had twelve hour time cycles. The night began at six p.m. and went till six a.m. It's all based of twelve hours in a day and twelve hours in a night.

"I, the Lord God, govern all days and all nights. I govern every hour of the day and every hour of the night. If you are a child of God, all of your time is My time. All of your days and all of your nights are mine. Not just one hour a day, or two hours a day, or 2.4 hours a day or two hours a week – whatever time you think that you are giving Me – IT'S ALL MINE ANYWAY!! I WANT ALL OF YOUR TIME!! I want all of it. I don't know where you learned that concept of giving Me just a tithe of your time. I DON'T WANT JUST TEN PERCENT OF YOUR TIME. I WANT ALL OF IT! ALL OF IT.!!!"

"It is a **covenantal relationship**. You see, when you give Me your life, you give Me all of your days and all of your nights until I take you home. That includes every twelve hours in the day and every twelve hours in the night – every waking moment – every sleeping moment! IT'S ALL MINE! So let us do away with this false teaching of a tithe of your time. No, No, No ...I WANT IT ALL!"

"And, this day, right now as you are reading this book, I want any child of God that is serious about their walk with Me to repent of this sin and give Me – now-- one hundred percent – all of your time. Hand it over to Me, the Lord Your God, and say, 'Lord God, here is all of my time: my days, my nights, my waking hours, my sleeping hours, all my days from now until the day you take me home. Lord God, I give them all to you. They are not mine to decide what to do with. I relinquish them all to My Master and My Lord and My Savior – I give them all to you this day. What do you, Lord, want me to do with My time? What do you, Lord, want me to do with all of my remaining days upon this earth?'"

"Forgive me, Lord, for presuming upon your time, for doing what I've wanted to do all these years, and thinking that I'm entitled to always doing what I want. I repent this day, Lord God Almighty, for doing what I've wanted to do with ninety percent of my life. God, I give you one hundred percent of all of my time from now on. And each day I will arise and say, 'Lord, what do you want me to do with the time that you give me, this day? What do you want me to do with the time and the breath that you give me today?'"

Each day is a gift from God, and we should be about our Father's business of what He wants us to do with each and every gift that He gives to us. And yes, there will be times of refreshing, and times of fun, and fellowship, and entertainment, and all of those things that we so love to do; but, there will also be times of sacrificing our time, and giving up of our time to serve others in many different facets of life.

Christianity is all about the cross! It's not the death of one man – it's the death of all men! And if you're serious about taking up your cross, Jesus said, *"Whoever desires to come after Me, let him deny himself, and take up his cross, and follow Me."*(Mk.8:34) Jesus also said, *"He who finds his life will lose it, and he who loses his life for My sake will find it."* (Mat.10:39)

It is in these times of sacrifice that you will gain a much greater blessing. It will be in times of serving others – be it in soup kitchens to feed the poor, or to shelter the homeless, or volunteering in the nursery caring for babies, or going on missions trips, etc. I believe God is going to increase this ministry within the body of Christ: to feed the poor, to shelter the homeless, and to help them get their life back, so that they can be a benefit to society again, and no longer be rejected, or feel unwanted by anyone.

There is going to be greater releasing of the ministry of "helps" within the body of Christ in the days ahead as we give all of our time to the Lord and ask Him what we should do with our days. Because, I know if you ask Him, He will put it on your heart to go and be a of all! The greatest in the kingdom will be a servant of all.

ne, not to be served like all other kings; but He came to serve ...id be the servant of all. He paid the ultimate price, and He was willing to do the lowliest of tasks in His earthly walk and ministry. He would do things that no other people would expect Him to do. And when He washed the disciples feet – one of the lowliest things He could ever do being a king of the world, and a king of the universe – He washed their feet-- an act of great servanthood and submission, showing all His disciples that He came to serve the world and be a servant of all. He was a different kind of King!

Another servant in God's kingdom who understood this principle was God's servant Moses. And even Moses stood at the "Promised Land" only to see it on the first day of the **eleventh** month, of the fortieth year. (Deut. 1:1-3) It was only an **eleven** day journey from Horeb to Kadesh Barnea to get to this "Promised Land".

"But My children, they failed to do what I asked them to do. They walked in unbelief and disobedience. Most of them never entered this 'Promised Land' that I promised to My servant Abraham."

Along with this idea of "incompleteness", we see that Jacob's family without Joseph – after he was sold into slavery in Egypt and thought to be dead to His Father – there was left an "incomplete" family. Also, Jesus had originally called twelve disciples; but after Judas Iscariot hung himself for betraying Jesus there was an "incomplete" apostleship. Only **eleven** disciples even heard the "Great Commission" from Jesus at Galilee. (Mat. 28) Only **eleven** apostles were there to hear of the Lord's resurrection, and were rebuked by Jesus for their lack of faith.

The number eleven also carries with it the ideas of "disintegration" and "disorganization" – the ideas of something breaking down. Scripturally, we see these ideas in the Old Testament in Jeremiah chapter 39, when Jerusalem fell to the Babylonians in the **eleventh** year of King Zedekiah. The city wall was broken through and the entire city was sacked. Most of the people were exiled to Babylon by King Nebuchadnezer.

Jehoiakim, King of Judah, reigned **eleven** years. *"He did evil in the eyes of the Lord."* (II Kings 23:26, 27; II Chron. 36:5) King Zedekiah, also King of Judah, reigned in Jerusalem for **eleven** years. *"He did evil just as Jehoiakim had done."* (II Kings 24:18, 19; Jer. 52:1-3) Then the city fell. The king was captured and taken to Babylon where His sons were

408

killed in front of him, and then his eyes were gorged out. The
him with shackles of bronze and he later died in prison.

The number **eleven** also carries the thoughts and ᴵᵈᵉᵃˢ
"lawlessness", "disorder", and also the "antichrist". The Antichrist is
the **eleventh** horn to arise in Daniel's dream of the "Four Beasts" in
Daniel chapter 7:8. The little horn symbolizes the last great ruler in this
world – the antichrist, or the man of lawlessness. (II Thes.2:3, 8)

I John 2:8 says, *"Dear children, this is the last hour; and as you have heard that
the antichrist is coming, even now many antichrists have come. This is how we know
it is the last hour."*

An enemy of Israel, the Philistines, their rulers bribed Delilah
with **eleven hundred** shekels of silver to gain the secret of Samson's
great strength. There were **eleven hundred** shekels of silver associated
with Micah's Idols in Judges 17:18. God instructed Moses to make a
set of **eleven** curtains to be the entire covering over the Tabernacle of
Moses. There was a set of five joined to a set of six, all combined
together, for a total of **eleven** curtains in all. Jesus is our covering for
all **"lawlessness", "disorder", and the "antichrist".**

Within these eleven curtains, there were a set of **five** and a set
of **six.** I want to give you another simple mathematical equation that
will signify this very clearly for us… **5 + 6 = 11.** Remember, **five** is the
number of Satan's fivefold kingdom; plus **six**, the number of fallen
man equals **eleven**, which is the number of "lawlessness and sin", the
"antichrist", and "disorder".

Along with these ideas of lawlessness and sin, in Judges 17:6
we read, *"Everyone did as he saw fit."* If man attempts to "add to" of
"take away from" God's divine law and order, or His divine kingdom,
and His standards are rejected, it will always result in despair, disorder,
and death. There will always be a moral disintegration of society ending
in chaos. I'd like to give you two more equations that will show us this
very clearly.

The first equation is **10 + 1 = 11**: The Number 10 is the
number of God's Divine Law; plus 1, if we add anything to it, equals
11, which is the number of "lawlessness, disorder, and disintegration."

The second equation is **12 − 1 = 11**: The Number 12 is God's
Divine Government; minus 1, if we take anything away from it, equals
11; the same number of "lawlessness, disorder, and disintegration."

We cannot add anything to God's Divine Holy Word! We can't take away anything from it. If we do, there is a very severe penalty for it at the end of God's holy word.

"Church of the Living God: You are guilty this day of 'adding to' and 'taking away' from My Divine Law and Order, and My government in the earth. YOU MUST REPENT THIS DAY FOR ADDING TO AND CORRUPTING MY DIVINE HOLY ANOINTING OIL and My DIVINE WORD," says the Lord Your God! "It's the same thing that Satan tried to do in the Garden. He tried to "add to" and "take away from" God's divine word to Eve. He presented a question: Did God say? **Did** … God say? Instead of, God said. He added one word; and look where that has gotten us. My warning was very severe. At the end of My Holy Scriptures I declared in My word: Do not add to … Do not take away from … or all the plagues that are contained therein will be added to you." (see Rev.22:18-19)

"This day, you wonder why the church is as she is. You wonder WHY YOU HAVE NO POWER! You wonder why you have NO ANOINTING. You wonder why you don't see the fullness of My kingdom in the earth. You wonder why you don't see more miracles and the power of God displayed within My body. You wonder why people are not coming to the light. It's because they walk in darkness."

"IT IS BECAUSE YOUR LIGHT IS ABOUT TO GO OUT! YOU ARE NOTHING BUT A SMOLDERING EMBER! It is time, church of the Living God: You must repent this day … REPENT!! AND THEN AND ONLY THEN, I WILL COME AND I, THE LORD GOD, I WILL TRIM YOUR WICKS ON YOUR LAMPSTAND SO THAT YOU WILL SHINE THE FULLNESS – THE SEVEN FOLD SPIRITS OF GOD-- IN THE EARTH ONCE AGAIN. YOU MUST REPENT THIS DAY!! <u>REPENT FOR ADDING TO MY HOLY WORD AND FOR TAKING AWAY FROM MY HOLY WORD!!</u>"

"Satan added one word. Did… God say? All of mankind has added much more than that. They have tried to add volumes to the word of God when NOTHING else needs to be added! I have given My divine word in the earth. It is the Holy Scriptures. It is all that 'I AM'. The word became flesh and dwelt among us. It is 'Emanuel': God with us! I need nothing added to Myself. I need nothing else added to who 'I AM'. 'I AM' already full. 'I AM' already complete! 'I

AM' already the God of ORDER. I need nothing else added to who I am… period! I am already the 'I AM, that I AM, that I AM'. I am already full and complete. Thanks, but no thanks to all of mankind; I need nothing else added to My essence – to My being."

"It is you, all of mankind, who must allow Me to come and take away from you and add to you – all of My Divine Word – take away from your Adamic nature, all that is in lawlessness, and sin, and disorder, and disintegration. You must allow Me, the 'I AM, that I AM', to take away from you and to give you all of My Kingdom."

"If you add the number **one** to **eleven**, the number is the number of God in all of My fullness. If you allow Me to add **one** to you, I can make you into a **'twelve'** – the Kingdom of God! If you'll realize that you have nothing in yourself and that you have become poor: *Blessed are the poor in spirit for theirs is the Kingdom.*" (Mat. 5:2)

"If you can get that revelation that you have nothing to give. Your good works are as filthy rags. Your own righteousness is as filthy rags. You have nothing to give Me. All that I want is just you. The only thing that you could ever give Me that I don't already have is-- YOU! Give ME your life and all that it is, today, and I will make you into a 'twelve'. I will give you the Kingdom of God."

Jesus paid the full price for all of our "sin" and all of our "lawlessness". He paid a full price for all the "disorder" that we see in this world. He paid a full price for all the "breakdown" and the "disintegration" that we see all around us in our world today.

He became our sin for us. He became lawlessness for us. He became an **"eleven"** for us, and took it all on the cross at Calvary's tree. Forsaken of the Father, He died and went to hell for us; so that we could be complete, so that we would no longer live a life of lawlessness, so that we could have order, and so that we could be "built-up" no longer having a "break-down" or a "disintegration" in our lives to where everything's falling apart. Jesus became an **"eleven"** for us. And within this chapter, we will search the scriptures and I will show you in the Old Testament and in the New Testament that God is the same yesterday, today, and forever.

Joseph had **"gone on ahead"** for his brothers in the Old Testament.

Jesus "went on ahead" for his brothers in the New Testament.

We must "go on ahead" for our brothers in this day and in this hour.

411

Will you come with me to **"GO ON AHEAD"?** Will you have the faith to turn the page? Will you have the faith to give God all that you are – all of your life, all of your time, all of your dreams, your hopes, your future, your entire life-- whatever that may be? Will you have the faith to give God all of that?

If you give God all that you are and all that you have; God will give you **all** that He "IS" and **all** that He has. That's **covenantal relationship!** That is the deal that God has given us. That is the shed blood on Calvary's tree. Will you sign the contract with your blood, symbolized by your life, and give God all that you are? If you do, God will turn your **"eleven"** into a **"twelve"**!

The Eleventh Son of Jacob
(Genesis 30)

JOSEPH... He is an Old Testament type, picture, and foreshadowing of all the life of Jesus Christ, and Him crucified, and Him risen. What Joseph is in the Old Testament, Jesus is in the New. There are many similarities between the two lives of these two men; and as you see the life of Joseph unfold in the Old Testament, the reader should keep in mind that it is all a foreshadowing of the life of their savior – Jesus Christ. For when one looks at the life of Joseph they can learn many principles about his life that apply to their life today, and we will see later on how you, too, are a New Testament reality of an Old Testament type. We will see how you too, are a "JOSEPH".

It all started with a dream. God gave Joseph a very powerful dream that he was perhaps not meant to share with anyone else. It was a revelation to Joseph himself of the plans and the purposes of God and the will of God for his life.

Joseph, as a young man of seventeen, had a dream. In fact, he had two dreams but they both carried the same meaning. We get the revelation of this dream in Genesis chapter 37. Listen as Joseph describes his dream: *"We were binding sheaves of grain out in the field when suddenly my sheaf rose and stood upright, while your sheaves gathered around mine and bowed down to it." His brothers said to him, "Do you intend to reign over us? Will you actually rule us? And they hated him all the more because of his dream*

412

and what he had said. Then he had another dream, "listen" he said, "this time the sun and moon and <u>eleven</u> stars were bowing down to me."

When he told his father as well as his brothers, his father rebuked him and said, "What is this dream you had? Will your mother and I and your brothers actually come and bow down to the ground before you? His brothers were jealous of him, but his father kept the matter in mind."(Gen. 37:7-11)

From that moment on his brothers had plotted to kill Joseph; not only to kill him physically, BUT TO ALSO KILL THE DREAM! So that dream, the plans, and the purposes of God would not come true in the earth. They would not bow down to this younger brother Joseph. They would not bow down to any authority that may be placed over them.

In fact, they were older, they were wiser – they thought. Even the firstborn, Reuben, stepped in and exercised some wisdom while he tried to save Joseph's life. He talked all the other brothers into not killing Joseph immediately. It bought him some time; so they just threw him into a dry cistern – just an old pit-- until they could decide exactly what to do with him.

They dipped his robe of "many colors" that his father Jacob had given to him; that symbolized the favor of the Father; the full spectrum blessing of the Father that had been upon Joseph's life. The other brothers knew that Joseph was the favored son that was symbolized in this coat. The others didn't get a coat from their father. They didn't have this coat of many colors. They didn't have the favor of the Father and this full spectrum blessing! They hated this coat just as much as they hated Joseph. So, they de-robed him. They took it away from Joseph. They said, "Let's dip it in goat's blood, and we will show it to Father and tell him that a ferocious animal has attacked him and has devoured him. That's what we will tell Father." So, they all agreed and that's what they did.

And in the meantime, a band of Midianite merchants had come traveling by. Judah said to his brothers, "Let's not kill him; after all, he is our own flesh and blood. He is our brother. Let's just sell him into slavery; and then we'll be done with him. We'll never see him again. They'll take him away to a far off land. We won't have to put up with this favored son anymore; and we'll be much the richer. We'll have all this silver that we receive for selling him." That seemed to be a much better idea. So, they sold Joseph into slavery to this band of merchants,

413

bound his feet in shackles and his neck in irons, and then carted him off to the land of Egypt.

But, that wasn't the end of the story. The brothers took the robe home and showed it to their father Jacob. They lied about all that had happened. And they convinced the Father that this favored son – this **eleventh** son – was dead and gone. They even had his robe to prove it. This father – he mourned the death of his son for many days. He wept and he sobbed, and he cried. You see, Joseph was also the first born of Rachael. And Rachael was Jacob's beloved wife. Rachael was the love of Jacob's life. He had worked many, many years to finally gain the hand   of this young girl. And when she was barren and could have no children, God answered her cry. Joseph meant all the more to Jacob, and especially after he lost his beloved wife. Rachael had passed away giving birth to her second son Benjamin. So, Jacob had already endured such great heartache. The memory of Rachael lived on in Joseph. The memory of his beloved lived on. That's why Joseph meant the world to Jacob, not that he didn't love his other sons; he just carried a little more favor. A little more of Jacob's heart was connected to the heart of Joseph.

So, Joseph gets sold into Egypt and we pick up his story – not sold just once but twice. He gets sold again to a man named Potiphar, one of Pharaoh's officials, the captain of the guard.

Joseph's brothers tried to steal the favor of the Father upon Joseph's life by taking his robe away from him; but that was only a symbol in the natural of what was already on Joseph's life in the spiritual. They could not take the favor of the Father away from him. It was eternal. It remained. The life of Joseph continued to be blessed. Everything that Joseph touched, God's blessing was upon it – everything! So, in the household of Potiphar everything became blessed. Everything that Joseph touched.

Potiphar's house was increased and it was blessed of the Lord. Potiphar began to recognize this fact and he knew it was because of this **eleventh** son of Jacob – all because of this Hebrew slave, and because of the God that he served. Potiphar knew it! So, he put Joseph in charge of everything – everything-- in his entire household. He trusted Joseph. He gave him everything he had. Joseph had it all!

But, Joseph was falsely accused of a crime that he did not commit. The enemy came in and used Potiphar's wife to falsely accuse Joseph of making advances towards her, and they threw him in a lowly dungeon-- into the pits of hell to remain, perhaps indefinitely, to die. He was sentenced to a life of death in a dungeon – the very pits of hell-- indefinitely – until… until … what? … you might ask.

UNTIL GOD INTERVENES!   UNTIL GOD STEPS IN! Because Joseph had a dream; and that dream – that purpose – that plan of God-- it will not and cannot be thwarted. It cannot be changed. It cannot be interrupted. It cannot be stopped in the earth.

God had a destiny for Joseph. He had a dream. He had a plan. He was the **eleventh** son of Jacob; but he was also a **"son"** of the Most High God. God had a plan and a dream for His son; and the piece that he gave to this son was an anchor so that this son could hold on to it. Even in times when he thought that this plan would never work out – would never be fulfilled – would never be accomplished. I'm sure there were days that Joseph thought that God had forgotten him. And this dream that he had: that it was just a joke; that he had been mistaken; that he was wrong; that it meant nothing. It was just another dream. Joseph was sold as a slave, shackled in chains of "irons", symbolic of taking upon the judgment of God. He endured a punishment for a crime that he did not commit. But God began to intervene and set in motion a series of events to elevate Joseph from the pits of hell to the palaces of Egypt – from the last in command to the second in command. And he would use a supernatural gifting and a supernatural way to fulfill such a plan.

While Joseph was in prison, two other men were also sentenced there. If you remember the story, the cup bearer and the baker, both in the service of the king, were sent there for something that they had done wrong. Both these men had dreams; and while they were there, it just so happened, that there was a man there that could interpret these dreams: one good and one bad. One was to live, and one was to die. Joseph gave them the accurate, correct interpretation and didn't hold anything back. He recognized in his heart and said out of his very own lips, "Are not the interpretations of dreams – are they not all God's?   Is not God the interpreter of dreams?" Joseph knew where his gifting had come from. He knew that it was not in his own power or strength that he would reveal these mysteries.

So, the cupbearer was restored to his high position next to the king. But the baker was hanged; receiving the death penalty just as Joseph had foreseen. Joseph had asked the cupbearer, "When all goes well with you, remember me … mention me to Pharaoh … for I have done nothing to deserve being put here." But the cupbearer had forgotten all about Joseph. He was forsaken and forgotten.

For over two years from that point he was forgotten and left in this prison. And then one day, Pharaoh, the king of Egypt, had a dream. There was not one in all the kingdom who could give Pharaoh the answer as to the meaning of his dream. He called all his magicians and wise men, but no one had an answer for him.

And then the cup bearer's memory was jogged a little bit and he remembered this Hebrew slave that was rotting away in the dungeon – in the very pits of hell. Immediately, Pharaoh called for Joseph. They cleaned him up and changed his clothes for he was about to come before the King.

Pharaoh had been greatly troubled by his two dreams; burdened by God Himself, because this dream carried with it the fate of a nation, and even the fate of the world. It carried with it grave consequences if this dream was not interpreted correctly. Pharaoh needed to know: what does this dream mean? Their very lives were at stake; but not only the life of Pharaoh, but the lives of his entire kingdom – and for that matter-- the entire world!

But Joseph's giftings – they were tested. They were refined. They were polished. Where? …In the very pits of hell. In his days of trials and testings he was "refined in the fire", and now he has been brought out for such a time as this.

This is Pharaoh's dream: *"He was standing by the Nile, when out of the river there came up seven cows, sleek and fat, and they grazed among the reeds. After them, seven other cows, ugly and gaunt, came up out of the Nile and stood beside those on the riverbank. And the cows that were ugly and gaunt ate up the seven sleek, fat cows. Then Pharaoh woke up."*

He fell asleep again and had a second dream: Seven heads of grain, healthy and good, were growing on a single stalk. After them, seven other heads of grain sprouted – thin and scorched by the east wind. The thin heads of grain swallowed up the seven healthy, full heads. Then Pharaoh woke up …" (Gen.41:1-7)

Then Joseph said to Pharaoh, *"The dreams of Pharaoh are one and the same. God has revealed to Pharaoh what he is about to do. The seven good cows are seven years, and the seven good heads of grain are seven years; it is one and the same dream. The seven lean, ugly cows that came up afterward are seven years, and*

416

so are the seven worthless heads of grain scorched by the east wind: They are seven years of famine.

Seven years of great abundance are coming throughout the land of Egypt, but seven years of famine will follow them. Then all the abundance in Egypt will be forgotten, and the famine will ravage the land. The abundance in the land will not be remembered because the famine that follows will be so severe. The reason the dream was given to Pharaoh in two forms is that the matter has been firmly decided by God, and God will do it soon. " (Gen. 41:25-32)

Seven years of abundance followed by seven years of famine. The survival of the entire known world was at stake. They needed a plan. They needed to know what to do. Where did this plan come from? Through a lowly Hebrew salve with a special gifting to interpret dreams.

Pharaoh had not seen such wisdom and revelation anywhere in his lifetime. He thought who could I put in charge of such a plan? Who could I trust? Who could I give such responsibility to? He placed his signet ring on Joseph's finger, gave him new robes of fine linen to wear, and he placed a gold chain around his neck, and declared to Joseph – he said, "All the kingdom I give unto you. You are second only to me. People will not raise hand or foot unless you say so." (Paraphrased)

Pharaoh also put Joseph in charge of this great plan to store up grain during the seven years of abundance, and to keep it in storehouses in all the different cities so that in the years of famine they would have something in reserve to sustain them. They stored up so much Joseph stopped keeping records. It was beyond measure!

Joseph went from the pits of hell to the palaces of Egypt, to "second-in-command" of the entire kingdom, but our story doesn't end there. The years of abundance came to an end, and they entered into the years of famine. These years of famine were severe throughout the land, and Egypt began to feel the effects of what was happening. People from all over the kingdom of Egypt would come to one man to buy grain so that they could make bread to sustain them through these times. They came to ONE MAN – the **eleventh son of Jacob!** And not only those in Egypt but the famine had spread throughout all the world, even to effect Joseph's brothers, his father, and mother in the land of Cannan.

417

So Jacob sent his sons to buy grain in the land of Egypt because he had heard they had the only grain available. It was their only hope; their only source of life. Joseph's brothers came to him to buy grain; but, this time Joseph used greater discernment and greater wisdom than he did before. Remember, he shared his dream in a time when maybe he should not have. Since then, he had gained greater wisdom, greater understanding, and greater knowledge. He was "refined in the fire". He had spent times in the pits of hell. But he had ascended to the throne for such a time as this!

He made his brothers go through several testings. He sent them back to his Father to get the youngest son – Benjamin, because that was his true brother, the one brother that he himself had mourned over – the younger son of Rachael. He wanted to make sure that this brother was okay; that this brother would be taken care of; and that this brother would be seen with his own eyes. He wanted to see his beloved Benjamin alive. Joseph put his brothers to the test so that they wouldn't be up to any more of their trickery and their deception.

His brothers came back, and this time, when they were all there, all **"eleven stars"** were there to bow down to this king, this ruler, this governor, this second in command of all Egypt. It was in that moment that Joseph was reminded of his dream. He had forgotten about it up until then. Instead of being bitter and angry, and harboring resentment in his heart, he had to remove himself for a moment, then he wept and he sobbed by himself because of what had just happened.

He could have thrown them into prison. He could have been bitter and angry, and immediately thrown them into the very dungeon that he was sent to. But Joseph didn't do that. He only exercised God's love and God's grace, and God's mercy. He recognized the plan of God in his life and he said to his brothers, who didn't recognize him because it had been twenty three years later since they had seen their brother. Joseph had changed. He wasn't that seventeen year old young man. After twenty three years, he said, "It is me, Joseph". And also, recognizing the plan of God in his life, he said, *"It was not you that has sent me here; but God sent me ahead of you to preserve for you a remnant on earth and to save your lives by a great deliverance."* (45:7)

Joseph sold them grain in that day so that they would not die. But he didn't just stop there. He showered them with blessings, upon blessings, upon blessings. He gave his brother Benjamin five times what he gave his other brothers and even added to that three hundred shekels of silver. He sent back to his father twenty donkeys. Ten loaded with all the best things of Egypt – all the best that Egypt had to offer. The other ten donkeys were loaded with grain, bread, and other provisions for their journey back to Egypt.

Joseph had sent word with them to invite them all to come live with him and he would give them land and possessions, and shower them with all the blessings of the kingdom. So, Jacob and all his brothers, realizing they hadn't much of a future where they were, traveled to the land of Egypt and lived there under the rulership of their son Joseph. These **"eleven stars, the sun, and the moon"** included, had come down to Egypt to bow down to this **eleventh** son of Jacob. God spoke to Jacob and said, "Do not be afraid, for I will bless you and make you into a wealthy, blessed nation in this land." (See, Gen.46:3)

And as Joseph is an Old Testament type of Christ, Jesus is the reality of that same life in the New Testament. Joseph was **"sent on ahead"** and endured great hardship and persecution at the hands of his own family. And through it all he was elevated to a position of great power and authority. No one saw it coming. Joseph couldn't ever have tried to fulfill that dream on his own. No one could. But God did it in His way and in His time.

Joseph had **"gone on ahead"** to save not only his family, but also the future of the young nation of Israel. He not only saved all of Egypt, he saved Israel, and all the other countries on the face of the earth. Just as Joseph had "gone on ahead" for his brothers and he is a type of Christ in the Old Testament, Jesus also had "gone on ahead" and endured great persecution for the sake of his brothers – for his family – and for all the world.

Jesus now sits at the right hand of God, second in command next to the father, to give out his "grain" and His "bread" in measureless supply to all the world – to every nation, every tribe, every tongue, and every people. He holds the keys to the storehouses of heaven just like Joseph held the keys to the storehouses of Egypt. "Keys" are a symbol of power and authority.

It is in this day and in this hour, that there is a spiritual famine in the land. And just like Joseph held the "keys" in his day, Jesus holds the "keys" in our day. He holds all power and all authority – second in command next to the Father. He is the triune God: Father, Son, and the Holy Spirit – the three-in-one God. He holds the keys to all the storehouses – plural. Not just to give out "grain" and "bread" but to give out all that God is and all that He has!

Joseph was the **eleventh** son of Jacob. Joseph was an "eleven" – an eleventh son; but firstborn of Rachael. Jesus was the firstborn of God, the only begotten of the Father. He had "gone on ahead" – endured the cross, went to hell, died for us and He is the "firstborn among many brethren". He was resurrected from the dead, "the firstborn", meaning that there are many more yet to follow. Jesus has "gone on ahead" for us. He lives so that we too might live. He has given us the "keys" to the kingdom. We are now "second in command" of all the storehouses of heaven and it is our job, in this day and in this hour, to give out "grain" and "bread" and all that God "IS" from all the storehouses of heaven--in a measureless supply – an unlimited supply-- out to a starving world.

Joseph was the **eleventh** son of Jacob. He is an Old Testament type of Christ. In the next section, we will see how Jesus became an **"eleven"** for us and that He is the "eleven curtains".

Eleven Curtains
(Exodus 26)

JESUS – HE IS THE ELEVEN CURTAINS! He is the complete covering for "lawlessness", "sin", "disintegration", and "disorder". He is the complete covering for a fallen world. He is the complete covering against the antichrist. He is the eleven curtains!

Jesus became "lawlessness and sin" for us – a sinless man, holy and righteous, born to the virgin Mary, condemned to die, and went to the cross for us. And then He didn't stop there; He descended into the lower regions of the earth; went to hell and took the keys of death, hell, and the grave back from Satan himself; ascended back into the earth realm; appeared to many for forty days and forty nights; and then ascended into the heavens to be seated at the right hand of God the Father.

He took upon Himself all of our sin, all of our iniquity, and died on an old rugged cross so that we wouldn't have to. He became an **"eleven"** in our place. A number symbolic of "lawlessness", "disorder", "sin", "rebellion", and "disintegration" – all the qualities of the kingdom of darkness and the kingdom of the antichrist, a kingdom

420

in direct opposition to God's Kingdom. He covered it all! He is the "eleven" curtains!

"*Surely He has borne our griefs and carried our sorrows; yet we esteemed Him stricken, smitten by God, and afflicted.*

But He was wounded for our transgressions, He was bruised for our iniquities; the chastisement for our peace was upon Him, and by His stripes we are healed.

All we like sheep have gone astray; we have turned, everyone, to his own way; and the Lord has laid on Him the iniquity of us all. He was oppressed and He was afflicted, yet He opened not His mouth; He was led as a lamb to the slaughter.

And as a sheep before its shearers is silent, He opened not His mouth. He was taken from prison and from judgment, and who will declare His generation? For He was cut off from the land of the living; for the transgressions of My people He was stricken. And they made His grave with the wicked – but with the rich at His death, because He had done no violence, nor was any deceit in His mouth.

Yet it pleased the Lord to bruise Him; He has put Him to grief. When You make His soul an offering for sin; He shall see His seed, He shall prolong His days, and the pleasure of the Lord shall prosper in His hand.

He shall see the labor of His soul, and be satisfied. By His knowledge My righteous Servant shall justify many, for He shall bear their iniquities. Therefore I will divide Him a portion with the great, and He shall divide the spoil with the strong, because He poured out His soul unto death, and He was numbered with the transgressors, and He bore the sin of many, and made intercession for the transgressors." (Isaiah 53: 4-12)

Just like Joseph, Jesus had "gone on ahead" for the lives of His brothers, His family, for us His descendants, for nations, and for the entire world. He was persecuted, beaten, tortured, sold for silver, endured the pits of hell, died for us, and then ascended into heaven, and is now seated at the right hand of God, so that all men could be saved! Jesus is second only to the Father. He took the "keys" back from Satan himself: the keys to death, hell, and the grave so that these would no longer have any power over all of mankind.

"*Whosoever calls on the name of the Lord shall be saved.*" (Acts 2:21)

"*...whoever believes in Him should not perish, but have everlasting life.*" (Jn. 3:16)

He has all power and authority over everything. He is the KING! He has "gone on ahead" for us! He died in our place and came back to life so that we too may live! "*He is the firstborn from among the dead.*" (Col.

421

1:18) *"He is the firstborn among many brethren."* Meaning that there are many more to follow. He paved the way for us. He is the Way, the Truth, and the Life! He took back the "keys" to the storehouses of heaven.

Adam gave it away. Jesus bought it all back. Now He has made everything that we need available. All that He "IS" and all that He has is available to us today; because, Jesus became our sin and our iniquity; because Jesus became "lawlessness" and "sin"; because Jesus became an "eleven" for us; we can enter into God's kingdom and experience all the fullness of God!

Jesus is the reality of the Old Testament type and foreshadowing that is seen in Joseph's life. Joseph is an Old Testament type of Christ. He was the **eleventh son of Jacob**; a number symbolic of all "lawlessness and sin, and disorder". Jesus became that **eleven** for us; and it is pictured for us in the Tabernacle of Moses!

As we look back in the Old Testament in the book of Exodus, we see in every detail of this tabernacle a portrayal of the life of Jesus Christ our Messiah. So, in this portion, I would like to look at all the "tent-like" coverings that were draped over the frame of the Most Holy Place and the Holy Place: the two innermost chambers where only the priest could enter. This tent-like structure was made up of four different, separate, layers. We will go through each one so that you can see the different aspects of Christ revealed in each layer, and why this number **"eleven"** is so important to us today!

The First Layer or covering was made of fine white linen with a total of "ten" curtains altogether. "Ten" is the number of the Ten Commandments and represents the Law Covenant between God and man. We see here the fact that Jesus is the perfect, righteous, sinless, man who kept the entire law and all the commandments of God in His earth-walk in their entirety. All the moral law, the civil law, and the ceremonial law were all fulfilled in the life of Christ. He is "Emmanuel": God with us!

These ten curtains were made of white, fine linen as described in Exodus 26:1. The clean, white, fine linen is a symbol of righteousness; first the righteousness of Christ as the pattern, and then secondly, to us – those who are in Christ – the righteousness of the saints. But it's not a self-righteousness which is only as good as filthy rags (Is.64:6), but one of faith – a righteousness that is imputed by God alone. This fine linen was the clothing of the priesthood. (Exodus

28:39-43) We are called to be kings and priests unto our God, and to wear the same garments that they did in the Old Testament. But to us it's symbolically in a spiritual sense!

The verse in Revelation 3:5 says, *"He that overcomes the same shall be **clothed** in white raiment."* Also, Isaiah 61:10 reads, *"He has **clothed** me with garments of salvation and **arrayed** me in a robe of righteousness."*

This white fine linen was also to be designed with *"...blue, purple, and scarlet thread; with artistic designs of cherubim you shall weave them."* (Ex.26:1)

Blue is the symbol of heaven. Jesus is the Lord of Heaven. (ICor.15:47; Jn.1:1-3; 14-18) The Children of Israel were directed to make tassels on the corners of their garments which contained a "blue" thread as a reminder of the commandments of God—the word from heaven.

Purple is the color of royalty and kingship. Jesus is the royal man—the King of kings and the Lord of lords. Interestingly, purple is made by the mixing of the blue and the red together. Jesus is the God-man in one person: fully God and fully man. (Lk.1:30-33; Rev. 19:11-16) This qualifies Jesus to be the only mediator between God and man.

Scarlet or red is the color of blood and is the symbol of sacrifice and humanity. They stripped Jesus of His own clothes and gave Him a scarlet robe. (Mat.27:28) *"Without the shedding of blood; there is no remission of sins."* (Heb.9-22) Jesus was and is the only true "lamb" for the sacrifice. All the animal blood of the Old Testament only foreshadowed the blood that Christ would shed in the New Testament. He is the final, perfect, and total sacrifice for all of our sin! Only His blood has the power to redeem man 100 percent!

Another point of interest here is that these four colors parallel the four gospels and the different aspects of Christ's life that are presented in each gospel. White is the "sinless man" that we find in the book of Luke. Blue is the "heavenly-man" portrayed in the gospel of John. Purple is the "royal-man" that we see as the King in Mathew. And scarlet is the "servant-man" that is revealed in the book of Mark.

These white, fine linen curtains were to have artistic designs of cherubim. Here we find a picture that does not represent angels; but these cherubim are symbolic of the fullness of the Godhead in bodily form. The Father, the Son, and the Holy Spirit all coming together into the earth and being involved in the life of Christ in His birth, ministry, life, death, burial, resurrection, and ascension.

If you walked into the Holy Place as a priest and looked up at the ceiling, you would see these heavenly, beautiful, inwrought, cherubim with wings in all of these pretty colors. It is here that we can see this picture in Psalms 91:4, *"He shall cover you with His feathers and under His wings you shall take refuge."*

It is dwelling in the "Secret Place" of the Most High God. It is the fullness of the Godhead! All that God is and all that He has, is a covering over you in this place. He is "El Elyon". He is "El Shaddai". He is "Jehovah Rapha". He is "Jehovah Nissi". He is "Jehovah Addonai". He is "Yahweh". He is "Jehovah Jirrah", "Jehovah Mekadesh", "Jehovah Shalom", and "Jehovah Tisidkenu". He is "Jehovah Rohi". He is "Jehovah Shammah". He is all these things! And all these things are His coverings over you, if you dwell in the "Secret Place" of the Most High God!

The Tabernacle of Moses – it's all a picture – it's a type of Christ – but it's also a pattern and a blueprint for the believer today. And as you, as His Royal Priesthood, if you will enter the Holy Place and then the Most Holy Place, you enter into the largest covering-- the greatest umbrella-- on the face of the planet.

This is entering into "Covenantal Relationship" with the Most High God. All that He "IS" – is yours in this covenant. Psalms 91:14 says, *"Because he has set His love upon Me; therefore I will deliver him; I will set him on high because he has known My name."* When you come into covenantal relationship, you know God by all these names. You know Him as El Elyon. You know Him as El Shaddai. You know Him as Jehovah Rapha – and all of these names that take on the personalities, the characteristics, and the functions of God. It's the most complete covering and umbrella in the entire universe. This is "abiding under the shadow" of the Almighty. If you give God all that you've got – He gives you all that He's got! And, that's not a bad deal.

The second layer of this tent-like structure that was over the Holy Place and the Most Holy Place was called a "curtain". We see in Exodus 26:7, *"You shall also make curtains of **goats hair**"* to be a tent over the tabernacle. You shall make **eleven** curtains. So we see that these curtains were **eleven** pieces joined together into **one**. The number eleven here is very, very significant, and also the material and color used.

Eleven being the number of "lawlessness and disorder" and associated with "sin and rebellion", Jesus is here pictured as the covering for all of this. He is the covering for what the number eleven symbolizes.

Also, here, we see that this curtain was made of goat's hair. The goat was one of the animals used for sacrifice, primarily in connection with the sin offering on the "Day of Atonement". The goat was also used in the three main feasts of Passover, Pentecost, and Tabernacles. Jesus is the perfect "lamb" of God. He is the perfect sacrifice.

In number and in the material used we see here a picture of how the Lord Jesus Christ became our sin offering and took upon Himself the wages of our sin and became death for us. The color black symbolizes death. These curtains were most likely black in color, characteristic of most of the goats in that region as seen in the Song of Solomon 1:5. It is in stark contrast to the fine, white, linen that is underneath it! II Cor. 5:21 says, *"For He made Him who knew no sin to be sin for us, that we might become the righteousness of God in Him".*

Also, in the length of these curtains we can see the life of Christ. They were to be made thirty cubits long. A priest had to be thirty years of age to begin their ministry. (Numbers 4:3) Jesus was thirty years old when He began His ministry which lasted only three years until the age of thirty three. This curtain of goat's hair was eleven curtains put together – one more than the fine linen curtain that was underneath it. The bottom curtain was made up of only ten curtains. So we get a picture of the top curtain being eleven – so 1/11 of that curtain extended beyond the ones below – only 1/11 was ever seen because the rest was covered with the other two coverings on top of it; so only 1/11 was ever seen. Why is this significant? Only 1/11 of Jesus life was seen in public ministry; just three years of His total thirty three years of life. The other thirty were hidden from view. We see the life of Christ unveiled in this picture of these curtains in the tabernacle!

This particular layer was also highly significant that God, Himself, specifically stated there was a set of five and a set of six that were to be joined together into one. Why is there the use of these numbers? I believe that five – as we have seen in chapter 5 – is symbolic also of Satan's kingdom and six is the number of fallen man. So here we have another equation: **5 + 6 = 11.** Five, being the number of Satan's kingdom, plus six, the number of fallen man, equals eleven – the number of lawlessness, sin, disorder, disintegration, and the anti-Christ. Jesus became an eleven for us and covered it all.

The third covering was a covering of ram's skins. It was to be dyed red. (Exodus 26:14) It is symbolic of sacrifice and blood. Here we have a picture of the ram's skin. It was used in the trespass offering, the burnt offering, and the peace offering, found in the book of Leviticus. It is also called the "ram of consecration" in Exodus 29:15. The ram was also used in the consecration of the priest so that he could minister. (8:22)

Also, the first place we see the ram in the bible is at Mount Moriah, when Abraham was asked to offer up Issac, his only son, upon the altar of God. God supplied a ram to be offered in his place. It is a foreshadowing of Jesus Christ who became the "Lamb of God" and shed His blood on Calvary's cross to be our substitutionary ram.

Perhaps the most interesting thing to note about this third covering is that there are no recorded measurements. It signifies to me that this blood covering – this sacrificial death is limitless. Jesus' blood covers it all! It covers all sin! I John 1:9 says, *"if we confess our sins, He is faithful and just to forgive us of our sins and cleanse us from all unrighteousness."* The blood that Jesus shed on the cross at Calvary covers a multitude of sins. It covers all of our sin!

The fourth and final layer or covering in this tent-like structure was made of badger skins. (Exodus 26:14) This layer, also, had no measurements. It was the outer covering. It covered everything else. It was to be the protection against the elements of desert life – the winds, the storms, the heat, the sun, and the cold-- all of these things. It is a picture of God being everything for us. The "I AM" that "I AM" in unlimited quantities. This is the covering that we have over our lives today if you are in covenantal relationship with God.

Within this covering we also see that, in the Septuagint, it translates it "as the skins of a blue color". It could have been dyed. Some translate it as the "skins of a porpoise". We don't know for sure; but nevertheless, we see this blue color associated with this final covering. Blue is the color of heaven. It is all of Heaven coming down into the earth! Jesus prayed, *"for Thy Kingdom come, Thy will be done on earth as it is in heaven."* Heaven's coming down! Heaven is coming down!

We see this truth here in this fourth covering – this fourth layer of the tent of the "Tabernacle of Moses." It is significant that badger skins were also used to protect all the pieces of furniture and articles of the tabernacle while they were in transit. These badger skins were not considered a precious fur; there was no beauty to behold in them. Only a look from the inside is the true beauty discovered.

(Isaiah 53: 1-3) *"When we see Him there is no beauty that we should desire Him."* (Isaiah 52:14) *"His visage was marred more than any man and His form more than the sons of men."* To those outside of Christ, there is nothing attractive about Christ. But to those who know Him, they see His beauty and His glory from the inside. Those that dwell in the Secret Place of the Most High God see the fine, white, linen curtain with the blue, purple, and scarlet inwrought cherubim. They see the true beauty of Christ and He becomes "all together lovely". (Song of Solomon 5:16)

"But the natural man does not receive the things of the Spirit of God; for they are foolishness to him; nor can he know them, because they are spiritually discerned." (I Cor. 2:14)

All of these four coverings are four separate layers that signify specific details about the life of Christ, but they all form one covering. Jesus became an **eleven** for you! He became the blackness of sin – the blackness of death for you. He became the blood sacrifice that was shed on Calvary's cross so that you would not have to. He ascended up into heaven. He became the blueness of heaven so that heaven could come down into the earth and bless you. He, also, is the white of His righteousness in you.

Jesus is the totality of all these coverings. He is the tent. He is the tabernacle. He is all these things. And when you come into a "Covenantal Relationship" with God, He becomes the greatest, most complete, umbrella covering over your life that you could ever know. All that He IS and all that He HAS – becomes a covering over your life; so that all you need is available at all times whenever you need it.

This is what it means to: "Abide Under the Shadow of the Almighty". God had a plan for His only begotten son. He had a dream. He had a purpose. Men tried to kill that dream and stop the plan of God from happening. But in so doing, they only helped to fulfill it! The plan of God cannot be thwarted – it cannot be changed.

Jesus Christ came to this world not to be king so that everyone would bow down to Him. He came as a baby to die for you and me. He came not to live in a palace, but He was sentenced to death-- to the pits of hell-- and died; so that you and I could live. He relinquished His entire life to the will of the Father, and He prayed this prayer: "Not My will; but Yours be done." He gave up everything for you and me, and for all the world. He lived a perfect sinless life – fulfilled the entire law – became sin for us, became lawlessness, disorder, incompleteness, and disintegration; so that He could bring to us, holiness, obedience, order, completeness, wholeness, and life for all of humanity. He reversed it all! He reversed the curse! He became an **eleven** for us!

He had "gone on ahead" – died and endured a punishment that we should have endured. We should have died for our own sin. *"The wages of sin is death; but the gift of God is eternal life in Jesus Christ our Lord."* (Rom. 6:23)

If you will call upon the name of the Lord, you will be saved. If you confess your sins, He is faithful and just and will forgive you of your sins and cleanse you from all unrighteousness. He will be your covering. He will be your eleven. He has already taken your place on the cross at Calvary. He has already become an eleven for you. All you need to do is by faith call upon the name of the Lord and appropriate what He has done. *"Believe on the Lord Jesus Christ and you will be saved."* (Acts 16:31)

If you have not done so, pray this simple prayer: My Father, who art in Heaven, Hallowed be Your Name. Your Kingdom come, your will be done on earth as it is in Heaven. Give me this day my daily bread. Forgive me of my debts, as I forgive my debtors, and do not lead me into temptation, but deliver me from evil. For Yours is the kingdom and the power and the glory forever and ever. Amen.

If you have prayed this simple prayer that the Lord Jesus – Himself – had instructed us to pray, you are forgiven. Your slate has been wiped clean. And just like the fine, white, linen curtain on the first layer in the Tabernacle of Moses – just like that – you have become wrapped in robes of righteousness. You have put on the garments of salvation because salvation has come to your house today. Salvation has come! Jesus has become an eleven for you. If we add one to it, 11 + 1, equals the kingdom.

"Blessed are the poor in spirit for theirs is the Kingdom of heaven." (Mat. 5:3)

When you realize there's nothing that you can give God – nothing that you have to offer Him except your life – yourself—you truly become poor! And if you give Him simply that, we can add a one to your eleven. **Eleven** plus **one** equals twelve… **(11+1=12)!!!**

This day, **all** of the kingdom is available to the poor in spirit. "Blessed are the poor in spirit for theirs is the Kingdom." This day I challenge you to read further and discover what your inheritance is as a descendant of the Most High God.

These Are the Days of My Remnant
(Exodus 26: 12, 13)

"The remnant that remains of the curtains of the tent, the half curtain that remains, shall hang over the back of the tabernacle." "And a cubit on one side and a cubit on the other side, of what remains of the length of the curtains of the tent, shall hang over the sides of the tabernacle, on this side and on that side, to cover it."

The Remnant that remains, it is the half curtain that remains. It is the excess, the remainder, the leftovers, the reserve, or the residual. It hung on the back and the side walls of the Most Holy Place – the deepest chamber in the Tabernacle of Moses. It seemed to have no other purpose, no other function; but just to hang in God's presence year, after year, after year, after year. This remnant, as it hung on the back wall of the Most Holy Place, it became saturated in the power, and the glory, and the presence of the Most High God. If this remnant could speak, it would cry out, "Holy, Holy, Holy, is the Lord God Almighty!"

Even in Isaiah's vision, he said, "I saw the Lord sitting on a throne, high and lifted up, and the train of His robe filled the temple." The seraphim cried out, "Holy, Holy, Holy, is the Lord of hosts, the whole earth is full of His glory." (Isaiah 6:1-3)

"Nothing else can remain in the glory of God. No flesh will glory in My Presence," says the Lord. "You are to be holy even as I am Holy. My desire for you is that you be saturated in My Power and in My presence. My desire for you is that you would even smell like God and carry His fragrance." II Cor. 12:14 says, "We are the fragrance of Christ."

"It is in the 'Secret Place of the Most High God' – the inner most chamber – the Holy of Holies – this is the place that I have called you, My church, My bride, to come to. Press in past the veil into the

429

very presence of the Living God – into the glory realms of the Most High."

In this book, this has been our destination – the Holy of Holies. We have a little ways yet to go; but in this chapter, in speaking about the eleven curtains, the leftovers, the remnant, the residual...

"THE TWELVETH PIECE HANGS IN THE HOLY OF HOLIES!"

"You are the twelfth piece," says the Lord God Almighty. "You are My Remnant," says the Lord Your God. "You are the Remnant that hangs in the Most Holy Place that is to be saturated with the power and the presence of the Living God. And in these Glory Realms there is no sin; there is no flesh. Everything here – it is holy! Even the atmosphere – it is holy. My desire for My people is that they are holy even as I am holy. And that may seem like a lofty, high, expectation to some; but what I declare in My word – have I not made a way for you to accomplish all that I desire? All that I ask of you – Jesus is the Way, the Truth, and the Life! Jesus has made a way possible for you to live in the 'Glory Realms' of God. It is not some far off unattainable goal or projection. It can be a reality in every believer, in every life, in this lifetime as you walk out God's plans, your dreams, and the purposes of God in your life today." Halleluiah! Glory to God!

"In this day, and in this hour, I am calling forth My Remnant from throughout the earth – from all the four corners of the globe. This Remnant has been hanging in the Most Holy Place for quite some time. These have learned the secrets of waiting in My presence – of being saturated with My power – of soaking in My Glory."

"These are the days of My Remnant," says the Lord God Almighty. "The world – including the church needs what they have! They carry the power, and the presence, and the glory of God. All that He is – that's what they have and they give off the fragrance of Christ. I am calling them forth, in this day, and in this hour. There are pieces of My Remnant all over the world, tucked away, hidden, and kept. They have been the leftovers. They have had no place; seemingly no purpose; even at times shunned by the church; considered too radical; too zealous; misunderstood and persecuted by their brothers. At times they have even been thrown into the pits, left alone and forgotten, rejected by the status-quo. The church has had no place for these. But while enduring the pits of hell, while in this prison, God has been refining them. They have been through the fire and they have come out singing with the fourth man in the fire!"

"They have also been set on fire with the glory of God. Remember the burning bush before Moses? It was caught on fire with the glory and not consumed. You see, all men are trees – symbolically. You are oaks of righteousness. You flourish like the palm tree. Israel is an olive tree. You have been grafted in. I am the vine – you are the branches. You are My Trees! My Bushes! My Branches! And My desire is to set you on fire with the Glory of God. I am calling forth My Remnant from the four corners of the earth in this day and in this hour, to be set on fire with the glory of God. You are a **'Burning Bush'!!!!** YOU ARE A BURNING BUSH! SET ON FIRE WITH THE POWER AND THE PRESENCE AND THE GLORY OF THE LIVING GOD."

"You will display My power in the earth in this day and in this hour. You have been saturated in My glory. You have been saturated in My presence," says the Lord. "You have been **'SOAKED TO THE BONE'** with the Rains of My Presence. You have hung on the back wall of the Holy of Holies for such a time as this!"

"These are the Days of My Remnant!" says the Lord. I am calling them out from different cities, different countries, different continents, from all over the earth – all speaking different languages but being united in one spirit – having perfect fellowship and perfect harmony. There will be an anointing that falls when they meet together. Why? Pieces coming together as one! They've been tucked away, hanging in the Holy of Holies, living in the Glory of God... pieces ... all coming together ... as one. The power of this Remnant will be in their unity and their oneness!"

Psalm 133 again, *"Behold how good and how pleasant it is for brethren to dwell together in unity. It is like the precious oil upon the head, running down on the beard, the beard of Aaron, running down on the edge of his garments. It is like the dew of Hermon, descending upon the Mountains of Zion."*

"Here unity is combined with anointing! As My Remnant comes together as one, My anointing increases; it is multiplied; it becomes greater, and greater, and greater, and greater. *'It is like the dew of Hermon...'* The dew of Hermon is water – another symbol of My

431

Holy Spirit. It is descending upon the mountains of Zion. What is Zion? It is the city of the Living God."

"IT IS WHERE I LIVE!   It is My habitation; and it is there, where I live, that I command the blessing: Life forevermore! LIFE forevermore! LIFE-- nothing but life. There is only life where I live," says the Lord. "There is no death where I live. There is no death where I live!" Halleluiah! "Mount Zion is coming down! Mount Zion – the city of the Living God – it is coming down into the earth. The Tabernacle of God is now among men. Heaven and earth are merging. They are becoming as one. It's the Lord's Prayer: Thy Kingdom come, Thy will be done; on earth as it is in Heaven."

"I am calling them forth, in this day and in this hour. REMNANT! REMNANT! Come Forth, in Jesus Name.   I have a plan. I have a purpose for you," says the Lord. "You have been shunned by your brothers. You have been put in the pits of hell. You have endured the very fires of God. This day, you are coming out of the fires, and you will dance with the fourth man in the furnace. You will carry the power and the presence of the Living God in the earth, in this day and in this hour."

"ALL OF HEAVEN – MOUNT ZION – WILL BE CARRIED THROUGH YOU!" says the Lord God Almighty. You will usher in the Kingdom! My Remnant, My Remnant: You will usher in the Kingdom of God in the earth – all that it is. All that it is! You will bring it down into the earth. Thy Kingdom come; thy will be done on earth as it is in heaven. Heaven is coming down," says the Lord God Almighty. "Heaven is coming down because you, My Remnant, have paid the price; because, you have died to yourself – completely – fully – and gone to the bottom of the sea. It is in this place – the Holy of Holies – where no flesh will glory in My presence. Your flesh has died completely. It is impossible for any flesh to be in the glory of God. Because in the glory realms, the burning fire of God – which is His glory – it is all completely consumed. There is nothing left of you. Nothing left!"

"Blessed are the poor in spirit; for theirs is the Kingdom." "When you have nothing left to give, I the Lord God will give you all that I have! It is in this place, the Holy of Holies and the glory realms of God, that I give you all of My Kingdom," says the Lord, "all of My Kingdom; not just half – but all!"

"Remnant Come Forth! Remnant Come Forth! You are My Josephs," says the Lord. "You have been persecuted by your brothers. You have been thrown into the very pits of hell; but it is there that I have refined you. It is there that I have trained you. It is there that I have had you hidden from the rest of the world. It is there that I have had you tucked away; all the while, dying to yourself – to your plans, your future, your goals, your hopes, and your dreams. Even your godly dreams, I have rolled in death to them; so that you would know that you cannot accomplish the will of God in your life on your own."

"Joseph could not do it! Jesus could not do it!"

"You cannot do it; will not do it. It is there that I have rolled in death even to your **God given dreams**. Why? So that you would know – **you cannot fulfill them!** And that you would stop trying. All the ways and the means of man's plans must come to an end. They must die. You cannot fulfill the God given dreams and plans for your life in the natural, in the carnal, in the flesh, in your strength, in your wisdom, in your knowledge, with your money, or with all of your resources. Because if you think you can: IT'S BACK TO THE PITS FOR YOU!"

"I must bring complete death to the dream – death in the natural, death in the carnal, death in the flesh. You are as My Josephs," says the Lord. "And until you are ready, you will not come out of your pits and your dungeons – UNTIL GOD INTERVENES!! Until God begins to move! Until God is ready to fulfill His dream in your life, you will remain in these pits. But I want you to know it's not forever. It is until you are ready; until you have been refined enough; until you have trained enough; until you have soaked enough; until you have been saturated enough. And in due time, even as I called Joseph out of that pit; so too, I will call you forth and fulfill the dream and the plans of God, the purposes of God, and the will of God in your life."

"And you will be exalted in that day; as Joseph was exalted to the right hand of the Father. This will be your high position! As Joseph was exalted and Jesus was exalted; so, you too, will be exalted to the right hand of God-- second in command over all the Kingdom. It will be in that time and in that day, that I will place upon your finger the ring of the King, and a robe of the King, and a chain of gold around your neck. These are all symbols of My power and My authority that you will have in the earth."

433

"This robe is a "coat of many colors." It is symbolic of the full spectrum blessing and favor of God Most High. You will hold the "keys" to the storehouses of heaven! You will have all authority and all power, and to give out grain to a starving world; but not only grain – ALL THAT I AM-- FROM ALL THE STOREHOUSES! The storehouses of grain, the storehouses of water, the storehouses of blessing – anything that you can think of – all that I AM! It's a full spectrum blessing! It is the 'coat of many colors'! It is all the storehouses of heaven."

"This is what I am calling My church to. This is the place that I am calling them to. You are to be as My Josephs. You are to "GO ON AHEAD" for your brothers and sisters. You are to "go on ahead" for the rest of the world. Yes, even at times to endure great persecution by the hands of your brothers, but it is so that they may live. Christianity is all about sacrifice. It is the giving up of one's self for the life of another." *"Greater love has no one than this; than to lay down one's life for his friends."* (Jn.14:13)

Someone has to pay the price. Joseph did. Jesus did. What about you? Will you pay the price that God is asking you to pay and give all of your life, all of your time, your resources, your dreams, your hopes, your future, all that you are, and die completely to yourself and go to the bottom of the sea-- be STRIPPED OF ALL YOUR NATURAL ROBES?

Joseph was stripped of his coat of many colors in the natural. Will you be stripped of your own "natural robe" to gain the robe of the King? We must follow in Joseph's footsteps. We must be stripped of our glory to gain the King's glory! Then we will possess the keys to the storehouses of heaven, to give out all that God has and all that God is to a starving, lost, hungry, and dying world. God has an unlimited supply in His storehouses of heaven, and heaven is coming down! Heaven is coming down! Heaven's coming down!

Will you be a "ladder" from earth to heaven? Will you be a "vessel of gold" to carry the power and the presence of the Living God? Will you be a "Jacob's Ladder" to bring down mighty answers from heaven? Will you live in the "Secret Place of the Most High God" and be saturated in the Holy of Holies? Will you be counted among this Remnant?

"These are the days of My Remnant," says the Lord. "For I am calling them forth in these days, to be My Josephs in the earth, to be second in command of all of My Kingdom, to bring down the Kingdom of Heaven into the Kingdom of the Earth, and command all the armies of heaven to come down and fight in the earth. These are the days of My Remnant. Will you be counted among this Remnant? Will you pay the price-- whatever the cost-- to have **"gone on ahead"** for the sake of someone else? Will you be a Joseph in My Kingdom?" says the Lord God Almighty.

Eleven Days
(Deut. 1:2)

It was only an eleven day journey from Horeb to Kadesh Barnea by the Mount Seir Road – from Egypt to the Promised Land. They could have entered their new country – their new homeland – on the twelfth day by direct route! They sent in twelve spies, one from each tribe, to scout out and explore the land. Only two, Joshua and Caleb came back with a good report. The rest grumbled and complained. They said that the people were too big, too strong, and too numerous. The cities were too large and the walls were too tall. They gave reports, also, of the "giants" living there. They failed to believe their God and all of His promises that He had given to them concerning the land, even when God's presence would go before them. Was not God able to do the impossible? Was anything bigger or stronger than the Lord God Almighty?

They doubted God. They doubted His word. They doubted His promises. They did believe a bad report instead. They saw what God did for them in Egypt. They had seen the cloud by day and the fire by night. They had seen the Red Sea open up before their very eyes. But, they did not believe or trust in the God of Abraham, Issac, and Jacob. As a result, God said not one of this evil generation would enter into this Promised Land except for Caleb and Joshua – the two spies that had given the good report. All the rest of them would die in the wilderness wandering for another forty years.

God had shown them His presence, His providence, and His patience even in times of extreme rebellion. He gave them manna from heaven, water from the smitten rock, quail in abundance to eat, divine strength, and divine health along the way. Even their clothes and their sandals never wore out after forty years. They saw God descend down upon Mount Sinai in the billows of smoke and fire, thunder, and lightning as He gave His laws to Moses for the people of this new nation to teach them how to live and to walk with their new God.

They tested God, however, ten times; (Numbers 14:22) constantly grumbling about their situations and their circumstances, and rebelled against the Lord their God. Before Moses had even gotten down out of Mount Sinai, the people had already made a golden calf to worship. When Moses had seen what they had done, he threw down the tablets in anger and shattered them into pieces. The Law was broken on the first day! But God remained faithful to His covenant people because He had made a promise to their father Abraham.

One of the Ten Commandments was to have "…no other gods before Me". They were not to worship as all the other nations had worshipped their gods. They were to smash all of their sacred stones, break down all of their altars, cut down all of their "Ashera" poles, and burn their idols in the fire. The Lord had said to them, *"For you are a people holy to the Lord your God. He has chosen you out of all the people on the face of the earth to be His people, His treasured possession." (Deut. 7:6)* They were to have one place of worship – the dwelling place of "Yeshua" – the Tabernacle of Moses.

God had given them His word – His revelation! It is known today as the Torah: the first five books of the bible. Within it were blessings and cursings. If they would obey the voice of the Lord, God would send blessings and life and "open heavens". If they disobeyed, only cursings and death would follow. God had fought for them against their enemies as they remained faithful to this covenant. But as they rebelled and sinned against the Most High consequences always followed.

They were nomadic travelers looking for a resting place – a place to settle -- a place to call home – a country of their very own. God promised Abraham to make him into a great nation with a land of their very own, with God – himself – as their King.

It was just an **eleven** day journey. On the twelfth day, they would be there! They would be in! But only two from this first generation would ever enter this land because of their disobedience and unbelief at the commands of the Lord. Everyone twenty years of age and older would die in the desert, never possessing or experiencing the full blessing and inheritance that they could have seen. Even Moses would only see the Promised Land from a distance.

What was physical for them is now spiritual for us. There still a land that God is trying to get us to – not just a "Promised Land" for when we die, but one for the here and now! This is when we need it the most and can use it for the most good. We need to enter this land today!

This whole "wilderness" story is a metaphor for our spiritual state of existence today. What is the condition of our soul? What does our "land" look like? There is a "Promised Land" on the inside of each and every one of us down deep in our inner most being – spiritually – that God wants us to enter into – now! Not when we die – but today! They could have entered into it thirty nine years earlier, if they would have simply believed God and taken Him at His word.

Just like us today, we don't have to "wander in the wilderness" in the dry desert places of life; but we can enter a land flowing with streams, and pools, and fountains of water, if we will just listen, believe, and do what the Lord tells us to do. Where there's water--there's life! Jesus came to give men life and life more abundantly. There's nothing but life in this new land, if we have the faith to enter it.

The church hasn't come into her fullness or into her full inheritance yet. In many ways, the church today has "wandered in the wilderness" just like that first generation of the Children of Israel. We have been wandering for many generations never knowing our full rights and privileges as sons and daughters of the Most High God. There are many among us today that have died in the "wilderness".

We have come through eleven chapters in this book. I have led you, now, to the border of this "Promised Land" – your native homeland. This is where your original descendants are from. Do you have the faith to believe God and enter this new land?

DO YOU HAVE THE FAITH TO BELIEVE GOD TO ENTER THIS LAND? WILL YOU BELIEVE A GOOD REPORT AND NOT A BAD ONE? Will you have the courage to move forward, and enter this land? Your response determines your future! You can "wander in the wilderness" all your life and never experience living in the land flowing with "milk and honey" - a land where you "lack nothing". (Deut.8 ... a description of the Promised Land) You can keep on doubting-- keep on disbelieving-- if you want to. You can die in the wilderness like so many others before you.

There is a "wilderness journey" for all of us; but how long this journey takes is up to you! We have to walk it out day by day. We have to believe and trust God. We must obey God. We have to grow in times of testing. We must stand firm and strong; unshakable, unmovable, and believe God and take Him at His word. *"God is not a man that He should lie, nor a son of man that He should change His mind. Does He speak and then not act? Does He promise and not fulfill?* (Numbers 23:19 NIV)

Doubt is like the "surf of the sea". It tosses us here and there. James describes it and says, *"let not that man expect that he will receive anything from the Lord. He is a double-minded man unstable in all his ways."* We must walk by faith, not by sight. We must believe God and take Him at His word.

"There is a land that is flowing with milk and honey that I want you – My people – to possess in the here and now – not in the life here after. You have been brought to the boarder of this land. Will you now have the faith to enter this land? It is a spiritual land. It is on the inside of you. Remember this scripture verse: The Kingdom of God ... is where? ... The Kingdom of God is within you! The 'Promised Land' is within you. It is a spiritual state of existence or state of being that any child of God can enter into. It is a land that is flowing with nothing but life, and life more abundantly. It is a land flowing with streams of water, fountains, and pools – all symbolic of My Holy Spirit and My presence. It is a land flowing with oil and new wine – symbolic of My anointing. It is a land flowing with an abundance of bread, and grain, and wheat, and barley – all symbolic of the 'bread from heaven' – the seventh day manna – Jesus! He is our bread. He is our grain. He is our wheat and barley!" *"Man shall not live by bread alone but man lives by every word that proceeds from the mouth of the Lord."* (Deut.8:3)

Have you been "wandering in the wilderness" for a very long time, thinking in your heart and believing that there's got to be more to all of this? ...More to your faith ... more to God ... more to the Kingdom ... more to life ...? If that is you, I challenge you this day, to believe all that I have told you in this book up to this point! Search it out in the scriptures! Pray through it to see whether it is from God. Take God at His word. Believe on the Lord Jesus Christ! Believe the "good report" and come with me. Read on and let's enter chapter twelve. And by faith, spiritually, enter this "Promised Land", this "country," that God has reserved for every one of His children. It is part of your inheritance. Will you believe a "good report"? Will you have faith in God and take Him at His word? Will you have the courage to read on and enter your new "homeland"?

It Is The Eleventh Hour
(Mat. 20:1-16)

Jesus' Parable: The Workers In The Vineyard

"For the Kingdom of Heaven is like a landowner who went out early on the morning to hire laborers for his vineyard. Now when he had agreed with laborers for a denarius a day, he sent them into his vineyard. And he went out about the third hour and saw others standing idle in the marketplace, and said to them, 'You also go into the vineyard, and whatever is right I will give you'. So they went. Again he went out about the sixth and ninth hour, and did likewise. And about the eleventh hour he went out and found others standing idle, and said to them, 'Why have you been standing here idle all day?' They said to him, 'Because no one hired us! He said to them, 'You also go into the vineyard and whatever is right you will receive! So when evening had come, the owner of the vineyard said to his steward, 'Call the laborers and give them their wages, beginning with the last to the first.' And when those came who were hired about the eleventh hour, they each received a denarius. But when the first came, they supposed that they would receive more; and they likewise received each a denarius. And when they had received it, they complained against the land owner, saying, 'These last men have worked only one hour, and you made them equal to us who have borne the burden and the heat of the day.' But he answered one of them and said, 'Friend, I am doing you no wrong. Did you not agree with me for a denarius? Take what is yours and go your way. I wish to give to this last man the same as to you. Is it not lawful for me to do what I wish with my own things? Or is your eye evil because I am good? So the last will be first, and the first last. For many are called, but few chosen."

The Kingdom of Heaven is like a landowner who went out early in the morning to hire workers to labor in his vineyard. He hired them in the third hour (9:00a.m.), the sixth hour (12:00 noon), the ninth hour (3:00p.m.), and the eleventh hour (5:00p.m.). But each time, every single one, they were all standing around doing nothing. The landowner asked, "Why have you been standing here idle all day?" He

439

seemed to be surprised at what he saw. Then their reply back was, "Because no one has hired us."

"Church of the Living God: YOU TOO, HAVE BEEN WAITING FOR PAYMENT! You have had the mentality of 'what is in it for me?' WHAT'S IN IT FOR ME? You have only wanted payment to work in this vineyard. You have only wanted your wages and what would benefit you. There has been no sacrificial labor! I have been looking and searching for people who will come and work in My vineyard; who will not ask for ANY WAGES; who will not ask for payment; but simply work to honor the landowner because they have been asked to work; and because, they have been called out to labor in these fields."

"THE FIELDS – THEY ARE WHITE UNTO HARVEST! Pray to the Lord of the Harvest to send out laborers into this harvest field. Who will go? Who will go and work these fields, even in the heat of the day? Who will work these fields all day long – for long hours if they have to, but not be concerned about their wages, or their gold, or their silver, or what is in it for them?"

"This day, I am calling out My Remnant in the earth. I am calling forth workers to labor in this harvest field, but I am calling those that will understand the Kingdom of God – who will understand that this Kingdom is based upon sacrifices – who will understand that Christianity's symbol is the cross! It's not the death of one man; it's the death of all men! You give up your life. 'He who loses his life for my sake will find it.' (Mat.10:39) The way up is down! The greatest in the Kingdom will be the servant of all. The last shall be first and the first shall be last. These are some of the principles in My Kingdom," says the Lord.

"It is the Eleventh Hour! It is the Eleventh Hour!"

"In the parable of the ten virgins, at the midnight hour the cry rang out: 'Here's the bridegroom. Come out to meet Him!' That midnight hour is not a literal time of day, but a figurative symbol of the fullness of time when the Lord Your God – Jesus Christ – is going to return. It is a time that only the Father knows. No one else knows the day or the hour. (Mark 13:35) A time when no one knows, I the Lord God, am returning to this earth to receive My bride unto Myself. It is the 'Wedding Supper of the Lamb'."

It is the eleventh hour. Time is running out. We don't have forever to do the work that the Lord has called us to do. We must be about our Father's business. *"Seek first the Kingdom of God and His righteousness and everything else shall be added unto you."* (Mat. 6:33)

"These are the days of My Remnant. And it is the eleventh hour; and I am calling them forth in this day and this hour. Time is running out, and I am calling them forth. Who will work in My harvest field? Who will work in My vineyard; just to honor the King; just to honor the landowner," says the Lord God Almighty. "I am calling forth My Remnant in these days-- My Remnant-- from all over the four corners of the earth."

"What I am about to do, in this day and in this hour, is unlike any other revival that has ever taken place. No eye has seen, nor ear has heard, nor has entered into the heart of man what I have prepared for those who love Me. This Revival will be the greatest revival that the world has ever seen. It will be a sovereign move of God with many prominent people involved in this revival; but still a sovereign move of God. It will not be just a one man show. This move will be within My bride-- within My people."

"My Power is Returning to My People," says the Lord. "My Power is returning to Jerusalem. In the days of King David, the Ark of the Covenant was returning to Jerusalem. It was the symbol of the throne of God – His power and presence – in the earth. The 'Ark' of God is returning to Jerusalem in this day, and in this hour. The power and the presence, and His anointing that should have been within My Bride all along and has not – it is returning in this hour."

"My people, who have been called by My name who have humbled themselves and sought My face – it is these… (II Chron. 7:14) (a very prominent verse in many revivals for a reason.)

"If My people will humble themselves and seek My face … it is in the humbling, it is in the dying to self and giving up of one's life for someone else. To go up, you have to go down. You have to go to the depths of the sea. You have to go to the death of yourself. This is the Revival that I am bringing," says the Lord.

"A Tsunami Wave of My Spirit is sweeping over the entire globe. It is coming swiftly, powerfully, and furiously… nothing will stop this revival that I am bringing. You can only prepare for the impact!"

Word For America

"A Tsunami of My Spirit is about to hit the east coast of the United States of America and sweep across this great land – from east to south and then sweep across into the west and then up north into Canada and then down into Mexico. The entire eastern Hemisphere will be affected by this revival," says the Lord God Almighty.

"America, America, prepare for the impact. Prepare for a tsunami of My Spirit," says the Lord, "for it is about to hit the east coast. Shock waves will be felt throughout this country – wave, upon wave, upon wave, upon wave will come. It will be relentless. It will come from person, to person, to person – from church to church, to church – from region to region and from state to state."

"With this tsunami will come a tremendous shaking in the land. I, the Lord God, I will shake everything. Nothing will be left. Every stone that has been laid by the hands of men will be torn down. Only those stones that are laid by the hand of God shall remain. Because, I am the Lord God. I am the architect! I am the Builder! I am building My church. I am building My tabernacle. I am building My temple in this day, and in this hour. My people, they are My temple – individually and corporately – they make up the bride of Christ-- individual temples making up a larger house of the Living God."

"This shaking will be unlike any other shaking that has ever been felt in the earth or in the body of Christ. This shaking will be violent and it will be severe. Lines will be drawn. Sides will be taken. Some will reject, but more will come in."

"The battle cry of this revival will be: Choose this Day Whom You Will Serve! If God be God serve Him! If Baal be God serve Him. It is a showdown of the ages. It's like Elijah on top of Mount Carmel. You cannot serve two masters. The days of sitting on the fence are over!"

"I, the Lord God, I say unto you, America: Choose This Day whom you will serve! If God be God serve Him. Serve God! Take Him at His word. Listen, Believe, and Do! Walk in obedience to whatever the Lord your God may say to you—specifically. My sheep know My voice; they hear My cry. They harken their ears unto the Lord God and His voice. Whatever I may say unto you – this is what I require. But to hear My voice, you must come to the 'Secret Place' of the Most High God. You must come back to a 'Covenantal Relationship' with Me!"

"America: I Am Calling You Back! Back to the foundations of what this country was built upon – the truth of My word. Your 'light' has gone out, and darkness has overtaken you. But I have heard the cries of My Remnant," says the Lord. "The Tide has shifted! I have heard from heaven and I am sending down My answer. There will be a shaking in the land, followed by tremendous blessing. But you must endure the shaking before the blessing may come. Some may have thought it was too late for America. I want you to know today that I have heard the cries of My Remnant, and America – She will shine her light once again. She will be a 'lighthouse' to the nations once again. She will shine with a flame of My fire and burn hot with the glory of God. She will be a 'Burning Bush' for Me, and her 'trees' will not be consumed. But her trees will shine out bright with the Glory of God!" Halleluiah! "She, once again, will affect nations for the kingdom of God. And the nations will come to her light and kings to the brightness of her rising."

"America is Rising once again. America is on the rise-- if they endure the shaking-- if they listen to the Most High God. If they humble themselves before My mighty hand." *"If My people who are called by My name, will humble themselves and pray, and seek My face, and turn from their wicked ways; then will I hear from heaven, and will forgive their sin, and will heal their land. Now My eyes will be open and My ears attentive to the prayers offered in this place."* (II Chron.7:14 NIV)

"America – will you listen to what the spirit of the Lord is saying to you in this day and in this hour?" **"IT IS THE ELEVENTH HOUR!"** "Time is short. Will you have ears to hear what the Spirit of the Lord is saying to you in these days?"

Chapter Twelve

I Give Unto You- The Kingdom

"Blessed are the poor in spirit,
for theirs is the kingdom of heaven."
Mat. 5:3

"In the beginning of all time, when I spoke and light was. I formed the sun and the earth and created all the things that you see. Even from the very beginning, I set into motion the earth's orbit and its rotation to the exact degree of its tilt. Twelve hours would govern the day and twelve hours would govern the night. It would take the earth one complete rotation to get through these twenty four hours. And each day that goes by, it's all governed by a multiple of twelve."

"It took three hundred sixty five days for the earth to orbit around the sun --this great fire ball-- one time. So, in those three hundred sixty five days, it was divided into twelve months to make one complete year. Twelve hours rule the day. Twelve hours rule the night. Twelve months govern the entire year as man would know it to be-- in your calendar."

"I AM THE LORD GOD! I GOVERN ALL TIME, AND ALL DAYS, AND ALL YEARS from the very beginning to the very end. I govern it all. I am the ruler of the universe. I made it all and I still govern it all. I still keep the earth in its orbit. I still hold the earth to a perfect degree's angle to the sun. I still govern the stars, and the moon in its orbit around the earth. I still govern and rule ALL THINGS!" "TWELVE IS THE NUMBER OF THE FULLNESS OF TIME!"

They could have entered the promised land on the twelfth day. It was the fullness of time! I wanted them to enter on that day, but they would not believe the word of God that was spoken to them; and so, all but two had to fall in the desert. They would wander another forty years before they would enter the promised land of God.

"Even as I govern the entire universe, I also govern the entire earth and the affairs of men. And even from the beginning I chose one man and made a covenant with him that he would be a father of many nations and that kings would come from him.""KINGS WOULD COME FROM HIM!"

"These kings would govern the affairs of men in the earth. But, you see, I the Lord God, I was establishing My government in the earth. It was originally to be a theocracy that I the Lord God would be their king. But they wanted to be like all the other nations of the earth, so they asked Me for a king and I gave them their first man–king."

446

"But through this one man, Abraham, I chose him above all the others on the face of the planet. He was from the righteous line of Seth, a direct descendant of Adam. And in the appointed time, I came and spoke to him and made a covenant with him. I made him a promise that I fully intended to fulfill and will fulfill."

Sin entered in. Sarah was barren. They had no children. They thought, "How could this promise of God be fulfilled? I can't be a father of one child, let alone the father of nations." Sarah said, "Here, sleep with my servant Hagar, and maybe this promise can be fulfilled through her." So then, they had an Ishmael – flesh line – carnal line – man's line.

"When Abraham was one hundred years old, Sarah gave birth to Issaic – the promised son – the spiritual son. Both these sons – from them would come rulers. Ishmael would also have twelve rulers for his sons. They would set up kingdoms in the earth and through Issaic would come Jacob. And then through Jacob and his twelve sons, I would begin the young nation of Israel to show Myself to the world. It was not My intention that Abraham would have an Ishmael. It was not My intention that that line would be fruitful and multiply. But it was not Ishmael's fault. It was not Hagar's fault. So, I the Lord God, who is rich in mercy, and goodness, and loving-kindness, I would also bless the line of Ishmael. And you see, even today, the line of the flesh and the line of the spirit are still warring against each other."

"FOR THE FLESH ALWAYS SETS ITSELF UP AGAINST THE SPIRIT – THEY ARE IN OPPOSITION TO ONE ANOTHER – ALWAYS!"

"And from this one man, Abraham, I called him to be the father of many nations. He believed God and it was reckoned to him as righteousness. He had a measure of faith. Even though they made mistakes, based upon his measure of faith-- that's all I need is a measure of faith – for someone to believe the word of God. I brought forth his Issac – his promised son. Through him would come the twelve tribes of Israel, for Me to establish My government in the earth. And through them, like it or not, through this one nation, I would bless all other nations on the face of the earth. Through them I would show My goodness, my mercy, and My loving-kindness. Through them, through this righteous line, would come the King of all kings and the Lord of all lords – the greatest King of all."

"It was through this one king, the greatest King of all kings, that all the nations of the earth would be blessed. This one King, He came down into the earth. This one king came as a baby born in a manger in Bethlehem City. They (Israel) were looking for a flesh king, not a spiritual king. They were still looking in the flesh. They wanted him to set up their kingdom in the earth. They wanted this king to establish their own country and overthrow the Roman government and be the greatest kingdom in the earth once again. It was grand and glorious in the days of King Solomon. That was a flesh-picture of a spiritual reality, a shadow of what was to come. But sin and idolatry caused King Solomon's reign to come to an end. The glory of Solomon's kingdom was only a taste of the kingdom that this king would bring."

"Jesus said, 'My kingdom is NOT of this world.' It's not 'of' this world. It did not originate in this world. It is not formed in this world. It is not formed in the mind of man or the flesh. It is a spiritual kingdom that I am beginning now!"

"When Jesus was born that very day of the Virgin Mary and He was placed in a manger, in that moment, THE KING TOOK HIS THRONE!" HALLELUIAH! "THE THRONE OF GOD WAS ESTABLISHED IN THE EARTH in that stable, in a manger. They had no room in the inn. They had NO ROOM for this king; because this king was a different kind of king. Jesus said, 'My kingdom is not "of" this world.' He didn't mean that it still would not be "in" this world."

This king began to grow, and mature, and walk in the ways of his father. He came to this world with a purpose-- with a mission. It was different from man's purpose – from man's desire – from man's ways. It was in the complete opposite of what man wanted him to do. Why? Because, He was establishing a spiritual kingdom different from what they knew; longer lasting than what they knew; bigger than what they could ever imagine!

Jesus came to this earth to establish His government not in just one single location, or just in one nation – which is what they wanted. They wanted to be the supreme nation on the face of the earth. They wanted the power for themselves. They wanted to rule and reign over all the earth and be supreme!

Jesus' kingdom would be supreme and it would rule over all nations – all peoples – all tribes – and all tongues. And though you

448

couldn't see it with the naked eye, it would be more glorious than even King Solomon's kingdom – more glorious than even King Solomon's Temple.

Jesus said, "I will bring down every stone of this temple and rebuild it in three days." He wasn't speaking in the flesh – or the carnal – He was speaking in the spiritual. He would tear down the old system that all pointed to Him, and make a new covenant with His people that was based upon simply their faith. No more sacrifices. No more blood of bulls and goats. But He would be the final "Lamb of God", the perfect sacrifice for all sin, so that all of mankind could be reunited with their heavenly father.

Jesus chose twelve men – twelve disciples – twelve apostles. That's it – only twelve! He poured himself into those twelve men. It is interesting, the number twelve again. Why twelve? Twelve is that number of God's divine government. We see it here repeated from the Old Testament – twelve tribes of Israel – the government of God – natural government – to twelve apostles – spiritual government. There was a shifting. It all changed at the cross!

God is still establishing His government in the earth today. It never stopped! It still continues on, but it's a spiritual kingdom not a flesh kingdom. We have to start thinking in the spiritual. Jesus' earth walk could only be in one place at any one time. He said, "I must go so that the Holy Comforter may come." Jesus came to die. That was totally against all of man's thinking. His disciples thought, "Lord, Lord, No – No! You can't let this happen! It will put an end to it all! Let's rise up. We are behind you. We will fight for you. We will draw swords." But, you see, that's not the kingdom that Jesus was bringing.

"I have come to die, but in so doing, I am guaranteeing that My Kingdom can and will be established in the earth. Why? Because, when I die and I go to hell for you and descend into the lower regions of the earth, I am taking back the keys. Keys are a symbol of power and authority. Adam gave it away. But I AM TAKING IT BACK! So, as Jesus went to the cross, then went to hell, He took back all the authority and the power that Satan held over all of mankind and over all the world."

Then Jesus came back and appeared to His twelve apostles. They voted in one more later. There was only eleven at the time. Judas was replaced with Mathias because Judas hung himself for betraying Christ.

449

"I want you to know today – the days of the apostles did not stop at the cross. One was lost. He was an apostle of the flesh. After the cross, another was appointed; and is not Paul even referred to as the 'Apostle' Paul! THESE ARE THE DAYS OF MY APOSTLES – TO ESTABLISH MY GOVERNMENT IN THE EARTH. I have given some to be apostles, some to be prophets, some to be evangelists, pastors, and teachers. It's My five-fold ministry to establish My divine government in the earth. It is a New Testament scripture. The 'Acts' of the Apostles have not stopped! The book of 'Acts' has no formal ending. Why? IT IS TO CONTINUE!"

"I, the Lord God, I still have a government. Anointing flows down from top to bottom. Just like you would pour out a pitcher of oil and gravity would pull it down from its highest to lowest point. As I pour out My Spirit in the earth through My spiritual kingdom, it will all come down out of heaven through My son Jesus, to My five-fold ministry, and then into the body of Christ. You cannot bypass the government of God. You cannot bypass five-fold ministry in the earth. Why are you lacking? Why are you in want? Because, you have not gone by the plan. You have not gone by the blueprint. You have not gone by the protocol. You have to do it God's way-- not man's way."

"It is not by might nor by power; but by My Spirit," says the Lord. "The kingdom that I bring can only be spiritually discerned. It can never, ever, ever, ever, be discerned by the flesh or by the carnal. For this kingdom to come, the flesh had to be ripped, and torn, and beaten, and crucified." And thank the Lord – thank God – that He took it upon Himself instead of us! He made a way where there was no way. So, that now – spiritually – you're flesh can be beaten, can be torn, can be crucified, can be done away with, and taken out of the way so that there will be no hindrance, no obstacle, no dividing wall between you and your God. It can all be taken away. But remember your greatest enemy is through your flesh – through your carnality – through your Adamic nature that you were born into.

By calling upon the name of the Lord and asking God for forgiveness for all of your sins and giving Him your entire life – that begins a process of all of your flesh being burned up by the glory of God. You see, because the glory of God is an all consuming fire. God manifested Himself on Mount Sinai. It was covered in His Glory; and to the people, it was a burning inferno. God is an all-consuming fire; and what that means is that – spiritually – He will burn up all that is

450

from and what remains of your Adamic nature. He will burn up all of your flesh – all of your carnality. But the only way that He can do that, is if you get into His presence. The very presence of God will burn up all flesh. No flesh can remain in God's glory. Nothing else can be exalted or lift itself above God and His glory. It can try in the earth. It can try in the natural. It can try in the flesh. It can try in any other and all places, except for in the presence of God. That's why it's so important for even the bride of Christ to get into the "Secret Place" of the Most High God; because, in the "Secret Place" there is the presence and the glory of God.

Church of the Living God: We've got to get to the "Secret Place." We have to get into the glory – the very presence of the Living God. There is a third realm of God that the church has largely forgotten all about. We've been satisfied to hang out in the "Holy Place" with all the gifts of the Spirit, with all the fruits of the Spirit, with the seven-fold spirits of God, the Candlestick (lampstand), the Table of Showbread, the Golden Altar of Incense – praise and worship-- and the art of intercession. But Church of the Living God, there is a third chamber that we have largely forgotten about. We talk about going in behind the veil. We sing songs about going in behind the veil; BUT WE HAVE NOT YET EXPERIENCED IT! WE HAVE NOT LIVED IT! WE HAVE NOT ATTEMPTED IT! WHY? Because, IT COSTS TOO MUCH!!! WILL YOU STEP IN BEHIND THE VEIL? IN THE VERY SECOND THAT YOU DO, ALL OF YOUR FLESH – ALL OF YOUR CARNALITY-- WILL BE BURNED UP IN AN INSTANCE! It will all be gone! You're body will not be able to take it. You will only be able to fall on your face, and weep and cry in the holiness of God. The glory of God is all that God is! It is His holiness, His righteousness, His goodness, His mercy, His longsuffering – all of who He is. When you step in to the pure, pure, pure, holiness of the Living God, you're body will not be able to take it. You'll fall on your face and cry out, "Holy, Holy, Holy, is the Lord God Almighty. I am a man of unclean lips and I am in the midst of a people, including myself, with dirty hands and soiled robes." This is the reaction of man's flesh when he enters the glory, when he goes in behind the veil.

So until you are having services and meetings where everyone winds up prostrate on the floor weeping and crying, you have not entered the glory. You can dance. You can praise. You can worship.

But that is all at the golden altar which is on the other side of the veil. You can enjoy that blessing and do that for hours upon hours; but it's all on the other side of the veil. Church: I know this a hard word; but it is the truth nevertheless. There's more! There's more! And if you want to see more, and if you want to experience more – individually and as a body – I admonish you to open your mind and open your heart to the word of the Lord – this day.

Allow God to come and burn up all of your flesh, which includes: carnal thinking, man's ways, man's wisdom, man's knowledge, and man's understanding. Remember, our minds must be renewed with the word of God. Romans 12:1, 2 says, "to be a living sacrifice". That sacrifice still has to be burned up. It has to be placed on the brazen altar of God which is in the outer court. But, now we've stepped on in and gone through the protocol of the King. We've spent time in praise and worship, but I'm calling you past the golden altar. I'm calling you to a place where your nose is touching the veil of the Living God. I'm calling you to a place in your heart to where you will say, "Yes, Brother Dave, I am ready to go with you behind the veil." And if that is you, I encourage you to dig down deep in your heart and in your soul, to search everything that there is and say, "Yes Lord, I'm ready to come in behind the veil--into the glory realms of God."

Because, when you do, life will not be the same. You will not be the same. Everything will change. If you are ready for that, come and go with me – have the faith to turn the page.

Apostolic Authority: Fullness and Power

"**All power** in heaven and earth has been given unto Me; therefore, GO! GO! GO! GO and make disciples of all nations teaching them to observe all that I have commanded you – ALL that I have commanded you. Jesus uttered those words at 'The Great Commission', and not many may realize that He was giving them the permission, the entitlement, not just in word only but in reality, to exercise His authority and to use His name in the earth."

"THAT AT THE NAME OF JESUS, EVERY KNEE SHALL BOW, EVERY TONGUE SHALL CONFESS THAT JESUS CHRIST IS LORD." HALLELUIAH!

In Jesus' earth walk, He not only told them, He demonstrated His authority in the earth. He not only said He had it in heaven and earth – HE DEMONSTRATED IT BEFORE THEIR VERY EYES. He had all authority – ALL AUTHORITY! I want you to grasp that word "all." Jesus, himself, was fully God coming down into the earth. So when you look at Jesus, don't think of Him as in any way less than God the Father. Don't think of Him in any way as not having all the power of God. He was God. He is God, and He always will be God. He was the fullness of God in bodily form. He was there in the beginning at creation. He made it all. He rules over it all. And He governs it all still today. Adam gave away the earth in the garden. It was on loan from God. Many may not realize Adam gave all of his power and authority over to Satan himself when he sinned in the garden. He gave it all away. He had it all, but he gave it all away.

You see, in scripture, Jesus is the second Adam – the second son of God. Adam was the first son. Jesus was the second son. And it is through the second son and His sacrifice that He buys and redeems all of the power and authority that Adam used to have, so that you and I can get it all back.

In Jesus' earthly ministry He exercised power and authority over everything: sickness, disease, conditions, the paralyzed, the blind, even the dead He raised back to life. Evil spirits had to obey His voice and listen to what He told them to do. Even the elements-- the waves and the wind – He created them – they still have to listen to Him even today. He had all authority over everything – the invisible world and the visible world. Because Jesus died and went to heaven and He has sent the Holy Spirit—the Holy Comforter who is also fully God-- to dwell in the believer's heart and life, it is through God's Spirit that we too can extend and use God's power and authority in the earth today. It is God's plan to use His people to expand His government in the earth. He has no other way to carry it out. He wants to use us – His bride – in the earth today.

Some may not like to hear that, but God wants to use you! And sometimes you have to become the greatest answers to your own prayers. Above anything else, God wants to change you, so that you would be formed into the likeness and into the image of God's son Jesus Christ. Not that we would all be "cookie-cutter" Christians and all be the same. No! God has made us all individual with different talents, giftings and abilities. You can still be uniquely you, but be fashioned in the likeness of God and take on His attributes, His nature, His virtues, all of His character and all of His qualities can be molded and shaped uniquely into the very fabric of your being; so that you will be unmistakably you, but that you'll also be unmistakably God!

IT DOESN'T MATTER WHAT IT WAS, IT HAD TO OBEY THE VOICE OF THE LORD. EVERYTHING HAD TO OBEY THE WORD OF GOD IN THE EARTH. Jesus' words were not just ordinary words spoken by any ordinary person. Jesus' words were power! Jesus' words were life! Jesus, He spoke three words. He said, "Lazarus, come forth!" And a dead body had to obey. It had to listen. It had no choice. It was the same voice that spoke, "light" and light was. He was there at creation. Everything was made by Him. It was all formed by Him. He created it all and He rules it all by His word. This kingdom that He is establishing in the earth – this spiritual kingdom – it is all governed by His word! It's all written down for us from Genesis to Revelation. We have it to read, to meditate upon, to memorize, and to study. Jesus is the word – fully in body. The word became flesh and dwelt among us-- John chapter one.

I want you to get this thought: Jesus is the word! His word is the standard for which He runs His spiritual kingdom in the earth, but He has given this word to His kings – small "k" – you and me. Revelation 1:6 says that we are "kings and priests" of God. You are a king in God's kingdom. What does that mean? It means that God has left this earth as the King of all kings, and He has put you and me in charge of establishing His kingdom in the earth today. And you may not realize that, no one may have ever told you that before; but you are a king! It does apply to females as well. Remember, there is no gender in God's sight. It is a circumcision of the flesh – male and female. Women are royalty too!

You have been called of the Most High to be a king and priest in His Kingdom. What does that mean? It means to carry out His power and His authority, and His word, in the earth. You have been called to handle the word of God correctly. *"For out of the abundance of the heart the mouth speaks!"* (Mat. 12:34) You are to speak forth the word of God in the earth. Its **bread and wine**! The "bread" is the word that you are speaking, and the "wine" is under the influence of the Holy Ghost. Halleluiah! Glory to God! The two are to be in fifty-fifty perfect balance. You are not to have one without the other! Too much of one without the other, you're out of balance. Too much wine not enough bread – out of balance. It's the Table of Showbread – there were both present. It is at the Lord's Table. It is communion! When you enter into a covenantal relationship, what do you partake of? You partake of BREAD AND WINE! It's fifty-fifty balance-- Word and Spirit!

"It should be a reminder to us, of this covenantal relationship that we have entered into, that you are to go and make disciples of all nations. But you are to go in the power of My Word – My Bread and My Wine – My Spirit."

Jesus came to this earth to die. That was His mission. That was His goal. That was the will of the Father that He submitted to fully and wholeheartedly. He said, "I must go so the Holy Comforter may come." His whole purpose was to take back the keys from Satan himself, then go back and ascend to the Father, so that the Holy Spirit could now dwell in the hearts of men.

You see, before, flesh and spirit could not dwell in the same place at the same time; the two are incompatible. The flesh must be taken out of the way. The penalty for sin had to be paid. It was paid in full at the cross by Jesus Christ and Him crucified. He paid the debt that you and I owed, so that we wouldn't have to pay it. But now spiritually, He has made a way for your flesh to be taken out of the way – for your "veil" to be torn in two. Flesh is a separation between you and God. The "veil" was a separation between the "Holy Place" and the "Most Holy Place."

"YOU'RE VEIL CAN BE TORN, AND TAKEN OUT OF THE WAY! THE VEIL IS A SYMBOL OF FLESH – CHRIST'S FLESH AND YOUR FLESH!   HIS WAS TORN SO THAT YOURS WOULDN'T HAVE TO BE."   GLORY TO GOD! HALLELUIAH!

The covenant that you are entering into, when you partake of the bread and the wine, you are entering into a serious covenant that says that you will obey the word of the Lord. It's not in your own flesh, it's not in your own strength, or in your own power. Your "veil" must be torn in two. Your flesh-- it must be crucified! It must be burned up – done away with. The flesh and the spirit cannot remain in the same place at the same time.

We are entering into the glory realms of God, into a place where all of your flesh will be completely incinerated. That may be scary to some, but sound inviting to others. In areas where you have

455

been struggling and striving and you can't get victory over your flesh, I've got good news for you. Come with me past the veil into the glory realms of God, for it is in this place that all flesh will die. It will be the complete death of you and the full life of God. And if you can submit to that word, all of Jesus Christ's authority – the fullness and power that He carried in His earth walk-- becomes available to you and to every believer. When we use the term "apostolic authority", all believers can walk in apostolic authority – the authority that was given to the original twelve apostles. That is what is meant by that term. So, anyone reading this book, you can't rule yourself out. There is no excuse. There is no reason why all of us cannot walk in apostolic authority; however, not all will be apostles. There are specific people that God has called to hold these specific offices in God's five-fold ministry. I don't want you to be confused about these thoughts.

All that we see Jesus doing in His earthly walk and as we read in the book of Acts, we see time and time again, the affects of His power and authority. But it was not in Peter, it was not in Paul, it was not in Philip, it was not in Stephen; it was a power and authority that was given to them that was supernatural! Jesus sent them out to preach the word of God in the earth, but He did not send them alone. He gave them the power of His Holy Spirit that is fully God, and is also for us today. Jesus has asked us to do the very same thing: to go and make disciples of all nations, baptizing and teaching them to observe all that He commands. But He doesn't send us out alone. He sends us the Holy Comforter, who is fully God to live in us as His dwelling place!

If you are a believer and have accepted Christ as your savior and repented of your sins, you have become a temple of the Living God. You have become a dwelling place of the Most High God. He has begun to take up residence in you – your vessel – your house. And from the day He comes in, He doesn't leave it the same. He begins to clean up this house and sets it in order.

Allow God to come in and clean up your house – every room-- from the kitchen, to the dining room, to the garage, to the closets. Allow Him access to everything in your life and your heart. He won't barge His way in. He will always ask your permission. He says, *"I stand at the door and knock, if any man hear My voice I will come into Him and eat with him and sup with him, and he with Me."* (Rev.3:20) He'll stand and He will ask your permission. He will knock on your heart's door. He will say, "Can I come into this closet? Can I clean it out?"

I admonish you this day: Give Him permission to go through every room of your house-- your whole life. He said that He was going away to prepare a place for us; while we must prepare a place here for Him to live. If we want to live with Him forever and ever in heaven in His mansion, we have to make a place here for Him to live and to dwell in our hearts and in our lives.

If you do and if you can, He will come in and begin to turn your life around. He will change everything that there is about you. All of your flesh will be crucified. All of your carnal nature will be changed from an Adamic nature to a godly nature, and He won't stop until He is completely finished. The work that He has begun in you; He will complete it until it is full-- until it is perfected-- until it is finished. That is the work of the Lord. That is the work of the Holy Spirit in your life and in the heart of every believer. He will not stop until He brings you into the fullness of God – into all that He "IS" – into a twelfth day -- into a "Promised Land" to where you receive your complete, full, inheritance – until you receive all that you are entitled to.

When you realize there is nothing you can give God based upon your good merits, or your good works, or your righteousness, and the only thing you can give God is your life and your heart, and ask forgiveness and repent of your sins – when you realize that-- and that you are poor-- Jesus said in His Sermon of the Mount, the Beatitudes, *"Blessed are the poor in spirit for theirs is the Kingdom."* (Mat.5:3) When you come to that realization, He gives you His entire Kingdom! He gives you all that He "IS" with all of His Kingdom authority and all of His Kingdom fullness and power.

God is still trying to establish His Kingdom here in this earth. He started it the day He was born in a manger in Bethlehem. Of this kingdom, there would be no end. It is an eternal Kingdom! It is one that continues on through our lifetimes, in this millennium, but also into the millennium to come. And the good news is that this Kingdom has no end to it. It's eternal! But some of us only look to the afterlife when we die and go to heaven; then we will experience the kingdom of God. That is true; but it's only half true, and a half truth is a whole lie. Because the reality of it is, God began a kingdom over two thousand years ago, and that kingdom has never stopped. He has been trying to establish it in the earth for all these years. **And He is still establishing it today!**

And some may have a problem with that, and right away they close their minds and their hearts. It comes under different names and different terms. I'm not talking about a physical kingdom. I'm talking about a **spiritual kingdom** that God wants to establish and advance. And you and I are "kings" and "ambassadors" of this new Kingdom. It's the only way that God has to establish it here in the earth. You and I … **YOU AND I… ARE ALL HE HAS! HE NEEDS YOU; AND YOU NEED HIM!** HE IS LOOKING FOR A FEW GOOD MEN AND WOMEN!

If I can use that slogan, "He's looking for a few good men" (and women) to help establish His Kingdom in the earth today; so that we would do the works of Christ through the power of His Holy Spirit. We are called to exercise His power and authority over the invisible and the visible, so that people will still know today that Jesus has the power and authority to forgive sins and that Jesus was who He said He was. **AND HE STILL IS WHO HE SAYS HE IS!** AND HE IS STILL ALIVE TODAY! And He is living in and among his people in the hearts of every believer. But instead of a dwelling, or a tabernacle, or a temple made by human hands, HE IS BUILDING A TEMPLE THAT IS MADE BY THE HANDS OF GOD!

HE IS BUILDING IT **ONE STONE AT A TIME!** AND YOU ARE A **LIVING STONE** THAT IS BUILT UP INTO A **SPIRITUAL HOUSE** UNTO GOD. FOR YOU HAVE COME TO MOUNT ZION – IT IS THE CITY OF THE LIVING GOD – IT IS A **NEW JERUSALEM** IN THE EARTH. IT IS A "Promised Land" that He has given to each and every believer on the face of the planet. It is our entitlement. It is our inheritance! IT HAS NOW BECOME RIGHTFULLY OURS! And you may not know this, but somebody died and he has left it all! He died for it all! And He gave it ALL TO YOU! – ALL THAT HE HAD!!!

He is El Elyon: the Possessor of Heaven and Earth. He owns it all. And He is also El Shaddai: the All-Sufficient God capable of giving everything to His people – all that they need. He is ready, able, and willing to give it all – to you! All that He "IS"-- is at your disposal.

In the physical, it is like someone has left you an inheritance or an estate. They died and they deposited twenty billion dollars into an

458

account for you – **AND NOBODY TOLD YOU THAT IT'S IN YOUR NAME!** HALLELUIAH!

I'm here today, and am writing this book, to tell every believer on the face of the planet that this is your inheritance. **You've got it all! All that God is, and all that He has is yours!** But it's not just for you to horde it up and soak it in and use it all for yourself. You know this kingdom, is based upon a law – "give and it shall be given". So, all that you receive, you're going to give it all back out to the rest of the world. But you can't out give God. The more you give; He's going to give back. And to the measure that you give, is the measure He will give back to you!

So, if you want more, you've got to give more!! Halleluiah! You can't out give God!! Physically, mentally, spiritually – in every dimension and aspect of life – if you want to experience more of God – **GIVE GOD MORE OF YOU!** Give God all that you are and all that you have: all your dreams, your hopes, your future, your goals, your family, your money, your finances -- everything! Give it all over to Him. Halleluiah! And to the measure that you use, He will use that same measure to pour back into your life.

If you want to live and walk in apostolic authority, fullness, and power; if you want to walk in the same richness and anointing that Jesus Christ, Himself walked in during His earth walk on this planet, **GIVE GOD ALL YOU'VE GOT!** GIVE IT ALL!! Give Him your past, your present, and your future. Trust God with all your tomorrows. Give Him all that you are, then He will give you all that He is – the I AM, that I AM, that I AM! He owns it all and He wants to give it all to the child of God who will simply give Him everything that they are and everything that they have.

So if you will, you will walk and see in your lifetime, the very works of Christ displayed before your very eyes. You will see the lame to walk, the blind to see, and the deaf to hear; not only spiritually, but physically as well. You will see the very works of Christ being carried out in the earth.

"All authority has been given unto Me in Heaven and in earth. Therefore, now go! Go! Go and make disciples of all nations – **all nations**-- baptizing them in the name of the Father, and the Son, and the Holy Ghost; teaching them to observe all that I have commanded you – **ALL** that I have commanded you!"

459

"For this day, if you become poor – I will make you rich. Blessed are the poor in spirit, for theirs is the Kingdom. If you realize you've got nothing to give, but you and your life – this day I give unto you THE KINGDOM."

"I GIVE UNTO YOU – MY KINGDOM!"

The Horn of the Wild Ox
(Psalms 92:10)

"You have exalted my horn like that of a wild ox; fine oils have been poured upon my head."

"This verse speaks of unlimited anointing. The anointing that I bring that was upon My son Jesus, that He gives to His descendants is an unlimited anointing – where all things are possible through God. All things are possible with God. ALL THINGS ARE POSSIBLE!! I want you to understand that word "**all**" again – **All** things are possible! That means that there is no limit to what I, the Lord God, can do in the earth. **NO LIMIT!**"

"I only need just one person – one child of God – who will come into a covenantal relationship with Me, and give Me all that they are, and all that they have; and then, I the Lord God will give them all that I have and all that I AM."

This is the revelation and the mystery: the same anointing that God – Himself – carried in the earth is available to every believer, every child of God, who will simply listen and obey what the Lord tells them to do. The one who will simply come into a covenantal agreement and sign the contract with their blood – their life – they get it all!

"The Horn of the Wild Ox" speaks of an unlimited anointing. And you may ask yourself, "How does he get that out of that?" But here, I will show you how.

"The Horn of the Wild Ox" – in this verse, it is combined with fine oils being poured upon the head. Fine oils is the anointing of the Holy Spirit, that is being poured out down from heaven that Jesus died for, so that His same anointing can come to every man – every women – and every child.

460

"The "Horn" is a symbol of strength, power and defense. The "Horn" is also a vessel that was used to contain the oil. Remember the Prophet Samuel's horn of oil to anoint King David. The horn is obtained only through the death of the animal or the sacrifice of the animal. It is only through this process that the horn is obtained! This unlimited anointing is obtained through the sacrifice of the "lamb." Jesus' death makes it all possible for the anointing to come to us. You are the vessel that holds the oil. You are the **horn** for the oil! The death of you brings the anointing of God. Jesus is described in scripture as being like many different animals with different symbolisms used in each example. Sometimes He is a lamb, sometimes He is a lion, sometimes He is portrayed as an eagle, sometimes an ox, a ram, or even a goat. Here Jesus is portrayed as a "Wild Ox".

"Wild" means: free to flow and move in the anointing of God as He has created you to be; not domesticated, or controlled, or manipulated by man; but to flow and live in the Spirit as God intended, not how man thinks you should flow. **The anointing is not for you – it's for God;** to be used for His service to help others. Always maintain a servant's heart and mind when flowing in the anointing. You do get to enjoy the byproducts however. There is no greater blessing than to minister to someone else and be used by the Lord!

The "Ox" is a symbol of servant hood, and is a beast of burden. The "Ox" is subjected to forced labor and is the servant of man. It has no will of its own. It pulls the plow in the field and is yoked up together with other oxen to work that field. The ox doesn't just go where it wants to go, but is directed by someone else. Proverbs 14:4 says, *"… but from the strength of an **ox** comes an abundant harvest."* We must have the anointing of God with a servants heart and mindset to work the fields and bring in an abundant harvest. Jesus was and is the ultimate servant. He came to this world not to be served, but to serve. Most kings have servants and want to be served most of the time. They could live a life of nothing but luxury; but not this King! This King came to demonstrate the ultimate in servanthood! Jesus said, *"But he who is greatest among you shall be your servant. And whoever exalts himself will be humbled, and he who humbles himself will be exalted"* (Mat. 23:11,12) It's the exact opposite of the world's way of thinking.

Jesus carried upon His life an unlimited anointing. He was given the Spirit without measure – without limits. *"For He whom God has sent speaks the words of God, for God does not give the Spirit by measure."* (John

3:34) There was no end to it. It was limitless in quantity and in application. There was nothing that Jesus could not do. There were certain things that He didn't do, and an appointed time for everything that He did do. He only walked in the will of the Father. He only did what He heard the Father saying to Him. He yielded His own will even to the death on a cross; because, He came to give His life as a ransom for many and to redeem man and pay the price for sin. But in so doing, in His death, He made the way possible for His full anointing to be given to us.

Jesus' ministry in Isaiah 61 is meant to continue on through us. "The Spirit of the Lord is upon me, for He has anointed me to preach good news to the poor, to bind up the brokenhearted, to set the captive free." All of these things is meant to be carried out through our own lives. So Jesus' ministry in His earth-walk should be extended through His descendants – all of the tremendous miracles that He preformed – the healings – the deliverances – even raising the dead. Even that can be carried out through the child of God who will simply believe and have the faith to believe the word of God.

The single most basic guideline for this anointing is that all things are possible.

"…WITH GOD ALL THINGS ARE POSSIBLE." (Mat. 19:26)

"I, the Lord God, I am only limited by what a child of God will believe. I can do anything. I can do everything as it is according to My word – as it lines up with My written word from Genesis to Revelation. **MY WORD – it is power and it is life!!** *If you abide in Me, and My words abide in you, you will ask what you desire, and it shall be done for you.' (Jn. 15:7) 'You do not have because you do not ask.'* (Jas. 4:2) If you will simply ask of Me will I not open up the floodgates of heaven and pour out a blessing upon you; so much so, that you'll not be able to contain it all. You have not because you ask not."

Part of your inheritance is the anointing of Christ. The same anointing that Jesus had upon His life is available to every child of God on the face of the earth. It is unlimited! It is never ending! All things are possible!

"I, the Lord God, will not act alone. The things that I can do, I will not do. Why? Because, it goes against My justness, My righteousness, and it goes against My Word. I am obligated by My word," says the Lord God Almighty. "Adam gave it away. Jesus

462

bought it back. Potentially, for the child of God – to ask of Me-- it's an "if" and "then" promise. It's conditional. All the things that I desire to do in the earth, I must do **through** My people – through My children-- who will humble themselves and come into a covenantal relationship. "If" you do this … "then" I will do this. II Chron. 7:14 says, *'If My people who are called by My name will humble themselves and pray and seek My face, and turn from their wicked ways, then I will hear from heaven, then … I will forgive their sin and will heal their land … then I will restore them.'"*

"It's 'Secret Place Living' … if you will come into the secret place … if you will allow all of your flesh to be burned up … if you will go through each progressive step in the "Tabernacle of Moses" … go through the protocol of how I, the Lord God, have designed it to be – not man's way – but God's way. If you come God's way, I will open the windows of heaven and I will pour out a blessing. If you come God's way and humble yourselves and seek My face, give Me your life and turn from your wicked ways, then I will hear from heaven."

"Psalm 91 reads, *'Because you have made the Lord your God your dwelling place … and you love me and honor Me. I will answer.'* (v. 9,14,15) It's an 'if' and 'then' promise."

"You've got to get to the 'Secret Place'. You've got to give Me everything you've got. Then I can give you all I've got, and that includes My anointing! The same anointing My son carried in this world. It is for you, this day," says the Lord God Almighty.

"The Horn of the Wild Ox" – Jesus came to be the servant of all. You have to begin to have a servant mentality like Jesus did. You have to be willing to wash other people's feet and do perhaps the dirtiest of jobs all for the sake of others. *"Greater love has no one than this, than to lay down one's life for his friends."* (Jn. 15:13) You have to be willing to lay your life down as Christ did for the sake of someone else. That is the ultimate servanthood mentality, where you're not thinking of yourself, but you're only thinking of others.

What will you believe God for in your life? What do you think God can do in your life? He is limited only by what you will believe that He can do. If there is no faith, there will be no answer. *"But without faith it is impossible to please God."* (Heb. 11:6) *"For he who doubts is like a wave of the sea driven and tossed by the wind…(here and there, to and fro), for let not that man expect that he will receive anything from the Lord."* (Jam. 1:6,7) God never rewarded unbelief. God never excused doubt. He would always call the people on this important issue. Why? He is trying to build faith. Faith can increase, just like anointing can. Anointing can increase. It should always be progressively increasing in the child of God's life – never decreasing-- just like faith. Faith begins with a small measure that is appointed to every man at birth. It is only a measure. It is a seed. It is supposed to grow. That seed is planted in the heart of man and it is supposed to grow. How does it grow? *"Faith comes by hearing and hearing by the word of God."* (Rom.10:17)

It's supernatural. Faith comes from God. It is a gift from Him. It is increased by Him, through your responsibility of hearing the word either written or Rhema; and it is to cause faith to grow. It is not supposed to stay the same amount, quantity or application. It is supposed to grow, and it is intended to become the largest tree in the garden – the mustard tree that the birds of the air can come and nest in it. New life can come and be birthed from it! (see Mat. 13)

I charge you this day: How much of God's anointing is upon your life? Have you exhausted His limits? Have you exhausted His supplies? Do you have the anointing of Jesus Christ Himself? Is it being demonstrated in your life? If not – there's more to get. There's more that the Lord Your God has for you. It should be an ever increasing, progressive, impartation to every believer – every child of God. Always increasing – never decreasing – as long as you "abide in the vine" and you stay in your covenantal relationship, listen to the voice of the Lord your God, and obey Him to the best of your ability.

Yes, you will have struggles. Yes, you will fail at times. Yes, you will make mistakes. But as long as you "abide in the vine" and "stay on the wheel", He will bring you into ever increasing quantities, amounts, and applications of the same anointing that God himself has – the same anointing His son, Jesus, had in the earth. Because remember, Jesus was fully God in the earth. He is the second person of the trinity. He had the Spirit of God without measure in His life – able to do all things! He is the Master Potter ready to mold you and shape you into His image.

This same anointing that comes from God, when all that God "IS"-- is available to you – even His anointing is available. Even His faith is available to you! Faith is supernatural. It's not natural – never will be. It is not from this earth. It's not from the carnal. It's not from the flesh. It is a gift from God, and it is meant to be increased in your life. You can walk with the same faith that God Himself has and

464

possesses because faith is part of what God has; and if He's going to give us all that He has in amounts, quantities, and applications – it includes His faith! Faith is supernatural. Faith is heaven sent. Faith originates in God's essence and His being. It is to be given to us in limitless measure. And I know that may be a new concept to many, but we are to be formed into the image of Christ in every way, in every aspect, in every virtue, and that includes having the faith of Jesus Christ – Himself. It is available to the child of God who will simply come into covenantal relationship, believe God, take Him at His word, and give God everything that they are and all that they have!

If you give God everything that you are, God will give you everything that He "IS" and He will show Himself to be "the I AM, that I AM, that I AM." All that He "IS" – is available to you today; and that includes His unlimited anointing-- "The Horn of the Wild Ox"-- and His unlimited faith. You are the vessel to hold the oil of the Holy Spirit that contains the anointing of Jesus-- free to move in it as God intended you to with a servant's heart. What can you believe God for? **"If I give them faith – with that comes everything else."** If it lines up with His written word and you fulfill your obligations to it – it's guaranteed! *"God is not a man that He should lie, nor a son of man, that He should change His mind. Does He speak and then not act? Does He promise and not fulfill? (Num.23:19)* But He will perform His word in the earth. He watches over His word to perform it.

Remember the fruit on the vine! It's only natural that the fruit will grow to maturity – to where someone can pick it and eat it. It holds true in the supernatural and spiritual as well. The word of God is a seed. He planted it in your heart. You grew into a vine. Now He is producing on your vine – mature fruit – which is the fulfillment of His word in your life. For every promise of God from Genesis to Revelation, there is a mature fruit waiting to be developed on your vine! Halleluiah!

Do you have the faith to believe God that He would pick you to pour out all that He "IS" upon you? You may not think you're worthy of that, but none of us are worthy. Jesus made a way where there was no way. It is through His sacrifice – His torture – His beatings – His crucifixion – and His death – that makes a way for the veil of our flesh to be torn in two – from top to bottom – in its completeness – in its totality – so that we can enter into the glory realms of God – twenty four hours a day, seven days a week, every day of our life. We can now go in and experience the glory realms of God – all that He "IS"!

"But for that to happen, you too, must take up your cross and follow Jesus. 'Take up your cross' means: it's the death of you! Allow God's Spirit to come and crucify the old man – the old Ishmael's – the lines of the flesh – to make you into a promised son from the line of Isaac. That you'll walk in My Spirit. You'll live in My Spirit. You'll have your being in My Spirit and the dwelling place of God has now come to live on the inside of you."

Will you prepare a place in your heart and in your life to where you become a house – a habitation – a place for God to live and dwell? Will you allow Him complete access to every room of your house? If you will, come and go with me for I will take you to a higher place – where even the eagles are afraid to fly!

JACOB'S LADDER
(Genesis 28:10-22)

"Come up! Come up! Come up! Come up to a higher place in Me," says the Lord. "The Way has been made. The veil has been torn in two. Come in and enter the 'Secret Place' of the Most High God – the 'Most Holy Place' in the Tabernacle of Moses. Come up to a higher place in Me," says the Lord. "I am calling My church to arise and come up higher and know the resurrection power of their risen savior – Jesus Christ; to live on the other side of the resurrection. Resurrection means: to ARISE; or to come up. With resurrection power comes life. It means death to the old and life to the new. I have come to give men life, and life more abundantly. When you come, and you die to yourself, and you take up your cross, and you follow Me, I the Lord God, by My Spirit, I bring complete death to the old – for behold the new has come. It's New life that I bring," says the Lord God Almighty.

Paul's heart's desire was that he would know the sufferings of Christ, the fellowship of His sufferings, and the power of His resurrection, being conformed to His death. (Phil. 3:10)

"To know the resurrection power of Christ means to walk in newness of life, where the old man is dead and gone, and the new man is alive and well. The word Resurrection means: to arise, or to come up. I, the Lord God, I'm calling you – My church – My believers – to come up to a higher place. I'm calling you, individually, to come up to a higher place. I'm calling you to come up into the third heavens of the Living God; but to do that; you won't even have to leave the earth. Why? Because heaven's coming down! Halleluiah! Heaven is coming down into the earth realm. The two are merging together. They are becoming one!"

"Jesus prayed, 'Our Father in Heaven, hallowed be Thy name. Thy Kingdom come, Thy will be done on earth as it is in heaven.' My will is always accomplished in heaven – always – it is My perfect will. But Jesus instructed His disciples to pray: 'Thy will be done **on earth** as it is in heaven.'"

Jacob saw a glimpse of this in his dream. He stopped for the night because the sun had set. Taking one of the stones there, he put it under his head and lay down to sleep. He had a dream in which he saw a ladder resting on the earth with its top reaching to heaven and the angles of God were ascending and descending on it. There above it stood the Lord and He said, "I am the Lord, the God of your father Abraham and the God of Isaac. I will give you and your descendants the land on which you are lying … all the people on earth will be blessed through you and your offspring. I am with you and will watch over you wherever you go, and I will bring you back to this land. I will not leave you until I have done what I have promised you."

When Jacob awoke from his sleep, he thought, *"Surely the Lord is in this place. This is none other than the house of God; this is the gate of heaven. He called that place 'Bethel', which means 'house of God'."* (v.16,17,19)

Jacob had a dream. He saw a ladder – a "WAY" that had been made for the angels of God to make it from heaven to the earth and back again; and at the top of this ladder, stood the Lord. And the Lord, interestingly enough, said again, "I am the Lord. I AM – the Lord!" It was the same revelation that God had given Moses at the "Burning Bush". He is the "I AM", that "I AM", that "I AM". When God says, "I am the Lord", He is saying: "I AM – I EXIST – I AM HERE – I AM always here." It points to His existence and His very being – all that He "IS". So all that God "was" and "IS" was at the top of Jacob's ladder. He said, "I AM – the Lord. I am the same God of your father Abraham, and the God of Isaac. I'll give you and your descendants this land on which you are lying." God was saying, "I'll be a God of My word! What has been promised you – I'm going to deliver. I AM A GOD OF MY WORD!"

"I cannot be separated from My Word – because My word – it "IS"! It's a promise. I am My word! The two cannot be separated. So all that I have promised you and your forefathers, Isaac and Abraham, it shall come to pass in the earth." But it was not only for Jacob, it was for everyone and anyone who would come into a covenantal relationship with this same God.

So, when you come into covenantal relationship and you've come into the "Secret Place", you've signed a contract in your blood. It's a Jacob's ladder! All of Heaven is at your disposal. God made a "WAY" for heaven and earth to merge – to come together. That "WAY" is Jesus Christ. He is the ladder! He is the instrument. He is the vessel so the two can become one. He was the two coming together in bodily form during His earth-walk.

But you are being transformed, fashioned, formed, shaped, and molded into His same image – to be like Him. So, a part of who you are – part of your identity in Christ is – that you become a "Jacob's ladder" as well. You also become a means for which heaven can come down and you can come up to a higher place; not only for you, but for the lives of everyone around you. You can experience it yourself and know God's resurrection power. What is of the earth realm in your life come up into the third heavens as high as you can go in God. Also, you can experience heaven on earth; heaven can come down into the earth realm. You don't have to wait to die to experience a piece of heaven down here in the earth. Heaven can come down in your life today – the goodness of God, the love of God, the mercy of God – all that He "IS". The angels of God are waiting to be ministering spirits sent out to you, and to bring down heaven's mighty answers for your life!

Psalms 91 says, *"He shall give His angels charge over thee, to keep thee in all thy ways."* When you dwell in the "Secret Place" of the Most High God and you "abide under the shadow of the Almighty", under His "wings" you shall take refuge. "Under His WINGS" – you shall take refuge. At times in the Old Testament, God would show Himself in a "theophany". You didn't know whether it was an encounter with one of God's angles or with the Lord – Himself. It's the fullness of the Godhead – all that He "IS". You abide under His "Shadow". You abide under the greatest umbrella-- the greatest coverings-- in the entire universe. And where you go – He goes! You take Him with you. You don't have to leave the "Secret Place". You don't have to go in and then come back out again. Some would say, "to be so heavenly minded you're no earthly good." That's a lie from the pits of hell!

YOU CAN LIVE IN THE SECRET PLACE OF THE MOST HIGH – EVERYDAY of your entire life! You can behold the goodness of the Lord and His beauty. Why? Because, you dwell in His temple. Why? **Because the temple has now become you!** And you can experience all that He "IS" – everyday of your life. And you can help others get from where they are and experience God's resurrection power and arise up into the heavens and experience heaven here in the earth. All of heaven can come down for them too. **You can be a "Jacob's Ladder" for someone else!** You can be the vessel, the ambassador, of this heavenly kingdom.

Hell is not just for eternity! Some people live in a hell on earth. Their lives are so bad they think their life is not worth living anymore. That's a hell on earth! But you can come along and say to them, "You don't have to live this way anymore. You don't have to live here in this hell anymore."

You see, lies bring bondage and when they live a lie, they live behind hells gates. But you've been given all the power and all the authority to kick in hell's gates and say to them, "Come, go with me – will you come to a higher place? Will you believe the truth from Genesis to Revelation? Speak to them the truth of God's word. And if they will believe the truth and come with you, they can arise and go up higher into a higher place. They will get out of their hell on earth and start living on the other side of the resurrection power of Christ.

If they will believe-- they can choose not to. They can choose to stay right where they are; and many will. But as you speak the word of God to them, and it may take time, it may take more than once-- it will be a process. You can minister to someone for years, and then finally one day, faith will come. Something will be sparked on the inside of them and they'll say, "Yes, I will believe." And they will begin to come out of their hell on earth. And the more they believe the more they'll come up. The more they believe, the more they will arise!

How high they go depends on them. The sky is the limit. Halleluiah! Do you want to come to the third heavens? Do you want to come up where the eagles are afraid to fly? Do you want to come up and experience all of heaven's glory? If you do, I know the WAY!!!

It's easier to show someone the way and how to get there if you've been there yourself. My first advice is to get there yourself. And

469

if you're living behind hell's gates in any aspect of your life, you have to be set free. You can be a believer, but still be locked behind hell's gates in certain areas of your life.

Satan could be holding you in a sickness, with a disease, or a condition. He may be holding you mentally. But I'm here to tell you today, you don't have to live there anymore! Diseases are not part of God's kingdom! Any conditions you may have are not part of God's kingdom! Any mental torment or anguish you may be going through is not part of God's kingdom!

Believe God's word today regarding your situation, and the truth shall set you free. The gates of hell are unlocked! They only appear to be closed. It only appears like this is all there is. This is as good as life gets. That's all based on a lie. Satan is the "father of lies". He always speaks his native language. The truth is: the gates of hell are unlocked! Jesus took the keys back from Satan himself; and He has given them, now, to the church. He said to Peter, *"Upon this rock, I will build My church and the gates of hell shall not prevail against it."* (Mat.16:18) "To you I give the keys!"

He was giving the keys – a symbol of His full power and authority. Keys are to lock and unlock – to bind and to loose – to exercise God's authority in the earth. It's all been given to the church today; and therefore, to every believer. So, we need to use them!

To know the fellowship of His sufferings and the resurrection power of God, you must believe His word. Then, and only then, you can ARISE with resurrection power and get out of the hell that you may be living in and come up to a higher place in God!

Heaven and earth – they can merge together. A "WAY" has been made. Jesus is the "WAY, the TRUTH, and the LIFE". He is all these things. We are formed in His image. Will you, too, be a ladder from earth to heaven and from heaven to earth? Will you be a "Jacob's Ladder" for someone else? Where you can speak the word of God to them and if they believe on the Lord Jesus Christ, they can be saved in every aspect of life: spiritually, mentally, and physically, and be released from their captivity.

The Spirit of the Lord is upon Me; for He has anointed Me to preach good news to the poor and to set the CAPTIVE FREE! The anointing of Christ will be upon you to set the captive free! And when you do, you'll kick in hell's gates – speak the word of God to the captives – then set them free! If they will believe the word of God, you can say to them, "Come hold my hand. I will believe with you, together, and we will go to a higher place. Then ascend up into the third heavens; but you'll never have to leave this world, because the two are coming together. They are joining – they are merging. They are becoming one! "Thy Kingdom come. Thy will be done; on earth as it is in heaven."

Jesus is the WAY! He is the Ladder! And in Christ, we too become a ladder for someone else. Will you be a ladder, this day, from earth to heaven? Will you give God all that you are and all that you have? If you do, all of Heaven is at your disposal.

It's a "Jacob's Ladder"!

It's "Secret Place" living!

It's also, a "New Jerusalem"!

From the "Secret Place" To the "New Jerusalem"
(Revelation 21)

When you come into the secret place of the Most High God; it's a four square room. Its dimensions were ten, by ten, by ten cubits. When you come in here, it is the throne of God in the earth – the King of all kings and the Lord of all lords seated on His throne. The golden Ark of the Covenant – its cover was the mercy seat – and the mercy seat was where the King sat. It's the throne of God in the earth. It was where God would live. It was the Lord's house. It was the dwelling place of the Most High God. The priest could only go in there once a year after sacrificing the animals, for himself, then for the nation. But now, the veil has been torn. Jesus' flesh has been rent. The "way" has been made for you to come in every day, every moment, and every hour. This "Secret Place" today – spiritually – is where any believer has made their house into a home where the King of Glory can come in. Who is this King of Glory? Who is this King of Glory? Open wide your ancient doors and let the King of Glory come into your heart to make His home, His abode, His habitation, His dwelling place, His tabernacle of the Most High God, on the inside of you.

If you have made your being, your spiritual house, a home for the Most High to come and live, and dwell – your life has become a "Secret Place" of the Most High God; which is simply this: a place where God lives! And if you have done simply just that; you also, have made your heart and your life into a "New Jerusalem"!

The "Secret Place" was a four square room. It was 10 x 10 x 10 cubits. The "New Jerusalem" is a four square city. It is twelve thousand stadia, by twelve thousand stadia, by twelve thousand stadia. (One thousand four hundred miles) It's as long, as it is wide, as it is high. It's the Kingdom of God coming down into the earth. It is all of heaven – all that God "IS" and all that He has – coming down into the earth realm. It's a "Jacob's Ladder." It's a "Secret Place of the Most High God." They are all connected. These thoughts and ideas, they're all related.

So, wherever you go – God goes! He goes with you. This Kingdom of God is a traveling kingdom, and it's wherever a child of God "IS". Someone who has given God **everything** that they are and all that they have, and have come into **covenantal relationship** – that's a "New Jerusalem"!

The Kingdom of God comes down into the earth in all of its fullness, in all of its glory, in all of its majesty, in all of its power, and in all of its greatness – it comes down into the earth. Some would say it's only for the future millennial reign of Christ. Some would say it's for when we get to heaven; but I am here to tell you today that this vision the Apostle John was shown, is a "NOW" vision! It is for today, and it is for you!

So, we need to take a second look at this term "a New Jerusalem." Revelation 21: 1-27 says, *¹ "Now I saw a new heaven and a new earth, for the first heaven and the first earth had passed away. Also there was no more sea. ²Then I, John, saw the Holy City, the New Jerusalem, coming down out of heaven from God, prepared as a bride adorned for her husband. ³And I heard a loud voice from heaven saying, 'Behold the tabernacle of God is with men, and He will dwell with them, and they shall be his people, and God himself will be with them and be their God. ⁴ He will wipe every tear from their eyes. There will be no more death or mourning or crying or pain, for the old order of things has passed away.'"⁵*

"He who was seated on the throne said, 'I am making everything new!' Then He said, 'Write this down, for these words are trustworthy and true.'"

⁶"He said to me: 'It is done. I am the Alpha and the Omega, the Beginning and the End. To him who is thirsty I will give to drink without cost from the spring of the water of life. ⁷He who overcomes will inherit all this, and I will be his God and he will be My son. ⁸But the cowardly, the unbelieving, the vile, the murderers, the sexually immoral, those who practice magic arts, the idolaters and all liars – their place will be in the fiery lake of burning sulfur. This is the second death.'"

[9]"One of the seven angles who had the seven bowls full of the seven last plagues came and said to me, 'Come, I will show you the bride, the wife of the Lamb.' [10]And he carried me away in the Spirit to a mountain great and high, and showed me the Holy City, Jerusalem, coming down out of heaven from God. [11]It shone with the glory of God, and its brilliance was like that of a very precious jewel, like a jasper, clear as crystal. [12] It had a great, high wall with twelve gates, and with twelve angels at the gates. On the gates were written the names of the twelve tribes of Israel. [13]There were three gates on the east, three on the north, three on the south and three on the west. [14]The wall of the city had twelve foundations, and on them were the names of the twelve apostles of the Lamb."

[15]"The angel who talked with me had a measuring rod of gold to measure the city, its gates and its walls. [16]The city was laid out like a square, as long as it was wide. He measured the city with the rod and found it to be twelve thousand stadia in length, and as wide and high as it is long. [17]He measured its wall and it was one hundred forty four cubits thick, by man's measurement, which the angel was using. [18]The wall was made of jasper, and the city of pure gold, as pure as glass. [19]The foundations of the city walls were decorated with every kind of precious stone. The first foundation was jasper, the second sapphire, the third chalcedony, the fourth emerald, [20]the fifth sardonyx, the sixth carnelian, the seventh chrysolite, the eighth beryl, the ninth topaz, the tenth chrysoprase, the eleventh jacinth, and the twelfth amethyst. [21]The twelve gates were twelve pearls, each gate made of a single pearl. The great street of the city was of pure gold, like transparent glass."

[22]"I did not see a temple in the city, because the Lord God Almighty and the Lamb are its temple. [23]the city does not need the sun or the moon to shine on it, for the glory of God gives it light, and the Lamb is its lamp. [24]The nations will walk by its light, and the kings of the earth will bring their splendor into it. [25]On no day will its gates ever be shut, for there will be no night there. [26]The glory and honor of the nations will be brought into it. [27]Nothing impure will ever enter it, nor will anyone who does what is shameful or deceitful, but only those whose names are written in the Lamb's book of life."(NKJV)

Revelation 22:1-6 says, [22]"And he showed me a pure river of water of life, clear as crystal, proceeding from the throne of God and of the Lamb. [2]In the middle of its street, and on either side of the river, was the tree of life, which bore twelve fruits, each tree yielding its fruit every month. The leaves of the tree were for the healing of the nations. [3]And there shall be no more curse, but the throne of God and of the Lamb shall be in it, and His servants shall serve Him. [4]They shall see

His face, and His name shall be on their foreheads. ⁵There shall be no night there: They need no lamp nor light of the sun, for the Lord God gives them light. And they shall reign forever and ever. ⁶Then he said to me, 'These words are faithful and true.' And the Lord God of the holy prophets sent His angel to show His servants the things which must shortly take place." (NKJV)

"Now, I, (John) saw a new heaven and a new earth, for the first heaven and the first earth had passed away." (Rev.21) When this kingdom comes, and thy will be done on earth as it is in heaven, life will not be the same. The earth will not be the same, and heaven will not be the same. Why? Because, heaven comes down into the earth and the two mix together creating an entirely new dimension of life beyond anything that we have known or could ever imagine. *"I am making everything new!"* *"And there was no more sea"*… you can remember from previous chapters, the horse and the rider had been hurled into the sea. When a "New Jerusalem" falls there are no enemies here. There is no need for any place to even throw them. When this kingdom falls there is no more sin. Because in this kingdom, there are no enemies. They are all completely destroyed.

"I saw the Holy City, the New Jerusalem, coming down out of heaven from God, prepared as a bride beautifully dressed for her husband." (v.2 NIV) This city is a picture of the bride. And where is the bride now? The bride is us! The bride is still in the earth! This is heaven coming down into the earth. It's a "Jacob's Ladder." It's all that God "IS" being united – merging – with His bride. They can now live together!

There was a loud voice from the throne saying, *"Now the dwelling of God is with men, and He will live with them. They will be His people, and God Himself will be with them and be their God."* (v.3) It's the dwelling place of Jehovah! It is the dwelling place of the Most High coming down and Him living in and among His people, establishing His Kingdom in the earth. And in this kingdom, *"He will wipe every tear from their eyes. There will be no more death, or mourning or crying or pain, for the old order of things has passed away."*(v.4)

"He who was seated on the throne said, I am making everything new. It is done. I am the Alpha and the Omega, the Beginning and the End." (v.5,6) Jesus makes all things new! The old passed away. When Jesus comes into your heart and life He makes everything new – everything! Verse 7 says, *"He who overcomes will inherit all this, and I will be his God and he will be My son."* Part of your inheritance is a "New Jerusalem". You are

entitled to it. You are entitled to know about it. You are entitled to know that God is establishing it still in the earth today – that it is for now – it is for today! It is a "now" vision. It is a "now" word. And it is applicable to your life today!

"But the cowardly, the unbelieving, the vile, the murderers, the sexually immoral, those who practice magic arts, the idolaters and all liars – their place will be in the fiery lake of burning sulfur. This is the second death." (v.8)

"All people that are not in a covenantal relationship with Me will never enter into this New Jerusalem. This is God's everlasting kingdom. He began it when He was born and was placed in a manger on His very first day. And it has continued till today and it will continue on. It is a never ending kingdom. It is an everlasting kingdom and this is a picture of it for you – today."

One of the seven angles said, *"Come, I will show you the bride, the WIFE of the Lamb."* (v.9) It's the **"wife"** of the Lamb! **It's the two coming together!** This is the marriage... the consummation... the coming together! **It's the "WIFE" of the Lamb!** We do not have to wait till we die to experience the "Marriage Supper of the Lamb". Halleluiah! Glory! Halleluiah! In this vision, John saw a picture; at first, it is mentioned that this is the **bride** beautifully dressed for her husband. But, then after it becomes the dwelling place of God in the earth it is written in verse 9, *"I will show you the **wife** of the Lamb."* The marriage has taken place ... in a "New Jerusalem"!

In the days of Queen Esther, the queen married the king. She had to, so that she could become the queen. She was welcomed by the king raising his scepter to her as a sign of approval to enter into his presence. She was granted up to half the kingdom – whatever she wanted – up to half. It's a picture of the bride of Christ becoming the Queen – becoming royalty – and now, for us, we can receive up to **all** the kingdom. Why? Because, King Zerxes was still alive and they shared the royalty. Today, the King has died. He has died and left His entire inheritance to His Queen! That's us! **The church today, in symbolic language, is Queen Esther; when she has come into a covenantal relationship!** In the physical realm, it is compared to even marriage itself between one man and one woman. When the bride of Christ comes into a covenantal relationship with God and they sign the contract – it's just like a marriage in the earth! It is legal. It is binding.

475

It is eternal. It is meant to be forever. The queen comes into a legal standing – by right, by family, and by royalty. **All of the King's Kingdom is given to the Queen!** The bride of Christ, today, needs to realize and come into her full identity, that she is the **"QUEEN"!** When she agrees to the covenant-- I want you to understand this-- when she agrees to the agreement and the "new covenant" is simply this: Jesus said at the last supper that this bread represents My body that was broken for you. Eat it in remembrance of ME. And this cup is the cup of My new covenant blood that was shed for you – drink this in remembrance of ME. **When you partake of that communion at the Lord's Table, you are entering a legally, binding contract.**

Just after God made His covenant with Abraham, the King–Priest Melchizedek brought bread and wine to Abraham. It was a "theophany." He had no beginning and no end. It was God, Himself, coming to seal the deal with bread and wine. When you partake of the bread and the wine, you are not only remembering the Lord's death until He comes, you are saying, "Yes, Lord. Yes. I will fulfill my responsibilities. I will fulfill My end of the bargain. I will obey **all** of your word from Genesis to Revelation and simply allow you to be the King of my life, and I will submit to your authority, and I will become your servant forever."

Then, the Lord says to us today, **"Up to all the Kingdom will I give unto thee. What is your request?"** It is because you are in a **covenantal relationship** that you can ask whatever you wish and it shall be done according to God's written word. All power and all authority has been given unto you – the bride; but when you come into **covenantal relationship**, the bride becomes the **"Queen"!** The bride becomes the **"WIFE" of the Lamb,** here and now, and you get everything else!

And then in verse 10, John gets carried away in the spirit to a *"mountain great and high"*; and the angel showed him the *"Holy City, Jerusalem, coming down out of heaven."* This bride has now become queen. This "City" is a picture of the "Queen" living where the King lives.

Verse 11: *"It* (the Queen) *shone with the glory of God."* The "Queen" shone with the *"brilliance"* that *"was like that of a very precious jewel, a jasper clear as crystal."* The "Queen" shone with the glory! This is intended for today. This is intended for the church of the Living God in today's world – to shine with the glory of God. And as we shine with the glory, the bride becomes the queen. And this "Queen" is

476

intended for every believer all across the globe to the four corners of the earth, to the north, the south, the east, and the west.

You see, this city, has three gates on each side: three gates on the east, three on the north, three on the south, and three on the west. This kingdom is to stretch across the entire face of the planet – the whole earth is to be filled with the glory of God. That's a "New Jerusalem"-- a worldwide New Jerusalem, full of believers from all peoples, from all nations, tribes, and tongues. That's the **"New Jerusalem"** in the earth. **It is the bride of Christ experiencing the glory of God –ALL that God IS**. It is people returning to a **covenantal relationship** with their creator. And each of these twelve gates was made of a single pearl, and each gate was guarded by an angel, and written on the gates were the names of the twelve tribes of Israel. In this city, there is nothing but truth! To enter this city you must pass through the **gates of truth.** A whole pearl is a symbol of all truth and nothing but the truth. **It's a whole pearl!** It's a whole truth! Jesus made reference to pearls in Matthew 7:6, *"Don't cast your pearls before swine."* Don't cast your precious beautiful pearls – which is the truth of God's word, and the mysteries that God reveals to you – don't just throw them around lightly and mishandle them or misuse them. Treat them like pearls that you would bind together and carry around your neck as a precious necklace. You would value them very highly.

Here we see, the "Queen" with a pearl necklace around her neck – three on the east, three on the north, three on the south, three on the west. It's a pearl necklace of truth that is around the Queen's neck!

The angels are placed by each gate to not allow any lies, any deception, or no shadow of turning. There is no falsehood here that could ever even enter into this city. Only the truth of God's word dwells in this city. His word lives here. He lives here. He is the word. It's Psalms 91:11; *"For He shall give His angels charge over you, to keep you in all your ways."*

The names are written upon each gate of the twelve tribes of Israel. It's because it all began with one family. That number twelve – there were twelve sons of Jacob. They became the twelve tribes of Israel. It was "natural" Israel in the earth; and God has a plan for natural Israel; but He also has a plan for "spiritual" Israel. This is "spiritual" Israel coming down into the earth. It's God's government –

477

His fullness – all that He "IS"! It is God establishing His kingdom in the earth today – His spiritual nation – His spiritual country.

The "New Jerusalem" has the number twelve stamped all over it. There are twelve gates, twelve pearls, twelve angels, twelve tribes of Israel, and twelve foundations. The names of the twelve apostles of the lamb were on the twelve foundations. The wall's measure one hundred forty four cubits thick (200 feet) – **that's 12x12** – it's the **exponential power** of God that was within these walls that surrounds this city. He is the refuge. He is the fortress. Psalm 91:2, *"I will say of the Lord, He is my refuge and my fortress."* When you run inside the gates of the "New Jerusalem", you have run inside of God-Himself. **The "New Jerusalem" – it is God; in all of His fullness. He is the city!** When you run inside a gate, you have to pass a whole pearl – which means the whole truth and nothing but the truth-- that resides in this city. **God is the Word!** The word became flesh and dwelt among us. Jesus made a way. He is the Way, the Truth, and the Life. The word and God are inseparable. They are one and the same. This is a picture for us that was given to the Apostle John of what God intended for His people to experience and to live out day by day in our world **today** – now! Not later! But now!

"The wall was made of jasper, and the city of pure gold, as pure as glass."(v.18) Gold speaks of the divine nature, kingdom glory, and the kingship. It's the two merging together. It is His Queen taking on the divine nature becoming as pure gold, as pure as glass (v.21); transparent, with no impurities in it whatsoever. It's so pure you can see through it! It is the Queen taking on the divine nature – the purity of God Himself!
"Foundations of the city walls were decorated with every kind of precious stone ... jasper, sapphire, chalcedony, emerald, sardonyx, carnelian, chrysolite, beryl, topaz, chrysoprase, jacinth, and amethyst."

Isaiah 61:10 says, *"...and as a bride adorns herself with her jewels ..."*

The very foundations of this holy city, the New Jerusalem – this Queen is adorned with these many precious stones – every single foundation. Each tribe of Israel in the Old Testament had an identity. That identity was represented in a precious stone that was placed upon the breastplate of the high priest –very close to the heart of God. There were twelve precious stones – each representing a tribe of Israel. Each of these stones represents a tribe of Israel; but this time it's

478

"spiritual" Israel. The number sealed is twelve thousand from each tribe for a total of one hundred forty four thousand. That's not a literal number! The number sealed, twelve thousand from each tribe, it is spiritual Israel. Twelve is the number of fullness. Twelve is the number of the Kingdom of God. It is the number of all that God **"IS"**! It's a never ending kingdom. 12 x 12 = 144. It speaks of the exponential power of the gospel to bring in descendants of Abraham that will outnumber the stars and will outnumber the sands of the sea! It is a number representing the idea that there are so many you can't count them all. And each and every one, as innumerable as that number is, there is a precious stone decorating each foundation of this New Jerusalem. **You are one of these precious stones!** If you are a believer in Christ and have come into covenantal relationship, you are a beautiful **precious stone** on the very foundations of this New Jerusalem. **There is a stone for every believer past, present and future that has ever come into the Kingdom of God!** You are precious to God. You are valuable. You are priceless. There is no measurable value placed on you. God sent His son to die for you. He paid the highest price for you. Jesus died and gave His life for you. That's how precious you are to God. **And you are on the foundation. Relationship is what it's all built upon.** You have been decorated as one of the precious stones on the foundations of the New Jerusalem.

There is no temple in this city for the *"Lord God Almighty and the Lamb are its temple."*(v22) *"The city does not need the sun or the moon to shine on it, for the glory of God gives it light, and the Lamb is its lamp."*(v23) The glory of God illuminates this city. There is no night time here. There is no darkness. There is no Satan. There are no lies; no deception. There is only day. There is only light. There is only the glory of God – nothing else can remain!

"The nations will walk by its light, and the Kings of the earth will bring their splendor into it."(v24) Even the kings – the natural, physical kings of this earth, in the here and now, can enter into this spiritual kingdom – this New Jerusalem. It doesn't matter what anyone's status in life is, if they are a king, a president, a prime minister, a cabinet member, a senator, or a representative. They could be a governor or a mayor, whatever position they may hold in this life; it does not matter their age – from a college graduate to an elementary school student – all

people from all nations, all tribes, and all tongues, young and old, male and female, can enter into this New Jerusalem!

"On no day will its gates ever be shut," (v25) this city is always open to any and all new comers, to all who will hear, to all who will harken unto the voice of the Lord and who will live by truth. They can enter into this city at any time.

"Nothing impure will ever enter it, nor will anyone who does what is shameful or deceitful, but only those whose names are written in the Lamb's book of life." (v27)

If you have called upon the name of the Lord, Jesus Christ as your savior, you can enter into this city. You can come into the glory realms of God. I want you to know that there is more that God has for you. You may not have been told the entire truth and nothing but the truth. There is still a third chamber of the Tabernacle of Moses that some have never entered into. This third chamber is the same thing as the "New Jerusalem" in Revelation 21; **and it is for every believer!**

In chapter twenty two, there is a river *"flowing from the throne of God and of the Lamb down the middle of the great street of the city."* (v1) And *"on each side of this river stood the tree of life; bearing twelve crops of fruit, yielding its fruit every month."* (v2) "Fruit" is the fulfillment of the word. It is the word of God being fulfilled in the lives of every believer. And it's meant for every month, every day, every season – these trees, they never stop bearing fruit. The word keeps on being fulfilled. You become a "tree of life" bearing fruit so that others can eat from your tree!

"And the leaves of the tree are for the healing of the nations." (v2) This river will flow out of this city and will touch the entire world. The leaves from these trees are for the healing of the nations. There is no disease here. There is no sickness here. There is no death, no mourning, no crying or pain. Only complete healing is in this city. Only complete health and life are in this city.

If you are sick now. If you need healing in your body, you need to run inside the gates of the "New Jerusalem". Get into the glory realms of God, for Jehovah-Rapha lives there. All that God "IS"- lives there! God is the great physician. He is the great healer. The truth of His gospel is, *"...by His stripes we are healed."* (I Peter 2:24) Get into the "Secret Place" of the Most High God! Get into covenantal relationship with Him! Believe God's word. There is healing in Jesus' name. There is health in Jesus' name. There are miracles in Jesus' name. There is deliverance in Jesus' name.

Jesus completely reversed the curse that was incurred by Adam, and did away with it to where there would be no more curse. (Rev. 22:3) The curse is reversed through Jesus Christ our Lord and savior. Every curse that was brought upon us by Adam, the fall of man, and this world, can be reversed, now, through Jesus Christ and His blood that He shed on Calvary to radically change our situations and our lives – today in the here and now! When we need it the most; not in the life after – not after we "cross on over"-- but now! We need all of this now – to where we can put it to the greatest use and benefit! God wants to equip us now! He wants to give it all to us now! Halleluiah!

"The Kingdom of heaven suffers violence, and the violent take it by force." (Mat.11:12) It's an offensive kingdom; not a defensive kingdom. *"The very gates of hell shall not prevail against it."* That's offensive! We are to go to the very gates of hell and kick in those gates to set the captive free. As we kick in hell's gates, we speak the truth to that someone and say, "You don't have to live here anymore." And we say, "Come with me – let's go to a higher place!" We take them up, with the resurrection power of the risen Christ – up into the third heavens and you don't have to leave this world to do that. Heaven is coming down! Heaven and earth are merging! **They can become a permanent resident of the "New Jerusalem" in the earth!**

This kingdom is expanding. There are people coming into it all the time – Refugees – from other nations in the spirit realm. You can inform them that they are descendants of Jesus Christ of Nazareth. This is their true spiritual origin. This is where they come from, and that they are from the spiritual country of "Israel" with a capital city of the "New Jerusalem". **You can inform them that they have now come home!** This is your inheritance! This is your "Promised Land". This is your new country. A land full of promises! You are originally from here, you just didn't know you were from here! Your descendants are Jewish! Your descendants are from a Jewish carpenter named Jesus Christ of Nazareth!

Your citizenship, also, is in this new country! Heaven has come down into the earth. You are a citizen of God's Kingdom in the earth. And as a citizen, you are entitled to all of its rights and privileges! You are entitled to protection from the King and His armies. All the armies of heaven are at your disposal to protect the homeland. They will fight

481

and they will not relent until every enemy is defeated. They will fight against all invading armies and invading forces. If you are sick with cancer, it is an invading army and it cannot come into this country. The King and all His legions of angels will fight against this invasion, and they will not lose. They never lose. Cancer cannot enter a "New Jerusalem". Any and all diseases, any and all conditions – they will and must be defeated. It is your right to have divine protections and coverings from your King – the King of Kings and the Lord of Lords! When you come into the "Secret Place", you come in under the shadow of the Almighty. You are under the greatest umbrella – the greatest covering-- in the entire universe. You are under the protections of the Most High God.

And in this new kingdom, there are new laws that govern this kingdom. They are written out for you in the books from Genesis to Revelation in the entire word of God. This is the law. These are the laws that govern this country. They were written by the King himself. **This supernatural law supersedes all other natural laws on the face of the planet.** It supersedes all scientific law and medical understanding. It does not matter if there is no organ there. The king will speak the "word" and He will make one! **All things are possible in this kingdom.** Miracles are in this kingdom! Healing and health are in this kingdom. Salvation and deliverance are in this kingdom. **All that God is – is in this kingdom!**

A "New Jerusalem" is a place where the King is allowed to be King. Man stops trying to tell God what to do and just simply allows God to be the King of His own country, and recognizes the fact that He rules and He reigns, and issues out His decrees. And His law is law – it is truth – period. And His subjects – His servants – come into this kingdom and will simply obey the King's word – whatever He says! Whatever He tells them to do – they will do. They give the King their life – all that they are and all that they have. They "abide in the vine", run inside the gates and they live there in the City of God. That's a "New Jerusalem"!

And also, for you to be a citizen of this country – this new kingdom, you must learn the language. The language of heaven is spoken here. The language of God is spoken here. The language of the King is spoken here. This language is also written down for us from Genesis to Revelation. It's the language of the King! It existed in eternity past before there ever was the concept of languages.

482

Remember, God is the word. Jesus is the word. They are inseparable! **God's language existed before it was ever written down!** He has always spoken the same language!

So, for you to live here, **you can only speak the King's language.** No other languages are recognized here. All other languages are considered foreign. So, anything that doesn't line up with the word of God, it is as if you are speaking a foreign language; and it will be considered only "**babble**" in this country. It is the reverse of the "Tower of Babble" where God confused all the languages. Only what the King says is recognized here. What He says goes! It's irreversible! It cannot be changed! God is unifying them today – people from all nations, all tribes, from all peoples, and tongues. They can all understand what the King is saying to them; but it's by God's Spirit. The Holy Spirit says one thing in the earth today. He is saying it and speaking it in every known language on the face of the earth, but He's saying it through all these different languages in such a way that everyone will understand it in their own language. But if you take all of those languages away God is saying the same thing. He is speaking one thing to His bride – His worldwide bride. If you take away the ability to communicate through language, in the spirit, people from all nations, all tribes, all peoples, all tongues – they all would understand what the King is saying. It's universal. That is the unity of the bride of Christ.

Psalms 133 says, *"How pleasant it is for brethren to dwell together in unity. It is like the precious oil upon the head..."* It is precious when the bride dwells together in unity. Jesus prayed before He left this world – His final prayer was, "I pray that they can be one even as I and the Father are one!" It was not an unattainable prayer. Jesus meant for that to be fulfilled.

When the bride comes together, it is a beautiful thing. "His visage was marred more than the sons of men." Jesus gave up His beauty. **The bridegroom gave up His beauty and He gave it all to His bride!** And she is beautifully adorned with precious pearls, jewels, gold, jasper, and the radiance of pure light! This is the **beauty** of the bride, when she **comes into her identity** and recognizes who she is and comes into a **covenantal relationship** with her King. **She becomes the Queen!** In doing so, she **experiences the glory of God!** Halleluiah!

Psalms 133:1, 2 *"Behold, how good and how pleasant it is for brethren to dwell together in unity; It is like the precious oil upon the head, running down on the beard, the beard of Aaron."*

When the bride dwells together in unity, anointing is increased in exponential fashion … "one puts a thousand to flight, two puts ten thousand to flight". It's psalm 91! "Thou a thousand may fall at your side, and ten thousand at your right hand…" (v7) Why? Because it is you that has slain them! It is the **"Warrior Bride"** of Christ coming into her **identity** – into who she is! Anointing is increased corporately! It is imperative-- it is crucial-- that the bride of Christ puts aside all of their differences, all of their denominational lines, all of their arguing and bickering over the doctrines of men, and realize that they are all **one bride**, and it will always be one bride.

"I charge you this day, church of the Living God: You must put aside everything that divides, everything that hinders, every obstacle for the sake of the Kingdom. It is one Kingdom – one spiritual nation under God, indivisible, with liberty and justice for all. Where the Spirit of the Lord is, there is liberty. God is trying to bring freedom in the midst of His body – in the midst of His bride. Will you put aside all of your differences that some may have gone on for generations? It's time to lay them down at the foot of the cross, then take up your crosses, and die to yourself. Allow the fires of God to burn on the inside of you so that all of your flesh, all of man's ways, man's wisdom, man's knowledge, and man's carnality may be burned up – burned to a crisp; so that you can enter into the "glory realms" of God."

The "New Jerusalem" is illuminated by the glory of God. There is no sun or moon to shine on it. There is no need for them. Only the light of God illuminates this city. If you're going to enter this city, you're going to enter the glory! So, you'll need to prepare for what you are about to experience. **This is a now word!** This is a **now vision!** This is for you – today! This word is for the bride of Christ – today! If you want more of God and you say you want more of God, and you want Him to increase in your life; in order for that to happen, you must decrease! There must become less of you, and then more of Him will come. You say you want more of Him? Well, **He wants more of you!**

There is still yet more for me to tell you. Will you have the faith to come with me and turn the page? We are about to enter into the "glory realms" of God!

The Glory Realms of God
(Isaiah 60:1-3)

"In the 'New Jerusalem', there is no sun nor moon, for the glory of God illuminates the city. I am the sun. I am an all-consuming fire," says the Lord God Almighty. "In human terms, if you look upon the sun in the natural, it is the greatest fire-ball that you could ever see. It is millions of miles away, yet it can still be unbearable in the heat of summer. To give you something to relate to, My glory is greater than the sun. And in the spirit realm, absolutely everything gets incinerated in this realm! I want you to understand that. There is no place for even a speck of flesh – a dust speck – a speck of carnality. This is what is in a 'New Jerusalem'. This is what was in the "Secret Place" of the Most High God. This is what was in the "Burning Bush". It also rested on Mt. Sinai, filled the tabernacle, and then later filled the temple – it's the glory of God!"

Adam experienced God's glory in the garden. He lost it all. Jesus bought it all back; and we as believers in Christ are able to experience the glory of God all over again, and go back to the "Garden of Eden" and walk with God in the "cool of the day." God lived in the garden with man. Sin caused a separation. Until Jesus, man could not dwell in the same place that God did. Jesus came, paid the penalty for sin, and made a way for man to be reunited with his creator. So, now, the two can live in the same place at the same time, in the same dimension. Heaven and earth, through Jesus Christ, have become one! They have become reunited. We as believers need to understand that basic – basic – truth. It's the Lord's Prayer very simply stated. He taught them to pray in this way: "Thy Kingdom come, Thy will be done on earth as it is in heaven."

Jesus knew then that heaven and earth were coming together. He was trying to teach His disciples the very same truth. They didn't understand it, and some believers today – over two thousand years later – still don't understand this simple basic truth. God began His kingdom as a baby in a manger. It is to continue on forever and ever. It is a kingdom without end. It is an everlasting kingdom!

When we speak of the "Glory Realms of God", we are speaking about all that God IS-- His total essence-- everything that you could ever list or imagine about God all combined together, speaks of the glory. So all that He "IS"-- He wants to give to His children. And Jesus has provided a way for that to happen. When we walk in obedience to the Lord's word and His will in the earth, and we come into a covenantal relationship, that is dwelling in the "Secret Place" of the Most High God. That is the "Glory Realms"! It is a "Jacob's Ladder". That's heaven and earth coming together. It is an "open heaven". It's Deut. 28 – the obedience chapter. God will create an "open heavens" for us. And it's also a "New Jerusalem"; where all of heaven comes down into the earth. IT'S ALL THAT GOD IS!

Jesus had it all. He left it all; gave His life for it all. **And He left it all to you!** So, ALL that God is, is your inheritance. It's everything that He IS! It is His Holiness, His righteousness, His patience, His faith, His anointing, His longsuffering, His forgiveness, His love, His grace, His mercy, etc. You see, you take on the image and the likeness of Christ. That's what it's all about; that we become like Christ. We take on His divine nature that's symbolized in the precious metal gold. So in the "Secret Place" there was a vessel of **gold** – the Ark of the Covenant. When we come into "covenant" with God, **we become an "Ark" – a vessel of gold**-- for Him. And you see that Ark would move from place to place; so wherever that Ark moved, the glory of God would move with it. We become **transporters of the "glory"** of God in the earth. Wherever we go – God goes! And us being kings (small k) in His kingdom, we are establishing His kingdom in the earth wherever we go. It's an "Open Heaven"! It's a "Jacob's Ladder"! It's a "Secret Place" of the Most High! It's a "New Jerusalem"! So, wherever you go, you'll establish a "New Jerusalem" in the earth. At every prayer meeting, at every worship service, at every church service, it can become a "New Jerusalem". But when this occurs, I say this as a word of preparation, the glory of God is going to fall. And when that does, it's like having the sun right in the room with you. It will absolutely consume all flesh – all carnality – all of the Adamic nature. It will be a "New Jerusalem" that will fall in the earth!

There will be no disease, no death, no sickness; no condition will be able to stay in that realm. Sicknesses and diseases will literally begin to fall off of people, because they cannot stay in the glory of God. It's guaranteed! **It cannot stay!** Everything that is of the flesh, everything that is of the fall, everything that has been given to us through our Adamic nature that we have inherited through him – all of this is reversed through Jesus Christ. So, all sickness and disease must go, all sin and all flesh must go, all carnality must go, all of our Adamic nature must go, all demons must go, evil spirits, principalities and powers, rulers, spiritual wickedness in high places, and Satan himself must go! Halleluiah! A "New Jerusalem" is a picture of that. There is no "darkness" there! There is no "night" – symbolic of Satan himself. He is the darkness. He is the lies. He likes to keep everything hidden – including this revelation!

When you enter the glory realms of God, you enter the "IS" realm of God. All of His word from Genesis to Revelation – "IT IS"! Remember, you can't separate God from His word. He is the word. The word – "IT IS"-- not "going to be". "IT IS! NOW! All that 'I AM'…'**IS**'… YOURS… NOW… FOREVER! Present tense!"

Too many times we pray and we're always hoping. We're always longing. It always seems so far into the future. Sometimes it seems like God will never answer. But in "Secret Place" living – it's the "glory realms" of God. When we come into that covenantal relationship, you know God and God knows you. *"Because, you have made the Lord thy God … your dwelling place…"* (v9) It's Psalms 91! "I will answer and I will hear from heaven and I will honor you because you have honored Me. And you know My name. You know who I AM! It's covenantal relationship! You know GOD! He is El Elyon – the possessor of heaven and earth. He owns it all! He is El-Shaddai! You know Him by name. You know His name. He is El-Shaddai! He is the all – sufficient God capable of giving <u>all</u> that His people need. He owns it all, and He wants to give it all to the child of God who will come into this covenantal relationship."

"Because he loves Me," says the Lord. "I will deliver him; I will set him on high, because he has known My name. He shall call upon Me, and I will answer him; I will be with him in trouble; I will deliver him, and honor him. With long life I will satisfy him, and show him My salvation." (Psalms 91:14-16) God will show you His salvation. He will "save" you in every aspect of life; not only spiritually; but mentally, emotionally, and physically as well.

487

"I will not share My glory with another. I will not – ever – ever share My glory with another. No flesh will glory in My presence. Church of the Loving God: You will not glory in My presence. You will not be exalted. Man will not be exalted; man's wisdom, man's knowledge, or man's understanding. People in high positions will not be exalted. If you want more of Me and you want all I've got, I say this with a word of warning, You have to be serious about what you ask for. "The greatest in My Kingdom shall be the servant of all." It's an inverted triangle. The greatest is on the bottom. Church of the Living God: You must be ready to repent for trying to glory in My presence; for trying to exalt yourselves and lift each other up and put man in the high places. Everything – absolutely everything-- that tries to set itself up against the knowledge of God and exalt itself – every mountain is coming down! Every stone in this spiritual temple that is not laid by the hand of God – every stone laid by the hands of men – it must come down."

"I am bringing a shaking to My church – worldwide-- such as the world has never seen. Why? **Because, My church is too full of themselves!** They are the Laodicean church that thinks that they have everything. They have it all; seen it all, bought it all; and have accumulated wealth and riches. They have God completely figured out. But I want you to know today; that God's reply is: they have become wretched, poor, miserable, blind, and naked. They are naked! When Adam was naked in the garden, he lost his glory; and God had to sacrifice an animal to clothe him and Eve. It was through the sacrifice of the lamb – Jesus Christ – that we can be clothed once again with the garments of God. We can be wrapped in robes of righteousness, put on the garments of praise for a spirit of heaviness; we can put on the full armor of God. All of these things, we can be dressed in the attire of the King, the Priest, and the Prophet. All the garments – My clothing mentioned in scripture – are putting on God – an active choice that requires some energy on our part. We must put Him on! And along with that, I am coming back for a bride that is without spot or wrinkle. She is clothed in white raiment. She is clothed in white – like the garments of the priesthood."

"I've called you to be a royal priesthood to carry out all the spiritual duties of the tabernacle – each and every step to get you to the "Secret Place" of the Most High God. Spiritually – it's all meant for you today. And if you will do simply just that, and you will come into the third chamber of the tabernacle of Moses, you will have entered into the 'glory realms' of God."

And I will end this the way we began, with Psalms 91:1: *"He who dwells in the secret place of the Most High, shall abide under the shadow of the Almighty."* If you come to the glory realms of God, into the Secret Place, you come under the largest umbrella and greatest protections in the entire universe. All that God "IS" – is at your disposal. When you come into a covenantal relationship – **you become the QUEEN** of the King. And it is in this **covenantal relationship** that the queen looks at her spouse and says, **"Honey I need you." Then the King looks at the Queen and says, "Honey, I need you too."** That's Covenantal Relationship!

God has no other plan. He needs us as much as we need Him to carry out His mission, His purposes, and His plans in the earth. We are many things. We are **sons and daughters** of the Most High. We are **kings** in His Kingdom. We are **priests** in His service. We are **prophets** to speak out His word in the earth. We are **warriors** dressed in the full armor of God ready to fight and do spiritual warfare to advance His Kingdom. We are **the Bride** of Christ beautifully adorned. We are the **Queen** of the King that has signed the contract. We are an **Ark** of the Covenant; vessels of gold to carry His glory throughout the earth. We are a **Jacob's Ladder** to bring heaven down into the earth, and to get others into heaven's realm. We are many things symbolized throughout the scriptures.

I want to leave you with this closing thought. The glory of God was revealed to Moses in a burning bush. The fire of God was upon this bush but the bush was not consumed. It was a picture of humanity being the bush, being the wood, the trees – a picture of humanity with everything else consumed that could be consumed – and all that was left was **a humanity with no carnality.** Nothing else could be burned. So I leave you with these thoughts: You are, also, a **"BURNING BUSH"** for the Lord God Almighty!

"I, the Lord God, will set you on fire for Me, and you will light and set your world on fire with the glory of God."

In some places, men are symbolized as trees in scripture. They are oaks of righteousness, trees of the fields, palm trees, cedar trees, vines and branches. When wood in the tabernacle was used, it speaks of the humanity of Christ. He was the God-Man in the earth – fully God yet fully a man. The "Ark of the Covenant" was a box of wood that was overlaid with gold. It's a picture of Christ's divine nature coming together with His human nature – as one – forming one vessel.

"You'll be a **'burning bush'** for Me. It's the divine and the human coming together as one – in you. I desire that they be not luke warm; but either cold or hot. Come and enter the glory realms of God so that I can set you on **fire** with the **glory** of God, and **where you go – I go!**"

"You will shine My glory out into the world.
You'll have become a Burning Bush for Me!
You'll blaze with My Glory …
You'll burn with My Holy Passion – My
Holy Zeal – a fire for Me!
You'll set the world on fire!"

Isaiah 59:19 "… men will fear the name of the Lord, and from the rising of the sun they will revere His glory."

Isaiah 60:1-3 "Arise, shine; for your light has come! And the glory of the Lord is risen upon you. For behold, the darkness shall cover the earth, and deep darkness the people; But the Lord will arise over you, and His glory will be seen upon you. The gentiles (nations) shall come to your light; and kings to the brightness of your rising."

"NATIONS WILL COME TO YOUR LIGHT! NATIONS WILL COME TO THE GLORY."

"Church of the Living God: There's more! There's more that I have for you. Come in behind the veil. Come into the glory realms of God. This is the place that I am calling you to. And if you will say, 'Yes Lord. Yes, I will come.' You will establish My 'New Jerusalem' in the earth today. Thy Kingdom come, Thy will be done on earth as it is in heaven."

If you will, Jesus' prayer will be fulfilled in the earth today. His Kingdom will come and His will shall be done in the earth and our world will not be the same. The light and the glory of God will illuminate it. And the nations shall walk by its light and the kings of the earth will bring their splendor into it.

Every nation on the face of the earth will be changed by the glory of God! Jesus' Kingdom will come and His will shall be done. Every knee shall bow and every tongue confess that Jesus Christ is Lord of all! He is the Lord of Glory! He is Lord over all the universe! **Can we allow Him to be King of His own world?**

490